COMMENTARIES

ON

THE LAWS

OF THE

ANCIENT HEBREWS;

WITH

AN INTRODUCTORY ESSAY ON CIVIL SOCIETY AND
GOVERNMENT.

BY

E. C. WINES.

THE LAWBOOK EXCHANGE, LTD.
Clark, New Jersey

ISBN 978-1-58477-527-0

Lawbook Exchange edition 2006, 2019

The quality of this reprint is equivalent to the quality of the original work.

THE LAWBOOK EXCHANGE, LTD.
33 Terminal Avenue
Clark, New Jersey 07066-1321

*Please see our website for a selection of our other publications
and fine facsimile reprints of classic works of legal history:*
www.lawbookexchange.com

Library of Congress Cataloging-in-Publication Data

Wines, E. C. (Enoch Cobb), 1806-1879.
 Commentaries on the laws of the ancient Hebrews : with an
introductory essay on civil society and government / by E.C. Wines.
  p. cm.
 Originally published: New York : G.P. Putnam, 1853.
 Includes bibliographical references.
 ISBN 1-58477-527-0 (cloth : alk. paper)
 1. Jewish law--History--To 1500. 2. Jews--Politics and government--
To 70 A.D. I. Title.

BM520.52.W56 2004
296.1'8--dc22   2004058297

Printed in the United States of America on acid-free paper

COMMENTARIES

ON

THE LAWS

OF THE

ANCIENT HEBREWS;

WITH

AN INTRODUCTORY ESSAY ON CIVIL SOCIETY AND
GOVERNMENT.

BY

E. C. WINES.

NEW YORK:

GEO. P. PUTNAM & CO., 10 PARK PLACE.

1853.

C. W. BENEDICT,
STEREOTYPER AND PRINTER,
201 William Street.

PREFACE.

NEXT to the birth and mission of Jesus Christ, the exist
ence and institutions of the Hebrew people are the most
important event in universal history. The founder of Judaism and the founder of Christianity are the two persons,
whose lives and labors have most extensively and powerfully influenced the progress and destiny of the human
race. The truths which they revealed, the doctrines which
they taught, have entered as the profoundest element into
the civilization of mankind. While saving individuals, they
have been the true power of nations, acting at once as the
most vivifying and the most conservative principle in human
affairs.

It is only with the institutions of the former of these
illustrious personages, that the present work is concerned.
The polity of Moses has a twofold importance. It is important, first, from the perfection of wisdom, in which the
work was accomplished; but still more important, secondly,
from its consequences to the world. These consequences
continue to this moment, and will continue through all

coming time. Christianity itself sprang from the bosom
of Judaism. Without the religion of Moses, the religion
of Christ never would have been given to the world. It
is, therefore, in a certain sense, undoubtedly true, that we
owe to the Mosaic code the greater part of the light, which
we this day enjoy. Especially are we indebted to this code
for a precious truth, which reason, left to itself, has never
yet discovered; I mean the doctrine of the unity of God.
By the possession of this truth, a large portion of the human
family have been happily rescued from the errors and immoralities, to which the belief in many gods invariably
leads.

The following treatise is an attempt to analyze, and to
develope systematically, the civil polity of the inspired
Hebrew lawgiver. The civil government of the ancient
Hebrews was the government of a free people; it was a
government of laws; it was a system of self-government.
It was not only the first, but the only government of antiquity, to which this description is fully applicable. To
Moses, a man of the most direct, firm, and positive spirit,
belongs the honor of being the founder of this sort of
government. His constitution was pervaded with popular
sympathies and the spirit of liberty. The best wisdom of
modern times in the difficult science of legislation was anticipated by Moses. The moderns are not real discoverers;
they have but propagated and applied truths and principles, established by the first, the wisest, the ablest of
legislators. In an age of barbarism and tyranny, Moses

solved the problem how a people could be self-governed, and yet well governed; how men ·could be kept in order, and still be free; and how the liberty of the individual could be reconciled with the welfare of the community.

The true character of the Hebrew constitution is not well understood. Nor is the want of full and accurate information concerning it matter of wonder. The cause of this ignorance has* been suggested by Salvador. During the long period, when the words people, law, equality, national utility, intellectual superiority, independence, and regular legislation, scarcely found a place in any living language, how could Moses find his true place and his just estimation? The people were too ignorant to study him, and their tyrants would have felt their pride and oppression rebuked by his ardent republicanism. But times are changed. Everywhere the need of a better and juster political organization is felt. Everywhere there is developed a strong tendency towards popular freedom and power. Everywhere an irresistible impulse is urging na-.tions to substitute for the arbitrary, capricious, and incon-stant government of men, the just and stable government of laws. The more this state of things developes itself, the more the principles of reason, justice, equality, liberty, and public utility, take possession of men's minds, and assert their power over human affairs, the more will the polity of the Hebrew commonwealth become an object of study, of interest, of admiration, and of imitation. And the more this constitution is studied, the more will it be

recognised as a free constitution; a constitution embodying all the great principles of political wisdom; a constitution, on several points, in advance even of the age in
which we live.

The basis of the following inquiries into the polity and
laws of the ancient Hebrews was a course of lectures, delivered in several Theological Seminaries, and in many of
the principal cities of the Union. Ten years ago, the
author was invited to deliver one of a course of lectures
before the Mercantile Library Company of Philadelphia.
Archbishop Hughes had already given a lecture of the
same course on Pope Pius VII. As the learned prelate
had selected, for eulogy, a dignitary of the Romish church,
that circumstance led me to choose, for the theme of my
discourse, a dignitary of the church universal. Accordingly, I took "Moses and his Laws." The lecture was
well received by the public, and brought a formal invitation from many of the leading citizens of Philadelphia,—
divines, lawyers, savans, and others,—that I would extend
the discussion, and give a series of discourses on the same
subject. In making the necessary preparation to comply
with this invitation, I became enamored of the theme.
The investigation became a labor of love with me. The
increasing light, afforded by my researches, led me, at
different times, to rewrite and enlarge the discussion; till,
at length, it came to be embodied in a very extended
series of lectures. The substance of these lectures, in
courses more or less comprehensive, wes given, as above

stated, in various Theological Seminaries, by invitation
from the Trustees and Professors, and in many other places,
at the request of citizens of the highest respectability. In
this form, the author's illustrations of the constitution and
laws of Israel had the good fortune to meet the approbation of gentlemen, both in church and state, whose good
opinion might well be an object of pride to persons of
literary pretensions, far higher than his.

The present work is complete in itself. It has a beginning,
a middle, and an end; in other words, it 'is characterized by
unity of design. It is an analysis of the political constitution, the jus publicum, of the Hebrews. It treats of a
particular department of the Hebrew institutions; but there
are other parts of those institutions, which it does not touch.
Hebrew jurisprudence, properly so called, a wide, rich, and
inviting field, it does not enter upon at all. This is reserved
for a separate work. My lectures embraced the latter class
of topics, as well as the former. Ample materials, therefore,
have been collected for the illustration of the private law of
the Hebrews; and these materials have been, to a considerable extent, arranged for publication. Should the present
work meet with favor, another, if life and health are spared,
will in due time follow. The second volume will contain a
detailed elucidation of the jurisprudence of Moses. His
whole system of laws will be reduced to a classification,
formed on the basis of Blackstone's division of the laws of
England. Each individual enactment will be examined,
with reference both to its intrinsic character and the reasons
on which it was based; whether those reasons relate to the gen-

eral wants of humanity, or to the adaptation of the code to times and circumstances. A prominent design of this work will be to institute comparisons, all along, between the jurisprudence of Moses and the jurisprudence of other enlightened nations, both ancient and modern. A sufficiently extended research into the laws and constitutions of the civilized world might make this one of the most interesting, instructive, and useful features of the proposed treatise.

The greatest difficulty I have encountered in the preparation of these sheets for the press, is the want of books. There are many works, of high respectability, relating to Hebrew history and law, not found, as far as I know, in any of the public or private libraries in the United States. The works of this kind, which are found in our libraries, are very widely scattered. I have sometimes had to travel hundreds of miles to examine a single book, and have been well repaid for my labor. My cordial thanks are due to various library associations, and not a few private gentlemen, for the loan of books. Among the former I would name Harvard University, the Boston Athenaeum, Columbia College, the Franklin Library Company of Philadelphia, and the Mercantile Library Association of New York. This last named institution has been particularly liberal, allowing me to take any number of books, and keep them any length of time free of cost; and has even offered to purchase such works as I might want, which are not already in its extensive, well selected, and invaluable library. And, with respect to future researches, my special thanks are due to David Banks, Esq., of New York, for his generous offer of the unlimited use of his very extensive collection of law books, ancient and modern, foreign and domestic.

It would be easy to make here an ambitious display of learning in an enumeration of the works examined in the progress of these inquiries; but that would serve less the purposes of utility, than of pedantry. The authorities relied upon are pretty copiously referred to in the accompanying notes; for I hold it to be a chief element of value in any scientific or philosophical work, to point out to those who may wish to extend their researches in reference to the topics treated, the sources of that increased light, which they desire.

The author cannot pretend to anything like perfection, or freedom from error, in his treatment of a subject so ancient, so extensive, so difficult, and involving so laborious a search into constitutions and laws, as the polity of the Hebrew commonwealth. He has diligently sought for TRUTH; and, in respect to fundamentals, he believes that he has found it. Let the candid reader weigh the evidence adduced, and judge for himself. At any rate, whatever estimate may be placed upon his own individual labors, if his work shall have a tendency to awaken in any minds an interest in Biblical studies; to remove from them sceptical doubts concerning the divine origin and authority of the Old Testament scriptures; to impress them with a sense of the dignity and value of those ancient compositions; and to convince them of the world's obligation to the Bible in promoting the civil liberty and social happiness of mankind,—he will feel, that he has not labored in vain.

EAST HAMPTON, L. I., March, 1853.

ADVERTISEMENT BY THE PUBLISHERS.

In his Preface, the author states, that the following treatise was originally written in the form of lectures, and delivered to students in Theological Seminaries, and to miscellaneous audiences, in many of our cities. In this form, his Commentaries on the Laws of the Hebrews everywhere met with acceptance, and were applauded by competent judges. In sending the work forth in a printed volume, the publishers deem it proper to accompany it with a few of the recommendations bestowed upon it, when given as lectures. They ought to state, however, that some of the opinions appended were given, after examining the manuscript as prepared for the press.

From the Hon. Benjamin F. Butler, *of New York.*

" The lectures of Professor Wines on the polity of the Hebrew Commonwealth are distinguished by a most thorough acquaintance with the subject, and by the clear and strong light in which they place the divine mission of the great Hebrew lawgiver, and the incomparable wisdom and usefulness of his institutions. They are full of important and valuable information to all classes."

From HIRAM KETCHUM, ESQ., *of New York, after examining portions of the work, as prepared for the press.*

" IT is a great work ; profoundly philosophical; and clear as crystal. I feel persuaded that it will have an extensive sale. It will be sought after by the legal as well as the clerical profession."

From the HON. WILLIAM KENT, *of New York.*

" THE lectures of Mr. Wines on the laws and polity of the Hebrews appeared to me very learned and able. They have given him a high character among scholars and students of history."

From GEORGE WOOD, ESQ., *of New York.*

" DEAR SIR :—I have read with pleasure the manuscript of your Essay on Civil Society and Government. I have been gratified with finding that your views concur in the main with my own. I think the publication of the work might be very useful. There is a portion of the religious class of the community, who have imbibed very erroneous notions upon some of the subjects on which you treat, and I think the general perusal of your production will have a tendency to prevent the spread of those errors.

" I am, Sir, with great respect,

" Your obedient servant,

" GEORGE WOOD."

N. Y., 30th June, 1851.
The Rev. E. C. Wines.

From the HON. MITCHELL KING, *of Charleston, S. C.*

" THE philosophical views which Professor Wines takes of the Hebrew institutions, the order and connexion in which he groups them, and the many striking analogies which he traces between them and our own laws and customs, are in the highest degree instructive and interesting."

From the late JUDGE WOODBURY, *of N. Hampshire.*

" PROFESSOR WINES's lectures on the Jewish polity are highly interesting, and in my opinion calculated to be useful."

From the late JEREMIAH MASON, *of Boston.*

"I HAVE been much instructed by Mr. Wines's lectures on the Hebrew polity and laws."

From the REV. DR. WOODS, *of Andover.*

" I HAVE heard all Professor Wines's lectures on the Mosaic institutions, and have wished that they might be extended much further. From the beginning to the end, they exhibit marks of extensive, patient study, and of profound, discriminating thought. They are, I think, sound in principle, and strong and conclusive in argument. The style in which they are written is perspicuous and forcible, and often rises to animation and eloquence. The lectures cannot fail to be profitable to any who love to think; but they are specially adapted to be interesting to men engaged in the professions of law and theology, to the different classes of students, and most of all, to those who are seeking for a clear insight into the Mosaic scriptures, and who wish to see the various principles involved in them clearly stated, and triumphantly vindicated against the subtle objections and profane sneers of infidel philosophy."

From the REV. DRS. POND, SHEPARD, *and* SMITH, *Professors in the Theological Seminary, Bangor, Me.*

" HAVING had the privilege of attending Professor Wines's full course of lectures on the institutions of Moses, we cannot forbear expressing how much we have been interested and instructed. Mr. Wines discusses the subject ably, clearly, and forcibly. He thoroughly vindicates the Jewish lawgiver from the objections of infidels, and shows how much the world, in all subsequent ages, has been indebted to his writings."

From Rev. G. W. Bethune, D.D. *of Brooklyn, N. Y.*

" The lectures of Professor Wines on the Jewish polity are conceived in a liberal and philosophical spirit, and are written with thorough scholarship and learning. They are elaborate, comprehensive, and interesting, showing great research and aptness in the lecturer. His plan is novel, and his inferences logically drawn, and practically useful."

———

From the Rev. Dr. J. W. Yeomans, *of Pennsylvania.*

" Professor Wines presents, in a compendious and impressive form, a philosophical view of the Hebrew polity, which makes the legislation of Moses appear, as it truly is, the most wonderful and instructive system of legislation the world has ever seen."

———

From Francis L. Hawks, D. D., *of New York.*

"From the examination I have been able to give the work of Mr. Wines on the laws and polity of the Hebrews, I think that it is characterized by signal ability, and that its publication cannot but be useful."

TABLE OF CONTENTS.

CHAPTER VIII.

CHAPTER IX.

BOOK II.

ORGANIC LAW OF THE HEBREW STATE.

CHAPTER I.

CHAPTER II.

CHAPTER III.

CHAPTER IV.

CHAPTER V.

CHAPTER VI.

CHAPTER VII.

CHAPTER VIII.

CHAPTER IX.

CHAPTER X.

INTRODUCTORY ESSAY

CIVIL SOCIETY AND GOVERNMENT.

THE design of this introductory essay is to inquire into the origin and foundation of civil society and government; to unfold the nature, sources, and sanctions of political power; and to establish some general principles of polity, law, and administration.

Next in importance to the science of religion, which teaches our relations to the Creator, and the science of morality, which explains our relations to our fellow men, is the science of government, which unfolds our relations and duties as members of civil society. There is, indeed, a beautiful alliance between theology, ethics, and jurisprudence. These sciences have a common origin, a common basis, and a common end.* The science of legislation, in effect, embraces our relations to God, to individual man, and to society. It includes within itself the most important principles of religion, morality, and law. No subject can more worthily engage the attention of a rational being; a being who has the happiness of himself and his species at heart.

* Translator's Pref. to Burlamaqui's Principles of Natural and Politic Law.

2

The true origin of civil government and its ultimate foundation, undoubtedly lie in the will of God. Government is, therefore, a divine institution. Reason, revelation, and the best human authority, concur in enforcing this conclusion. Let us interrogate each of these teachers in turn.

What, in the first place, is the testimony of reason, that faculty of the soul, whose high office it is to investigate the mutual relations of things, to compare these relations together, and thence to infer just principles for forming our belief, and guiding our conduct?

The exact point we are now in search of is, whether it be the will of God, that laws should be instituted among men; the manner of their enactment will be inquired into hereafter.

1. The aptitude of our nature for government is a clear indication of the divine origin of government.* Man is endowed with understanding and choice, sensible of pleasure and pain, and adapted to be moved by the expectation of rewards and punishments. The possession of such powers and susceptibilities indicates a purpose, just as the structure of the eye and the ear shows that these organs were designed for sight and hearing. For why should the Deity give us a nature so exactly suited to the reception of laws, if he had intended that none should ever be made for us? This would be creating so many useless faculties; it would be instituting an admirable system of means to no end; and it would, therefore, signify a waste of contrivance, inconsistent with absolute perfection.

2. An examination of human nature, in another aspect of it, will evince, that man was made for society, and consequently for government and law; for without these society cannot exist.† Two leading principles enter as elements into

* Burlam. Prin. Nat. Law, Part ii., Chap. 2.
† See Bishop Butler's Sermons on Human Nature.

the soul of man;—self-love and benevolence. Self-love is the affection which one has for himself. This prompts us to take care of ourselves, our life, our health, our private interest. Benevolence is a disposition to friendship, compassion, love, kindness. It is an affection whose aim and end is the good of others. There can be no doubt of the existence of such a principle in human nature. So natural is it for man to be attracted towards man, that the bare fact of having trod the same soil and breathed in the same climate becomes, not unfrequently, the occasion of contracting close intimacies and friendships; the occasion, I say; for the real tie is not the slight relations alluded to above, nor any others like them; but the prior, original, deeply-seated disposition and bias of our nature to love one another.

But if there is no doubt of the existence of this principle in man, there is quite as little, that its office is to incite us to seek the welfare and happiness of society, just as it is the office of self-love to incite us to seek our own good.

Besides benevolence, there are other principles in human nature, which, being adapted to promote the good of society, are a clear indication that man was designed for society by the Creator. Such are the desire of esteem from others, the love of society for its own sake, and the indignation we feel against successful vice. These affections have a direct relation to others. They incline us to a behavior beneficial to others. Their tendency is to public good; that is to say, the good of man in society. Why should God implant in us principles having an immediate respect to society, why make us social beings, if he did not intend us for the social state? To affirm that he did, would be to charge him foolishly.

There is still another principle in human nature, which points the same way. I refer to that faculty by which men distinguish between their own actions, approving of some, and disapproving of others; the faculty of conscience.

That this faculty tends to restrain men from doing mischief to each other, and leads them to do good, is too manifest to need being insisted on. Here, then, in the conscience, we have another principle of our nature, which has quite as close a relation to public as to private good. The existence of this principle in the inward frame of man is a clear proof that the Creator intended us to be instruments of good to one another by living in society, and by instituting and obeying such laws as are essential to the being and welfare of civil communities.

3. The divine origin of government may be argued, analogically, from the constitution of the material universe. Look at the harmony of the visible creation. See its beauty, regularity, order. Every object is relative to a certain end, and these particular ends, though endlessly diversified, are so combined as to conspire to one general design. Notwithstanding the amazing variety, there is no confusion. The parts of the universe are so proportioned and balanced, that while each preserves its proper form, place, and motion, together they make an harmonious and beautiful whole.*

Such is the order which the Supreme Wisdom has established in the physical world. Can we contemplate this admirable constitution, and persuade ourselves, that the Deity has abandoned the moral world to chance and disorder? A wise being, in all his actions, proposes a reasonable end, and appoints the means necessary to effect it. The end which God has in view with respect to his creatures, is their perfection and happiness; and his plan must include every thing essential to such a design. Most evident is it to every reflecting mind, that the only agency adequate to the end in view, is the institution of civil society and government. Had the constitution of man been merely physical, God himself would have done whatever was expedient for the perfection of his work ; as, in fact, we see he has in the case

* Burlam. Prin. Nat. Law, Part ii., Chap. 1.

of the bee, the beaver, and the other creatures, whose motions are governed by pure instinct. But man is an intelligent being. He is capable of deliberation and choice. The means, therefore, by which the Deity designs him to be conducted to his end, must be adapted to his rational nature, which, as we have before shown, eminently fit him to become the subject of government and law.

4. These considerations acquire new force, when we attend to the consequences of the opposite doctrine. What would become of man, were every individual complete master of his own actions? Caprice and passion would then be his chief rules of conduct. In that case, most of our faculties would become quite useless. The powers of reason, judgment, reflection, prudence, conscience, and liberty of choice, form the true dignity of our nature. But to what purpose should we be endowed with these noble faculties, if we were always to yield to first impressions, and allowed ourselves to be evermore hurried away by the impulses of instinct or the force of blind inclinations? In the case supposed, the most exalted powers of the soul would not only be rendered futile, but would become hurtful by their very excellence; since the higher any faculty is, the more does the abuse of it become dangerous.*

To leave men wholly to themselves, is to leave an open field to the passions. Universal license would inevitably draw after it universal licentiousness. Injustice, violence, and perfidy would run riot. Without government, mankind would never emerge from the state of barbarism; nay, they would not even rise above the condition of wild beasts; and universal war, which Hobbes imagined to be the necessary consequence of the bad principles of human nature, when not held in check by despotism, would, indeed, become a terrible reality. We must, therefore, have recourse to other ideas. We must conclude, that God, having created man for

* Burlam. Prin. Nat. Law, Part ii., Chap. 2.

happiness, having implanted in. him a desire for it, having subjected him to the necessity of living in society, and having also inspired him with the love of order, intended, at the same time, that he should be subjected to the restraints of law.

5. This last observation contains a thought which deserves to be expanded into a distinct argument for the divine origin of government.

As there are, in physical science, certain axioms, which serve as the basis of all its deductions, so likewise, in moral and political science, there are certain elementary principles, which constitute the foundation of ethics and jurisprudence. These, in both cases, are termed first truths, because they carry their own evidence along with them, and form the ultimate basis of all reasoning. They are the dictate of pure reason, independently of all ratiocination. Hence, by an original law of our nature, we yield our assent to them the moment they are announced.

These first principles being discovered, all the consequences flowing from them by fair deduction, are as certain as the principles themselves. It is only necessary, that the premises and conclusions be properly connected; the whole business being to deduce the one from the other by a train of logical reasoning.

That the ultimate end of man is happiness: that happiness cannot consist in things inconsistent with his nature; that, to attain happiness, not only present good and evil must be considered, but also their consequences; that it is unreasonable to pursue a present good, which must issue in a greater evil, but quite reasonable to bear a present evil, which must issue in a greater good; that a higher good ought ever to be preferred to a lower one; and that order is more excellent than disorder; these are all first truths. They are of a nature to compel our assent.* They have the

* Burlam. Prin. Nat. Law, Part ii., Chap. 2.

same self-evident clearness and force, as the axioms of mathematical and physical science; such as that the whole is greater than any of its parts; that things which are equal to the same things are equal to one another; that every effect must be preceded by an adequate cause; and the like. These principles form a body of maxims, drawn from the nature of things. Being engraved on our heart by the Creator, whatever lessons they inculcate are a clear indication of his will. Whither, then, do they look? Plainly, to the establishment of civil government, as indispensable to the attainment of man's ultimate end. That end is happiness; for that was he formed and fashioned; and to that does he direct all his actions.

The true happiness of every being consists in the proper perfection of its nature. The road to a just development of human nature and the road to happiness are one and the same. When a particular system of means is adapted to perfect our nature, and another is not, it is evident that we are bound to choose the former and reject the latter. This is the clear verdict of reason; and the language of right reason is the voice of God. Now, nothing is more certain than that civil government is essential to the perfection of man's nature. It is, therefore, a necessary means to the attainment of his proper happiness. But that, as we have seen, in subordination, doubtless, to the divine glory, was the final cause of his creation. When reason, then, informs us, as she does, that the discipline of laws is an essential condition of human happiness, it is God himself who speaks to us in this inward oracle. Thereby he gives us clearly to understand, that government, being adapted to our nature and our needs, is, at the same time and for the same reason, agreeable to his will.

6. The contemplation of human society, as an able living divine* has well observed, leads directly to the contempla-

* See Rev. Dr. Lothrop's Sermon on the Death of the late Harrison Gray Otis.

tion and acknowledgment of God as its author. We look around us, and behold a vast multitude, whom no man can number. Their voice is like the sound of many waters, their movement like the roll of mighty thunderings. Of this mighty throng, we see each one thinking, contriving, and working chiefly for himself. When we consider the variety of human interests, the force of human passions, and the prevalence of human depravity, we wonder that chaos does not come back upon the social world. Yet, comparatively, it is but seldom that convulsions disturb the elements of social order. Men for the most part take their proper places in society with ease and contentment. This result is not achieved wholly by man's wisdom. It is produced, rather, by God's providence, appointing alike the good and the evil, which befal the individual and the race. Thus does the contemplation of society conduct our thoughts to God as its author; the being, who, amid all the fluctuations of human affairs, presides over mortal destinies, and reigns with an equal supremacy, in the armies of heaven and among the inhabitants of earth. Now, since human society is so manifestly embraced within the comprehensive purpose of the Creator, whatever agencies are essential to its successful working must be agreeable to his will. Of these agencies, government is clearly one ; and, indeed, it holds a conspicuous place among them.

7. Consider the nature and uses of civil government; and you shall confess its origin to be divine. A nation is a wonderful and a fearful thing. "A mighty moral mass, immortal in mortality." How much weakness to be helped ! How much ignorance to be taught ! How much misery to relieved ! What vast capacities to be developed and disciplined ! What complicated interests to be adjusted ! What folly, madness, and crime to be held in check ! What a sum of good to be achieved, and of evil to be prevented ! "Can there be any human measure of national

responsibility ? Can there be anything, short of creation, so
pregnant in results, as the national organization ? What
hand, unequal to the one, could have been trusted with the
other ? Who, that refers the first to God, will, in the other,
stop with man ? Where is the wisdom, short of God's, that
shall devise ? Where are the sanctions, short of God's, that
shall authenticate ? Where is the power, short of God's,
that shall sustain ? "*

8. I conclude this branch of the general argument in
support of the divine origin of government with a few
beautiful reflections of a heathen philosopher, bearing upon
the subject. " Nature," says Seneca,* " to make amends to
man for denying him those natural arms which she has
given to wild beasts, has endowed him with two things
which make him greatly their superior; I mean reason and
sociability. By these he who alone could make no resistance, becomes master of the whole. Society gives him an
empire over other animals. Society supplies him with
remedies in his diseases, assistance in his old age, and comfort in his pains and anxieties. Society enables him, as it
were, to bid defiance to fortune. Take away society, and
you destroy the union of mankind, on which the preservation and the whole happiness of life depend." Thus it
appears, that society is among the most precious of those
blessings, for which we are indebted to the divine benevolence. And can we believe, that the wisdom of God has
denied that which is essential to the enjoyment of a gift,
which his goodness has bestowed upon us ?

Such is the voice of reason in regard to the origin and
foundation of civil government. Let us now proceed to
inquire, secondly, what is the teaching of revelation on this
point ?

* Bishop Doane's Orat. before the N. J. Society of the Cincinnati, entitled
Civil Government a Sacred Trust from God.

* Cited in Barbeyrac's Int. to Puffendorf's Law of Nature and Nations.

Here the Bible holds a language both clear and emphatic. Its doctrine is, that God is the universal governor; that civil government is a sacred trust from him; that he rules in and by the civil magistrate; and that civil obedience is a religious obligation, a tribute due to heaven, because he ministers in the person of the ruler. The proof-texts, affirming these positions, are numerous, in both the Old Testament and the New. But we must content ourselves with a very few citations.

It is no dubious or feeble support of this theory, that the Spirit of inspiration has dignified magistrates with the title of "gods;" as he clearly has in Ps. 82: 1. "God standeth in the congregation of the mighty; he judgeth among the gods." The import of such an appellation deserves to be seriously weighed. It is a title which cannot imply less, than that civil rulers are invested with a divine authority, and are, in the exercise of their magistracies, the representatives and vicegerents of the divine majesty. Such seems to be our Savior's interpretation: "He called them gods, unto whom the word of God came." What is the meaning of the declaration, "the word of God came to them," if not, that they hold their commission from him?

The wisdom of God,—that divine being, who is elsewhere called the Word of God, and who is affirmed to be from the beginning, to be with God, and to be God,— declares, by the mouth of Solomon: "By me kings reign, and princes decree justice: by me princes rule, and nobles, yea, all the judges of the earth." What can be the meaning of this, but that the authority of all civil governors, whether in a monarchy or a republic,—patriarchs, kings, sultans, presidents, judges,—is in consequence of the appointment of God, who has been pleased to regulate and administer human affairs in this manner? Does it not indicate his presence and presidency in the enactment and execution of laws? It would be a frigid interpretation to say, that God reigns by kings and governors in the way of tolerance alone, and by merely withholding his interference. It is rather by the solemn institution and decree of his sovereignty.

Passing by innumerable other scripture testimonies to this point, which it were tedious to cite, we come to the celebrated passage in Paul's letter to the Roman Christians, in which the illustrious apostle discusses the subject of civil government in a full and formal manner, and declares his opinion in the most explicit terms. " Let every soul," says this inspired Christian philosopher and statist, " be subject unto the higher powers. For there is no power but of God; the powers that be are ordained of God. Whosoever, therefore, resisteth the power, resisteth the ordinance of God; and they that resist shall receive to themselves damnation (condemnation, punishment). For rulers are not a terror to good works, but to the evil. Wilt thou not be afraid of the power? Do that which is good, and thou shalt have praise of the same; for he is the minister of God to thee for good. But if thou do that which is evil, be afraid; for he beareth not the sword in vain. For he is the minister of God, a revenger to execute wrath upon him that doeth evil. Wherefore, ye must needs be subject, not only for wrath, but also for conscience' sake. For this cause pay ye tribute also; for they are God's ministers, attending continually upon this very thing. Render, therefore, to all their dues; tribute to whom tribute; custom to whom custom; fear to whom fear; honor to whom honor."*

Here the Bible theory of civil government is set forth with great perspicuity and power. The scriptural argument for its divine origin and sanction might be safely rested on this citation alone. It would be difficult to find, in the whole compass of human literature, a more pregnant passage; or one containing views on government more solid, rational, and conservative. It exhibits a complete theory

* Rom. 13 : 1–7.

of civil polity, in its fundamental principles; a theory which commends itself to every sober understanding and enlightened judgment by the common sense excellence of its leading maxims. The main points in the social theory of St. Paul, as here developed, are these following:—That government is a divine appointment, vs. 1, 2, 4, 6; that the civil magistrate is the minister of God, his representative and vicegerent, and that under every form of polity, vs. 4, 6; that the end of government is the good of the governed, vs. 3, 4; that the magistracy is invested with all needful power both of rewarding and punishing, vs. 2, 3, 4; that obedience to the civil power is a religious duty, vs. 1, 2, 3, 4; that conscience, more than fear, ought to constrain us to obedience, v. 5; that punishment is in its nature vindictive; it is a vindication of justice, and therefore not wholly for the determent of others from the like crimes, and still less for the mere reformation of the criminal himself, v. 4; and that those who serve the state in the magistracy are entitled, in return, to support and honor, from those over whom they are placed, v. 7.

We are, next, to inquire, what is the voice of human authority as to the divine origin and authority of government?

The theory, which traces the institution of society and government up to the will of God, and which we have shown to be suggested by reason and confirmed by revelation, has united the voices of the best and wisest of men in all times and countries. The idea was very general in ancient times, that divine authority was indispensable to the establishment of laws over a people. We see this very plainly in the care taken by all the lawgivers of antiquity to impress upon those for whom they legislated the belief that they were under a divine inspiration. Nor was this idea confined to rude and barbarous tribes, but appears to have been most widely diffused in those nations where the refinements of civilization had made the greatest advances; as among the

Persians, Egyptians, Greeks, and Romans. This was a fiction, no doubt; but the universality of it, and the ready assent which mankind yielded to it, may be received as evidence of the truth, so clearly made known in the Scriptures, that "the powers that be are ordained of God;"* i. e. that civil laws have their origin in his will, and their sanction from his authority.

There is a general concurrence among moral and political philosophers in the doctrine, that civil government is founded on the will of God. Bishop Horsley speaks of "the principle of subjection" to civil power as "a conscientious submission to the will of God."† "The reason why we should be subject to magistrates," says Calvin, "is because they are appointed by the ordinance of God. Since it has pleased God so to administer the government of this world, he who resists their power, strives against the divine ordinance, and so fights against God. Because to disregard his providence, who is the author of civil government, is to go to war with him."‡ "That all lawful dominion, considered in the abstract," says Archbishop Bramhall, "is from God, no man can make any doubt."§ On this subject the profoundly philosophic Bishop Butler speaks thus: "Civil government is that part of God's government over the world, which he exercises by the instrumentality of men. Considering that all power is of God, all authority is properly of divine appointment; men's very living under magistracy might naturally have led them to the contemplation of authority in its source and origin, the one supreme authority of Almighty God."|| "All dominion over man," says the great Edmund Burke, "is the effect of the divine disposition. It is bound by the eternal laws of him that

* Rom. xiii., 1.
† Sermon 44, Rivington's edition, 1824, cited by Bishop Doane.
‡ Commentary on Rom. xiii., 1.
§ *Serpent Salve.* "Archb. Bramhall's Works," vol. iii., p. 317, cited by Doane. || Sermon before the House of Lords.

gave it, with which no human authority can dispense; neither he that exercises it, nor even those who are subject to it. * * * * * We are all born in subjection, all born equally, high and low, governors and governed, in subjection to one great, immutable, pre-existent law, prior to all our devices and all our contrivances, paramount to all our ideas and all our sensations, antecedent to our very existence, by which we are knit and connected in the eternal frame of the universe, and out of which we cannot stir. This great law does not arise out of our conventions or compacts; on the contrary, it gives to our compacts and conventions all the force and sanction they can have."

Besides the writers whose opinions are here adduced, many other illustrious masters of political science, as Plato, Heraclitus, Aristotle, Cicero, Grotius, Puffendorf, Burlamaqui, and Blackstone,† have represented civil government as founded in the will and purpose of the Deity. Nor is this a slender support. For, although it were impious, as well as irrational, to attach to mere human opinions any thing like infallibility, yet deference to the authority of good and great minds is but the testimony of a reverent and grateful spirit to high intellectual and moral worth. Indeed, with the bulk of mankind, authority seems little less than a necessity. The light which they find not in themselves, they instinctively seek in others. The existence of oracles, from ancient Dodona to modern Rome, attests this fact.

* WORKS, v. iii., p. 116, *Little & Brown.*

† Most of these, with others, are cited by Barbeyrac in his Introd. to Puffendorf, Plato says: "All laws came from God; no mortal man was the founder of laws." Aristotle adopted the theory of his master, Plato. Heraclitus, in Stobaeus, affirms, "All human laws are nourished by one divine law." Cicero delivers the opinion that "law is nothing else but right reason, derived from the Divinity, and government an emanation of the divine mind." Special citations are not needful from the other writers named in the text, as their political writings are pervaded with this sentiment.

Our earliest opinicns are all formed in this way. In child-hood the voice of the parent is the voice of God. Nor is authority, at any period of life, to be looked upon as incom-patible with free thinking. Doubtless, it is capable of being abused; as what good thing is not? Yet when rightly used it is a law to the seeing, as well as a guide to the blind. While it forms, as it were, a safe-conduct to persons of dor-mant intellect, it affords, at the same time, to the awakened but unsettled mind a centre of reference amid the multitude of its own thoughts, a centre of rest amid the conflict of its own volitions.*

Thus it appears, that reason, revelation, and the best human authority bear concurrent testimony to the divine ori-gin and foundation of civil polity and laws. But the divine basis of government, and the divine right on the part of any particular individuals, of instituting and administering gov-ernment, are questions totally distinct in their nature; though they have often been confounded by such advocates of arbitrary power as Sir Robert Filmer, and by such tyrants as King James the second. Neither is every divine institu-tion of exactly the same sort. God has instituted a Church, a ministry, a Sabbath, and a special public worship of him-self. He has also instituted civil society and civil govern-ment; but in another manner. The former of these institu-tions are by positive enactment, the latter, by deduction of right reason. To a knowledge of the former as of divine authority, we are conducted by revelation alone; to a know-ledge of the latter as originating in the divine will and en-joying the divine sanction, we are conducted by the light of nature, as well as by the light of revealed truth.

"The powers that be are ordained of God."† Undoubt-edly they are. But let us beware of drawing false inferences

* See Rev. Mr. Hedge's Oration before the Phi Beta Kappa Society, Harvard University.
† Rom. xiii. 1.

from the use of the word "ordained" in this passage. The
reference is rather to the sanction, than the source, of civil
authority. The term is not designed here to instruct us as
to the immediate origin of civil power, but rather to inform
us, that government is agreeable to the will of God, as being
an essential agency in carrying out his purpose with respect
to human happiness.

God has "ordained" certain things as the conditions of
health, reputation, and success in business, as truly as he has
" ordained the powers that be." And we discover these
several divine ordinances in the same manner, viz., by the
use of enlightened reason. God has also " ordained" baptism, preaching, and the sacramental supper. But both the
mode of ordination and the manner of discovering it, are,
in the two classes of cases, quite different. In regard to
these last-mentioned " ordinances," and various other divine
appointments, it is revelation alone, that enables us to know
what is the will of God. But concerning many things we
have no such mode of ascertaining the purpose of Deity;
and yet may the divine will be as clearly known in these,
as in the other cases. " Not those things alone are from
God," says Puffendorf, laying down a just principle with
great clearness and felicity of diction, " not those things
alone are from God, which he institutes and ordains by his
own immediate act, without the concurrence or interposition
of men ; but those likewise, which men themselves, by the
guidance of good reason, according as the different circumstances of times and places required, have taken up, in order
to the fulfillment of some obligation laid upon them by God's
command."*

When God created man, he established certain immutable
laws, commonly called the laws of nature, by which man
was to regulate his conduct in all things. These laws were
to serve him as guides in the pursuit of happiness. That

* "Law of Nature and Nations," L. 7. c. 3, § 2.

man might be enabled to discover and apply the laws of nature, he was endowed by the Creator with the faculty of reason. Among the laws or principles of reason here referred to, are these following:—That we should live honorably; that we should hurt nobody; that we should render to all their dues; that we should seek the good of our fellows: and, to this end, that we should institute societies, establish governments, and ordain laws. And all these, society, government, law, are, at the same time, truly divine and truly human institutions. They are divine, inasmuch as they are essential agencies in carrying out the divine purpose in the creation of man. They are human, inasmuch as they are instituted and administered by men, without any special and immediate interposition of the Deity.

This view of civil government, as at the same time of divine and human appointment, is agreeable to the explicit teaching of God's word. It harmonizes in a simple, natural, and satisfactory manner, two passages of scripture, which, to superficial thinkers, would seem at variance with each other. St. Paul declares, "The powers that be are ordained of God."* St. Peter exhorts: "Submit yourselves to every ordinance of man."† The former of these inspired writers represents government as an ordinance of God; the latter, as an ordinance of man. What have we here, then? One divine inspiration contradicting another divine inspiration? Not in the least. Are the two apostles inconsistent with each other in their doctrine? No, in no wise. They look at government from different stand-points. They exhibit it in different relations. St. Paul would hold up to our view, and enforce upon the conscience, the divine sanction of all government; St. Peter, the duty of obedience to the actually existing government. The reference of Paul is to the remote and ultimate foundation of civil polity; the reference of Peter to that which is more directly and immediately so.

---

* Rom. xiii. 1. † 1 Pet. ii. 13.

3

34 INTRODUCTORY ESSAY.

The one contemplates government in the root; the other in the bough; the one, in the fountain; the other, in the stream. Archbishop Bramhall and Bishop Sanderson harmonize these passages in the following manner. Says the former of these prelates: "The essence of power is always from God; the existence, sometimes from God, sometimes from man."* The latter going more fully into the subject, holds this language: "The substance of the power of every magistrate is the ordinance of God; but the specification of the circumstances thereto belonging, as in regard of places, persons, titles, continuance, jurisdiction, subordination, and the rest, is a human ordinance, introduced by custom or positive law."†

Pertinent to this point, and throwing light on the twofold origin of government here contended for, are the following reflections from that eminent prelate, Bishop Horsley: "The principles which I advance, ascribe no greater sanctity to monarchy, than to any other form of established government; nor do they at all involve the exploded notion, that all or any of the sovereigns of earth hold their sovereignty by virtue of such immediate or implied nomination, on the part of God, of themselves personally, or of the stocks from which they are descended, as might confer an endless, indefeasible right on their posterity. In contending that government was coeval with mankind, it will readily be admitted, that all particular forms of government which now exist are the work of human policy, under the control of God's overruling providence; * * * * * but it is contended, that all government is in such sort of divine institution, that, be the form of any particular government what it may, the submission of the individual is a principal branch of that religious duty which each man owes to God. In governments, of whatever denomination, if the form of gov-

* WORKS, v. iii., p. 317.
† "Serm. ad Magistr." p. 110, cited by Bloomfield, on 1 Pet. ii. 13.

ernment undergo a change, or the established rule of succession be set aside by any violent or necessary revolution,
the act of the nation itself is necessary to erect a new sovereignty, or to transfer the old right to the new possessor.
* * * * * * * Of all sovereigns none reign by so fair and
just a title, as those who can derive their claim from such
public act of the nation which they govern. * * * * The
obligation to obedience proceeds, primarily, from the will of
God; secondarily, from the act of man."* Dr. Jortin,†
another eminent and learned divine of the Church of England, has embodied the same opinion in one short, but luminous sentence : "Government, both in Church and State, is
of God; the forms of it are of men."

Hence, although the ultimate source of civil government
is the divine will, the immediate source of it may be, and
certainly is, quite another thing. God has instituted no particular species of civil polity for all mankind, nor invested
any particular persons with authority over their fellows.
All forms of polity, not subversive of the true ends of government, the preservation, perfection, and happiness of man,
are agreeable to his will. All civil rulers, kings, consuls,
senators, presidents, governors, representative assemblies,
and the whole body of the people exercising the functions
of sovereignty, are equally his vicegerents, his ministers,
ruling in his place, bearing the sword for him.

It is, therefore, quite proper to inquire into the origin of
political government and the sources of political power, as
things of human contrivance and purpose, without any reference to that divine sanction, which, by the law of nature,
as well as the law of revelation, will inevitably attach itself
to political institutions, as soon as they are formed and put
into operation. Nor is such an inquiry justly open to the
charge of irreligion. For, as Puffendorf has truly observed,

* Sermon 44, Rivington's Edition.
† Cited by "Dr. Miller on the Christian Ministry," c. 1.

"he who affirms sovereignty to result immediately from compact, doth not in the least detract from the sacred character of civil government, or maintain that princes bear rule by human right only, not by divine."*

It is proper here to distinguish between natural society and civil society. If it be contended that no such distinction has ever existed in point of fact, this, if true, does not hinder from making it an object of thought. When God made man, he made him for society. He endowed him with sociability. He subjected him to the necessity of living in community. But he gave no man civil power over other men. The family is, indeed, a divine institution; and the father is, by divine right, invested with a power of command over his children. But parental authority is not civil authority. Nor is it, perhaps, possible now to determine how far the existence of civil laws, and consequently of civil society, would have been necessary, had man never fallen. So far, at least, is certain, that the necessity of civil laws results, if not wholly, yet in good part, from the wickedness of mankind. The sense of obligation to divine law is not enough to keep men from injustice. Hence human law must supervene to hold their bad passions in check. Public force must take the place of individual conscience. Men must be restrained in the use of that liberty, which but for their depravity, they might, perhaps, have enjoyed without curtailment. Natural society, then, is a state, where, so far as civil authority is concerned, all are equal, all independent, all free; a state, where none possess the right to command, and none are under the obligation to obey. Civil society destroys this equality, abridges this independence, curtails this freedom. It may be defined to be, the union of a multitude of people, who agree to live in subjection to government, in order to secure, through its protection and care, the happiness for which they were created, which they natu-

* "Law of Nature and Nations," L. 7, C. 3, § 1.

rally desire, and which they cannot procure in any other way.

The actual commencement of civil communities, as an historical fact, is forever lost in the darkness of antiquity. Some plausible guesses are all that the most sagacious minds have ever been able to achieve in their search of it. Some attribute the origin of civil society to parental authority; some, to mutual distrust and dread; and some, to ambition, supported by force of arms, or force of genius. These are the principal conjectures of writers concerning the origin of political unions. There is nothing in them, on which the mind can settle, in the conviction that it has attained to truth. It is quite probable, that, in the first institution of civil societies, mankind sought relief from vio- lence and injustice, rather than the several advantages arising from established laws, such as commerce, letters, sciences, arts, and the various other social improvements, in which a high civilization consists. It is equally probable, that pater- nal authority, with the many advantages flowing from the family relation, suggested the first idea, and afforded the earliest model of political organizations. It is still more probable, as appears from the history of Nimrod, that am- bition had no little agency in the early establishment of governments among men. But, however these things may be, all the analogies of human affairs attest, that the bodies politic first formed were not such as we see now existing. All human institutions are imperfect in their beginnings. Improvement is ever a work of time. The progress from rudeness to perfection is commonly by slow degrees. Gov- ernment does not form an exception to this rule. Civil law at first was very imperfect. Jurisprudence was not formed into a regular system at once. No human sagacity could foresee everything; and new occasions would continually demand the enactment of new laws. The earliest states, therefore, were, in all probability, small in extent, and simple in polity. Kings were mere chieftains, possessing very limited powers. They were often appointed to act simply as arbiters in disputes, or leaders in war. Hence, in the most ancient histories, we sometimes read of several kings in the same nation at the same time. A small city, a town, a few leagues of territory, were honored with the name of kingdom. There were no less than thirty-one kings in the little territory of Palestine, at the time of the Hebrew Conquest.*

But such questions afford matter rather of curious speculation, than of practical utility. The point of real importance is : What is the true source of political government? What the true basis of political power? What the true foundation of political sovereignty?

Nor let any one imagine, that these are adjudicated questions. The fact is quite otherwise. Not only is the original institution of government veiled in darkness, but the legitimate sources and limits of its authority are matters yet in dispute. The late Alexander Everett, a statesman and scholar of no mean repute, in an Essay on the Life and Writings of Rousseau, says : "The theory of a social contract, though somewhat plausible at first view, does not bear the test of examination, and is rarely admitted at the present day by competent judges."† A declaration this the more remarkable, as it is unsustained by a single word of argument, and is in direct contradiction to the express doctrine of the constitution of Massachusetts, of which state Mr. Everett was a citizen. The Bishop of New Jersey, in an able, and for the most part, admirable oration, pronounced before the New Jersey Society of the Cincinnati, and entitled "Civil Government, a Sacred Trust from God," declares, that "the social compact, which men talk of, was never entered into."‡

* Josh. xii. 24. Homer mentions several kings of the Pheacians, Odyss. L. 8, vs. 40, 41. Goguet (Origin of Laws, B. 1.)

† Essays of Alexander Everett.   ‡ P. 14.

He, too, contents himself with the naked assertion, without adducing a single proof or authority to support it. A distinguished divine of Boston, in a discourse before the Massachusetts Legislature on the Religious Theory of Civil Government, has, not obscurely, broached the doctrine, that the Divine will is the immediate source of civil power; that it is anti-christian to regard the people as the fountain of civil authority; and that the theory of civil society, known as the social compact, is, to use his own words, "negatively atheistic."*

There is, perhaps, a growing indisposition in the clergy to admit the doctrine of the social compact, as the true theory of civil government. This has arisen from an apprehension,—a mistaken apprehension certainly,—that the tendency of the theory is to undermine, or, at least, to weaken the religious obligation of civil obedience. There is no doubt, that much that is erroneous concerning both the nature and the sanctions of civil government, is taught under the name of the social compact. Some, for instance, suppose and teach, that civil society, in its associated capacity, can possess no power, which does not, while the state of nature lasts, actually belong to men, in their personal capacity. They suppose and teach, that individuals can give to the community no power which they do not individually possess. From such a view of the social compact it would follow, that, as no individual has the right to take his own life, civil society can have no such right. There has been, be-, cause there could be, no grant of such power from the persons composing the state. Thus, the fact that suicide is a sin, becomes an argument against capital punishment.

But this, as will appear in the sequel, is an abuse of the doctrine which we are considering. The theory as thus presented, is distorted either by ignorance or cunning. When correctly exhibited, it inculcates no such view as this. It

* Rev. Dr. Alexander H. Vinton's Election Sermon, 1848, passim.

does not deny that civil government is an ordinance of God. It does not repudiate a religious sanction as attaching to civil authority. It does not question the doctrine, that obedience to civil laws is a religious duty. It does not in the least detract from the dignity and sacredness of civil government as a divine institution. It does not deny the divine right of government; but it does deny the divine right of kings, considered as persons, and not as powers. It denies an original divine title to civil power, in any man, or any set of men. It denies the divine right of an absolute and unquestionable administration of government. It hurls its iron gauntlet against such a comprehensive charter of despotism as this doctrine would establish. It thunders its defiance against the monarchs who would thus create a saturnalia for themselves, laying the cost of it in human blood and freedom.

Let us inquire into these things. There can be but two theories on this subject. The sovereign authority in a state must be derived directly either from God or the people. Observe, that the question here is not concerning the remote origin of government. It is not concerning the ultimate foundation of government. It is not concerning the sanction of government. All these are, in the strictest sense, divine. The question is concerning the proximate source of civil power,—whether it is in God, or in the will and act of the nation.

It must be kept in mind, that there are but two possible sources of civil power, viz., God and the people. The question is, from which of these does the magistrate immediately receive his authority? Not, surely, from God. God does not designate the rulers of nations by special revelation; neither does he set distinguishing marks of dominion upon some men, and of subjection upon others. "He does not," as Sidney has forcibly said, "cause some to be born with crowns upon their heads, and others with saddles on their backs."*

There must, therefore, be a real and proper sense in which it may be affirmed, that the people are the fountain of political power;† that political sovereignty resides in them, as its spring and source ;‡ that the immediate original of sovereign authority is in human covenants ;§ that it is competent for the people to retain, or to transfer it; that, in short, they are the sole judges of the forms they will give to their commonwealths, and of the powers and limitations of power which they will establish in them.

My ideas on these points can be best explained by an imaginary case. Let us suppose a hundred persons to have taken possession of an unappropriated island. Each is, by supposition, independent of the others. They stand upon a footing of entire equality. The old maxim,—"*par in parem non habet imperium*,"—equals have no authority over one another,—is in full force. No one of the hundred possesses any right of command over the others; no one of them is subject to any obligation of obedience. This, then, is the state of nature; wherein all are in the full enjoyment of what is called natural liberty ; that is to say, the right of doing each what he pleases; subject only to the restraints imposed by the law of nature.

Manifestly, this is a state of things not long to be endured while human passions continue what they are. The power of acting as each one thinks fit, is inconsistent with security in any of the enjoyments of life.¶ It will soon, therefore, be found expedient, if not imperative, to enter into some compact, whereby individuals may be protected in those absolute rights which are vested in them by the immutable

* Discourses on Government, Chap. 3, Sect. 33.
† Adams' Defence of American Constitutions.
‡ Burlamaqui's " Politic Law," Part 1, Chap. 6.
§ Ibidem.
¶ Blackstone's Commentaries, Book 1, Chap. 1.

laws of nature. In other words, it will become necessary to institute civil society.

What, under these circumstances, will be the probable course of things? First, these isolated individuals must agree, each with each, to join in one firm and lasting society, and to concert the measures of their mutual safety and welfare. Here will be the germ and first rudiments of a state. The next step will be to agree upon some form of polity. Here, it is quite plain, they may settle their new commonwealth upon any basis and give it any form they like best. They may institute a monarchy, an aristocracy, a democracy, or a government compounded out of all three. This labor done, the state begins to assume a definite and fixed form. A further advance will be the choice of such magistrates as may have been agreed upon. A covenant— it matters not whether it be express or implied—between the governors and the governed, whereby the former bind themselves to take care of the common defence and welfare, and the latter to yield obedience to them in the exercise of their rightful authority, gives completeness and perfection to the state.* This last covenant includes the subjection of the will of each individual member of the society to the will of the head, so far as the public good requires; whether such head be a single person, one or more councils of sages, or the assembled people.† And thus it is, that a regular state and a perfect government are formed.

The state has now become, by this submission and union of wills, a moral person; invested with personal attributes; enjoying personal rights; subject to personal obligations; and capable of deliberating, resolving, and acting in a personal capacity. It is no longer a mere multitude. It is not an assemblage of individuals without any common will. It is a body politic. It is a society animated by one soul,

---

* Puffendorf's " Law of Nature and Nations," Lib. 7, C. 2.
† Burlamaqui's " Politic Law," Part 1, Chap. 4.

which directs all its motions and makes all its members act with a view to one and the same end,—the public utility. Neither is the personality of the state in the least affected, whether this union of wills be brought about by the appointment of one man to be the sovereign, by the institution of a council or councils of senators, or by a majority of voices in a general assembly of the people. It is still a unit, and not an aggregate. It is an organized product, having an internal vitality, working its own growth and ripeness, though dependent, all the while, in its organic capacity on that great Being, who is the founder of nations, no less than the Creator of man.

Now, in the case which I have supposed, the origination of the society, the form of polity, the choice of magistrates, the powers confided to them, the qualifications for office, the conditions of surrendering it, the duration of the magistracies, and, in brief, the entire constitution of the state, are the direct result of the action of the people. Is not the popular will, then, the immediate origin of the government? Is it not the direct source of power in those who administer it? When a man gets from me something to which he had before no claim, and which he could not have obtained otherwise than through me, then am I, clearly, the immediate source of that possession to him. Suppose A buys a piece of land of B. The title being before truly in B, B is to A the immediate source of his right to the property in question; and this, notwithstanding the general right of property has its foundation in the will of God. So if a dozen men of the hundred become, through the action of the hundred, invested with a right of command, which before they possessed not, then are the hundred the immediate fountain of such their authority, though it be admitted, as it freely is, that the will of God is the remote source and the ultimate basis of it.

This, now, is the social compact. Mr. Locke is not, as

many suppose, the author of this theory of government. On the contrary, its essential principles have been held by the most illustrious political philosophers of all ages.

Plato defines a law to be "a public ordinance of the body of the state;" meaning thereby, the whole people. He makes the foundation of the state to be "a tacit agreement between each member and the whole community," and declares that "they who refuse to submit to the laws, violate the agreement."*

Aristotle founds his politics on nearly the same principles with those of his master. "The civil law," he says, "is that which takes place amongst a number of free persons, who are members of the same community, in which they live on a footing of equality, either pure and simple, or proportionable."†

Apuleius, from the authority of Plato himself, defining the Platonic commonwealth as the most perfect model of government, calls it "a union of many men, in which some govern and some are governed, but all agree and mutually assist each other, guiding themselves in their duty by the same laws."‡

Livy declares "the force of the supreme command to be built upon the consent of those who obey."§

Cicero, with his usual exactness and felicity, defines a state to be "a multitude of people, united together by common laws, a common interest, and a common consent."‖

To the same effect is the definition of Puffendorf. It is this: "A civil state is a compound moral person, whose will united and tied together by those covenants, which before

---

* De Leg. L. 1. See also "Dacier's Life of Plato," pp. 90, 91 ; Barbeyrac's Historical and Critical Account of the Science of Morality, § 21.

† Barbeyrac's Historical and Critical Account of the Science of Morality, § 24.

‡ Puffend. "Law of Nature and Nations," Lib. 7. c. 2.

§ Hist. Lib. 2, c. 59.   De Rep. L. 3.

passed among the multitude, is deemed the will of all, to the end that it may maintain the common peace and security."*

Grotius declares his opinion concerning the original of government thus: "Men, not influenced by the express command of God, but of their own accord, having experienced the weak defence of separate families against the assaults of violence, united themselves in civil society, the effect of which was civil power, styled, on this account, by St. Peter, the ordinance of man."†

Montesquieu, quoting Gravina with approbation, says: "The conjunction of the particular forces of individuals constitutes what we call a political state. The particular forces of individuals cannot be united without a conjunction of all their wills. The conjunction of those wills is what we call the civil state."‡

Blackstone, though he rejects the theory of an actually existing unconnected state of nature, nevertheless admits an "original contract of society," concerning which he makes the following observation; "This contract, though perhaps in no instance has it ever been formally expressed at the first institution of a state, yet in nature and reason must be always understood and implied, in the very act of associating together: namely, that the whole should protect all its parts, and that every part should pay obedience to the will of the whole; or, in other words, that the community should guard the rights of each individual member, and that, in return for this protection, each individual should submit to the laws of the community."§

The elder Adams, one of the most solid and sagacious of political writers, in his Review of "Nedham's Right Consti-

* "Law of Nature and Nations," Lib. 7, Cap. 2.
† "Right of War and Peace," Lib. 4, § 7.
‡ "Spirit of Laws," B. 1. c. 3.
§ Comment. Bk. 1. c. 6.

tution of a Commonwealth," among many other things to the
same effect, has the following : "If ever that excellent
maxim, that the fountain of all just power and government
is in the people, was fully demonstrated and exemplified
among men, it was in the late American revolution, when
thirteen governments were taken down from the foundation, and new ones erected wholly by the people, as an arch-
itect would pull down an old building, and erect a new
one."*

It would be tedious to proceed with these citations, though
to multiply them were an easy task. For not only the
authors above-cited, but also Harrington, Milton, Bacon,
Sidney, Locke, Barbeyrac, Burlamaqui, Turgot, Neckar, and
our own statesmen and publicists almost without exception,
have held to the doctrine of the social compact, as the true
theory of political organizations.

It is objected to this theory of a social compact, that it is
"historically untrue."† That depends upon the meaning we
attach to the phrase, " historically untrue." If by this expression be meant simply, that there is no authentic account
of the first governments instituted among men, in which the
social compact can be historically traced, I assent to the proposition. But then, for the very same reason, every other
theory of civil society must be also "historically untrue ;"
for the origin of all the earliest polities is involved in the
same impenetrable darkness of antiquity. If, on the other
hand, it be intended to assert, that no civil community has
ever been instituted on the basis of express compact, we will
interrogate history on that point.

But before entering on this inquiry, let it be observed, that
none of the advocates of the social compact, in presenting
their ideas concerning the first formation of governments,

* " Defence of American Constitution," v. 3. p. 365.

† Dr. Vinton's Elect. Sermon on the Religious Theory of Civil Government, p. 16.

are to be understood as writing, or intending to write history. They have but propounded a philosophical theory in a lively way. Every state must have had a beginning; and since it is impossible to conceive how any union could be formed without covenants, we must believe, that such covenants were, tacitly, if not formally, entered into in the institution of commonwealths. To express this conviction in a graphic manner, theoretical writers have imagined what might have happened, and what substantially must have happened, when men first formed themselves into political unions. "Nor is there anything to hinder," as Puffendorf has truly said, "but that the original of some things, not committed to the monuments of time and history, may be traced out by the disquisitions of reason."* But probably neither Locke, nor Sidney, nor any other rational writer, supposed there was once a time when no such thing as society existed; and, that, from the impulse of reason and the sense of their own wants, individuals met together in a large plain, entered into an original formal contract, and chose the tallest man present to be their governor.

Thus much by way of apology for certain writers, who have not always, perhaps, been sufficiently careful to distinguish between actual history and what they have themselves rationally imagined. Let us now glance at the social compact in an historical point of view. Let us inquire whether, in point of fact, states have ever been formally established upon this basis.

The reader is first invited to the study of a piece of history, to which he will, perhaps, hardly expect to have his attention called; but which, on examination, will be found, unless I am mistaken, both pertinent and instructive. It is contained in the nineteenth chapter of Exodus, where the historian gives an account of the origin of the Hebrew government. Unless my analysis of the transaction there re-

* "Law of Nature and Nations," Lib. 7, Cap. 2, § 8.

corded be erroneous, we shall find in it the substantial elements of the social compact. Proceed we to this analysis.

Moses is solemnly summoned to Mount Sinai.* There he receives a commission to propose Jehovah to the Hebrew people, as the civil head of their state.† Descending from the mount, he assembles the head men, called " elders of the people." In due form he submits the proposition to the convention as from Jehovah.‡ Thereupon the meeting formally gives its assent, in the name and behalf of the nation.§ Moses then re-ascends the mount, and returns "the words of the people to Jehovah;" that is, carries their official reply to him, a reply made by the people through their representatives, the " elders."‖ Having thus received formal assurance of the willingness of the people to meet his proposal, Jehovah completes the covenant by acceding to it in a manner equally formal. This he does by replying to Moses, as the nation's plenipotentiary and representative. " Lo I come unto thee in a thick cloud, that the people may hear when I speak with thee."¶

Now, what have we here? To all intents and purposes, the social compact. Here is a multitude of people, each covenanting with each to unite together and form a civil community to be governed by common laws. Here is a partial settlement of the form of the commonwealth. Here is an assent by the people to the rule of a lawgiver and head, formally proposed to their election. Here is a covenant between the sovereign thus chosen and each member of the society, in which the former promises protection, and the latter submission and obedience. Hence Jahn denominates this transaction " a great and solemn compact."** between Jehovah, as sovereign, and the Hebrew people, as subjects.

* Verse 3.   † Verses 3–6.   ‡ Verse 7.
§ Verse 8,   ‖ Verse 8.   ¶ Verse 9.
** Hebrew Commonwealth, chap. 2.

Hence, Dean Graves* speaks of it as a "solemn compact," on which, he says, " was founded the Jewish government." Hence, Lowman calls it the " original contract of the Hebrew government."† Hence Michaelis‡ and our own Dr. Spring,§ speak of the election of Jehovah to be the king of the Hebrews, as the voluntary act of the Hebrew people. Hence, also, Warburton says, that " the crime of idolatry is always represented by the sacred writers as, in a peculiar sense, the transgression of the covenant;"‖ that is, the original compact of government between God and the Hebrew people. And hence even Bossuet¶ himself, though the apologist and apostle of despotic power, says, that " the law of Moses is a true social compact," (véritable contrat social); and that " all who have spoken accurately of the law, have regarded it, in its origin, as a solemn pact and treaty," (pacte et traité solennel). It was thus that idolatry became, in the Hebrew state, a civil crime ; the crime, in fact, of treason ; for as God was, by the compact which we have been considering, constituted king of the Hebrews, a defection from him was a defection from their rightful sovereign.**

Here I cannot but recal a conversation which I had some years ago, with that eminent scholar and statesman, the late John Quincy Adams. In it, he drew, with a luminousness and power peculiar to himself, a contrast between the Hebrew government and the other ancient oriental polities. Point by point, did he unfold, with copious eloquence, the differences between them. But that which he chiefly insisted on, was the fact, that all the rest were founded on

* " On the Pentateuch," Pt. 2, Sec. 3.
† " Civil Government of the Hebrews."
‡ " Commentary on Laws of Moses," Vol. 1, Art. 34.
§ " Obligations of the World to the Bible," Lect. 3.
‖ " Divine Legation," B. 5, S. 2.
¶ "Politique Sacrée," Liv. 1, Art. 4.
** Jahn's Hebrew Commonwealth, chap. 2. Dr. Vinton himself says : " The Theocracy was elective." Elect. Serm., p. 18.

4

force, this only on consent. I have regretted since, that I did not ask him to commit those views to writing; and I cannot but indulge the hope, that the subject will somewhere be found alluded to at least, if not handled at length, in his posthumous papers.

The reader's attention is invited, in passing, to one point of special interest in the narrative, which I have been analyzing and commenting upon. The seventh verse of the chapter states, that "Moses called for the elders of the people," and laid the divine proposal before them. It is immediately added, in the eighth verse: "And all the people answered together, and said, all that Jehovah hath spoken we will do." How did the people answer in this case? No otherwise than by their representatives, the "elders." This is the first intimation we find in history of the doctrine of popular representation. Does it not prove Montesquieu* to be mistaken in the supposition, that representation is an improvement in the art of government, invented by the moderns, and unknown to the ancient world? The first act in the institution of the Hebrew state opens upon us, with this doctrine, to all appearance, in full play. On the practice of representation in the Israelitish government, I shall have more to say in a subsequent part of this work. The error of Montesquieu in saying, that "the ancients had no notion of a government founded on a legislative body composed of the representatives of the people," will then more plainly appear.

Proceeding in our research, we come down to the Roman commonwealth. The original of the Roman government was, clearly, in a voluntary convention among equals. First, a number of men flock together on the banks of the Tiber, with the design of forming themselves into a civil society. Here, obviously, there must have been a tacit, if not a formal covenant between them to that effect. Then,

* "Spirit of Laws," B. 11, C. 8.

they deliberate about the form they shall give to their new government, and agree upon establishing a monarchy. This done, the work is completed by electing Romulus for their king, and investing him with the sovereignty; a procedure which necessarily implies a mutual promise, viz., of protection on the one hand, and of obedience on the other.* Here, then, we have a state manifestly founded on voluntary convention; and the theory of the social compact has, in the Roman polity, a solid historical basis to rest upon.

The Venetian state had a like origin. It began by the union of several persons, before free and independent, among whom, previously to compact, there was neither superiority nor subjection.†

The same is true of the founders of Carthage. They also were freemen. They were wholly independent of one another. The footing on which they stood was that of entire equality. And the government which they set up, was by their own consent. It was the result of deliberation and compact.‡

Something like this is related by Herodotus to have happened even in Persia, during the interregnum which preceded the elevation of Darius to the throne. The nobles debate on the comparative advantages of democracy, aristocracy, and monarchy; and the monarchical principle triumphs by the majority of voices.§

Bracton was an eminent British lawyer, who wrote under Henry III. He lays it down as a principle of the British constitution, that the king is subject to the law. The reason which he assigns as the basis of this maxim is, that "the law maketh the king."‖ From this he draws the inference, as solid as it is liberal, that "he is not truly king, where will and pleasure rules, and not the law." Two centuries

* Livy, Lib. 1. Dionys. Halicarn. Lib. 2.
† Locke on Civil Government, Chap. 7, § 110.
‡ Justin. Lib. 3, Cap. 4.   § Herod, l. 4. c, 44.
‖ Cited by Blackstone, Commentaries, Book 1, Chap. 6.

later, Fortescue, having first accurately distinguished between a government introduced by conquest and violence, and a government arising from mutual consent, affirms, that the British monarchy belongs to the latter of these two species of polity. He then proceeds to lay down the principle, that "the king of England must rule his people according to the decrees of the laws thereof."* To obviate all doubt on this question, it is expressly declared by statute 12 and 13 William III., C. 2, "that the laws of England are the birth-right of the people thereof; and all the kings and queens, who shall ascend the throne of this realm, ought to administer the government of the same according to the said laws." Blackstone declares, that this is not only consonant to the principles of nature, of liberty, of reason, and of society, but has always been esteemed an express part of the common law of England, even when prerogative was at its highest. The same great authority pronounces the coronation oath, prescribed by the laws of England to the British sovereign on ascending the throne, to be, most indisputably, a fundamental and original express contract.†

Such are the opinions which have been held by the ablest British lawyers, jurists, and statesmen, concerning the nature of the British constitution. They agree in representing the government of their country as a government arising from mutual consent; a government based upon compact; a government drawing its life and energy from the popular will.

It has always been the doctrine of the English whigs, that the foundation of the English government was a contract, expressed on one side by the coronation oath, and on the other by the oath of allegiance; that the duties of this contract were mutual; and that a sovereign who grossly abused his power, might lawfully be dethroned by his

* Cited by Blackstone.
† Commentaries, Book 1, Chap. 6.

people. And is this a mere partizan theory? No! It was solemnly acted upon by the British nation, when James II. was hurled from the throne which he had forfeited by .his tyranny, and the crown was placed upon the head of William of Orange. This was not done by an act of mutiny and violence, but by a formal vote of the estates of the realm; the tory party joining with the whig party in giving the doctrine a practical embodiment in the fundamental law of the land. In this very thing, and in this alone, consisted the essence of the great revolution of 1688. No towns were sacked, no fields were wasted, no blood .was spilt, in that revolution. All that was apparent in it, was a slight deviation from the usual order of succession to the crown. That was the extent of what appeared to the eye. But in that deviation, trifling as it seemed, there is a distinct proclamation of the doctrine, that the British sovereign is in reality elective by the British people. It announced that the strife between the popular element and the despotic element in the government, which had lasted so long, and been so prolific in seditions, rebellions, plots, battles, sieges, impeachments, proscriptions, and judicial murders, was at an end; and that the former, having at length fairly triumphed over the latter, was thenceforth to be permitted freely to develop itself, and become predomii nant in the English polity.*

· How stands this question as connected with the history of government in the nations of continental Europe? The crusades, combining with other causes, broke down the system, and destroyed the power, of feudalism. As the fierce authority and independent jurisdiction of multitudes of baronical chiefs gave way, the people, on the one hand, and kings, on the other, rose into importance. Power, authority, political sovereignty, gradually centralizing themselves,

* See the first vol. of Macauley's History, on this subject.

came at length to be settled in fewer hands indeed, but
under greater limitations and with better guaranties. It resulted, at last, that there arose real nations and real governments. The form was, without doubt, in every instance,
kingly. But these monarchies, springing from the wreck
of the feudal system, were at first quite different things
from what they afterwards became. They were originally
representative. The great principle of popular consent was
recognized as the foundation of rightful authority. Monarchy, as a form of polity, was the expression and embody-
ment of the nation's will. The doctrine that the king held
his power, not by consent of the people, but by a divine
right personal to himself, sprang up afterwards. It did not
belong to the political creed of that age. An error of later
growth, it has filled Europe, in later times, with popular
commotions and popular revolutions; but it is now well nigh
extinguished. Russia, it is true, is an example of absolutism,
of gigantic proportions, still remaining in Europe; but, with
this exception, the only kind of monarchy recognized as
legitimate by enlightened European opinion, is that which
makes the sovereign simply the chief magistrate of the
nation, the representative of the majesty of the state, the
embodiment of the will and wisdom of the people.*

But, leaving these ancient and foreign examples, let us
come to our own times, and, as it were, to our own hearths.
Here a clearer light shines upon the true origin and nature
of civil government. Times and seasons are in the hands
of God. Infinite wisdom, combined with infinite power,
sustains, moves, guides, and governs all things. The affairs
of all ages, though produced immediately by the voluntary

* On the subject of the foregoing paragraph, see an able address entitled
" The Social System," by Daniel D. Barnard, L.L.D. " The limitation of the
regal authority was a first and essential principle in all the Gothic systems
of government established in Europe ; though gradually driven out and
overborne by violence and chichane, in most of the kingdoms on the Continent." Bl. Com. B. 1. c. 7.

agency of innumerable actors, nevertheless fulfil the divine counsel, and carry forward the divine plan. Great and manifold were the purposes, which the divine providence comprehended in the discovery of America and the planting of the British colonies on its shores. Certainly, not among the least of these purposes, were improvements in the science and art of governing; the discovery of new principles of civil polity, the freer and more energetic application of principles known before. Previously to the colonization of America by Englishmen, shafts of light on the subject of government had been poured down upon some generous and gifted souls. Such shafts of light and power we find in the works of Bacon, Harrington, Sidney, Milton, Locke, Grotius, Puffendorf, and Montesquieu. But as the sunlight is often seen amidst streams of vapor drawn from the earth and rising into clouds, so the conceptions of the greatest geniuses on theories of government were obscured by folds of vaporous prejudice, gathered from existing monarchical institutions. But when the sun of American freedom culminated, the mists of prejudice melted away, and the true theory of political organizations appeared like a " glorious landscape amidst clear shining after rain."*

The very first chapter of New England history opens upon us with a bright light shining upon the subject of our inquiry. Before the pilgrim fathers disembarked from the Mayflower, on the eleventh of November, 1620, off Cape Cod, they framed and subscribed a formal social compact. Here is an extract from that instrument: " We, whose names are under-written, * * * * * do, by these presents, solemnly and mutually, in the presence of God and one of another, covenant and combine ourselves together into a civil body politic, * * * * and by virtue hereof, to enact, constitute and frame such just and equal laws, ordinances, acts, constitutions, offices from time to time, as shall be thought most

* Cheever's Journal of the Pilgrims, Pref.

meet and convenient for the general good of the colony; unto which we promise all due submission and obedience. In witness whereof we have hereunder subscribed our names."* To this remarkable document were appended the names of thirty-two persons, that is, of all the male adults on board the ship; the whole number of souls on board being a hundred and one. Here the supposition made a little while ago of a hundred persons taking possession of a desert island, and, by compact, forming themselves, under the necessities of the case, into a civil state, is fulfilled almost to the letter.

The theory of the social compact forms the basis of the civil polity established by every state in the American union, and is fully embodied in the constitution of the general government.

The constitution of Massachusetts is very explicit. It declares : " The body politic is formed by a voluntary association of individuals. It is a social compact, by which the whole people covenants with each citizen, and each citizen with the whole people, that all shall be governed by certain laws for the common good." †

The constitution of New York, framed in 1777, declares : " No authority shall, on any pretence whatever, be exercised over the people or members of this state, but such as shall be derived from and granted by them." "The style of all laws shall be as follows; to wit : ' Be it enacted by the people of the state of New York, represented in senate and assembly.' All writs and other proceedings shall run in the name of the people of the state of New York." ‡

The constitution of New Jersey, adopted in 1776, holds the following language : " Whereas all the constitutional authority, ever possessed by the kings of Great Britain, over

* *Idem*, pp. 30, 31.

† Constitutions of the United States, Carey, Stewart and Co., 1791, p. 4.

‡ *Idem*, pp. 49, 57.

these colonies or their other dominions, was, by compact, derived from the people, and held of them, for the common interest of the whole society;—allegiance and protection are, in the nature of things, reciprocal ties, each equally depending upon the other, and liable to be dissolved by the other's being refused or withdrawn." It further affirms, that, since the compact has been broken by the king of Great Britain, " all civil authority under him is necessarily at an end, and a dissolution of government in each colony has consequently taken place."*

The constitution of Pennsylvania, ratified September 2, 1790, says : " All power is inherent in the people ; and all free governments are founded on their authority, and instituted for their peace, safety, and happiness. For the advancement of those ends, they have, at all times, an inalienable and indefeasible right to alter, reform, or abolish their government, in such manner as they may think proper."†

The constitution of Delaware, framed and adopted in 1776, asserts: " All government, of right, originates from the people, is founded in compact only, and instituted solely for the good of the whole."‡

The constitution of Maryland affirms the same doctrine in the same words. It adds : " The right, in the people, to participate in the legislature, is the best security of liberty, and the foundation of all free government."§

To Virginia belongs the immortal honor of being the first of the colonies, in obedience to the recommendation of the continental congress of May 15th, 1776, to renounce the colonial name and condition, and to form herself into a free, sovereign, and independent commonwealth. Her constitution was adopted the day after the Declaration of Independence. The members of the convention who framed it,

* *Idem*, p. 61.　† *Idem*, p. 76.　‡ *Idem*, p. 82.　§ *Idem*, pp. 92, 93.

speak of themselves as "the delegates and representatives of the good people of Virginia," and say that, as such, they "do declare the future form of government of Virginia to be," &c., &c.*

The constitution of North Carolina, adopted in 1776, utters the sentiment of that state in the following terms: "All political power is vested in, and derived from, the people." "Allegiance and protection are, in their nature, reciprocal, and the one should of right be refused, when the other is withdrawn."†

The constitution of South Carolina, formed in 1790, says: "All power is originally vested in the people; and all free governments are founded on their authority, and are instituted for their peace, safety, and happiness."‡

The constitutions of New Hampshire and Georgia contain no declaration of rights, but the delegates who framed and adopted them, speak of themselves as "empowered by the people," and as acting by virtue of the powers vested in them by the people in what they did.§

Here we have, from eleven of the thirteen original colonies, explicit declarations of the doctrine of the popular sovereignty. Here we have eleven old governments abolished by the people, and new governments instituted in their place on the basis of express compact. Here we have a perfect exemplification of the maxim, that the popular will is the fountain of all just power and authority, in the state. Connecticut and Rhode Island retained the same constitutions which they had before. There was not the same necessity for altering them as existed in the other colonies. The charters of these two colonies reserved to the crown no control over the internal policy emanating from the colonial legislative bodies, nor even any share in the executive power. The acts of their legislatures did not

* Constitutions of the United States. Carey, Stewart and Co's. ed. p. 112.
† *Idem*, pp. 116, 119.   ‡ *Idem*, p. 135.   § *Idem*, pp. 1, 136.

require the royal sanction, and their executive officers were chosen by the colonists themselves. Nothing, therefore, was wanting to their convenient action as states, but the casting off of their dependence on Great Britain.

But not only are the constitutions of the several states based upon the principle of the social compact,—the constitution of the United States itself, that master-piece of political wisdom, is neither more, nor less, nor other, than the social compact. "We, the people of the United States;" it declares, " in order to form a more perfect union, establish justice, insure domestic tranquillity, provide for the common defence, promote the general welfare, and secure the blessings of liberty to ourselves and our posterity, do ordain and establish this constitution for the United States of America."* The people ordain and establish a supreme government! Sublime conception! Glorious truth! Now, for the first time in the history of the world, so distinctly and broadly announced as the only legitimate basis of civil society, the only just foundation of political government.†

But, although the doctrine that the original of all just government is in the people, has been more emphatically asserted, and more comprehensively acted upon, by the American republics, than by any other nation, yet has the doctrine at all times maintained a struggle, more or less vigorous, more or less successful, against the doctrine of a divine right to absolute power. It is the struggle between these two principles,—the principle of the social compact and the principle of absolutism in government,—which has caused most of the revolutions of modern times. It is this struggle which has made a battle-field of almost every plain

---

* *Idem*, p. 163.

† It is not, of course, meant here, that this principle was not as distinctly asserted in the state constitutions adopted before the formation of the federal constitution ; but that it was reserved for America to proclaim it in a more distinct and emphatic manner than any previous government had ever done.

in Europe. It is this struggle which has brought to the
scaffold, a Hamden, a Sidney, a Russel, an Emmett, and a
whole army of political martyrs, second in dignity only to
that other illustrious throng of Christian witnesses, who
have sealed their testimony with their blood. It is this
struggle, which three years* ago lighted a train in the city
of Paris, that has exploded beneath almost every throne in
Europe, laying some of them in ruins, and so shattering
others, that, despite the eclipse which, for the moment,
obscures the prospect of the popular cause, they will never
be able to regain either their former power or their former
splendor. ' It is this struggle, which drove the Pope from the
Vatican in the livery of a servant; which has despoiled him
in a great measure of his temporal power, except as it is
defended by foreign bayonets; and which has made to
tremble even the foundations of his spiritual dominion.

The principle of absolutism,—that dogma of centuries,—
has, I believe in God, received its death-blow. Mind has
been stirred. Thought has been awakened. Inquiry has
been set on foot. Railroads are everywhere constructed,
on which ideas travel, even more than men and merchan-
dize. Nations are thus intermingled and interlaced in an
unprecedented manner. Every man has an interest in
every other man. Every man feels, that he has a relationship to the whole of humanity. It is a curious fact, that in
proportion as this sentiment of union and brotherhood
among nations extends its sway, there springs up, in each
individual mind, the sense of personal dignity and personal
responsibility. In former ages, men were like herds of
cattle. They worked in masses. They were a part of the
freehold. They had a master, an owner. They were
kindred to the brutes. Now, each one says, or feels : "I
am somebody. I am not a chattel. I have a mind, a soul,
a conscience. I am a free agent. I can think. I go erect.

* This was written in the early part of 1851.

I am not prone, like the beasts. No man owns me. No man is my master." What a power there is in this! It has lifted crowns from the head of princes. It has wrested the sceptre from the grasp of kings. It has made thrones topple and fall.

The slumber of ages is broken. The masses have discovered, that political sovereignty is in them; that no man has the right, irrespective of the assent of the governed, to rule his fellow-men. The iron barrier, which hitherto has shut them out from their rights, if not yet broken down, has been terribly shattered. The dawn of a rational freedom is visible above the political horizon. The potentates, who feel the ground giving way under them, and power stealing from their grasp, chafe and roar and gnash their teeth. By combined and extraordinary efforts, by a lavish expenditure of blood and treasure, they have succeeded in giving a check to the onward progress of events. They have produced an apparent quiet, and flatter themselves, that the spirit of liberty is crushed. Vain toil! Delusive confidence! The seeming calm is but the stillness which precedes the earthquake or the hurricane. There is a power behind the throne greater than the throne. It is the power of individual man; the power of a newly awakened consciousness of manly dignity; the power of a felt personal responsibility; the power of a great and vital truth, long smothered beneath the abuses of ancient dynasties, but now breaking through the pressure, and asserting its vivifying force.

Writers speculate on coming events, and wonder whether the people of Europe are prepared for the enjoyment of liberty and the exercise of self-government. Perhaps they are not prepared. Probably they are not prepared. It would be strange if they were prepared. They must be schooled to this end. They must be prepared for it, as the Israelites, as our fathers, as all others in this fallen world have been prepared for freedom, by a baptism of suffering.

But prepared or unprepared now, both liberty and self-government will at length come. It is not in the people, but the principle, that I confide. Principles, founded in truth, are stronger than men. They are stronger even than men's vices. They seem to be invested with a portion of that omnipotence, which belongs to him who ordained them. The great principle of popular right and popular sovereignty, in some form or other, is predestined to a universal triumph. It may achieve this triumph in one century, or it may not achieve it in five; but its ultimate success is as certain as its truth. God never made a truth, into which he did not put a power, that sooner or later would cause it to prevail. Despotism, therefore, will have to bow before the majesty and supremacy of the people. Even the frozen gates of Siberia shall yet dissolve and disappear beneath the genial warmth of the sun of freedom. Tyranny, with its chains and its blood, will every where come to an end. Humanity will recover her rights. And an enfranchised world shall yet exult in the liberty and happiness, for which it has sighed and struggled through many a weary century of injustice and oppression.

We are now, I think, prepared to say, whether or not the theory of the social compact is "historically untrue." We have traced this compact in the Israelitish government. We have traced it in the institution of the Roman monarchy and the Venetian and Carthagenian republics. We have seen it, in the opinion of such men as Bracton, Fortescue, and Blackstone, entering, from the first, as a vital element into the constitution of Great Britain; and we have seen it, as it were, by the entire British nation formally ingrafted into the fundamental law of the realm, in the transfer of the crown of England from the head of James II, to that of William of Orange. We have found it to underlie the monarchies of continental Europe, which sprang up after the overthrow of the feudal system. We have beheld it, after a long eclipse, re-appearing, and successfully vindicating its truth and power in the European revolutions of these later ages, and in the general substitution of constitutional monarchies for the iron despotisms of the seventeenth and eighteenth centuries. We have followed it in its passage over the ocean billows, in the brave hearts and strong arms, which the immortal Mayflower bore to this western clime. And we have heard it distinctly proclaimed by thirteen sovereign States and one great republic embracing them all, as the only just foundation of political government, the only true spring and source of political power. "Arbitrary power," says Burke, "is a thing which neither any man can hold, nor any man can give. No man can lawfully govern himself according to his own will ; much less, can one person be governed by the will of another." And again: "Law and arbitrary power are in eternal enmity. Name me a magistrate, and I will name property. Name me power, and I will name protection. It is a contradiction in terms, it is wickedness in politics, it is blasphemy in religion, to say that any man can have arbitrary power. In every patent of office, duty is included. For what else does a magistrate exist ? To suppose for power, is an absurdity in idea. Judges are guarded and governed by the eternal laws of justice, to which we all are subject. We may bite our chains, if we will ; but we shall be made to know ourselves, and be taught that man is born to be governed by law ; and he that will substitute will in the place of it, is an enemy to God."*

The allegation, that the theory of the social compact is "historically untrue," seems to me so far from being a fact of history, that there is no constitutional government in the world, nor ever has been, which is not, or was not, based upon such compact. Every such government, whatever its form, is created by the act of the people, is continued by the

* Works, v. 7, pp. 118, 119, Little & Brown.

will of the people, and represents the august majesty of the people. Hence, perhaps, that apparently paradoxical maxim,—"rex est populus,"—the king is the people. It matters not whether a formal convention can be traced in the inception of the government, nor whether, in point of fact, any such formal convention ever passed. It is enough that we find a people actually living under established laws, and peacefully pursuing their several vocations under their protection. The covenants, constituting the social compact, must, in such case, be pre-supposed. Whether these covenants were formal or implied, express or silent, does not alter the essential nature of the transaction. The doctrine of tacit covenants, is by no means a novelty to statesmen and civilians. The whole system of the common law, with its rich train of blessings, is built upon nothing else but the doctrine of silent covenants.*

The persons who instituted the bodies politic, known as the commonwealths of Virginia and Massachusetts, did so by express compact. But their descendants, without such formality, do, by silent acquiescence in the established order of things, as really contract, as the original founders. Furthermore, since every civil community is fixed in a certain locality, it is considered a law in all states, that whoever

---

* "The re-union of families, by whatever means it was brought about, could not have taken place but by an agreement of wills on certain general objects. When we view society as the effect of unanimous concord, it necessarily supposes certain covenants. These covenants imply conditions. It is these conditions, which are to be considered as the first laws, by which societies were governed. These [covenants] also are the origin of all the political regulations, which have been successively established. It was not necessary, that either the first covenants, or the conditions on which they were founded, should be express. It was sufficient, in many cases, that they were tacitly understood. * * * * The first laws of society were naturally established by a tacit consent, a kind of engagement, to which men are naturally very much inclined. Even political authority was established in this manner, by a tacit agreement between those who submitted to it and those who exercised it."—*Goguet's Origin of Laws*, B. 1.

comes within the proper limits of such a community to reside, does, by this very act, surrender his natural liberty, and silently consent to the government there established. Hence Puffendorf lays down the principle, that they who join themselves to a state already settled, are not less parties to the social compact, than they who, by assembling and uniting themselves together, formed it at the beginning.*

Does any one say,—"Whither shall I go, if I do not consent to the social compact?" The answer is: "You must go where there is no civil society." Is it replied,—"That is impossible?" I admit it. But it is just such another impossibility as stealing with impunity. The necessity of living under government, and the necessity of respecting the rights of property, are conditions of humanity, originating in the will of the Creator; and both conditions spring from the same benevolent regard to the welfare and happiness of his rational creatures.

But the objection, that the theory of the social compact is historically untrue, is not the only one, that has been urged against it. It is alleged, that the theory is anti-christian; that it leaves no place for the idea of an organic unity in the state; that it is productive of injustice towards minorities; that it makes the relation between the rulers and the ruled a purely commercial one; that it makes revolution the rule of political life, and obedience the exception; and that it converts capital punishment into a mere aggression upon individual right.†

Let us examine these several additional grounds of objection to the doctrine of the social compact.

It is alleged, that the theory is anti-christian and semi-atheistic, leaving no place for the divine element in government, so much insisted upon by St. Paul, and other inspired writers. It is even alleged to be infidelity's great battering-

* "Law of Nature and Nations," Lib. 7, Cap. 4, § 20.
† "Religious Theory of Civ. Government." *Passim.*

ram, with which she has beaten down the firm bulwarks of society, as in the bloody and detestable French revolution of the last century.*

This objection, if founded in truth, decides the question. The old theory of Filmer, which makes the sovereignty of a nation a personal divine right, must be revived. King James's dogma, that "it is presumption and sedition to dispute what a king may do in the height of his power," must be enforced. Mankind must bow, with what grace they may, to a doctrine which extinguishes their rights, and makes all resistance to the powers that be rebellion against God. For, of necessity, the sovereign authority of a state must either be derived from the people; or it must belong by an original divine right, to some particular person or persons in the state; or it must be usurped, and wrongfully held by force of arms against the consent and choice of the nation.

But, in truth, the objection is founded in a fallacy. The fallacy consists in a misapprehension of the mode in which the divine will concerning government is ascertained. If God, by an express revelation, designated the persons in every state to whom the supreme authority should be entrusted, then the objection would hold. But the divine right of government is not so ascertained. It is originally through the suggestion of reason, that the will of God concerning government discovers itself. Independently of revelation, we know with certainty, that it is the divine will that government should exist, since the end for which mankind was created could not otherwise be attained. But God permits men freely to institute such polities as they please, and to invest whom they will with the sovereignty; and his sanction is given to all forms of government, all systems of law, and all modes of administration, which do not contravene the end, for which he made man. Therefore, since the

* "Religious Theory of Civil Government." Pp. 17, 18, 19, 20, 21.

author of our being has been graciously pleased to allow so much freedom to his rational creation, no theory of government, which is not subversive of justice and human happiness, can be anti-christian or atheistic.

The social compact, says the objection, is anti-christian; negatively atheistic; infidelity's battering-ram. How does this statement tally with the fact, that since the doctrine of the popular sovereignty has gained so general a prevalence, society has been steadily advancing in religion, morals, science, letters, art, jurisprudence, philanthropy, refinement, and whatever else constitutes the true dignity and happiness of man? The social, moral, and religious progress of our race, has never been so conspicuous, as during the last half century. The world has never before been so active in doing good. The zeal of science, the activity of commerce, the comprehensive and far-reaching enterprises of capital, are rivaled by the ardor, the energy, and the breadth of its benevolent undertakings. Philanthropy has sought out the lurking places of vice, shame, want, and misery, and is intent on elevating all the most degraded members of society in their physical, intellectual, and moral condition. And religion, awaking as from the slumber of centuries, and catching her inspiration from ancient prophecy, has started upon the sublime and glorious enterprise of evangelizing the world. Surely this does not look as if the canker of irreligion were at work in the very heart of our social systems, in the very frame and texture of our political organizations. Where is there less of infidelity, where more of spiritual religion, where a higher reverence for law, than in the great North American republic? Yet here the social compact is the only recognized basis of civil society.

As it respects the terrible scenes of the French revolution, it was not the theory of the social compact, it was not the doctrine of the popular sovereignty, that produced them. It was the depraved heart of the nation. It was the formal

abrogation of the Christian religion. It was the deification
of human reason. It was the writings of a Diderot and a
Voltaire, not those of a Locke or a Sidney, that wrought the
mischief. The truth is, it is in no case the government that
makes the manners, but always the manners that make the
government. The real nature of a government can never be
known from the name it bears; for, as the people are, such,
by an inevitable law, will the government be, call it by what
title you will.

Again it is said, that the theory of the social compact
leaves no place for the idea of an organic unity in the state.*
But why not? One of the essential covenants of this compact is, that each member of the body politic submit his
individual will to the will of the recognized head of the
state; whether such head be one man, one or more councils
of sages, or the assembled people, acting in an organic capacity. And what other definition can be given of organic
unity? When each member of a civil society submits his
will to the will of a man, of a council of senators, or of an
assembly of the people, whatever this person, this council,
or this assembly resolves, in matters relating to the common
safety, is deemed the will of all in general, and of each in
particular. It is a fundamental principle, a principle universally recognized and acted upon in civil affairs, that,
when I have delegated my power to another, his act and
choice must be interpreted as mine. A society such as that
described above, and exactly such an one is formed by the
social compact, being actuated by one soul and possessing
one will, is a true moral person, concerning whom it seems
quite proper to predicate organic unity. It is not, indeed,
a unity such as the world has so often seen, in which vast
multitudes of human beings are delivered up to the arbitrary
will of one man. It is a unity, effected by the abolition of
every thing of the nature of caste; a unity, founded on the

* "Religious Theory of Civil Government," p. 30.

principlè of political equality; a unity, where the same
fundamental rights are recognized as belonging to all—the
same fundamental duties as binding upon all; a unity, without either hereditary dignities or hereditary inferiority; a
unity, in short, in which the whole people forms the state,
contrary to what happens in despotic governments, where
the monarch is the state, as Louis XIV, of France, distinctly avowed himself to be.

It is further objected, that the theory of the social compact, resolving all law into the majority of wills, leaves the
minority without remedy for the wrongs, that may be inflicted upon them.* What redress may be open to the minority,
or what restraint may be laid upon the power of the majority, can, in any given case, be known only from an examination of the internal structure of the state. The social
compact leaves a wide range for the details of political
organization. It will admit quite as many checks and balances as any other theory of government. The establishment of three independent branches of power—executive,
legislative, and judicial—having its foundation in nature, is
the most effectual contrivance, ever yet devised by the wit
of man, to restrain the tyranny of majorities, and protect the
rights of minorities. Accordingly, nowhere else is either the
restraint or the protection as effective as under the English
and American constitutions, where this three-fold distribution
of power obtains, and where, also, the principle of the social
compact, is most operative. But granting the truth of the
objection, has it never occurred to writers who urge it, that
the only difference between a government admitting and a
government rejecting the principle of the social compact
would be, that in the former the minority, and in the latter
the majority, would be without redress of wrong?

Another objection to the doctrine of the social compact
is, that it makes the relation between the governors and the

* *Idem*, p. 20.

governed a purely commercial one, and so tends to detract
from the proper sanction of civil power.* Such an objection is more likely to lower the standard of commercial
virtue, than to raise that of political virtue. It does not
seem wise to discriminate between the sanctions annexed to
moral duties. It is a dangerous, as well as unscriptural,
distinction, which the church of Rome has made between
mortal and venial sins. " Obey magistrates," and " defraud
not," are laws enacted by one and the same authority. The
violation of the latter, there can be no doubt, is just as abhorrent to the supreme lawgiver, as the violation of the
former. Blackstone expressly lays down the doctrine, that
the obligation of a contract is equal, in point of conscience,
to the obligation of a law.† And in the suggestion made
above, viz.: that both obligations emanate from the same
source, we have the reason of this equality.

It is further objected to the theory of a social compact,
that it makes revolution the rule of political life, and obedience the exception.‡ Not so. God made man to be happy.
To that end he wills both the institution of government and
the permanence of government; and the latter equally with
the former. Neither one man nor a whole community of
men has any the least right herein to thwart his design.
But frequent revolutions in government would as effectually
defeat the benevolent purpose of the Creator as the want of
all government. The stability of law is quite as essential to
human happiness as the existence of law. The same light
of reason, therefore, which gives us to understand, that it is
God's will that government should be, tells us with equal
clearness, that it is his will that government should be permanent.

Besides, the Deity himself, whose work is ever perfect,
has made provision against frequent revolutions of society,

---

* "Religious Theory of Civil Government," p. 23.   † Commentaries.
‡ *Idem*, p. 29.

in that element of man's nature, which makes him cling to whatever enjoys the sanction of age. The old is always venerable in the eyes of the multitude. Ambitious leaders, and still more those who seek to become leaders, may plot to overturn the established order of things; but the masses are rarely moved to revolutionary action, till the pressure of public wrong has become insupportable. It must be a great occasion that can induce a whole people to unite in subverting their government; especially, when it is a government of their own choice, a government instituted and administered by themselves.

The theory of the social compact undoubtedly throws much light on the nature and the respective provinces of rebellion and revolution. While it as strongly condemns the former, as any other theory of government can, it is the only theory, which asserts the right of down-trodden humanity to resort for relief to the latter.

The very end of government,—the preservation, perfection, and happiness of man,—imposes an obligation of obedience to the sovereign authority, so long as it acts with moderation and equity. It is this obligation of obedience, founded in the will of God, because founded in the nature and fitness of things, which constitutes the whole force of civil society, and consequently the entire felicity of the state. Whoever, therefore, rises up against the sovereign power to destroy it, is guilty of the greatest crime that can be committed, since he seeks to subvert the foundations of the public felicity, in which that of every individual is included.

This is rebellion. But if the supreme power degenerate into tyranny, if they who hold it are manifestly aiming to destroy the liberties of the state, it is the doctrine of the social compact, that the people have the right to rise in their majesty, and to demand from their tyrants the surrender of trusts, forfeited by abuses of so flagrant a character.

This is revolution. It is a remedy, not only justifiable when all others fail, but demanded by the very same reason on which government itself is founded,—a regard to the welfare and felicity of mankind. A strict observance of law, on the part of rulers as well as people, is essential to the happiness of nations. To resist a tyrant, who knows no law but his own will, is not rebellion, but revolution. It is not lawless violence, but lawful self-defence. It is not an invasion of the prerogative of one, but a vindication of the prerogatives of millions. It is not a right merely, but a duty.

Finally, it is objected that, on the principle of the social compact, capital punishment is an aggression upon individual rights, a bloody, popular revenge.* This objection, like the preceding, overlooks the end for which God wills the institution of government,—the safety, peace, and happiness of his rational creation. In ordaining this end, he must, of necessity, have ordained the means. The necessary agencies and appliances of government are as much an ordinance of heaven as government itself is. As to what instrumentalities are necessary to enable government to answer the end of its institution, right reason, whose function it was, originally, to discover the congruity of law to the divine will, is the sole judge. Hence, the members of a civil state, who have united together, on the principle of compact, express or implied, the more effectually to carry out the purpose of the Deity in ordaining government, are, by the very constitution and nature of things, clothed with full power to institute such rewards and punishments as, in the enlightened use of their faculties, they may deem essential to the end in view. Nay, they not only have the power, but they are under the obligation, of annexing to their laws such sanctions as will effectually restrain the bad

* *Idem*, pp. 32, 33.

† See " Social Contract," Chaps. 4th and 5th.

passions of men, though these sanctions may include the loss of property, liberty, and life itself. The maxim, "*salus populi suprema lex*," is as applicable to the punitive, as it is to any other department of government, and as applicable ' to. a government which embraces, as to one which repudiates, the principle of the social compact. The use of capital punishments, therefore, is as much within the limits of legitimate authority in a state formed on the basis of compact, as in a state established on the opposite principle of absolutism.

Rousseau, indeed, assumes, that, as the waters of a spring cannot rise above their source, so the power of the magistracy, being derived from the people, cannot rise higher than the power of the people in their individual capacity.* From this assumption the inference is drawn for him, (he does not draw it himself,) that, as no man has the right to commit suicide, civil society can have no right to take away human life in punishment of crimes.† The principle relied

---

* See "Social Compact," Chaps. 4th and 5th.

† Rousseau expressly disclaims this inference. He says : " It hath been asked, how individuals, having no right to dispose of their own life, can transmit that right to the sovereign ? The difficulty of resolving this question arises only from its being badly expressed. Every man hath an undoubted right to hazard his life for its preservation. Was a man ever charged with suicide for throwing himself from the top of a house in flames, in order to avoid being burnt ? * * * * To prevent our falling by the hands of an assassin, we consent to die on becoming such ourselves. * * * * Add to this, that every malefactor, by breaking the laws of his country, becomes a rebel and a traitor, ceasing from that time to be a member of the community, and even declaring war against it. In this case, the preservation of the state is incompatible with his ; one of the two must perish ; and thus, when a criminal is executed, he doth not suffer in the quality of a citizen, but in that of an enemy. His trial and sentence are the evidence and declaration of his having broken the social compact, and that, of consequence, he is no longer a member of the state.' —" Social Cont.," Chap. 5. These are, certainly, false and insufficient grounds ; but they show, that the author was not prepared for the consequences of his own doctrine. He was, beyond a

on to support this conclusion is, that the master cannot confer upon the servant a right which he himself has not.
They who oppose the conventional origin of government,
hold the theory of a social compact responsible for an
infidel sophism of one of its advocates. Rousseau has many
great truths and admirable reflections in his treatise on government, just as the rationalistic interpreters have, by their
deep learning, thrown a strong light on many obscure
places of Holy Writ. But I should as soon think of taking
the latter for my guides in studying the doctrine of atonement, as the former in framing a theory of civil polity.

I have called the argument attributed to the Genevan
philosopher a sophism. It is nothing more. It overlooks
the twofold origin of government, explained in a former
part of this essay. It leaves wholly out of view the divine
element of law, which the social compact admits as readily
as any other theory of government. In this connexion, I
cannot but refer again to the distinction, so plain and solid
in itself, and so well stated by Bishop Sanderson and Archbishop Bramhall. Says the former of these prelates: "The
substance of the power of every magistrate is the ordinance
of God; but the specification of the circumstances thereto
relating is a human ordinance, introduced by custom or
positive law."* Says the latter: "That all lawful dominion,
considered in the abstract, is from God, no man can make
any doubt. But the right and application of this power and
interest, in the concrete, to this or that particular man, is
many times from the grant and consent of the people. So
God is the principal agent; man, the instrumental. God is
the fountain, the root of power; man, the stream, the bough,

doubt, an enemy to capital punishment, except, perhaps, in the most
extreme cases; for he adds in the same chapter: "There is no malefactor,
who might not be made good for something, nor ought any person to be put
to death, even by way of example, unless such as could not be preserved
without endangering the community."

* "Sermon ad Magistros."

by which it is derived. The essence of power is always from God; the existence, sometimes from God, sometimes from man."*

The sum is: God ordains government to secure the rights of man,—"life, liberty, and the pursuit of happiness." He equally ordains the means necessary and fit to attain that end. He does not designate the means. He could not do so, for the plain reason, that the means will vary in different ages, climates, and states of society. He leaves it to men, whom he has endowed with reason for this, among other purposes, to choose such means as to their wisdom may seem suitable and sufficient. It is the will of God, that the rights of property shall be guarded; but whether this shall be effected by blows, restitution, imprisonment, servitude, or even death, is left to the calm and conscientious judgment of men. It is the will of God, that human life should be secure; but in what manner this security shall be attained, whether by exile, perpetual confinement, deprivation of life, or other penalties, inflicted on those who invade it, man's wisdom is the sole judge. Neither forms of government, nor theories of government, make any difference. The magistrate, whether he be an hereditary prince of the thousandth generation, or the elected chief of a community, whose members but yesterday formed themselves into a civil state by voluntary compact, is the minister and vicegerent of God; and his sword of power is bathed in heaven.†

From this inquiry into the true theory of civil society, there result certain general principles of government and law, which I propose, briefly, to unfold. Perhaps I should express my meaning better, if I were to say, that these principles are embodied in the foregoing discussion, and that I desire to group them together, and present them, in a summary way, to the reader's view.

* Works, vol. 3, p. 317.
† Isaiah xxxiv. 5

1. Human society is, originally and in itself, a state of equality, freedom, and independence.* In this primitive state, which we can conceive of as an object of thought, even though we reject it as an actuality, no man has an original and inherent right of command over his fellows. No man possesses any title to sovereignty. Men are free and equal; and each is as independent of the others, as they all are dependent on God.

2. The institution of civil society, by establishing a sovereign power having the right of command, abridges this liberty, equality, and independence.† The change, however, does not subvert natural society, but rather perfects it. Civil society is natural society, so modified as to have a recognized head and established rules of intercourse. Civil liberty replaces natural liberty. By this means, mankind more certainly attain, and more securely hold, that happiness, which was the final cause of their creation,—in subordination always to the divine glory.

3. States, when formed, having each a common will, as well as a common interest, acquire certain personal attributes. They become, in effect, moral persons; and are to be looked upon as such. Hence arise new relations among men, viz.: the relations which exist between the several civil societies, into which they have formed themselves. States have with respect to each other the same rights and obligations as real persons. Their intercourse is to be regulated by the same ethical principles as the intercourse of real persons. That great moral maxim, whose transcendent beauty and importance have given it the appellation of the golden rule,‡ is as applicable in the one case as in the other.

4. The question of the form of government has much engaged men's thoughts and pens. The highest efforts of genius have been expended on the study and elucidation of it.

* " Burlam. Pol. Law," Part 1, chap 3.
† Ibidem.   ‡ Matt. 7, 12.

There are commonly reckoned three simple forms:—monarchy, or the government of one; aristocracy, or the government of the worthiest; and democracy, or the government of the people. But these three simple forms are capable of indefinite combination with each other; and thence have resulted that endless diversity of polities, which have existed in the world.

A two-fold inquiry has arisen in regard to political organizations, viz.: 1. What is the most legitimate form? 2. What is the best form? From principles established in this essay it results, that all forms, founded on popular consent, and tending to promote the general happiness, are equally legitimate. The best form is another question. Liberty, the source of the most precious blessings, has two enemies in civil society,—licentiousness and tyranny.* To guard against these enemies is the height of both human prudence and human felicity. To effect this, a polity must be so constituted as to banish the one, without introducing the other. Such a temperament, excluding alike lawlessness and oppression, is the perfection of a civil constitution. `But it is a temperament which neither a pure despotism nor a pure democracy affords. The former is too violent, and tends to tyranny; the latter is too weak, and tends to anarchy. It follows, that that form of polity is best, in which the principle of monarchy and the principle of democracy are so blended as to banish both these foes to true freedom. Such a combination secures that happy balance in the state, which is most essential to the stability of the government and the welfare of the people.

5. A spirit of moderation is the spirit which should characterize both legislators and legislation.† And the broader the territories of a state are, and consequently the greater the diversity of its interests, the more need there is that mo-

* " Burlam, Pol. Law," Pt. 2, chap. 2.
† " Montesq. Sp. Laws," Bk. 29, chap. 1.

derate councils should prevail. Political good commonly lies between two extremes. This is, preëminently, the case in our country. A spirit of compromise, of generosity, of candor, of nobleness, of brotherhood, of mutual deference and concession, is the proper spirit of the American Republic. It was in this spirit that our constitution and our union were formed; and in this spirit alone can that constitution and that union, which are the spring of all our enjoyments, be maintained and made perpetual.

6. Government should be characterized by a spirit of equity as well as of moderation. The laws ought to be equal in their operation. Justice requires that there should be neither partial exemptions nor partial burdens. Taxation should bear with equal weight on all. The path to public trust and honor should be open to all. The same legal process should impend over all for a violation of the laws. Law should be the buckler of the peasant, as well as the defence of the noble; the inheritance of the poor, as well as the patrimony of the rich; the staff of honesty, and the shield of innocence; not the two-edged sword of craft and oppression.* These ideas have gone into the universal mind of America.† They are the vital element, the soul, of our political system. They are to us, in civil science, what the axioms of Euclid are to geometry—truths which no one questions; the basis of our more recondite political theorems; the starting point of higher investigations.

Not so, however, in most other countries. The laws of all despotic states, and even of England, afford many examples of the violation of the great principle, that both the burdens and the privileges of the state should be equal to all.‡ It is the policy of the aristocracy, in the European monarchies,

* Lord Brougham's Rep. on L. Ref. to the Br. Parl.
† Park Godwin's "Review of the Last Half Cent." in N. Y. Ev. Post.
‡ See an able Paper on this subject, appended to Mr. Combes' "Travels in the United States."

to preserve great estates, and, as a consequence, the great power and influence which attend them, in the same family. Hence the great inequality and the great injustice of the laws in those proud monarchies. The process of law which would enter a poor man's hovel, and drive him out of it, falls dead at the gate of a nobleman's palace. But this iniquity cannot stand for ever. The towering structure of aristocratic pride and power must give way, and the nobler and fairer edifice of truth and justice will rise majestically upon its ruins.

7. The administration of justice ought to be impartial, speedy, uniform, economical, free from perplexing technicalities, according to established forms of procedure, and as near to every man's door as circumstances will permit. All should have it, without going far to seek it, without waiting long to obtain it, and without paying an exorbitant price for it.

8. The well-being of the entire body of the people is the central doctrine, the one paramount law of political philosophy. " Salus populi suprema lex." To this great end, this predominant idea, should all the laws be relative. The fundamental principle of law is benevolence.*

9. The style in which the laws are written is not beneath the attention of legislators. It should be concise, simple, clear, and explicit.† It should excite in every mind the same ideas ; and this because the object is to establish justice and teach duties—not to furnish specimens of rhetoric. The Roman laws of the twelve tables were models of conciseness.‡ The boys in school were required to commit them to memory. The Mosaic legislation is marked by a like brevity. It consists of a " series of laconic regulations, directly opposite in form to the endless iterations and syno-

---

* Spring's " Obl. of the World to the Bible," Lect. 3.
† Montes. " Sp. Laws," Bk. 29, Chap. 16.   ‡ *Ibidem.*

nymies of modern statute books."* The early laws of New
England were clothed in a diction, curt, bold, clear, and
straightforward—a reflection of the men who made them.

The composition of laws should be exact, as well as brief.
Montesquieu instances a law of the emperor Honorius as
wanting in this quality.† The imperial edict makes it
death to "molest" a freedman. Now, the "molestation"
felt by a person, in a given case, depends upon his sensibility. Thus it would happen, that an act done to A, would
be quite innocent, which, when done to B, would be a capital crime. A rescript of Cardinal Richelieu is open to the
same objection.‡ The Cardinal agreed, that a minister
might be accused to the king. But the accusation must be
respecting a "matter of moment," otherwise the accuser
was to be punished. Now, a "matter of moment" is altogether relative; the phrase has no intrinsic meaning. The
permission, therefore, was, in effect, a prohibition against
uttering any truth against the ministers of the crown. That
it should have this operation, was, probably, the design of
the wily politician.

10. Laws ought to arise out of circumstances and be
relative to certain definite ends.§ By overlooking this principle, the Romans not only committed a ridiculous blunder,
but subverted justice in one of the laws of the twelve
tables. This law ordained, that, if a thief was caught with
the stolen article before he had conveyed it to a hiding
place, he should be scourged with rods and condemned to
slavery ; but that, if he was not detected till some time
afterwards, he should only be condemned to a recompence of
double the value of what he had stolen. Now, the time of
detection could not possibly alter the nature of the crime.
Neither would the Roman jurisprudence ever have made so

* "Princeton Bib. Rep." for Jan. 1848,   Art. The Mos. Leg
† "Sp. Laws," Book 29, Chap. 16.   ‡ Ibidem.
§ Ibidem, Book 29, Chaps. 13, 14.

unmeaning a distinction, if it had not borrowed the law from the Spartan legislation. In the code to which it originally belonged, whatever we may think of its morality, the policy of it was unquestionable. Lycurgus wished to make the Spartans cunning and dexterous. To this end he ordained, that children should be practised in thieving. If caught in the act, they were punished; if they had the art to avoid detection, they were applauded. The punishment was not for the theft, but for the want of adroitness in concealing it. No such end being proposed by the Roman legislators, the law was, in their jurisprudence, a simple burlesque upon justice.

The principle now under consideration is of the utmost importance in interpreting the legislation of antiquity. The more the manners and circumstances of the people differ from our own, which will generally be in proportion to their remoteness from us in time and space, the more will it be necessary to keep this principle in view, in the study of their institutions and laws. If, besides this, a civil polity propose the accomplishment of certain great purposes peculiar to itself, the principle rises to a transcendent importance as a guide in the interpretation of the laws, which are relative to those special ends.*

11. Laws, and not men, are the rulers, in every justly constituted state. The difference is broad and impassable between a government of will and a government of law. Where the leading principle of a polity is, " stat pro ratione voluntas," it is of little moment what name it bears, or under what forms it exists and acts. Hence such an unlimited democracy as that of Athens, in which the people ostracised illustrious citizens for acts which they had never before declared illegal, was as absolute a despotism as that of Nero. In practice, it always proved itself as bloody,

---

* This last remark has an important bearing on the interpretation of the Hebrew legislation, as will more fully appear as we proceed in our inquiries.

cruel, and tyrannical. In full accordance with this view is
the principle before cited from Bracton, as an element, or
doctrine, of the British Constitution, viz.: that "the law
maketh the king;" and the further principle, which the
same eminent jurist derives as an inference from the preceding one, viz.: that "he is not truly king, where will
and pleasure rules, and not the law."*
Tyranny is quite as likely to exist under an unrestrained
democracy, as under an unrestrained despotism. Liberty,
true liberty, is encompassed with dangers, and that from
within, as well as from without. Its greatest peril is that of
running into licentiousness, just as liberality is apt to degenerate into extravagance. Licentiousness is an excess of
liberty, and tends to its destruction. "A particular man
may be licentious, without being less free, but a community
cannot; since the licentiousness of one will unavoidably
break in upon the liberty of another. Civil liberty, the
liberty of a community, is a severe and restrained thing;
implies, in the notion of it, authority, settled subordinations,
subjection, and obedience; and is altogether as much hurt
by too little of this kind, as by too much of it. And the
love of liberty, when it is indeed the love of liberty, which
carries us to withstand tyranny, will as much carry us to
reverence authority and support it; for this most obvious
reason, that the one is as necessary to the very being of
liberty, as the other is destructive of it. And, therefore, the
love of liberty, which does not produce this effect, the
love of liberty, which is not a real principle of dutiful behavior towards authority, is as hypocritical as the religion,
which is not productive of a good life. Licentiousness is, in
truth, such an excess of liberty, as is of the same nature
with tyranny. For what is the difference between them,
but that one is lawless power, exercised under pretence of

* Bracton's "Treatise on the Laws and Customs of England," cited by
Blackstone.

authority, or by persons invested with it; the other, lawless power, exercised under the pretence of liberty, or without any pretence at all. A people, then, must be always less free, in proportion as they are more licentious; licentiousness being not only different from liberty, but contrary to it, a direct breach upon it."* "Government, as distinguished from mere power, free government, necessarily implies reverence, in the subjects of it, for authority or power regulated by laws, and a habit of submission to the subordinations in civil life, throughout its several ranks ; nor is a people capable of liberty, without something of this kind. But, it must be observed, this reverence and submission will at best be very precarious, if it be not founded upon a sense of authority being God's ordinance, and the subordinations of life, a providential appointment of things."†

12. Magistrates ought to consider, and ever to bear in mind, that they are God's representatives and vicegerents. The tendency of this consideration will be to make them circumspect, just, diligent, and merciful, in the exercise of their magisterial function. Their power is a trust from heaven, as well as from earth ; a high, holy, fearful trust. They are God's ministers, not man's masters; his ministers for the good, not the oppression, of the governed. The trial of their fidelity at the bar of their constituents is sometimes dreadful ; the account to be rendered at the tribunal of the supreme judge, from whom even more than from men their authority comes, will be far more so. " If they are faithful, heaven has nothing that he will not lavish on them through eternity. If they are faithless, there is no pit in hell too deep and dark for their eternal exile from all peace, all rest, all joy. Forever mindful, then, should they be of their sacred trust. Forever mindful, that they hold it for God's children upon earth. Forever mindful, that they hold it under most

---

* " Bishop Butler's Sermon in the House of Lords."
† *Idem.*

severe accountability to him. They are to govern by the law. They are to seek no good but theirs who are entrusted to their care; no other glory than his, who put them thus in trust."*

What can more animate an upright and conscientious magistrate to do his duty, than the consideration, that he is delegated of God to the work of the magistracy, and that he must one day appear before him to give an account of his administration? To this principle do the sacred writers constantly appeal, for the purpose of engaging magistrates to fidelity in the execution of their trust. "Judge righteously," says Moses, "between every man and his brother, and the stranger that is with thee; for the judgment is God's."† "Take heed," says Jehoshaphat, "what ye do; for ye judge not for man, but for the Lord, who is with you in the judgment. Wherefore now let the fear of the Lord be upon you: take heed and do it: for there is no iniquity with the Lord our God."‡ "God standeth in the congregation of the mighty," says the psalmist; "he judgeth among the gods [magistrates.] How long will ye judge unjustly, and accept the persons of the wicked?"§ The motives here urged to a faithful discharge of official duty on the part of magistrates, to the exercise of prudence, moderation, justice, clemency, and diligence in their public relations, are, that their seat is the throne of God; that their decisions are the utterances of the divinity; that their decrees are the edicts of heaven; that, in short, they are ministers of the divine equity and goodness, and, "if they fail in their duty, they not only injure men by criminally distressing them, but they even offend God by polluting his sacred judgments."‖

13. The duties of citizens to their rulers are honor and obedience.¶ They are to look upon their office as a dele-

* "Bishop Doane's Orat., entitled, Civ. Gov. a Sac. Trust from God."
† Deut. i. 16, 17.   ‡ 2 Chron. xix. 6. 7.
§ Psalm lxxxii. 1, 2.   ‖ Calv. Inst. Ch. Rel. B. 4, C. 20.
¶ Fuller's Works, V. 3, pp. 670, seqq.

gation from God, and upon themselves as God's ministers. On this account they are to esteem and reverence both their function and their persons. As they are to feel an attachment to government as government, irrespective of the men who administer it; so they are to feel an attachment to magistrates as magistrates, irrespective of the party to which they belong. If I honor the ruler of my people, because he belongs to my party, and not because Christ enjoins it, I may be a good partisan, but I am not a good Christian. Without honor, reverence, esteem, attachment, there can be no true obedience. Constrained obedience is no obedience. I deliver up my purse to a robber at his command; but there is not one grain of honor or obedience in the act; there is a simple yielding to a power which I cannot resist. To call such an act obedience would be as great an abuse of language, as to speak of obedience to a falling tree or stone, in reference to the motion by which I avoided being crushed by their momentum. There is an element in obedience, over and above mere outward compliance, whether as due to parents, masters, or magistrates. Moreover, the obedience rendered to magistrates must be rendered as due to God, whose representatives and delegates they are. He who resists the magistrate, resists God. Let him who adventures such an act, tremble at his own rash daring. An unarmed minister of the law may seem a despicable thing. But an affront offered to him, in his ministerial capacity, is an affront offered to God himself, who is armed with the terrors of omnipotence.* Korah and his company thought little of the power of Moses; but they found whom they had offended in despising him, when the rent earth closed over their miserable remains, engulfing them within its dark and frightful caverns.

14. Finally: Civil government is man's best friend and

* Calv. Inst. Ch. Rel. B. 4, C. 20.

benefactor. "It is equally as necessary to mankind," says Calvin, "as bread and water, light and air, and far more excellent. For it not only tends to secure the accommodations arising from all these things, that men may breathe, eat, drink, and be sustained in life, * * * *; its objects also are, that idolatry, sacrileges against the name of God, blasphemies against his truth, and other offences against religion, may not openly appear and be disseminated among the people; that the public tranquillity may not be disturbed; that every person may enjoy his property without molestation; that men may transact their business together without fraud or injustice; that integrity and modesty may be cultivated among them; in short, that there may be a public form of religion among Christians, and that humanity may be maintained among men."*

Wise laws and a due administration of them are essential to the peace, order, and safety of every community. Law is at once the measure and the defender of right. It prescribes to every man a course of conduct which entitles him to the protection of society. It is, indeed, a master; but a master that is itself under the government of reason and benevolence. Its commands are founded on the welfare of those to whom they are addressed. But it is also a guardian, as well as a master. "Life, liberty, and the pursuit of happiness,"† are under its protecting care. It keeps watch and ward, by night and by day, over our persons, our property, our reputation, our morals, our entire well-being. Were its protection withdrawn, no man would remain for a day in his present possessions, no man would be secure for an hour against personal violence. Strength would take the place of right. Lands, tenements, goods, moneys, property of every name and kind, would lay open to a thousand invaders. The hand of every man would be against that of

---

* Calv. Inst. Ch. Rel. B. 4, C. 20.
† Const. United States.

every other. The fountains of the great deep, in the moral world, would be broken up. All things would rush to confusion and ruin; and the world itself would soon become one vast aceldama—a field of blood. Of law, then, to borrow the sublime personification of Hooker—" Of law there can no less be acknowledged, than that her seat is the bosom of God, her voice the harmony of the world. All things in heaven and earth do her homage; the very least as feeling her care, the greatest as not exempt from her power. Both angels and men, and creatures of what condition soever, though each in a different sort and name, yet all, with one uniform consent, admire her as the mother of their peace and joy."*

Here ends the inquiry into the origin and nature of civil society, and into the sources, sanctions, and boundaries of political government. Let us now briefly retrace our steps, survey the ground over which we have travelled, and gather up and present, in one comprehensive view, the results of this discussion. If I have not missed my aim, the following leading positions, among others of less prominence, have been established in the course of these inquiries.

Civil government is a divine institution. In favor of this view we have the concurrent testimony of reason, revelation, and the wisest human authority. The testimony of reason we have in the original aptitude of our nature for government; in the possession by man of conscience, benevolence, desire of esteem, and love of society, qualities clearly suited to promote the good of civil communities, and therefore a plain indication that it is the Creator's will that such communities should exist; in the admirable order and harmony of the material universe, evincing, analogically, that it is not the design of the Deity to abandon the moral world to chance and confusion; in the fact that, were such indeed

* Eccl. Pol. B. 1.

the divine purpose, our highest faculties—reason, reflection,
prudence, conscience, the power of suspénding our judgment, and liberty of choice—would be in vain, and caprice
and passion would become the governors of human conduct;
in the undoubted truth, that God's end in creating man—
the perfection of his nature and the happiness of his being
—would be defeated by the non-existence of civil government and law; in the actual condition and history of civil
society, which is such as to lead the mind directly to the
contemplation of God as its author; and in the actual
benefits flowing, as it were, in a full and perpetual stream,
from civil polity and law. The testimony of revelation we
have in numerous explicit passages, affirming, or implying,
the divinity of government; particularly, Ps. lxxxii. 1;
Prov. viii. 15, 16; Rom. xiii. 1-6; Tit. iii. 1; 1 Pet. ii. 13, 14;
and many others. The testimony of wise and good men we
have in the recorded opinions of such writers as Calvin,
Archbishop Bramhall, Bishops Butler and Sanderson,
Burke, Plato, Aristotle, Cicero, Grotius, Puffendorf, Montesquieu, Blackstone, and a host of others, dead and living,
of scarcely inferior note.

But as government is a truly divine, so is it, also, a truly
human institution. It has a twofold origin—one in the will
and purpose of the Deity, the other in the act and choice of
men. The divine will is its remote source and ultimate
basis; human covenants its direct spring and immediate
foundation. This view harmonizes two passages of holy
writ, which appear to be in contradiction to each other—one
of which, in explicit terms, affirms government to be an
"ordinance of God;" the other, in language equally distinct,
affirms it to be an "ordinance of man."

Hence, it is proper to inquire into the origin of civil
government, as a thing of human contrivance and design.
A distinction is to be made between natural society and
civil society. Natural society is a state wherein all are on a

footing of equality, freedom and independence. If this state
has never, in point of fact, existed among men, still it may
be conceived of in the mind, as an object of philosophical
speculation. Civil society, on the other hand, is the union
of a multitude of people, who agree, whether expressly or
tacitly it matters not, to live in subjection to government,
for certain great and beneficial purposes, not otherwise
attainable.

The basis of this subjection to government is a social
compact, " by which the whole people covenants with each
citizen, and each citizen with the whole people, that all shall
be governed by certain laws for the common good."* The
substantial elements of the social compact may be distinctly
traced in the Hebrew, Roman, Venetian, Carthagenian, and
English constitutions. They may be traced in the monarchies of continental Europe, which arose on the ruins of the
feudal system. But the principle of the social compact has
received its largest development, and been permitted to
work out its results with the greatest freedom in the new
world. This theory forms the basis of the civil polity
established by every State in the American Union, and is
fully embodied in the constitution of the general government. And it is the great and vivifying truth of popular
sovereignty, embodied in the doctrine of the social compact,
which has produced the European revolutions of our day,
and brought about the general substitution of constitutional
monarchies for the iron despotisms of the seventeenth and
eighteenth centuries.

Various objections have been urged against the theory of
a social compact—such as that it is anti-christian and negatively atheistic ; that it is destructive of the idea of an
organic unity in the state; that it subjects minorities to the
cruelty and injustice of majorities ; that it degrades into a
mere commercial relation that which exists between the

* Const. Mass.

rulers and the ruled ; that it makes revolution the law of
political life ; and that it converts capital punishment into
a bloody, popular revenge—a mere aggression upon individual right. These objections will not bear examination.
They are all founded either in very fallacious or very
imperfect notions as to the true nature and operation of the
doctrine of a social contract.

Our inquiries into the origin, nature, power, and sanctions
of civil society and government, draw after, or include in
them, certain general principles of polity and law, of no
little importance as guides to legislators, statesmen, jurists,
and citizens. They are such as these following :—1. Human
society is, originally, a condition in which all are equal,
free, and independent. 2. Civil society curtails this
equality, liberty, and independency; and so modifies natural
society as to give to it a recognized head and established rules
of intercourse. 3. States are moral persons, enjoying, with
respect to each other, the same rights, and subject to the
same obligations as real persons. 4. That form of polity
may be accounted best, which most effectually excludes
tyranny, without introducing anarchy. 5. The true spirit
of legislation is the spirit of moderation. 6. Government
ought to be just, granting no partial exemptions and imposing no special burdens. 7. The administration of justice
ought to be cheap, speedy, equal, uniform, and unembar-
rassed by perplexing technicalities. 8. The well-being of
the people is the central doctrine of political philosophy ;
benevolence the guiding and controlling principle of civil
law. 9. The style in which the laws are written, ought to
be exact, brief, and clear. 10. Laws should arise out of
circumstances, and be relative to specific ends. 11. Laws,
and not men, are the rulers in every justly constituted state.
12. Magistrates should ever bear in mind, that they are
God's ministers to the people for good ; and this, not that
they may be puffed up with pride, but that they may be

circumspect, active, just, and merciful in the exercise of their office, imitating and reflecting, as far as they may, God's providence in their care of God's children. 13. Citizens must render honor, esteem, and obedience to magistrates, as the representatives and vicegerents of the supreme and universal king. And, 14. Law is man's truest friend, and, next to the divine providence, from which indeed it cannot be rightfully separated, his greatest benefactor.

———

Having thus developed the true theory of civil society and government, it may not be amiss to call the reader's attention, in a few paragraphs, to the results of this theory, when applied as a principle of practical legislation. The American Government and Union are founded upon the principle of the social compact, or, which is the same thing expressed in other words, upon the doctrine of the sovereignty of the people. This theory has had freer scope in America than has elsewhere ever been accorded to it for working out its legitimate results. The results, then, providentially achieved through the agency of the American Union, will afford a decisive test of the excellence of the theory as a basis of civil polity. Let us glance at these results.

In eastern fable the world is a harp. Its strings are earth, air, fire, flood, life, death, and mind. At certain periods, an angel, flying through the heavens, strikes the harp. Its vibrations are those mighty issues of good and evil, which mark the destiny of our race. At one time, tempests, earthquakes, inundations, war, famine, and pestilence follow the mystic touch. At another, all nature is dressed in smiles and roses. The earth is covered with waving grass and luxuriant harvests. The fields are gay with bloom. The air is filled with fragrance. Rich flocks and herds crown the hill-tops, and spread themselves out over the valleys. And laughter rings out its merry peals on the glad ear of hope.

This is the fable. The moral is plain. The mighty tract of human affairs is marked by great epochs. Time is full of eras.

The mystic harp was touched, when the pilgrims set foot on Plymouth Rock. Its quivering strings discoursed their most eloquent music. The burden of the notes was,—human freedom; human brotherhood; human rights; the sovereignty of the people; the supremacy of law over will; the divine right of man to govern himself. The strain is still prolonged, in vibrations of ever-widening circuit. That was an era of eras. Its influence, vitalized by the American Union, is fast becoming paramount throughout the civilized world. Europe feels it, at this very moment, to her utmost extremities, in every sense, in every fibre, in every pulsation of her convulsed and struggling energies.

The great birth of that era is practical liberty;—liberty, based on the principles of the Gospel; liberty, fashioned into symmetry and beauty and strength by the moulding power of Christianity; liberty, which "places sovereignty in the hands of the people, and then sends them to the Bible, that they may learn how to wear the crown."* And what a birth! Already is the infant grown into a giant. Liberty, as it exists among us, that is, secured by constitutional guaranties, impregnated with Gospel principles, and freed from alliance with royalty, has raised this country from colonial bondage and insignificance to the rank of a leading power among the governments of earth.

The union of these States under one government, effected by our national Constitution, has given to America a career unparalleled, in all the annals of time, for rapidity and brilliancy. Her three millions of people have swelled, in little more than half a century, to twenty-five millions. Her one million square miles have expanded into nearly four millions. Her thirteen States have grown into thirty-one.

* Mathew's "Bible and Civil Government," Lec. 1.

Her navigation and commerce rival those of the oldest and most commercial nations. Her keels vex all waters. Her maritime means and maritime power are seen on all seas and oceans, lakes and rivers. Her inventive genius has given to the world the two greatest achievements of human ingenuity, in the steamboat and the electric telegraph. Two thousand steamers ply her waters; twenty thousand miles of magnetic wires form a net-work over her soil. The growth of her cities is more like magic than reality. New York has doubled its population in ten years. The man is yet living, who felled the first tree, and reared the first log-cabin, on the site of Cincinnati. Now that city contains one hundred and fifty thousand souls. It is larger than the ancient and venerable city of Bristol, in England.

The universal Christian education of our people is a precious blessing, for which we are indebted to our civil constitution and our union under it. Herein we enjoy an honorable distinction over all other nations. It is not in depth and vastness of learning, that the peculiarity consists. The Bacons, Hookers, Miltons, Souths, Baxters, Howes, Taylors, and Owens, of the mother country, in former times, have but few representatives among us at the present day. But what is wanting in depth, is made up in breadth. The few are less learned, but the masses are more enlightened. Diffusion, expansion, universality, is the great principle of American knowledge. This it is, which distinguishes ours from all other lands. It is the country of the free school and the free press, the country of the cheap book and the cheaper magazine and newspaper. The million are readers here. To satisfy so vast an intellectual craving, the press pours out its thousands of volumes daily. Many of these are trashy and worthless. But the great majority are not so. They embrace works of the highest value, in all the departments of knowledge, "issued and re-issued," as Mr. Godwin has well said, "till one doubts, whether the world can contain them all. Yet is there no cessation to the labors of the compositor and pressman; for what books fail to hold, is uttered in the periodical and the newspaper, which, like motes in the sunbeam, fill the whole air."* America prints and publishes twenty-seven hundred newspapers,—full one half of the whole number issued on the terraqueous globe.

Under the broad ægis of the American union, life is secure, property is secure, reputation is secure, the fruits of industry are secure, up to the point and beyond it, that such security is enjoyed under any other of the governments, now existing among men.

Such has been our career; such the results of our union under a free constitution. In resources, present and prospective; in available talent; in popular education and intelligence; in religion and piety; in practical philanthrophy; and in indomitable energy, to which obstacles are but incentives ;—in all these attributes and possessions, we would not, at this moment, exchange conditions with the proudest nation on the globe. We are not afraid of comparison with the oldest and the mightiest. Though the splendor of courts is unknown to us, though no patrician palaces or royal galleries adorn our soil, yet we would not part with our republican simplicity, our republican freedom, our republican virtue, and our republican prosperity and happiness, for all that Europe boasts of ancestral dignity and modern magnificence. What a vivifying effect has freedom had upon us! In every sense, we are a positive people. Negatives have no place in our nature. Every man, every organization, is instinct with earnest vitalities. Science is here in order to art. Art is the handmaid of utility. Philosophical speculation itself is valued only as it leads to practical issues. Life is a great school, in which the problems to be solved are realities, not abstractions. Thought, deci-

* " Review of the Last Half Century."

sion, action, are the grand elements of our character as a people. Here, then, are other excellent and admirable results of our system of government.

Our example has been a beacon light, and a centre of influence, to the whole American continent. When the nineteenth century opened, the United States were the only republic in this western world. What astonishing changes have taken place since! How sublime has been the advance of liberty! There is but one country,—Brazil,—from Behring's Straits to Cape Horn, in which the monarchical form of government still prevails. All the rest, except Canada, have, in imitation of the United States, by successive throes, cast off colonial dependence and bondage. There are pregnant indications, that a similar destiny awaits the only remaining monarchy; that, ere the lapse of many years, the empire of Brazil will be blotted from the map of America; and that the imperial crown and purple, as appertaining to this continent, will be known only as among the things that were. Here is another splendid result of the American union.

The influence of our institutions has not been confined to the climes of the setting sun. Contemporaneous with these transactions in the western world, great movements have been going on, and great results have been effected, in other parts of the globe. As far back as 1787, the emperor Joseph II, of Austria, observed, that the American revolution had given birth to reflections on freedom.* The fact, which that intelligent and sagacious monarch discerned at so early a day, now stands out, with the clearness of sunlight, to the observation and knowledge of the whole world.

The people of Europe have deeply felt this influence. It has modified their sentiments, opinions, and actions. High thoughts, high hopes, high aspirings have been kindled in men's bosoms, and deeds of noble daring prompted, by the

* Mr. Webster's Letter to Baron Hulsemann.

example of American liberty. During the entire period, which has elapsed since the adoption of our federal constitution, there has been a perpetual restlessness on the part of the people, and a perpetual struggle on the part of power to retain and enforce its rule. Revolutionary agitations have never ceased. But they burst forth with a violence, unknown before, in the great crisis of 1848. Then kings fled. Tyrannical ministers fled. The Pope fled. It seemed as if the whole system of aristocratic and arbitrary rule was about to fall into irretrievable ruin. Great was the tumult of kingdoms, deep calling unto deep, with responses loud and portentous. There is a lull in the storm at present; but the tempest is not over. There is a suspension of the volcanic action; but the lava boils and rages, deep in the bowels of the fiery mountain. It will burst forth in due time. There will be an eruption of popular sentiment and popular power, which will bury despotism deeper than the lava and ashes of Vesuvius buried the cities of Herculaneum and Pompeii.

A significant token of the influence of American ideas on European affairs is the fact, that even the Emperor of Austria, in lately giving a new constitution to his subjects. has introduced into it, doubtless from an outward pressure compelling him to do so, several of the great principles of civil liberty, embodied in our polity.* A still more significant token we have in the present condition of the papacy. Never before, since Luther hurled his iron gauntlet at the door of the Vatican, has Rome tottered and reeled, as under the heavings of the political earthquake of 1848. The papacy, though not dead, is dying. Like an expiring giant, it puts forth gigantic energies, even in the death-struggle. Its latest usurpation, the daring attempt to re-establish its ecclesiastical rule, and cast the fetters of its worn out superstition, over gospel-enlightened England, is

* Mr. Webster's Letter to Baron Hulsemann.

not the effect of conscious life and health, but rather a spasm of waning vitality.

But American thought, American genius and American freedom have extended their influence far beyond the confines of European life and society. Turkey, Egypt, Barbary, and a long belt of the western coast of Africa, have felt their genial power. The Sultan has established religious liberty by law, as the fruit of American missionary zeal. Persia owns the healthful pressure of American intelligence and American piety. The wild Indians of our own continent, the roving hunters and herdsmen of Asia, the imbruted savages of Africa, the cannibal barbarians of Polynesia, and the stolid and changeless dwellers in the flowery land, have all been breathed upon by the influences of a higher life, emanating from this Christian republic.

Here, again, do we behold the noble fruits of our national constitution and our national union, in shaking the thrones of despotism, in liberalizing the political systems of foreign lands, in widening the domain of civil freedom, and in extending the blessings of Christian knowledge and civilization to the very ends of the earth.

There is another glorious issue of our free and common government. It has made our country the true Bethesda,— a house of mercy for the suffering of all lands. It has made of it a new land of promise, to which the oppressed and stifled millions of Europe are rushing, like the tides of the ocean, to breathe the air of hope and freedom. And let them come! God forbid, that our beloved country, whose boast it is to be free and happy herself, should ever cease to afford to the sons and daughters of sorrow, fleeing from the wrongs and miseries of European despotism, a hearty welcome and a happy home! Let us not drive back from our shores one such refugee, to perish in the flood, or starve in the lap of an unnatural mother. Rather, let us extend to all a Christian welcome and a Christian care. Let us freely

7

bestow upon them the blessings of a Christian press, a Christian ministry, and a Christian education, teaching them to practise the duties of citizenship here, and to aspire to the honor of a nobler citizenship above. That we have the ability to exercise such a ministry of love and mercy, is due to our union in a federal government. Palsied be the hand, that would sunder a bond, which confers so beneficent, so godlike a power! Congealed be the fountain of life in him who would tear from his country's brow so bright a jewel, so resplendent a glory!

All these are results of our union, already achieved. But the hopes which it inspires are still more sublime and animating. It was a saying of Archimedes, that, if he had a place to stand on, he could move the world by the mechanical power of the lever. The dream of the ancient philosopher is the realization of our youthful republic. Standing upon the soil of freedom, and using the lever of Christian civilization, she has a place whereon and a power wherewith, not only to move the world, but to transform it from a desolate wilderness into the garden of the Lord, covering it with the light of truth and the beauty of goodness. There are two principles,—American principles preeminently,—which may be made to mould and sway the destinies of this earth. They are popular constitutional government and universal Christian education. The light of these principles, shining upon the nations in our example, will be like the sun in the firmament at high noon,—bright, glowing, penetrating, and vivifying. If we are true to our position and to the trust which it involves, these principles will move on, with a constantly accelerated progress, till they shall have completed the circuit of the earth;—dropping everywhere, in their course, the inestimable blessings of true liberty,—liberty based on the Bible, and vivified by its living power.

Such are the results of the American union; such the

hopes which it inspires; such our mission as a nation; such the part assigned us by providence, in the great work of improving human affairs.

Our path of duty is straight onward; and it is as clearly defined to the view, as the milky girdle of the heavens, in a cloudless night. We must stand by the constitution of our country. If that perish, our happiness perishes with it; the hopes that swell the hearts of millions perish; the sublime enterprises of Christian philanthrophy are arrested; and the chariot wheels of the gospel, that are now rolling on to the conquest of a world, are stopped, turned back, and made to recede far within the line, to which they have already advanced. We must stand by the laws of our country, indignantly frowning upon all sentiments and utterances of revolutionary violence. We must stand by the rulers of our country, honoring them as the ministers of God to us for good. We must stand by the union of our country, regarding it as the spring of our blessings, the palladium of our freedom, the sheet-anchor of our felicity, and the star of hope to the oppressed and down-trodden nations. We must stand by the schools of our country, multiplying and purifying these fountains of popular knowledge and virtue. Above all, we must imbibe the spirit, and think the thoughts, and pray the prayers, and live the life of Christ; for then are we the best citizens, when we are the best Christians. A free government, a free gospel, a free education, a free press, an open Bible, a reverence for authority, a willing subservience to law, and an enlightened, earnest, active piety, are the great and fitting elements of American institutions and American character.

As a nation, we hold a trust of mightiest significance. We hold it in the sight of suffering and struggling humanity. We hold it in full view of the illustrious dead, whose spirits are hovering over us, and whose affections are breathing around us. Let us catch the inspiration of their sentiments and example; and go forth, like men, to the fulfilment of our trust. Let us feel that we are ONE PEOPLE; having a common history, a common end, a common character, a common freedom, and a common destiny. Let us cling, with a firm grasp, to the union of these states, and to the principles on which it is founded. Let us give to these principles, under the stripes and stars of our common flag, a broader development, a higher activity. Let us transmit them to our children, as we received them from our fathers, entire, and untainted,—to be by them, in like manner, under the shield of the national banner, handed down to theirs, as a precious and perpetual inheritance. Then shall the republic be preserved, united and flourishing, to the latest period of time; and the civilization, the prosperity, the happiness, flowing from our glorious CONSTITUTIONAL UNION, as from a perennial spring, shall outstrip our fondest anticipations, and more than realise the brightest vision of bard or prophet.

Spirit of Washington! breathe upon our hearts, inspire our councils, and guide our policy!

BOOK I.—PRELIMINARY.

CHAPTER I.

Introductory Observations—Nature and Plan of the Work—Claims of the
Hebrew Law to our Study and Regard—The Question whether the
Mosaic Laws were binding upon other Nations than the Hebrews con-
sidered.

THE present and the future, justly perhaps, challenge our
chief attention; yet the past is not without a claim upon it.
As wisdom will not die with us, so neither is its birth a
thing of to-day. Brave men, according to the sentence of the
Roman poet,* lived before Agamemnon. The wise preacher
expresses a similar sentiment in another form of words:
"That which has been shall be," says he, "and there is
nothing new under the sun."†

History is philosophy teaching by example. But, unless
its lessons be correctly read, they will have little value.
History is, eminently, a work of interpretation. But the
interpretation will vary with every degree of knowledge
and skill in the interpreter. A chief function of the philosophical historian, is to trace out the great parallelisms of
opinions, manners, usages, and institutions in the different
periods of civilization, and to show how the records of the
past may be translated into the conceptions of the present.
Principles, substantially the same, are often disguised to us

* Horace.   † Ecclesiastes, i. 9.

by the changing forms in which they are clothed. An ancient law, custom, opinion, mode of action, or form of speech, then becomes truly intelligible to us, when we know what it corresponds to in the present state of society, when we can trace it to some living experience of our daily life, or some universal principle of our common humanity.*

The past is a dim page; and its obscurity is increased by every increase of distance from ourselves. There are many sources of error in our study of remote antiquity;—the loss of not a few of its most precious records, the fragmentary nature of its remaining annals, and the strange shapes into which its opinions and usages were cast. But the greatest source of misconception, and consequently of misinterpretation, lies in the transfer of modern ideas to those distant ages. The revolutions of time and empire are accompanied by the still more important revolutions of thought and opinion; and each succeeding age is apt to apply its own ideas to the interpretation of all the ages that have gone before it. If we would grapple successfully with the study of antiquity, this prejudice must be overcome; otherwise we shall rush upon error, and lose ourselves in a labyrinth of false conclusions. Yet the past must be read in the light of the present; and, as that light increases, the past will need to be continually re-read. In our study of it, as before intimated, we encounter only relics and fragments. It is only by repeated trials and by the occasional use of skilful conjecture, that the disjointed members can be ultimately arranged into something like the coherence of their original structure.

The design of the present treatise is, to investigate, open, and apply the political and moral lessons of a very interesting and instructive portion of universal history;—the polity and laws of the Hebrew people. For the correct understanding and explanation of this subject, the materials

* Prospective Review for February, 1848.

are more ample, as well as more reliable, than for the study
of any other history of as high an antiquity.

Learned men have occupied themselves in tracing, with
no little labor of research, the migrations of particular races
of men; the several seats into which nations have passed;
what were the Pelasgic, the Dorian, the Ionian colonizations; what the Phenician; by what track, and through
what stopping places, the Celts came into Europe; how the Punic race, quitting Asia, strayed to Ireland; and whence came
the Aztecs, and other aboriginal tribes of the western world.
To the elucidation of such themes has been applied, I say
not unworthily, the genius of a Balbi, a Malte-Brun, a
Bochart, a Le Clerc, a Niebuhr, a Pinkerton, and a Prescott.
But mind has its migrations not less than body.

"Mind is like a volatile essence, flitting hither and thither,
  An active, versatile agent, untiring in the principle of energy."

Thoughts colonize, as well as races. Ideas, like families,
have a genealogy and a propagation. To trace these
spiritual migrations, colonizations, genealogies; to ascertain
when and where the notions, which have most widely
affected mankind, sprang up, and how and whither they
have been propagated: to find out the birthplace of a great
idea; to follow it down in its passage from age to age, from
country to country, from race to race, from tongue to tongue,
from author to author; to trace principles in the revolutions,
to which they have given birth;—this, surely, were a work
not less worthy and instructive than the other. It is to a
labor of this kind that I now address myself.

What can afford nobler themes of study than the master
minds of our race, as seen in the thoughts created by their
genius, and the institutions established by their wisdom?
And what mind is more worthy to engage the profound
attention of our age, than his, whose high mission it was,
under Providence, to found a model government, combining

in a remarkable degree, liberty and law, the freedom of the individual with the welfare of the community? The polity established by Moses will be found, on examination, as venerable for its wisdom as it is for its antiquity. The best subsequent civilization has been built upon that ancient law. The Hebrew lawgiver is, in many respects, the man for the present. He belongs not solely to the past, as too common prejudice imagines. The great principles of public and private law, which he not only developed in theory, but reduced to practice, are so many lessons of inspired wisdom, so many lights of experience, to guide the labors of statesmen and legislators to the end of time. These lessons have a special pertinence and value at the present time (1850), when nations are in the birth-pangs of liberty.

It is proposed in the following treatise, to institute some inquiries into the foundation and structure of the Hebrew commonwealth, and into the nature and operation of the laws, which Moses, by divine command, delivered to his countrymen. We are entering, the reader will perceive, upon the study of a civilization which preceded the Grecian by nearly a thousand years. The Hebrew civilization was the earliest that history has recorded, in which the human faculties had free play. It was the earliest civilization which was based upon a true faith, a just science of politics, and a right philosophy of life.

Two systems of civilization,—the Asiatic and the Egyptian,—preceded the Hebrew culture.* The former had its foundation in the spiritual element of our nature; the latter, in the sensitive element. The leisure afforded by the shepherd life of Arabia and India, led to the observation of nature, and induced a contemplative habit of mind. On the other hand, an early devotion to agriculture directed the

* See on this subject Salvador's "Essay on Civilization before Moses," introductory to his "Histoire des Institutions de Moise et du Peuple Hebreu."

Egyptian mind to things of practical utility. The study of the seasons, the labors demanded by the cultivation of the earth, the necessity of providing against the overflowings of the Nile, the forethought and contrivance thus imposed upon men, and the early discovered convenience of an interchange of superfluous commodities, opened a career to industry, commerce, and the arts, which essentially modified the Egyptian civilization. The merchants of Egypt imported into their country the speculations of Asia, as well as its riches ; and the sages of Memphis learned the philosophy of those Indian gymnosophists, whose wisdom they ever held in the highest esteem. But, notwithstanding the strong infusion of Indian into Egyptian philosophy, the latter did not cease to be essentially physical.

The speculative opinions of these countries gave shape and color to their political institutions. The Indian philosophers, devoted to meditation, endeavored to reduce the practical affairs of life to the fanciful ideas, which they had formed of the harmony of the universe. In this spirit, they directed their social organizations. With them religion was the mother of politics. The Egyptian philosophers reversed this process. Receiving their first impulse from physical utility, they accommodated their religious faith and their civil institutions to their grosser material necessities. Contrary to what happened in the former case, the theology of the Egyptians flowed from their politics.

These two methods of procedure, though unlike in their principle, encountered, in their application, the same fruitful source of error. Physical wants are almost as difficult to determine with exactness, as those which belong to our mental or moral nature. The senses have their illusions not less than the intellect and the heart; and there is almost as much controversy about the useful and the hurtful, as there is about the just and the unjust. It happened, that the contemplative philosophers made a fatal, because groundless, application of their speculative notions to the social order; and that the physical philosophers, mistaking the real wants of humanity, invented an incoherent and grovelling mythology, which gave an ill-advised direction to men's minds.

At the same time the passions of individuals, as usually happens, obtained a mastering influence over these political organizations. The men, capable of taking the lead in public affairs, are always but a small part of the whole. These master spirits united together; formed themselves into a body; and, preferring their private interests to the interests of the public, they framed both their civil and ecclesiastical polity with a view to the promotion of their own personal ends. Hence resulted, both in India and Egypt, the establishment of privileged classes, called castes. These were composed of persons, who, pretending to be of a superior nature to the common herd, monopolized science, legislation, religion, honors, and riches. They neglected nothing that could strengthen and extend their own power. The ignorance and superstition of the people were reduced to a system. Idolatry reigned in all its hideous deformity. The multitude prostrated themselves before vile and loathsome objects. Human victims were offered up to impure and malignant deities. Religion was made to consist in rites the most puerile and extravagant. In short, an unrelenting and iron despotism, civil and ecclesiastical, held all men beneath its crushing power.

In the midst of this deplorable superstition and tyranny, there appeared a man, endowed with a noble genius; deeply versed in all the wisdom and all the folly of those times; strong in the energy of his own thought; and expressly raised up and qualified by Heaven to become the reformer of his age. That man was Moses, the inspired Hebrew law-giver. By the wisdom of his policy and the vigor of his genius, he overthrew the whole degrading apparatus of political juggglery and priestly despotism. He reduced the speculative ideas of his own and the preceding ages to a single sublime principle of simplicity. He recognized the welfare and happiness of the people as the one supreme law of political philosophy. He impressed a new character upon his age and species. He gave a new impulse to man, both in his individual and social energies. And he fixed upon his labors the indestructible seal of a divine wisdom and beneficence.

The code of Moses substituted, for the ecclesiastical despotism of Egypt, a moderate democracy; a government, based upon the natural superiority of intelligence; a civil constitution, freely accepted by the nation subjected to its authority. The world has since traversed an immense circuit of political ideas. But it is now coming back to the principles of government, announced by the inspired lawgiver of Judea.

To trace the labors of this man, in their progress and results; to unfold the system of government and law, which he instituted; to compare it with the other schemes of civil polity and jurisprudence, which have prevailed in the world; and to show how far the later systems have been modified and improved by the earlier,—is the purpose of the following work. That some method may be observed in the prosecution of this design, I have arranged my materials under six general divisions, each of which will form a distinct book.

The first book will embrace a variety of topics, collateral to the general subject of the work, and having important relations to it.

The second book will treat of the organic law of the Hebrew state. Herein the great principles, on which Moses founded his civil polity, will first be pointed out; and then it will be shown, how these principles were applied, in framing the constitution of the state, and in administering the affairs of the government.

The third book will unfold the rights and duties of persons in the Hebrew state.

The fourth book will exhibit a detail of the various regulations of the Mosaic code relating to property.

The fifth book will treat of the criminal jurisprudence of Moses.

The sixth book will be devoted to an elucidation of the. Hebrew sumptuary and sanitary laws, and of such other miscellaneous regulations, as do not appropriately fall under any of the preceding divisions.

Throughout the entire discussion of my subject, it will be my endeavor, on the one hand, to clear away from the Mosaic institutions the misconceptions of ignorance, and, on the other, to vindicate their wisdom and humanity from the malignant sneers of unbelievers and the specious but flimsy sophistries of misnamed philosophers. The whole tribe of infidel writers have fallen upon these institutions, and, as Warburton* strongly expresses it, have dipped their pencils in sulphur, in order to delineate them with horns and tails. Voltaire calls the Mosaic constitution a detestable polity. Bolingbroke and Spinoza brand it with names almost equally hard. Morgan does not scruple to characterize it as a refinement upon the superstition of Egypt. He unblushingly pronounces its laws unjust, cruel, tyrannical, and barbarous.† While the whole tribe of German rationalists, transcendentalists and pantheists affect to regard the Mosaic history as a tissue of fables, gross in conception, clumsy in execution, and revolting in morals.

How far these grave charges, proceeding from men, who have assumed the office of public teachers, either spring from ignorance of the Mosaic institutions, or are founded on

* Divine Legation, B. 5. § 1.
† Lowman on the Civil Government of the Hebrews, C. 1.

such a predisposition to censure and condemn, as dares first to falsify, in order afterwards to treat them as criminal and ridiculous, will, I trust, sufficiently appear, in the progress of these inquiries.

The intelligent reader will have noticed, that, in this attempt to elucidate the polity and laws of the ancient Hebrews, the classification of Sir William Blackstone has been adopted, as far as it is applicable to the subject in hand. In these researches, it is proposed to consider, in succession, the several enactments, or, at least, the several classes of enactments, in the Hebrew code. It is proposed to inquire into the ground, or reasons, on which the laws were based; whether those reasons have respect to the relation of the laws to the general wants of humanity, or their relation to the times and circumstances, in which the code had its origin. It is proposed, further, as opportunity offers, or occasion may seem to require, to institute comparisons between the legislation of the Hebrews and the legislation of other enlightened nations, both ancient and modern.

If the results, to which my investigations have conducted me, are not fallacious, the discussion, on which we are entering, will exhibit Moses as a man of magnanimous soul, and a legislator of consummate ability. It will evince the credibility and truth of his history, and vindicate his claim to a divine legation. It will establish an immeasurable superiority in the Mosaic institutes of government over all other ancient polities. It will exhibit them as embodying all the elements of the most refined and exalted statesmanship, and as entering deeply into the subsequent legislation, philosophy, literature, morals, and general civilization of mankind. It will prove the error of those philosophers, who have denounced the Jewish lawgiver as the apostle of despotism. It will, on the contrary, demonstrate the fact, that it is to his admirable legislative policy the world is indebted for its first ideas of constitutional republican liberty. In

110   COMMENTARIES ON THE

fine, it will show, that civil liberty, founded on equal rights,
guarded by written constitutions, and acting through the
popular will, was a blessing unknown to all antiquity,
beyond the single commonwealth, founded by that illustrious man, who, impelled by a lofty faith and a generous
patriotism, nobly declined the honors of a throne to lead
forth his enslaved countrymen to freedom and independence
and regulated government; among whom he sought no
other preëminence, than preëminent toil and devotion to his
country's welfare.

The Hebrew law has special claims upon the attention of
the antiquary, the theologian, the moralist, the lawyer, the
statesman, and the friend of popular liberty.

The mere lover of antiquarian research will here find
much to gratify a liberal curiosity. No other body of laws,
of an antiquity at all comparable to that of the Hebrew
code, has come down to us entire.* What a Greek would
call ancient was quite modern to a Hebrew. The Dracos,
the Solons, and the Lycurguses were many centuries posterior to the Jewish legislator. With the exception of the
Egyptian monarchy, of which we have little authentic information, reaching back to the exodus of the Israelites,
scarcely a few fragments of the laws of the contemporaneous
states,—as the Assyrian, Phrygian, Lydian, and Trojan,—
remain to the present time. Not only have those mighty
empires themselves fallen; but their institutions,—their
entire systems of government and administration, their
municipal, civil, ecclesiastical, military and moral laws,—
have perished also.† They are buried in a total darkness,
and the knowledge of them is obliterated from the memory
of men. But the Hebrew code has descended to us entire.
It has the completeness and clearness with which it came
from the hand of the lawgiver. It has survived the ravages

* Michaelis' Commentaries on the Laws of Moses, Art. 1.
† J. Q. Adams' Letters to his Son, p. 34.

of time, and remains as a venerable and precious relic of the most ancient legislative wisdom. This consideration alone renders the Mosaic law very remarkable, and invests it with a peculiar interest and charm to the lovers of antiquarian lore.

But this law has immeasurably higher claims upon the attention of the theologian. It is important for him to study it, first, that he may become acquainted with its divinity. The theological principles and purposes of the Jewish law constitute a remarkable and important branch of it. The primary truth of its theology, the truth which underlies the whole system, the truth which it is the leading object of the system to unfold and enforce, is that great doctrine, which forms the basis of all true religion—the self-existence, eternity, unity, perfections, and providence of Jehovah, the creator of heaven and earth. Setting itself in opposition to the universal religious belief and practice of mankind, at the time of its promulgation, it rejected and denounced all false gods; all image-worship, whether the object of adoration was intended as a representation of the true God, or of idols; and all the absurdities, pollutions, impieties, and abominations of idolatry, of every name and sort. Nor was this all. The law of Moses revealed, in type and shadow, the whole mystery of redemption, through the sacrificial death and the intercession of Jesus Christ. It prepared the way for the introduction and universal diffusion of that more spiritual religion, which was promulgated in the gospel. This is largely proved by the author of the Epistle to the Hebrews. Still further: Not only did the Mosaic law maintain the radical principles of true theology, not only did it prepare, by its typical representations, for the introduction of the gospel and the establishment of Messiah's kingdom, but, by the spirituality, breadth, and strictness of its moral precepts, it probed the human heart to the core, and laid bare the depths of its depravity. Thus did it expose to man his moral weakness, his inability to obtain eternal happiness on the ground of his own merit, and his need of a justifying righteousness out of himself. Thus did it shut him up to the faith of the gospel, and serve as " a schoolmaster to bring him to Christ."*

There is a second reason why the theologian should become well versed in the Mosaic law ; and that, not merely as containing a body of divinity, but also as developing a system of civil legislation. It is, that he may be able to vindicate the divine original of the law. He ought to make himself acquainted with the circumstances of the Jewish people, and with the ideas and usages of those distant ages, to the end that he may know the reasons on which the laws were grounded, and the objects they were designed to subserve. No otherwise can he become prepared to offer a solid and rational defence of the system, as of divine origin and authority. Several of the statutes of the Hebrew code, —for example, those relating to usury, to the fallow of the seventh year, to commerce, to the periodical remission of debts, &c.—have been assailed as destitute of the essential elements of general legislative policy.† Others,—as those relating to war and penal justice,—have been held up to execration, as breathing a cruel, vindictive, revengeful spirit. Others,—as those relating to polygamy, divorce, slavery, and blood-avengement,—have been denounced and decried as contravening the principles of immutable morality. While others still,—as, for instance, the statutes relating to meats, to the mode of cutting the hair and beard, to the boiling of a kid in the dam's milk, to the sowing of mixed seeds, to the combination of flax and wool in the same garment, &c. &c.—have been profanely ridiculed, as too trivial to proceed from the Divine Being. It is impossible to make a satisfactory defence of these and other like

* See Dean Graves's Lectures on the Pent., Pt. 1.

† Michaelis' Commentaries on the Laws of Moses, Art. 2.

statutes, without a competent knowledge of the causes, relations, and objects of the Hebrew polity. Whoever, therefore, would successfully vindicate revelation against sceptical cavils, and meet the learning of infidelity with a counter learning of religion, must make himself well acquainted with the Mosaic institutions.

The moralist, not less than the divine, will find the Mosaic code replete with principles and maxims, which will repay an attentive study of it. Where, in the whole compass of human literature, can a summary of moral duty be found, comparable to that contained in the decalogue? Here are the seminal principles of all virtue, piety, filial duty, justice, truth, benevolence, and internal purity. The law of Moses enjoined supreme love to God, love to our neighbor equal to that which we bear ourselves, reverence for old age, forgiveness of injuries, the rendering of good for evil, mutual kindness, compassion towards the unfortunate, and a generous hospitality. It earnestly enforced the conviction, that God requires of his rational creatures, not a mere external service, but an internal worship; desires duly regulated; and a benevolence expansive, ardent, and active. It taught, that ritual observances could not obtain pardon without repentance, nor repentance without reformation. It represented outward legal rites as designed to symbolize and recommend inward holiness, and the love of God as a practical principle, stimulating to the cultivation of purity, justice, humanity, mercy, and truth.* In a word, the gospel itself has scarcely a single moral precept, which had not been already promulgated in the Mosaic institution. In its moral teachings, Christianity does little more than give a greater breadth to principles, which Judaism had formed into a body of practical ethics, more than a thousand years before Socrates and Plato flourished.

A knowledge of the Mosaic laws will be useful to the

* Graves on the Pentateuch, Pt. 1.

8

lawyer, as well as to the theologian and the moralist. Every motive that can prompt him to the study of the Grecian and Roman jurisprudence, will, with at least an equal force, recommend the Hebrew jurisprudence to his attention. The mere technical lawyer may rest satisfied with a knowledge of the laws actually in force in the courts, where his practice lies. But he who aspires to a knowledge of the philosophy of law, will find it necessary to extend his view to the legislation of other climes and other ages. To him who knows nothing beyond the limits of his own country, or of the nations nearest to it in time and situation, many things in law will seem necessary, which yet, in other circumstances, are not so. He will not perceive the variations of legislative policy, which difference of climate, difference of manners, difference of purpose, and a hundred other circumstances must occasion. Then only will he become sensible of these things, and begin, without much perplexity, to philosophize, like Montesquieu, on the laws of his country, when he compares a variety of laws that are strange, and seem at first, perhaps, almost absurd.* But what system of laws offers to our consideration a greater number of new views, in this respect, than that of Moses? Remounting to the highest antiquity, framed in a distant quarter of the globe, and adapted to a climate, a people, and a purpose, differing in several important particulars, from any thing known among the western nations, it offers to the legal mind of Europe and America a study, as interesting as it is curious, as useful as it is recondite.

But further: There are some of the Mosaic laws, which are still in force, to a certain extent, and to which reference is often made in actions at law. The law respecting forbidden degrees of affinity in matrimonial alliances, is the strongest example of this.† This law has been formally incorporated into the jurisprudence of some Christian states;

* Michaelis Com., Art. 1.   † *Ibid.* Art. 2.

and even where this has ñot been done, it is generally
regarded as embodying, in reference to the points which it
embraces, the dictates of philosophical morality, as well as
the decisions of the divine sovereignty. In regard also to
the punishment of murder, Moses is often quoted, and his
authority, at least, in the opinion of many lawyers, as well
as divines, has still, with us, the force of law. How frequently, likewise, is he appealed to, when the question is
concerning divorce, or the punishment of seduction? In
these and other cases, where his authority is acknowledged,
or his rules and maxims of law are appealed to, in our
courts, it is necessary for a lawyer to understand his laws,
in all their bearings. I may add, with Michaelis, that it is
generally the most important, and, at the same time, the
most difficult points of law, which give the civilian and the
advocate, who are learned in the Mosaic laws, the best op-
portunities of making a distinguished figure.

Statesmen and legislators, equally with theologians, moralists, and lawyers, will find the study of the Mosaic legislation
a rich source of knowledge and wisdom. I have before spoken
of the high antiquity of this code, and claimed, that, on that
account alone, it is well worthy of our study. But a consideration of this nature forms neither its only nor its highest claim to our attention and regard. It contains, undeniably, the germ of almost everything precious in modern
civilization. It is a common fountain, from which, as will
appear in the sequel, the most enlightened nations of subsequent ages have drawn their best principles of political, civil,
and criminal law. It abounds in shining specimens of philosophical statesmanship and legislative policy. In short, it is
a system of legislation, which embodies and applies, with an
admirable skill and efficiency, most of the great principles of
just, wise, and equal government.

This leads me to the last observation, which I have to make
in submitting this detail of the points of chief attraction in

the Mosaic polity, viz. : that it is a legislation, which addresses itself with peculiar force to the earnest scrutiny and the
grateful affection of the friends of human rights and constitutional liberty. The book, which contains the record of it,
might fitly be made the text-book of the nations now struggling for the supremacy of the popular principle in government. The early colonists of New England proposed to
govern themselves, for a time, by the Hebrew laws. This
resolution of theirs has caused many a smile at their supposed
simplicity and rudeness. Most unjustly! Those clear-head-
ed and strong-hearted puritans distinctly saw and deeply
sympathized with the spirit of freedom, which runs through
those institutions. It was this quality in the laws of Moses,—
their decided friendliness to civil liberty, which secured the
affection and imitation of our forefathers. The principle of
habeas corpus was not in the Mosaic code. But as this is a
writ, designed to secure the citizen from unjust and illegal
imprisonment, and as imprisonment was a punishment unknown to the Hebrew law, there was no occasion, and, indeed,
no place for it there. With this exception, there is not, I believe, a single fundamental principle, which enters into the
constitution of a free State, which will not be found to have
been incorporated into the polity of the Hebrew commonwealth. That government is instituted for the good of the
many, and not of the few,—for the happiness of the people,
and not the advantage of the prince and the nobles ; that the
people, either directly or by representatives, should have a
voice in the enactment of the laws ; that the powers of the
several departments of government should be cautiously balanced ; that the laws should be equal in their operation, without special burdens or special exemptions ; that the life,
liberty, and property of no citizen should be infringed, but by
process of law ; that justice should hold an even balance,
neither respecting the persons of the rich, nor yielding to the
necessities of the poor ; that judicial proceedings should be

public, and conducted in accordance with established rules; that every man who obeys the laws, has a right to their protection; that education, embracing a knowledge of the laws, the obligations of citizenship, and the duties of morality, should be universal, and that whatever is valuable in political and social institutions, rests upon the intelligence and virtue of the people :—these great and vital principles of civil liberty were as fully embodied in the Hebrew constitution, as they are in the freest constitutions now existing among men.

By the governments of most ancient empires the people were regarded as of very little importance. Every where, even in States which boasted of their freedom, the masses were degraded, brutalized, and oppressed by arbitrary power. To this rule the Jewish republic formed an illustrious exception. Liberty to the masses, general competence, physical comfort, ease of mind, repose and opportunity of reflection, moral and religious instruction to all classes, equal laws, equal rights, equal justice,—these were the paramount objects of the Hebrew constitution, so far as its political relations were concerned. These features mark its kindred to our own, and set it widely apart and distinct from all other governments, which existed with it, and for many ages after it. It is not in Greece that liberty was cradled. This idea is, indeed, taught to our youth in the halls of learning, and proclaimed to our people from the halls of legislation. But it is none the less an error. Far other and higher is the origin of a blessing, so intimately interwoven with the welfare and progress of man. It was not the wisdom of Greece, speaking in the halls either of philosophy or legislation, but the wisdom of God, speaking from heaven through his servant Moses, which first taught mankind the doctrine of popular rights. Nothing can be wider of the truth than the idea, that it is in the political forms and usages of the Grecian and Roman commonwealths, we are to seek the origin and elements of our own republican institutions. No; it is rather

in that admirable frame of government, given by the oracle
of Jehovah, and established by the authority of the Supreme
Ruler of the World, that we find the type and model of our own
constitution. Even the Declaration of American Independence,—that terrible handwriting on the wall of despotism,
which has troubled the thoughts of many a tyrant,—that glorious pledge of liberty to the oppressed of every clime, was
but an echo from the deep thunders of Mount Sinai.

There is a question of considerable importance, which it is
proper briefly to consider in this introductory chapter, viz. :
whether the civil laws of Moses are binding upon us? The
Mosaic laws are commonly divided into moral, ceremonial,
and judicial or civil. Concerning the first two classes, no
doubt can arise in any mind. The moral laws are clearly of
perpetual obligation. The ceremonial laws were as clearly
abolished by Christ. But how is it with the civil laws?
Have they been abrogated? or are they still in force?

There have not been wanting writers of high authority,
who have held, that legislators ought to adhere closely to the
Mosaic laws, as being the wisest that can be framed. Nor is
this opinion without a plausible ground of support. The argument affirming it runs thus: God was the lawgiver of the
Hebrew people; but God is an infinitely wise law-giver;
therefore a body of laws emanating from him must be the
wisest that can be. This reasoning is plausible; but it is
fallacious. It overlooks a material distinction;—the distinction between laws intrinsically the wisest, and laws which
are the wisest only when viewed as relating to times and circumstances. Laws may be perfectly wise, when framed with
reference to one state of society, which would be unwise and
absurd, if framed with reference to another condition of things.

Civil laws, whatever be their source, to be adapted to the
wants of any given community, must arise out of circumstances, and be relative to certain specific ends; which ends,

under other circumstances, it might be the height of folly to pursue. When Solon was asked whether he had given the best laws to the Athenians, he replied: "I have given them the best that they were able to bear."* Sage response! Is it not of much the same nature with that declaration of divine wisdom to the Jews, which has so perplexed biblical inquirers, —" I gave them also statutes that were not good,"† that is, laws not absolutely the best, though they were relatively so. Montesquieu,‡ with that penetration which belongs to all his philosophical reflections, has observed, that the passage, cited above, is the sponge that wipes out all the difficulties, which are to be found in the law of Moses. This view of the meaning and force of the passage is confirmed by the words of our Savior. He has told us, that Moses tolerated divorce among the Jews, because of the hardness of their hearts.§ It is reasonable to conclude that he permitted the continuance of other social evils on the same principle. It is implied in our Lord's declaration, that, if the Jews of Moses' time had been less hard-hearted, that is, less prejudiced, less wedded to old notions and usages, several of his statutes would have been different from what they were. Is it not also involved, that the excellence, which Moses claims, and most justly, as belonging to his laws, is, as it respects some of them at least, a relative rather than an absolute excellence? Considerations of political expediency were often of prevailing force with him in framing his laws.

A wise legislator, whether divine or human, in framing a new code of laws for a people, will give attention to considerations of climate, of religion, of existing institutions, of settled maxims of government, of precedent, of morals, of customs, and of manners.‖ Out of all these there arises a general tone, or habit, of feeling, thinking, and acting, which constitutes what may be called the spirit of the nation. Now, a

* Plutarch's Life of Solon.   † Ezek. xx. 25.
‡ "Spirit of Laws," B. 19. C. 21.   § Mat. xix. 8. Mark x. 5.
‖ Mich. Com. Art. 8.

lawgiver shows himself deficient in legislative wisdom, who makes laws which shock the general sentiment of the people, laws which are at war with prevalent notions and rooted customs, laws which strip men of long established and favorite rights. Nations in general cling tenaciously to what is old. True legislative wisdom, therefore, will abide by established laws, when it can, even though satisfied, that other laws are better in themselves, and, but for the force of custom in favor of the old, would be more expedient. A wise lawgiver, who desires to see ancient usages replaced by new and different ones, will not attempt to change such customs at once, by direct legal enactments, but will seek, by the introduction of judicious provisions into his code, to lead the people to change them themselves.

Balbi, a citizen of the Republic of Venice, being at Pegu, was introduced to the king. In the interview which followed, he informed the monarch, that they had no king in his country. The latter instantly burst into a laugh, which ended in such a fit of coughing, that it was a long time before he was able to resume the conversation.* What wise man, in framing a code of laws for such a people, would propose the constitution of the United States as the basis of it? The establishment of a popular government would be the greatest calamity that could happen to such a nation. The best laws cannot at once be given to a people that has long been under bad ones. Their minds must be prepared for the reception of the best laws by the discipline of others, which are as good as they can bear. The pleadings of the Roman advocates at the civil tribunal of Varus were so odious to the Germans, that they cut out their tongues, crying,—" Viper, don't hiss."† There was nothing with which Mithridates so much reproached the Romans, as the formalities attending their proceedings at law.‡ And the Parthians could not endure the polished and easy manners of one of their kings, who had been educated at

* Montesquieu's Sp. of Laws, B. 19. C. 2.   † *Ibid.*   ‡ *Ibid.*

Rome. The virtues of refinement and affability, because unknown to that savage nation, Tacitus says, were regarded by
them as new vices.

The principle that laws must be relative to circumstances,
that they must grow out of the state of society, and be adapted
to its wants, is founded in reason, and confirmed by experience. It is, therefore, a just and solid principle, and must
commend itself as such to every enlightened judgment. But
it involves this clear and certain inference, that God never
intended the Mosaic laws to bind any nation but the Hebrews;
and that it would be quite foolish to detach particular parts
from the rest, and to attempt the ingrafting of them on other
systems, to which they must prove incongruous. The fundamental principle of the Hebrew polity,—the suppression of
idolatry and the maintenance of the worship of the one true
God,—so diverse from that of every other government ever
known among men, could not but enter essentially into the
frame of the laws. Besides this, the circumstances of climate,
soil, situation, political relations, character and power of the
neighboring nations, customs, mode of life, prevalent notions,
as to honor and disgrace, and the nature and severity of punishments, species and sources of crime, kinds of disease, &c.
&c., would modify a divine, quite as much as they would a
human legislation ; and still more, perhaps, in proportion to
its superior wisdom. If God were now, by special revelation,
to enact a code of civil laws for every nation on the globe,
it is not likely, that any two of them would agree in every
particular. It is certain, for example, that in such a code,
framed for the United States, there would be wanting the old
Hebrew laws respecting divorce, polygamy, blood-avengement, usury, the double portion of the first-born son, the exclusion of daughters from the inheritance, the marriage of a
deceased brother's childless widow, and the sumptuary laws
in general ; for none of the reasons, on which these laws were
based, has any existence among us; and to separate a law

from its principle, is like sundering the body from the head or the heart. No part of the Mosaic legislation is more excel-lent or admirable than the statute respecting the distribution and tenure of lands. Yet there is, probably, not a nation upon earth, at the present time, into whose civil code such a law could be introduced, without a violation of justice, and without shaking society to its deepest foundations. Where is the nation, now existing, that has its entire territory unappro-priated? But where this is not the case, with what justice could an equal partition of the land be made? Yet this was the first great principle of the Hebrew agrarian; and, in a nation situated as the Hebrews were, at the formation of their code, it was equitable and wise. The second fundamen-tal principle, which was equally just and beneficial, was an absolute prohibition of the sale of land in perpetuity. Yet, wise and righteous as this principle was in the Hebrew polity, what greater hardship could a lawgiver put upon those mem-bers of the state, who, when he framed his laws, were desti-tute of landed property, than that to which such a provision would subject them?

Moses himself, it is quite evident, was often compelled, by the force of circumstances, to admit into his code, laws, which under a different state of things, he would gladly have seen replaced by others. The law requiring a man to marry the widow of a brother, who had died without issue, is an instance in point. It is plain, as we shall see hereafter, that Moses cared very little for the execution of this law, and only gave place to it among his statutes as a piece of ancient Israelitish manners, and because he did not wish to shock the prejudi-ces of his countrymen by abolishing it. Throughout his le-gislation there are traces of the influence of a more ancient system of laws,—a lex non scripta, or jus consuetudinarium, —of much the same nature and force as the common law among us. Moses, as any wise legislator would do, (and cer-tainly he was all the wiser for being inspired,) paid no little deference to this law of custom. Sometimes he confirmed it, as it stood; sometimes he improved it by amendments; sometimes he restricted its operation; and sometimes he annulled it altogether.*

But more than this: The purely civil laws of Moses could be repealed or changed, as the altered state of the commonwealth required or justified, even during the continuance of the Mosaic government. For example, Moses's first law against usury forbade the taking of interest from the poor Israelites only;† his second law on the subject extended the same prohibition to the whole nation.‡ His statute, forbidding to kill animals for food in private, and enjoining to bring all such to the altar and offer them to Jehovah,§ remained in force only during the abode in the wilderness. It was formally repealed on entering the promised land.‖ The punishments originally annexed to the violation of laws, must be increased in severity, when, as often happens in the progress of society and of crime, they become too mild to secure obedience to the civil rule. Hence the penalty for theft, which Moses had fixed at a fourfold or fivefold restitution,¶ was increased to a sevenfold restitution in the time of Solomon.** The highest fine imposed by Moses in punishment for crime, was about fifteen dollars. What would that be, when the increasing wealth of the nation had proportionably diminished the value of gold and silver?

There is, indeed, an expression attached to many of the Mosaic laws, which, at first blush, would seem to make them absolutely unalterable. The expression is,—" a statute to you forever, throughout your generations."†† The question is: Is this form of words to be taken literally, or metaphorically?

* Mich. Comment. on the Laws of Moses, Art. 3.   † Exod. xxii. 25.
‡ Deut. xxiii. 19.   § Levit. xvii. 3–7.   ‖ Deut. xii. 20, 21.
¶ Ex. xxii. 1.   ** Prov. vi. 31.
†† Ex. xxvii. 21.   xxx. 21.   Lev. iii. 17.   vi. 8.   vii. 36.   x. 9.
xvi. 7.   xxiii. 14, 21, 31, 41.

Does it mean always, or only a great while? The words are annexed to the prohibition against the killing of animals in private, which, as we have seen, was subsequently repealed by Moses himself.* This makes it certain that the latter is the true meaning of the expression. It simply marks the distinction between permanent laws and those regulations which were made for a limited time. It signifies a law, which was to continue in force, till regularly abrogated, or modified.

The views, above presented, warrant the conclusion, that the Mosaic laws do not bind, and were never intended to bind, other nations. But this does not detract from the value of the Hebrew jurisprudence, as a philosophical and practical study, any more than the fact, that the Roman and British laws are not obligatory on us, detracts from the value of the Roman and British jurisprudence. We are at liberty to borrow what is good in the laws of other nations, however remote from us in time or space. My neighbor's lantern may be very useful to me, though I do not follow by its light exactly the same path which he pursued. In like manner, the laws of a foreign state may afford a highly advantageous light, though we do not copy everything which they contain. It is impossible to survey the legislative policy of the Hebrews without feeling the highest admiration of its wisdom, equity, and benevolence. It was a policy, directed not to foreign conquest, but to the culture and benefit of their own territory; a policy founded on the arts of peace. "If we were better acquainted with the comprehensive and far extended legislative knowledge of this people, very probably our own political system, so far at least as connected with agriculture, and as directed to the peaceful increase of our internal strength as a nation, might receive material improvement."

* Levit. xvii. 7. Deut. xii. 20, 21.

CHAPTER II.

Moses as a Man and a Lawgiver.

THE proofs of the divine mission of Moses will be submitted, and objections against it examined and refuted, in a subsequent part of this work. The object of the present chapter is to study the character of Moses, and to unfold the leading qualities of his mind and heart, irrespective of that supernatural illumination and guidance, which he enjoyed in the execution of his office.

It appears to be a fundamental principle in the divine administration never to do in an extraordinary way that which can be equally well accomplished in an ordinary way. But the heavens above us do not more exceed in height the earth on which we tread, than the methods of the supreme wisdom transcend the utmost stretch of human policy. There is an unseen but almighty hand behind the scenes of providence, which brings them forward, directs, adjusts, moulds, or removes them, according as the accomplishment of his purposes demands. By the cruel edict, which required the Hebrews to cast all their male children into the river Nile, Pharaoh intended to check the growing greatness of a nation, whose numbers he began to dread. But he who sitteth in the heavens, and laughs at the impotent malice of his enemies, nay, who even turns it as a two-edged sword against themselves, had far other purposes to answer through its agency. It was designed as the occasion of the adoption of Moses by no less a personage than the daughter of the reigning sovereign ; and this to the intent, that the future leader and lawgiver of the Hebrew people might be educated in a manner suited to fit him for his responsible office.

But is there no fear, that the child, breathing only the atmosphere of the court, almost from the first hour of its being, will lose all fellow-feeling for his countrymen, and become an Egyptian in everything but blood ? No ! The supreme wisdom is never defective, nor once inconsistent with itself. By a contrivance, no doubt suggested by the divine mind, the mother of Moses becomes his nurse. Thus the first words he hears is the story of his country's wrongs ; the first sentiment he feels, sympathy for the sorrow of his brethren, mingled with indignation against their oppressors.

Inspiration apart, Moses possessed all those endowments and qualities, which form the consummate statesman and chief magistrate :—an intellect of the highest order : a perfect mastery of all the civil wisdom of the age : a penetrating, comprehensive, and sagacious judgment: great promptness and energy in action : patriotism, which neither ingratitude, illtreatment, nor rebellion could quench, or even cool : a commanding and persuasive eloquence: a hearty love of truth: an incorruptible virtue: an entire freedom from selfish ambition: an invincible hatred of tyranny and injustice: a patient endurance of toil: a courageous contempt of danger: and a greatness of soul, in which he has never been surpassed by the most admired heroes of ancient or modern times. Comprehensiveness, grasp, force, sagacity were the predominant characteristics of his mind ; magnanimity, disinterestedness, an enthusiastic devotion to liberty, and an ardent but rational piety, the leading qualities of his heart.

The truth of this observation may be easily evinced.

Of the greatness and vigor of his intellectual endowments, his own writings afford ample proof. Never was the art of writing little and saying much displayed in higher perfection.

A perfect idea is given of the ground that philosophical history ought to cover, including not only the causes and current of events, but also the progress of society, manners, government, art, and religion, which prevailed in those early ages. True, most of his pictures are but sketches; but every touch reveals the hand of a master, and rarely do we feel any material deficiency. How vividly, and with what calm sublimity, do a few strokes of his pencil place the deluge before us! And whenever he favors us with a finished portrait, with what divine charms and graces does he invest it! Witness the history of the venerable patriarch, who won the exalted titles of the friend of God and father of the faithful. What grandeur of conception! What elevation of sentiment! What dignity of style! What simplicity and truthfulness in the narrative! What strength and beauty of coloring! What exquisite tenderness and pathos! Witness also the inimitable story of Joseph, the most faultless character, perhaps, in human annals, he alone excepted, who was holy, harmless, undefiled, and separate from sinners. The strange and stirring incidents of his life, and the high and generous qualities of his nature, are drawn in characters, which must challenge the praises and secure the affections of mankind, and which make us feel, that rivalry is forever distanced, and all attempts at imitation nugatory and hopeless.

The poetic talent of Moses, in its perfection one of the noblest gifts of God, is a striking evidence of his mental superiority. Read the noble lyric ode, in which he celebrates the passage of the Red Sea; or that, yet more powerful, in which he bids a last farewell to his countrymen. Among the Psalms, the plaintive elegy, beginning, "Lord, thou hast been our dwelling place in all generations," is ascribed to him; and none of all the number, exceeds it in mournful and affecting beauty.*

That Moses was master of all the civil wisdom then extant, we have the testimony of the proto-martyr Stephen, who says

* Christian Examiner for Sept. 1836.

of him, that he was " learned in all the wisdom of the Egyptians."* It is the acute and solid observation of Bishop Warburton† on this passage, that when the wisdom of a nation is spoken of, that which is characteristic of the nation must needs be meant; when the wisdom of a man, that which is peculiar to his quality and profession. On both grounds, civil or political wisdom must be here intended. It was for that the Egyptian nation was principally distinguished; and in that also must have consisted the eminence of one, who had a royal adoption, was bred up at court, and became at length the leader and lawgiver of a numerous people."‡

---

* Acts vii. 27.   † Divine Legation of Moses, B. 4. § 6.

‡ The knowledge of Moses, however, was not limited to subjects connected with government and law. He was "learned in *all* the wisdom of Egypt." He was master of her science as well as of her statesmanship. A remarkable proof of this we have in the history of the golden calf. The narrative states, that he burnt it in the fire, ground it to powder, and made the children of Israel drink of the dust. " The manner in which this was done is a proof of the extraordinary skill in the metallurgic arts possessed by the Egyptians; and, through their instruction, by the Hebrews. Modern chemistry employs tartaric acid, and reduces gold to powder. Stahl, one of the ablest chemists, informs us that natron, which is very common in the east, will produce the same effect; and, if the metal be previously heated, the effect is sooner produced. Hence Moses, in the first instance, cast the image into the fire, and then made it potable. Now one of two consequences must follow; either he performed a miracle, or he possessed very extensive scientific attainments. There is no account of any miraculous intervention of providence in the story; it then was the result of natural means, but such as none but a very well informed chemist could have known or used. No alternative, then, is left us, but a positive denial of the facts, or an admission of the knowledge of Moses. * * * * There is another small item of evidence here, to establish the fact of Moses's knowledge. He strewed the gold dust on water, and made the children of Israel drink of it. He was perfectly acquainted with the scientific effect of what he had done. He meant to aggravate the punishment, and impress upon their recollections the never to be forgotten memory of their disobedience, and to this latter end, he made their own sense of taste to minister; for of all detestable drinks, none is more so than that of gold thus rendered potable."—*Hawks on the Monuments of Egypt*, pp. 270, 271.

An intelligent infidel writer has borne eloquent testimony to the high intellectual qualities of the Hebrew sage. "The Jewish law," observes Rousseau,* "is a standing proof of the superior genius of the great man, by whom it was dictated; and though the vanity of philosophy and the blind prejudice of party see nothing in his character but a fortunate impostor, the true politician admires, in his institutions, that sagacious and comprehensive power of mind, which must ever lay the lasting foundation of human establishments." Bossuet† also, an authority of another order, after saying that the Jewish lawgiver was instructed in all the wisdom, human and divine, with which a great and noble genius could be adorned, adds the following observations: "Inspiration only carried to the highest point of certitude and perfection, that which had been sketched by the usage and the knowledge of the sagest of empires." Moses unquestionably belonged to that distinguished few, of whom Bolingbroke‡ has observed, that it has pleased the author of nature to mingle them, from time to time, at distant intervals, among the societies of men, to maintain the moral system of the universe at a certain point, though, doubtless, far below that of ideal perfection.

A natural explanation of the high intellectual development of Moses is afforded by the narrative of his early life. Adopted as her own son by the daughter of Pharaoh, the young Hebrew grew up in the midst of the wisest spirits of the nation. Endowed with a quick and penetrating genius, he readily mastered whatever of science and learning constituted the civilization of Egypt. Second in rank only to the reigning sovereign, and born to mould, direct, and govern his fellow men, there cannot be a doubt, that he was called to important public trusts before prudence dictated his retirement from the Egyptian court; and that, in discharging these trusts, he gained a familiar acquaintance with practical

* Social Contract, B. 2, c. 7. † Discours sur l'Histoire Universelle.
‡ Cited by Adams in his Defence of American Constitutions.

statesmanship. Later in life, while keeping the flocks of his father-in-law Jethro, he had ample opportunity for perfecting his knowledge by meditation, in the valleys of Horeb and Sinai, and along the shores of the Red Sea. Solitude, the observation of nature, and continual communion with God and his own thoughts, carried his enthusiasm to the highest pitch, and impressed upon his imagination that strong poetic tincture, which was reflected in his whole life. The burning bush of Horeb was a fit emblem of that inner flame of mingled patriotism and piety, which penetrated and irradiated all the faculties of his soul.

The soundness of Moses's judgment was evinced, as on various other occasions, so especially in the admirable measures which he employed to quell the rebellion of Korah, to soothe the agitations of the multitude, and to reconcile the people to the elevation of Aaron to the priesthood.*

The promptness with which Moses decided, and the energy with which he put his determinations into execution, are fearfully illustrated in the course which he pursued, when, on descending from the Mount, he found that the people had made a golden calf, with the design of returning to Egypt under its conduct. Having burnt the idol in the fire, ground it to powder, strewed it upon the water, and caused the children of Israel to drink of it, in derision of its divinity, he took his station in the gate of the camp, and cried :—" Who is on Jehovah's side ? To me !" The sons of Levi promptly answered to the challenge, and were ordered to go in and out from gate to gate throughout the camp, and to slay every man his brother, and every man his companion, and every man his neighbor. The order was faithfully executed, and there fell of the people that day about three thousand souls.† This salutary severity had the desired effect. The murmurs of the people were thoroughly allayed, and all thought of going back to Egypt was for the time laid aside. How finely

* Num. xvi.   † Ex. xxxii. 26–29.

do the strength and ardor of Moses's patriotism shine out in the sequel of this very history! No sooner is the needful work of punishment ended, than we find this devoted lover of his country returning to Jehovah, and giving vent to the deep and agonized emotions of his soul: "O, this people have sinned a great sin, and have made them gods of gold; yet now, if thou wilt, forgive their sin; and if not, blot me, I pray thee, out of thy book."* Most truly has it been said,† that there is nothing in all the scriptures more calmly majestic than the divine reply: "Whosoever hath sinned against me, him will I blot out of my book."‡

In the same passage, in which St. Stephen attests the wisdom of Moses, he says, that he was "mighty in words and in deeds."§ Here we have a clear testimony to the eminence of Moses in eloquence. When Moses received his commission to become the leader of his countrymen, he did undoubtedly excuse himself on the ground, that he was not eloquent.|| This plea might have been based upon some impediment in his speech; but it is more probable, that it proceeded from a modest diffidence, which is so often the attendant of true merit. However this may have been, there is reason to believe, that the impediments, of whatever sort they were, were gradually overcome, and that Moses became as eminent in oratory, as he was in all the other great and commanding qualities of a civil leader. Certainly he had the mental gifts, which eloquence requires, for he was a poet, and dealt in the living images and passionate sentiments, which fire the hearts of congregated thousands.¶

Along with a powerful understanding to plan, and an inflexible will to adhere to his resolves, Moses possessed a mighty heart to bear him through an enterprize, the most difficult, perhaps, ever undertaken by man. To present in detail the proofs of his magnanimity and freedom from personal

---

* Ex. xxxii. 31, 32.   † Ch. Exam. for Sept. 1836.   ‡ Ex. xxxii. 33.
§ Acts vii. 27. || Ex. iv. 10.   ¶ Ch. Exam. for Sept. 1836.

ambition, would be to transcribe no small part of his history.
That he dwelt in a palace, that he basked in the sunshine of
royal favor, that he was surrounded with the splendors and
luxuries of a court, with perhaps a prospect of wearing the
diadem himself, and yet that even there, in the midst of all
that was flattering to the pride and seductive to the baser
passions of human nature, his heart beat in sympathy with
his country's wrongs, and his thoughts were all engaged about
the methods of its deliverance,—these circumstances are of
themselves a sufficient proof of moral greatness. Encompassed by every species of allurement, he forgets not, for a
single moment, that his brethren are groaning beneath the
pressure of a bitter servitude.

Nor was it in a single great act of self-devotion, such as
that of renouncing his brilliant prospects of wealth and power,
that his generosity shone out. No! It was the living, guiding, moulding principle of his whole life. And though he
met with no grateful return, though he heard not one word of
thankfulness, where he heard a million of complaint and up-
braiding, his spirit of self-sacrifice endured to the last, nor
abated a particle of its vigor. His post was not one that
common ambition would have coveted. It brought with it no
superiority of comfort, or luxury, or visible splendor. Even
his dress, Josephus testifies, was that of a common man; and
in all other respects he behaved like one of the common people, nor sought to distinguish himself from the multitude.
Though his many shining qualities obtained for him an
unbounded influence in the state, yet never in a solitary instance, did he use it for his own individual advantage, or that
of his family. He provided no places of honor, trust, or
profit for his children or his kindred. In the choice of a successor, he thinks not of his family or his tribe, but of his
country. Public office he looks upon, not as a means of
wealth or personal gratification, but as a solemn trust, to be
executed for the benefit of the governed. Merit is the sole

claim to magistracy, which he recognizes as valid ; all others are, in his esteem, lighter than vanity.

Josephus* relates, that, during the childhood of Moses, Pharaoh, holding him in his arms, placed the crown of Egypt upon his head. Instantly the young hero tore it from his temples, cast it on the ground, and trod it beneath his feet. This fiction,—for it is probably nothing more than a fiction, —is admirably imagined to set forth, in vivid colors, one of the predominant qualities of his great soul,—a deep detestation of that tyranny, which but too often accompanies the possession of kingly power.

A strong proof of this disposition in Moses we have in an incident related in the second chapter of Exodus.† Upon a certain occasion he saw an Egyptian beating a Hebrew. With the impetuosity of a generous and impulsive nature, he launched upon the assailant, and, in the struggle which ensued, the latter was slain. A close inspection of the narrative renders it probable, that this man was not a simple citizen, but an agent of the Egyptian tyranny; a circumstance, which, if it does not justify, serves at least to palliate the conduct of Moses.‡

A story of kindred significance we find narrated in the same chapter of Exodus.§ Scarcely had Moses, in his flight from Egypt, reached the borders of Midian, when he saw several shepherds chasing some young women from a well, where they were watering their flocks. Instantly, without a thought of their number or his own danger, he flies to the succor of the injured and weaker party, and, single-handed, beats back the assailants, leaving the place in the sole occupancy of the young shepherdesses.

Such were all the instincts of his nature. The injured ever found in him a ready helper ; the injurer, an uncom-

* Antiquities of the Jews, L. 2. c. 5. † Vv. 11, 12.
‡ Salvador's " Histoire des Institutions de Moise," Introduction.
§ Vv. 15–17.

promising foe. Tyranny he abhorred; while the just and the right were with him little short of a passion.

Such was Moses, the illustrious agent employed by providence to lead forth the chosen tribes from the hard bondage of Egypt to the enjoyment of independent and constitutional government in the land of promise. And it must be confessed, that all his great endowments were not more than enough for the task to which he had been called. The Israelites were a stubborn people; now first forming into civil society; greatly licentious; and the more so because they were just emerging from a state of slavery. Upon all the principles of human calculation, their passage through the wilderness would be attended with unparalleled difficulties. A country without water, without vegetation, without any of the ordinary means of subsistence, was to be traversed. Powerful enemies were to be met and overcome. A spirit-broken people was to be braced up to bold and decisive action; and an ungovernable people was to be reduced and brought under the restraints of law and order.*

But, more than all, and worse than all, the many ten thousands whom he commanded, were madly in love with the idolatries of Egypt. Hence, on every little distress, " Let us go back to Egypt," was their never-ceasing cry. It was not merely the flesh-pots,—the fish, the cucumbers, the melons, the leeks, the onions, and the garlic,†—it was the spiritual luxury of Egypt, her superstitions, with which the people were so debauched; a debauchery, which neither gentleness nor severity, neither the mild beams of mercy nor the glittering sword of vengeance, neither the blaze of miracle nor the terrors of prophetic denunciation, could ever wholly overcome; a debauchery, of whose malignant virus the nation was at last purged only in the fiery furnace of a seventy years' captivity.

How much did the position of Moses differ from that of

* Chr. Examiner for Sept., 1836.   † Num. xi. 5.

all other legislators !* Lycurgus, Draco, Solon, and Numa, in the midst of men already in subjection to laws and possessed of a country, are borne, as it were, by the ordinary current of events, to their elevated functions. Zaleucus, Pythagoras, Zoroaster and Confucius, peacefully dictate sage maxims to their fellow citizens. Even Mahomet, after fifteen years meditation in solitude, presents a modified code to people already living under established laws. But Moses, after a forty years' absence, re-enters Egypt, a stranger to his own countrymen, and without any the least physical force at his command. The people, whom he is to form into a nation, are without a country. Before he can propose to them a system of laws, it will be necessary to conquer a country. It will be necessary to conquer their oppressors. It will be necessary to conquer themselves; to conquer the deep depression that has seized upon their spirits ; to triumph over a frightful crowd of opposing circumstances.

Insurmountable, to human apprehension, are the difficulties which surround the Hebrew lawgiver ; and the most fearful of them are those which he has to contend with in his own countrymen. There is neither union nor confidence among them. There is neither courage nor self-respect. Long centuries of slavery and misery have extinguished such sentiments. From this people he can expect nothing. Yet without this people he can do nothing. What remains to him ? Before he gives them freedom, he must make them capable of freedom. He must restore to them those elements of humanity which they have lost. He must give back to them the qualities which a long barbarism has smothered. He must rekindle in them hope, courage, generosity, self-respect, and enthusiasm. With noble bearing did our intrepid chief meet and conquer every difficulty. Dying,

* See on the subject of this and the following paragraph a tract by Schiller on the Mission of Moses. It is rationalistic in its tone, but contains many excellent reflections.

he bequeathed to his countrymen a constitution of government and a body of laws, embracing most of the great principles of political wisdom, and entitled to be regarded in its leading features as a model of free institutions for all after ages.

At the advanced age of one hundred and twenty years, while yet his eye was not dim, nor his natural strength abated, Moses paid the common debt of nature, and was gathered to his fathers. More than thirty centuries have since fulfilled their cycles, and are numbered with the years before the flood. Yet the influence of his genius and writings survives, as vigorous and benign in its action at the present moment, as when his compatriots felt the first gush of grief at his irreparable loss. To whom else of all the illustrious dead has such a thing happened? What other legislator of ancient times is still exerting any considerable influence in the world? What philosopher, what statesman, of antiquity, can boast a single disciple now? What other voice comes down to us with equal power over the stormy waves of time? Though the daily sacrifice has ceased, and the distinction of the tribes is lost; though the temple has not left one stone upon another, and the altar fires have been extinguished for ages, yet wherever a Jew is found,—and he is found wherever the foot of an adventurer treads,—he is a living monument of the power, which the great Hebrew statesman still has over the minds and hearts of his countrymen.*

Nor this alone. The whole civilized world has felt, and feels, and to the end of time will continue to feel, the quickening power of his genius and example. Who knows not, and, knowing, owns not, the obligations of mankind to his inspired writings for their silent, but mighty influence, in promoting science, taste, and literature; in purifying the social institutions; in destroying the cruel and debasing

* Christian Examiner for Sept., 1836.

superstitions of paganism; in enlarging the domain of civil liberty; in securing the rights of conscience; in invigorating both public and private morals; in allaying and rooting out abuses of government; in giving a healthful tone to legislation; and in infusing the purest, the most elevating, and the most conservative elements into human civilization. Of all the great men, who have played their part on the broad theatre of human action, Moses is the one, who has exerted the most pregnant influence on the destinies of mankind, and on the direction and progress of civilization. His lofty intellect, his greatness of soul, his preëminent virtue, and his unequalled services in the cause of true religion and of republican constitutional liberty, place him at the head of those illustrious benefactors of mankind, who here and there, though at intervals too distant from each other, embellish the canvass of history.

It is sometimes alleged, that Moses borrowed his institutions from Egypt. This is said for the purpose of derogating from his merit as a lawgiver, and especially from his reputation as an inspired lawgiver. But from what fountain did Egypt herself, in all likelihood, draw her best principles of law? There is a common fact in the history of the Hebrews and the Egyptians, hitherto so much overlooked, that I do not remember to have seen it adverted to by any writer, which, nevertheless, sheds an important light on this subject. By an extraordinary concurrence of circumstances, an Israelite, some centuries prior to the age of Moses, had been raised to the primacy of Egypt. For eighty successive years Joseph swayed the destinies of that empire; and an inspired writer has told us, that he taught her senators wisdom.* It cannot be doubted, therefore, that many of the wisest maxims of Egyptian policy were due to the genius of that illustrious minister, and to the special divine guidance vouchsafed to him in his administration.

* Psalm cv. 22.

But suppose it to be true, that some, or many, of the civil laws of Egypt were embodied in the Hebrew code, what inference, derogatory either to the genius or the inspiration of Moses, would such a fact warrant? Did any body ever suppose it detracted from the merit of the Roman jurisprudence, that the twelve tables were framed by a commission, which had been appointed by the senate to examine the laws of other nations? And how would such a fact militate against the inspiration of the lawgiver? The spirit of God might as well prompt him to take from the legislation of a foreign state that which was valuable, and with which he and his people were already acquainted, as to dictate laws entirely new, and till then unknown. The former is as natural and legitimate a province of inspiration as the latter. Besides: Let all that is alleged be granted; it still remains true, that, in their fundamental principles, the two constitutions were the antipodes of each other. Egypt was a despotism; Judea a republic. The people of the former were slaves; the people of the latter, freemen. In Egypt the prince governed, or the priesthood through the prince; in Palestine the nation. The Egyptian government was founded on force; the Hebrew government on consent. The former was a government of will; the latter, a government of law. In Egypt an iron system of caste crushed every opening faculty and every generous aspiration of man's nature; on the banner of Palestine flamed, in living letters, liberty, equality, fraternity.

Be it that the institutions and manners of his age exacted their tribute from the Jewish lawgiver in modifying his system of legislation. It is what I have admitted and even contended for in the preceding chapter. Still, the results which he achieved, are none the less great; none the less original; none the less stupendous. The greatness of Egypt, far from diminishing, serves only to enhance the real glory of his labors. Egypt has fallen; and the most learned researches have hitherto shed but a feeble light on her civilization. But Moses lived; and his name and works are known and honored among all nations. Though neither brass nor marble has preserved to us the shape and stature of his outer man, the finer elements of his soul, the form and lineaments of his inner being, stand revealed to us, in all their fair proportions, in the monuments which his genius has left behind him. Though his body has long since been mingled with its kindred dust, yet all of him, as Tacitus has elegantly said of Agricola, all of him, which gained the love and admiration of his cotemporaries, still subsists, and will for ever subsist, preserved in the minds of men, the register of ages, and the records of fame. Even the pyramids have not availed to preserve the Pharaohs from forgetfulness. Those proud monarchs have sunk to the common lot of oblivion, inglorious and unremembered. But Moses, by his worthy deeds and his immortal writings, has triumphed over the injuries of time.

CHAPTER III.

Uncertainty of early Profane History.

THE credibility of the historical books of the Old Testament, and those of Moses in particular, has been called in question, on the ground, that they contain statements at variance with the historical records of the learned heathen nations of antiquity. Thus the pretence of ancient history is made a plea for infidelity ; and by many no argument against revelation is thought more plausible than its contrariety to some of the averments of early profane story. How little force there is in this argument will appear in the present chapter, the purpose of which is to show, that there is no certain credibility in those ancient histories, which contradict the Bible. This chapter will be followed by another, whose aim will be to prove that all the marks of historical truth are found in the record of Moses. In this endeavor I must gratefully acknowledge my indebtedness to the learned industry of Bishop Stillingfleet, to whose admirable Origines Sacræ, I would refer those persons, who desire to see the argument presented in all its breadth and strength.

It is related of Sir Walter Raleigh, who added to the graces of a courtier and the bravery of a hero the higher accomplishments of a learned historian, that, in despair of arriving at the truth of an event, which happened under his own window, he committed to the flames some of his most valuable manuscripts on historical subjects. It is but a few years ago, that an important appropriation bill was lost in the expiring throes of an annual session of the American congress. On the re-assembling of that body the following year, gentlemen of undoubted probity and honor gave such conflicting accounts of the causes of the failure of the bill, as were, in no small degree, calculated to impair our confidence in the general credibility of human testimony. The writer retains a vivid recollection of the painful emotions and reflections, which that event excited in his mind. It brought forcibly to remem brance the observation which Addison puts into the mouth of Sir Roger de Coverly, in the Spectator, that it is not mere-ly that on most questions much may be said on both sides, but that the real obscurities on many subjects of an historical character are such as to pain and perplex every honest in-quirer.

Who wrote Junius? Who discovered the differential calculus? Who killed Tecumseh? Who commanded the American forces at the battle of Bunker Hill? Who was the hero of lake Erie? On what day were the signatures affixed to the declaration of American Independence? What was the original policy of the American cabinet in reference to the employment of our public ships in the last war with Great Britain? Did Napoleon poison his sick soldiers at Jaffa? Was the beautiful Mary, perishing on the scaffold under the insatiate envy of her virgin rival, guilty or innocent? These, and a thousand other questions, are still unadjudicated in the great court of modern history.

How, then, can we hope to penetrate the abyss of time, and bring forth to the light the mysteries, which lie concealed within its profound recesses? We look back upon the con-fused traditions of the first ages of the world, as upon some distant ocean; but shadows, clouds, and darkness brood over its troubled surface; and if an occasional glimmer of truth appear, it is but a rush-light, too feeble to reveal to us events in their true relations to each other. In all that relates to the

birth and infancy of our race, its social relations, its progress
in art and learning, and the achievements and monuments of
genius, in those distant ages, profane history is either a total
blank, or so obscured in the exaggerated imagery of epic
poetry and the wild and dreamy myths of gods and demi-
gods, as to be no better than a mere ignis fatuus in directing our steps in the search after historical truth.

There is, then, no ground of assent to any ancient histories,
which give an account of things different from that contained
in the Bible. The truth of this proposition will be proved by
three arguments: First, from the obvious inability of these
histories to give an authentic account of the earliest transactions of mankind. Secondly, from the confusion and ambiguity of the accounts, which they profess to give. And
thirdly, from the manifest partiality of the historians to their
respective countries, and their manifest inconsistency with
each other.*

The first general argument is drawn from the plain inability of any ancient history to afford a creditable narrative of
the first ages of the world. If this point be established, it
will of itself demonstrate the incompetency of those records to
overthrow or invalidate the facts of sacred history. The inability or defect, here referred to, is twofold. It is both
general and special; general, in so far as it is common to all
ancient histories; special, in so far as it is peculiar to the
history of each of the several nations, whose pretensions are
highest on the score of antiquity.

The general defect, the defect common to the history of all
ancient nations, is the want of authentic early records. If a
nation has no certain mode of preserving its traditions, if it
has no permanent and safe depository of historical truth, and
if, in addition to this deficiency, its people are subjected to
the necessity of constant bodily labor, and of frequent removals from one place to another, it is clear that lapse of time

* Stillingfleet's Origines Sacræ, Book 1, Chap. 1.

will introduce many corruptions into its history. This may happen, nay must happen, through the imperfection of men's memory, through the ignorance and barbarism of rude ages, and still more, perhaps, through the dishonesty of those, whose interest lies in a deviation from the original tradition.

The above is undoubtedly a true description of the state of most ancient nations in their infancy. Their poverty laid them under the necessity of incessant physical toil; and their ignorance of the true principles of agricultural science, and the best modes of agricultural practice, led to the adoption of a wandering manner of life. The conflict with want and necessity was unceasing. Men had neither the leisure nor the opportunity to cultivate arts and sciences. But without these, the memory of their former state must gradually fade away, and at length be lost in mere fable. And this, in fact, was the case with most of the earliest nations. A sufficient proof of this is the silly fiction, not uncommon with ancient tribes, that they sprang from the soil, on which they lived. What credible account of the first ages can be looked for from nations, so defective in the knowledge of their own origin?

A consideration of the several methods, employed by mankind, for conveying knowledge to one another, will still further evince the want of permanent historical records of an early date. These methods are chiefly three: words, symbols, and letters.

Spoken words were undoubtedly the earliest means in use of communicating ideas. But words are of so evanescent a nature, men's memories are so treacherous, and their minds are so clouded by ignorance, prejudice, and interest, that nothing can be more uncertain than the reports of oral tradition.

The second method of conveying knowledge was by means of representative symbols. Such were the Egyptian hieroglyphics, which were, partly at least, of a symbolical nature. The defectiveness of hieroglyphics as an instrument of communicating knowledge, may be inferred from the following circumstances: 1. The time and labor necessarily consumed in the invention of them. 2. Their obscurity and ambiguity, after they had been invented. 3. Their limited extent, as compared with the whole field of human thought and knowledge. And 4. The fact that the use of them must have been confined to the favored few, who had leisure and ability to master their occult significations and refined mysteries. The variety of interpretations, to which they were liable, and their consequent uncertainty, are aptly illustrated in the different opinions of the ancients as to the meaning of a golden hieroglyphic, consisting of two dogs, a hawk and an ibis. Some understood the dogs to represent the two hemispheres; others, the two tropics. By some the hawk was supposed to signify the sun; by others the equinoctial. By the ibis some thought the moon to be intended; others, the zodiac. And if, as modern researches have shown, hieroglyphics were representatives sometimes of ideas, and sometimes of sounds alone, this is a new source of perplexity. It makes the language which they speak still more ambiguous, and increases the confusion and uncertainty of their reports.

From the imperfection of the foregoing methods of communicating ideas, it is evident, that, before there can exist any certain medium of conveying the knowledge of past to coming ages, some way must be found out, whereby, as has been aptly said,* men's voices may be seen, and their fingers made to speak. This can be done only by means of a phonic alphabet; that is, by the invention of certain characters, which shall represent all the articulate sounds of the human voice, employed in spoken language. Well has Galileo called this important discovery " admirandarum omnium inventionum humanarum signaculum," the masterpiece of all the wonderful inventions of human genius. If there were no other proof of the obscurity and deficiency of ancient history than the uncertainty as to the inventor of letters,—the only effectual mode

* Stillingfleet's Origines Sacræ, B. 1, C. 1.

of preserving and transmitting knowledge, that alone would
be a demonstration of it. There was hardly an ancient nation of any note, which did not put in its claim to this honor.
The Jews attributed the invention of letters to Adam, or
Moses; the Egyptians, to Hermes; the Phenicians to Taautus;
the Greeks, to Cadmus; and the Romans, to Saturn.

So much for the general deficiency of ancient histories,—
the want of permanent and authentic early records for the
perpetuation of historical truth. Let us proceed now to a
closer study of the particular histories of the several nations,
which enjoy the most distinguished reputation both for antiquity and learning. There are four of these,—the Phenicians, the Egyptians, the Chaldeans, and the Greeks. It is
proposed to inquire into the credibility of their early records,
as also into the ages of their most distinguished historians.

We will begin with the history of the Phenicians. The
most celebrated historian of this people was Sanchoniathon.
His history of Phenicia, in nine books, was translated into
Greek by Philo Biblius. The age of this writer is a question,
which has been much in debate among chronologists. Porphyry, the subtlest antagonist of christianity in the primitive
ages, too learned to be satisfied with the idle pretensions of the
Greek historians, laboriously sought after the most ancient
records, that he might have something wherewith to confront
the antiquity of the scriptures. He could find no other profane author as old as the Phenician historian. Yet he acknowledges him posterior to Moses; and he even grounds an
argument for the truth of some of his statements on their
agreement with those of the Jewish historian.*

When did this man flourish, with whom no other ancient
writer, even in the estimation of Porphyry, can vie in age?
The learned Bochart† makes Sanchoniathon cotemporary
with Gideon; that is, nearly two hundred years later than

* Euseb. Præp. Ev. L. 10. C. 8.
† Geog. Sac. in Stillingfleet, Book 1, Chap. 2.

10

Moses, and only sixty-five years before the destruction of Troy. Scaliger* and Stillingfleet,† with greater reason, bring him still lower down, even to the time of Solomon, or one hundred and fifty years after the destruction of Troy. This opinion is founded mainly on the fact, that Sanchoniathon speaks of the building of Tyre as an ancient event; but, by general consent, this event happened about the time of Gideon.

Having thus, as far as we are able, cleared the age of Sanchoniathon, let us inquire into his credibility as an historian. He professes to have drawn his history from three sources:—the records of Jerombaal, priest of the god Jao; the annals of the several cities; and the sacred inscriptions in the temples.‡ Who this Jerombaal was, is a vexed question among the learned. Bochart conjectures, that he was the same as Gideon, both because the latter is called in scripture Jerubbaal, and because soon after the death of Gideon the Israelites worshipped Baal-berith, by which he thinks is probably meant the idol of Berith, or Berytus, the place where Sanchoniathon lived. Porphyry commends Sanchoniathon for his fidelity. Philo, his translator, styles him a learned and inquisitive man. Theodoret thinks his name signifies a lover of truth.§

Of his fidelity we have no means of judging, since the records are lost, out of which he professes to have taken his history. But the fragments of his writings, still extant, give us no very exalted idea either of his love of truth, or his diligence in seeking it. All that remains of his history of Phenicia, is the first book, transcribed into Eusebius. This relates to the Phenician theology. It is a confused jumble of incongruities, absurdities, and fables. The most valuable thing in it, and almost the only one that is clear and con-

* Not. in Frag. Græc., p. 40 in Stillingfleet.
† Origines Sacræ. Book 1, Chap. 2.
‡ *Ibidem.*   § *Ibidem.*

sistent, is a confession, that idolatry had its origin in a deification, after death, of men, who had performed some useful actions, while living. What can there be in such a writer, capable of giving a moment's uneasiness to a rational mind, whatever contrariety there may be between his statements and those of sacred story?

We proceed now to the Egyptian history. Stillingfleet* has quaintly, but not without truth, observed, that the Egyptians were a people, so unreasonably given to fables, that the wisest action they ever did, was to conceal their religion; and the best office their gods had, was to hold their fingers in their mouth, to command silence to their worshippers. This nation boasts an antiquity extending back to tens of thousands of years before the creation of the world. The thirty-one dynasties of their most celebrated historian, Manetho Sebennyta, embrace a period of more than fifty thousand years.† Let us a little sift this high-sounding claim of antiquity. Their most famous historian, as observed above, was Manetho. He was high priest of Heliopolis, in the time of Ptolemy Philadelphus. He flourished, therefore, less than three hundred years before Christ. He composed his history at the request of Philadelphus; and, in an abridged form, it is still extant.‡

It is manifest, that the credibility of Manetho will depend on the credibility of the records, which he used in compiling his history. He professes to have copied it from certain pillars, inscribed before the flood by the first Egyptian Hermes, and afterwards found by the second Hermes, in the land of Seriad. Who this Hermes, Thoyth, or Mercury (for

* Orig. Sac., B. 1, c. 2.

† The exact number is 53,535.

‡ "These dynasties are yet preserved, being first epitomized by Julius Africanus, from him transcribed into Eusebius's Chronica, from Eusebius, by Georgius Syncellus, out of whom they are produced by Joseph Scaliger, and may be seen both in his Eusebius and his Canones Isogogici."—STIL-LINGFLEET.

he was called by these several names) was, is a question hope-
lessly buried up in the mists of ancient allegory. The accounts
respecting him are so strangely contradictory, that some have
doubted whether any such person ever existed. Cotta, in
Cicero de Natura Deorum, brings forward no less than five
Mercuries, expressly for the purpose of establishing his
academical doctrine of withholding assent. The Egyptians,
according to Diodorus, represent him to have been a sacred
scribe to Osiris, and the tutor of Isis.* How he could have
stood in such relations to these personages, and yet lived
before the flood, is a mystery which they do not explain, and
which, without such explanation, is quite incomprehensible.

But let us look somewhat more closely at these Mercurial
pillars. Manetho vouches the credibility of his history from
the fact, that " he took it from some pillars in the land of
Seriad, on which they were inscribed in the sacred dialect
by the first Mercury, and after the flood were translated out
of the sacred dialect into the Greek tongue, in hieroglyphic
characters, by Agathodæmon, the second Mercury, the
father of Taut."†

Would it be possible for an author more effectually to
blast his own reputation for credibility, than Manetho has
done in this passage? For, in the first place, where is this
land of Seriad, in which the pillars were found? Scaliger,‡
after a laborious search, acknowledges his inability to find
its locality. It is manifestly a utopian region. Secondly,
what likelihood is there, that these pillars could have with-
stood the rush of waters, which overthrew the most solid
edifices, and reduced whole cities to heaps of ruins? Thirdly,
how was it possible for Hermes, who lived in the beginning
of the first dynasty, to write in advance the history of so
many thousand years? Fourthly, what other writer has ever

* Stillingfleet, Orig. Sac., B. 1, c. 2.
† Euseb. Chron., in Still., B. 1, c. 2.
‡ Not. in Frag. Maneth. in Euseb. cited by Stillingfleet.

mentioned the co-existence of a sacred and common dialect in Egypt? There was, as is well known, a difference between sacred and common writing; but no trace, elsewhere, of a difference between the sacred and common language.* Finally, what shall we say to the translation of this history into Greek so soon after the flood? Where, and how did the author obtain his knowledge of Greek? Was the Greek language so much in request at that early period? On the contrary, is it not plain, both from Herodotus and Diodorus,† that the Greeks were not allowed any commerce with the Egyptians, till the time of Psalmmeticus, which was as late as the twenty-sixth dynasty of Manetho, and more than a hundred years after the first Olympiad?

Besides, how can a writer, of the age of Ptolemy Philadelphus, deriving his knowledge from records manifestly the most vague and uncertain, and writing, too, under circumstances and for a purpose, as will presently appear, well calculated to throw suspicion upon his statements, be reasonably confronted with Moses?‡ Infidelity is welcome to all the strength it can derive from such a labor. Nothing, surely, but a deep consciousness of the inherent weakness of its cause, could make it catch at such straws, or induce it to regard them as affording the least support to its impious assumptions.§

The Chaldean history next claims our attention. The Chaldeans were, without doubt, a people of high antiquity. They were the first nation, that was formed into a regular

* Hengstenberg's " Egypt and the Books of Moses," p. 244.

† Herod. L. 2. Diod. L. 1, C. 67.

‡ "It is evident from what remains of him in Eusebius's Chronica, that he not only flourished in the time of Philadelphus, but writ his history at the special command of Philadelphus, as manifestly appears by the remaining epistle of Manetho to him, still extant in Eusebius."—STILLINGFLEET.

§ I have spoken of Manetho, as if he were a true historical personage. Of this, however, there is much doubt. Hengstenberg, in his Books of Moses, has argued strongly, and to most persons probably convincingly, in support of the opinion, that the whole story of Manetho is a mere fable.

government after the flood. For the knowledge of this fact, however, we are more indebted to scripture history, than to any undoubted historical records of their own. Their vanity led them to exaggerate their antiquity to an extent, quite equal to that of the Egyptians.*

Their historian of highest repute was Berosus. He was, as we learn from Josephus,† a priest of Belus, and a native of Babylon. Having become an adept in the Chaldean learning and philosophy, he removed to the Grecian island of Cos. Here he opened a school of astronomy, and was the first to bring the Chaldean astrology into repute among the Greeks.‡ Dr. Anthon§ makes him contemporary with Alexander. Herein he is certainly at fault in his chronology. Tatian, in a fragment preserved in Eusebius, informs us, that Berosus wrote the Chaldean history in three books, and dedicated it to Antiochus, the third from Seleucus.‖ This must have been Antiochus Theos, whose reign commenced in the twenty-second year of Ptolemy Philadelphus. Vossius, from a passage in Pliny, proves, that the history of

* " Even among these, who enjoyed all the advantages of ease, quiet, and a flourishing empire, we find no undoubted or credible records preserved, but the same vanity as among the Egyptians, in arrogating antiquity to themselves beyond all proportion of reason or satisfaction from their own history, to fill up that vast measure of time with ; which makes it most probable what Diodorus (Bibliothec. l. 1,) observes of them, that in things pertaining to their arts they made use of lunar years of thirty days ; so they had need, when Tully (de Divin. l. 1,) tells us, that they boasted of observations of the stars for 470,000 years. It had been impossible for them to have been so extravagant in their accounts of themselves, had they but preserved the history of their nation in any certain records."—STILLINGFLEET.

† Contra, App., L. 1.

‡ The Athenians erected a statue to his memory with a gilded tongue ; " A good emblem," says Stillingfleet, " of his history, which made a fair and specious show, but was not that within, which it pretended to be; especially where he pretends to give an account of the most ancient times.

§ Class. Dict. Art. Berosus.

‖ Euseb. Præp. Evang., L. 10, in Still., B. 1, c. 3.

Berosus could not have been given to the world much, if any, before the twenty-second year of Philadelphus.* It was during the reign and at the instance of the same prince, as is well known, that Manetho, the Egyptian historian, composed his history.

This is a point of no little importance to be cleared, as will appear from the following considerations.

Ptolemy Philadelphus was a great patron of letters. Among the most princely, as well as useful instances of this patronage, was the translation which he caused to be made of the sacred books of the Jews into the Greek language, commonly called the Septuagint. This great work, as Vossius† has shown, was executed in the early part of Ptolemy's reign. In this opinion of Vossius the learned Jesuit Petavius‡ concurs. Then it was that this authentic history of the creation and first ages of the world was, for the first time, produced to the view of mankind. Such a work, containing as it does, a narrative of the peopling of the world, the flood, the confusion of tongues, the dispersion of mankind, the formation of civil societies, the origin of idolatry, the selection of a particular nation to be the people of the true God, its investiture with peculiar privileges, its admirable system of civil laws, and its wonderful and miraculous history, such a work, I say, it will readily* be imagined, must have created no small stir among the scholars of that age. The desire would naturally be excited, in the nations of most distinguished repute for learning and antiquity, to produce somewhat from their own annals, with which they might confront these strange and startling revelations. Then it was, as we have seen above, that Manetho and Berosus published their histories to the world. It thus appears, that these two distinguished histo-

* Voss. de Hist. Græc., l. 1, c. 13.	Plin. Hist. Nat. l. 7, c. 57, in Still.

† De Hist. Græc., l. 1, c. 12.

‡ Notes on Epiphanius, in Stillingfleet, B. 1, c. 3.

rians flourished at a period later even than that of the translation of the Old Testament into Greek ; by which, indeed, it seems highly probable, that they were incited to put forth their respective relations.

Thus much to show the incompetency of the Chaldean history to give an authentic account of the first ages of mankind. It cannot be denied, and there is certainly no disposition in any friend of divine revelation to deny that the fragments of Berosus in Josephus, Tatian, and Eusebius, are of considerable value and importance, not only as throwing light upon the history of the Babylonish empire, but also as confirming the truth of the scripture history. All that is maintained is, that the Chaldean history is of no such authority in respect to ancient times, as to be entitled to credit, when it comes in conflict with the historical statements of holy writ.* I conclude with an observation of

* A caviller might object, that there is an inconsistency in the text, which represents profane historians as confirming the truth of the scripture history, when the relations of the former accord with those of the latter, while it affirms, that they are not entitled to credit, when their statements conflict with those of holy writ. But there is no real inconsistency. Let us illustrate the case by facts. Diodorus says, that Babylon was not yet founded, when Ninus conquered Mesopotamia, and that Nineveh was not built, till after he had subdued the Babylonians. The scripture, on the other hand, asserts, that both these cities were built centuries before the events mentioned by the Greek historian. Now all must feel, that the authority of Diodorus on this point is as nothing, when compared to the authority of Moses. Again : From the 47th chapter of Genesis, we learn, that Pharaoh purchased of his subjects the right of possession to their land, with the exception of the land of the priests, which he bought not ; and that the land was parcelled out to its former possessors, who paid for the use of it a fifth part of its yearly produce. Such is the statement of Moses. Now for the testimony of profane historians. According to Herodotus, (B. 2, c. 109,) the king divided the whole land among the Egyptians, collecting from each individual a yearly rent. According to Diodorus, (l. 73,) all the land in Egypt belonged to the priests, or the kings, or the military caste. According to Strabo, (17, p. 787,) the Egyptians, who were employed in agricul-

Strabo,* one of the most grave, solid, and judicious of heathen
writers. Speaking of the antiquities of the Medes, Persians,
and Syrians, he says : " These nations have not obtained
any great credit in the world, by reason of the simplicity
and fabulousness of their historians."

Let us descend now to Greece and her historians. That
country was the great metropolis of ancient art and learning.
The seat of letters and philosophy, when at the zenith of her
glory she attracted to herself, as to a common centre, the
gaze and admiration of the world. She was the shrine, at
which taste and genius worshipped. Her very decay attests
her former magnificence. Her very ruins are models of
taste. Her broken marbles still constitute a well-spring of
inspiration to genius. But what is the ability and merit of
her historians, as to giving an account of the most ancient
times ? Did they, by the depth and compass of their researches, arrive at greater certainty, than other nations were

ture, held their land subject to rent. Here is an important point of agreement between sacred and profane history, viz., in the statement of the fact,
that the cultivators of the soil in Egypt were not the owners of it. Do we
not feel, instinctively, that these profane writers, deriving their knowledge
from entirely independent sources, confirm by their testimony the truth of
the scripture history ? There is, indeed, a discrepancy between the two
accounts. Moses limits the ownership of the land to the kings and the
priests ; Diodorus extends it to a third order in the state, the military caste.
Now, if there were no means of reconciling this apparent contradiction,
we could not hesitate as to which authority is most entitled to credit. But
Herodotus has enabled us to clear up the difficulty. According to him, the
land of the soldiers differed from the land of the peasants in being free of
rent ; but otherwise it belonged to the kings. The use of the land exempt
from public burdens was instead of pay. From this it is plain, that
Diodorus was led into the error of supposing that the military order owned
their land, by not sifting the matter to the bottom. He observed, that the
tenure in their case was different from that of the peasants, and erroneously
concluded, that they were proprietors, when in point of fact they were but
tenants.

* Lib. 11.

able to attain? No, in no wise. Stillingfleet* evinces the defect and insufficiency of Grecian history by three arguments: First, that the earliest writers among the Greeks were poetical and fabulous. Secondly, that their most ancient historians are of suspected credit and authority even among themselves. And thirdly, that their best authors either candidly confess their ignorance of the early ages, or clearly betray it.

First: Their most ancient writers were poetical, and most manifestly fabulous. Strabo† undertakes to prove, that prose is a mere imitation of poetry; of course it would follow, that poetry must have been written before prose. At first, he says, poetry only was in request; afterwards, in imitation of that, Cadmus, Pherecydes, and Hecatæus wrote their histories, observing all the laws of poetry, except its measures. It is most undoubted, that poetry was first in use among the Greeks. When they began to emerge out of barbarism, all the philosophical and moral instructions they received, were delivered in verse. Plutarch‡ instances this in Orpheus, Hesiod, Parmenides, Xenophanes, Empedocles, and Thales. Hence Heinsius§ observes, that the poets were anciently called teachers. Hence also the same word in Greek, and afterwards in Latin, denoted poems and precepts of morality.‖ It is not certain when poetry first came into use among the Greeks; but it is certain, that it was employed not solely for instruction. Strabo¶ says, it was used "the more gently to draw people on to idolatry." He adds:** "It is impossible to persuade women and the promiscuous multitude to religion by mere dry reason, or philosophy; but for this there is need of superstition, and this cannot be advanced without some fables and wonders. The

---

* Orig. Sac. B. 1, C. 4.   † Lib. 1.
‡ De Pith. Orac. p. 403, in Stillingfleet.
§ Diss. in Hes. c. 6.   ‖ *Ibid.*
¶ Lib. 1.   ** *Ibid.*

thunderbolts, shields, tridents, serpents, and spears, attributed to the gods, are mere fables; and so is all the ancient theology; but the governors of the commonwealth made use of these things the better to awe the silly multitude, and to bring them into better order." Eratosthenes, a writer of such solid parts and attainments as to have gained the title of another Plato, condemns the ancient poetry as old wives' tales, without real learning or truth.[*]

Secondly : The earliest historical writers of Greece are of suspected authority among their own countrymen, and mutually distrust and discredit one another. Strabo[†] calls them mere writers of myths. Diodorus[‡] condemns as fabulous Cadmus, Hecatæus, and Hellanicus. Strabo[§] speaks of Damastes Sigeensis as unworthy of credit. Yet he is followed by Eratosthenes, Dionysius of Halicarnassus, Plutarch, Pliny, and other approved writers.[||] His testimony is also taken by Aristeas Proconnesius, whom Stillingfleet[¶] regards as the Sir John Mandeville of Greece, and whom Strabo[**] pronounces inferior to no one in jugglery, probably because it was commonly reported, that he had the power to let his soul out of his body, and bring it back again at will.[††]

But further : What credit can be given to the historians, who are perpetually criminating one another, and whose writings are filled with mutual charges of error and deception ? Josephus[‡‡] informs us, that Hesiod is accused of falsehood by Acusilaus; Acusilaus, by Ephorus; Ephorus, by Timæus; and Timæus, by those who followed him. In the

[*] Stillingf., Orig. Sac., B. 1, c. 4. [†] Lib. 1
[‡] In Stillingf., Orig. Sac., B. 1, c. 4. [§] Lib. 1
[||] Voss. de Hist. Graec., l. 4, c. 5, in Orig. Sac., B. 1, c. 4.
[¶] Orig. Sac., B. 1, c. 4. [**] Lib. 13.
[††] "Yet this juggler did Celsus pitch on to confront with our blessed Savior, as Hierocles did on Apollonius : so much have those been to seek for reason, who have sought to oppose the doctrine of faith."—STILLINGF.
[‡‡] Con. App. L. 1.

midst of such contradictions, where shall we fix our belief?
Upon all in common? That were to believe, that black is
white, and white black. Shall we believe one, and reject
the others? What evidence does that one give, why he
should be believed more than the rest? None at all. It is,
then, clearly impossible to find any undoubted certainty
concerning the first ages in any of the Greek historians.

This will be still more apparent, when it is added, on the
authority and according to the conclusive reasoning of Vossius,* that the highest antiquity of the historical writers of
Greece does not much exceed the age of Cyrus and Cambyses. Of many even of these nothing now remains but
their bare names. A catalogue of them may be found in
Vossius De Historicis Graecis. Such are Sisyphus Cous.
Corinnus, Eugeon Samius, Deïochus Proconnesius, Eudemus
Parius, Democles Phigaleus, Amelesagoras Chalcedonius,
Xenomedes Chius, and several others. Of all these historians, not even the subjects on which they wrote are known.
Of others, whose better fortune it was to have not only
their names, but the subjects of their histories, handed down
to posterity, nothing is extant, till the time of the Persian
war.† Cadmus of Miletus wrote the Antiquities of Ionia.
Acusilaus treated on Genealogies. Pherecydes Syrius composed the History of the Gods. Pherecydes Lerius wrote
on the Attic Antiquities. Hecatæus published a Description of Asia; and Hellannicus, the Originals of Nations, and
Founders of Cities. There was a history of Persia, Greece,
and Egypt, written by Charon Lampsacenus; of Lydia, by
Xanthus; of Corinth, by Eumelus; of Scythia, by Anacharsis; of Phrygia, by Diagoras; of Chaldea and Persia, by
Democritus; and of Sicily and Italy, by Hippys. Where
now are all these works? Swallowed up in the all-devouring
gulf of time.

* De Hist. Graec., in Stillingf., B. 1, c. 4.
† Stillingf., Orig. Sac., B. 1, c. 4.

Thirdly: Even the historians, whose works have come down to us, either candidly confess their ignorance, or palpably betray it. Thucydides,* the most solid, truth-loving, and accurate of the Greek historical writers, not only confesses, but proves, the impossibility of an exact account of the times preceding the Peloponesian war. He says, that all he could find in the ancient state of Greece, was a great deal of confusion, unquiet stations, frequent removals, continual piracies, and no settled form of commonwealth. Plutarch,† a later writer of distinguished learning, sagacious judgment, and sincere love of truth, pretends not to go farther back than the age of Theseus. Before that time, he says, as geographers in their maps, when they have gone as far as they can, fill up the empty spaces with impassible mountains, or frozen seas, or devouring sands, so those who give an account of ancient times are fain to insert some wonderful and tragical stories, which have neither truth nor certainty in them.

Thus we perceive, that those who were best able to judge of the credibility of the early Grecian annals, could find in them no sure footing to stand upon. But those writers who have not the candor to own their ignorance, very plainly discover it. Herodotus‡ denied, that there was an ocean encompassing the land, and condemned the geographers for asserting it. Aristotle thought, that the Indies were joined to Europe near the Straits of Gibraltar.§ Alexander wrote to his mother, that he had found the sources of the Nile in

* Lib. 1.   † In Stillingfleet, L. 1, c. 4.

‡ Lib. 2, C. 5. " Herodotus himself hath stood in need of his compurgators, who yet have not been able to acquit him of fabulousness. * * * Herodotus was not first suspected of falsehood in these latter ages of the world, but even among the Greeks themselves there have been found some that would undertake to make good that charge against him. * * * Josephus thinks he was deceived by the Egyptian priests in things relating to the state of their affairs."—STILLINGFLEET.

§ In Stillingfleet's Orig. Sac., B. 1, c. 4.

the East Indies.* Many of the learned Grecians imagined,
that the sun with a great noise descended into the ocean every
night.† Yet when these crude ideas prevailed, learning
was at its height in Greece, and discoveries were daily made
by means of the wars, which were carried on abroad.
What credible account of the earliest ages can we expect
from men, who were so ignorant of the state of the world in
their own times? Is it easier to pierce the darkness of antiquity, and bring up the verities of history from its cavernous
recesses, than to explore the surface of the earth, and ascertain the facts of geography, which are always within our
reach?

So much for the first argument against the credibility of
profane history, when its statements are repugnant to those
contained in the Bible. The facts of sacred history are in
no danger of being discredited with candid and enlightened
minds on any such grounds as these. These facts stand
fixed and immovable as mountains of brass. Like the rock,
that defies the fury of the waves, they remain unaffected
and serene, amid the assaults of sophistry, ridicule, and
falsehood.

The second general argument is drawn from the confusion and ambiguity of ancient profane histories. Proceed
we now to a consideration of this topic.

We have seen how deficient the early profane historians
were in authentic records, out of which to construct their
several narratives. But if the case had been otherwise, if
the materials, which they used, had been full and reliable,
still, if the accounts of ancient times, given by them, were
perplexed, confused, and ambiguous, this circumstance
would be as fatal to their credibility, as the want of records.
That their accounts were of the character here supposed,
will appear evident from this consideration, that their chronology was altogether vague and uncertain. Scaliger has

* Stillingfleet's Orig. Sac., B. 1, c. 4.   † *Ibid.*

well denominated chronology the life and soul of history,
without which, it is a rude and undigested mass, having
neither life nor form. The defectiveness of the chronology
of the ancient heathen nations shows itself chiefly in two
things,—the uncertain length of their years, and the want
of fixed periods, or epochs, to which to refer the various
transactions, embraced in their annals. Let us briefly par-
ticularize under each of these heads.

First: The uncertain and variable length of their years.
A year is a system of days, and is capable of as great
variety in duration, as there are methods of joining days
together. If the years of ancient nations were of unequal
lengths,—sometimes lunar, sometimes solar, sometimes thirty
days, sometimes four months, sometimes three hundred and
sixty days, and sometimes three hundred and sixty-five days,—
and if the historians are accustomed to speak of years, without
distinguishing between the several kinds, and without letting
their readers know which kind were meant, it is plain, that
this must introduce inextricable confusion into their accounts
of early times, and make the credibility of those accounts
more than a matter of doubt. That there was, in point of
fact, this inequality of duration in their years, is proved by
many and unimpeachable testimonies. Plutarch, in his Life
of Numa, says: "The Egyptians had at first a year of one
month, and afterwards of four months." Varro,* cited by
Lactantius, speaks of the Egyptian year of thirty days, as a
thing certain and undoubted. Diodorus, Solinus, and
Augustine,† mention the year of four months, as used in
computing time by that people. That they had also the
solar year, the year formed by the passage of the sun through
the twelve signs of the zodiac, is evident from the history of
Joseph, since the seven years of plenty and the seven years
of famine in Pharaoh's dream must have been of this kind.

Plutarch‡ accounts for what he calls "the infinite number

* Stillingfleet's Orig. Sac. B. 1, c. 5.   † *Ibid.*   ‡ Life of Numa.

of years" in the Egyptian computation by the fact, that they
reckoned months for years. Stillingfleet,* using this principle for a guide, has, with great labor and learning, reduced
the vast number of Egyptian years to something like reason
and probability. But which ever way we take them, the
authority of Manetho is discredited. When Manetho wrote
his Dynasties, the Julian year of three hundred and sixty-
five days was in use in Egypt. Now, either by his fifty odd
thousand years he meant Julian years, and then his history
must be looked upon as fabulous; or he meant years of
months, and then he is open to the charge of intentional
deception. In either case, he is an unsafe guide in historical inquiries; and his statements are not entitled to the
least weight, when ever they happen to be repugnant to
those of Holy Writ. And here I may observe, by the way,
that it appears to have been the policy of the Egyptian
priests to mislead and deceive the credulous Greeks, in the
accounts which they gave of their national antiquities; a
thing which, by reason of the different kinds of years in use
among them, they could the more readily do, without being
impeached of direct falsehood; since their statements, though
not true in the sense in which they were understood, were
yet true in a sense known only to themselves.

There is good reason to believe, that the Chaldeans also,
as well as the Egyptians, had years of unequal duration.
This has been conclusively shown by Bishop Stillingfleet in
the fifth chapter of the first book of his Origines Sacræ, to
which the reader, who would see the argument handled at
length, is referred.

Secondly: The defective chronology of the ancients appears from this, that they had no fixed periods, or great
epochs, of an early date, to which they could refer the
events recorded in their histories.

Such fixed periods are essential to the clearness and cer-

* Orig. Sac. B. 1, c. 5.

tainty of historical narrations. Diodorus * takes notice of this in speaking of the history of his own country. These are his words: "There is no certainty in the ancient Grecian history, because they had no certain term, from whence to deduce their accounts." This view of the matter is most just and rational. For, if there be no fixed points of time to determine the succession of ages, and to measure the events which occur in the intervening spaces, we shall be perpetually tossed upon an ocean of uncertainties, without any solid foundation, whereon to ground any account of ancient times. "The ancient accounts of the world," says Stillingfleet,† "were merely from year to year, and that with abundance of obscurity, uncertainty, and variety; sometimes going by the moon, and therein they were as mutable as the moon herself, how to conform the year regularly to her motion; and it was yet greater difficulty to regulate it by the course of the sun, and to make the accounts of the sun and moon meet. There was so much perplexity and confusion about the ordering of a single year, and so long in most nations before they could bring it into any order, that we are not to expect any fixed periods, by which to find out the succession of ages among them."

The Egyptians are commonly believed to have been best skilled in the computation and adjustment of times. Yet they were long in finding out any certain course of the year, and reducing it to a systematic form. Even after they had learned to regulate the year by the course of the sun, they made it consist of only three hundred and sixty days. Such a division of the year must, in process of time, be the occasion of very great confusion, since the months would be continually changing their places, so that a month, which was once in the summer, would come at length to be a winter month, and vice versa. This explains the fable told by the Egyptian priests to Herodotus,‡ that in the times of their

<hr/>

* In Still., B. 1, c. 6.   † *Ibid.*   ‡ Euterpe.

11

early kings, the sun had twice changed his rising and setting. It was not the sun, but their months, that had changed, by reason of the defective adjustment of their year. The observation of this effect led the Egyptians, after a great lapse of time, to add five days to their year. Yet even so it was still deficient by one fourth of a day. Whether they ever intercalated a day in their civil year has been a question much debated among the learned, and especially by Scaliger and Petavius. It seems probable, that they never did, as Censorinus,* who lived in the third century of the Christian era, says expressly, that in his time the civil year of the Egyptians had three hundred and sixty-five days only, without any intercalation. The result of Stillingfleet's learned and able examination of this subject, so far as the Egyptians are concerned, is, that "they had anciently no certain periods to govern themselves by in their computation of ancient times." "Nay," he adds, "the Egyptians have not, as appears, any certain epochas to go by, elder than the Egyptian years of Nabonassar, and afterwards from the death of Alexander, and Ptolemy Philadelphus, and Augustus's victory at Actium."

Passing from the domain of Egyptian into that of Grecian history, we find ourselves plunged into still deeper uncertainties. Here, until the Greeks began to reckon by olympiads, we have no fixed periods, no certain epochs, to serve as a pole star to guide us in the vast ocean of Grecian antiquities. The early accounts of Greece are most imperfect and fragmentary. Varro in Censorinus divides the whole succession of Grecian history into three parts, two of which he accounts as mythical and fabulous, and the third only, beginning with the olympiads, as historical. Some writers, as Scaliger, Heeren, &c. name the second period, extending from the siege of Troy to the olympiads, heroic, considering it historical in respect to persons, but

* De Die Nat. c. 18.

fabulous in respect to actions. Some of the learned Greeks,
—as Apollodorus, Dionysius, and others, who were skilled
in astronomy—labored, with commendable zeal, as Stillingfleet* says, " to find out some certain periods to fix on in the
time before the olympiads." Supposing them, by their astro-
nomical calculations, to have truly assigned the destruction of
Troy to 1184 B.C., what a vast tract of time there is before
the Trojan war, whose history is wholly fabulous! And as
to the series of events in the interval between that epoch
and the olympiads, it is all confusion and uncertainty.

Great is the ambiguity in the accounts of the foundation
and early history of the several states of Greece. Matters
are here so perplexed, confused, and uncertain, that their
own ablest chronologists give over the reduction of them to
any certain form. Dionysius, of Halicarnassus, considers
Argolis as the most ancient of the Grecian kingdoms. He
places the foundation of it a thousand years before that of
Attica. Yet he makes the Arcadians, who boasted that they
were older than the moon, younger than the Athenians by
nine generations, that is, according to the Grecian computation, nearly three hundred years. What is still more remarkable, he makes Phthiotis under Ducalion younger than
these same Arcadians by forty two generations, or more
than a thousand years.† Most justly has Scaliger‡ pronounced these accounts inconsistent and impossible. The
greater part of historians differ from Dionysius, in considering Sycion as the oldest of the Grecian states. Varro, as
we learn from Augustine,§ commenced his history with the
foundation of this kingdom. But here, too, the accounts are
confused and contradictory. Pausanias gives a list of
Sycionian kings, without any succession of times among
them. Africanus and Eusebius differ from Pausanias in
respect to these names.‖ But what is strangest of all is,

* Orig. Sac., B. 1, c. 6.   † Ibid.   ‡ De Hist. Græc.
§ De Civit. Dei, l. 16, c. 2.   ‖ Orig. Sac. B. 1, c. 6.

that Adrastus, who is the twenty-third king of Sycion in the list of Africanus, is said by Homer* to have been the first. So perplexed and uncertain is the account of ancient times among the Greeks, before they began to reckon by olympiads. Not without the greatest reason does Diodorus deny all certainty to the ancient Grecian history, assigning as the cause the fact, that they had no certain term, from whence to deduce their accounts. It is true, that the succession of times and events becomes comparatively clear and consistent after the system of olympiads commenced. But this was not, as Scaliger has clearly shown, till the year 776 B.C.†

Such was the crude state of chronological knowledge in the early ages. There would seem to have been no branch of learning, in which the ancients were less skilled; and yet there is no branch more essential to the exactness and credibility of historical relations.

Another circumstance which tended, in no slight degree, to the confusion and ambiguity of early profane history, was the uncertain signification of the characters in which the records were made. "It is well known of the Egyptian priests," says Stillingfleet,‡ "that the sacred characters of their temples were seldom made known to any but such as were of their own number and family, or such others as by long converse had insinuated themselves into their society, as some of the Greek philosophers and historians had done. That the Phenician priests had their peculiar and sacred characters too, is evident from the words of Philo Byblius concerning Sanchoniathon, if we take Bochart's exposition of them. He tells us, that his history was compared with the inscriptions in the temples, written in Ammunean letters, which are known to few. The same author tells us, out of Diogenes Laertius, of a book of Democritus concerning the sacred characters in Babylon, by which it is evident,

---

* Ill. l. 2.   † De Emend. Temp., l. 5.

‡ Orig. Sac., B. 1, c. 5.

that the Babylonian priests had their sacred characters too ; and also of a testimony of Theodoret in respect to all the Grecian temples, that they had some peculiar characters, which were called sacred. But that learned author thinks, that there is no necessity of understanding it peculiarly of the Grecians, because the Greek fathers called all the heathens by the name of Greeks ; but if so, the testimony is larger, and amounts to an universal testimony of the heathen temples."

The third general argument to evince the want of credibility in the history of the most ancient times, is drawn from the manifest partiality of the historians to their respective countries, and their inconsistency with each other.

It requires but a slight acquaintance with the historical writers of antiquity to be convinced, that a chief object of almost every one of them was to enhance the glory of his own country, and that too many of them were little scrupulous as to the means by which that end should be attained. Hence the high-sounding claims to antiquity put forth by the Egyptians, Chaldeans, Greeks, and various other nations. The errors, inconsistencies, contradictions, and mutual charges of deception, of which the historians are guilty, have already abundantly appeared in our preceding inquiries. These, if it were necessary, might be still further evinced by a comparison of what has been written by Manetho, Herodotus, Diodorus, and Eratosthenes concerning the Egyptian History ; by Herodotus, Diodorus, and Africanus concerning the Assyrian history; by Herodotus and Clesias concerning the Persian history ; and by all the Greeks concerning themselves. The want of credibility in the ancient histories, on this particular ground, is strikingly set forth by the learned British antiquary, Bishop Richardson.* He says, that, after a diligent study of the History of Persia, as written by native Persian authors on the one hand, and by the Greek historians

* Observations on Ezekiel cited in Hale's Analysis of Chronology.

on the other, he was scarcely able to recognize any identity between their respective accounts.

Thus much to show the uncertainty of early profane histories. What credit can such vague, confused, and contradictory reports have with intelligent and candid readers, when their statements conflict with those of sacred history? The credibility of the historians on doubtful points is quite destroyed by their evident inability to give an authentic account of the earliest times; by the confusion, inconsistency, and ambiguity of the accounts, which they have given; and by their manifest and blinding partiality to themselves. To demonstrate the credibility of the Mosaic history, as contained in the Pentateuch, will be the object of the following chapter.

CHAPTER IV.

Credibility of Moses as an Historian.

I PROCEED to the execution of the design announced at the close of the last chapter, viz.: to evince the trustworthiness of the Mosaic history. Moses was an historian, as well as a lawgiver; and it concerns us to settle his credibility in that character. If his testimony cannot be relied on, if his commonwealth, like the utopian republics of Plato, Harrington, and More, be but an ingenious romance, though the study of it may amuse an idle hour, it becomes comparatively valueless, as a practical guide in legislation.

There is an antecedent probability, that the supreme ruler of the world should have caused an authentic history of the first ages to be written.* It is reasonable to suppose, that

* See on this subject Stillingf. Orig. Sac. B. 2, c. 1.

events, so remarkable and important as those contained in the Pentateuch, should not always be left to the uncertainty of oral tradition, but should be embodied in permanent records, to be preserved to the memory of posterity. That a firm belief as to future events,—a point of no little importance to mankind,—be established, it must be settled in our belief, that all past events have been managed by divine providence. Upon what basis can such a conviction rest, other than that of some credible record of former ages? Without something of this kind, the mind of man will be at sea upon an ocean of uncertainties. And, as it is antecedently probable, that God would cause such a record to be made, it is, in like manner, antecedently probable, that he would cause it to be made in such form, that it might be conveyed, with equal certainty, to the whole race of mankind. It must, therefore, be held agreeable to reason, that God should have employed some suitable person to write an authentic history of his dealings with men, during the primitive ages of the world.

The question now before us is, did God, in point of fact, cause such a record to be made? And this question branches itself out into two others, viz.: First, is Moses the author of the books, which commonly go under his name? Secondly, is the history contained in these books, worthy of credit? Is it a credible account of the events which it narrates? It is the purpose of the present chapter to assert and prove the affirmative of these questions.

Beyond a reasonable doubt, Moses is the author of the history, commonly ascribed to him. Here, it is proper to observe, that we must not look for evidence of this fact, different, either in kind or degree, from that which the matter to be proved admits.* It would be unreasonable to demand mathematical demonstration, in a matter admitting only that kind of proof, which is called moral certainty. Does any man question the fact, that Euclid is the author of the geometry,

* Ibid, B. 2, c. 1.

going under his name, merely because a proposition, affirming such authorship, cannot be established by a demonstration, similar to those which he employs in proving his theorems? All the hellebore in the three Anticyræ would not suffice to cure such a person. In point of fact, the weightiest actions of men's lives are, for the most part, based upon no other foundation, than this moral certainty. Why do I invest thousands of dollars in the purchase of a certain estate? Because I believe, on moral evidence, that the title is good. Why am I braving the perils of the deep in a frail bark, for purposes of gain, or health, or pleasure? Because I am morally certain, that there are such places as London, Paris, Naples, Calcutta, and Canton. Indeed, we must either deny altogether, that there is any such thing as historical verity, or we must admit, that moral certainty is a valid ground of assent to historical relations.

We are not now inquiring into the divine legation of Moses, that is, whether he was commissioned and inspired of God, in the giving of his laws, and the writing of his history. That question will form the subject of a future chapter in this treatise. In an inquiry into a written divine revelation, there are two distinct questions to be considered, viz. first, whether the writing be genuine and authentic, that is, whether it was written by the person whose name it bears, and whether it relate matters of fact, as they actually occurred; and, secondly, whether the matters recorded are of true divine revelation.[*] If we would avoid plunging into an inextricable labyrinth, we must carefully attend to this distinction, when we seek, either to understand for ourselves, or to explain to others, the ground of a belief, that any particular writing is the word of God. The first of these points,—viz. the genuineness and authenticity of the Mosaic record,—is the special subject of our present inquiry.

In conducting this investigation, the first proposition to be

[*] Stillingfleet's Orig. Sac. B. 2, c. 1.

proved, is that the history contained in the Pentateuch is, undoubtedly, the composition of Moses.

Here the reader's attention is called, at the outset, to the nature and form of this writing. Two distinct elements are observable in it;—one, a set of laws forming a complete ecclesiastical and civil code; the other, an historical detail of the principal events, connected with the promulgation of the laws.* The two elements are combined in a manner quite extraordinary. The laws do not stand insulated by themselves, neither are they embodied in a systematic form, like the institutes of Lycurgus, or the pandects of Justinian. But, however paradoxical the assertion may seem, they are both separated and connected by the historical narrative. " It is a code of laws in a frame of history."† There are continual transitions from history to law, and from law to history. They are everywhere grafted, the one into the other; and there is such a mutual connexion and dependence, that the two parts seem to grow together, like the several branches of a tree. It is material to keep this fact in memory, as important use will be made of it, in the progress of this argument. With this preliminary observation, I proceed to exhibit the proof of the proposition now in hand, viz.: that Moses is the author of the books commonly attributed to him.

The argument here is similar to that which would be employed in evincing the genuineness of any other ancient writing. Let it be proposed, for example, to prove the genuineness of Cæsar's Commentaries ; and let the most acute deist or rationalist frame his proofs to establish the fact, that Cæsar is the author of that writing. Every one of them, mutatis mutandis, would be pertinent in an argument to prove that Moses is the author of the Pentateuch. Nor would this even exhaust the proof; for, superadded to all the considerations that could be adduced in support of the former of these prop-

* Edwards' Works, v. 9, pp. 130, seqq.

† Bib. Rep. Jan. 1848.

ositions, are several new and distinct topics of arguments, of invincible force in favor of the latter.

In the general argument evincing the credibility of Moses as an historian, the second proposition to be proved is, that his narrative is authentic as well as genuine, that is to say, its statements are in accordance with fact and reality. In other words, the history was not only written by Moses, but it contains a true relation of events really occurring, and set forth as they occurred.

The attributes of genuineness and authenticity are not always found united in the same work. The history of Telemachus, by Fenelon, is a fictitious narrative, but it was written by the man whose name it bears ; it is, therefore, genuine, but not authentic. The book, entitled Travels of Ali Bey, is a true account of a journey through several eastern countries, by a European scholar, under an assumed name; it is therefore, authentic, but not genuine. The genuineness and authenticity of the Pentateuch, however, are inseparable attributes. The former involves the latter. They are so interwoven and blended together, that, although they may be separated in thought, they may be most conveniently considered in connexion. They will, therefore, be so treated in the following inquiries.

Let us first examine the external testimony, by which the truth and genuineness of the Mosaic history are supported.

That the Pentateuch existed in its present form, from the close of the Babylonish captivity to the coming of Christ, that it was written by Moses, and that it contained a true record of the transactions and occurrences, which it relates, is the voice of all antiquity. The first question to be considered, then, is, whether the book was compiled from vague and indistinct traditions, on the return of the Jews out of their captivity, and palmed upon the nation, as the genuine work of their ancient lawgiver ? Various considerations might be urged to show the falsity of this suspicion ; but I shall confine myself to three, both for the sake of brevity, and because they are in themselves decisive.

The first consideration, showing that the Pentateuch was not compiled at the close of the captivity, is the fact, that the book of the law of Moses was a thing by no means unknown to the Jews, during the captivity. Distinct and repeated allusions are made to it in the prophecies of Daniel. See Dan. vi. 5; ix. 10–13; xi. 22–32. From the first of these passages it is manifest, that the law of Moses was known to the heathen themselves; and from all, that the Jews, at least the better informed among them, were quite familiar with it. The publicity, nay, even the notoriety, which the book of the law had obtained among the heathen, is still more apparent from the letter of Artaxerxes, authorizing Ezra to go up to Jerusalem at the head of such of his countrymen as were willing to accompany him, to reform the government and beautify the temple and city of their fathers: " Artaxerxes, king of kings, unto Ezra the priest, a scribe of the law of the God of heaven. * * * *. According to the law of thy God, which is in thine hand. * * * *. And thou, Ezra, after the wisdom of thy God, that is in thine hand, set magistrates and judges, which may judge all the people, that are beyond the river, all such as know the laws of thy God; and teach ye them that know them not." See the whole letter of Artaxerxes to Ezra, (Ez. vii. 12–26) of which the above passages are but brief citations. From the prophecies of Haggai (ii. 11–13,) it appears, that the priests in Jerusalem had the book of the law, before Ezra came to them, in virtue of his commission from the great king; even when they first came out of the captivity. The same may be inferred from a statement contained in Ezra iii. 2. It is also quite clear, that, not more than a dozen or fifteen years after Ezra first went up to Jerusalem, Nehemiah, then cup-bearer to the great king in Shushan, or Susa, was well acquainted with the book of the law of Moses. See Neh. i. 7–9. From all this, two things are plain—1st, that a writing under the name of the book of the law of Moses, existed and was widely known, both among Jews and heathen, during the captivity; and 2ndly, that Ezra enjoyed an extensive and distinguished reputation, as "a ready scribe" in that law. Such a reputation, it is well known, is of slow growth, and is long in coming to that breadth and height, which the fame of Ezra had evidently reached. Either of these considerations would prove, much more do both together evince, that the copy of the law, which Ezra took with him to Jerusalem, and which became the basis of his numerous and salutary governmental reforms, could not have been a writing, forged out of his own brain, or even compiled by him from floating and uncertain historical traditions.

The second proof, on which I rely to establish the same conclusion, is of still greater strength. It is the fact, that the code, which Ezra enjoined, and which the people received, so far from containing only such provisions, as were suited to the temper and agreeable to the wishes of the nation, required sacrifices, of the gravest and most painful kind; sacrifices, which no wise governor would have ventured to impose, and no people would have consented to make, but in obedience to a law, whose authority was beyond dispute.* To instance only one particular of this sort. The law forbade intermarriages, on the part of the Jews, with idolatrous nations. This prohibition had been infringed in numerous instances, during the dispersion of the Jews.† Ezra, armed with the authority of what claimed to be the code of Moses, entered upon the reformation of the national manners in this respect, with a boldness and zeal worthy of the occasion and of himself.‡ The greatest alarm and consternation seized upon all classes, on discovering the vast numbers involved in the transgression, and the high rank

* Graves on the Pent. Pt. 1, Lect.

† Ez. ix. 1, 2; x. 13.   ‡ Ez. ix. 3, seq.

of many of the offenders; for many of the priests, Levites, and princes of the congregation were among them.* Nevertheless, the history informs us, that Israel, with one voice, said, "Let us make a covenant with our God, to put away all the strange wives, and such as are born of them, according to the counsel of my lord, and of those that tremble at the commandment of our God, and let it be done according to the law."† A commission was, accordingly, appointed to investigate the matter, and the inquiry proved to be of such extent, in consequence of the multitude of persons involved in the guilt, that three months were consumed in the prosecution of it.‡ Does this seem like obedience to a code of doubtful authority? Has it the air of submission to a newly formed compilation of traditionary laws? Would any sane man invent or forge such a statute, under the circumstances, and if there had existed a degree of folly, equal to such an attempt, could it have met with any response, other than that of scorn and contempt? In a word, this fact seems to me a decisive proof, that the code, received and acknowledged by the Jews, on their return out of captivity, was the identical code, received and acknowledged by them, before the dissolution of their government; and that it was not then invented, modified, compiled, or recast, but was embodied in the well known and authentic records of the state, i. e. in the Pentateuch, as we now have it.

There is still a third argument, in support of the same view, of greater cogency, than either of the foregoing ones. It is well known, that a bitter enmity existed between the Jews and the Samaritans, from the very beginning of the captivity down through all the subsequent history of the nation. It would be in contradiction of every principle of human nature to suppose, that the Samaritans would receive, as authentic, a law and a history, invented or compiled by the Jews, so long after the commencement of the original feud.

* Ez. x. 1, 9.   † Ez. x. 3.   ‡ Ez. x. 16, 17.

Yet, what was the code of the Samaritans? The Pentateuch, the whole Pentateuch, and nothing but the Pentateuch. This was always held by them to be the genuine work of Moses; was received as true and authentic; and was reverenced as of divine original and authority. Could there be a more certain proof, could mathematical demonstration itself more indubitably establish the fact, that the copy of the law, used by Ezra, was not a writing forged by him, and foisted upon his countrymen, as the original and genuine production of their ancient lawgiver?

But Ezra did not go up to Jerusalem, till seventy-nine years after the edict of Cyrus, and the first return of the Jews to their own country. It may, therefore, be pretended, that the Pentateuch was compiled by the Jews at Jerusalem, during the interval, which elapsed between their first return and the coming of Ezra. This hypothesis is encompassed with even greater difficulties than the other; for it has all that belonged to that in full force, accompanied by some others, peculiar to itself. The three considerations brought forward above, and insisted on as overthrowing the supposition, that Ezra forged the Pentateuch, are as decisive against the supposition, that it was compiled or invented by the Jews, previously to his coming to them. But, superadded to these considerations are the following ones, which are pertinent here, and of invincible force. The returned Jews in Jerusalem had a copy of the book of the law, as appears from the prophecies of Haggai,* which were delivered thirty-six years, before Ezra went up to that city. But Ezra, a noted scribe in the law of Moses in Babylon, went up to Jerusalem, with the express design of teaching the people there this very law;† and the copy, which he used, he did not receive from his brethren in the holy city, but carried it up with him in his hand.‡ If the copy in possession of the Jews had been forged or compiled by them, it would

* Hag. ii. 11–13.　　† Ez. vii. 25.　　‡ Ez. vii. 14, 25.

necessarily have differed from that carried up by Ezra. But there is not the slightest token of any such difference, nor any trace of the conflict, which must have ensued, upon the discovery of it. On the contrary, princes, priests, Levites, and people receive Ezra's copy of the law, as of unquestionable authority, and submit to it without opposition, though such submission, as we have seen, involved sacrifices the most distressing, on the part of great numbers of the people, many of whom were of high rank and authority. But again : Seventeen years subsequent to Ezra's commission from Artaxerxes to go up to Jerusalem, Nehemiah was deputed by the same prince to follow him as governor of Judea.* He also, it is quite apparent, possessed and carried with him a copy of the law of Moses, distinct from both the others, and derived from neither, but from an independent source.† Yet there was no discrepancy or conflict between them. The three copies appear to have agreed in every particular. Ezra, Nehemiah, and the princes of the people went on harmoniously, as well as zealously, in the work of civil and ecclesiastical reform ;—a reform of great breadth and thoroughness, since it embraced the following specifications:—the engagement of the people in a solemn covenant to walk in God's law, as given by Moses ; the renunciation and avoidance of all intermarriages with idolatrous nations ; the rigid sanctification of the Sabbath ; the observance of the sabbatical year and the non-exaction of debts therein ; the payment of a tax of a third of a shekel yearly for the service of the temple ; the bringing of the first-fruits of the ground, of their sons, and of their cattle, to the house of the Lord ; and the giving of tithes to the priests and Levites of all the proceeds of the land.‡ These details cover no inconsiderable part of the Pentateuch, as we now have it; and the fact, that the three independent copies of the law under consideration concurred in them, shows both that

* Neh. ii. 8. † Neh. i. 7-9. ‡ Neh. x. 29-37.

those copies must have had a common source, and that neither of them could have been compiled at or subsequently to the time of the first return of the Jews out of their captivity. Moreover, it is certain, that, in the time of Esther, who became queen of Persia the very year, in which Ezra was commissioned to go up to Jerusalem, the entire people of the Jews, dispersed throughout the vast extent of the Persian empire, agreed, without controversy or any difference of opinion, in acknowledging one and the same law; and this fact was notorious to the heathen themselves.* This alone is a demonstrative proof of the existence of the book of the law, before the dispersion, in the same form, as it existed during the continuance and at the close of the captivity; for, how could any one part of this widely scattered people forge a code of laws, and embody it in a fictitious or newly compiled history, and get all the rest to acknowledge both, as genuine and authentic? But further still: some of the persons, present at the laying of the foundation of the second temple, had seen the first in all its glory; and therefore must have lived before the captivity, and must have known the laws and customs of their nation at that time.† Now, could these persons have been imposed upon by any attempt to fabricate, as the public code of the national religion and government, a compilation till then wholly unknown? If the book, now put forth as the old, well known, and genuine law of Moses, had been a new made code, with all the history foisted in by some daring hand, would they not certainly have known, and as certainly have exposed, with scorn and indignation, the fraudulent proceeding? There cannot be a doubt of it, in any fair and reasonable mind.

Wherefore, I must hold it for proved, that the Pentateuch, which we now have, is the same book and in the same form, as the Pentateuch of the Jews, previously to the Babylonish

* Esth. iii. 8.   † Ez. iii. 12.

captivity. This brings us up to nearly six hundred years before the Christian era.

A train of reasoning, not unlike the foregoing, will establish the existence of the Pentateuch, in its present form, at the time of the separation of the tribes and the formation of the two kingdoms of Judah and Israel, through the obstinate fatuity of the son and successor of Solomon. From that point, the interests of these two kingdoms lay in diverging lines; and we find it to have been the steady policy of the kings of Israel to alienate their people, as far as possible, from the religion and worship of Judah; a policy adopted by the very first of these monarchs,* and pursued by him and his successors, with unscrupulous boldness. To the prosecution of this policy, the Pentateuch interposed the most formidable obstacle. It set itself, in the strongest and most direct manner, against the design of these sovereigns. Now, on the supposition of the truth of the hypothesis, which assigns a date to the compilation of the Pentateuch, subsequent to the separation of the tribes, the kings of Israel would certainly know, that the book was not in existence at the time of the separation; they would certainly know when and for what intent it was compiled; and they and all their people would certainly have rejected it, as the most barefaced, clumsy, and ridiculous attempt at imposition, ever engendered in the teeming brain of human folly. If, then, it appear, that the Israelitish monarchs, and the people whom they ruled, acknowledged the Pentateuch as the common code of the whole nation, before the separation, such acknowledgement, on their part, must be held to be the clearest possible proof of its existence, at the time when that event occurred, in the same form, in which it was found at the commencement of the captivity. That they did recognize its genuineness and authority, there is evidence sufficient to satisfy every candid inquirer. For,

* 1 Kings xii. 26–33.

12

In the first place, if they opposed and rejected the authority of the Pentateuch, every trace of such opposition and rejection has disappeared from the records of history. As such a thing is scarcely within the range of possibilities, this must be regarded as a negative proof, of no inconsiderable force. Secondly, at the very time when the kings of Israel were seeking to undermine the influence of the Pentateuch, and to destroy its authority, they studiously imitated, in their idolatrous worship, the festivals, fasts, sacrifices, and various rites of that very code. Thus it is said of Jeroboam, that he "ordained a feast in the eighth month like unto the feast which is in Judah."* They carefully preserved the forms of the ritual, while they as carefully sought to rob them of all their true power and worth. Nothing could be more natural than such a procedure, on the part of the politic princes, who knew, that their subjects had been long accustomed to reverence and obey the code, as of divine original; nothing more unnatural and even insane, on the supposition, that it was an imposition, flagrant in itself, and injurious to their interests. Thirdly, an incident occurred in the reign of Hezekiah, which not only affords a full testimony to the authenticity of the Pentateuch itself, and the acknowledged authority of the laws contained in it, but which also incontestibly proves, that the kingdom of Israel, not less than the kingdom of Judah, recognized it, as containing the genuine and authoritative record of the law of Moses, the national code of the whole Jewish race. That monarch, in his pious zeal for the restoration of a pure worship according to the Mosaic ritual, with the minutest requirements of which he sedulously complied, appointed a solemn passover, to which he not only invited his own subjects, but made proclamation also "to Ephraim and Manasseh and all Israel, from Beersheba unto Dan, that they should come to the house of the Lord at Jerusalem, to keep the passover unto the

* 1 Kings xii. 32.

Lord God of Israel."* In this proclamation he exhorted the ten tribes to turn again to the Lord God of Abraham, Isaac, and Jacob, and not to trespass and be stiff-necked as their fathers were, but to yield themselves to the Lord, and enter into his sanctuary.† "So the posts passed from city to city, through the country of Ephraim and Manasseh, even unto Zebulun."‡ Would any prince, not bereft of reason, have ventured upon such a procedure, if the authority of the code, on which it was founded, had not been acknowledged by the persons, to whom the proclamation was made? The success of the measure was exactly such as might have been anticipated, on the supposition of such acknowledgement; but wholly inexplicable, on any other. Many, through an impiety and contempt, engendered by long neglect, mocked at the messengers of Hezekiah; but many others of the revolted tribes "humbled themselves and came to Jerusalem."§ Is not this a clear proof, that the authenticity and authority of the Pentateuch were recognized by those tribes? But, fourthly, strong as this argument is, there is another still more cogent. Let it be remembered, that the kingdom of Israel existed as an independent state for 268 years, at the close of which period it was subverted by the Assyrians, and many of the people carried into captivity. The Samaritans succeeded to the ten tribes. They were a mixed race, composed partly of Israelites, and partly of foreigners, whom the king of Assyria had sent to occupy the lands of those who had been removed. Now, upon the supposition, that the ten tribes, during their separate existence, rejected the Pentateuch, what is the state of the case? Why, that for 268 years the Israelites combatted, as a known forgery, and then all at once their descendants and successors received, and ever afterwards acknowledged, as of divine original and authority, the code of another nation, between whom and

* 2 Chr. xxx. 1. † 2 Chr. xxx. 7, 8.
‡ 2 Chr. xxx. 10. § 2 Chr. xxx. 10, 11.

themselves, both before and after the reception of it, the bitterist enmity always existed; and yet, that every trace of their original and long continued rejection of the code has faded from the memory of mankind, and been obliterated from the records of history. He who can believe that, is prepared to swallow the greatest conceivable absurdities, provided only they be thought to impugn and weaken the authority of divine revelation.

Wherefore, I conceive it to be proved, that the Pentateuch existed, in its present form, at the separation of the tribes and the formation of the two independent kingdoms of Judah and Israel, which event happened 979 years before the birth of our Savior.

Let us advance a step higher. What reason is there to believe, that the composition of the Pentateuch is at least as old as the establishment of kingly government among the Hebrews? Dean Graves has suggested an argument in support of this view, which seems to carry with it an unanswerable force.* The argument is, that the civil form of government, exhibited in the Pentateuch, is not regal. So far from this, it notices the regal form as an innovation, which should be introduced in an age subsequent to the establishment of the original polity; an innovation, too, far from being pleasing to God. But further and stronger still: The code of the Pentateuch imposed numerous restraints upon the kings, which abridged their prerogative, curbed their power, and put fetters upon their ambition. Moreover, it required, that the reigning sovereign should keep always by him a copy of the law, imposing these stern and irksome restraints; that he should consult it daily ; and that he should make it the steady rule of his private life and his public administration.† Now, if the Pentateuch was forged or compiled, after the establishment of the regal form of government and during its continuance, this must have been done, either, first, by the king

---

* On the Pent., Pt. 1, Lect. 1.   † Deut. xvii. 16, seq.

himself, or at his instigation ; or, secondly, by some person, or persons, who probably wished to weaken his authority, and curb his ambition. It is impossible, that the latter supposition should be true, for whoever happened to be king at the time, when the fabrication was made, would certainly know the real character of the writing; and would, with equal certainty, reject it. And the former supposition is so improbable, that it cannot for a moment be admitted, without direct and irrefragable proof of its truth ; for what king ever did, or would, make a fictitious code of laws, which condemned the kingly form of government, which rebuked and denounced all regal tyranny, and which confined the royal prerogative within the narrowest compass compatible even with the name of king ? This is an improbability so great, that it may well be regarded as amounting to a moral impossibility. This is a decisive answer to the argument of those who hold, that the Pentateuch was first compiled in the reign and by the authority of king Josiah. It is equally decisive against another suspicion, entertained by some, that Samuel was the author of it. Let it be remembered, that, when the people asked a king of Samuel, he opposed their demand, on the ground, that the appointment of a man to be king would be a rejection of Jehovah as their sovereign; he painted, in vivid colors, the oppressions, to which they would be subjected, under the regal government ; he told them, that they were rushing into a servitude, which would prove intolerably burdensome; he warned them to desist in time, for that they would assuredly repent of their rashness.; and, when he found all his remonstrances unavailing, he labored to impose restraints upon the future sovereigns, which would at least mitigate, if they did not avert, the mischiefs, which he apprehended from their rule.* Is it credible, that Samuel would have ventured upon such a course, if he had not felt himself entrenched behind the authority of a code, revered by the

* 1 Sam. viii. 11–18.

people as the work of their ancient lawgiver? Or, if he had fabricated the Pentateuch, would not the imposition have been detected by Saul, who was at bitter enmity with the prophet during a great part of his reign, and was a man by no means wanting in the requisite ability? And still more, would not Solomon, the monarch famed in every age and region of the world for his wisdom and sagacity, have penetrated and exposed the odious cheat; Solomon, who, in so many instances, flagrantly violated the law of Moses, and must have felt his fame wounded by its stern and indignant rebuke ?[*]

Wherefore, there is no reason to doubt, and every reason to believe, that the Pentateuch existed in its present form, prior to the establishment of kingly government among the Hebrews.

We have now reached a very high antiquity in our argument, and are come within 400 years of the foundation of the Hebrew state, according to the chronology of Usher, or within 500 years, according to that of Josephus, Jackson, and Russel.[†] Throughout all this period, the peculiar polity, established by Moses, was in force. No occasion arose for the invention or compilation of a new code. No special interest can be conceived, likely to be promoted by such a fabrication. And no man, or body of men, appears upon the stage, of an influence and authority sufficient to ensure its reception among the people. It is true, that during this period the Israelites often transgressed the law, and thereby brought upon themselves grievous calamities; but they as often repented of their sin, owned the justice of their punishment, and returned to their former obedience. Would a fabricated code be likely to secure such respect and submission? It cannot be pretended. "That prosperity should corrupt a nation, is credible; that calamity should rouse them to repentance, is also credible; but that they should ascribe their calamities to the violation of a law, whose authority they had never ac-

* Graves on Pent. Pt. 1, Lect. 1.   † Smith's Heb. People, C. 3.

knowledged, and that, in the midst of vice and corruption, a new code should be fabricated, condemning that vice and corruption, and be imposed upon the nation as the known law of their fathers, without opposition, is surely most improbable and strange."*

Thus have we traced back the Pentateuch, all along the stream of history, to the age of Moses himself. From these facts and reasonings, the conclusion seems fully warranted, that such as we have it now, such it came from the hand of that illustrious law giver, historian, and prophet.

But strong as the foregoing proofs are, they do not constitute the whole strength of even the external evidence. The Pentateuch is not the only book belonging to the sacred literature of the Jews. There are numerous other tracts, some of them of no inconsiderable compass, written by a great number of authors, embracing a great variety of subjects, and composed at different times along a tract of more than a thousand years, reaching from Moses to Malachi. Now all these manifold writings are crowded with allusions, quotations, and abridged histories, taken out of the Pentateuch.† These references and citations are thickly scattered throughout the whole of the Old Testament. There is hardly one important statement in the Pentateuch, there is scarcely a chapter from the beginning of Genesis to the end of Deuteronomy, which is not in this manner referred to or cited. Many of the places are mentioned very often, and the citations are of great length, and embrace a great number of minute details. The references are to the creation; the first marriage; man's dominion over the creatures; the grant of herbs and plants for meat; the garden of Eden; the violation of the covenant; the curse denounced against Adam and the serpent; the flood; Noah's character; the residence of the ancestors of the Jews beyond the Euphrates; numerous particulars in the

* Graves on Pent. Pt. 1. Lect. 1.   † Edwards's Works, v. 9. pp. 132, seqq.

lives of Abraham and the other patriarchs; Melchizedek as
both a king and a priest of the true God; the great fertility
of the land of Sodom, and the great wickedness of the inhabitants; the sudden destruction by fire of the cities of the
plain; the two wives of Jacob as building the house of Israel;
all the leading events in the life of Joseph; Tamar's bearing
Pharez to Judah; the famine that compelled Israel and his
family to seek bread in Egypt; the Israelites multiplying
there, and the Egyptians dealing subtilly with them; their
bondage in Egypt; the kind of service required of them;
the circumstances attending their egress out of Egypt, their
wanderings in the wilderness, and their settlement in the land
of Canaan, with hardly a single exception; and other particulars recorded in the Pentateuch, too numerous to specify.*

Now, upon this state of the case I argue thus : Here we
have innumerable references to the facts contained in the
Pentateuch; references made by many different writers, in
may different ages. Hence the Israelitish nation must have
had, from the origin of their commonwealth, a great, standing, and authoritative record of these facts; and this record
must have been the Pentateuch itself. For, if there had
been no such history to serve as the common guide of all
these authors, it must have been morally impossible for them,
in such a vast number of allusions and quotations, and these
extending to such a multitude of minute details, to avoid innumerable inconsistencies with each other. And, even if we
may suppose the existence of the tracts independently of the
history, can we believe that the wit of man is equal to the task
of framing a fictitious history, in which all these manifold
references, citations, and rehearsals, dispersed through the
works of so many authors, writing for so many different objects,
and in so many different styles and ages, should be introduced

---

* See these references drawn out in full, covering many pages in the 9th
volume of President Edwards's Works, in his Notes on the Bible, pp. 133–
142.

and harmonized without a single jar, and with such an air of
verisimilitude and originality, that all the world should mistake the fabrication as the common fountain and source of
the very books, out of which it was formed? Can there be
any absurdity equal to the absurdity of such a supposition?
Consider! "All these multiplied and various compositions
unite in presupposing the existence and the truth of the Pentateuch, and uniformly refer to and quote it as the only true and
genuine account of the ancient history and known laws of the
Jews. They recite its facts; they refer to its laws; they cele-
brate its author; they appeal to the people, to the kings, to
the priests; they rebuke and threaten them for neglecting the
law of Moses, as contained in the Pentateuch; and, what is
most decisive, they never once give the least hint of any rival
law, of any new compilation, of any doubt as to its authenticity."*

Such is the argument, embodying the external historical
proofs of the genuineness and authenticity of the Pentateuch.
The sum is this. The evidence for the existence of this writing, all along down from the return of the Jews out of captivity to the present time is so strong, that none dispute it. At
this point we enter upon debated territory. Yet the Pentateuch could not have been compiled at this time, but must
have been the same writing, which the Jews received as the
law of Moses before the captivity, because it was evidently
well known both to Jews and heathen during the captivity;
because the law enforced by Ezra required sacrifices of the
people, to which they would never have submitted but in obedience to a code of established and unquestionable authority;
because many persons, who were present at the laying of the
foundation of the second temple, had seen the first, and must
have known the law then in use, and therefore could and
would have detected and exposed a fabricated code; because
three distinct copies of the writing can be traced, manifestly

* Graves on Pent. Pt. 1, Lect. 1.

not borrowed from each other, yet all agreeing in their statements; and because the Samaritans, the bitter enemies of the Jews, as well before as after the captivity, acknowledged it as of divine original and authority. Again, our copy of the Pentateuch must have existed prior to the division of the tribes into the separate kingdoms of Israel and Judah, because the monarchs and people of the former, not less than those of the latter, owned its authority as the code of the whole Jewish race before that event, notwithstanding it was repugnant to their interests as an independent state, and interposed the greatest obstacle to the peculiar policy, adopted from the first and steadily pursued to the end by the Israelitish kings. Further, the Pentateuch, as we have it, must have preceded the establishment of monarchy among the Hebrews, because it not only does not exhibit a regal form of government, but expressly opposes that description of polity, noticing it as an innovaton that would arise in the progress of ages, and seeking, by various admirable enactments, to counteract its innate tendencies to despotism and tyranny. And further still, this venerable writing must be coeval with the origin of the Hebrew state, because, during the interval which elapsed between the first formation of the government and the establishment of monarchy, no change was made in the form of polity, no occasion arose for fabricating a code, no conceivable interest could be promoted by such a procedure, and no man or body of men appear to have possessed an influence sufficiently commanding to give currency to the imposition. Superadded to all these considerations, is the still more forcible fact, that a long catalogue of Jewish writers, stretching from the age of Moses himself down to the birth of Christ, have acknowledged and cited the Pentateuch, in every possible form of acknowledgement and citation, as the true and authentic history and code of their nation; and that, among the many disputes and differences of opinion which the Jews have had about the Mosaic law, there never was any such dispute or difference as this, whether Moses was the author of the writing, or whether it contained a credible account of the foundation and early annals of their state; even the Sadducees, learned men and free-thinkers, who rejected all the other books held sacred by their countrymen, acknowledging the Pentateuch as genuine and divine. The world may be challenged to produce a chain of evidence, of equal strength, in support of the genuineness and authenticity of any other ancient writing.

Nor let it be objected, that the Pentateuch lacks confirmation from contemporaneous profane authors. If any such existed, their writings have long since perished. There is no contemporary literature. Can we look for such testimony from the Greeks? Thucydides* has declared, that even respecting his own countrymen he could find no authentic records, prior to the Peloponesian war. Can we expect it from the Romans? They had scarcely begun to be a people, when the empire of Jerusalem was destroyed, and the nation reduced to captivity. Not a fragment of any contemporaneous record has floated down the stream of time. Every other chronicle has been swallowed up and lost in the gulf of ages. Centuries elapsed after the exodus of Israel, before Homer, or Hesiod, or Manetho, or Berous, or even Sanchoniathon wrote. There are, therefore, no profane histories with which to compare the Pentateuch. Its credibility must stand or fall, on evidence entirely independent of either favoring or opposing testimony of this kind. Yet such profane testimony as the nature of the case admits, we have in several pagan authors. Diodorus Siculus, Strabo, Longinus, Juvenal, Tacitus, and others, mention Moses by name, and quote from his writings, just as we appeal to any of these authors and their works.

There is another species of external testimony to the genuineness and authenticity of the Pentateuch, by which these

* Lib. 1.

qualities, as pertaining to that writing, may be proved with equal certainty. I refer to the argument from public monuments and actions. The strongest species of historical evidence lies in commemorative rites and festivals. No ingenuity of a false logic, no mystification of an insane philosophy, no bitterness of malignity against unpalatable truths, no demoniac desire to overturn men's dearest hopes and aspirations, can either break or evade its force.

The nature and force of this evidence may be illustrated in an example taken from our own history. On the 4th day of July, 1776, the British colonies of North America declared themselves free and independent States. Ever since that event, an annual festival has been observed to keep alive the memory of it in the mind and heart of the nation. Let us suppose the declaration of independence not to have been made, nor a separation from Great Britain effected, nor a distinct government established, at that time. Could the festival have been instituted then? Reason and common sense reply:—"It is impossible."

Let it be supposed then, secondly, that these States have continued to our day in the condition of British colonies, and that some one starts up on the morning of the 4th of July, 1852, and summons the people to the celebration of the national jubilee, instituted, according to his proclamation, seventy-six years before, and ever since faithfully observed, to commemorate an event, which by the hypothesis, never occurred, viz.: the resolution of our forefathers to shake off the yoke of British tyranny, and their subsequent victory over British valor? Would any body believe him, or pay the least attention to his summons? Such an hypothesis would, if possible, be more absurd than the former. Let a man make such an attempt with respect to Austria or Russia. Let him undertake to persuade the people of those countries, that a hundred years ago they raised the standard of revolution, dethroned their sovereigns, and replaced their monarchical

with democratic institutions, and that ever since, they had
celebrated those vast achievements by commemorative festivals renewed from year to year. What would be the issue of
such an attempt ? The author of it would either be laughed
at as a harmless fool, or pitied as a wretched maniac. No
words could set the absurdity of it in a more glaring light,
than the very terms in which the supposition itself must be
made.

It is, then, impossible, in the nature of things, that a national commemorative festival should ever arise, except upon
a basis of truth. Such an institution presupposes, involves,
and demonstrates the reality of the events, which it commem-
orates.

Were there, then, any public monuments among the Jews,
any national commemorative actions, coeval with the origin
of the Hebrew State, and des ned to preserve the memory
of the events recorded in the Pentateuch ? Yes, such public
monuments and actions there were in great number. For
example, the passover ; the pentecost; the feast of tabernacles ;
the dedication of the first-born, both man and beast; the
consecration of one entire tribe to minister in holy things ;
Aaron's rod that budded ; the pot of manna ; the brazen serpent; the pile of stones at Gilgal ; the day of annual atonement;
the new moons ; the sabbaths ; and even the daily sacrifices.
So long, therefore, as each returning vernal equinox brings
anew into requisition the unleavened bread, so long as the
passover, the pentecost, and the day of atonement continue to
be celebrated by the scattered remnant of Jacob's sons ; so
long, indeed, as there shall remain historical evidence of the
past existence of these and other Jewish festivals and monuments ;—so long may we be sure of the reality of the events
which they commemorate. So long may we be sure that
the Israelites were slaves in Egypt, and that they were delivered by the miraculous exertion of an almighty power. So
long may we be sure. that God divided the Red Sea for their

accommodation; that he spake the law in thunder from Sinai; that for forty years he led the people by a cloudy and fiery pillar, the never-failing symbol of his presence; that he satisfied their hunger with bread that nightly fell around their camp, the product of his creative energy; that he preserved from decay the garments that covered their nakedness; that he parted the waters of Jordan and led them dry-shod over its pebbly bottom; and that he finally planted them securely on the territories of their enemies and his, in the land that he had promised to their fathers. On the national monuments and festivals of commemoration, we may plant our faith in the truth and authority of the Pentateuch, as upon an impregnable fortress; and the storms of an infidel philosophy may spend their rage upon us in vain.

Having thus considered the two branches of external evidence, the testimony of history and the testimony of monuments, I pass to an examination of the internal evidence in favor of the genuineness and authenticity of the Mosaic record. Let it be observed here, in passing, that Moses was every way qualified to write the history of the Pentateuch. He was, as we have seen in the second chapter of this book, a man of solid intellect, acute perceptions, calm judgment, great learning, unparalleled disinterestedness, and much experience in public affairs. In regard to every thing related in the last four books of the Pentateuch, his knowledge was ample and exact, since he was himself a chief actor in the transactions, which he records. The only doubt that can arise, as to the fullness of his information, relates to the events of former times, contained in the book of Genesis. Here, setting aside divine revelation, and insisting only on what may be demanded in an uninspired historian, Moses had sources of information more direct, copious, and reliable than were open to the most learned of his contemporaries in other nations, not excepting the Egyptians themselves. Lamech, the father of Noah, was fifty-six years contemporary with Adam, and Noah's son, Shem, survived to the time of Abraham. Thus it appears, that this patriarch received, or might receive, whatever knowledge Adam conveyed to his posterity, through only three intermediate links. From his time, there was an unmixed lineal descent from father to son, in the Jewish nation, and consequently an unbroken tradition of former times. The chief cause of the confusion and uncertainty in the traditions of other nations, was the frequent intermixture of families and races. But divine providence, as if purposely to satisfy mankind of the capacity of the Jewish nation to preserve the tradition of the first ages entire, prohibited their mixture with the people of other nations. From the time of Abraham, then, to that of Moses, how easily and naturally might the general tradition of the ancient history be preserved pure and authentic, when the families, in which the tradition was lodged, all belonged to the same nation, and were united by the bond of a common religion, and for a considerable part of the time by the scarcely less powerful tie of a common adversity.

The first internal proof of the genuineness and authenticity of the Pentateuch is drawn from the nature of its contents. This writing is not a mere history, but contains the entire civil and ecclesiastical code of the Jews; it was the grand and sacred rule, the constitution and foundation of their State. And, so far as it is historical in its character, the series of events, which it records, is by no means of the common order; neither did the events happen thousands of years before the time of Moses; nor yet were they such, that his countrymen would be likely to feel little or no interest in them, other than the interest of mere curiosity. Quite the reverse of this was the true state of the case. The facts themselves were most extraordinary and conspicuous; they happened, for the most part, under the immediate observation of the persons to whom the relation was addressed; and they were of the deepest moment, both to the nation at large and to every individual in it. Now, if the Pentateuch is not what it purports to be,

either it is a fictitious narrative and code, forged by Moses
himself, or it was compiled and palmed upon the nation as
his, in a subsequent age. Let it be considered, then, how
strange, how public, and how momentous the main facts narrated in the Pentateuch were, affecting every order in the
State, and every interest of society. And let it be considered,
further, how constantly Moses appeals for the truth of his relations, to the personal knowledge of those whom he addresses.
" Your eyes have seen all these things," is the confident tone
in which he speaks to his countrymen, and challenges a denial of his statements.

Suppose these relations to be false; could Moses, by any
possibility, have induced his countrymen to believe that they
were true? Could he have made them believe, that they
had all been slaves in Egypt, and that a royal edict of destruction had been issued against their male infants, if they had
never experienced the bitterness of servitude, nor felt the
pangs, occasioned by the cruel mandate? Could he have
gained any credit to the statement, that they had wrought at
making bricks and building treasure-cities in Egypt, if they
had never groaned under the tyranny, which imposed these
tasks upon them? Could he have persuaded them, that the
first-born of the Egyptians had all been slain in a night, in
their very presence, as it were, if no voice of parental lamentation, consequent thereupon, had ever reached their ears?
Could he have made them believe, that the Red Sea had
opened to afford them a passage, if its waters had opposed an
invincible barrier to their progress? Could he have produced in them the conviction that the law of God had, in
their presence, been published in an audible voice, from the
summit of the burning mountain, if they had never seen the
flashes, nor heard the thunders that issued from the thick
darkness that enveloped it? Could he have induced the belief, that the violation of that law had been punished with
desolating plagues, if none of all their company had perished

by such a visitation? Could he have persuaded them, that, during all their wanderings and encampments in the wilderness, a miraculous cloud had covered them by day, and a miraculous fire had illuminated their dwellings by night, if they had experienced neither the cooling shelter of the one, nor the pleasant companionship of the other? Could he have made them believe, that for forty years they had been fed with manna, which fell around their camp, while in reality they had eaten nothing of the kind?

If we can suppose an effrontery, sufficient to publish such a stupendous series of falsehoods, possible, and Moses to have been guilty of it, could he have escaped the punishment, which a conduct, unparalleled in guilt and folly, would have richly deserved? Were not the contemporaries of Moses prone to transgress his laws? Did they not often fall into idolatry? Had there been the least suspicion of imposture in his writings, would the ringleaders in these revolts have declined so excellent a plea for their apostasies? Would not the charge of forgery, made good against Moses, have afforded a solid ground for the rebellion of Korah and his company? In short, is it to be imagined that, when there were so many envious of his eminent position, and ready with the charge, that he " took too much upon him," Moses would have adventured any thing into the public records, which was not indisputably true? Surely, the man who can digest such a mass of absurdities, need never again open his lips to ridicule the credulity of those who believe, with the magicians of Egypt, that they see the finger of God in the wonders above detailed, and hear the voice of God's messenger in the utterances of the Hebrew prophet and lawgiver.

These considerations make it certain, that Moses himself could not have palmed upon his countrymen a fictitious history and a forged code of laws. The fabrication, therefore, if the Pentateuch be a fabrication, must belong to an age subsequent to that of Moses. Let us assume this hypothesis, and

13

subject it to the test of examination. Let us see whether it is a probable supposition, or whether, on the contrary, it is not encompassed with absurdities and impossibilities.

It is acknowledged, that forged writings have been repeatedly palmed upon the world; and, in some instances, with temporary success. It is impossible to say, that in no case has the design completely succeeded. But it is so difficult to secure a perfect verisimilitude; it is so hard to avoid having some allusion, date, or characteristic circumstance, nay, many such, out of joint with the times, at which the forgery is placed; it is so almost impossible to conceal all traces of the particular design of the fabrication; and there have been so many instances of detection, as to render it probable, that no imposition of this kind has ultimately eluded discovery and exposure. It is, besides, a consideration of no little force here, that forged writings have usually been of such a nature as not materially to affect the interests of mankind;—mere literary productions, under the venerable name of some ancient author. But the Pentateuch, it must be remembered, is a history of events the most extraordinary and important; and not only so, but it exhibits also a constitution of civil government, and a complete body of ecclesiastical and municipal laws.

Now, by the hypothesis which we have assumed for the sake of argument, this writing, with all its history, laws, constitutions, and minute and endless regulations, relating to persons, property, morals, crimes, sacrifices, public worship, and all the diversified interests of society, is a forgery, invented and compiled in an age posterior to that of Moses, foisted upon the Jews as the authentic and genuine work of that lawgiver, and so universally received, honored, and obeyed as such, by the Jewish nation, that no record, tradition, fragment, or vestige of whatever kind, of any other law, is now in being; and the memory of such prior and different code, if it ever existed, has entirely faded and disappeared from the records of the human race.

Who, upon this hypothesis, were the persons that first published to the Jews this fictitious history and counterfeit law? At what age did they live? When was the fabrication made, and the cheat put upon the nation? Was it while the memory of Moses's name and deeds was still recent, or afterwards? Certainly not at the former period, for then all things were too fresh in the recollection of men to admit the possibility of a forgery of this nature. Moses himself might as readily have played upon the credulity of his countrymen, as any of his immediate or early successors. Therefore, the imposition must have been accomplished in an age long posterior to the time of Moses. In that case, had the law exhibited in the Pentateuch been observed before, or not? If not, then the nation, at the time of its promulgation, would know it to be a cheat, and would reject it as such. If it had been observed before, had such observance been continually down from the time of Moses, or not? If continually down, then the law must have been of his framing, and the hypothesis falls to the ground. If not continually down, then the nearer the forgery was to his time, the more difficult it would be of execution. For so the real institutions of Moses would be fresh in men's memory, and they would be able to detect, and would certainly repudiate, all counterfeits.*

Innumerable and insuperable difficulties press upon this hypothesis. We have seen some of them; let us glance at others.

If the Pentateuch is a fabrication, the author of it put a key into the hands of those upon whom he sought to impose it, which would enable them, with infallible certainty, to detect the imposition. He makes the writing speak of itself as com-

* See the reasoning of this paragraph presented in a more extended form, and with great power, in Still. Orig. Sac. B. 2, c. 1.

posed by Moses ;* he makes it say, that a copy was from the first preserved in the ark ;† and he makes it obligatory on the king to have a copy always by him.‡ Now, when the author of this counterfeit history first brought it forward, it would be known by all, that there was no copy in the ark ; none in the hands of the king ; and none in the hands of any body else. This shows, that the writing could not be a forgery, but must have been the genuine work of Moses ; for, if it had not been his, its own declarations would have interposed an effectual bar to its reception.

The Pentateuch vouches its own credibility by public actions, observed at stated times.§ It narrates various important events, and states, that, at the time when they occurred, certain observances were instituted to preserve the memory of them to posterity. For example, it relates the destruction of the first-born of the Egyptians, and declares that to commemorate this event, the first-born of Israel, both of man and beast, were forever afterwards to be consecrated to the Lord.¶ Let us now recur to the hypothesis, that the Pentateuch is a forgery. When the fabrication was first published, every person in the nation must have known, that there was no such rite or custom in existence among them, as the consecration of the first-born to Jehovah. Yet this was as much a part of the original matter of fact, as the destruction of the Egyptians. Would they not, then, knowing one essential part of the statement to be false, conclude the other to be false likewise, and reject the whole as a fable, and one, too, of an extremely clumsy construction? If I were now to invent some strange story about the first settlement of this country, I might perhaps gain some credit to the tale among weak-minded persons. But if I were to add, that at the time when the alleged fact took place, it was solemnly appointed to be commemorated

* Deut. xxxi. 9. † Deut. xxxi. 26. ‡ Deut. xvii. 18, 19.
§ See "Leslie's Method with the Deists," on the argument from monuments.
¶ Ex. xiii. 15.

in all future time by indelibly branding a certain mark upon
the forehead of every male child, the most credulous person
in the world would laugh the story to scorn, because every
man he met would be a visible and standing confutation of it·
And if, not content with inventing a single fact, I should
fabricate a series of the most public and remarkable occurrences, vouch their credibility by an extended system of commemorative festivals and observances, and publish the whole
as an authentic history in the name of Christopher Columbus,
expecting to get it received as such by my countrymen,—
could any words sufficiently express the folly of such an attempt? One universal scream of ridicule would be the only
response it could meet. Yet exactly such an attempt,—
absurd, incredible, impossible as it is,—a certain class of
writers would have us believe, was not only made, but succeeded, in the case of the Pentateuch.

But more and worse. The Pentateuch is not a mere
history; it is a code of laws likewise; a code, as all admit,
acknowledged and adopted by the Jews, as the civil and
ecclesiastical constitution of their state. By the hypothesis
under consideration, this code is a fabrication, a forgery.
Originally, therefore, the Jews were under a different law,
and this was foisted upon them by an impostor. Now, it is
as easy to impose a fabricated code on one nation as another,
and in the present age as any preceding one. Let any one,
then, ask himself, whether it would be possible now to invent
a set of acts of congress, and get them received by the whole
American people, as the established laws of the republic,
known and obeyed as such, since the origin of the government down to the present time? Does this strike the reader
as absurd and impossible? Not less absurd and impossible is
the supposition of forgery in the present case. The impostor,
who imposed the code of the Pentateuch upon the Hebrews,
must have made them forget all the ancient constitutions of
their state, and believe, that they and their forefathers had

lived under a system of laws and institutions, which, in point
of fact, had never been known or heard of, till then. Is such
a thing conceivable? Is it within the bounds of possibility?
The very polity and laws of the ancient Hebrews, as exhibited in the Pentateuch, might just as readily be imposed
upon the American people at this moment, to the exclusion
of all existing statutes, and the whole nation made to believe,
that they are the only system of ecclesiastical and civil law
ever known among them, as they could be imposed upon the
Hebrew people, in any age subsequent to that of Moses, on
the hypothesis that they were a forgery.

No other instance is adduced out of all history, none is
even pretended, of a forged code of laws, purporting to be
brought to light after a long interval, palmed upon the
nation as the genuine work of their ancient legislators, and
actually adopted by them, as the rule of their civil and religious institutions. It is impossible in this way to alter the
fundamental laws of a state, after long settlement, as every
candid person must see and own, on the slightest reflection.
Such a procedure would produce endless confusion of interests and rights, overturning, as it must, all the established
relations of property, and changing all the old institutions
and usages of society. Men would not submit to the change.
A striking fact illustrative of this point occurs in Roman
history. Long after the death of Numa, a body of laws was
found in his grave. It seems to have been believed, that
these laws were of his composing. Yet, notwithstanding the
veneration in which his memory was held, the senate, judging them contrary to the existing laws, ordered them to be
burnt. They would not even allow the public to know the
nature and purport of them, lest the state should be unsettled by it.*

A writing may be forged, and gain a temporary success, if
it relates to matters not of general interest; but when it con-

* Stillingfleet, Orig. Sac. B. 2, c. 1.

cerns the rights, privileges, and government of a nation, there will be enough, whose interest will lead them to prevent imposture. Men are quicksighted in what relates to their estates and freeholds. It is certain, therefore, that any attempt of the kind supposed, would fail, and would be laughed at as the last abortive folly of a crazed imagination. Men were not simpletons in ancient times, any more than they are now. They had their senses, as well as we. They were as much alive to their interests, and as clear-sighted in the discernment of them. They were as tenacious of their rights, and as unwilling to be deceived. No man, therefore, could forge, and no man did forge, the Pentateuch. The very supposition of such an imposture is a libel upon the intelligence of antiquity. It is tantamount to a charge of idiocy against the whole Jewish race. And if nations, in their associated capacity, could bring an action for slander, such an action could be sustained by the house of Israel against any man, who should charge them with being so far "non compotes mentis," as to have allowed a forgery of the kind in question to obtain the least credit or currency among them.

The second internal proof of the genuineness and authenticity of the Pentateuch, is drawn from the minuteness and particularity of the narrative, and from the general tone and style of the composition, which is remarkable for its artlessness and simplicity. The entire structure of the work is totally unlike the general detail of a remote compiler; its whole manner the direct opposite of the labored artifice of fiction and forgery. This argument is of greater force in such a writing as the Pentateuch, than it would be in most other compositions; for the author, if he were an impostor, must have felt that he was engaged in an undertaking of the greatest difficulty; an undertaking requiring no ordinary ingenuity and no common caution; an undertaking, indeed, never before attempted, and little likely to succeed; and this

consciousness must have occasioned a feeling of constraint
and anxiety, which would be sure to betray itself in the execution of his self-imposed task. But, in point of fact, from
the beginning to the end of the five books of Moses, there is
not the slightest appearance of any such feeling in the writer.
He descends to the minutest details in describing the materials and workmanship of the tabernacle and its furniture,—
the altar, the lavers, the ark, the dress of the priests, the
curtains and their borders, the pillars, the sockets, the rings,
the loops, the tenons, &c., &c. There is the same minuteness of detail in laying down rules for the sacrifices, in distinguishing between clean and unclean meats, in pointing
out the various ways of contracting and removing ceremonial
impurity, and in describing the symptoms and the cure of
leprosy, both of persons and of houses. Again, the same thing
is observable in the geographical enumerations of the Pentateuch, and in its accounts of the marches and encampments
of the Israelites. In regard to all these matters, the details
are numerous and exact in the highest degree; and many of
them are repeated again and again. But throughout the
whole there is not the least appearance of art, or caution, or
dread of discovery. Now, all this is most natural and
probable, on the hypothesis that the Pentateuch is what it
purports to be, and Moses the writer of it; but most unnatural and improbable, on the hypothesis that an impostor in
a distant age was the author of the writing. It is the way
of forgers and impostors to deal in vague generalities. They
studiously avoid minuteness of detail, for that greatly multi-
plies the chances of discovery. But the author of the Pentateuch appears perfectly careless in this matter. He says
what he has to say, in the most inartificial and guileless
manner imaginable, interweaving laws with history, and
piling details upon details, without the least apparent solicitude as to whether his statements should be believed or not.
Could he have done this, if he had not known, that what he

wrote was true, and if he had not felt, that it would be
unhesitatingly credited by the persons, to whom it was addressed ?

The third internal proof of the genuineness and authenticity of the Pentateuch, is drawn from its impartiality. When
we see a writer manifestly actuated by a design to aggran-
dize himself, to advance his family and posterity, or,—which
is a fault highly characteristic of the Greek historians,—to
raise the credit and fame of his own nation, we may suspect
him of leaving the beaten way of truth, to tread the devious
paths of deceit. But there is no ground to suspect the
author of the Pentateuch of any such personal, domestic, or
national bias. On the contrary, never has any other historian
displayed the quality of impartiality in so eminent a degree
as this writer. See how he speaks of the near relatives of
the lawgiver. The faults of Aaron and Miriam, his brother
and sister, the fault of Nadab and Abihu, his nephews, and
the rebellious conduct of his own tribe, in common with that
of the other tribes, on the return of the spies, are spoken of
in terms at once plain and severe. Little is said of his wife,
except that her name was Zipporah, that she was an Ethio-
pian woman, and that as such she was an object of contemp:
and hatred.*   His own sons were left in the meanest sort of
attendance upon the tabernacle, no provision being made for
the civil advancement, either of them or their posterity. Quite
as little does the author of the Pentateuch flatter the nation
of the lawgiver. It could have formed no part of his design
to enhance their reputation in the world, since he describes
their frowardness, unbelief, murmurings, disobedience, and
rebellions, in such vivid colors as might almost warrant the
suspicion of an intention to vilify their national character.
He sets forth also, with great particularity, the faults and
foibles of the patriarchs, their ancestors, without seeking in
the smallest degree to disguise or extenuate them. Several

* Num xii. 1.

of these ancestors he describes as having been guilty of gross crimes; and upon all, with the solitary exception of Joseph, he charges weaknesses and imperfections, which a zealous partizan would have studiously concealed. But the impartiality of this writer is most conspicuous in his manner of speaking of the lawgiver himself. Without the least reserve he interweaves the history of his failings with that of the failings of his nation. Had he entertained the design of causing his memory to be held in superstitious veneration by his countrymen, how easy had it been to leave out those passages which mar the perfect symmetry of his character, and obscure the brilliancy of his reputation, as in fact has been done by the Jewish historian Josephus. But he appears perfectly indifferent in that regard, or rather, I may say, he studiously depresses the honor of men, his own as well as that of others, that he may magnify the power of God, and exalt his goodness towards a disobedient and rebellious people. And all this he does, not in an affected strain of rhetoric, but in a style natural and unadorned. The low design of pandering to the taste of the multitude with rhetorical phrases, was manifestly beneath his ambition. Like Paul, he held in contempt that excellency of speech, on which the ancient rhetoricians so prided themselves. He displays no vanity of composition, no anxiety about the elegance of his periods. He writes without effort and without art. Yet, had it been his design to produce a splendid piece of writing, he shows plainly enough, that he might have pursued it with no mean success. "In the triumphant hymn, which he has inserted on the deliverance of the terrified Israelites from the host of Pharaoh, we discover a boldness and sublimity of composition seldom excelled. In the address to the assembled nation, supposed to be delivered by Moses shortly before his death; in the blessings promised for obedience, and the curses denounced against offenders; and especially in the song he taught the people, recapitulating the wonders of God's providence which they had witnessed, and the judgments they might expect; we discover a judicious selection of striking circumstances, strong imagery, pathetic appeals to the tenderest feelings, and the authoritative language of the legislator and the prophet combined so aptly, as prove the writer fully capable of commanding most powerfully the attention, and interesting the heart.*" Nevertheless, though evidently so well qualified to produce a beautiful, eloquent, and engaging composition, and to embellish it with every artistic excellence; he has written the Pentateuch in such a way as to show conclusively, that this was no part of his design. He seems, indeed, to have thought that truth itself is invested with such inborn majesty and perfection, as to command both the submission of our understanding and the affection of our heart.

The fourth internal proof of the genuineness and authenticity of the Pentateuch, and the only remaining one, to which the reader's attention will be called, is drawn from the intimate knowledge, which the writer everywhere displays of Egypt, its climate, soil, productions, manners, customs, religion, government, arts, and civilization. It is true, indeed, that an argument of directly the opposite purport, an argument in derogation of the claim of the Pentateuch to be considered as a true and genuine history, has been reared on the author's alleged ignorance of these very things, and his consequent blunders in his Egyptian references. But this, like all other attacks directed against the evidences of divine revelation, has but added strength to the bulwarks of our faith, by calling to its aid the best powers of its adherents, who have, with pious industry, explored the whole subject, and brought back, as the result of their learned labors, the certainty, that the writer of the Pentateuch, so far from being chargeable with ignorance on this score, was

* Graveson Pent. Pt. 1, Lect. 2.

perfectly familiar with the whole circle of Egyptian manners, arts, and learning. In this field Hengstenberg has particularly distinguished himself. To his admirable work, entitled "Egypt and the Books of Moses,"* in which the subject is treated in detail, the reader is directed for full satisfaction. All that can be attempted here is a few brief references to some of the more striking points.

The author of the Pentateuch says of the Egyptians, that they made the lives of the Hebrews bitter with hard bondage, in mortar and in brick.† Upon this statement, he has been charged with ignorance of Egyptian usages, and with transferring to the valley of the Nile what really belonged to Babylonia. But the explorations of Egyptian monuments, made during the present century, cause the charge to rebound upon those who have brought it. Champollion speaks of a tomb of brick at Sais, and a temple of the same material at Wady Halfa. Rosellini‡ says, that ruins of great brick buildings are found in all parts of Egypt, and whole pyramids of brick at Dashoor. Wilkinson§ also attests the use of crude bricks, baked in the sun, to have been universal in upper and lower Egypt, both for public and private buildings.‖

In the enumeration, which the author of the Pentateuch has made of Pharaoh's present to Abraham, asses, sheep, and camels are included.¶ On this, also, has been founded

* Translated by an eminent American scholar, Prof. Robinson, of Middlebury College.

† Ex. i. 14.

‡ I Monumenti dell' Egitto e della Nubia, ii. 2, p. 249. This reference, as also most of those which follow in the remaining part of this chapter, except the biblical references, are taken from Hengstenberg without verification, the authorities not being at hand where the author writes.

§ Manners and Customs of the Ancient Egyptians, London, 1842, vol. ii. p. 96.

‖ Hengstenberg's "Egypt and the Books of Moses," pp. 1, 2.

¶ Gen. xii. 16.

the charge of ignorance and error. These animals, it is alleged, were not found in Egypt. But the monuments exhibit
numerous representations of both sheep and asses, proving
conclusively, that they were found there, and that in great
abundance. Camels, it is true, have not yet been found
delineated on the monuments. But the strongest inference,
which that fact will warrant, is, that they were not numerous. Even such an inference is not certain; for not only
are many objects, known to have existed among the ancient
Egyptians, as the wild boar and the wild ass, for instance,*
wanting in their paintings; but some are wanting, in which
Egypt certainly abounded, of which class fowls and pigeons
may serve as an example.† The reader's attention is called,
in passing, to a singular omission in Pharaoh's present, viz.
the horse. This omission affords an undesigned, but on that
account all the more cogent evidence of the antiquity and
genuineness of the Pentateuch. The horse was native to
Egypt, and found there in the greatest abundance. The
reason of the omission of this animal from Pharaoh's present, therefore, could not have been in the giver, but must
have been in the receiver. Now it is certain, that, down to
the time of Joshua and the Judges, little or no use is made
of the horse by the patriarchs or their descendants. In all
the descriptions of the riches of Palestine, contained in the
Pentateuch, though camels, oxen, sheep, goats, and asses are
enumerated, no mention is made of the horse. Would not
a fabricator, who lived in the times of the kings, and after
horses had become common in Palestine, have mentioned
that animal? Beyond a doubt he would; for it is not likely,
that he would know at what time the horse was introduced;
and it is still less likely, that he would have managed his
forgery with so much circumspection for the sake of preserving historical consistency.‡ To my mind, this is a very

---

* Wilk. vol. iii. p. 21.   † Ibid. p. 35.
‡ Hengstenberg's "Egypt and Books of Moses," pp. 3-7

strong argument in support of the genuine historical character and Mosaic origin of the Pentateuch.

The dream of Pharaoh's chief butler, as narrated in the Pentateuch,* has been supposed to show the narrator's ignorance of the agriculture of Egypt. The dream implies the existence of the vine in that country. Now Herodotus says expressly, that no vines grew in Egypt, and Plutarch affirms, that wine was neither drunk nor offered in sacrifice, till the time of Psammeticus, who was contemporary with Josiah. These, it must be owned, look like formidable testimonies. Yet even if there were no counter testimony, wherewith to rebut them, I would still adhere to the conclusion established in the last chapter, i. e. that no such superior credibility belongs to ancient profane history, that it is to be believed in preference, when its statements conflict with those of sacred writ. But, fortunately, there is no lack of proof in this case, to convict of error the heathen historians, and to vindicate the truth of the Mosaic record. Both Hellanicus and Diodorus not only attest the cultivation of the vine in Egypt, but ascribe to that country the origin of the vine-culture. Herodotus even may be confronted by Herodotus;† for out of other parts of his writings, an argument of no little force, might be constructed, to prove that the vine was cultivated in Egypt at a very early day. But all this, however important it might be under other circumstances, is to little purpose now, since the monuments show, conclusively, both that the vine was cultivated and wine made in the land of the Pharaohs. This fact is fully established, through the labors of Champollion, Rosellini, and Wilkinson. Champollion‡ says, that there are found, in the grottoes of Beni Hassan, representations of the vine, the vintage, the putting up of the wine in bottles or jars, the transportation into the cellar, &c., &c. Rosellini§ devotes

* Gen. xl. 10. seq.   † Herod. ii. 42 and 144.
‡ Champ. 51.   § Rosell. vol. ii. pp. 365, et seq.

a whole section to grape gathering and the art of making wine. Wilkinson* gives the engraving and description of an Egyptian vineyard, and the different kind of labor bestowed upon it.† Joseph, according to the Pentateuch, is placed by Potiphar over all his substance, both in the house and in the field ;‡ and, after his exaltation, he himself has a man over his house.§ A custom peculiarly Egyptian, as the paintings abundantly attest.||

The shameless impudence of Potiphar's wife is related by the author of the Pentateuch.¶ This is a touch of Egyptian manners, true to the life. Nowhere was the marriage vow less regarded. The wife of one of the kings, according to Herodotus,** was untrue to him. He wished to take another. He began the search for a woman, who had proved faithful to her husband. It was long before he found such an one, and when he did, he took her without hesitation for himself. Herodotus describes the great corruption of manners with respect to the marriage relation. The monuments do not give a favorable testimony to the Egyptian women. They represent them as addicted to excessive drinking, so as often to be unable to walk, or even to stand alone.††

The author of the Pentateuch is charged with error in representing Joseph as being admitted into the presence of a lady of such rank as the wife of Potiphar,‡‡ since, as is alleged, none but eunuchs could enter the apartments of the women. But the author knew better what to say than his critics. The blunder is with them, instead of him. They have transferred a custom of the East to the banks of the Nile, while he has spoken of Egyptian manners just as they were, thereby showing that intimate acquaintance with his subject, which it is so difficult for a forger to attain. The

---

* V. 2. pp. 143, et seq. † Hengsten. pp. 12–18
‡ Gen. xxxix. 4, 5. § Gen. xliii. 16, 19. xliv. 1.
|| Hengsten. p. 25. ¶ Gen. xxxiii. 7, et seq.
** ii. 111. †† Wilk. v. 2. p. 167. Hensten. pp. 25, 26.
‡‡ Gen. xxxix. 11.

monuments, according to Wilkinson,* represent the women of Egypt as living under far less restraint, than that to which they were subject in more eastern countries, or even in Greece itself. Ladies and gentlemen are delineated as mingling together, in their festive entertainments, with all the freedom of modern European intercourse.†

Joseph, when called before Pharaoh, is represented in the Pentateuch as shaving himself.‡ This was a purely Egyptian custom. Herodotus§ mentions it as such; and the sculptures confirm his representation. According to Wilkinson,‖ the Egyptians were so particular on this point, that "to have neglected it was a subject of reproach and ridicule; and whenever they intended to convey the idea of a man of low condition, or a slovenly person, the artists represented him with a beard."¶

The Pentateuch describes the labors of Joseph in building store-houses, and storing up corn against the famine.** The paintings on the monuments give a vivid representation of the whole scene, showing how very common the store-house was in Egypt. It appears from the paintings, that they kept an account of the amount of grain stored in the magazines, for at the side of the windows of one of them there are characters indicating the quantity deposited therein."†† This throws light on the statement, that Joseph gathered corn as the sand of the sea, "until he left numbering."‡‡

The author of the Pentateuch speaks of famine as visiting Egypt and the adjacent country of Palestine at the same time.§§ This fact has been seized upon by the enemies of revelation, and made the ground of a charge of ignorance in the writer of the natural condition of Egypt. The fertility

---

* V. 2. p. 389.   † Hengsten. p. 26.
‡ Gen. xli. 14.   § ii. 35.   ‖ V. 3. p. 357.
¶ Hengsten. p. 30.   ** Gen. xli. 48, 49.
†† Rosel. v. 2. p. 324, seq. ‡‡ Gen. xli. 49. Hengsten pp. 34, 35.
§§ Gen. xlvii. 13.

of Egypt depends upon the overflowings of the Nile ; the fertility of Palestine, upon rain; causes, apparently, quite diverse the one from the other. This certainly has a suspicious look. But it only needs a little deeper study of the subject to change the suspicion into an opposite certainty. The author's representation is in harmony with the meteorological phenomena in the case, and the reproach of ignorance recoils on those who make it. That the rise and overflow of the Nile depend upon the rains which fall upon the Abyssinian mountains, is noticed even by Herodotus. These rains, it is now well ascertained, proceed from clouds formed upon the Mediterranean Sea, and have the same origin as the rains which fall in Palestine.* Thus it appears that, contrary to what would at first be supposed, the fertility of Egypt and the fertility of Palestine have a common source ; and the accuracy of the Pentateuch is fully vindicated. Had the author's knowledge of Egypt been less, had it been grounded on mere hearsay, instead of actual observation, he would probably have represented the matter in conformity with the demand of his calumniators, and so have proved his ignorance to be equal to theirs.†

The Pentateuch describes Joseph, his brethren, and the Egyptians as sitting at an entertainment.‡ Another touch peculiarly Egyptian. While the orientals, the Hebrews included, were accustomed to recline at their meals, the habit of the Egyptians, according to the monuments, was to sit.§ Rosellini‖ describes a painting, in which each of the guests sits upon a stool, which, he says, in accordance with their custom, took the place of the couch.¶

The Pentateuch speaks of the steward of Joseph as designating a certain cup of his master's as that out of which he divineth.** The practice of divining by cups is mentioned

---

* Le Pere, Descr. v. 7. p. 576.   † Hengsten. pp. 35, 37.
‡ Gen. xliii. 32.   § Wilk. v. 2, p. 201.
‖ Vol. 2. p. 439.   ¶ Hengsten. pp. 37, 38.   ** Gen. xliv. 5.

by Jamblicus,* as among the superstitions of Egypt; and it appears from a passage in Norden's Travels,† that the custom has descended through all the intervening ages, down to our own times. In a remote extremity of Egypt, a powerful Arab chief addressed one of the party thus: "I know what sort of people you are. I have consulted my cup," &c.‡

The references of the author of the Pentateuch to the geographical relations and features of Egypt, though not numerous, are such as to evince his accurate knowledge of the topography of the country. It is true, that they are scattered, incidental, and undesigned; but all the more certain is the proof thence afforded, that the writer's knowledge was not laboriously gathered for the occasion, nor received at second hand, but was original, derived from personal observation, and of such compass and exactness as to free him from all apprehension of falling into errors. On the whole, they add no little strength to the internal evidence of his credibility as an historian. But to bring out this argument in its just force would require more space than can be spared for the purpose. The reader is, therefore, referred to the work of Professor Hengstenberg on Egypt and the Books of Moses, where he will find it treated at large on pp. 42–61.

The Pentateuch narrates, as a consequence of famine, the sale to the sovereign of all the lands of the people of Egypt; the reservation of the lands of the priests, because, having food assigned them by Pharaoh, they were under no necessity of parting with them; and the parcelling out, when the famine was over, of the same territory to its former owners by lease, on condition of a yearly rent of one-fifth of the produce, to be paid into the royal treasury.§ What, now, is the testimony of profane writers? According to Herodotus,‖ an ancient king had divided the whole land among

* Part 3. § 14. p. 68.   † V. 3. p. 68.   ‡ Hengsten. pp. 38, 39.
§ Gen. xlvii. 13, 26.   ‖ B. 2. c. 109.

the Egyptians, giving to each a square portion of equal excellent, and receiving from each a yearly rent in return. According to Diodorus,* all the land in Egypt belonged either to the kings, or the priests, or the military caste. According to Strabo,† the Egyptians, who were engaged in agriculture, held their land of the sovereign, and paid rent. According to the monuments, as we learn from Wilkinson, only kings, priests, and the military order were land owners. All these profane authorities concur with holy writ in the main fact, viz. ; that the cultivators were not the owners of the soil. On one point, indeed, there is an apparent disagreement. The Pentateuch limits the ownership of land to the kings and the priests ; Strabo extends it to the military order as well ; and herein his authority is confirmed, by the sculptures.‡ But Herodotus§ furnishes a key, whereby this apparent discrepancy can be reconciled. It is in the statement made by him, that the land of the soldiers differed from that of the peasants in being free of rent ; otherwise, he says, it belonged to the kings, and was given by them in fee to the soldiery. But there is still another point of disagreement between the Pentateuch and these profane authors. Moses asserts an original possession of the soil of Egypt by the cultivators, and a transfer of the title to the king under extraordinary circumstances ;¶ Herodotus knows nothing of this, but represents the king as the original proprietor. Now this contradiction, so far from invalidating the credibility of the Pentateuch, serves rather to confirm it, since it presents in a strong light the superior knowledge of the author, which extends back to a period not even approached by the knowledge of profane writers. Here is an historical fact, stated by the Pentateuch, and vouched in the most ample manner by these writers, viz. ; the possession by the king of all the land of Egypt not owned by the priests.

* 1. 73.   † 17. p. 787.   ‡ Wilk. v. 1. p. 263.
§ B. 2. c. 141.   ‖ Gen. xlvii. 19, 20.

How did this fact orignate ? How came such a condition of
things to exist ? Egypt was not obtained by conquest ; and it
is, therefore, wholly inconceivable, as being contrary to all
the analogies of history, that the king should have been the
original proprietor. The author of the Pentateuch solves
the problem, in a manner both natural and probable; the
profane authors leave it not only unexplained, but inexplicable. Can any ingenuous mind fail to recognize, in this
accurate acquaintance with the condition of Egypt, in the
most remote ages, a strong proof of the credibility of the
writer, who exhibits it ?*

The author of the Pentateuch speaks of the embalming
of Jacob as occupying forty days, and the mourning for him
by the Egyptians as lasting seventy days.† The view given
by classical authors—Diodorus,‡ Herodotus,§ and others—
of the general usage of the Egyptians, on both these points,
agrees with this statement exactly. Again, the author
represents the funeral train, which accompanied the corpse
of Jacob to Canaan, as coming to the threshing floor of Atad,
beyond Jordan, and mourning there with a great and sore
lamentation.‖ This was, as we learn from other sources,
eminently an Egyptian custom. The classical writers show
that the Egyptians appointed for themselves a very sol--
emn mourning for the dead, especially for those of high
rank.¶ There is another touch in this history of the mourning for Israel, which evinces the author's intimate acquaintance with Egyptian peculiarities. He represents Joseph
as speaking to the house of Pharaoh, and saying, "If now
I have found grace in your eyes, speak, I pray you, in the
ears of Pharaoh," &c.** Why did not Joseph go directly to
the king with his request, as at other times ? Doubtless, because propriety, agreeably to the Egyptian conception of it,
required the head and face to be shaven, and none were

---

* Hensten pp. 62–70.   † Gen. l. 3.   ‡ 1. 91, 72.
§ 2. 86.   ‖ Gen. l. 10, 11.
¶ Herod. B. 2. c. 85.   Diod. B. 1. c. 91.   ** Gen. l. 4.

permitted to appear before the king unshorn.* But, on the other hand, the laws of mourning forbade the use of the razor, while the mourning continued.† How natural, under these circumstances, the application to Pharaoh through others, which, under other circumstances, would most naturally have been made in person! In the same history, the author distinguishes between the elders of the house of Pharaoh and the elders of the land of Egypt;‡ that is, between the court-officers and the state-officers. A distinction highly characteristic of Egyptian usage, and noticed by profane authors. The court of the king was composed of the sons of the most distinguished priests; while the state-officers were taken from other orders of society.§ Such incidental and undesigned allusions as these to peculiar customs, may well arrest attention. They are the signature of truth. The knowledge of an impostor, writing in a distant age and country, would not be likely to be so minute and accurate; neither would it manifest itself in a way so simple and natural. Such a knowledge we should expect to find in Moses, but in no one else, by whom the Pentateuch could possibly be composed; and the fact, that the writing does actually on almost every page, exhibit this knowledge, is a strong argument in support of its Mosaic origin.‖

The author of the Pentateuch describes the fear of Pharaoh lest the Israelites should multiply, and, when war fell out, should join the invading force, and fight against the Egyptians.¶ A most reasonable apprehension; for the inhabitants of the adjacent deserts are the natural enemies of Egypt, and when these find allies among the Egyptians themselves, the country is in the greatest peril. That this is not an imaginary danger, the history of the Bedouins in Egypt abundantly proves. These have made common cause with the foreign

* Gen. xli. 14.   Wilk. v. iii. pp. 357, 358.
† Herod. ii. 35.   ‡ Gen. l. 7.   § Heeren, Ideen, S. 337.
‖ Hengsten. pp. 70–78.   ¶ Exod. i. 10.

invaders against all the powers that have successively held possession of Egypt,—the Arabs, the Saracens, the Turkomans, the Memlook sultans, and the Osmanlies. The view given by the Pentateuch of Pharaoh's dread of the Hebrews is, therefore, in perfect accordance with the state of things in Egypt. So also does the method which it represents him as adopting to prevent their increase, accord with the known severity of those proud sovereigns towards foreigners, the objects of a boundless hatred and contempt.*

According to the Pentateuch, Pharaoh made the life of the Israelites bitter with hard bondage in mortar and brick, and one of the ingredients in the manufacture of the bricks was straw.† The recent scientific explorations in Egypt show, that chopped straw is found in the composition of the ancient Egyptian bricks.‡ Straw was used, according to Rosellini,§ to give greater firmness and durability to the bricks, they being for the most part not burned in the fire, but dried in the sun. A picture has been found in a tomb at Thebes, of which Rosellini‖ furnishes a drawing, and which he does not doubt is a picture representing the Hebrews engaged in making brick. "Of the laborers," he says, "some are employed in transporting the clay in vessels, some in intermingling it with the straw, others are taking the bricks out of the form and placing them in rows, still others, with a piece of wood upon their back and ropes on each side, carry away the bricks already burned or dried. Their dissimilarity to the Egyptians appears at the first view; the complexion, physiognomy, and beard permit us not to be mistaken in supposing them to be Hebrews. Among the Hebrews, four Egyptians, very distinguishable by their mein, figure, and color, are seen," &c. &c. One of the most interesting points in this picture is the intermixture of Egyptians with the

---

* Hengsten. pp. 79, 80.   † Ex. i. 14, v. 7.   ‡ Rosel. vol. 2, p. 252.
§ Vol. 2, p. 259.   ‖ Vol. 2, pp. 254, seq.

Hebrews in their servile labors. It throws light upon an extraordinary circumstance connected with the exode, the fact, namely, that the Israelites were accompanied by a mixed multitude of Egyptians.* They were described by the author of the Pentateuch as a rabble, a populace, hewers of wood and drawers of water, that is, as very poor, as the lowest servants. Just such people, native Egyptians, we should expect to find in Egypt, as the result of the system of caste; and just such, both classical authors and the monuments testify existed there in great numbers.† Regarded as unclean, they were debarred all intercourse with their brethren, and not permitted so much as to enter the temples. These the picture places on a level with the hated and despised foreigners. What more natural than that, sharing with the Hebrews a common misery, many of them, at least, should choose to be partakers of their pilgrimage?‡

The Pentateuch represents the mother of Moses as taking a chest of papyrus, smearing it with bitumen and pitch, putting the child in it, and then placing it among the reeds on the edge of the Nile.§ The mention of these materials,— papyrus, bitumen, and pitch,—shows the author's acquaintance with Egypt. Pitch is found in Egyptian objects belonging to the most remote times.‖ Bitumen was a chief ingredient in embalming.¶ The papyrus plant was used in Egypt, and only there, in the manufacture of various articles, as mats, chests, baskets, sandals, and even boats; and that at an early day, as the sculptures testify.** In the most ancient of these, the papyrus is found with writing upon it.††

According to the Pentateuch, Moses carried a rod as his

---

* Ex. xii. 38.   † Herod. B. 2, c. 47. Wilk. v. 1, p. 285. Heeren, S. 150.
‡ Hengsten. pp. 81–86.   § Ex. ii. 3.
‖ Hengsten. p. 87.   ¶ Diod. 19, 99.
** Wilk. v. 3, pp. 62, 146. Herod. 2, 96. Plut de Is. et Osir. p. 395, according to which Isis is borne upon a boat of papyrus. Rosel. II. 3, p. 124.
†† Wilk. 3, 150. Hengsten. pp. 86, 87.

inseparable companion,* and each of the magicians did the same.† The monuments‡ show that persons of rank, both priests and nobles, were accustomed to carry a staff, when they went abroad.§

The name of the Israelitish officers, whom the task-masters of Pharaoh placed over them, was, according to Hengstenberg, "the writers."‖ And this designation he pronounces highly characteristic of the state of things in Egypt. There was a time, when the argument against the authenticity of the Pentateuch, derived from the supposed non-existence of the art of writing in the age when it purports to have been written, was deemed very cogent. But the time is gone by, when any weight can be attached to such reasoning. The monuments prove conclusively, that in no country of the ancient world was facility in writing so great, in none were the materials for writing so perfect, and in none was the passion for writing so incorporated into the habits and business of the people, as in Egypt; and that, too, at a period anterior to the time of Moses, and even of Joseph. In this opinion scholars best qualified to judge upon the subject, concur,—as Wilkinson,¶ Rosellini,** Salvolini,†† Gesenius,‡‡ Ewald,§§ and others. "We must shut our eyes against the clearest light," says Rosellini,‖‖ "if we would deny that the art of reading and writing was generally studied and practised in ancient Egypt, to as great a degree at least as it now is among us." So that it turns out, that the many passages in the Pentateuch, implying a great extension of the art of writing among the Hebrews in the time of Moses, are founded in truth, and just

---

* Ex. iv. 2.   † Ex. vii. 12.   ‡ Wilk. v. 3, p. 386.

§ Hengsten. p. 88.   ‖ P. 89.   ¶ Wilk. 3, 152.

** V. II. 3, p. 272, seq.   †† Campagne de Rhamsés, p. 123.

‡‡ Appendix to his Hebrew Gram. published a short time before his death.

§§ His latest work, Geschichte des Volkes Israel, V. 1, pp. 68-71.

‖‖ V. II. 3. p. 239.

make known what could not have been otherwise. Thus, instead of invalidating, they confirm the narrative. They witness not against, but for its Mosaic origin, and its entire trustworthiness.*

The Israelites were directed, when they came into the promised land, to erect great stones, and write upon them all the words of the law. The stones were to be prepared for receiving the inscriptions by "plastering them with plaster."† In this mode of preparation there is a clear Egyptian reference. It appears from the testimony of Wilkinson,‡ that sandstone and even granite were often covered with a kind of stucco, before the inscriptions or paintings were made upon them.§

According to the Mosaic law, when stripes were inflicted, the guilty person was to "lie down and be beaten."‖ This was precisely the Egyptian mode. Wilkinson¶ describes a picture of an Egyptian bastinado, in which the culprits, men and boys, were laid flat on the ground, while the punishment was administered.**

The insolent pride and insane obstinacy, which the Pentateuch ascribes to Pharaoh, representing him as saying, "Who is Jehovah, that I should hear his voice?" and as preferring to go to destruction, with his land and people, rather than yield to the divine command,†† are, as fully shown by the monuments‡‡ in various ways, in accordance with the genuine spirit of the Egyptian sovereigns. These sovereigns were accustomed to style themselves "kings of the whole world,"§§ and they even carried their arrogance to such a pitch as to claim divine honors.‖‖

The author of the Pentateuch represents Jehovah as threat-

* Hengsten. pp. 89–91.   † Deut. xvii. 2.   ‡ V. 3, p. 300.
§ Hengsten. p. 91.   ‖ Deut. xxv. 2.   ¶ V. 2, p. 41.
** Hengsten. p. 92.   †† Ex. v. et seq.
‡‡ Champollion, p. 227.   §§ Ibid. p. 231.
‖‖ Ibid. 257. Rosel. v. I. 1, p. 115. Wilk. v. 1, p. 43. Hengsten. pp. 94, 95.

ening, that blood should be in all Egypt, both in wood and
in stone,* that is, as our translators have rightly supplied,
vessels of these materials. A remarkable expression, containing a wholly unpremeditated and most important Egyptian reference, viz. to the custom of filtering the turbid water
of the Nile in vessels of wood and of stone, chiefly the
latter.† The knowledge, exhibited by the author, of the
common method of purifying water in Egypt, is not so important as the manner of the exhibition. He does not, as
Hengstenberg aptly expresses it, obtrude his knowledge.
He supposes that a mere hint is enough for his immediate
readers, who were themselves acquainted with the peculiarities of Egypt.‡ These two little words "wood and stone,"
thus inartificially introduced in this connexion, certainly
afford both a striking and a strong proof, that Moses is the
author of the Pentateuch.

The same verse§ contains a direction to Moses to take his
rod and stretch out his hand upon the waters of Egypt, upon
its streams, upon its canals, upon its pools, and upon all its
collections of waters. Here is a classification of the waters
of Egypt, accurate to a tittle. The streams are the arms of
the Nile. The canals are the artificial ditches which abounded in Egypt. The pools are the stagnant ponds formed by
the Nile, of which there are many. And the collections of
water are all the other standing water, the lakes and puddles
at a distance from the Nile.‖

According to the Pentateuch, Moses was directed to go to
Pharaoh in the morning when he went out to the water, and
to meet him on the banks of the Nile.¶ This is an entirely
artless and undesigned allusion to a prominent superstition of
Egypt,—that of worshipping the Nile as a divinity. In the
most ancient times divine honors were paid to this river by

* Ex. vii. 19.

† Mayr, Reise, Th. 2, S. 19, Le Bruyn, v. 2, p. 103. Thevenot, v. 1, p. 245.

‡ Hengsten. pp. 110, 111.   § Ex. vii. 19.

‖ Hengsten. p. 111.   ¶ Ex. vii. 15, viii. 20.

the Egyptians. Herodotus[*] speaks of the priests of the Nile. Plutarch[†] makes it identical with Osiris. Lucian[‡] calls it a common divinity of all the Egyptians. Heliodorus[§] names it the Egyptian Jupiter. The monuments[||] corroborate this testimony of the classical writers. One of the paintings represents Remeses II. as offering wine to the god of the Nile, who, in the hieroglyphic inscription, is called " the life-giving father of all existences."[¶]

The Hebrews dwelt in that part of Lower Egypt which borders on the Red Sea. According to the representations of the Pentateuch, Pharaoh was able, on the instant, to bring into the field almost the entire martial power of his kingdom.[**] This seems incredible to a person unacquainted with the disposition of the military forces of Egypt; but to one who knows the state of things on this point, nothing can be more natural and probable. It was precisely on this border, the most exposed of all the parts of Egypt, that, according to the accounts of profane authors, almost the entire military power of Egypt was concentrated. Herodotus states, that sixteen districts were allotted to the military order within the Delta, while, in all Middle and Upper Egypt, only two districts were in possession of the soldiers.[††]

From an industrious and learned survey of all that appears in the Pentateuch on the subject, Hengstenberg[‡‡] arrives at the conclusion, apparently a just and solid one, that the only force, with which Pharaoh pursued the fleeing Israelites, consisted of chariots and chariot-warriors. Cavalry, in the modern acceptation of the term, there was none; and infantry, under the circumstances, could not have taken part in the pursuit. Now, how does this representation, made by

* B. 2, c. 90.   † De Is. et Osir. p. 363.
‡ Jupiter Tragoed. Opp. v. 2, 699.   § Aeth. 9, 435. 5, 203.
|| Champollion, In den Briefer aus Egypten, S. 121.
¶ Hengsten. pp. 112–114.   ** Exod. xiv.
†† Heeren. S. 37.   ‡‡ P. 134, seq.

the author of the Pentateuch, agree with the information derived from ancient profane writers, and from the recently discovered monuments of Egypt? In the most exact and remarkable manner. Homer* represents chariots as constituting the principal strength of the Egyptian army. Champollion, drawing his inference from the monuments, says of the war chariots :† "This was the cavalry of the age; cavalry properly speaking did not exist then in Egypt." Rosellini‡ informs us, that, whenever the armies are represented on the great monuments of Egypt, they are composed of troops of infantry and ranks of chariots. Wilkinson,§ though not admitting that the Egyptians had no horsemen at all, yet agrees with Rosellini in the main point, viz. that their principal military force consisted in chariots.‖

The author of the Pentateuch¶ represents Miriam, after the triumphal hymn on the passage of the Red Sea had been sung by Moses and the children of Israel, as taking a timbrel, and all the women as following her, and the whole train as answering the men in responsive notes, " Sing ye to Jehovah," &c. The monuments** reproduce this scene in all its parts. Separate choirs of men and women are represented on them, singing in alternate responses; the timbrel, or tambourine, is represented as the instrument of the women, as the flute is that of the men; and the playing of the tambourine, unaccompanied, as here, by other instruments, is represented in connexion with singing and the dance. Further, it appears from the monuments, that music had eminently a religious destination in Egypt;†† that the timbrel was specially devoted

---

* Il. 9, 383.   † P. 442 of German Transl. of his Letters.
‡ V. II. 3, p. 232.   § V. 1, pp. 288, 335.
‖ Hengsten. pp. 132–136.   ¶ Ex. xv. 20, 21.
** Champ. S. 53, der Briefe.   Wilk. v. 2, pp. 253, 254, 314.   Rosel. II.
3, p. 37 seq.
†† Rosel. II. 3, p. 78.

to sacred uses ;* and that religious dances were performed in the worship of Osiris.†

The author of the Pentateuch, in Numb. 10, speaks of two silver trumpets, used for calling the congregation together, for giving the signal to break up the camp, for use in war, and for festal occasions; and in Lev. 25, of another kind of trumpet, by whose blast the year of jubilee was proclaimed. From Josh. 6 : 4, it appears that this last was of a crooked form, since it is there called interchangeably a trumpet and a horn. The other sort, therefore, was the straight trumpet. The monuments show, that trumpets were used in Egypt for military purposes as far back as the earliest times of the Pharaohs.‡ The crooked trumpet, indeed, is not found on them; but Eustathius§ mentions an instrument of this sort, whose invention he ascribes to Osiris, and which he says was used for assembling the people to sacrifice. It is very observable, that the straight trumpet only was in general use in both nations, and especially that in both it alone was employed in war.‖

But I have already exceeded the space proper to be devoted to this branch of my subject, and, tempting as the field is, must withdraw the hand. The Egyptian references detailed above are but a portion, and that by no means the larger portion, of such references contained in the Pentateuch. Indeed, these allusions are incomparably more numerous and direct than any one had supposed, till they were brought to light by the learned industry of Hengstenberg. Both the Egyptian references here given, and those which are omitted, everywhere exhibit a writer possessed of the most ample and exact knowledge of Egypt in its topography, climate, soil, tillage, productions, animals, resources, arts, superstitions, laws, manners, customs, and civilization. Much light has

---

* Wilk. V. 2, p. 316.   † Rosel. II. 3, p. 96.   Hengsten. pp. 136, 137.
‡ Wilk. v. 1, p. 297.   § On the Iliad, v. 4, p. 65.
‖ Wilk. v. 2, 260, 262.   Hengsten. pp. 137, 138.

been thrown upon all these points by the late researches of English, French, Italian, and German archæologists; but not one of their innumerable discoveries comes into conflict with any of the statements contained in the books of Moses. One of the most enlightened, discriminating, and cautious of these scholars,—Sir Gardner Wilkinson,—bears this distinct and important testimony: "Wherever any fact is mentioned in the bible history, we do not discover any thing on the monuments, which tends to contradict it."[*] No; in all the references to Egypt contained in the Pentateuch, though so many and so various, though scattered through every part of the writing, and mixed up with almost every topic which it embraces, there cannot be detected a single element, which is not clearly and decisively Egyptian. Could a fictitious narrative, fabricated in a remote country and a distant age, accomplish such a result? "Credat Judaeus Apella!" But even this statement does not bring out the argument in its strongest light. It is not so much the extent or the accuracy of the writer's knowledge of Egypt, as it is the manner in which he brings it out, that seals the trustworthiness of the narrative. This is always so incidental, so unpremeditated, so undesigned, so perfectly inartificial, and so destitute of all explanatory remarks as not necessary for his immediate readers, as to constitute an indubitable signature of truth. Such a manner would be quite natural in Moses, but most unnatural, and indeed impossible, in a mythic historian. It is a manner which cannot be assumed by an impostor. We have here, then, both in the Egyptian knowledge of the author and in the manner of its exhibition, a strong internal proof of the credibility of the Pentateuch, of its composition in the age of Moses, and consequently of its Mosaic origin. He who is not convinced by it of the genuineness and authenticity of the work, is certainly very far removed from credulity; but then he stands at an equal distance from that intelligent candor, which feels and owns the force of truth.

* Anc. Eg. 1. 34.

CHAPTER V.

Divine Legation of Moses.

THE divine legation of Moses is a legitimate inference from the argument contained in the last chapter. If the credibility of the Pentateuch be once admitted, then it follows, as a matter of course, that, in establishing the Hebrew constitution, Moses was the accredited minister of Jehovah; since, throughout the entire writing, he constantly claims to have acted in that capacity. Here I might rest the proof of the divinity of Moses's mission; but, that nothing may be wanting to the foundation of our faith, I propose, in the present chapter, to adduce three additional topics of argument to establish the point in hand, to wit, the theology, the morality, and the miracles of the Pentateuch.

The theology of the Mosaic code attests its divine original. This is the first proposition to be illustrated. Here, as the basis of the following argument,* the principle is assumed, that a religious element belongs to the original constitution of man. It is instinctive with him to fear the power, to reverence the authority, to propitiate the favor, to lean upon the help, and to imitate the conduct, of some superior being. He is thus impelled, by a law of his nature, to worship a divinity.

* For many of the thoughts, and some of the expressions, contained in this argument, the writer acknowledges himself indebted to the ingenious anonymous author of the Philosophy of the Plan of Salvation, to which work the reader is referred.

Accordingly, we find no nation, either of ancient or modern times, sunk so low in the scale of rational existence, as to be without some notion of a god, some rites of worship, and some sentiments of religion.

Now, it belongs to the essential nature of religious worship to assimilate the moral attributes of the worshippers to those of the object of worship. The heathen themselves recognize this principle. "The sum of religion," said Pythagoras, "is to be like him whom thou worshippest." "Think of Buddah," say the priests of that pretended deity, "and you will be transformed into Buddah." This is consonant to the highest reason. The heart seeks to be in favor with its god; and what more natural means to that end, than the imitation of his qualities and actions,—the assimilation of our character to his ? The god, whom we worship, must constitute our ideal of perfection; and the nearer we approach our ideal, the higher, in our own estimation, will be the degree of excellence which we have reached. Every act of worship, there- fore, every prayer, every devout aspiration, every serious thought of the divine nature, must tend to make us one with our god, and to transfer to ourselves the impress of his char- acter.

The history of idolatry confirms this reasoning. The gods of Egypt were unwarlike; as a natural consequence, the ordi- nary policy of Egypt was peaceful. Odin and Thor, those sanguinary deities of the north, turned their worshippers into bloodhounds, to whom war was their native element, and the scent of carnage more grateful than incense. One of the hero- gods of the Northmen is represented, in their wild mythology, as having committed suicide; and his followers, who had failed to die in battle, imitated the horrid deed, lest a natural death should abridge their pleasures in the halls of Valhalla. Venus, that impersonation of sensual pleasure, was the chief divinity of the Cyprians and the Corinthians. What followed ? The persons highest in honor in those places were prostitutes, who exercised their vocations within the very temples of the goddess; and lust and sensuality held an undivided empire over all hearts.

Idolatry had overspread the earth, and was the universal religion of mankind, when the law was proclaimed from Sinai. Would the reader learn its influence? Let him listen to the testimony of two of the most distinguished moralists among the ancients. Plato says: "The histories of the gods ought not to be rehearsed in public, lest they should influence the youth to the commission of crimes." Seneca says: "How great is the madness of men! They lisp the most abominable prayers; and if a man is found listening, they are silent. What a man ought not to hear, they do not blush to relate to the gods. If any one considers what things they do, instead of decency, he will find indecency; instead of the honorable, the unworthy; instead of the rational, the insane."

The labor of unfolding, in detail, the nature, extent, tendencies, and results of the ancient idolatry, is reserved for a subsequent part of this work.* But it may be observed, in passing, that all history abounds with testimonies, similar to those cited above. There was scarcely an object, element, or living creature in nature, good or bad, which did not receive a heart-debasing and life-corrupting worship. Dead men, celestial luminaries, light, air, wind, fire, hills, streams, groves, beasts, birds, reptiles, plants, darkness, storm, pestilence, the fates, the furies, and other like objects, were deified, and adored by terrified and trembling votaries. By a system of worship, so blind and degrading, reason, truth, and virtue were well nigh obliterated from the human heart; and, in their place, folly, falsehood, and vice reigned with almost undisputed sway. Not only in the ruder and more uncivilized, but even in the most enlightened and polished nations of gentile antiquity, immoralities the most revolting, and crimes the most unnatural, were sanctioned by the example, and conse-

* See the Chapter on the Hebrew Theocracy in the Second Book.
15

crated in the worship of the gods. Lewdness was practised in the temples, and human victims bled upon the altars of these impure and sanguinary deities.

An important inquiry arises here ; an inquiry of such magnitude, that its solution involved the moral destinies of the human race It is, whether man, by his own unaided efforts, was able to overthrow so vast a system of error and corruption, and to replace it with the reign of truth and purity? A candid survey of the difficulties to be overcome, taken in connexion with the condition and powers of human nature, must induce the sad conviction, that no such ability inhered in man, that no such means were within his grasp.

What would be the very first step in such a labor? The production of a perfect God ;—the creation of an object of worship, pure, holy, just, wise, good,—in short, possessing all the proper attributes of divinity in an infinite degree. And by what agent must this idea of a perfect being be originated and developed? By imperfect man,—a being of high native endowments, undoubtedly ; but with a blight resting upon all his powers,—the reason, the understanding, the will, the affections. Here is a plain impossibility. The stream cannot rise higher than the fountain ; much less can the finite originate the infinite, the impure the pure, the creature of an hour, the uncreated and eternal one. Man could not invest his deities with a holier character than belonged to himself. He could transfer his own imperfect attributes to them, and that was the limit of his power in respect of making gods. A sagacious and philosophic heathen has perceived and expressed, in one brief but pregnant sentence, the whole truth in reference to this matter. "Instead of the

* See on the subject of ancient idolatry Maimon. de Idol. Euseb. Praep. Evang. L. 1. C. 9. Leland's Adv. of Rev. Pt. 1. Bryant's Analysis of Mythology. Cic. de Nat. Deor. Voss. de Idol. Selden de Diis Syriis. Graves on the Pent. Pt. 2. Lect. 1. Josephus con. Apion. And the classical writers passim.

transfer to men of that which is divine," says Cicero, "they transferred human sins to the gods, and then experienced again the necessary reaction."

But suppose this first obstacle overcome, and a suitable object of worship imagined and unfolded. Another difficulty, of scarcely inferior magnitude, would instantly start up in the path of him, who should undertake the more than Herculean task of uprooting idolatry, and replacing it with a holier worship. How to persuade men to forsake their follies, and embrace the truth? "Hic labor, hoc opus est." The mere revelation of a proper object of worship is not enough. Such revelation must be accompanied with a power sufficiently great to arrest men's attention, to convince them of the impotence of their idols, to induce them to forsake those lying vanities, and to worship the holy being, made known to them. But such a power as this belongs to God alone, and can be wielded by none but those whom he employs and commissions.

Of all this, the following is the sum. Man's nature is religious. He instinctively worships some being, whom he regards as God. It is the nature of religious worship to assimilate the character of the worshipper to that of the being worshipped. The objects of worship, everywhere throughout the ancient world, were corrupt and corrupting. In order to man's moral improvement, he must have a holy object of worship. It is obviously impossible for an imperfect and sinful man to originate the idea of a perfect and sinless god. And even if this impossibility could be overcome, man does not possess the power necessary to eradicate idolatry, and replace it with a better worship. Men must, therefore, have forever remained wicked idolaters, unless God had interposed for their deliverance. But God did interpose. This is evident from the fact, that there is a large portion of mankind who have renounced idolatry, and now profess and practise a purer faith. This reformed worship is coeval with the Hebrew polity. The gods, whom men invented and set up, were as imperfect and wicked as themselves; and from the nature of the case, they could not be otherwise. Moses, on the contrary, revealed a holy and a perfect God. How pure, how amiable, how sublime, how transcendently glorious the character, with which this God is invested by the Hebrew lawgiver! "I am that I am"* is the mysterious and awful title, under which he declares to the children of men his self-existence and eternity. His unity is announced, with majestic brevity, in the sentence, "Jehovah, our God, is one Jehovah:" † His creative power, in the sublime record, In the beginning God created the heaven and the earth: ‡ His sole and supreme dominion, in the declaration, "Jehovah, he is God in heaven above, and upon the earth beneath; there is none else:" § And his moral perfections of wisdom, justice, holiness, truth, goodness, and mercy, in such noble and glowing expressions as these following:—"Ascribe ye greatness to our God; he is the Rock; his work is perfect; for all his ways are judgment; a God of truth, and without iniquity, just and right is he;‖ glorious in holiness, fearful in praises, doing wonders;¶ merciful and gracious, longsuffering and abundant in goodness, keeping mercy for thousands, forgiving iniquity, transgression and sin."** To this self-existent, eternal, only, omnipotent, supreme, wise, just, holy, true, and merciful God, Moses everywhere ascribes a providence, both sovereign and universal, which he represents, not only as directing the government of the universe by general laws, but also as superintending the conduct and determining the fortune of every nation, of every family, and of every individual of the human species. How striking is the contrast, which this sublime delineation of Jehovah as the maker, proprietor, and sovereign of the universe, in-

---

* Ex. iii. 14.   † Deut. iv. 39.   ‡ Gen. i. 1.
§ Deut. iv. 39.   ‖ Ibid. xxxii. 3, 4.   ¶ Ex. xv. 11.
** Ex. xxxiv. 6, 7.

vested with every conceivable excellence, presents to the
grovelling mythology of the most enlightened portions of
the ancient world, in which the objects of religious worship
were pictured with the passions and vices of the fierce and
licentious chieftains of the primitive ages. And Moses not
only revealed a perfect God, and published a true theology,
but he also accompanied the revelation and the publication
with such an exhibition of supernatural power, as to enable
him to overthrow the system of idolatry, and establish the
better faith upon its ruins.

From all this it follows, as I conceive, by direct and
inevitable inference, that Moses held a divine commission,
and that in founding his constitution of government, and
proclaiming its laws, he acted as the legate and minister of
Heaven. The Pentateuch, so diverse from all the productions of philosophic genius, and so superior to them, presents
a remarkable phenomenon in the intellectual and moral history of our race. If we admit the inspiration of its author,
the phenomenon is at once explained; if we deny his inspiration, no rational solution of it can be offered. The publication of such a theology, in such an age,—a theology, which
put to flight the darkness and the error of polytheism, when
polytheism had covered the earth with the temples and the
altars of its monster gods,—cannot be satisfactorily accounted
for without allowing, and is satisfactorily accounted for by
allowing, the truth of the Mosaic history, and the establishment of the Mosaic constitution by divine authority.

The morality, not less than the theology, of the Hebrew
code, proves the divine mission of the lawgiver. This is the
second point to be opened in the present argument. The
first thing, which attracts our attention here, is the decalogue,
or ten commandments. These constitute a summary of
moral duty, of unequalled excellence and breadth ; a summary,
containing the seminal principles of all human virtue; a
summary, so comprehensive and perfect, that it cannot be

improved by any conceivable addition or subtraction. The precepts of the decalogue alone, it has been well and truly said by Goguet,[*] disclose more sublime truths, more maxims essentially suited to the happiness of man, than all the writings of profane antiquity together can furnish. The more one meditates upon them, the brighter and more striking does their wisdom appear. Vain would be the search among the writings of profane antiquity, not merely of the remote antiquity when the law was published from Sinai, but of the most refined and philosophic ages of Greece and Rome, to find so broad, so complete, and so solid a basis of morality as the decalogue exhibits. [†]

It is related of a distinguished lawyer,[‡] who had been sceptical on the subject of divine revelation, that he undertook the study of the Old Testament, with a view of satisfying himself as to the validity of its claim to be an inspired writing. When he came to the decalogue, and had given it an attentive perusal, lost in admiration of its superhuman perfection, he exclaimed, " Where did Moses get that law ?" To the resolution of that question, he applied the powers of an acute and discriminating mind, vigorous by original endowment, and disciplined to exactness by the study of the law and the practice of the legal profession. The result was the removal of every sceptical doubt, and the attainment of a clear and earnest conviction of the divine original of the law.

And how, indeed, could an enlightened and candid examination of the decalogue have a different issue ? The first four commandments inculcate that profound and penetrating sentiment.of piety, which forms the only immovable foundation of human virtue. This part of the decalogue enjoins " the adoration of the one true God, who made heaven and earth, the sea, and all that in them is ; who must, therefore,

* Orig. of Laws.   † J. Q. Adams's Letters to his Son.
‡ Tract 321 of Am. Tr. Soc.

be infinite in power, and wisdom, and goodness; the object
of exclusive adoration; of gratitude for every blessing we
enjoy; of fear, for he is a jealous God; and of hope, for he
is merciful. It prohibits every species of idolatry; whether
by associating false gods with the true, or worshipping· the
true by symbols or images. Commanding not to take the
name of God in vain, it enjoins the observance of all outward
respect for the divine authority, as well as the cultivation of
inward sentiments and feelings, suited to this outward reverence; and it establishes the obligations of oaths, and, by
consequence, of all compacts and deliberate promises; a
principle, without which the administration of laws would be
impracticable, and the bonds of society must be dissolved.
By commanding to keep holy the Sabbath, as the memorial
of the creation, it establishes the necessity of public worship,
and of a stated and outward profession of the truths of religion, as well as of the cultivation of suitable feelings: and it
enforces this by a motive, which is equally applicable to all
mankind; and which should have taught the Jew, that he
ought to consider all nations as equally creatures of that Jehovah whom he himself adored; equally subject to his
government, and if sincerely obedient, equally entitled to all
the privileges his favor could bestow."*

The fifth commandment enjoins, as next in importance to
the duty of worshipping the creator, that of honoring our
earthly parents, as those to whom we owe the greatest of
earthly obligations, and are bound by the strongest of earthly
ties. And while the obligation of honoring father and
mother is alone specifically named, there can be no doubt,
that the principle of the law was meant to be extended to all
the duties arising out of our domestic relations, and indeed
to all "the duties belonging to every one in their several
places and relations, as superiors, inferiors, or equals."† So
Philo Judaeus ‡ interprets. "In the precept, ' honor your

* Graves on the Pent. Pt. 2. Lect. 2.
† Sh. Cat. Ans. to Ques. 64.   ‡ Opp. p. 590.

parents,' (he says) are many laws, prescribing the duties of the young to the old, of subjects to magistrates, of servants to masters, and of those who have received benefits to their benefactors."

After this there follow four precepts, designed to restrain us from injuring our neighbor in his person, his property, his conjugal rights, and his good name. Here, the reader will observe, injuries to our neighbor are classified by the decalogue. The classification is into offences against life, chastity, property, and character. In each of these classes, the greatest offence is made the object of an express prohibition. Thus murder is forbidden as the greatest injury to life ; adultery, as the greatest injury to chastity ; theft, as the greatest injury to property ; and false witness, or perjury, as the greatest injury to character. But the greater must be understood to include the less ; and on this principle both Jewish doctors and Christian divines have, with one voice, interpreted these laws. Agreeably to this view, the command, "Thou shalt not kill," forbids, not simply the act of taking away life, but all injury of every kind to life or limb, all violence, all hatred, all resentful passion, and every thing which tends to beget and foster that malignant and revengeful temper, which constitutes so material a part of the guilt of murder. Anger and railing are expressly affirmed by our Savior to be violations of the fifth commandment.* In like manner the command, "Thou shalt not commit adultery," forbids not merely the specific act named, but also, as Philo† explains, "all irregular desire and licentious indulgence," and, as a far greater than he has said, even an impure "look."‡ So of all the rest. The principle is,—and every intelligent and candid reasoner will admit its soundness,—that each of the commandments must be understood to prohibit, not only the extreme injury named, but every inferior degree of it as well, every injury kindred to it in nature, every thing, in

* Matt. v. 22.   † Opp. p. 592.   ‡ Mat. v. 28.

short, calculated to prompt and lead to the commission of it ; and at the same time to inculcate the practice of the contrary virtues, and the cultivation of counteracting dispositions. This view of the spirituality and comprehensiveness of the decalogue is confirmed by the nature and form of its closing precept. All the great interests of piety being provided for in the first four commandments, all the domestic duties being secured in the fifth, and all the essential enjoyments of life being guarded from voluntary injury in the four succeeding ones, the tenth goes to the very source of human actions—the heart—and positively forbids all those desires, those inward motions of the soul, which are the spring of every violation of the rights of our fellow-creatures.

Where, in all the writings of antiquity, whether in the codes of its legislators or the ethics of its philosophers, can a system of human duty be found, comparable to this ? In different countries,—and those, too, esteemed civilized and refined—Babylon, Persia, Egypt, Phoenicia, Carthage, Greece, and Rome,—theft,* piracy,† adultery,‡ crimes against nature,§ exposure of infants,‖ and human sacrifice,¶ either separate or combined, have been familiarized by custom, and authorized by law. Look at the real institutions of Lycurgus, the most renowned of heathen lawgivers,** and the imaginary institutions of Plato, the most enlightened of heathen philosophers.†† Impurity the most brutalizing sanctioned, and cruelty the most unnatural enforced, by legal enactments ! Behold the mild Trajan and the amiable Cicero,‡‡ one of them exhibiting, and the other defending,

* Plut. in Lyc. † Thucyd. L. 1. c. 5. ‡ Plut. in Lyc.
§ Virg. Ec. 2. Plut. in Lyc. Leland's Adv. of Rev. Pt. 1. c. 7. Pt. 2. c. 3.
‖ Plut. in Lyc. Ter. Self-Tormentor. Plat. de Rep. L. 5. Arist. Pol. L. 7. c. 16. Cic. de Leg. L. 3. c. 8. From the authority last cited it appears, that the practice was enjoined by a law of the twelve tables.
¶ Magee on Aton. & Sac. vol. 1. pp. 88, seq.
** Plut. in Lyc. †† Plat. de Rep. L. 5. ‡‡ De Fin. L. 3.

the murderous combats of the gladiators! Hear even the
virtuous Cato,—for so he was styled by the ancients,—coolly
applauding public houses of prostitution, * and heartlessly
declaring, that an old plough and a worn-out slave ought to
be treated in the same manner! "The Greeks (we are told
by an inspired writer) sought after wisdom." † But did they
find it? Let the leading dogmas of their various schools of
philosophy answer. The epicureans made pleasure the chief
good, and virtue that by which it could be most successfully
attained. The academicians knew not whether virtue is pre-
ferable to vice, or vice to virtue; nor did they suppose that,
amid the endless varieties and conflicts of human opinion,
anything could be decided with absolute certainty; that is,
they held that truth, in the strict sense, is unattainable. The
stoics taught, that man is bound to act conformably to his
nature; that the great object of human pursuit is conformity
to nature; and that this is the origin and foundation of all
moral obligation. ‡

Such was the legislation, and such the philosophy, of profane antiquity. The question of the sceptical lawyer returns
upon us, "Where did Moses get his law?"—a law, as we see,
incomparably superior to all that was produced by the civil
and philosophic wisdom of the most enlightened ages and
nations of the ancient world. Moses lived at a very remote
period in the history of mankind, a period comparatively
barbarous and unenlightened; yet has he given to the world
a law, in which all the learning and sagacity of subsequent
ages have not been able to detect a single flaw. Where did
he get this law? Could he, by his own independent and unaided powers, soar so far above all his cotemporaries and
compeers, as to devise it himself? This cannot, with any
show of reason or probability, be pretended. The source,
then, whence it emanated, is open as the day. It came direct

* Hor. Sat. L. 1. S. 2.　　　† 1 Cor. i. 22.
‡ Spring's Obl. of the World to the Bib. pp. 159, 160.

from the infinite intelligence, and is an undoubted seal of the divine mission of him, through whose agency it was enacted, and by whose pen it was published to the world.

Here I rest the argument for the supernatural illumination and guidance of Moses in the enactment of his code, so far as it depends upon the consideration of the moral principles embodied therein. It does not seem to me needful, for the purpose I have in view, to urge it beyond this point. The reader who would see it fully elucidated, may consult the second lecture of the second part of dean Graves's admirable work on the Pentateuch. There he will find the following positions firmly established, viz. that the law of Moses " enjoined love to God with the most unceasing solicitude, and love to our neighbor as extensively and forcibly as the peculiar design of the Jewish economy and the peculiar character of the Jewish people would permit; that it impressed the deepest conviction of God's requiring, not mere external observances, but heartfelt piety, well regulated desires, and active benevolence ; that it taught sacrifice could not obtain pardon without repentance, or repentance without reformation and restitution ; that it described circumcision itself, and by consequence every other legal rite, as designed to typify and inculcate internal holiness, which alone could render men acceptable to God ; and that it represented the love of God as designed to act as a practical principle stimulating to the constant and sincere cultivation of purity, mercy, and truth." Certainly it is not a forced conclusion, which the learned author draws from these premises, that a moral system so perfect, and promulgated at so early a period, strongly bespeaks a divine original.

I observe again, that the divine legation of Moses reposes with a firmness and stability that nothing can shake, on the miracles which he performed by the command of God. Every ancient lawgiver, of any eminence, claimed to have received his ordinances from some divinity,—a Jupiter, a

Minerva, an Apollo, a Mercury, a Vesta, or an Egeria. Moses, also, with a greater distinctness and emphasis than any of them, asserted his inspiration by Jehovah, the true God, in the laws which he ordained and·published to his countrymen. And, that which none of the others could do, Moses proved the authenticity of his claim by a succession of the most stupendous miracles;—miracles done in open day, palpable to the senses, repeatedly involving one nation in unparalleled perplexity and distress, and supplying the necessities of another, in a manner quite beyond and above all the ordinary methods and resources of nature;—miracles, which could neither be forged, counterfeited, nor gainsayed;—miracles, whose reality is at this day attested by proofs a thousandfold clearer and stronger than any that make us believe, that Cæsar crossed the Rubicon, and seized upon the liberties of his country,—that Hannibal traversed the Alps,—that Scipio conquered Carthage,—or, indeed, that any other unquestioned and unquestionable fact of ancient story was, as it has come down to us in the record that contains it.

The human mind, apparently by an original law of its constitution, demands the evidence of miracles, that is, the doing of things above the reach of nature, in proof of a divine commission to establish a new religion. These are the necessary credentials of a messenger of Heaven, without which his claim to such a character is instinctively rejected, and with which it is as instinctively acknowledged with reverence and submission. Through miracles, the authority of such a claim entrenches itself in the deepest convictions of men; and nothing can dislodge it, but the production of a contrary conviction, that the miracles themselves are the effect of imposture and illusion. Miracles believed constitute the ultimate basis of every received system of religion in the world; miracles disproved would be the inevitable destruction of every such system.

Accordingly, we find that the first and main endeavor of

the enemies of revealed religion has always been to discredit the evidence and authority of its miracles, either by establishing the falsity of the record, or by showing the miracles themselves to have been mere scientific devices, invented to impose on the credulity of ignorance and the weakness of enthusiasm. But every such attempt has only recoiled upon its authors, evincing at the same time their impotence, and the impregnable strength of the citadel, which they had undertaken to demolish.

The miracles of Moses differ from the pretended miracles of false religions in three particulars,—their authenticity, their nature, and their end.

They differ in their authenticity. The credibility of the history, in which the miracles are related, was proved in the last chapter; and this, of course, involves the truth, as well of the miraculous, as of the common events of the record. The inquirer will probably be satisfied with the proof, which has been exhibited; the caviller, by none that can be exhibited. Still, let the two following considerations be added, as confirmatory of the reality and truth of the miracles recorded in the Pentateuch. The one of them is largely and forcibly opened by dean Graves in his Lectures on the Pentateuch,* and the other, with no less ability, by the acute and philosophical Leslie, in his Short Method with Deists. †

Superadded to the important fact, that the miraculous events of the Pentateuch are interwoven in one detail with the common ones, with the same marks of candor, artlessness, and truth, is the further and more important consideration, that the common events, sundered from the miracles, are disconnected, unnatural, inexplicable, improbable, and even wholly incredible; but combined with them, the entire series. becomes natural, consistent, and every way probable. Let a single illustration of this position suffice; and for this purpose, take the exodus itself, with the circumstances attending

* Part 1, Lect. 5.   † Passim.

it. The common facts here, as contradistinguished from the miraculous events by which they were accompanied,—facts admitted by all, unbelievers as well as believers,—are such as these following: A numerous nation is held in the most abject political slavery, by the proudest and mightiest monarchy of earth. For entire centuries, they have worn their chains, nor made one effort to burst them asunder, and assert their freedom. The vindication of their liberty by force is an enterprise so utterly hopeless, that no thought of it has ever been entertained. The Israelites are without arms, without spirit, without military knowledge and discipline, without martial resources of any sort; while their masters and oppressors abound in all. At length, however, headed by a stranger,—for Moses has been forty years away from Egypt,—and he armed only with a simple staff, they demand leave of the haughty and powerful sovereign to emigrate in a body, from his territories, with their wives, their little ones, their flocks, their herds, and all their possessions. The loss of this people will be to him the loss of the greatest instrument of his power, luxury, and pride. Will he let them go? Will he, in this easy manner, part with their invaluable service? We shall see. The request for permission to depart is made in the name of Jehovah, who is not only the sovereign of the universe, but also the tutelary God of the Hebrews. To this request, with the swelling insolence of conscious power, the monarch replies, " Who is Jehovah, that I should obey his voice to let Israel go? I know not Jehovah, neither will I let Israel go."* Thereupon, he endeavors still further to break the spirit of the people by increasing their burdens.† A short time elapses, and what happens? No sword is lifted, no spear is poised, no bow is bent, no arrow is sped, no dart is aimed, no human force of any kind is exerted. Yet the proud monarch is humbled. ‡ He yields to the demand, which

---

* Ex. v. 2.   † Ex. v. 5-9.   ‡ Ex. xii. 31.

before he rejected with scorn. Nay, more ; he not only lets
Israel go, but both he and his people, terrified and panic-
struck, unite in urging them to hasten their departure. *
And they go, loaded with treasures bestowed upon them
by their mercenary lords. In the act of departing, the
Israelites demand (not " borrow") of the Egyptians gold and
silver and jewels and raiment.† This treasure the divine
providence awards to them, in recompence for the service
rendered in their long and bitter bondage. The Egyptians
grant everything that is asked ; ‡ and the Israelites begin
their emigration, six hundred thousand men on foot, besides
women and children, and a mixed multitude of Egyptians,
as well as flocks and herds and much cattle. §

Can any thing be more unnatural, improbable, and incredible, on the supposition, that there were no supernatural
causes in operation to work out these results? Can any
thing be more natural, probable, and even certain, if we admit
the reality of the miraculous plagues recorded in the Pentateuch? An analysis of the relation of almost every miracle
to the common events connected with it, would afford a similar result. Does not such a fact furnish strong presumptive
evidence of the truth of the miracles ?

The second additional consideration to prove the authenticity of the Mosaic miracles, referred to above, is that which
Dr. Leslie has handled, with such masterly ability and such
unanswerable force, in his Short Method with the Deists.
This ingenious author proves the truth of the miraculous
events of the Pentateuch by applying to them four rules,
which, whenever they can be truly applied to any matters of
fact, exclude every rational doubt of their reality. The first
rule is, that the facts be such, that men's senses can judge of
them. The second is, that they be performed publicly, in
the presence of witnesses. The third, that public monuments
be set up, and public actions be appointed to be performed,

* Ex. xii. 33.   † Ex. xii. 35.   ‡ Ex. xii. 36.   § Ex. xii. 37, 38.

in memory of them. And the fourth, that these monuments and actions be established and instituted at the time of the facts, and thenceforward continued without interruption. The first two rules make it impossible to impose a false fact upon men at the time when the alleged fact is said to happen, because every body's senses would contradict it. Thus, for example, if I were to publish to the people of New York, that I yesterday divided the Hudson river in the presence of the whole city, and that they all passed over dry-shod, I could not get a single individual to credit the statement, for the simple reason, that every man, woman, and child, would know that they had neither seen the stream parted, nor had themselves crossed over its bed, in the manner alleged. The last two rules render it equally impossible to impose a false fact upon the credulity of any subsequent age, when the generation in which it was said to occur, has passed away; because, whenever the alleged fact is related, since the statement of the fact is accompanied with the declaration, that public monuments of it still remain, and public actions have ever been, and still are, statedly performed to commemorate it, the forger puts it in the power of every one to detect and discredit his fabrication, there being no such public monuments existing, and no such public actions done, as he alleges. To recur, in illustration, to the former example. Suppose I were to pretend, that the miracle of dividing the Hudson was performed on new year's day by the first Dutch governor of New York, and were to add to the story the allegation, that a vast hall had been erected, at the time when it occurred, of stones obtained from the channel of the river; that a festival of a very peculiar kind, instituted to commemorate the miracle, had ever since, even down to the present time, been celebrated in the hall the first day of every year; and that the door of the hall is never, on any pretext, opened at any other time, or for any other purpose. Is there a person living credulous enough to believe the story? Would not every child even, on hearing it, say, —"I never saw the hall, of which you speak; I never witnessed, nor saw the person that has witnessed, the festival, which you describe; and I never heard of any building in New York, which is opened but once a year."

Now, how do these four marks of authenticity apply to the miraculous events of the Pentateuch? In the most exact and wonderful manner. Consider! Could any thing be more public, or more within the cognizance of men's senses, than the miracles ascribed to Moses?—as the plagues of Egypt, the passage of the Red Sea, the pillar of cloud and fire, the giving of the law, the healing of the waters of Marah, the manna, the quails, the preservation of their garments, the cures effected by the brazen serpent, the destruction of Korah, Dathan, and Abiram, the bringing the water out of the flinty rock, &c. &c. If these things had not happened, as they are recorded, could Moses have obtained credit for them among the men of that generation? Not a whit more than I could obtain credit from the people of New York in asserting, that I had parted the waters of the Hudson in their presence, and led them all dry-shod over the river to Jersey City. Thus the reader perceives the entire applicability of Leslie's first two rules to the Mosaic miracles.

But are the other two rules equally pertinent? We may answer, without the least hesitation, yes; they have both an equal applicability in themselves, and an equal force and conclusiveness, when actually applied. There is scarcely a miracle in the record, which was not attested by public monuments set up, or public actions performed, or both combined, to commemorate it. For example: The two tables of stone, preserved in the ark, were a monument of the miraculous giving of the law at Sinai.* The pot of manna kept in the same, was a monument of the miraculous food in the wilderness.† Aaron's rod that budded, also pre-

* Deut. x. 5. † Ex. xvi. 33.

17

242 COMMENTARIES ON THE

served in the ark, and the censers of Korah and his party, formed into plates for overlaying the altar, were monuments of the miraculous destruction of the rebels.* The brazen serpent, kept, till it was destroyed by Hezekiah, as having become an object of idolatrous veneration, was a monument of the miraculous cures wrought upon the people, when bitten by the fiery serpents in the wilderness.† The heap of stones at Gilgal, taken from the dry bed of the Jordan, was a monument of the miraculous passage of that river by the chosen tribes.‡ The reasoning of Leslie§ on this last monument,—and it is equally applicable to all the others,—has an irresistible force, and is quite unanswerable. "To form our argument," he says, "let us suppose that there never was any such thing as that passage over Jordan; that these stones at Gilgal were set up on some other occasion, in some after age; and then, that some designing men invented this book of Joshua, and said it had been written at that time, and gave this stonage at Gilgal for a testimony of its truth. Would not every body say, 'We know of this stonage at Gilgal, but we never before heard of this reason, nor of this book of Joshua. Where has it been all this time? And when and how came you, after so many ages, to find it? Besides, this book tells us, that, after this passage over Jordan, it was ordained to be taught to our children from age to age, and therefore, that they were always to be instructed in the meaning of this monument. But we were never taught it, nor did we ever teach our children any such event.' Thus impossible would it be to gain credit for a fact thus circumstanced, after the period when it was supposed to take place."

But the proof of the reality of the Mosaic miracles is still stronger; for the public commemorative actions of the Jewish nation were far more numerous than the public monu-

* Num. xvi. 39, 40, xvii. 10.   † Comp. Num. xxi. and 2 Kings xviii.
‡ Josh. iv. 20–23.   § Short Method with the Deists, p. 14.

ments set up among them; insomuch that, as dean Graves *
has truly observed, we may almost be said to have two histories of Moses and his miracles,—one in the written record of
the Pentateuch, and the other in the institutions, ceremonies,
and festivals of the Hebrew people. The consecration of the
tribe of Levi to the religious service of the nation was commemorative of the miraculous destruction of the first-born of
the Egyptians.† The passover was commemorative of the
several miraculous events preceding and accompanying the
exode.‡ The pentecost was commemorative of the miraculous promulgation of the law.§ The feast of tabernacles was
commemorative of the miraculous supplies, guidance, and
protection, which the Israelites enjoyed throughout all their
journeyings and encampments in the wilderness.‖ Nay, the
entire Jewish ritual, with all its sacrifices, sabbaths, new
moons, and feasts of various name, was, either directly or indirectly, commemorative of the miraculous deliverance out of
Egyptian bondage, and the various other miraculous interpositions of divine providence in behalf of this people, whereby
they were shielded, sustained, guided in the right way, and
finally established in the promised land, a free and independent nation.' In this manner, the whole series of signal miracles, from the first, which Moses wrought in the presence of
Pharaoh, to the last, which brought them safely over Jordan,
was recalled to the memory of the Jews, and attested as authentic and indubitable, yearly, monthly, weekly, daily, almost hourly, as long as a vestige of their religion remained.
Attested, I say, as authentic and indubitable; for, could an
impostor, in a remote age, invent these miracles, and get the
whole Jewish race, not only to believe the facts themselves,
but also, which would be more difficult, that both they and
their ancestors had, from time immemorial, been in the habit
of celebrating various festivals, and performing various pub-

* On the Pent. Pt. Lect. 6.　　† Comp. Ex. xiii. and Num. iii. and viii.
‡ Ex. xii.　　§ Deut. xxvi. 5–10.　　‖ Lev. xxiii. 40–43.

lic actions, in memory of them? That would be just such
another impossibility as for me now to get the people of New
York to believe, not only that the first Dutch governor divided
the waters of the Hudson river, and led their ancestors over
on dry ground, but also, that an immense building, erected,
at the time of the miracle, of stones procured from the bed of
the stream, is still standing, that it is opened only once a
year, and that, on this occasion, they themselves do, as their
ancestors did before them, participate in a commemorative
festival, marked by peculiar and remarkable ceremonies.

Thus are the miracles of Moses guarded against the charge
of falsehood at every point. They could not be imposed
upon the Jews in the age of Moses; for they were of so public a nature, and so completely within the cognizance of
men's senses, that, unless they were real, they could not have
gained the credence of a single person; much less, of an entire nation. They could not be imposed upon the Jews in
any subsequent age; for, in order to this, at the very moment
when the miracles were first told to them, they must have
been made to believe, that their ancestors for ages back had
known them, that they themselves had been taught them in
infancy, and that they were surrounded with public monuments, and in the habit of performing public actions, comme-
morating them; which is impossible.

The miracles of Moses differ from the pretended miracles
of false religions in their nature, as well as in their authenticity. Both in their intrinsic properties and their external
circumstances, the difference between false miracles and true
is as great as the difference between darkness and light.
Counterfeit miracles are apt to be trifling in their character,
as the cutting of a stone with a razor, the suspension of a
coffin in the air, or some other inanity. Mohammed himself
set up no claim to the power of miracles; and those which are
ascribed to him,—as his conversation with the moon and his
night journey from Mecca to Jerusalem and thence to heaven,

—are ridiculous legends, which are rejected by the more sober and reflecting of his own followers. The marvellous adventures of the heathen deities are not only trivial and absurd, but often degrading and immoral also. Such are the
stories of Mercury's stealing sheep, and of Jupiter's trans-
forming himself, now into a bull, and now into a shower of
gold, the more readily to compass a base gratification. But
the miraculous interpositions of divine power recorded in the
Pentateuch are uniformly marked with a grandeur worthy
of the creator of the world, before whom the gods of the mythologists, not excepting even their supreme Jupiter, dwindle
into vanity and emptiness. Let him who would mark the
characteristics, which distinguish true religion from false, and
real miracles from lying wonders, compare the manner in which
the ten commandments were proclaimed from the fiery summit
of mount Sinai, by the voice of Jehovah, in the hearing of more
than two million souls, with the studied secresy and mystery
and mummery, with which the oracles of the pagan gods were
delivered. Here the divine voice, issuing from the visible
glory, was distinctly heard by the assembled nation, promul-
gating the moral law, with every circumstance, which could
impress the deepest awe upon even the dullest minds. How
solemn, how awful was this manifestation of the Deity, and
how well suited to make indelible impressions upon the
imaginations and souls of the mortals, to whom he revealed
himself, in a law worthy of the sublimity which invested its
promulgation, a law perfect and glorious as its author. The
entire annals of paganism may be challenged to furnish a
parallel to this scene.

The miracles of Moses differ from the miracles of priestcraft
in their end, quite as much as in their authenticity and their
nature. The pretended miracles of paganism were without
point or meaning; but those of Moses interpreted, at the same
time that they confirmed, his doctrine. Every miracle had its
lesson. Along with the almighty power which produced it,

each revealed a principle, which was thenceforth to take the place of the miracle, and render a similar interposition of the Deity ever afterwards unnecessary. In illustration of this point, let us glance at the series of miracles, which preceded and accomplished the exodus of Israel.

Idolatry, as observed above, had now spread its infection throughout the entire mass of mankind. In this false and corrupt system of religion Egypt stood preëminent. Herein she was the teacher of other nations ; and her pernicious influence had extended itself far beyond her territorial limits. The whole virus of polytheism seems to have collected itself in this polished and cultivated people. It had, obviously, become essential to the religious interests of mankind, that a striking display should be made of the folly and futility of idolatry, as well as of the existence and power of the one living and true God. It is a partial and imperfect view of the miracles wrought in the field of Zoan, which those take, who regard them as limited in their design to the deliverance of the chosen people out of Egyptian bondage. This they were undoubtedly intended to effect ; but a further and more important purpose was, to confound the impure idolatry of Egypt, and to make such a revelation of the infinite, eternal, and unchangeable Jehovah to the Israelites, as would be sufficient to call forth and confirm their faith in his being, wisdom, power, holiness, justice, goodness, and truth. That the plagues of Egypt had this breadth of design, that in them God was engaged in opposing and defeating the power of the Egyptian idols, is distinctly announced by himself in the declaration,* "Against all the gods of Egypt I will execute judgment." The same thing appears from the remark of Jethro,† the father-in-law of Moses, on hearing a recital of them : "Now I know that Jehovah is greater than all gods ; for in the thing wherein they dealt proudly, he is above them." Nothing, therefore, can be more certain than that the controversy was less with

* Ex. xii. 12.   † Ex. xviii. 11.

the sovereign than with the idols of Egypt; and that the miracles, in breaking his power and subduing his will, were intended to confront and put to shame the gods in whom he trusted. Unless we take this broad view of the subject, the miracles, though they remain stupendous exhibitions of divine power, lose their peculiar appropriateness and significancy.

With this principle for our guide, let us briefly examine the system of miracles, employed to humble the pride of the Egyptian monarch, in confounding and defeating the power of the Egyptian gods, and so to effect the exodus of the chosen people from the Egyptian dominions.

The first in the series was manifestly aimed against one of the prevalent forms of Egyptian superstition, that of serpent worship. No fact of ancient history is better attested than that in Egypt the serpent was an emblem of divinity, and that its worship formed a conspicuous part of her idolatry.* The second time that Moses and Aaron appeared before Pharaoh, he demanded a miracle† in proof of a divine mission. Aaron cast down his rod, and it became a serpent.‡ The king's magicians imitated this miracle, "for they cast down every man his rod, and they became serpents."§ Either by sleight of hand they substituted serpents for their rods, or Jehovah, for a wise purpose, changed them into serpents. So far the contest between the true God and the false gods seemed equal; or, if there was any advantage, it appeared rather on the side of the idols. But what followed? "Aaron's rod swallowed up their rods."‖ This result clearly proclaimed the superiority of the invisible God of the Hebrews over the serpent-gods of the Egyptians.

The second miracle,—which was the first plague,—was directed against the worship of the Nile, and intended to disprove the divinity of that river. The miracle consisted in smiting the waters of the river, and turning them into blood.¶

* Deane on the Serp. in Smith's Heb. Peop. p. 38.
† Ex. vii. 9.   ‡ Ex. vii. 10.   § Ex. vii. 12.
‖ Ex. vii. 12.   ¶ Ex. vii. 20.

The Nile, it is well known, was a chief deity of the Egyptians.* Indeed, Moses was commanded to meet Pharaoh, "early in the morning as he went forth to the water,"† that is, just as he was preparing to bring his daily offering to the false god. At this point of time, when the Nile was receiving, or about to receive, the religious homage of Egypt's haughty sovereign, all its waters were turned into blood, and the fish that was in the river died, and the Egyptians could not drink of the water.‡ How manifestly did Jehovah here execute "judgment against the gods of Egypt !"§ What could be better suited than this miracle to cover with confusion the whole system of Egyptian idolatry ?

The next plague was intended as a confutation of reptile worship, a practice in which Egypt had, at a very early period of her history, obtained an infamous notoriety. This miracle consisted in bringing up frogs from the Nile and all the waters of Egypt, in such numbers, that the loathsome creatures penetrated everywhere, even into the houses, and into the bed-chambers, and into the beds, and into the ovens, and into all the receptacles of provisions.‖ Must not this have been felt as a signal and most painful rebuke of the particular species of superstition, against which it was directed ?

The third plague was still more loathsome. The miracle consisted in smiting the dust of the earth, so that it became lice, covering man and beast throughout all the land of Egypt.¶ This miracle was aimed against the entire system of idolatrous worship; since, as no priest could officiate in the temples with so impure an insect on his person, not a single religious rite could be performed during the continuance of it. "To conceive the severity of this miracle," observes

* Herod, c. B. 2. 90. Cic. de Nat. Deor. Plut. de Is. et O. ir. p. 363. "The monuments bear witness to the same effect as the ancient authors." Hengsten. Eg. and Bks. of Mos. p. 113.

† Ex. vii. 15.   ‡ Ex. vii. 20, 21.   § Ex. xii. 12.
‖ Ex. viii. 3.   ¶ Ex. viii. 17.

Stackhouse,* " as a judgment on their idolatry, we must recollect their utter abhorrence of all kinds of vermin, and their extreme attention to external purity, above every other people, perhaps, that have ever existed. On this head they were more particularly solicitous, when about to enter the temples of their gods; for Herodotus informs us, that the priests wore linen garments only, that they might be daily washed, and every third day, shaved every part of their body, to prevent lice, or any species of impurity, from adhering to those who were engaged in the worship of the gods. * * * * Hence we find, that, on the production of the lice, the priests and magicians perceived immediately from what hand the miracle had come; for it was probably as much from this circumstance, as from its exceeding their own art to imitate, that they exclaimed, ' This is the finger of God.' "

The fourth plague was the miracle of flies, " a grievous swarm, coming into the house of Pharaoh, and into his servants' houses, and into all the land of Egypt," so that " the land was corrupted by the swarm of flies."† It is probable, that this miracle was designed as a curse on the animal worship of Egypt. " A poisonous fly resting on all animals without distinction must have exhibited the weakness of these imaginary gods, and the folly of their worship, in the most affecting manner."‡ But further : There is reason to think, that the instrument, by which this plague was inflicted, was itself regarded with idolatrous veneration. Baal-Zebub, " the lord of flies," was the tutelary deity of Ekron,—a city of the Philistines, which was near the confines of Egypt,—and was worshipped there as a fly-god, the defender of the people against this noxious insect. It is probable, that a like superstition prevailed in Egypt. The guardian god of lower Egypt was adored under the symbol of a winged asp. In this form

* Hist. of Bib. Vol. 1, p. 473.
† Ex. viii. 24.   ‡ Smith's Heb. Peop. p. 40.

Wilkinson * found it sculptured in one of the royal tombs at Thebes. The deity showed himself utterly incapable of protecting his worshippers against the power, that was thus grievously afflicting them, and pouring contempt upon the whole system of animal worship. Here, again, we have Jehovah " executing judgment against the gods of Egypt,"† and " in the thing wherein they dealt proudly" showing himself " above them.‡"

The fifth plague, like the preceding one, was designed to show the folly and falsity of the brute worship of Egypt. The miracle consisted in bringing " a grievous murrain," a contagious, inflammatory, and very fatal disease, " upon the horses, upon the asses, upon the camels, upon the oxen, and upon the sheep."§ The severity of this miracle, as a vindictive stroke, aimed against the abomination of animal worship, may be estimated from the fact, that the death of a single one of the sacred animals was looked upon by the Egyptians as a great public calamity. How terrible, then, must have been their consternation at seeing them perish by thousands! What severer judgment could the God of the Hebrews have executed against the gods of the Egyptians ? How humbling were such visitations to the pride of a nation, claiming preeminence over all others in power and wisdom! How strong their tendency to wean the people from their absurd and impure theology!

The next miracle,—the plague of boils,‖—deserves to arrest our most serious attention. "Hitherto the judgments of God had been chiefly directed against the objects of idolatrous worship ; this affected the most cultivated and powerful supporters of this idolatry."¶ The reader is requested to notice particularly the means, which the Lord directed Moses to employ to produce this plague,—"handfuls of ashes of the

---

* Anc. Eg. Vol. 5, pp. 45, 84.   † Ex. xii. 12.

‡ Ex. xviii. 11.   § Ex. ix. 3.

‖ Ex. ix. 8–12.   ¶ Smith's Heb. Peop. p. 41.

furnace, sprinkled toward the heaven in the sight of Pharaoh."*
THE furnace. What furnace? The answer to this question is
important; for on it the force and significancy of the miracle
mainly depend. The Egyptians, like the orientals, believed
in the existence of an evil principle, which they adored under
the name of Typho. This malign deity was worshipped with
human sacrifices. The fact is mentioned by several ancient
authors; but Plutarch,† from Manetho, describes the manner
of the worship. "Formerly in the city of Idithya," he says,
"they were wont to burn even men alive, giving them the
name of Typhos, and, winnowing their ashes through a sieve,
to scatter and disperse them in the air." This was done to
propitiate the cruel deity, and that evil might be averted from
every place, whereon there fell a single particle of the ashes
of the human victims consumed upon his altars. These altars,
there is every reason to suppose, were "the furnace" of the
sacred text, and these ashes were the ashes which Moses was
directed to sprinkle by handfuls towards heaven, in the sight
of Pharaoh; for what occasion would be more likely to call
into requisition the horrid rites above described, than the
appalling visitations, under which Egypt had been now for
some time suffering? The ashes, from which the Egyptian
court and hierarchy were hoping for relief and victory, cast by
Moses into the air, instead of preventing evil, became a new
source of it, for it turned to boils and blains on the persons
of king, priest, magician, and people. Thus the rites of this
Egyptian Moloch proved a curse rather than a blessing to his
worshippers, and the power and supremacy of Jehovah were
incontestably established. The triumph was complete; and the
Egyptians could not but see and own, that there was neither
might, nor wisdom, nor understanding, nor counsel against
the Lord.‡ Does not this miracle, thus explained, make God's
controversy with the idolatry of Egypt clear as a sunbeam?

---

* Ex. ix. 8.

† De Is. et Osir. in Smith's Heb. Peop. p. 42.   ‡ Prov. xxi. 30.

And does it not give a meaning, consistency, and force to the transaction, which would otherwise be wanting to it?

The seventh plague was a severe tempest, attended with lightning, thunder, hail, and rain.* This miracle carried the war upon the Egyptian superstition into a new department of it,—the vegetable kingdom. The wisdom of Egypt deified, not only beasts, reptiles, and insects, but trees and plants also. Among the vegetable gods of her impure and grovelling theology were, of trees, the peach, the pomegranate, the vine, the acanthus, the fig, and the tamarisk; and of plants, the onion, the garlic, the papyrus, and the ivy. If these were not all actually worshipped as deities, some of them were, and the others received a superstitious veneration, as sacred and divine. Here, then, in the wide-spread destruction, occasioned by this miraculous storm to the vegetable growth of Egypt, for " the hail smote every herb of the field, and brake every tree of the field,"† we have a fresh confutation of the Egyptian idolatry.

In the address which Jehovah, when about to inflict this plague upon Egypt, directed Moses to make to Pharaoh, there occurs an expression, which confirms the view here taken of the significance and intent of this whole succession of miracles : "That thou mayest know that there is none like me in all the earth."‡ Here there is a direct comparison between Jehovah and some other beings. To suppose between him and men would be jejune and frigid. It must certainly be between Jehovah and other gods. But if so, then the entire series of plagues was, as here contended, a controversy between true religion and false, a war carried on by the living God against the senseless and impure system of idolatry, weak in every thing, except its power to corrupt and destroy the souls of men. The account of this miracle contains also an intimation of the effect, which the issue of the controversy thus far had had on the Egyptians. Some are described as

* Ex. ix. 23, 24. † Ex. ix. 25. ‡ Ex. ix. 14.

"fearing the word of Jehovah," and, as a consequence, "making their servants and cattle flee into the houses;"* others as regarding not the word of Jehovah," and so "leaving their servants and cattle in the field."† From this statement, it is plain that there were some, we may reasonably suppose there were many, of the wealthy Egyptians, whose confidence in their idols had been thoroughly shaken, and who now believed that Jehovah, the God of the Hebrews, was the living and the true God.

The eighth plague had a similar object with the seventh, and was, as it were, the consummation of it. The miracle consisted in an unprecedented incursion of locusts, brought by a strong east wind.‡ "Very grievous were they. * * * They covered the face of the whole earth, so that the land was darkened; and they did eat every herb of the land, and all the fruit of the trees which the hail had left; and there remained not any green thing in the trees, or in the herbs of the field, through all the land of Egypt."§ Thus was completed the triumph of the God of Israel over the vegetable gods of Egypt. Some writers have supposed, that this miracle was directed especially against the worship of Serapis, whose function it was to protect the country against locusts.‖ If such was the office of this god, his impotence stood conspicuously revealed. At any rate, through the present and preceding penal visitations, Egypt saw all she held most dear and sacred on earth, crushed, broken, obliterated, and destroyed, by a power, which seemed armed against the entire range of her idolatrous worship. How galling to a nation so proud of her wisdom, her power, and her gods!

But a still more humiliating blow was yet to fall upon the pride of Egypt; a still more signal proof was to be given of the impotence and nothingness of her idols. One class of

* Ex. ix. 20. † Ex. ix. 21.
‡ Ex. x. 13. § Ex. x. 14. 15.
‖ Smith's Heb. Peop. p. 43.

her deities alone remained yet unabashed and untouched by
the power of Jehovah,—the heavenly luminaries. It is
against the divinity of these orbs, particularly of the most
resplendently glorious of them, that the ninth plague was
directed.* "The sun was worshipped throughout Egypt.
The sacred emblems of his influence and supremacy were
constantly in use. * * * * The moon was also worshipped
under the name of Thoth. * * * These sublime objects of
their idolatrous worship seemed to be too distant from our
earth, too great and too glorious, to be affected by any
power which Moses could wield. * * * * But Jehovah
had arisen out of his place to vindicate his insulted majesty.
* * * * In the accomplishment of this purpose, no object
was so high, no creature so great, as to withstand his will.
Moses was commanded to stretch out 'his hand toward
heaven, and there was a thick darkness in all the land of
Egypt three days.' So deep was the darkness that during
the whole of this time, 'they saw not one another.' So over-
whelming were the amazement and sorrow, that during this
period no man 'rose from his place.' Uncertain whether
they should ever again see the light, they lay paralyzed in a
darkness that could be felt. Here the triumph of the God of
Israel was complete, and the perfect vanity of Egyptian
idolatry demonstrated. Egypt, with all her learning and
prowess, supported by a gorgeous and almost boundless
range of idolatrous religion, is exhibited as convicted, punished, and without any power to escape, or any hope of
alleviation."†

Having thus "executed judgment against all the gods of
Egypt,"‡ and shown himself "greater than all gods," being
"above them in the thing wherein they dealt proudly,"§
Jehovah by the tenth and last in this terrible series of penal
inflictions, intended to teach the Egyptians, by causing the

* Ex. x. 21-23. † Smith's Heb. Peop. p. 43-44.
‡ Ex. xii. 12. § Ex. xviii. 11.

iron to enter into their own souls, that to him alone it belonged to execute judgment in the earth. On that direful night, when the first-born of every family in Egypt, "from the first-born of Pharaoh that was on his throne unto the firstborn of the captive that was in the dungeon,"* became a corpse, all the innocent Hebrew blood that had gorged the monsters of the Nile, was required, to the last drop, of Pharaoh and his people.

From all this the conclusion is, that the miracles of Moses were undoubtedly real, and that, as a consequence, his mission was certainly divine. For who but a man commissioned as God's vicegerent, could wield a power like that displayed in the plagues of Egypt, and the subsequent wonders of the Red Sea and the wilderness? Who but a true divine messenger could control the laws and elements of nature?

How stands the question, then, of the divine legation of Moses? Let me sum up the argument in one brief sentence. The general credibility of the Pentateuch, the publication of a theology worthy of the true God, the overthrow of idolatry, and the substitution of a better faith and worship in its place, the superhuman purity and excellence of his moral code, and the clear and well established power of miracles,—such is the array of proofs, which concentrate their force, in a blaze of demonstration, around the warrant of Moses to publish laws in the name of Jehovah.

* Ex. xii. 29.

CHAPTER VI.

Objections considered and answered.

NOTWITHSTANDING these clear and irrefragable proofs of a divine legation, the inspiration of Moses has been both denied and ridiculed by men, who claim the character and authority of philosophers and historians, and who arrogantly assume, as their exclusive right, the title of free thinkers; as if all the rest of the world, besides themselves, were fast bound in the chains of prejudice and priestcraft. These writers ground their denial of inspiration to Moses on certain internal evidences of imposture, contained in his laws themselves. They allege, that many of his statutes are trivial, absurd, and unworthy the wisdom and majesty of Deity; that the spirit of his legislation is sanguinary and cruel; that his code permits many things, now commonly regarded as social evils; that it recognizes what they are pleased to stigmatise as the monstrous principle of retaliation; that it omits the doctrine of future rewards and punishments; and that his laws respecting the extermination of the Canaanites violate the plainest dictates of religion, and the most sacred rules of justice.

Most if not all of these objections will be sufficiently refuted in that general exposition of the Mosaic code, which it is the object of these pages to offer; yet it may be well, in advance of such a confutation, which must of necessity spread itself over the entire treatise, and at the hazard of some repetition, to present in this place, a brief specific answer to the allegations above recited. This, therefore, is what I now propose to do. We will consider them in the order in which they are mentioned in the preceding paragraph. The first objection is based upon the alleged trifling nature of many of the Mosaic laws. Such are the laws against cutting the hair and beard after a particular manner ;* against boiling a kid in the dam's milk ;† against wearing garments made of linen and woollen mixed together ;‡ against the interchange of male and female attire ;§ against cutting the flesh ;‖ against receiving the price of a dog and the hire of a prostitute into the public treasury ;¶ against the sowing of mixed seeds ;** against worshipping in groves and high places ;†† and against the use of certain kinds of animal food.‡‡

All these laws, with others of an apparently like trivial nature, were aimed against the idolatrous customs, then prevalent in the world. Unless, therefore, idolatry itself, with all its horrid train of crimes and impurities, was a trifle unbecoming the care of God, the agencies adapted to its extirpation could not but be worthy of his contrivance and institution. Let us glance at a few of the practices, against which the laws in question were directed.

A particular mode of shaving the head and face were regarded by certain sects of idolatrous priests as essential to the acceptable worship of their gods.§§ By others it was supposed that the pursuits of husbandry would be rendered more successful by sprinkling the fields and gardens with the milk

---

* Lev. xix. 27.　　　† Ex. xxiii. 19, 34.　Deut. xiv 21.
‡ Levit. xix. 19.　　　§ Deut. xxii. 5.　　　‖ Levit. xix. 28.
¶ Deut. xxii. 5.　　　** Levit. xix. 19.
†† Ex. xxxiv. 13.　Deut. vii. 5.　‡‡ Levit. xi.
§§ Herod. L. 3, c. 8; also L. 4. c. 175.　Maimon. More Nev. Pt 3. ᴣ. ᴣ7.
See also Dr. Clarke's very instructive note on Lev. xix. 27.

of a goat, in which a young kid had been previously boiled.* Maimonides,† who, with an untiring industry, searched into every nook and corner of ancient history, for the purpose of bringing to light all the institutions and usages of idolatry, informs us, that the gentile priests used to wear garments made of a mixture of the produce of plants and animals, hoping thereby to have the beneficial influence of some lucky conjunction of the planets, and to derive thence a blessing upon their sheep and flax. From the same writer‡ we learn that another common custom of idolatry was for men, in the worship of several of their gods, to put on the garments worn by women, and women those used by men. He found an express precept in an old magical book, enjoining that men should stand before the star of Venus in the ornamented garments of women, and women in the armor of men before the star of Mars. The savage rite of cutting the flesh was generally practised by the ancient heathen nations, to pacify the infernal deities, and render them propitious to departed souls.§ Anubis, one of the principal Egyptian divinities, had the head of a dog,‖ and was worshipped under the symbol of that animal. Nothing was more common than to consecrate the wages of prostitution to the gods; and, indeed, this vile commerce was carried on within the very precincts of the temples, and under the sanction of the impure divinities, whose priests fattened on its unholy gains.¶ To worship in groves and

---

* See Cudw. on the Lord's Sup. and Spencer de Leg. Heb. cited in Dr. Clarke's note on Ex. xxiii. 19.

† De Idol. Also on Lev. xix. 19.   ‡ On Deut. xxii. 5.

§ See Magee on Aton. and Sac. vol. 1, p. 101.

‖ Anth. Class. Dic. Art. Anubis. This opinion, indeed, has been shaken by Wilkinson, (Anc. Eg. vol. 5, p. 260,) who has rendered it probable, that Anubis had not the head of a dog, but of a jackal. Still it remains certain, that the dog was a sacred animal with the Egyptians, and, as such, received a superstitious veneration. See Smith's Heb. Peop. pp. 39, 40.

¶ See Prof. Bush and Dr. Clarke on Levit. xix. 29; also Augustin de Civit. Dei, L. 18, c. 5.

high places was supposed to be peculiarly acceptable to the
false deities of paganism, and was certainly favorable to the
impurities, which were but too often found associated with
their worship. Particular citations here are unnecessary, as
all heathen antiquity is full of allusions to this practice.
Finally the old Zabii not only sowed mixed seeds and
grafted different kinds of trees upon one another as a religious rite, but used abominable filthiness at the time of
doing it.

Such were some of the cruel, absurd, and impure customs of
idolatry, against which the laws in question were directed,
and which, it cannot be denied, they were well adapted to
destroy. Doubtless, there were some things condemned in
these laws, which are in themselves innocent and harmless,
and which, if practised now, would not incur the divine dis-
pleasure, as worshipping God in groves, sowing mixed seeds,
wearing clothes of wool and flax mingled together, &c. But
in that age these things were so closely connected with others
which were evil, that, with a people of gross intellect, and
but little addicted to refined distinctions, the two could not
be disjoined, and the permission of the one would be likely
to draw after it the practice of the other.

A parallel to this procedure of Moses, we find in the conduct of the early protestant reformers. They waged war
upon a variety of usages, harmless enough in themselves, but
hurtful through their connexion with the papal system.
These usages were among "the monuments of idolatry,"
which must be overthrown at all hazards. Something analogous we have in our political history. The tax on tea was a
paltry thing in itself. Why was it refused, and the horrors of
civil war encountered, rather than pay it? Not, surely, on
its own account, but because of its relation to a system. This
was precisely the principle of these Mosaic laws. In condemning them, therefore, we condemn the principle of the

war of independence, and call in question its wisdom and necessity.

There is another class of the Mosaic laws,—the rites of purification,—whose divine original has been denied, on this same ground of triviality. But the extended system of ritual purification, established by these laws, embraced, among other purposes, one as noble and sublime, as any other in all the wide range of the Mosaic legislation. It was to convey into the minds of the Israelites the idea of the divine holiness; an idea, which, as far as we can see, could be infused in no other way. This has been clearly shown by the ingenious author of the Philosophy of the Plan of Salvation, to whose chapter on the development of the idea of holiness, the reader is referred. He will there see the argument handled at length, and with masterly ability. It must be presented here in a condensed form, and so shorn of a portion of its strength.

All the nations, by whom the Israelites were surrounded, worshipped unholy beings. How, then, were the chosen people to be made to understand and feel the holy character of God? Whatever may be the speculations of philosophers about innate ideas, it is yet true, that all acquired knowledge comes to us through the medium of the senses. By them the knowledge of external objects is conveyed to the mind; and these simple ideas serve as material for reflection, comparison, and abstraction. Thus the idea of power, among the Hebrews, was derived, through the eye, from the horn of an animal and the hand of a man; because, through these parts, their respective strength was mainly exerted. And hence the words horn and hand came to be used as abstract terms, denoting the general quality of power. Thus "a horn of salvation" means a mighty salvation; and "the power of the tongue" in Hebrew is "the hand of the tongue." So the same word, in that language, by a similar transfer of the

material to the immaterial, means both sunshine and happiness.

'These few instances will show how the abstract ideas of the
Hebrews were originated; viz. through the impressions made
by external objects on the senses.

Mark now both the fact and the principle. The fact is, that
the whole world of matter did not afford a single object, capable of conveying to the mind the idea of God's holiness. The
principle is, that the idea, having been first originated, must
then be thrown into the mind through the instrumentality of
the senses, by a process instituted for that purpose. Mark,
also, the correspondence between this principle, founded, as
it is, upon the laws of mind, and the system devised to
instruct the Israelites in the knowledge of God's moral purity.

Throughout the entire Levitical economy, purity is the predominating idea. This idea pervades all its ceremonies and
observances. The priests were to be purified, the sacrifices
were to be purified, the people were to be purified, the camp
was to be purified, every thing was to be purified and re-pu-
rified; "and each process of the ordinances was designed to
reflect purity upon the others; until, finally, that idea of
purity, formed in the mind, and rendered intense by the con-
vergence of so many rays, was transferred to God,—in whom,
as a moral being, it would become moral purity, or holiness.
Thus they learned, in the sentiment of Scripture, that God
was of too PURE eyes to look upon iniquity. That the idea
of moral purity in the minds of the Israelites was thus originated by the machinery of the Levitical dispensation, is supported not only by the philosophy of the thing, but by many
allusions in the Scriptures. Such allusions are frequent in the
writers of both the Old Testament and the New; evidencing
that, in their minds, the idea of moral purity was still symbolized by physical purity. The rite of baptism is founded
upon this symbolical analogy. In the epistle to the Hebrews,
St. Paul says: 'It was therefore necessary that the patterns

of things in the heavens should be purified with these;' i. e. with these purifying processes addressed to the senses. The plain instruction of which is, that the parts and processes of the Levitical economy were patterns addressed to the senses of unseen things in heaven, and that the purifying of those patterns indicated the spiritual purity of the spiritual things which they represented."

Undoubtedly the Levitical rites of purification had other purposes to answer, which this is not the place to unfold. But if the end here indicated were the only one, I put it to the candor of thinking men, whether a system of laws and observances, designed and adapted to originate the idea of moral purity, or holiness, and to transfer it to the object of religious worship, is justly open to the charge of frivolity. Ought it not rather to be numbered among the proofs of the divine origin of the Mosaic institutions? To my mind it furnishes presumptive evidence to that effect of no inconsiderable force.

The second objection to the divine legation of Moses is grounded on the inhumanity of the Mosaic code. The criminal jurisprudence of the lawgiver is here made the point of a fierce assault. The particular charge against this part of his polity is, that it is vindictive and cruel. How is this?

At the very threshold of the penal laws of Moses, we find civil liberty making a great stride in its work of human improvement. How much, and how justly, do we congratulate ourselves on that principle of our constitutional law, that no criminal attainder shall work corruption of blood! Yet this principle was embodied in the constitution of Moses, notwithstanding the opposite doctrine prevailed in the governments of the most polished nations of antiquity. His statute is expressed with characteristic clearness and brevity: 'The fathers shall not be put to death for the children, neither shall the children be put to death for the fathers; every man shall be put to death for his own sins."* This principle Moses in-

* Deut. xxiv. 16.

corporated into his code, in the face of prejudice, common opinion, immemorial usage, and the sentiment of inexorable and insatiate revenge. Undeniably, it is a specimen of legislative policy, which takes its author out of the crowd of ancient legislators, and places him on an eminence far above them all.

Loud complaint has been made against Moses on account of the number of crimes made capital in his code. But great injustice has been done him in this particular. The crimes punishable with death by his laws were either of a deep moral malignity, or such as were aimed against the very being of the State. It will be found, too, on examination, that there were but four classes of capital offences, known to his laws,—treason, murder, deliberate and gross abuse of parents, and the more unnatural and horrid crimes arising out of the sexual relation. And all the specifications under these classes amounted to only seventeen; whereas, it is not two hundred years since the criminal code of Great Britain numbered one hundred and forty-eight crimes punishable with death,—many of them of a trivial nature, as petty thefts and trespasses upon property. But "no injury simply affecting property could draw down upon an Israelite an ignominious death. The Mosaic law respected moral depravity more than gold. Moral turpitude, and the most atrocious expressions of moral turpitude,—these were the objects of its unsleeping severity."*

The principal punishments, known to the Mosaic code, were the sword, stoning, stripes, compensations, restitutions, reparation of losses, and fines. Our inspired jurist appointed no ignominious punishments for the living. Blows were not regarded in that light by the Asiatics; and burning, hanging, and burying beneath a pile of stones, which were of this nature, were, it is probable, according to the laws of Moses, inflicted after death, and are, therefore, to be looked upon as

* Spring's Obl. of the World to the Bible, Lect. 3.

posthumous disgraces. To his everlasting honor be it said, that Moses stained not his penal code with any of those torturous and lingering punishments, which have disgraced the jurisprudence of so many polished nations since his day,—as breaking on the wheel, impaling, flaying alive, roasting over a slow fire, drowning, exposure to wild beasts, and, above all, crucifixion, that horrid offspring of ancient barbarity, in which life and consciousness and intolerable agony were prolonged, not unfrequently to the third day, and sometimes even to the seventh. If, then, his penal inflictions must somctimes be admitted to be severe, at least human nature is never compelled to shudder at their cruelty.*

If Moses be blamed for admitting capital punishments into his code, he must even bear the reproach along with the purest, wisest, and most humane jurists of all ages. The great design of punishment he represents to be the protection of society and the vindication of law and justice. Transgressors must suffer, not simply, or chiefly, that they themselves may be amended, but, to use his own expressive language, that others " may hear, and fear, and commit no more any such evil."† He was quite unacquainted with a modern refinement of wisdom, which represents the reformation of the criminal as the only legitimate end of punishment. He had no sympathy with that mawkish philanthropy which pours forth such floods of tears over the fate of the hardened perpetrator of crime, that it has scarcely one left to mingle with those of the unhappy victims of his villanies. This is not the place to vindicate either the lawfulness or the policy of capital penalties. Let the jurisprudence of all christendom stand as their defence. It may, however, be observed, in passing, that such punishments are as conformable to right reason, as they are to revelation and the practice of enlightened legislators. The equity of putting a murderer to death arises from this, among

---

* " The law of the twelve tables is full of very cruel punishments."
Montesq. Sp. of Laws, B. 6. c. 15.   † Deut xix. 20.

other considerations, that the law by which he is punished was made for his own security. He has himself enjoyed the benefit of the law, which condemns him. It has been a continual shield over him all his life. Can he, then, in reason, object to it?*

The war code of Moses has also been made a point of attack by the enemies of revelation, and by some of its professed friends. How little do such persons know of it! How slender the ground for their assaults, which have sometimes been conducted with a ferocity equal to that which they charge against the Hebrew lawgiver! The Canaanitish wars, which formed no part of the general war system, will be considered in a subsequent part of the present chapter; and the other military laws of Moses will receive a full elucidation in one of the succeeding books of this treatise. The extraordinary mildness of these laws towards the citizen, their wise moderation towards the enemy, and their unexampled tenderness towards female captives, will then be made to appear, to the satisfaction, I hope, of every candid inquirer. It will be seen, that they offer, in these respects, a perfect contrast to the military laws and usages of other ancient nations, even of those which were renowned for their clemency and refinement. " Lex nulla victo parcit,"—no law spares the vanquished,— was the great military maxim of antiquity. It was the right of war, recognized by all nations, questioned by none; and often the conqueror pushed the exercise of this barbarous right to its utmost rigor. He sacked, demolished, burnt, and murdered, without pity for age or sex. Slavery was the mildest lot to be hoped for by those who had been unfortunate enough to survive the carnage of the combat. In this manner were treated Sidon by Artaxerxes Ochus; Tyre, by Alexander; the towns of the Marsi, by Germanicus; and Jerusalem, by Titus. " It was thus," indignantly exclaimed the authors of the Letters of certain Jews to Voltaire,† " it was thus that the

* Montesq. Sp. of Laws, B. 15. c. 2.   † Letter 3.

military laws of the Persians, the Greeks, and the Romans were mild, and those of the Hebrews barbarous."

How imperfectly do those understand the Hebrew legislation, who accuse it of inhumanity! Its distinctive character is gentleness and beneficence. No ancient legislation will bear a moment's comparison with it in this respect. It forbids to cherish sentiments of hatred and revenge.* It enjoins the forgetfulness of injuries, the cultivation of mutual love, and the practice of kindness even to enemies.† It commands respect and compassion towards the aged, the deaf, and the blind.‡ It enjoins that the traveller, uncertain of his route, be directed in the right way.§ It requires benevolence and generosity towards the poor, the widow, the orphan, and the stranger.‖ For them, the corners of the field were to remain unreaped, and the forgotten sheaf was to be left where it had fallen.¶ For them, the husbandman was forbidden to go over his corn patch a second time, or to twice glean the grapes of his vineyard and shake the boughs of his olive trees.** Servants, engaged in the preparation of food, and men, employed in gathering in the bounties of nature, had the legal right to taste the fruits and viands, about which they were busied.†† Even animals shared in the thoughts and the compassion of the Hebrew Lawgiver.‡‡ "These precepts are very touching. They are the finest political morality ; and not only very high morality, but very deep sentiment. A complete collection of the rules of this character, scattered through the Mosaic legislation, would form one of the most striking collections of kind, considerate, merciful maxims ever known.§§ And they would prove Moses to have been, not only a wise and benevolent

---

* Lev. xix. 17, 18.   † Ex. xxiii. 4, 5.   ‡ Lev. xix. 14, 32.

§ The Jews interpret the law contained in Deut. xxvii. 28, as extending to travellers. See the eleventh of the Letters of certain Jews to Voltaire.

‖ Lev. xxv. 35. Ex. xxii. 21. Deut. xxiv. 17.

¶ Lev. xix. 9. Deut. xxiii. 19.   ** Deut. xxiii. 19–21.

†† Deut. xxv. 4.   ‡‡ Deut. xxii. 6, 7. xxv. 4.

§§ Lect. 3 of Spring's Obl. of the World to the Bible.

legislator, but a man of feeling, delicacy, and refinement; a man of large and magnanimous spirit; a man who saw in every other man a brother, and with whom every human form, though unblest by fortune and unknown to fame, constituted a sure passport to his sympathy, his solicitude, and his love.

Surely, such a system of laws could never have been dic-tated by a barbarian legislator for a horde of savages. It is precisely in this point of humanity, that the Mosaic legislation leaves all other ancient constitutions far behind, and shines with a preëminently mild and genial lustre.

Another objection against the divine origin of the Mosaic legislation is grounded on its tolerance of various acknowl-edged social evils,—polygamy, slavery, extra-judicial divorce, and blood-avengement. "The laws of Moses (says the ob-jector) are not, at least some of them are not, the best, intrin-sically, that could be framed; therefore, the system is not of divine original." The premises in this argument are admitted; but the conclusion, it is contended, is illogical. The absolute perfection of every statute in a civil code is not the charac-teristic mark of inspiration in the lawgiver; but the highest excellence attainable under all the circumstances of the case. This is that infallible sign of the Divinity, which fails all mere human legislation; but it may be asserted, without qualifica-tion, of the political system of Moses.

When God assumed the relation of king to the Hebrew people, two general methods of administration were open to his election;—either to overrule the will by an act of omnip-otence, or to influence it by motives addressed to the under-standing and the conscience. In employing the former method, his power would be the chief attribute required; in the latter, his wisdom. That God chose to deal with his peo-ple as accountable agents, and that, notwithstanding the extraordinary providence by which they were conducted, and the constant blaze of almighty power that encircled them, the will remained ever free and uncontrolled, is a truth written upon every page of the history.

God, then, as temporal sovereign of the Israelites, having chosen this method of government, was under a sort of necessity of proceeding upon the same principles with any wise human legislator. Now, such is the invincible proneness of man's will to revolt against what directly opposes its prejudices, that prudent lawgivers, in framing laws in conflict with these prejudices, have always found it necessary to yield something to them in order to break and evade the force of human perversity.

Thus did our inspired lawgiver act with his people, who, if he had not indulged them in some things, would have revolted against all. Hence a partial toleration of some social evils, is no argument against a divine wisdom in the lawgiver; but is, on the contrary, an essential attribute of such wisdom, without which the signature of its divinity would be wanting.

To place this point in a stronger light, let us suppose that a perfectly wise man were now to receive full authority to legislate for China. Would he frame a code of laws for the government of that empire, irrespective of the ancient customs, the cherished opinions, and the deep rooted prejudices of the nation, which are strong in the gathered strength of revolving centuries? Such a procedure would stamp him as a fool, instead of a sage; and would inevitably defeat his best intentions. A truly wise lawgiver would study the character and circumstances of the people. He would respect, and, to a certain extent, even flatter their prejudices. He would limit, where he could not remove; modify, where he could not reverse; ameliorate, where he could not perfect; and so, by degrees, would prepare the nation for improvements in the system of government, more radical than he would venture to propose at first. No really wise legislator will make laws, which shock the general spirit of a nation.*

* Montesq. Sp. of Laws, B. 19, c. 11.

Even Rousseau perceived the force and acknowledged the justness of this principle. In his treatise on the social compact, he observes :* "The prudent legislator does not begin by making a digest of salutary laws, but examines first whether the people for whom such laws are designed are capable of supporting them. It was for this reason that Plato refused to give laws to the Arcadians and Cyrenians, knowing they were rich and luxurious, and could not admit of the introduction of equality among them. * * * * When customs are once established and prejudices have taken root among a people, it is a dangerous and fruitless enterprise to attempt to reform them." Again, in another place of the same treatise, he says :† "Legislation should be variously modified in different countries, according to local situation, the character of the inhabitants, and those other circumstances, which require that every people should have a particular system of laws, not always the best in itself, but the best adapted to the state for which it is calculated." If this celebrated infidel had been writing in defence of the actual procedure of Moses as an inspired lawgiver, he could not have uttered any thing more pertinent or forcible than these sentences. Moses, though a real and earnest, was, nevertheless, an enlightened and wise reformer. His policy was to correct errors gradually and with caution, rather than to attempt the sudden and violent eradication of them; to repair, strengthen, and adorn the political edifice, rather than to undermine its foundations, and triumph over its ruins. He well knew, that systems of government grow and assume form and solidity with time; that, however bad they may be, they come at length to be rooted in the customs, and often also in the affections of the people; and that to violently destroy the former shocks and deranges the latter, and so produces misery rather than happiness.‡ "The secret of great statesmen," says Nie-

* B. 2. C. 8.   † B. 2. C. 11.

‡ See President Sparks' Pref. to the Am. Ed. of Smith's Lects. on Modern History, for some excellent reflections on this subject.

buhr,* " is the gradual development and improvement of the several parts of an actual constitution; they never attempt to raise an institution at once to perfection." Nations are, for the most part, very tenacious of their customs, and very apt to revolt against violent innovations. Wise statesmen, therefore, do not change them suddenly, but lead the people to make the change themselves.†

The procedure of Moses in a mere human lawgiver would carry all voices, as the very perfection of political prudence. And shall that be charged as imposture in him, because he claimed to act under a divine guidance, which would be honored as consummate wisdom in a Solon, a Numa, a Chatham, or a Washington ? Yet this is what the infidel and the rationalist do in the objection which we are considering. Moses tolerated polygamy, divorce, slavery, and the avenging of blood in the death of the murderer by the nearest of kin to the slaughtered victim. But he evidently did not approve these things any more than the most humane and enlightened legislator of modern times. Why, then, did he permit them ? Because the abolition of them, at the time and under the circumstances of his legislation, would have endangered his whole polity. They had been practised the world over from time immemorial. They were inwoven in the whole framework of society. Their propriety and even necessity were unquestioned. And they had long since gained over to their support those master passions of the soul,—the ambition of lordship, the love of pleasure, and the thirst of gain.

Weigh these circumstances in a just balance, and cease to wonder, that Moses did not slay at a blow the whole brood, and to argue thence his fraud and charlatanry. Admire rather the generous philanthropy and heroic courage, which fired his spirit and nerved his arm in the work of reform. Mark the gentle but efficient skill, with which he takes out their sting,

* Lects. on the Hist. of Rome, p. 91.
† Montesq. Sp. of Laws, B. 19. C. 14.

restrains their excesses, mollifies their rigors, and almost reverses their properties; and then acknowledge, that the hand that accomplished all this must indeed have been guided by a wisdom more than human.

Again, the divine mission of Moses has been assailed and denied, because he admitted into his code the primitive and in early times universal principle of "like for like," technically called the "lex talionis." It is thus expressed in the 21st chapter of Exodus: "Thou shalt give life for life, eye for eye, tooth for tooth, hand for hand, foot for foot, burning for burning, wound for wound, stripe for stripe."*

It is admitted, that, as a law of private vengeance, none could be better fitted to destroy the peace and safety of society, and to sow the seeds of hatred, revenge, and all uncharitableness. But considered as the rule of official judgment in cases of personal injury, it appears in another light, and is to be judged upon principles different from those applicable in the former case.

Of penal laws, it is the most ancient on record; and it is, obviously, founded on pure natural equity. The divine government itself recognizes the justice of the principle. In the providence of God, crimes and punishments often correspond in the most remarkable manner. Indeed, it is an observation made long ago, that what mischiefs any one prepares against another, he, without knowing it, first contrives against himself.

However widely the lex talionis deviates from our penal laws, it accords not merely with the usages of the rude and barbarous nations of antiquity, but with the express statutes of nations accounted to have been highly civilized. It existed in great rigor among the ancient Athenians, and Solon even ordained, that whoever put out the eye of a one-eyed person, should for so doing, lose both his own. It constituted a part of the Roman laws of the twelve tables, so famous in antiquity; but the punishment was afterwards changed to a

* Vv. 23, 24.

pecuniary fine, to be levied at the discretion of the prætor.
"It prevails less or more," observes Dr. Adam Clarke, "in
most civilized countries ; and is fully acted upon in the canon
law in reference to all calumniators : 'If the calumniator fail
in the proof of his accusation, let him suffer the same punishment, which he wished to have inflicted on the man, whom
he falsely accused.' "*

In our exposition and defence of this law, it is, as already
hinted, important to observe, that it did not authorize the
retaliation of injuries by individuals, and so make each man
a judge and avenger in his own cause. Such a principle as
this never entered into the mind of the Hebrew lawgiver. It
is abhorrent to the whole genius of his legislation, and would
have been as earnestly repudiated by him, as it is by any one
of his assailants. In every instance of the application of the
principle of the lex talionis, it was the duty of a legal tribunal
to adjudge, and of the public executive power to inflict, the
punishment.

Another material observation is, that the person receiving
the injury retained always the natural right of remitting the
punishment, if the other chose to compound the matter by
apologies and pecuniary compensations. The law does not
peremptorily command an injured person to avail himself of
the right of retaliation, without any alternative. It only fixes
the punishment, to which the author of an injury must submit, if he cannot compound matters with the injured party.
Such satisfactions were in fact so common, that Moses found
it necessary to restrain the use of them, in the case of deliberate murder : " Ye shall take no satisfaction for the life of
a murderer."†

The law, as it stands in the Mosaic code, is probably to be
regarded as a mere declaration of the general principle, that
whoever has done an injury to another is bound to make
suitable reparation for the wrong which he has committed ;

* Com. on Levit. xxi. 24.   † Num. xxxv. 31.

—a principle essential to the safety and good order of society
—a principle, indeed, without which society could not exist.
But even if interpreted and administered literally, how favorably does it compare, on the score of liberality, with what
was, at no distant period, the law of our British ancestors!
It is not so very long, since both the theory and practice of
British jurisprudence might have been expressed, not in the
Hebrew formulary of "an eye for an eye," but in such maxims as "a man for a sheep," "a man for a guinea," nay, mark
it, ye who stigmatize the Mosaic law of retaliation as savoring
of barbarian rudeness, "a man for a twelve-pence-farthing!"

The usages which prevail at this day in several countries
of the east throw light upon the manner in which the law of
retaliation was, in all probability, administered among the
ancient Hebrews. Burkhardt* says that all insulting expressions, all acts of violence, a blow however slight, and the infliction of a wound causing a single drop of blood to flow,
have their respective fines ascertained. He gives an amusing
specimen of a kadi's sentence, which ran thus: "Bokhyt
called Djolan a dog; Djolan returned the insult by a blow
on Bokhyt's arm; then Bokhyt cut Djolan's with a knife.
Bokhyt, therefore, owes to Djolan,—

For the insulting expression,	1 sheep.
" wounding him in the shoulder,	3 camels.
Djolan owes to Bokhyt,	
For the blow on his arm,	1 camel.
Remain due to Djolan	2 camels and 1 sheep."

The baron de Montesquieu,† a writer whose humanity and
love of rational liberty are equalled only by the depth of his
genius, the solidity of his judgment, and the extent of his
juridical learning, affirms, that all the punishments inflicted
upon crimes, that attack the safety of the citizen, are a kind
of retaliation, by which society refuses security to a member, who has intentionally deprived another of his security.

* Cited by Bush on Lev. xxi. 24.   † Spirit of Laws.

These retaliatory punishments, he says, are derived from the nature of the thing, founded in reason, and drawn from the very source of good and evil. Thus a man deserves death when he has violated the security of society so far as to deprive another man of his life. So crime committed against the security of property should, most naturally, be punished with the loss of property. And this, indeed, ought to be the case, if men's fortunes were equal. It was the case in the Hebrew polity, where all the citizens possessed landed estates, of a less or greater extent. But, as in most states there are multitudes without property, and as those who have no property of their own, are generally the readiest to attack the property of others, it has been found necessary to substitute a corporeal for a pecuniary punishment. So, then, according to this profound jurist, the principle of the lex talionis is the principle of all those criminal laws, which are designed to protect the citizen from injury in his person and his property. It should be observed, in passing, that Moses is not the originator of the lex talionis; but that in admitting it into his code, he simply conformed to the common practice of the primitive ages.

It has often been alleged, that Christit* made war upon the lex talionis as of more than doubtful morality, and thus assumed an attitude of direct hostility to the law of Moses. Such an idea must have arisen from a total misconception of his words. It was against a perversion of the law, that Jesus levelled his reproofs. The persons addressed by Moses and by Christ belonged to distinct classes. Moses speaks to the perpetrator of the injury and tells him, that he was bound to give " eye for eye and tooth for tooth;" that is, to make satisfaction for wrongs and injuries committed by him. Christ, on the other hand, addresses the injured party, and forbids him, as an individual, to give vent to his vindictive

* In his Serm. on the Mount, Mat. v. 38, 39.

feelings,—abusing a rule of public justice to the indulgence of private revenge, and pleading it in justification of his vindictiveness. It would seem that in the time of our Savior, the jus talionis was confounded with moral principles, that is to say, it was held that the law of Moses, which was merely civil or penal, justified a person, in a moral point of view, in inflicting on another the same injury which he had received from him. The persons, who give this exposition to the law, do not appear to have recollected its true character as a civil or penal law, nor to have remembered, that the literal retaliation could not take place, until after the decision of a judge on a suit, brought by the person injured, and then was never to exceed the original injury.* Christ made no reference whatever to any action of a civil tribunal, whereas the sole reference of Moses was to this very thing. How absurd to allege a conflict between them, when their discourse does not even relate to the same matter; the reference of one being to a judicial decision, and of the other to private vengeance. Thus does every appearance of a want of harmony between the different parts of revelation vanish, when the principles of common sense and sober criticism are applied to their interpretation.

Another objection to the divine original of the law of Moses is, that it omits the doctrine of future rewards and punishments. This objection is unworthy of any man who claims the name of a philosopher. It is conceded, that Moses did not annex to his laws the promised joys and threatened terrors of eternity. And what inference is to be drawn from the omission? Had he introduced such sanctions, he would have been chargeable with a flagrant incongruity. In excluding them, he acted conformably to the nature of his mission. Who and what was Moses? The founder of a civil polity; a polity, no doubt, designed to keep up the knowledge and wor-

* Jahn's Bib. Arch. S. 256.

ship of the true God, in opposition to the absurd doctrines and impure rites of idolatry, and to foreshadow and introduce the christian dispensation; yet still, in the strict sense, a civil polity. And what proper connexion have the terrors of eternity with a code of civil laws? It thus appears, that the Hebrew legislator was restrained from annexing future punishments as sanctions to his laws, by considerations arising from the character of his mission, and the nature of the institutions, which he was commissioned to establish. But did not Moses, therefore, believe in such punishments? How absurd would such an inference be! As well might we lay the sweeping charge of national infidelity at the door of Great Britain and the United States, because the British parliament and the American congress do not enforce the enactments in their statute-books with such sanctions. But to proceed forth from this point, and argue, as Bishop Warburton* has done, an ignorance in the ancient sons of Jacob of a future world, shocks all our religious feelings. To a mind intent on discovering the truth, instead of defending a fanciful theory, and that will fairly survey all the grounds of an opinion in the premises, hardly anything can be plainer, than that the doctrine of a future life and of future retributions, was well known, and held with a firm grasp, by the patriarchs and their descendants; and by none of them, with a more living power, than by the great lawgiver and founder of the state.

"But although Moses does not annex the sanctions of a future life to the violation of his laws, there is a most remarkable peculiarity in his procedure with regard to punishments, which distinguishes him from all other legislators. It is this: He threatens the whole nation, if as a nation they should wickedly transgress his laws, with punishments in this life, which no human power could execute; but which the divine providence could, and certainly would, inflict upon the people and the land. No mere human legislator could have done

* Div. Leg. passim.

this; at least, could so have done it, as that the issue should
not expose to the people the emptiness of his threatenings. It
is the sure criterion of an immediate messenger from heaven,
enacting laws by command of the Most High."*

One further objection to the divine mission of the Jewish
lawgiver I notice. It may be expressed in the following sentences: " Moses could not have acted under a divine commission, or he would never have enacted laws involving a direct and manifest breach of the most sacred rules of justice.
What right had the Hebrews to injure the Canaanites, either
in their persons or their estates ? They had never been thus
injured by the latter ; and they could, therefore, have no plausible pretence, much less any just warrant, to make war upon
them, and strip them of their territories."†

So the case is often put. But the true question is not, what
right the Israelites had to the land of the Canaanites, nor
whether they had, in themselves, any right at all. It is,
whether God, as sovereign owner and ruler of the world, had
a right to punish their abominable wickedness by the agencies
actually employed, and whether it was the dictate of wisdom
and goodness to use such means for the abolition of idolatry ?
The crimes of the Canaanites were of such a nature, that no
pretence to freedom of thought and liberty of conscience
would, in any well-ordered human government, be allowed as
a justification of them, or as a bar to the infliction of condign
punishment. And shall it be said, that the supreme lawgiver
and judge is hindered by justice from recalling a life, which
has been forfeited to civil society, and which the civil law itself might take away by the hand of a common executioner ?

---

* Mich. Com. on the laws of Mos. Art. 8.

† Various answers have been given by different writers to this objection.
The most rational and satisfactory defence of the command to exterminate
the Canaanites, which I have ever met with, is the one offered in the text.
The reader will find it handled much more at large, in Lowman's excellent
chapter on the subject in his Civ. Gov. of the Hebrews.

Those who contend for such a doctrine, cannot, surely, be aware of the consequences, to which it would lead. If considerations of justice forbid the Deity to punish flagitious offenders by a forfeiture of the blessings of this life, the same considerations would operate as a bar to any penal inflictions whatsoever at his hand. So that, upon this principle, crime would enjoy a perfect immunity from punishment, so far as the divine government is concerned. Besides, what would be unjust in God, must be equally unjust in men; and hence it will follow, that all the laws of society to punish and restrain the most flagitious offenders, are nothing less than usurpation, and an unjust invasion and abridgement of personal liberty. And so the principle will end in the utter subversion of all government, human and divine; and, on pretence of maintaining the rights of justice, it will effectually and forever banish justice from the earth, aye, and from heaven too. It must, therefore, be held to have been just in God to punish the idolatry of the Canaanites, with the forfeiture of their estates, their liberties, and even their lives.

But granting so much, the objector still asks, " Why did not God punish the Canaanites by his own hand,—by earthquake, tempest, famine, pestilence, or inundation? Why should he commission the Hebrews to dispossess them of their lands, especially as such an example would be liable to the most dangerous abuses, and might be pleaded by every enthusiast or impostor, as a warrant for invading and robbing his neighbors, under pretence of religion, and in the name of the most holy ? A procedure of this nature has very little the appearance of wisdom, and still less of goodness."

Thus reasons the objector. In opposition to this logic, which wears an imposing air of humanity and regard to the divine honor, I maintain, that, considering the abolition of idolatry as one grand design of the Mosaic polity, the means employed for the accomplishment of that end, were the dictate of consummate wisdom and benevolence.

For, in the first place, we know that the most terrific visitations of divine providence had been tried without effect. Had not the whole antediluvian world, amounting probably to hundreds of millions of sinners, found one common grave in the waters of a universal deluge? Had not Sodom and Gomorrah, Admah and Zeboim, in this very land of Canaan, been whelmed beneath a fiery tempest for their crimes? Had not ghastly famine glutted its voracious appetite with tens of thousands of these idolaters, when it drove the Israelites down to Egypt for bread? And what the better were men for these direful punishments? Did they not, on the contrary, become daily more besotted and daring in their impiety?

But, in the second place, unfruitful seasons, sickness, whelming waters, and the blasting thunderbolt would be considered but as common accidents; or rather, they would be interpreted as proceeding from the vengeance of their demons, and so, instead of rooting out idolatry, would add fresh vigor to its growth.

And this leads to the third and principal observation, which I have to submit in this argument. It is this:—God gave the territories of the Canaanites into the hands of the Hebrews, coupled with a reason for the grant and a condition of its perpetuity, which were in themselves a public condemnation of idolatry, and a standing confutation of it. Both the reason and the condition are thus expressed in the 18th chapter of Leviticus: "The land is defiled; therefore I do visit the iniquities thereof upon it, and the land itself vomiteth out its inhabitants. Ye shall, therefore, keep my statutes and my judgments, and shall not commit any of these abominations; that the land spew not you out also, when ye defile it, as it spewed out the nations that were before you. For whosoever shall commit any of these abominations, even the souls that commit them shall be cut off."*

* Vv. 25–29.

Here both the right of possession and the obligation of surrender are very plainly set down. And how does the record
represent the matter? The Canaanites are expelled from
their country for their abominable idolatries. The Israelites
are put in possession of their lands, on profession of their
faith in the one supreme and living God, and are to hold
them only so long as they keep themselves from the like
abominations. And the power and truth of Jehovah are
pledged to the fulfilment of the promise and the exaction of
the forfeiture, in opposition to the power of all the idol gods,
worshipped by the neighboring heathen nations.

How admirable is the wisdom displayed in this arrangement! How far does it transcend all that mere human sagacity could have contrived! Natural evils of the most dreadful kind had been tried in vain. The corruption of men's
minds was such as to convert evils of this nature rather into
a means of strengthening than of destroying idolatry. What
remedy could be devised, adequate to the removal of the
evil? Human wisdom must here acknowledge itself completely at fault. But the things that are impossible with
men, are possible with God. He drives out a nation of idolaters from their possessions, and plants in them another, of an
opposite and purer faith. He makes the grant of these lands
to the latter perpetual, on condition of their adherence to the
faith and worship, on which it is founded. And by an extraordinary providence, maintained from age to age, he vindicates his own uncontrollable sovereignty and omnipotence,
over the pretended power of the whole rabble of heathen
divinities. What other confutation of the hopes of idolaters,
what other encouragement of the hopes of the worshippers of
the true God, can be imagined, comparable to this? Gratitude for innumerable deliverances and innumerable blessings; a contempt for idols, generated and strengthened by a
thousand manifest proofs of their utter nothingness; a solemn
dread of the vengeance of an ever present and almighty

power; the clearest calculations of interest; and the very instinct of self-preservation, the strongest that our nature owns,—were thus all enlisted in support of the doctrine of the divine unity, and became so many props and guaranties for the worship of the one true God.

As to the apprehension that such a commission from God as that which Moses held, will countenance the reveries of enthusiasm or the artifices of imposture, it is but a panic dread. So long as pretence and reality are not convertible terms, and the ideas suggested by them do not coalesce in one and the same thing, so long all such fears will be irrational and groundless. When any man will show me the same proofs of a divine mission, that Moses showed his countrymen, when for forty successive years I shall see the elements above, beneath, and around me contradicting the laws of nature in obedience to one who claims to act under a commission from the author of nature, and who alone has power to control, suspend, or reverse those laws, then will I open my ear to his doctrine, yield my conscience to his guidance, and to every contemptuous sneer and profane censure I will answer, in the adoring words of Eliphaz the Temanite :—" Shall mortal man be more just than God? Shall a man be more pure than his Maker?* Till then, I shall continue to regard the apprehension of danger to the peace and safety of nations, from the command of Jehovah to exterminate the Canaanites for their idolatries, either as the mere whimsy of a morbid imagination, or as one of the many hypocritical pretences, with which infidelity seeks to veil its hatred of God and religion.

Besides the objections considered above to the genuineness, authenticity, and inspiration of the Pentateuch, many others have been made. They are such as these following:

The moral and religious conceptions of more enlightened ages are often shocked by the doctrines of the Pentateuch.

* Job iv. 17.

Several of its statements are opposed to the facts and deductions of modern physical science.

Many of its representations of the Deity are unworthy of the true God, and imply very rude notions of his nature.

It is filled with contradictions and discrepancies.

The art of writing was unknown, or at least not in use, in the time of Moses; of course, he could not have been the author of it.

The style of the Pentateuch is too much like the style of the later Hebrew writers to admit the supposition, that its composition belongs to the high antiquity commonly ascribed to it.

The work relates events posterior to the time of Moses; how, then, could he be the author of it?

It uniformly speaks of Moses in the third person, and not in the first. This is a modesty unsuited to his official character.

The Pentateuch is replete with inconsistencies, incredibilities, and impossibilities;—as the whole of the ceremonial law; the rite of circumcision; the institution of the Sabbath; the laws respecting slavery; the distinction of meats; the number of the Israelites on their egress from Egypt; Pharaoh's command to destroy their male children; their tame submission to it, supposing it to have been really given; most of the events connected with their departure from Egypt; their spoiling of the Egyptians; the number of their flocks and herds; the amount of their wealth; their skill in the mechanic arts; the story about the quenching of their thirst at Marah and Horeb; the law against destroying all the inhabitants of Palestine at once, lest wild beasts should increase upon them; the command to destroy witches, &c., &c., &c.

All these objections, and others of a like nature, have been made by infidel and rationalistic writers; and they have been repeated and enforced by Dr. Norton, formerly professor of divinity in Harvard university, with much learning and ability, in an elaborate note appended to the second volume of his Genuineness of the Gospels.* Some of them are trivial and impertinent; some have no foundation in fact or reason; but others, it must be owned, offer to the candid inquirer difficulties of no inconsiderable magnitude. It does not fall within the province of the present work to reply to objections of this sort. The most of them have been refuted, again and again, by learned and able defenders of divine revelation.† My object in bringing them to the notice of the reader is to state a general principle concerning difficulties, which has an eminent applicability here. The principle is, that often, in things which are invested with the highest certainty, difficulties still inhere, which we find ourselves quite incapable of resolving to our own satisfaction.‡ This incapacity on our part is nothing more than the natural consequence of the limited powers of the human understanding, or the limited attainments we have made in the knowledge of the subject under investigation. It results from the principle just stated, that, when a truth is proved by solid reasons, the difficulties which may still inhere in it, ought not to weaken our conviction, provided they are difficulties, which only puzzle the mind, without invalidating the proofs themselves. There is a broad difference between seeing that a thing is absurd in itself, and not comprehending every thing that belongs to it; and a difference quite as broad between an unanswerable question in relation to a particular truth and an unanswerable objection against it. Multitudes there are, who confound these two sorts of difficulties, though no two things can be more distinct than they. Suppose, for example, that I were unable to answer the vulgar objection to the rotundity of the earth,

* Pp. 48–200 of the Add'l. Notes.

† See Hengsten. on Eg. and the Bks. of Mos., Jahn on the Lang. and Style of the Pent., Stuart on the Canon of the O. T., Graves on the Pent., and two elaborate Arts. in the Bib. Sac. for May and Nov. 1845.

‡ Burlam. Princ. of Nat. Law, c. 2.

that in that case the people on the opposite side must fall off;
would such inability stagger my belief of it, the proofs remaining as they are? Must not the proofs themselves be
invalidated, before I will consent to give up my conviction?
When I come to understand the law of gravitation, I can
explain the difficulty to the peasant's satisfaction, as well as
to my own. Now let us apply this illustration. Suppose it
to be objected to the law,—"Ye shall not round the corners
of your heads, neither shalt thou mar the corners of thy
beard,"*—that it is too trivial to have proceeded from God;
and suppose, further, that I am unable to assign any reason
for the introduction into the code of a statute apparently so
unimportant; should I, on account of my inability to answer
the objection, surrender my faith in the divine mission of the
lawgiver, while so many and so solid grounds of it remain?
The moment I come to know, that the law in question was
levelled against idolatry, and that it was both designed and
adapted to counteract that baleful system, the difficulty vanishes entirely. The difference, then, between an unanswerable
objection against a proposition and an unanswerable question
relating to it, seems to be this: An unanswerable objection
proves, that what was before taken for a truth cannot be true,
because the admission of it would involve some absurdity;
an unanswerable question proves only our ignorance of some
points connected with a known truth. The former is relative
to the substance of the matter; the latter is relative only to
our want of knowledge concerning it.†

---

* Lev. xix. 27.

† There are few persons, who have paid much attention to the study of
the O. T., and particularly of the Pentateuch, who will not fully sympa-
thize with the late Prof. Stuart in the following remarks, which occur in
the Introduction to his work on the Canon of the O. T. The learned
author has but given form and voice to feelings, which must be familiar
to the consciousness of every thoughtful and candid inquirer. "In the
early part of my biblical studies," he says, "some 30-35 years ago, when

NOTE ON BISHOP WARBURTON'S OPINION CONCERNING THE
IGNORANCE OF THE ANCIENT ISRAELITES OF A FUTURE
STATE OF REWARDS AND PUNISHMENTS.

The theory of this celebrated prelate having been alluded
to in the preceding chapter,* a brief glance at it, as we pass
along, may not be unacceptable to the reader. The object of
the fifth book of the Divine Legation, is to prove, "that the
doctrine of a future state of rewards and punishments is not
to be found in, and did not make part of, the Mosaic dispensation.† The following are the author's principal positions
on this subject: "In no one place of the Mosaic institutes, is
there the least mention, or any intelligible hint, of the rewards and punishments of another life."‡ Again: "The
Israelites, from the time of Moses, to the time of their captivity, had not the doctrine of a future state of rewards and
punishments."§ These expressions are sufficiently bold and

I first began the critical investigation of the Scriptures, doubts and difficulties started up on every side like the armed men whom Cadmus is
fabled to have raised up. Time, patience, continued study, a better acquaintance with the original scriptural languages, and the countries where
the sacred books were written, have scattered to the winds nearly all these
doubts. I meet, indeed, with difficulties still, which I cannot solve at once;
with some, where even repeated efforts have not solved them. But I quiet
myself by calling to mind, that hosts of other difficulties, once apparently
to me as formidable as these, have been removed, and have disappeared
from the circle of my troubled vision. Why may I not hope, then, as to
the difficulties which remain? Every year is now casting some new light
on the bible, and making plain some things, which aforetime were either
not understood, or were misunderstood. Why may not my difficulties be
reached by some future progressive increase of light?" For one, I can say
that my experience exactly corresponds with this; and I have attained to
that state of mind, in which, whenever a difficulty occurs, which I cannot
satisfactorily explain, I uniformly, and without hesitation, set it down as
relative to my own ignorance, and not to the substance of the thing itself.
* P. 275.　† B. 5, S. 1.　‡ B. 5, S. 5.　§ B. 5, S. 5.

energetic; but those which follow are still more so. "In none of the different circumstances of life, in none of their various casts of composition, do we ever find them acting on the motives, or influenced by the prospect, of future rewards and punishments, or indeed expressing the least hope or fear or common curiosity concerning them; but every thing they do or say respects the present life only, the good and ill of which are the sole objects of all their pursuits and aversions."* Again: "I infer, as amidst all this variety of writing the doctrine of a future state never once appears to have had any share in this people's thoughts, it never did, indeed, form any part of their religious opinions." "Their subterfuge is quite cut off, who pretend, that Moses did not indeed propagate the doctrine of a future state of rewards and punishments in writing, but that he delivered it to tradition. For we see he was so far from teaching it, that he studiously contrived to keep it out of sight, nay, provided for the want of it; and that the people were so far from being influenced by it, that they had not even the idea of it."†

These are strange and startling declarations. How clearly do they evince the blinding power of a predominant love of system over a genius of unsurpassed vigor and brilliancy! No intelligible hint of another life in the Mosaic writings! No trace of the doctrine of a future state in the Jewish scriptures before the captivity! No evidence of higher motives to virtue from Moses to Ezra than such as are connected with the present world! Let us look a little into the sacred books of the Israelites, to ascertain, if possible, whether the positions of this distinguished and learned prelate are sustained by them.

The eternity of the supreme being is distinctly taught in the Pentateuch. I AM THAT I AM‡ is the sublime title, under which he reveals himself. Now, in the very first chapter of Genesis, in the record of that great transaction, in

* B. 5, S. 5.   † B. 5, S. 5.   ‡ Ex. iii. 14.

which the history of our world begins, Moses says, "God created man in his own image."* Would it not be a frigid interpretation of these words, which would restrict their meaning to the mere assertion, that God had endowed man with a somewhat higher intelligence than other animals? Do they not more than hint the doctrine, that the soul of man is kindred to the Deity, not only in the possession of reason, freedom of will, and moral rectitude, but also of a nature adapted and destined to immortality? It seems to me, that any lower interpretation would eliminate all proper meaning from them, and reduce them to a piece of idle bombast. The soundest interpreters assign this force to the expression. Dean Graves† says: "The expression of the image of God plainly implies the idea of the soul's immortality." The same writer cites Abarbanel, Tertullian, Vatablus, Paulus Fagius, Edwards, Augustin, Poole, and Patrick as holding the same view.

In the second chapter of Genesis, we have an account of the trial of our first parents. The penalty of failure was to be death. Does not this clearly imply the promise of life as the reward of obedience? And the life, thus implicitly promised, must have been an endless one; otherwise death would have followed obedience as well as disobedience, and the distinction between virtue and vice would have been destroyed.

The third chapter contains a history of the fall of man. The execution of the threatened sentence is suspended, and a future deliverer and redeemer is promised. Thereupon Adam changed the name of his wife, and called her Eve, "because," says the historian, "she was the mother of all living."‡ This is a remarkable record. It deserves to be deeply studied. At first he had called her by a name, which signified simply a "female man." Now he changes that appellation to another signifying "life." Wherefore such a

---

* Gen. i. 27.   † On the Pent. Pt. 3, Lect. 4.   ‡ V. 20.

change? One should rather suppose, that he would now call her by a name denoting death. What rational explanation can be given of the change actually made, except that it is an expression of Adam's faith in the promise of a new and immortal life to be bestowed upon him and his posterity, through the intervention of the predicted deliverer?

In the next chapter the historian informs us of the offerings of Cain and Abel; of the rejection of the former and acceptance of the latter; and of the foul murder perpetrated, in consequence, upon Abel, by his elder brother. What do we see here? Virtue crushed, and vice triumphant; the good man perishing by violence, and his murderer, though driven from his home, and exiled from the place where the visible symbol of the divine presence dwelt, yet spared to found cities, and become the father of a numerous and flourishing posterity. If there is no hereafter, if death is the annihilation of our being, what a spectacle would this be to contemplate! The omnipotent judge punishing goodness, and rewarding crime! A righteous man perishing, because he had acted in a manner conformable to the will of God! Surely, the facts contained in this record very distinctly point to a future state of rewards and punishments. The writer to the Hebrews intimates as much, when he says of Abel, that "he being dead, yet speaketh."* Of what does he speak? Of the immortality of the soul and the retributions of another world. Very respectable commentators concur in this view of the transaction. Dean Graves† says: "We cannot conceive, that the circumstances attending this first infliction of death upon man, could have been ordered by providence so as to testify more plainly this great truth of a future state of recompense, had this been the sole purpose for which they were designed. To conceive, that a just and merciful God should openly approve the sacrifice of Abel, and yet permit him, in consequence of that very action, to

* Heb. xi. 4.   † On the Pent. Pt. 3, Lect. 4.

suffer a cruel death, which put a final period to his existence; while his murderer, whom the same God openly condemned, was yet permitted to live; all this is so monstrous, so contradictory to the divine attributes, as to prove, beyond possibility of doubt, that this event was permitted to take place, partly at least, in order to show, that death was not a final extinction of being, but on the contrary, a passage from this world to another, where the righteous should be recompensed for their adherence to the will of their heavenly father, in opposition to suffering and death, by a sure and eternal reward." Fagius* observes: "His blood poured forth witnesses that you put him to death. Let this comfort the righteous, who are slain for their justice, that they still live with God, and are his chief care." Taylor† says: "The patriarchs before and after Job, and the Israelites before Christ, had a notion of a future state. By sacrifices was plainly shown, that a way was open to the divine favor and acceptance; and the favor of God imports happiness; which to Abel, who was for that very reason, because he was accepted of God, unjustly slain, could be only in a future state; and dying on account of that faith, 'he speaketh' an invisible future state of reward." Doddridge‡ also interprets the words "he being dead yet speaketh," as referring to the testimony borne by his story to a future state. So Philo Judaus:§ "Abel, though cut off, lives. * * * This the divine oracle attests, for it expressly declares, he cries out against the criminal by whom he suffered: but if he no longer existed, how could he thus cry out? Thus the wise man, who appears deprived of this mortal life, lives an immortal one."

In the fifth chapter of Genesis, we have an account of the translation of the patriarch Enoch: "And Enoch walked with God; and he was not; for God took him."‖ If there is no future life, in which virtue receives its appropriate

* Cited by Poole in loc.   † Scheme of Scrip. Div. c. 24.
‡ Fam. Exp. on Heb. xi. 4.   § Opp. p. 127.   ‖ V. 24.

reward, what a picture does the sacred historian here offer us
of the God of the Hebrews! A man, illustrious beyond all
his contemporaries for piety, is cut off in the midst of his
days from all the honors and enjoyments of life, and rewarded with annihilation! What heart but must recoil from
a being, who recompenses the devotion of his servants with
the extinction of their being? Who can believe that Moses
teaches a doctrine so abhorrent both to reason and revelation? This record of the translation of Enoch, so far from
being a mere hint of another life, seems to me almost as
plain a revelation of it, as the declaration of the Lord of life
himself, "The hour is coming, in the which all that are in
the graves shall hear his voice, and shall come forth."[*]
Warburton,[†] to evade the force of this scripture, says, that
the fact that Enoch walked with God, and was not, because
God took him, is related with a studied obscurity and brevity, as if to conceal the idea of another life. To this Dr.
Graves[‡] well replies, that "it is related in exactly the same
style and manner as every other fact in this part of the
patriarchal history; and it is so plain, that the only possible
way of concealing or obscuring the information it contains,
would be entirely to suppress the fact. Enough is told to
justify the observation of the apostle, "By faith Enoch was
translated, that he should not see death; and was not found
because God had translated him; for before his translation,
he had this testimony, that he pleased God."[§]

A little farther on in the sacred narrative,[||] we come to
the great trial of Abraham's faith in the command to offer up
his son Isaac. We have the explicit testimony of St. Paul,[¶]
that he did this in the belief, that God would raise him from
the dead. Could such a thought have occurred to a mind in
utter darkness as to a future state, and to which death sug

* John v. 28, 39.   † Div. Leg. B. 5, S. 5.   ‡ On the Pent. Pt. 3, Lect. 4.
§ Heb. xi. 5. || Gen. xxii.   ¶ Heb. xi. 19.

gested no other idea, than that of an eternal sleep? It is impossible.

That Abraham and the other patriarchs, contrary to the theory of Bishop Warburton, were influenced in their conduct by the prospect of a future life, is a truth which rests for support on inspired authority. "By faith," says the author of the epistle to the Hebrews, "Abraham sojourned in the land of promise, as in a strange country, dwelling in tabernacles with Isaac and Jacob, the heirs with him of the same promise. For he looked for a city which hath foundations, whose builder and maker is God."* Again, speaking of the patriarchs in general, the same writer says: "These all died in faith, not having received the promises, but having seen them afar off, and were persuaded of them, and embraced them, and confessed that they were strangers and pilgrims on the earth. For they that say such things declare plainly, that they seek a country. And truly, if they had been mindful of that country from which they came out, they might have had opportunity to have returned. But now they desire a better country, that is an heavenly: wherefore God is not ashamed to be called their God; for he hath prepared for them a city."†

When God revealed himself to Moses in the burning bush, it was in these words: "I am the God of Abraham, the God of Isaac, and the God of Jacob."‡ According to the authoritative interpretation of our Savior,§ the doctrine not only of a future life, but even of a resurrection from the dead, is taught in this passage. It must, therefore, unless the divine expounder has put an erroneous construction upon it, be regarded as containing something more than a mere hint of another life. It is a distinct revelation of it.

Moses is commonly supposed to have been heir apparent to the crown of Egypt. Whether this be so or not, the highest dignities below the throne were open to his ambition;

* Heb. xi. 9, 10.   † Heb. xi. 13–16.   ‡ Ex. iii. 6.   § Mat. xii. 21, 32.

and boundless wealth, splendor, and luxury were his by prescriptive right. All this he renounced for reproach, exile, poverty, toil, privation, ingratitude, and death. Wherefore pursue a course, so irrational in the world's esteem, and so contradictory to its most cherished maxims? Because, according to the writer to the Hebrews,[*] he had respect to rewards unappreciated in the world's philosophy. Either, therefore, Bishop Warburton is mistaken, or St. Paul is; for they put forth diametrically opposite opinions on the question whether or not the Israelites were ever actuated by the prospect of future rewards and punishments,—the former teaching that they were not, the latter that they were.

Balaam was undoubtedly favored with a portion of the true prophetic spirit. His prayer " let me die the death of the righteous, and let my last end be like his," conveys a distinct allusion to the rewards of a future state of being.[†] " It imports," observes Dr. Graves,[‡] " a wish to die the death of the righteous, in order to enjoy the happiness of another life, which the righteous only can share." If anything could establish the correctness of this interpretation, it would be the unnatural and jejune construction which Warburton is compelled to put upon the passage. According to him, the prayer means, " Let me die in a mature old age, after a life of health and peace, with all my posterity flourishing about me; as was the lot of the righteous observers of the law."[§] Could any thing be more forced and frigid?

The Mosaic statute, repeated not less than four times in the Pentatauch,[||] prohibiting all recourse to wizards, witches, necromancers, and the like, viewed in connexion with the continuance of the superstition in spite of the rigorous enforcement of the prohibition, and especially in connexion with Saul's application to the witch of Endor to bring up

---

[*] Heb. xi. 26.　　　[†] Num. xxiii. 10.　　　[‡] On the Pent. Pt. 3. Lect. 4.
[§] Div. Leg. B. 5.　　　[||] Lev. xix. 31; xx. 6, 27. Deut. xviii. 11.

Samuel from the dead,* affords an incontestible proof, not only that the doctrine of the separate existence of the soul after the dissolution of the body formed a part of the popular creed of the Jewish nation, but also that the abuse of the doctrine constituted a prominent feature of the popular superstition.

The solemn Hebrew adjuration, which we find in 1 Sam. 25 : 6, and other places of the Old Testament,—" As Jehovah liveth and as thy soul liveth," contains a hint of immortality, by no means equivocal. Why this remarkable conjunction of terms ? Is it accidental ? Is it rhetorical merely ? Is it not rather intimated, in this wonderful association of the human spirit with the father of spirits, that as the one lives, so shall the other ? The being of the one is recognised as the pledge of the being of the other. In this language the divine spirit is so intimately connected with the human spirit, that the eternal existence of the former is made the immoveable ground of the eternal blessedness of the latter.

By the inspired teachers who succeeded Moses, and whose writings form a part of the sacred volume, the doctrine of another life was developed with continually increasing clearness and force. From the mind of David, the royal prophet and sweet singer of Israel, the contemplation of the future state of retribution seems hardly ever to have been absent. Let us glance at a few of the places in his pious and inspired hymns, in which this idea appears conspicuous.

In the 16th Psalm,† David uses these glowing expressions :—

" I have set the Lord always before me ; because he is at my right hand, I shall not be moved. Therefore my heart is glad, and my glory rejoiceth : my flesh also shall rest in hope. For thou wilt not leave my soul in hell; neither wilt thou suffer thy Holy One to see corruption. Thou wilt show me

* 1 Sam. xxviii.   † Vv. 8–11.

the path of life: in thy presence is fulness of joy: at thy right hand there are pleasures for evermore."

It is true that the psalmist here speaks in the person of the Messiah, and the words, "neither wilt thou suffer thy holy one to see corruption," are explained by Peter[*] as applicable to him alone. Yet, without doubt, he expresses his own full assurance of a future state, in which earthly sorrow shall terminate in heavenly joy, and momentary pain shall be rewarded with everlasting felicity.[†]

In the psalm immediately succeeding to this,[‡] the royal poet expresses himself thus:—" deliver my soul from the wicked, which is thy sword: From men which are thy hand, O Lord, from men of the world, which have their portion in this life, and whose belly thou fillest with thy hid treasure: they are full of children, and leave the rest of their substance to their babes. As for me, I will behold thy face in righteousness: I shall be satisfied, when I awake, with thy likeness." Here the psalmist draws an express contrast between the gross earthly pleasures of the men of the world and the pure celestial happiness of the righteous in another life. In opposition to those who have " their portion in this life, and whose belly is filled with hid treasure," he places all his felicity in the vision of God, anticipates the hour when he shall awake (i. e. from death to life) in the divine likeness, and expresses his assured confidence, that then he shall be satisfied with the fulness of joy, yea, with the exceeding abundance of eternal glory.[§]

In psalm 21: 1, the writer says, " Into thy hands do I yield up my SPIRIT, for thou hast redeemed [purchased] me, O Lord God of truth." These expressions represent death as the giving up of something that goes away at the bodily dissolution. Blind must he be, who, in such expressions, sees only nature, or, as the naturalist would say, a debt due to nature, and nothing of grace, nothing of covenant, nothing of the redemp-

---

[*] Acts ii.   [†] See Horne in loc.   [‡] xvii. 13–15.   [§] Horne in loc.

tion and immortality of the soul. The passage contains
clearly the idea of restoration, or the paying back of a deposit,
placed in the hands of Jehovah.

The forty-ninth psalm is a glorious testimony to the doctrine of a future state of rewards and punishments. The
psalmist commences with a solemn call to all the inhabitants
of the world to give ear to a lesson of divine wisdom. The
lesson is the folly of trusting in riches, for of wealthy transgressors he says :* "This their way is their folly : yet their
posterity approve their sayings. Like sheep they are laid in
the grave; death shall feed on them; and the upright shall
have dominion over them in the morning; and their beauty
shall consume in the grave from their dwelling. But God
will redeem my soul from the power of the grave ; for he
shall receive me." Here we have a contrast between sinners
who trust in their wealth and the upright. Both are, indeed,
subject to the power of death ; both shall be laid in the grave ;
both shall be re-animated and come forth out of the dust;
but the upright shall have dominion over the wicked in the
morning. Graves,† Patrick,‡ and Horne§ interpret "the
morning" here as denoting the resurrection. Horne's para-
phrase of the fourteenth verse is strikingly beautiful : "The
high and mighty ones of the earth, who cause people to fear,
and nations to tremble around them, must one day crowd the
grave; in multitude and impotence, though not in innocence,
resembling sheep driven and confined by the butcher in his
house of slaughter. There death, that ravening wolf, shall
feed sweetly on them, and devour his long expected prey in
silence and darkness, until the glorious morning of the resurrection dawn; when the once oppressed and afflicted righteous,
risen from the dead, and sitting with their Lord in judgment,
shall have dominion over their cruel and insulting enemies;
whose faded beauty, withered strength, and departed glory,

* Vv. 13–15.   † On the Pent. Pt. 3, Lect. 4.   ‡ In loc.   § In loc.

shall display to men and angels the vanity of that confidence, which is not placed in God."*

The main sentiment of the psalm which we have just been considering, is brought out with still greater distinctness in the seventy-third. The writer describes himself as brought into a state of the most anxious perplexity by a view of the worldly prosperity of the wicked; but the darkness, which for a time clouded his mind, was scattered by the light of religion, revealing the final doom of the ungodly and the future glory and felicity of the pious. He thus describes both the disease and the remedy :† "Verily I have cleansed my heart in vain, and washed my hands in innocency. For all the day long have I been plagued, and chastened every morning. If I say I will speak thus; behold, I should offend against the generation of thy children. When I thought to know this, it was too painful for me; until I went into the sanctuary of God; then understood I their end. Surely thou didst set them in slippery places: thou castedst them down into destruction. How are they brought into desolation, as in a moment! they are utterly consumed with terrors. As a dream when one awaketh; so, O Lord, when thou awakest, thou shalt despise their image. Thus my heart was grieved, and I was pricked in my reins. So foolish was I, and' ignorant; I was as a beast before thee. Nevertheless I am continually with thee: thou hast holden me by my right hand. Thou shalt guide me with thy counsel, and afterward receive me to glory. Whom have I in heaven but thee? and there is none upon earth that I desire besides thee. My flesh and my heart faileth: but God is the strength of my heart, and my portion for ever." How clear is the doctrine of a future life

* "Warburton interprets 'in the morning.' to mean, 'by the judgment of the law, which was administered in the morning hours.' What straits is a system driven to, to require such an interpretation!" Graves on the Pent.

† Vv. 13–26.

in these verses! How strong the psalmist's hope of a personal enjoyment of its blessedness! With what rapture and exultation does he dwell upon the blissful anticipation!

The list of references to another life in the book of Psalms might be greatly extended; but let these instances suffice. That Solomon, the pride of his nation and wonder of the world for wisdom, was acquainted with the doctrine of retribution in a future state, and that he held it to be the strongest foundation and sanction of virtue, the inspired productions of his pen afford decisive proof. In Proverbs 4: 18, he compares "the path of the just" to "the shining light, that shineth more and more unto the perfect day." Patrick, Poole, Doddridge, and Graves concur in interpreting these words as a beautiful description of the reward of virtue, increasing from day to day, till it terminates in endless glory. In the same book (8: 35, 36) wisdom is represented as saying, "Whoso findeth me findeth life," and "All they that hate me love death." Eternal life and eternal death are here, plainly, intended. The same must be understood in chap. 12: 28, where we are told, that "in the way of righteousness is life, and in the pathway thereof there is no death;" and in chap. 14: 27, where it is said, that "the fear of the Lord is a fountain of life, to depart from the snares of death." In these places, it is impossible to interpret the words life and death otherwise than as appertaining to a future state of being, because the wicked enjoy the present life as well as the righteous, and the righteous are subject to temporal death not less than the wicked. Still clearer, if possible, is the doctrine of future retribution in the thirty-second verse of this chapter: "The wicked is driven away in his wickedness; but the righteous hath hope in his death." If death is the annihilation of our being, the righteous are as much driven away as the wicked; and neither can have any well grounded hope in the mortal struggle. It is true, that Warburton interprets the expression, "the righteous hath hope in his death," as meaning, " he hath hope, that he shall be delivered from the most imminent dangers." But, so long as there is any ground whatever for the hope of escape from such perils, this feeling, as far as my observation has extended, is as strong in the wicked as it is in the righteous. Besides, this interpretation does violence to the language of the sacred writer. Hope in death is surely not the same thing as the hope of escape from death. The latter must rest upon some probable, or at least possible, grounds of escape; the former may and does exist in full strength, after all such grounds have been removed.

Passing now from the book of Proverbs to that of Ecclesiastes, if in the former we meet with only scattered and incidental notices of the doctrine of future retribution, in the latter we shall find this doctrine entering into the very substance of the writing, and constituting in fact its leading dogma. " The royal preacher expatiates on the transitory condition of mankind, if considered as confined to the present state of existence; the vanity and vexation of spirit attending all present human enjoyment; and the apparent inequality of providence, by which there appears one event to the righteous and the wicked. But in all the difficulties and perplexities, all the vanity and vexation of spirit, which this partial view of human nature implies, the royal preacher brings forward the prospect of a future life and just retribution, as the solution and the remedy, the consolation and the cure."* And he closes the whole discussion with these memorable words, intended to imprint upon the heart of his readers the great truth, which it had been his principal aim to unfold and enforce :† " Let us hear the conclusion of the whole matter : Fear God and keep his commandments : for this is the whole duty of man. For God shall bring every work into judgment, with every secret thing, whether it be good, or whether it be evil."

Miracle was superadded to verbal instruction to confirm

* Graves on the Pent. Pt. 3, Lect. 4.   † Eccl. xii. 13, 14.

the doctrine of the soul's continued existence after the death of the body, and of its capability of a blessed immortality. Three instances occurred of an actual resurrection from the dead, produced by the miraculous power of Elijah and Elisha, prophets of the most high God,—viz. the son of the widow of Zarephath,* the son of the Shunamite woman,† and the man let down into the sepulchre of Elisha.‡ "These miracles, combined with others of a different kind wrought by the same prophets, which must have excited general attention, could not fail of impressing extensively and deeply on the Jewish nation the opinion of the soul's surviving death, and being capable of a blessed immortality."§ But a miracle far more remarkable and illustrious, and tending more directly and powerfully to confirm the doctrine of a future state of existence, we have in the translation of Elijah.‖ "And it came to pass, as they¶ still went on, and talked, behold, there appeared a chariot of fire, and horses of fire, and parted them both asunder; and Elijah went up by a whirlwind into heaven. And Elisha saw it, and he cried, My father, my father! the chariot of Israel and the horsemen thereof! And he saw him no more." With such a record as this before him, how was it possible for a man of Warburton's genius, a doctor of divinity and a bishop in the established church of England, to avow the opinion that the Jews, from Moses to the captivity, "had not even the idea of a future state,"** and never "expressed the least hope or fear or common curiosity concerning it?"††

A very few citations from the subsequent prophets must close this already too extended note. In the fourteenth chapter of Isaiah, in a bold and sublime scenic representation, the invisible world is uncovered, and we see and hear

* 1 Kings xvii. 17–23. † 2 Kings iv. 33–36. ‡ 2 Kings xiii. 21.
§ Graves on the Pent. Pt. 3, Lect. 4. ‖ 2 Kings ii. 11, 12.
¶ Viz. Elijah and Elisha. ** Div. Leg. vol. 4, p. 344.
†† Div. Leg. B. 5, S. 5.

what is transacting there. Nebuchadnezzar, the fallen tyrant of Babylon, descends to the lower regions, whose inhabitants, aroused by his approach, come forth to meet him :* "Hell from beneath is moved for thee to meet thee at thy coming: it stirreth up the dead for thee, even all the chief ones of the earth: it hath raised up from their thrones all the kings of the nations. All they shall speak and say unto thee, Art thou also become weak as we? Art thou become like unto us?" Does not this whole representation prove, that the idea of a state of future retribution was familiar to the Jewish mind in the age of this prophet?

In his twenty-sixth chapter, Isaiah, celebrating the faithfulness of God to his people, says:† "Thy dead men shall live, together with my dead body shall they rise. Awake and sing, ye that dwell in dust: for thy dew is as the dew of herbs, and the earth shall cast out the dead." The interpretation of this passage is much disputed. Various senses are assigned to it by the commentators. Into these controversies I do not enter; nor is it needful that I should; for, whatever the specific reference of the prophet may be, the passage is a clear proof, that the doctrine of a resurrection of the dead was current among the Jews at the time when it was penned.

Passing by numerous other allusions to a future state, in this sublime and evangelic prophet, we come to his fifty-seventh chapter, " in which he describes, in terms the most clear and impressive, that strict retribution, by which divine justice will correct all the inequalities of the present life, and render to every man according to his works :"‡ " The righteous perisheth, and no man layeth it to heart: and merciful men are taken away, none considering that the righteous is taken away from the evil to come. He shall enter into peace: they shall rest in their beds, each one walking in his uprightness."§

---

* Vv. 9, 10.　　　　　　　　　† V. 19.

‡ Graves on the Pent. Pt. 3, Lect. 4.　　§ Vv. 1, 2.

I pass the references to a future state of rewards and punishments contained in Jeremiah, Ezekiel, and the minor prophets, though much might be gleaned from these writers, which would have a strong bearing upon the present discussion; and close with the sublime and awful description of the great and terrible day of the Lord, the day of final retribution, which we find in the prophecies of Daniel:* " I beheld till the thrones were cast down, and the Ancient of days did sit, whose garment was white as snow, and the hair of his head like the pure wool: his throne was like the fiery flame, and his wheels as burning fire. A fiery stream issued and came forth from before him: thousand thousands ministered unto him, and ten thousand times ten thousand stood before him: the judgment was set, and the books were opened. I saw in the night visions, and behold one like the Son of man came with the clouds of heaven, and came to the Ancient of days, and they brought him near before him. And there was given him dominion and glory, and a kingdom, that all people, nations, and languages, should serve him: his dominion is an everlasting dominion, which shall not pass away, and his kingdom, that which shall not be destroyed." "And at that time shall Michael stand up, the great prince which standeth for the children of thy people: and there shall be a time of trouble, such as never was since there was a nation even to that same time: and at that time thy people shall be delivered, every one that shall be found written in the book. And many of them that sleep in the dust of the earth shall awake, some to everlasting life, and some to shame and everlasting contempt. And they that be wise, shall shine as the brightness of the firmament; and they that turn many to righteousness, as the stars for ever and ever."

* vii. 9, 10, 13, 14. xii. 1-3.

CHAPTER VII.

Influence of the Laws and Writings of Moses on the subsequent Civilisation of the World.

A WORK like the Pentateuch, distinguished for its literary merit, its theology, its ethics, and the preëminent excellence of its system of civil institutions, could not fail to exert a wide and powerful influence on the opinions and practices of mankind. To trace and unfold this influence, as we find it modifying the religion, the literature, the philosophy, and the legislation of the world, since the age of Moses, is the purpose of the present chapter. As, however, it is not always easy to distinguish between the effect of the Pentateuch and of the other inspired writings, which form the canon of the Old Testament, I shall not be particularly studious of such discriminations, but shall treat of the influence generally of the Hebrew scriptures ; never forgetting, however, that the chief place, in such a review, is due to the books of Moses.

Moses made no secret of the high estimate, which he placed upon his labors, as a lawgiver. " What nation is there so great, that hath statutes and judgments so righteous as all this law, which I set before you this day ?"* is the confident tone, in which he claims the obedience of his country

* Deut. iv. 8.

men and the admiration of the world. It is a challenge which might still be made in reference to the greater part of the nations of the earth. Moses seems to have been impressed with the conviction, that his legislation was destined to exert a commanding influence on the progress of government and civilization. He evidently anticipated, that his laws would become known, and would be imitated, by other nations; and, ever upon the alert for motives to enforce the observance of them upon his own countrymen, he employs this expectation as an argument to that end. " Keep, therefore, and do them (he says), for this is your wisdom and youɪ understanding in the sight of the nations, which shall hear of these statutes, and say, surely this great nation is a wise and understanding people."*

The event was in harmony with the anticipation. Hardly any historical fact rests upon a more solid foundation than that the most celebrated nations and lawgivers of antiquity borrowed many of their wisest institutions from the laws of Moses. We have plain and certain proofs, that these laws were powerfully felt in modifying the religious sentiments, the philosophical opinions, the literary labors, the political maxims, the civil institutions, and the moral judgments and practices of mankind. The exhibition of these proofs is the labor now in hand.

The reader's attention is here, in a preliminary way, called to the geographical position of the country of the Hebrews, in its relations to the other countries of the eastern hemisphere. A glance at the map shows how admirably it was situated for becoming a central point of illumination, a fountain whence streams of knowledge might flow to a benighted world. The divine voice itself, in describing the boundaries of the promised land, says: " From the wilderness and Lebanon, from the river, the river Euphrates, even unto the uttermost sea, shall your coast be."† The western border of

---

* Deut. iv. 6.   † Deut xi. 24.

the Hebrews was the Mediterranean sea, by means of whose waters there was an easy access to the entire southern coast of Europe and northern coast of Africa. Their eastern border was the Euphrates, which, discharging itself into the Indian ocean, opened a way to the whole southern shore of Asia. In this commanding position, this city set on a hill, Jehovah, fixing the abode of his chosen people, set up a school for the instruction of the nations. Judea, enjoying the sacred light of revelation, became the great depository of religious, moral, and political knowledge for the world. And it was so central, and so easy of access, that light could thence be most readily made to radiate to every region of the globe.*

That the Hebrew institutions were not designed for the exclusive benefit of the Hebrew people, we know from the express declarations of holy writ. See in confirmation of this Ex. 9 : 16. 15 : 14 ; Num. 14 : 13–21 ; Deut. 4 : 6–8. 28 : 10. The prayer of Solomon at the dedication of the temple is particularly pertinent here. Therein that illustrious monarch prays, that " all the people of the earth may know thy name, to fear thee, as do thy people Israel."† And again, in his solemn benediction of all the congregation of Israel at the conclusion of his prayer, he makes request, that God would " maintain the cause of his people Israel at all times, that all the people of the earth may know that Jehovah is God, and that there is none else."‡ This last citation is the more important, as it contains a distinct recognition of the principles and objects of the Jewish law. According to this decisive testimony, these, from the very first, stood connected with the communication of the knowledge of the true God to all the people of the earth.

The Mosaic law tended to promote the instruction and improvement of mankind by exhibiting to all the nations in the vicinity of the Hebrews, and all that were affected by their

* Dr. Mathew's Bib. & Civ. Gov. pp. 103, 104.
† 1 Kings viii. 43. ‡ 1 Kings viii. 59, 60.

fortunes, the most striking proofs of the existence and power of the true God. Such, in the earlier ages, were the Egyptians, the Canaanites, and the Phenicians, renowned respectively for their wisdom, their military prowess, and their commercial enterprise. Such, in later times, were the Assyrians, the Persians, the Greeks, and the Romans who swayed successively the sceptre of universal empire. It is not, therefore, unlikely, as dean Graves * has suggested, that whatever knowledge of the true God was preserved among mankind, was derived from this source, or at least was from thence materially extended and improved.

A deep impression of the power of the true God was made on the mind of remote antiquity by the miracles wrought in behalf of the chosen people. This appears in the confession extorted from Pharaoh's magicians,—" this is the finger of God."† It is seen in the expostulations of the Egyptian people with their king on his obstinacy in refusing to let the Israelites go.‡· It is seen in the terror felt by the Canaanites on the approach of the Israelitish armies, when kings trembled on their thrones, and the hearts of their people melted, and there remained no more courage in any man.§ It appears in the passionate exclamations of the Philistines, three hundred years afterwards, when the ark was brought into the camp of Israel,—" Woe unto us, who shall deliver us out of the hands of these mighty gods ? These are the gods, which smote the Egyptians with all the plagues in the wilderness.‖ The effect produced on the mariners, when Jonah told them he was a Hebrew, and feared Jehovah, the God of heaven, who made the sea and the dry land, shows very plainly, that the displays of omnipotence, on behalf of Israel, were not unknown to the surrounding nations.¶ That also which was soon after produced on the Ninevites, when they learned that

---

* On the Pent. Pt. 3 Lect. 5.   † Ex. viii. 19.   ‡ Ex. x. 7.
§ Josh. ii. 9–11.   ix. 9–11, 24.   ‖ 1 Sam. iv. 8.   ¶ Jonah i. 10..

he was a Hebrew prophet, sent of God, evinces the same thing.*

How far the knowledge of the true God was diffused by these means, it is impossible at this distance of time, to trace with much distinctness. It cannot, however, be doubted, that the manifest and admitted superiority of Jehovah over the idols of the heathens, must have had a powerful effect in weakening their confidence in these false gods, and in leading thoughtful minds to favor a purer and more rational faith.

The reign of Solomon was eminently favorable to the spread of the religious ideas of the Hebrews. The magnificence of his temple, the splendor of his court, and the unrivalled fame of his wisdom attracted to his capital, from all quarters, men and women, illustrious for their rank and influence. Jerusalem became the Athens of its day; the centre of light to the surrounding nations; who were ambitious to sit at the feet of its renowned sage and sovereign. The queen of Sheba, with a very great company, and all the kings of the earth sought his presence to hear his wisdom.† Thus did the men, who swayed the destinies of their respective countries, become acquainted with the civil and religious institutions of Moses, and with the amazing history of the divine interpositions in favor of a people, professing the faith and worship of the true God. This knowledge, thus widely extended, constituted a leaven, which must have produced a great ferment in men's religious and political ideas, and must have tended, in no inconsiderable degree, to their instruction and reformation.

It was not, however, merely persons of this description,— princes and the ambassadors of princes,—who were drawn to Judea as the rich store-house of knowledge and wisdom. Before the reign of Solomon, a vast multitude of foreigners had been attracted thither, and without probably embracing the Jewish religion wholly, and becoming citizens in the full

* Jonah iii. 5-9.　　† 1 Kings iv. 29-34. x. 1-13. 2 Chron. ix. 1-12.

sense' by being circumcised, had renounced idolatry and become worshippers of the true God. Some idea of the total
number of this class of residents may be obtained from the
fact that no less than one hundred and fifty-three thousand
and six hundred of them were employed in the work of
building the temple. Their character for intelligence may be
estimated from the circumstance, that nearly four thousand
of them were fit to be made overseers of the work.* This is
a record in the history, brief and incidental it is true, and
therefore apt to be overlooked, like many others, as insignificant, which yet is of the high st importance, as showing,
that the Hebrews were far from being an insulated people,
unknown and unfelt by other nations. It proves, on the contrary, that they occupied a commanding position, that the
influence of their religion and laws was widely diffused and
powerfully felt, and that the tendency of their polity was to
disseminate light, and render the knowledge of the true God
increasingly conspicuous and increasingly operative.

Let any one duly consider these circumstances,—the immense influx of foreign residents into Judea, and the flocking
thither of the great and the learned for purposes connected
with the improvement of the mind and the amelioration of
government,—and he will readily conceive what a flood of
light must have been poured upon the nations from this central orb. But there was gradually introduced into the Jewish
history an element, which gave to the Mosaic laws and
writings a tenfold diffusion and power, and proportionably
increased the obligations of mankind to them. Commerce
first, and military subjugation afterwards, by degrees dispersed the Jews throughout the principal nations of the
world. Wherever they went, they appear to have won, by
their intelligence and their excellent moral qualities, no
small share of esteem and influence. · Many of them rose to
exalted stations in the respective governments, under which

* 2 Chron. ii. 17, 18.

they lived. Hecataeus attests the high estimation, in which they were held by Alexander the Great, who permitted them to hold the country of Samaria, free from tribute, for their fidelity towards him. Ptolemy Soter entrusted the fortresses of Egypt to their hands, as believing they would defend them faithfully and valiantly. Ptolemy Philometer and his queen Cleopatra committed their entire kingdom to the Jews, in appointing Onias and Dositheus generals of all their forces.

The affection of Ptolemy Philadelphus towards both the nation and the laws of the Jews is well known. He purchased the freedom of 120,000 Jewish slaves at an immense price, which he paid out of the royal treasures, and sent them back to their own country. He was delighted with the laws of Moses; pronounced his legislation wonderful; was astonished at the depth of his wisdom; and professed to have learned from him the true science of government.*

The chronicles of the kings of Assyria, Media, and Persia, afford additional testimony to the estimation in which the Jewish people were held by contemporary nations. The superior wisdom and virtue of the more cultivated Hebrews attracted the notice and regard of the Asiatic sovereigns, who elevated them to the highest civil dignities. Witness the case of those excellent men, Daniel and Nehemiah,—the former of whom became the prime minister and favorite of Darius, the Mede, and the latter held a responsible and confidential office under the Persian Artaxerxes. Witness also the elevation of the Jewess Esther to the throne of Persia, and of her noble-hearted and inflexible kinsman, Mordecai, to the primacy of the realm. During the reign of Artaxerxes, the Ahasuerus of the scriptures, " many of the people of the

---

* See all these facts, with the authorities on which they rest, in Josephus contra Apion.

land became Jews;"* that is, they renounced idolatry, and became worshippers of Jehovah. This is another incidental record of the highest significance and value, as evincing the power and influence of Judaism on the gentiles.

The majesty and providence of God extorted from successive Assyrian, Median, and Persian monarchs, public official decrees, recognizing his power and sovereignty in the most explicit terms; commanding all people, nations, and languages, to praise and extol and honor the king of heaven;† and to tremble and fear before him;‡ and denouncing the most terrible punishments upon such as should dare to speak any thing amiss against the God of Israel.§ And this reverence and worship of the true God was enjoined upon their subjects by these heathen princes, because, say they, " He is the living God, and steadfast forever; he delivereth and he rescueth, and he worketh signs and wonders in heaven and earth; his kingdom is an everlasting kingdom, and his dominion is from generation to generation.‖

Edicts to this effect were published by Nebuchadnezzar, Darius, Cyrus, and Artaxerxes. " Such public and solemn testimonies to the majesty of the God of Israel," observes Dr. Graves,¶ " must have contributed materially to check error and idolatry, in a country where the form of the government rendered the example and opinions of the monarch so powerful and operative. They must have gained the Jews, even in their captive and degraded state, much consideration and attention; and as such a state led them to take pride in their religious superiority,—the only superiority now left them,— and to exalt the divine original and wisdom of their religion; so these events must have gained their representations weight and credulity."

The oriental nations were the primeval seat and source of

---

* Esth. viii. 17.   † Dan. iii. 29. iv. 1, 37.   ‡ Dan. vi. 25–27.
§ Dan. ii. iii. iv. v. vi.   ‖ Dan. vi. 26, 27. iv. 3.
¶ On the Pent. Pt. 3, Lect. 5.

civilization and philosophy. The full effect of the Mosaic writings in checking idolatry and spreading the knowledge of true religion in those distant regions, cannot, at this late day, be clearly traced, nor duly estimated. But a remarkable instance of it occurs in the history of the Magian or ancient Persian religion.*

The Persians, in process of time, appear to have declined from that purity of doctrine and worship, which they had received from their pious ancestor Elam, and to have engrafted upon their national religion the superstitions of the Zabian idolatry. From this they were probably, in a good degree, recovered by the instructions of the patriarch Abraham. But they again lapsed from the purity of their primitive faith; and, although they never sank into the gross idolatry of other nations, they paid a superstitious reverence to the heavenly bodies and the elements of nature, particularly fire and the sun. They admitted into their religious creed the doctrine of two original and independent principles of evil and of good, so derogatory to the honor of the one supreme and universal lord and king.

From these corruptions—as observed by the author of Lectures on the Pentateuch—this religion was again purified by the celebrated Zoroaster. This illustrious person is represented by writers best informed in oriental literature and history, to have been cotemporary with Daniel ; and if not himself a Jew, yet perfectly acquainted with the Jewish scriptures ; to which, indeed, the distinguishing features of

---

* What is here delivered concerning Zoroaster and the Persian religion, is the valuable substance of dean Graves's dissertation on the subject in the 5th Lecture of his 3rd Part on the Pentateuch. The reader will find the topic much more extensively treated there, with copious references to the following authorities :—Hyde's Religio Veterum Persarum ; Lord's Religion of the Persees ; Prideaux's Connection ; Universal History, Pocockii Specimen Historiæ Arabicæ ; Maurice's History of Hindostan ; and Hottinger's Historia Persarum.

his reformation were, in a high degree, conformable. Hence his condemnation of two independent principles, and his assertion, that the supreme God was the universal creator of both good and evil. This dogma he evidently borrowed from the doctrine of Isaiah, which that sublime prophet introduces in such a manner as to prove, that it was particularly designed to rouse the attention of the eastern nations, and more especially Persia, to this important truth. The statement of the principle is in a prophecy relating to Cyrus the Great, the most renowned and powerful monarch, that ever filled the Persian throne: " I am the Lord, and there is none else; I form the light and create darkness ; I make peace and create evil ; I the Lord do all these things."*

This radical principle of true religion Zoroaster inculcates clearly and strongly. And in other subordinate particulars of his scheme, we find a conformity to that of Moses, too close to be accounted for, except on the supposition of a deliberate imitation. Thus, as Moses heard God speaking from the fire, Zoroaster pretended to do the same. As the Jews had their Scheckinah, or special presence of God, resting on the mercy-seat, so Zoroaster taught the magians to regard the sacred fires in their temples as emblems of the divine presence. As the Jews had frequently received fire from heaven to consume their sacrifices, Zoroaster pretended to the same. As the Jewish priests were of one tribe, so were those of the Persian prophet. As the former were supported by tithes and offerings, so were the latter. Many of the distinctions between things clean and unclean are preserved in the religious code of Zoroaster. His doctrine and religion he delivers as the doctrine and religion of Abraham ; so that his innovations had clearly for their object the bringing back of the magian religion to the purity, which it had originally derived from the instructions of that illustrious patriarch.

Some idea may be formed of the wide as well as the puri-

* Is. xlv. 5–7.

fying influence of this comparatively uncorrupted faith, obtained by Zoroaster from the books of Moses, from the extent to which the magian religion prevailed. We learn from Lucian, that, in his time, which was soon after the promulgation of the gospel, it was received by the Persians, the Parthians, the Bactians, the Arians, the Sacans, the Medes, and various other eastern nations. And even to this day, its doctrines are held by a large sect both in Persia and India; who, says Prideaux, worship in his language, practice his rites, and preserve his book with the highest reverence, as the sole rule both of their faith and manners.

So much for the influence of Moses and his writings on the religion of the ancient world. Let us now inquire into the extent of that influence on letters. That both ancient and modern literature is indebted to the Hebrew scriptures for many of its choicest beauties, is an opinion, which has been very generally entertained by the learned. In support of this opinion, we have the concurrent testimony of Jewish authors, christian fathers, pagan writers, and modern critics.

Aristobulus, an Alexandrian Jew, who lived about two hundred years after Plato, is said to have written a commentary on the books of Moses. This work is now lost, but some fragments of it are extant in Clemens[*] Alexandrinus and Eusebius.[†] Of Plato this Jewish author says : " He followed our institutes closely, and diligently examined the several parts thereof." Of Pythagoras he observes : " He translated many things out of our discipline into the opinions of his own sect."[‡] Josephus[§] likewise affirms, that " Pythagoras not only understood the Jewish discipline, but embraced many things therein contained."

---

[*] Strom. 1.   [†] Praep. Evang. L. 9. C. 6.

[‡] See Gale's Court of the Gentiles, B. 1. C. 2. Also Selden de Jure Nat. Hebr. L. 1. C. 2. It is due to truth to say, that Prideaux has thrown much doubt upon the genuineness of this commentary of Aristobulus, Pt. 2. B. 1.

[§] Contra Ap. L. 1.

The primitive christians strongly insisted on this point in their arguments and apologies for the christian religion. Thus Tertullian:* "I am fully persuaded, that holy writ is the treasury of all following wisdom. Which of the poets, which of the sophists is there, who did not drink altogether of the prophets' fountain? Thence also the philosophers quenched their thirst; so that what they had from our scriptures, that we receive back from them." Again Tertullian† observes: "The philosopher Menedemus, who was a great patron of the opinion of divine providence, admired that which the seventy related, and was in this point of the same opinion." Clemens Alexandrinus‡ styles Plato "the Hebrew philosopher," and again and again asserts, that "the Greeks stole their chief opinions out of the books of Moses and the prophets." Justin Martyr§ affirms concerning Plato: "He drew many things from the Hebrew fountains, especially his pious conceptions of God and his worship."‖ The same is declared by Augustin.¶

The testimony of pagan philosophers, critics, and historians is to the same effect. Hermippus,** a disciple and biographer of Pythagoras, says, that his master "transferred many things out of the Jewish institutions into his own philosophy." On this account he styles him "the imitator of the Jewish dogmas." Hence Grotius†† says: "According to the testimony of Hermippus, Pythagorean lived among the Jews." Numenius,‡‡ a Greek philosopher of the Pythagorean school, speaking of Plato, exclaims: "What is Plato, but Moses atticising?" Gale, in his Court of the Gentiles, has gone into an extended examination of the sentiments of Plato concerning God, his nature and worship, the production of the universe,

---

* Apol. C. 47.   † Apol. C. 18.   ‡ Strom. 1.   § Apol. 2.
‖ See Gale's Court of the Gentiles, B. 1. C. 2.
¶ De Civitat. Dei, L. 8. C. 11.
** See Ibid. Also Selden de Jur. Nat. Hebr. L. 1. C. 2.
†† Votum. p. 124.   ‡‡ In Gale, B. 1. C. 2.

the fall of man, &c. &c. In this review, he has pointed out many striking analogies between the opinions of that philosopher and the doctrines of holy scripture. The reader is referred, for full satisfaction, to the work itself; a few instances, as a specimen, follow. In his Phaedo, he speaks of a "divine word," transmitting to us a knowledge of the soul's immortality; where the allusion is probably to a scriptural tradition. In his Philebus, he says: "The knowledge of the one infinite being was from the gods, who communicated this knowledge to us by a certain Prometheus, together with a bright fire." Who can doubt the reference here to those original divine communications made to the patriarchs, and to the Scheckinah, that fiery symbol of the divine presence? Not less plain is the allusion, in Plato's first or self-existent being, to the sublime declaration of Jehovah,* "I am that I am."† In his Timaeus, Plato says: "After the father of the universe had beheld his workmanship, he was delighted therein." How indubitably does this flow from the divine record,‡ "And God saw every thing that he had made, and behold, it was very good."

Plato's way appears to have been to disguise what he received from the Jewish fountain, under the form of parable and allegory. Origen§ suggests the reason of this. "It was the custom of Plato," he says, "to hide his choicest opinions, under the figure of some fable, because of the vulgar sort, lest he should too much displease the fabulous people by making mention of the Jews, who were so infamous amongst them."‖ Plato himself owns as much in saying, that "what

* Ex. iii. 14.
† See August. de Civit. Dei. L. 8. C. 11, with Lud. Vives's Notes.
‡ Gen. i. 31.   § Cont. Cels. L. 4.
‖ Serranus, a learned French protestant divine, in his preface to Plato's works, assigns the same cause for his silence respecting the Jews. "These symbols," he observes, "Plato drew from the doctrine of the Jews, as all the learned early Christians assert; but he industriously abstained from making any mention of the Jews, because their name was odious among all nations."

the Greeks receive from the barbarians, they put into a better form or garb." Besides, there is little doubt, that Plato does, in point of fact, make distinct references to the Jews, under other names, as Phenicians, Syrians, Egyptians, Chaldeans, and Barbarians.*

Clearchus, a distinguished disciple of Aristotle, in a book now lost, but cited by Josephus,† says, that he had heard his master speak of a certain Jew, with whom, when he resided in Asia,, he had held frequent conversations. This person, Aristotle described as a man of wonderful learning, wisdom, temperance, and goodness; and said, that he [Aristotle] had received more knowledge from him, than he had been able to impart in return. A remarkable proof of Aristotle's acquaintance with the Mosaic law is adduced out of Arrian‡ by Prideaux.§ It is well known, that this philosopher had been the tutor of Alexander the Great. When Alexander went into winter-quarters, in Asia Minor, he ordered all the soldiers of his army, who had married that year, to return into Macedonia, spend the winter with their wives, and come back to him in the spring. This agrees with the Jewish law,‖ but not with the usages of any other nation known in history. Does it not afford probable ground for the conjecture, that Aristotle learned it from the Jew, with whom he so much conversed while in Asia, and that, approving it as an equitable usage, he had made it known to Alexander, while acting as his preceptor, who was thence induced to put it in practice upon this occasion?

That the Grecian critics were acquainted with the writings of Moses, is certain from the fact, that we find Longinus, in his treatise on the Sublime,¶ drawing from them in illustration of his subject. The same is true of the historians.

---

* See in confirmation of this many authorities in Gale, B. 1. C. 2.
† Con. Ap. L. 1.   ‡ Lib. 1.   § Connex. Vol. 1. p. 366.
‖ Deut. xxiv. 5.   ¶ Lect. 8.

Strabo* makes honorable mention of Moses as a lawgiver; and Diodorus Siculus† acknowledges him to be the first of legislators, from whom all laws had their origin.‡

Among distinguished modern critics and divines, who have held the opinion, that profane literature is greatly indebted to the sacred scriptures, may be mentioned Ludovicus Vives, the Scaligers, Grotius, Bochart, Selden, Usher, Cudworth, Stillingfleet, Witsius, Magee, and a host of others, of scarcely inferior note. Most of these authorities are cited in different parts of Gale's Court of the Gentiles. It would occupy more space than can be spared for such a purpose to introduce extracts from them all here. Let one or two suffice. Bochart's§ testimony is in these words: "Whatsoever was most ancient among the heathen, the same was fetched or wrested from our scriptures." Grotius‖ expresses his opinion thus: "That which the ancient philosophers drew from the theology of the Phenicians, and the poets from them, the Phenicians drew from the Hebrews." That the Phenicians were identical with the ancient Canaanites; that they were well acquainted with the Jewish doctrine and traditions; that, by reason of their devotion to navigation and commerce, they spread these ideas all along the shores of the Mediterranean sea, in Asia Minor, Greece, Italy, Spain, Africa, and numerous islands; and that the Jews themselves were known to other nations, under the names of Phenicians, Syrians, Assyrians, &c., has been proved at large by learned men.¶

The intellectual qualities and achievements of the Hebrew race were such as naturally to give them a commanding power and influence. The sublimity, splendor, and force of

* Lib. 16.   † Biblioth. Lib. 1.
‡ See Gale, B. 1, B. 2.   B. 3, C. 9.   § Phaleg. L. 1, C. 1.
‖ On Mat. xxiv. 38.

¶ See Boch. Phaleg. Lib. 4, C. 34; also his Canaan, Pref. and Bks. 1 and 2. Gale's Court of the Gentiles, B. 1, Chaps. 3–12. Josephus con. Ap. L. 1. Euseb. Prep. Ev. L. 1. Voss. de Hist. Graec. L. 3, C. 16.

the Hebrew genius have never been surpassed. In history, in statesmanship, in military renown, in poetry, in eloquence, in music, in architecture, in legislation, and in the true philosophy of life, the annals of Judea furnish names, illustrious beyond those of most other nations. As historians, Tacitus and Thucydides must yield the palm to Moses and the author of Samuel. Of how many important and interesting points of historical inquiry would the world be ignorant without the Pentateuch! Moses was the father of history. His power of condensation has never been surpassed. The first few chapters of Genesis furnish a connected history of two thousand of the earliest years of time. Unlike other ancient historians, Moses has no fabulous ages. There is, in his clear, consistent, and unmatched pages, no uncertainty, no fable, no conjecture, no chasm. In the writings of all other early historical inquirers, the first ages of mankind are like a distant ocean, whose troubled waters are overspread with shadows, clouds, and darkness; but the Mosaic history, to borrow the elegant simile of Bryant, is like a bright but remote object, seen through the glass of an excellent optician, clear, distinct, and well defined. The historic record of Moses is a treasure above the price of rubies. By its sure, serene, and steady light, we are conducted, through the long night of ages, back to the very threshold of creation, and placed beside the first human pair, in the garden of Eden. As military commanders, Joshua, David, and the Maccabees will compare favorably with the great captains of antiquity. Among legislators and statesmen, where shall we meet with higher civil qualities than those which gave such lustre to the names of Joseph, Moses, Samuel, David, Solomon, Daniel, Ezra, and Nehemiah? The music of the temple service, as arranged by David and Asaph, has never been surpassed in sublimity and richness. The architecture of the temple and palace of Solomon, as has been shown by learned men, was imitated by the most polished nations of antiquity.

Its influence has been traced in those elegant structures, whose very ruins attest the fine architectural taste and genius of the Greeks. Socrates, Cicero, and Seneca, the brightest names in the philosophic annals of Greece and Rome, pale before the sublime and sententious ethical wisdom of Solomon. Demosthenes is matched, if not overmatched, in oratory, both by the prophet, whose lips were touched with a living coal from the altar, and by the great apostle to the gentiles. In the higher walks of poetry, Homer, Milton, and Shakespeare are inferior to Isaiah and the author of the book of Job. In lyrics, Pindar and Sappho must yield the supremacy to Moses and David. "Compare the book of Psalms with the Odes of Horace and Anacreon, with the hymns of Callimachus, the golden verses of Pythagoras, and the choruses of the Greek tragedians; and you will quickly see how greatly it surpasses them all in piety of sentiment, in sublimity of expression, in purity of morals, and in rational theology."[*] Indeed, the lyrical compositions of the royal poet are marked by a depth of feeling, a strength of thought, a brilliancy of genius, a chasteness of diction, and a purity of taste, not surpassed by any writer in any nation or age of the world. In pastorals, Virgil and Theocritus are more than equalled by Solomon. In elegy, David is the superior of Bion and Moschus. The whole range of elegiac poetry offers nothing that can be compared with his sublime and exquisite lament over the death of Saul and Jonathan.[†] In deep and breathing pathos, Jeremiah distances all competitors, whether among ancient or modern bards. The sacred scriptures throughout are distinguished by a sublimity of genius, a vigor of conception, a wealth of thought, a splendor of imagery, and a grace and beauty of style, which give to the bible, though much of it was written in a comparatively rude age, an elevation and an excellence, which do not belong to the most admired productions of the human mind,

* Bp. Watson in Smith's Heb. Peop. p. 183.   † 2 Sam. i. 19–27.

in the most advanced and cultivated condition of human society. And the age of Pericles in Greece, of Augustus in Rome, of queen Anne in Britain, of Louis XIV. in France, and of the Medici in Italy, all have their counterpart, if not, indeed, their remote origin, in the brilliant reign of a Hebrew prince, whose renown for wisdom is not bounded even by the limits of civilization, but has penetrated the dark mass of barbarian rudeness and ignorance.

It would be strange, indeed, if a book so comprehensive, so weighty, so perfect, and so wonderful, as the bible, had had no influence on human thought and learning. In point of fact, its influence has been most penetrating and diffusive.

That the greater part of the myths, which make up the ancient pagan theology, were but corrupt imitations of scripture histories, has been abundantly demonstrated by learned men, as Selden, Bochart, Vossius, the Scaligers, Maimonides, and various of the Christian fathers. These authorities will be found cited at length by Gale in the second book of his Court of the Gentiles, and by Stillingfleet in the fifth chapter of the third book of his Origines Sacrae, to which the reader is referred for full satisfaction. From the remarkable correspondence of the heathen mythology with the scriptures, it is manifest, that the former is but a corruption of the latter. This is so plain and certain, that no one who has studied the subject will hesitate to assent to the remark of Bochart: "The agreement is so wonderful, that even to the blind it will appear, that the ancient framers of fables borrowed many things from the sacred writers."

That poetry was the earliest form of literature, is asserted by Strabo,* and proved by Vossius.† The early pagan bards were much indebted to the poetry of the scriptures. Linus, Orpheus, Homer and Hesiod, as well as others who followed them, drew copiously from the waters of the sanctuary

---

* Lib. 1.   † De Hist. Graec. Lib. 1, C. 1

Phenicia and Egypt were their preceptors; and these had both been under the tuition of Israel in the best part of their learning.* Some suppose Linus, the earliest of the Greek poets, to have been a Phenician by birth,† and to have flourished about the time of the expulsion of the Canaanites by the Hebrews under Joshua. If so, he must have known the wonders wrought by divine power in behalf of the chosen people, and the sublime doctrines of the Jewish lawgiver concerning the power and providence of Jehovah. The few fragments of his poems which remain, appear to have flowed from this sacred fountain. "It is easy," he says, in a golden line still extant, "for God to achieve all things; and with him nothing is impossible." Steuchus Eugubinus has drawn an elaborate parallel between the Mosaic and Orphic theology; in which he has shown the traduction of the latter from the former. According to him, the first part of the theology of Orpheus consisted in praises of the creator. The second treats of chaos, the formation of man out of the earth, the infusion of the rational soul by his maker, &c. &c. These and other topics are clearly derived from the Mosaic history, though they are overlaid with a veil of allegory, in which the lively imagination of the Greeks so much delighted. Justin Martyr‡ has preserved a fragment of Orpheus, wherein there appears to be something of the history of Abraham and the tables of the decalogue. Artapanus is cited by Eusebius,§ affirming that Moses was called by the Greeks Musaeus, and that he was the teacher of Orpheus. Upon this Witsius‖ observes, that it is not necessary to suppose Orpheus contemporary with Moses; but that the meaning of Artapanus is, that for whatever there is just and true in his theology, he is

* See on this subject Gale, B. 3, C.1; and Wits. Aegypt. L. 2, C. 14.

† "Linum a Phoenice venisse tradunt veteres." Wits. Aegypt. L. 2, C. 14.

‡ Cited by Gale, B. 3, C. 1.

§ Praep. Evan. L. 9, C. 27.   ‖ Aegyptiaca, L. 2, C. 14.

indebted to Moses. Witsius* is further of the opinion, that Moses is expressly mentioned and praised by Orpheus, under the epithet ὑδογενὴς, i. e. born of or produced by water, in allusion to his being taken out of the water by Pharaoh's daughter.† Homer, the prince of Grecian poets, was cotemporary with Isaiah,‡ or flourished only a short time before him. That he visited Egypt, and spent some time there, is an opinion, commonly entertained by the learned.§ Some even think, that Egypt was his native country.‖ Sir Walter Raleigh¶ was of the opinion, that he derived not a few of his fictions from scripture traditions, which he gathered up in Egypt. This he infers from the affinity of many of his expressions to scripture language; and he believes him not unacquainted with the books of Moses. Eugubinus likewise speaks of a "manifest concord" between the sublimity and religious rites of Homer and those of sacred scripture. The same general position as to indebtedness to the Hebrew sources seems true of Hesiod, his entire theogony being, apparently, but a corrupt imitation of sacred persons, actions, and stories.**

Nor was the obligation of pagan history to the Hebrew scriptures less than that of pagan poetry. One great design of Eusebius, in his Chronicon, is to demonstrate the high antiquity of the divine records, and the derivation of much of the matter of profane historians from the Hebrew writers; and this design has been learnedly and successfully carried on in modern times by Joseph Scaliger, Vossius, Bochart, Grotius, Witsius, Gale, and others. The scriptures contain a series of historical records of priceless worth. Half the ages of the world would be shrouded in impenetrable darkness,

---

* Aegyptiaca, L. 2, C. 14.   † Ex. ii. 10.

‡ Carion Chron. L. 2, in Gale, B. 3, C. 1.

§ See Grotius on Mat. x. 28, and Gale, B. 3, C. 1.

‖ Sanford Descens. L. 2, in Gale, B. 3, C. 1.

¶ Hist. Pt. 1, B. 1, C. 6.   ** Carion Chron. L. 2. Gale. B. 3. C. 1.

but for the light cast upon them by these venerable writings. The creation of the material universe, the formation, trial, and fall of man, the promise of a savior, the patriarchal age, the deluge, the foundation and settlement of the new world, the confusion of languages, the division of men into several communities, their dispersion into the various regions of the globe, the history of the earliest monarchies of earth, the call of Abraham, the selection of a particular nation to be the chosen people of God, their descent into Egypt, their residence there, their exodus out of the house of bondage, their establishment into a commonwealth, the momentous events of their subsequent history, the overthrow of their state, the progress and decline of Canaan, Persia, and Media,—all this, and much more, would, without the Hebrew scriptures, either be wholly lost to mankind, or buried in the mists of tradition and fable.

In regard to all these points, and many others, profane historians have drawn much of their matter from Hebrew sources, either directly, or through the Chaldeans, the Egyptians, and especially the Phenicians. If any one doubts this, let him read the 4th chapter of the 2nd book of Witsius's Aegyptiaca, the 3rd chapter of the 3rd book of Stillingfleet's Origines Sacrae, and chaps. 2–8 of the 3rd book of Gale's Court of the Gentiles. He will find there such an array of proofs, as must convince the most incredulous. There is scarcely any part of the sacred record, which, in a form more or less corrupted, has not found its way into the pages of profane story. Gentile writers, both Greek and barbarian, abound with references to the origin of the world, its creation by the power of God, its primitive chaos, its subsequent order and beauty, the production of light, the formation of man out of the dust of the ground, the infusion of the rational soul, man's creation in the image of God, the paradisiacal state, the fall, the tree of life, the depravation of man's will and affections, the flood, the dove and raven of Noah, the

tower of Babel, the golden calf, the supply of water in the
wilderness, &c. &c. It would detain us too long to exhibit
the proof of all this in detail. Let a few specimens suffice.
Moses affirms, that the world had a beginning.* This
all the poets, philosophers, and historians, who flourished
before the time of Aristotle, with one spirit and voice, as
Lactantius says, attest; and none more fully than Plato.
It was the common opinion of Greeks, Egyptians, Indians,
and the gentile nations generally; derived, beyond a doubt,
from the original fountain of divine revelation. Aristotle
was the first of the philosophers, who taught the eternity of
the world. To this he was impelled by a proud spirit of
speculation, a vain fondness of philosophizing, that made
him reject all traditions, which he could not bend to his own
reason.†
Moses makes God the creator of the world.‡ In like manner heathen writers ascribe the origin of the world to a real
divine efficience.§ Plato, in divers of his works,‖ speaks of
the supreme cause; of the cause of causes; of natural things
as not springing up of themselves, but as being the products
of God's workmanship; of its being unworthy of a philosopher to treat only of second causes, and leave out God, who
was the first and chief cause; of a first beauty, which is the
cause of all the rest; and of one supreme idea of good
(God), which gives being, virtue, and essence to all things
else, eternal in duration, infinite in power, and independent
in working. Homer says: "By Jove's nod the earth existed, and whatsoever the earth brings forth; the sea existed,
and whatsoever the sea produces; the air existed, and whatsoever the air sustains; the heavens existed, and whatsoever

* Gen. i. 1.
† See the authorities in proof of these positions in the Aegyptiaca of
Witsius, B. 2. C. 14, and in Gale, B. 3. C. 3.
‡ Gen. i. 1.   § See Wits. & Gale, as above.
‖ As in his Phaed. Tim. Theaetet. Soph. & Repub.

moveth in the heavens. All these works are wrought by the nod (i. e. the will) of Jove." Maximus Tyrius * discourses most elegantly and eloquently concerning God, representing him as the maker of all things by the simple exertion of his will. He speaks of him as the being, who marshalled the host of heaven, who guides the sun, moon, and stars in their orbits, who determines their rising and their setting, who distinguishes times and seasons, who governs the winds, who formed the sea and the earth, who pours out the rivers, who draws forth the fruits, who produces the tribes of animals, and, in fine, whose mind, simple, uncompounded, and incorruptible, is in no respect divided, but with incredible velocity, with a mere glance of the eye, adorns and makes glorious whatever it touches. From what fountain could these sublime and noble ideas of the divine power and providence be drawn, if not from scripture history or tradition? They are certainly emanations of celestial light.

The order of the creation, as narrated by Moses, is imitated by pagan writers. According to the Mosaic account, the heaven and the earth were the beginning of the creation; according to Plato, fire and earth were the elementary principles of things. What Moses calls *tohoo bohoo*, emptiness and confusion, the poets call chaos, a confused and shapeless mass. Moses represents a universal darkness as originally overspreading all things; Thales, the philosopher, taught that darkness preceded light. Moses speaks of the earth as originally surrounded by water ;† Thales, again, says that water was the first principle of things, and that God was that spirit that formed all things out of water.‡

Moses speaks of the spirit of God as moving, literally " brooding," upon the waters. The word expresses the tremulous motion of the hen, while hatching her eggs, and suggests the idea of incubation. This undoubtedly gave rise to the notion, so widely prevalent among the ancients, that the

* Dissert. 25.   † Gen. i. 2.   ‡ Cic. de Nat. Deor. L. 1. C. 10.

world was generated from an egg. The affinity of the Mosaic and pagan histories, and the derivation of the one from the other, are here apparent to every one, on the slightest inspection.* The Mosaic account of the creation, indistinctly understood, is, manifestly, the germ of all the above cited opinions.

Anaxagoras,† who was the first of the philosophers to teach distinctly the separate existence of one supreme and all-directing mind, spoke of the material world as originating from a chaotic mass, consisting of different kinds of particles, which afterwards combined in homogeneous masses; "an opinion," observes Dr. Graves,‡ "so similar to that of the Mosaic records, that we can scarcely doubt but that it was from them derived."

Moses states, that man was formed out of the dust of the ground.§ Numerous are the vestiges of this fact in pagan authors. By Sanchoniathon,‖ the oldest of profane historians, man is said to have sprung out of the earth. It is probable, that Plato alludes to this, when he mentions a Phenician fable touching the brotherhood of mankind, as having all had a common extraction out of the earth.¶ Socrates, Zeno, and Plato concur in affirming, that the genesis of men was from the earth.** The latter of these writers takes pains to say, that this ancient tradition, as he styles it, is worthy of all credit.

Moses affirms the direct infusion by the Deity of the rational soul into man.†† Herein also he is imitated by profane writers. Sanchoniathon, according to the version of Philo Byblius, states the same fact, in almost the same words. Orpheus says, that man was framed by God himself out of

* Wits. Aegypt. L. 2. C. 14.
† See Bruck. Hist. Philos. L. 2. C. 1. Sect. 20.
‡ On the Pent. Pt. 3. Lect. 5. Sect. 2.
§ Gen. ii. 7.   ‖ Gale, B. 3. C. 4.   ¶ In Gale, B. 3. C. 4.
** See the citations in Wits. Aeg. L. 2. C. 15.   †† Gen. ii. 7.

the earth, and received from him a rational soul.* Epichar-
mus, in Plutarch, teaches, that the soul came from God, and
was by him breathed into man. He adds, that at death each
part goes whence it had come, the earth returns to earth, and
the spirit ascends to God.† Grotius produces a like sentiment out of Euripides.

In the Mosaic history it is said, that God created man in
his own image.‡ Profane history has copied this. Plato, in
his Critias, affirms, that in the first men there was a portion
of God, a divine nature, which he denominates the old
nature.§ In his Republic,‖ he places the likeness to the
Deity in the soul, and indeed in the wisdom and probity of
the soul. In his Theaetetus, again, he makes the image of
God to consist in justice, holiness, and prudence.¶ In the
above instances, how admirable the correspondence between
sacred and profane story! In those which follow, the agreement is not less striking.

Moses relates that man, formed in the image of God, was
placed in Eden,** a garden of pleasures, where all was beauty, melody, serenity, fragrance, and delight. This blissful
state of man in paradise has been celebrated by heathen
poets, philosophers, and historians, under the name of the
golden age. Particular citations are here unnecessary.
Allusions to this happy period, and descriptions of it, pervade
the literature of pagan nations. Their writers kindle and
glow under the inspiring theme. They represent this primitive state of man as a state of unmingled happiness.
Innocence, peace, and joy are constant inhabitants of his
soul. External nature is in harmony with his pure mind.
Here are no pinching frosts, no burning heats, no stubborn
soil, no blasting winds, no devouring beasts, no thorns, weeds,
or brambles. Perpetual spring reigned. No labor of agri-

* Gale, B. 3. C. 4.   † Wits. L. 2. C. 15.   ‡ Gen. i. 27.
§ Gale, B. 3. C. 4.   ‖ Lib. 10.   ¶ Wits. Aeg. L. 2. C. 15.
** Gen. ii. 8.

culture was necessary. The unploughed earth yielded its delicious fruits. The gentle breezes fanned the spontaneous flowers. The rivers flowed with milk and nectar, and honey distilled from the rock. From the Mosaic paradise, without doubt, the ancient heathens borrowed their ideas of the gardens of the Hesperides, where the trees bore golden fruit; and probably also of the gardens of Adonis, a name which seems evidently derived from Aden or Eden.* The famed Elysian fields of the ancient mythology, with their glow of purple light, and their perpetual verdure and serenity, are a manifest, though corrupt imitation of the garden of Eden. This was the opinion of the great Bochart,† who derives the word Elysius from the Hebrew " alis,"—joyful,—by the not unusual change of a into e. Thus it appears, that the Elysian field signifies a place of delight or joy, a meaning entirely coincident with that of Eden, the garden of pleasure. How exactly do these heathen descriptions of the golden age, the Hesperian gardens, and the Elysian fields, reflect the beautiful and splendid images, which form the picture of the paradisiacal state.

Moses states concerning our first parents, that they were naked.‡ Plato, in his Politicus, speaks of men in the golden age as living in the open air, naked and uncovered. Moses mentions the conversation between the serpent and Eve.§ Plato speaks of men in the primitive times holding converse with beasts. The tree of life figures conspicuously in the Mosaic history.‖ There can be little doubt, that the ambrosia of the ancients, which made immortal, and their nectar, which made young, were but obscure and broken traditions of the tree of life. The temptation of Eve by an evil spirit, under the form of the serpent, is recorded by Moses.¶ Stillingfleet, in the 3rd book of his Origines Sacrae,

---

* See Gale's C. of G. B. 3. C. 4; Stillingf. Orig. Sac. B. 3. C. 3; and A. Clarke in loc.   † Can. L. i. C. 34.   ‡ Gen. ii. 25.
§ Gen. iii. 1.   ‖ Gen. ii. 9, iii. 22, 24.   ¶ Gen. iii. 1.

has shown, that there is an allusion to this story in Pherecydes Syrius's account of the war of the giants against Saturn. The reference is so manifest, that Celsus, the early antagonist of christianity, grounds upon it an argument to prove, that Moses corrupted and altered the heathen fables, for the purpose of framing his own history out of them.

The fall of man is narrated at length by Moses.* In his Critias, Plato, after discoursing of the "divine nature," which belonged to man in the golden age, adds : "This divine nature, being at length contempered with the mortal part in man, the human inclination or custom prevailed, even to the pestilential infection and ruin of mankind ; and from this fountain all evils rushed in upon men, who thereby lost the best of their precious things." To the like effect he discourses in his Theaetetus, declaring that man fell from his original rectitude, or likeness to God, into a kind of nothingness and inhumanity.† Whence could Plato derive such scriptural notions, if not from scripture itself, or at least from scriptural traditions? Origen does not doubt, that his opinions came from this source. He conceives, that Plato learned the history of man's fall from his intercourse with the Jews in Egypt, and that he describes it under an allegorical form in his symposiacs. Porus (Adam), feasting with the rest of the gods, and becoming drunk with nectar, goes into Jupiter's garden (Eden), and there is circumvented and led into sin by Penia (the serpent).‡

This parallel between sacred and profane history, as it respects the subject-matter of both, might be greatly extended, whereby it would yet more clearly appear, to what an extent the latter has borrowed its materials from the former. With these brief illustrations of the subject, however, the reader must be left to pursue the investigation for himself.

Chronology and geography have been, not improperly,

* Gen. iii.　　†Literally, manlessness, want of manhood.
‡ See Stillingf. Orig. Sac. B. 3, C. 3, and Gale B. 3, C. 5.

denominated the two eyes of history. Certainly, nothing is more essential to clear and correct historical knowledge, than that the events lie before us, in their due order of time, and their proper locality. In both these respects, the obligations of profane to sacred history can hardly be overestimated.

Ancient chronology, without the bible, would be involved in inextricable confusion. Chronological inconsistencies abound in the most authentic historians of antiquity. Sir Isaac Newton, by applying his powerful mind to the study of the scriptures, has detected great errors in the chronology of the ancients. It is only by a rigid adherence to the scriptural standard of dates and eras, as Dr. Hale* has well said, that the historical inquirer can hope to avoid the mazes, the deserts, and the quicksands of ancient and primeval chronology, in which so many adventurers have been swallowed up and lost, by following the ignus fatuus of their own imagination, or the treacherous glare of hypotheses. That the scriptural account of times is the fountain and measure of pagan chronology, has been evinced by Eusebius, Bochart, Melancthon, Preston, and others. Bochart affirms the derivation of the Chaldean chronology from the sacred annals of the Hebrews. He proves his assertion thus. Simplicius, the ablest of the ancient commentators on Aristotle, mentions a work of that philosopher, in which he states, that he had received from his pupil Alexander the records of the Chaldeans, on examining which he found, that the series of times extended through so many years; which, says Bochart, answers to the scripture account of times. One great design of Eusebius, in his Chronicon, was to prove the traduction of ethnic from sacred chronology. Melancthon speaks of it as "the singular glory of the church, that nowhere, in the whole mass of mankind, there can be found a more ancient series of empires and times; neither has any other nation such certain numbers of years passed, so exactly computed." But none have spoken

* New Analysis of Chronology.

more clearly on this point than Preston, in his third Sermon on the Divine Attributes. "I will add to this," he says, "but one argument for the authority of the scripture. Consider the exact chronology which is found in the scriptures, and the agreement of them with the heathen histories. In latter times there have been great confusions; but the greatest evidence that is to be found, is the table of Ptolemy lately found, which doth exactly agree with the scripture. He exactly sets down the time, that Nebuchadnezzar and Cyrus reigned; so also the time when Jerusalem was taken; which compare with the scripture, and you shall find these agree with Daniel and Jeremiah. And this is the greatest testimony the scripture can have from heathen men."*

Geography is the other eye of history. There is ample proof, not only that scripture geography preceded pagan, but that the latter was, in great part, derived from the former. Porphyry, in his fourth book against the christians, informs us, that Sanchoniathon gave an account of places conformable to that of Moses. A chief design of Bochart, in his Phaleg, is to evince the traduction of profane from sacred geography. He shows, that from Japhet (Gen. 10 : 2.) the Grecians referred their first plantations to Japetus; that from Javan (Gen. 10 : 2.) they derived their Ionians; that from Elisa (Gen. 10 : 4.) they derived their Elis and Hellas; that from Kittim they named a city in Cyprus Citium; and that from Tarsis (Gen. 10 : 4.) came Iberis, or Spain. Many other instances he gives to the same effect; particularly that from Misraim and Ludim, father and son, (Gen. 10 : 13.) Egypt and Ethiopia were originally called by those names. Conformably to this, Diodorus * speaks of the friendly intercourse kept up between the Egyptians and Ethiopians, and infers from it their near relationship. In this manner has this learned man and distinguished geographer demonstrated the identity of sacred and ethnic geography. In the preface to

* Gale's Court of the Gentiles, B. 3. C. 2.   † Lib. 3.

his Canaan, he gives his opinion very explicitly thus : " Moses, by divine revelation, approved himself more skilful in geography, than either Homer, or Hesiod, or any of later times among the Grecians. For he mentions more nations, and those more remote by far. Neither doth it suffice him to name them, but withal he opens their original ; showing us in what age, and from what place, and upon what occasion, each was dispersed into countries most remote, even from the Caspian and Persian seas to the extreme Gades ; and all this in one chapter." See further on this subject Gale's Court of the Gentiles, B. 3. C. 2, and Stillingfleet's Origines Sacrae, B. 3. c. 4 ; where it is shown, that sacred geography is not only the most ancient, exact, and certain, but also the fountain and measure of pagan geography.*

Having demonstrated the obligation of pagan religion, poetry, and history to the inspired oracles, I proceed to make manifest a like indebtedness on the part of pagan philosophy. This is a vast field, affording scope for an extended treatise in itself. A mere glance is all the attention that can be bestowed upon it in the present work.

The very term *sophoi*, wise men, philosophers, among the Greeks, Heinsius † deduces, without the least doubt of the truth of the etymology, from the Hebrew *sophim*, watchmen. He says, that both the Hebrews and the Phenicians, as well as the Greeks, called their learned men by this name, because they were accustomed to observe the motions of the heavenly bodies from elevated places.

But not to insist upon the etymology of a word, as of much weight in the argument, let us attend to other consid-

---

* "Moses is the only faithful guide in the history of the first peopling of countries. The tenth and eleventh chapters of Genesis diffuse more light on that subject, than all the writings of profane historians, which, on this head, are nothing but a heap of confusion, conjectures, and contradictions."

Gog. Orig. Laws, B. 1. c. 1. Art. 5.

† Exercit. Sacr. L. 1. C. 2.

erations. Three general circumstances may be mentioned, as affording strong presumptive evidence of the obligations of Grecian philosophy to the Hebrew scriptures.

The first circumstance, on which this conclusion rests, is the fact, that Egypt and Phenicia, themselves large recipients of the precious treasures of revelation, were, by common admission, the sources of Grecian culture and learning. Up to the period when the empire of Jerusalem was destroyed by Nebuchadnezzar, Europe had remained, to a great degree, sunk in barbarism and ignorance. At this time part of the Jewish nation was carried captive to Babylon, and another large portion took refuge in Egypt. These latter, after the restoration of their brethren by Cyrus, remained in their adopted country, where they built a temple, publicly exercised their religion, and flourished in such multitudes under Alexander and his successors, as almost to equal those of Judea in number, wealth, and influence. They even lost the use of the Hebrew, and adopted the Greek tongue,—a language, beyond all others, copious, expressive, and harmonious ;—qualities which caused it to become the universal dialect of learned men, both in the east and the west.

About the time of the Babylonish captivity, Greece began to emerge from the depths of ignorance and rudeness, in which her people had hitherto been sunk. A spirit of inquiry and research was awakened. Thales, Anaximander, Anaxagoras, Pherecydes, Pythagoras, Plato, Herodotus, and a host of other Grecian philosophers and historians, travelled into Egypt, Chaldea,* and Phenicia ; some of them residing in those countries for a long series of years. Here they became acquainted with the more cultivated and learned of the Jews ; saw their religion, and heard their conversations on the origin of the universe, on the power, sovereignty, spirituality and unity of the true God ; on the divine providence ; on moral

* See the Chron. Tables of Marshall, the Univ. Hist. and Bruck. Hist. Philos.

good and evil; on human duty; and on other topics, connected with religion and philosophy. It is not improbable
that some of them saw and read the sacred books of the
Hebrews, either in the original tongue, or the Greek translation,
made under Ptolemy Philadelphus.

The intercourse between Europe, Asia, and Egypt continued
to increase, and access to the sacred treasures of revelation
became more and more practicable and common. Mind was
stirred. Thought was developed. Inquiry became keen and
discursive. A thousand scattered rays, emanating originally
from the sacred volume, were concentrated, in a blaze of
light, on the little promontory of Attica. Literature, philosophy, and the fine arts spread rapidly over Greece, and were
cultivated with an ardor unknown in any other age or
country. Then did the Greeks, possessing the finest genius,
and blessed with the most delicious climate and picturesque
scenery, produce those immortal works in poetry, eloquence,
history, and philosophy, which have embalmed their memory;
which have become universal models of taste and composition; and which have constituted the solace and delight of
cultivated minds, in every age and nation of the world.

The second general circumstance, affording ground to infer
the derivation of pagan philosophy from sacred sources, is
the fact, that the earlier philosophers delivered their instructions, not in elaborate systems, which is the form they would
have taken, had they been the result of original thought and
investigation; but in pithy sayings and unconnected dogmas,
the very method they must have adopted, had they derived
their tenets from the broken fragments and records of Holy
Scripture.

The third circumstance is, that the higher we trace the
religious opinions of the philosophers, and the popular worship of Greece, the purer and more uncorrupted do we find
them. " The nearer we approach to the sources of eastern
tradition, the more conspicuous appears the radiance of that

heavenly light of original revelation, whose beams, though
clouded and dispersed, still contribute to enlighten and
direct mankind; the more clear traces do we discover of that
primeval and patriarchal religion, which acknowledged the
existence and inculcated the worship of the true and only
God. We find no mortals yet exalted to divinities, no images
in their temples, no impure or cruel rites."*

The testimonies of Jewish, pagan, and christian writers,
adduced in a former part of this chapter,† and the presumptive proofs here brought forward, are sufficient of themselves
to warrant the belief, that Greece, the parent of pagan letters
and arts, Greece, the common mistress and teacher of Europe,
owed the best part of her wisdom to Judea. But that which
affords incontestible proofs of this fact, is a comparison of
the maxims of her philosophers with the teachings of Holy
Scripture. This, however, is a labor too extensive for the
present work; and unless it is handled at length, it is better
not to touch it at all. Let the reader, who would see it fully
discussed, with all the authorities bearing upon it cited, consult the third book of the Aegyptiaca of Witsius, and the
whole of the second part of Gale's Court of the Gentiles. It
is quite possible, indeed, that it may never be fully known,
how far the Greeks and other heathen nations were indebted
to Moses and the prophets for their purest ethical doctrines,
their choicest poetic beauties, their finest rhetorical touches,
their loftiest flights of eloquence, their wisest maxims of
government, and their sublimest speculations concerning the
divine nature and human duty. Enough, however, is known
to afford solid ground for the opinion, that Judea was the
birth-place of letters, that her priests were men of learning,
that her Levitical cities were so many universities, that the
scholars of other countries lighted their torch in Zion, and

* Graves on the Pent. Pt. 3. Lect. 5, Sect. 2.
† Pp. 312 seqq.

that the altars of pagan philosophy caught their first spark
from the flame, that glowed within the temple of Jerusalem.*
It remains to trace the influence of the Mosaic legislation
on government and law in succeeding ages. Grotius, than
whom no man was more competent to express an opinion on
the subject, in his Truth of the Christian religion, says :
" The most ancient Attic laws, whence in after times the
Roman were derived, owe their origin to Moses's laws." He
expresses the same opinion in his treatise on the Right of
War and Peace : " Who may not believe, that, seeing the
law of Moses had such an express image of the divine will,
the nations did well in taking their laws thence ? Which
that the Grecians did, especially the Attics, is credible.
Whence the Attic laws and the Roman twelve tables, which
sprang thence, bear so much similitude with the Hebrew
laws." The similitude between the Grecian and Mosaic laws
has been noticed by many learned men besides Grotius ; as
Josephus, Clemens Alexandrinus, Augustin, Selden, Gale,
Cunaeus, Serranus, Sir Matthew Hale, and Archbishop Potter. This last mentioned writer, in his Grecian Antiquities,
has traced out many resemblances between the Greek and
Hebrew legislation. " The Athenians had a prescribed bill
of divorce, and so had the Jews. Among the Jews, the
father gave names to the children ; and such was the custom
among the Greeks. The purgation oath among the Greeks,
strongly resembled the oath of jealousy among the Hebrews.
The harvest and vintage festival among the Greeks, the presentation of the best of their flocks, and the offering of their
first fruits to God, together with the portion prescribed to the
priests, the interdiction against garments of divers colors,
protection from violence to the man who had fled to their
altars, would seem to indicate that the Greeks had cautiously
copied the usages of the Jews. And whence was it, that no
person was permitted to approach the altar of Diana, who

* Comp. Spring's Discs. on the Bib. pp. 41, 42.

had touched a dead body, or been exposed to other causes of impurity, and that the laws of Athens admitted no man to the priesthood, who had any blemish on his person, unless from the institutions of Moses? And has not the agrarian law of Lycurgus its prototype, though none of its defects, in the agrarian law of the Hebrews? Many of the Athenian laws in relation to the descent of property and the prohibited degrees of relationship in marriage, seem to have been transcribed by Solon from the laws of Moses. Sir Matthew Hale, in his history of the Common Law of England, affirms, ' that among the Grecians, the laws of descent resemble those of the Jews.' "* The law of the Areopagites against accidental manslaughter, which punished the offender with a year's banishment, is manifestly borrowed from the Mosaic law respecting the cities of refuge.†

That Plato's ideal republic was, in many of its principles, derived from the Hebrew constitution, is an opinion held by many, and, as would seem, on good grounds. His sacred college of conservators of the laws, composed of the principal priests, the elders of the people, venerable by age and virtue, and the chief magistrate as president, was a clear imitation of the Jewish sanhedrim. Not less clearly of Jewish origin was his law respecting the election and approval of priests, requiring that they be perfect and legitimate. From the same source, evidently, came his law excommunicating an offender, who had been guilty of striking his parent, and even forbidding any one to eat and drink with such a person, lest he should thereby be polluted. So manifest are the obligations of Plato to the Mosaic law, that Clemens Alexandrinus, apostrophizing him, exclaims, " But as for laws, whatever are true, as also for the opinion of God, these things were conveyed to thee from the Hebrews.‡

* Spring's Disc. on the Bib. pp. 94, 95.
† Petit de Legibus Atticis, in Gale, B. 3. c. 9.
‡ Gale, B. 3, C. 9.

If the Grecian laws can be traced to the Hebrew as their fountain-head, the Roman laws must, of necessity, confess a similar origin. The twelve tables, a work concerning which Cicero declares, that he prefers it alone to all the volumes of the philosophers, were confessedly borrowed from the Grecian legislation.

Through these channels, as well as more directly from the original fountain, the principles of the Mosaic code have found their way, to a less or greater extent, into the jurisprudence of all civilized nations. Sir Matthew Hale has traced the influence of the bible generally on the laws of England. Sismondi testifies, that Alfred the Great, in causing a republication of the Saxon laws, inserted several statutes taken from the code of Moses, to give new strength and cogency to the principles of morality. The same historian also states, that one of the first acts of the clergy, under Pepin and Charlemagne, was to improve the legislation of the Franks by the introduction of several of the Mosaic laws.* Dr. Olaus Rabenius, formerly professor of law and syndic of the university at Upsal, informed Michaelis,† that, until recently, the civil law of Moses had been a jus subsidiarum in Sweden, and that, although it is no longer cited in the courts, there necessarily remain, in the Swedish jurisprudence, many vestiges of its former authority. The civil institutions of the United States are pervaded with the spirit of the Mosaic legislation. Equality, liberty, general education, social order, peace, industry, union, and the reign of law are the sources of our prosperity and happiness. But these principles are the very heart of the Mosaic constitution. Upon the whole, the opinion of Milman, expressed in his History of the Jews, seems well considered and well founded, that the Hebrew lawgiver has exercised a more extensive and permanent influence over

---

* Spring's Obl. of the World to the Bib. p. 96.
† See Pref. to his Com. on the Laws of Moses.

the destinies of mankind, than any other individual in the annals of the world.

In a former part of this chapter I have spoken of the genius, taste, and literature of the ancient Hebrews. Will the reader pardon me for adding here, though it may not be exactly in place, that the page of history, science, art, and philosophy, is not unadorned with splendid Jewish names, that have figured since the canon of scripture was closed. Aben-Ezra, Abarbanel, Maimonides,—"the eagle of the synagogue,"—Buxtorf, Mendohlson, and Neander were men, of whom any nation might boast. The proudest glories of old Spain were in a great measure due to the talent, learning, and energy of the Hebrew race. Never did rulers make a greater mistake, than Ferdinand and Isabella, in expelling that people, one of the brightest jewels in their crown, from their dominions. Rarely has a sublimer moral spectacle been presented to the world, than that afforded by the departure, from every thing most dear to them, of so vast a multitude, in loyalty to the faith of their fathers. Spain had become to these people a second Palestine. Its charming climate, its fertile fields, and the unrivalled beauty of its landscapes, had caused them almost to forget their exile from the green vales and vine-clad hills of their revered fatherland. Yet, rather than renounce the religion, inherited from an illustrious line of ancestors, cheerfully, courageously, uncomplainingly, did they leave their quiet homes, their pleasant possessions, their hoarded treasures, and the sepulchres of their beloved dead,—the rich generously sharing their last dollar with the poorest of their brethren,—to seek a country, they knew not where ; to find a home, perchance, beneath the inhospitable billows, or on the more inhospitable shores, to which their shattered barks might be driven.

I cannot pass in silence a remarkable peculiarity in the fortunes of this remarkable people. While, under the pressure of causes far less, both in number and malignity, than those to which the Jewish people have been subjected, the descendants of other celebrated nations of antiquity have so degenerated, that we can scarcely recognize, in their present character, a single element of their ancestral greatness, the Israelites retain no inconsiderable portion of the genius, learning, skill, and enterprise of their remote progenitors. I cannot help sometimes picturing to myself what sort of nation they would form, if the scattered remnant of their tribes could once more be put in possession of their own country. They would carry there the liberal principles and indomitable energy of America, the commercial ability of England, the science of France, the learning of Germany, the arts of Italy, and the agricultural skill and industry of the dwellers along the shores of the Black Sea and in the fertile basins of the Danube and the Rhine. They retain, in their dispersion and after so many centuries of oppression, all the elements of greatness and of power, out of which to frame a model republic, and once again to become the light and glory of the world. Who knows whether providence has not some such splendid destiny in reserve for them? Surely, a preservation so signal cannot be without an ultimate object, equally remarkable. Would that the veil were removed from their hearts, and they could at length recognize, as one day they will assuredly recognize, in the pure and gentle Nazarene, their long expected Messiah! If the casting of them off be the riches of the gentiles, what shall the receiving of them be to the christian church but life from the dead ?

Why should a people, thus honored in their ancestry, their history, and their influence, be oppressed, enslaved, and maltreated by Christian nations? These live, as it were, upon the patrimony of Israel, and yet despise and revile the people, from whom they received their inheritance. Besides the rights of our common nature, which belong alike to all, the Israelite has a superadded claim to the consideration and gratitude of his fellow-men, arising from the lustre of his name, and from the unequalled benefits which his nation has conferred upon mankind. Yet in most countries of christen- dom he is denied the privileges, which are his birthright as a man. He is treated as if he had neither human rights nor human feelings. Ignorance, prejudice, and superstition sur- round him as with an adamantine wall of civil disabilities and social degradation. In Europe, in Africa, and in Asia I have myself seen him insulted and abused in a manner that caused the blood to tingle in my veins. Let us thank the God of Israel, that it is otherwise among us. Let us rejoice, that in this home of freedom and equality, persecution has never dis- turbed the descendants of the patriarchs in the peaceful retire- ment of their firesides, and that exclusion from political rights has not been practised towards them. Here Jew and Christian stand together upon the same platform of civil and social immunities. May we not hope, that, when Jehovah shall judge the nations, he will in mercy remember the land, which has afforded a refuge and a home to the sons of Jacob?

CHAPTER VIll.

Review of the leading Constitutions of Gentile Antiquity, with special reference to the Question, how far Civil Liberty was secured by them.*

THE obligation of mankind to the Hebrew legislation was considered in the last chapter. It cannot, however, be properly appreciated, without a brief inquiry of the kind proposed in the present chapter. A full analysis of even the leading constitutions of antiquity, would fill more of my space, than can be spared for such a purpose. A glance is all that can be attempted; but it will be sufficient to convince us, that nowhere, without the limits of Palestine, was there

---

* A great number of special references were prepared for this chapter; but, unfortunately, they have been mislaid and lost; and the authorities are not now before me for re-examination. Besides the more common ancient authors, as Aristotle, Plato, Xenophon, Plutarch, Herodotus, Thucydides, Ælian, Cicero, Livy, Tacitus, &c., the principal modern authorities consulted are Salvador's Histoire des Institutions de Moise et du Peuple Hébreu, Goguet on the Origin of Laws, Niebuhr's Roman History and Lectures, Adams's Defence of the Constitutions of Government of the United States of America, Montesquieu's Spirit of Laws, Potter's Grecian Antiquities, Puffendorf's Law of Nature and Nations, Barthelemy's Anacharsis, Heeren's Researches on Ancient Greece, Ferguson on the Roman Constitution, Gillie's Greece, and De Solme on the English Constitution. The last named of these works has been particularly useful to me in affording an insight into the structure and working of the Roman policy. I have borrowed much from him, sometimes using his very words, oftener condensing the substance of his observations.

to be found a rational, well poised and well guarded public freedom; and that all antiquity does not afford an example of a state, where the people enjoyed any just influence in the government, till we come to the Jewish republic. From the earliest ages, mankind have been, for the most part, governed by arbitrary power. Even where a seeming exemption from such rule has been secured by established laws, the laws themselves have been arbitrary and despotic; at one time extravagantly severe, at another as extravagantly indulgent, —the mere expression of individual authority and caprice. Thus, in every period of the world's history, the mass of human beings have been ruled either by arbitrary men or arbitrary laws.

This proposition, so far as it relates to oriental countries, needs no formal proof. Throughout the vast regions of Asia, despotism, absolute and unchecked, has been, at all times, the prevailing form of government. Dynasty has succeeded to dynasty, and empires have arisen upon the ruins of empires; but no change has elevated the people to a share in the government, or brought with it any improvement in their condition, except so far as such improvement has resulted from the character of the reigning sovereign. From Nimrod to Ninus, from Ninus to the subversion of the Persian empire by the victorious arms of Alexander, whenever the affairs of Asia rise to our view on the troubled bosom of history, some new scene of capricious or vindictive tyranny freezes us with horror, or fires us with indignation. An incident occurred in the history of Cambyses, which is a key to the polity of all the Asiatic nations. That prince wished to marry his sister, and consulted his ministers of justice on the lawfulness of the procedure. The interpreters of law could find no statute authorizing such an act, but they found one which permitted the kings of Persia to do whatever they pleased. What could the people be in a country where the sovereign, as was the case in Persia, kept sixteen thousand

and eight hundred horses for his private use ? Xerxes wrote
to mount Athos to get out of his way ; ordered the Helles-
pont to be scourged for daring to break in pieces his bridge
of boats ; and commanded, that the builders be put to death,
because their structure was unable to withstand the fury of
the tempest. Who but a tyrant, bereft of reason through the
intoxication of power, could have enacted such solemn pue-
rilities, such revolting atrocities ? Thus has it ever been in
the east. The many have been ground down into hopeless
degradation to pamper the pride of the few. Voluptuousness and luxury have reigned in the palaces of the nobles ;
poverty and wretchedness have deformed the hovels of the
peasants.

Leaving the countries watered by the Choaspes and the
Tigris, and directing our observation to that, which, by a happy metaphor, has been styled the gift of the Nile, we undoubtedly see a nation less devoted to war and conquest, and more
proficient in agriculture and the arts, as well as in civil polity
and law. Yet the people were equally without authority or
influence in the state. Of the despotism of Egypt, we need
no other proof, than her very ruins, those stupendous and imperishable monuments, whose stability rivals that of nature
herself. Under what other than a despotic government, could
have been constructed her pyramids, her temples, her palaces,
her lake Moeris, four hundred and fifty miles in circumference,
the sole product of human industry, and her mighty labyrinth,
before whose vastness and intricacy Herodotus stood confounded, and which, he assures us, must have cost more than
all the public monuments of Greece together. Where, but
under an iron despotism, could the revenues of a fishery,
amounting to more than a quarter of a million per annum,
have been appropriated to the ladies of the royal household
for the purchase of robes and perfumes ? The institution of
caste, or hereditary professions, which is of the essence of
despotic rule, prevailed in full rigor in Egypt. For the rest,

what sort of government was that, where the priests not only bound the conscience of the sovereign, but fettered genius by prescribing a model for every work of art; where involuntary accidents were punished as premeditated crimes; where theft was actually encouraged and rewarded by a contrivance of state; and where it was less dangerous to murder a man, than tó kill a cat, an ibis, a hawk, or an ichneumon,—the criminal, in this latter case, being invariably seized upon by the populacĕ and torn in pieces.

But not to detain the reader with these generalities, let us come to a closer study of the Egyptian institutions. The government of Egypt was theocratic. Its laws emanated from the gods. The power of causing the gods to speak, and the right of interpreting their utterances, belonged to the priests.

The state was divided into three principal castes,—the sacerdotal, the military, and the vulgar. The first of these represented intelligence, the second symbolized force, and the third found its analogy in matter. The king, in a change of dynasties, was always chosen from the first or the second class. He was a priest, or a captain; never a man of the people. The people had no voice in the election. The suffrages of the two privileged classes were not of equal weight and value. The priests, less in number than the warriors, balanced this disadvantage by the greater dignity of their rank. The vote of a priest of the first order was equivalent to the votes of a hundred warriors; of a priest of the second order, to those of twenty warriors; and of a priest of the third order, to those of ten warriors. If in any case the election was doubtful, the oracle, which spake only at the dictation of the priests, decided the question. If the king happened to be taken from the military caste, he was forthwith initiated into the sacerdotal caste, which spared no pains to keep him ever afterwards subject to their control. The sacerdotal class made the laws; interpreted them; pre·

served them in their own archives; and cautiously concealed them from all eyes. Thus all the great civil dignities of the state, all the magistracies, all the professions demanding intelligence, were filled by themselves; they could be filled by no others. The warriors, in time of peace, performed in rotation certain services near the person of the king. In time of war, they were assembled by his order, and were recompensed by sharing with the sacerdotal caste the honor of wearing certain badges of distinction. The people were a mere herd. They enjoyed neither honors nor possessions. Under secondary divisions, they comprised all who were devoted to agricultural, mechanical, and commercial pur suits.

Such was the distinction of persons under the Egyptian constitution. Let us now glance at the distribution of property.

The soil of Egypt was divided into three great portions. One of these belonged to the sacerdotal caste, and was not subject to taxation. Besides this, the priests received in the temples each his portion of wine and sacred viands, so that they had no need to consume upon their living any of their own private goods. Both the other divisions belonged to the king. One of them furnished him with the means of supporting his dignity and defraying the expenses of government. The other formed the appanage of the soldiers, to each of whom was allotted a certain portion of ground, which was exempted from public burdens. But it did not belong to him in fee simple, as the lands of the priests did to them. His domain could be changed, or even taken away from him wholly. The people had no landed estates of their own. They cultivated the lands of the king, the priests, and the warriors.

Such were the leading features of the Egyptian constitution. It contained no principle of national unity, since the same state comprehended classes as distinct as different races. It contained no principle of social equality, since all had not the right to do the same things, nor to reach the same civil dignities. It contained no principle of civil liberty, since men were not permitted to develope their faculties in the manner best adapted to their individual qualities, and most agreeable to their personal predilections.

But what shall we say of Greece? Were not Sparta and Athens blessed with free institutions? Did not civil liberty, in all its genial influences, find a home in those illustrious states? The genius of liberty did, indeed, for a time, hover over those sunny regions, like the dove above the waste of waters; but, like her, too, she found there no rest for the sole of her foot.

The great aim of Lycurgus, as of the Cretan lawgiver Minos, whose institutions he closely imitated, was to raise up a nation of invincible warriors. How far civil freedom, according to any just notions of it, was enjoyed by the Lacedemonians, will appear from a brief statement of some of the leading provisions of their political and social system. I shall not weary the reader with a detail of the institutions of Lycurgus; but present them merely in outline.

The essential defect of the political constitution of Sparta was the want of a proper balance of powers. The constitution, as it came from the hand of Lycurgus, recognized three orders in the government, viz. the kings, the senate, and the assembly of the people.

Monarchy, though retained in name, was virtually abolished. The authority of the kings was extremely limited. Their prerogative was confined to the high-priesthood, the chief military command, and the presidency of the senate. They were but the first citizens of the state; and their will, as it would seem, was far from having a predominating influence in the public affairs. They had no negative on the proceedings of the senate. As presidents of the body, they had simply a vote, like the other senators; or, as some say, two votes. This was the extent of their power, which, one may see at a glance, was weak and greatly circumscribed.

The senate, instituted by Lycurgus, consisted of twenty-eight members, besides the kings. They held their office for life. The whole executive power of the state was in the hands of this body. Almost the whole legislative power was entrusted to it likewise. As all laws must originate here, they had a perfect negative before debate. To the assembly of the people belonged the right of ratifying or rejecting laws proposed to them by the senate. But they must do this without debate. All deliberation was expressly forbidden to them. They could not even assign a reason for their vote. A simple aye or no was all that was allowed. Surely, the substance of political power was, by this arrangement, wholly taken away from the people; and only a faint shadow of it left to them. But perhaps they possessed an effective check in the privilege, accorded to them by the constitution, of choosing the senators? Not at all. The senators were, indeed, elective by the votes of the people in their legislative assemblies. But as their office was for life, and as the influence of kings and senators would be commonly used with great unanimity in favor of the eldest son, to fill up a vacancy made by the death of his father, and as the people were not permitted to debate, their choice was probably little more than a consent by acclamations to a nomination made by the senate; and so this body came to be much the same thing as an hereditary house of peers. The consequence of all this was to render the senators absolute masters of the legislature. Moreover, to the senate belonged the trial of the most important judicial questions, and particularly all such as were of a capital nature. Here, then, we have nearly all the powers of the state,—legislative, judicial, and executive, collected into one centre; and that centre an irresponsible body of nobles.

The government was little short of a pure oligarchy. The

power of the nobility soon exhibited itself as too strong and absolute. Plato says, that it was exercised with such violence and wantonness, that it wanted a bridle. And this curb was, in effect, subsequently imposed upon it by the appointment of five magistrates, called ephori; a magistracy, instituted to defend the rights of the people against the tyranny of the nobles, and furnishing the model after which that of the tribunes of Rome was afterwards formed.

Thus it is seen at a glance, how defective, how ill-balanced, how utterly wanting in popular sympathy, and how little likely to be permanent, this famous constitution was. It failed in the essential particular of the balance. Nor would it have lasted for any considerable period, but, on the contrary, would have been speedily annihilated, if it had not been accompanied and supported by a social system, which, while it strikingly displayed the genius and sagacity of the lawgiver, destroyed all the real merit of his celebrated institution, making of it one of the most horrible despotisms, that has ever cursed mankind. Some of the more important elements of this system were the banishment of gold and silver; the prohibition of travel and all intercourse with strangers; the interdiction of arts; the discouragement of science and letters; the public meals; the incessant martial exercises; and the doctrine, that parents should not be entrusted with the education of their own children, since every man was the property of the state. It is not the usual custom of legislators to regulate the manners by positive laws. But the code of Lycurgus embraced, not only the civil polity and general police of the state, but the private conduct of the citizens as well. Nothing was free at Sparta, not even the most indifferent actions. Food, dress, the style of architecture, the intercourse of a married man with his wife, the kinds of business, amusements, and the very topics of conversation, were all regulated by law. The clothing must be the same in summer and winter. The children were restricted to a single garment, and shoes and stockings were a luxury, which they were never permitted to enjoy. One slender meal a day was all that was allowed them. The food of all was coarse and spare; corpulency was a high crime. To the young grave questions were continually proposed, which they must answer quickly and justly, or they were beaten without mercy. Well did the witty Alcibiades, when certain Lacedemonians boasted to him of their contempt of death, reply,—"I do not wonder at it; it is the only means you have of freeing yourselves from the perpetual irksomeness and constraint, which are caused by the life you are obliged to lead."

To this austere life the Spartans were condemned, from the moment of their birth. The kings themselves enjoyed no exemption from it. Plutarch relates an incident, which affords a striking proof of this. King Agis had returned from an expedition, in which he had gained a brilliant victory over the Athenians. Desiring to sup with his wife, he asked, that his portion might be sent home. His request was denied, and he was obliged to go and eat his supper at the public tables. Piqued at this severity, he neglected the next day to offer the sacrifice usual on occasions of victory; and a fine was in consequence imposed upon him to punish his resentment.

The rigor of the Spartan discipline made the people contract a harsh, cruel, and even ferocious character. Proofs innumerable of this fact might be cited. Weak and deformed children they cast without pity into a deep cavern at the base of Mount Taygetus. The unrelenting severity of the Spartans towards their conquered enemies is well known. Witness their horrid barbarities in Athens, a city dear to all Greece. If the testimony of Xenophon is to be believed, they there put to death more persons in eight months of peace, than the enemies had killed in thirty years of war. How exquisite was their cruelty towards their four hundred thousand wretched Helots! Personal beauty in a slave was a crime punishable with death. Every slave received annually a cer-

tain number of lashes, just to remind him of his bondage and
his obligation to obedience. No master could give freedom
to a slave, however much he might desire to do so. A cap
and coat of dog-skin or sheep-skin was all the clothing they
were allowed. They were often compelled to drink to intoxication, and then to sing mean songs and dance ridiculous
dances, that so they might afford to the Spartan youth an exhibition of what drunkenness was. And what shall I say of
an institution, called by ancient authors the ambuscade? No
wonder that this institution gave to Plato a bad impression
of Lycurgus and his laws. Every year the governors of the
youth selected the boldest and most sagacious of them, fed
them like stalled oxen for some time to increase their ferocity,
armed them with daggers, and furnished them with several
days' provisions. Thus prepared and equipped, they were
sent to the fields, where they concealed themselves in the
day-time, to sally forth at night, and slaughter all the miserable Helots, whom they encountered.

But the very offspring of the Lacedemonians were the
objects of a most unnatural severity. At the annual festival
of Diana, all the children in Sparta were whipped till their
blood ran down upon the altars of the inhuman goddess.
The innocent victims often expired under this cruel ceremony,
while their own fathers and mothers stood by, exhorting them
to bear the scourging without uttering a single cry of distress,
or giving the least sign of pain. Brutality is too mild a term
for this pretended fortitude; nor do I know a word, which
will adequately express its dark and terrible enormity. Human nature starts back, petrified and aghast, from a spectacle,
than which incarnate demons could have contrived nothing
more monstrous and revolting. But I will not further pursue
the odious and sickening detail. Morality, humanity, and all
the comforts, refinements, elegancies, and pleasures of life
expired under this stern and frigid system. Every thing was
sacrificed to the one absorbing passion of military glory. To

call this people either happy or free, is an abuse of language. Their happiness was that of the tiger, watching, seizing, or devouring his prey; their liberty, that of a man chained in a dungeon,—the liberty of remaining as he is. Population, the surest criterion of national freedom and felicity, diminished to such a degree, that at length not more than one thousand families of the old Spartans remained, while nine thousand foreigners had come in, despite all their prohibitory laws.

Beyond a doubt, the constitution of Lycurgus preserved the independence of his country throughout a long series of ages. Beyond a doubt, it produced a race of warriors and politicians, brave, martial, prudent, firm in their maxims, constant in their designs, and skilled in the military art, above all the people of Greece. But here our admiration must pause. At this point our eulogy must turn to censure. In making his people such as here described, Lycurgus stripped them of all the gentler attributes of humanity, and made them put on the fierceness of wild beasts. From the best study I have been able to give to his polity, I cannot regard it otherwise than as a frightful and unrelenting despotism. There is no tyranny, like the tyranny of law. A despot may relent; but law is inexorable. A despot may die, and be succeeded by a prince of milder temper and juster views; but law is permanent, and knows no such fortunate casualties.

But does not Athens afford some relief to this picture? Undoubtedly she does; and yet her citizens can hardly be said to have enjoyed the blessings of true liberty. Her constitution was, without doubt, sufficiently popular; yet, like that of Sparta, it failed in the balance.

From the first, the Athenians were strongly inclined to democracy. Though their government was regal, absolute monarchy was unknown, as a legal constitution. The power of making laws never formed a part of the royal prerogative. Even Homer, in his catalogue of the Grecian forces at the siege of Troy, distinguishes the Athenians by the name of

"people." This designation makes apparent the early proclivity of the Athenians to democratic government, and shows,
that the principal authority was already in the hands of the
people. After the death of Codrus, the seventeenth king of
Athens, a dispute arose between his two sons, Medon and
Nelius, which gave the Athenians, impatient of the name of
king, a pretext for abolishing royalty. Jupiter was, by a
decree of the people, made sole sovereign of Athens. Medon
was chosen chief magistrate, with the title of archon. The
office was at first hereditary, and for life. Twelve hereditary
and perpetual archons followed Medon, and governed Athens
for a period of three hundred and thirty-one years. But the
perpetual archonship was too vivid an image of royalty to
suit the democratic temper of the Athenians. It was, therefore, abolished, and the term of office limited to ten years.
Even this limitation did not satisfy the Greeks, nor produce
tranquility. The restless spirit of democracy at length
reduced the term to one year, and substituted nine archons
in the place of one.

The archons were not all of equal dignity. The first in
rank represented the majesty of the state, was honored with
the title of archon, and gave his name to the civil year. The
second, under the name of king, was the head of religion.
The third was styled polemarch, and was chief of the military
affairs. The other six were called thesmothetes. They were
guardians of the laws, and acted as judges in the ordinary
courts of justice. Legislation was in the assembly of the
people. The archons were commonly chosen by lot; but
sometimes the people claimed the right of naming them.

The annual elections only increased the disorders of the
state. Liberty, as often happens, was confounded with
licentiousness. Intestine broils never ceased. Factions
arose every day. All order and harmony were at an end.
Athens was upon the brink of ruin. The turbulence of

democracy and the perpetual fluctuations of law became at length insufferable.

The people in their distress, applied to Draco to frame a new code of laws. Draco was a man of illustrious birth and distinguished virtue, but of little ability as a statesman. He was wholly unequal to the task of reforming a political constitution, and of introducing an improved code of jurisprudence. His temper was hard and austere. There appears to have been little in his laws remarkable, beyond the extreme rigor of their penalties. Every infraction of them was punished with death; a severity, which defeated the very end in view, since it rendered them incapable of execution.

Thus the remedy proved worse than the disease; and a few years afterwards, Solon, a man of true genius and statesmanship, was summoned, by the unanimous voice of his countrymen, to take the helm, and right the tottering ship of state. To this labor he addressed himself with consummate ability; but he was in the end obliged to confess, that the task was beyond his powers. His constitution, he said, was not the best in itself, but the best that the Athenians would bear. This acknowledgement is a key to his method of procedure. His endeavor was to adapt his laws to the people, rather than the people to his laws. His polity was exceedingly complex. Yet it failed to establish an equilibrium of powers, with adequate and effective checks upon each other. The balance was wanting. It is not necessary to go into a detailed analysis of his constitution. Suffice it to say, that, knowing how jealous his countrymen were of their liberty and independence, he bent his main endeavor to curb the restless spirit and restrain the overgrown power of democracy.

One of the checks, which he introduced into the constitution, was the division of all the citizens into four classes, upon a property basis, and the restriction of all the offices and dignities of the state to the first three, that is to say, to the rich; though he allowed to each of the members of the fourth class a vote in the assembly of the people. This would seem, at first view, an inconsiderable privilege; but it proved, in the end, to be a formidable power. As the right of trying appeals from the civil courts, the right of interpreting the laws, which had the defect of being written with much obscurity, and the right of peace and war, of making treaties, and of regulating commerce and finance, as well as the right of general legislation, were vested in this body, the people were absolute masters of the state. All authority was centred in them, and the government was a pure democracy.

Another check, which Solon, sensible of the evils of such a constitution, imposed upon the power of the multitude, was the institution of a senate of four hundred. This body he made the great council of the state, and clothed it with very high powers. The most important of its functions was the preparation of business for the assembly of the people. It was a law of Solon, that nothing should come before the people in their assemblies, which had not first been debated and approved in the senate. If this law had been always observed, it would have made the senate a balance of a very effective kind, and would have given greater steadiness to the public administration, and a more prolonged existence to the commonwealth. But the senate had no absolute negative; and without such a check, a popular assembly is as much disposed to overleap constitutional and legal barriers, as kings and nobles are. In effect, demagogues were never wanting at Athens, to remind the people, that all authority was lodged in their hands; and in point of fact, they claimed and exercised all the powers of the state, whenever they thought fit, brushing away the laws of Solon, like so many cobwebs.

A third check, introduced by Solon, was the re-establishment of the Areopagus, shorn of its ancient glories by the laws of Draco, with enlarged powers and dignities. This august court was made the guardian of the laws, the keeper of the public treasure, the superintendent of education and morals, and indeed the inspector-general of the whole state. So high was its reputation for wisdom and justice, that Cicero said, that Athens could no more be governed without the areopagus, than the world without the providence of God. From it alone there lay no appeal to the assembly of the people. This court was certainly a most important check to the rashness and haste of the multitude; nevertheless, even here, if the people chose to interfere, there was no balancing power in the constitution to restrain their despotic will. So that, as we still see, the whole power of the state was collected into one centre, and that centre was the people in their general assembly.

One further check Solon sought to impose upon the power of the democracy. "The urgent necessity for balances to a sovereign assembly, in which all authority, legislative, executive and judicial, was collected into one centre, induced Solon, though in so small a state, to make his constitution extremely complicated. No less than ten courts of judicature, four for criminal causes, and six for civil, besides the areopagus and general assembly, were established at Athens. In conformity to his own saying, celebrated among those of the seven wise men, that the most perfect government is that, where an injury to any one is the concern of all, he directed, that in all the ten courts, causes should be decided by a body of men, like our juries, taken from among the people; the archons only presiding, like our judges. As the archons were appointed by lot, they were often but indifferent lawyers, and chose two persons of experience to assist them. These in time became regular constitutional officers, by the name of assessors. The jurors were paid for their service, and appointed by lot. This institution of juries for the trial of causes is the glory of Solon's laws. It is that department,

356   COMMENTARIES ON THE

which ought to belong to the people at large. They are most
competent for this; and the property, liberty, equality,
and security of the citizens, all require, that they alone
should possess it. Itinerant judges, called the forty, were
appointed to go through the counties, to determine assaults,
and civil actions under a certain sum."

But, notwithstanding the checks and balances thus embodied in his constitution, the work of Solon proved a failure.
His two anchors, as he called the senate and the areopagus,
proved too weak to hold the vessel of state amid the storms
which assailed it. The former had no share in the legislative
department of the government; and the latter, itself dependent upon the people, could not resist the waves of popular
commotion. Within ten years from the establishment of his
constitution, Solon had the mortification of seeing Pisistratus
sole master of his beloved Athens, with a body-guard to
attend him, after the manner of the Persian sovereigns.

The question is, did this constitution, or could it, secure to
the citizens the enjoyment of civil liberty? We are constrained to answer in the negative. In a state, where the
whole body of the people, convened in general assembly, are
the legal sovereign, the government must be irregular, confused, contradictory, and often tyrannical. Unchecked by
an effective balancing power, lodged in fewer hands, a power
possessing an absolute veto, it is not properly the rule of a
sovereign, but of a mob; and it must partake, more or less,
of the fluctuations and injustice of mob law. This is the
judgment of reason; and it is verified in the history of
Athens. Not unfrequently the magistrates proceeded in much
the same manner as they now do among the Turks. Let the
following instance serve as an illustration. A barber in the
Piraeus, who had spread the news of the defeat of the Athenians in Sicily, on the authority of a person who came into
his shop, was put to the torture by command of the archons,

because he could not tell the name of the person who had communicated the intelligence to him.

The remark of Cicero was perfectly just, that the rashness and licentiousness of the popular assemblies ruined the republics of Greece ; to which Goguet, with equal truth, has added, "particularly that of Athens." The Athenians were always impetuous, always rash, always fickle, always, in a word, the sport of the demagogues who ruled them. This last expression is a key to the whole political history of Athens. A government, in which every citizen has the right to vote in making, interpreting, and executing the laws, must, it would seem, be the beau ideal of a free constitution. The argument in support of this view would run somewhat after this fashion : "A man who contributes by his vote to the passing of a law, has himself made the law. In obeying it, he obeys himself; he therefore is free." But this is not reasoning ; it is merely playing upon words. His vote is but one of a thousand, perhaps ten thousand. He has had no opportunity to examine, deliberate, state objections, suggest restrictions, or propose amendments. He has only been allowed to express his assent or dissent. And in doing this, it is a hundred to one but he has been led by some intriguing aspirant for power and place. The multitude, absorbed in the care of providing the means of subsistence, have neither the time nor the knowledge necessary for functions of this nature. Besides, nature, sparing of her gifts, bestows upon comparatively few an understanding equal to the complicated business of legislation. As a sick man trusts to his physician, and a client to his lawyer, so the greater part of a popular legislative assembly must trust to those who have more abilities than themselves. These, wholly taken up with the thoughts of their own power, live but to increase it. Versed in the management of public affairs, foreseeing the most important consequences of measures, and having exclusive control of the springs of government, they offer propositions,

make speeches, present facts and arguments which there is
no time to examine, conceal what is designed to promote their
own private views, by joining it to things which they know
will be acceptable to the people, employ skilfully all the common places of rhetoric, and so are enabled to gain over to
their side the majority of votes, in almost every proposal
which they make. So that, in the end, what is proclaimed
as the general will, is, in reality, nothing more than the effect
of the artifices of a few cunning men, who, exulting over
their success, deride in secret the sottishness of the people,
whom they had flattered in public, only to mislead and betray
them. This is an exact account of the manner in which the
public affairs were managed at Athens, where legislation
would often have been wiser and more beneficial to the state,
if it had been determined by the casting of dice, than by the
suffrages of the multitude.

The truth is, as Goguet has well said, we are too much accustomed to view the Athenians on their favorable side. We are
struck with the shining images of the history of Athens, and
imposed upon by its lustre. We are dazzled by the victories
of Marathon and Salamis, by the pomp of the spectacles, by
the taste and magnificence of the public monuments, by that
crowd of great men, who will render the name of Athens
forever precious and memorable. Nevertheless, when we
examine the interior state of this republic, far different scenes
present themselves. We see a state in incessant combustion,
assemblies always tumultuous, a people perpetually agitated
by factions, hurried away by first impressions, and abandoned
to the impetuous eloquence of unprincipled orators. Virtue
was proscribed at Athens, and the most eminent public services were not only forgotten, but often punished by the ostra-
cism. Well did Valerius Maximus exclaim, "Happy Athens,
after such unjust treatment, still to have found citizens, who
loved their country."

An absolute democracy, like that of Athens, and a representative republic, like that of Judea, are governments, as wide asunder as the poles. In Athens, the people held and exercised all power,—legislative, executive, and judicial,—subject to no effective restraint or responsibility. It was a government of will, rather than of law. Its leading principle was, "stat pro ratione voluntas." The only reason which it rendered for its actions, was, "sic volo, sic jubeo, sic veto." It was a despotism, as pure and absolute as that of Nero; and, in practice, it always proved itself as capricious and tyrannical. Licentiousness there was at Athens, without doubt; but not true civil liberty. These are so far from being identical, that the one is contrary to the other, and destructive of it.

The Roman constitution next demands our attention. The ghost of Romulus, we are told by Livy, soon after his disappearance from among men, revisited the distinguished senator, Proculus Julius, and addressed him thus: "Go tell my countrymen, it is the decree of heaven, that the city I have founded shall become the mistress of the world. Let her cultivate assiduously the military art. Then let her be assured, and transmit the assurance from age to age, that no mortal power can resist the arms of Rome." How faithfully Rome obeyed the spirit of this counsel, let her colossal power under the Caesars inform us, when the significations of her will were obeyed throughout the vast regions, that stretch from the Atlantic to the Ganges, and from Siberia to the Great Desert. Whatever other merit may be denied to regal, republican, or imperial Rome, none will ever dispute her title to be regarded as a perfect model of a predatory state.

How far civil liberty was secured by the Roman constitution, and what degree of power and authority in the administration of public affairs belonged to the Roman people, will appear in the progress of these inquiries.

A full analysis of the Roman constitution is not proposed. The innumerable stages through which it passed in its development, render such analysis a work of great difficulty, and would demand more space than can be given to this or any other of the topics embraced in this preliminary book. Nor is it required by the end I have in view; my object being rather to point out the defects of the constitution, so far as guaranties of public liberty were concerned, than to analyze the constitution itself.

The reader's attention is first invited to the constitution of the Roman comitia. The comitia were assemblies of the people, convened for the purpose of electing officers, or enacting laws. The comitia were not a simple body, nor did they vote in a uniform way. They were of three sorts, according to the manner in which the votes were taken. Sometimes they voted by curiae, sometimes by centuries, and sometimes by tribes.

But this needs explanation. It is to be premised, that the ancients did not vote as individuals, but as corporations. Thus the Athenians, from the earliest times, were accustomed to vote in tribes, four of which would be outvoted by six, although the number of individuals in the six might be much smaller than that of the four. This method of voting corresponds to that authorized by our constitution, whenever the election of a president of the United States happens to devolve upon the house of representatives. The representatives do not, in that case, vote in their individual capacity, but according to states; and a state with fifty representatives would have no more voice in the election, than a state having but a single representative.

It was in accordance with this principle, that all popular votes were given in ancient Rome. Yet, as already stated, there were different manners of voting. By the constitution of Romulus, the Roman people were divided into two tribes, called Ramnes and Tities, the former consisting of the original citizens, and the latter of the Sabines, who were subsequently incorporated into the body of the state. A constitution, which allowed only these two tribes to vote, would have given rise to difficulties, since it would often nappen, that one tribe wished a thing, which the other opposed, and hence would have resulted endless collisions and feuds. How was this difficulty obviated? In the following manner. Each tribe was divided into a hundred associations, called gentes; and each gens, again, consisted of several families, forming in itself a small state, with many peculiar rights, called jus gentium and jura gentium. They resembled the tribes of the Arabs and the clans of Highlanders of Scotland. But between the division into tribes and gentes, there was another, named curiae, of which there were ten in a tribe. They answered to the orders at Cologne, and to the classes in the Lombard towns. Each curia was a tenth part of a tribe, and, on the other hand, included in itself ten gentes. The membership of a curia implied special religious duties, and conferred the right of voting in comitia. Thus the curiae stepped into the place of the tribes. A third tribe under the name of Luceres, composed of Albans and other foreigners, was formed by Tullus Hostilius, and was admitted to the full franchise in the reign of Tarquinius Priscus. The number of tribes was afterwards increased by Servius Tullius to thirty.

Servius also made another division of the people, for political purposes, into six classes, upon a property basis. The first class consisted of persons, whose estates in res corporales, that is, land, slaves, cattle, metal, farming implements, and the like, amounted to about $2000; the second, to $1500; the third to $1000; the fourth to $500; the fifth to $250; and the sixth included all those whose property fell below the last named sum. The six classes were subdivided into one hundred and ninety-three centuries. Ninety-eight of these, a clear majority of the whole, were comprehended in the first class; twenty-two, in the second; twenty, in the third; twenty-two, in the fourth; and thirty, in the fifth; while the whole of the sixth class formed but a single century. As the voting was by centuries, the lowest class had but one vote, though no other class contained so large a number of individuals as this. The centuries composing the first class were entitled to a priority in voting. If they voted unanimously, as in fact they commonly did, the question was decided. In that case, the remaining centuries did not vote at all. If the votes of the first class did not determine the question, the other centuries went on voting, till a majority was obtained. As soon as that happened, the voting ceased. So that the great body of the Roman people, in the comitia centuriata, had the barren honor of a casting vote, in case of a tie in the ballots of the higher classes. If any thing in the nature of political power can be conceived more shadowy than this, I am at a loss to imagine what it is. The object of the whole institution seems to have been to give to a very small minority a decisive influence in the state. Wealth and birth had all the power, while numbers were of little account.

It has been mentioned above, that Servius Tullius increased the whole number of tribes to thirty, four of which belonged to the city, and twenty-six to the circumjacent country. This institution, however, must not be confounded with that of the three tribes named above. Each tribe had a magistrate called tribunus (tribune), chosen by the members of the tribe. The tribes were composed only of plebeians. At first the comitia of the tribes had no legislative power; they could only elect their own officers, and make arrangements concerning their local interests. An important power was conferred upon the assembly of the tribes by Servius, viz. the right of trying appeals from judgments of condemnation pronounced by a magistrate against plebeians. The patricians had long possessed the privilege of appeal, in such cases, to the assembly of the curiae. The functions of the comitia of the tribes were gradually enlarged, till at length they obtained an important share in the business of legislation.

Thus we have, in this constitution, three distinct species of popular assemblies,—the comitia curiata, the comitia centuriata, and the comitia tributa. The assemblies of the curiae and the centuries formed an aristocracy; that of the tribes, a democracy. As it was not with any precision determined by law what should be done in the several assemblies, and as the patricians and plebeians did not, therefore, balance each other by regular checks, the administration of the state became a continual scene of contradictions. The centuries alone, in which the high-born and the rich had an undoubted majority, as well as in the senate, had for a long time the authority of making laws. The plebeians denied the legislative authority of the senate; and the senate in like manner denied the right of the tribes to make laws. Justice required, that the plebeians should have a share in the enactment of laws. But, instead of becoming a co-ordinate branch of the legislature, instead of aiming at a concurrent authority with the senate and the comitia of the centuries, or, which would have been better still, with the senate and consuls, as distinct branches of the legislative department, they obtained a separate and independent power of legislation. Hence the intricacy of his constitution; hence three distinct sources of laws, decrees of the senate, acts of the centuries, and resolutions of the tribes;—a perpetual fountain of division and tumult.

The word liberty is one of those terms, which have been most misunderstood, or misapplied. Writers have represented, that no people can be free, who do not expressly enact their own laws. Thus Rousseau, in his Social Contract, says, that the people of England are much mistaken in thinking themselves free; they are free only during the election of members of parliament; as soon as these are elected, the people are slaves; they are nothing. He here commits the egregious blunder of confounding a mere function of government with a constituent part of liberty. The patricians and

senate of Rome, who were always the real masters of the
state, sensible that their own tyranny would be at an end
under a lawful authority entrusted to a single ruler, had the
address to persuade the people, that, provided those who exercised a despotic power over them, and who every day
heaped wrongs and insults upon them, were called consuls,
dictators, senators, patricians, military tribunes, or, indeed,
received any appellation other than that horrid and hated
one of king, they were free, and that these empty titles might
wisely be purchased at the price of every calamity. This
they were able to accomplish by occasionally performing the
illusory ceremony of assembling the people, that they might
make a show of consulting them. They made them believe,
according to the doctrine of Rousseau just cited, that liberty
consisted in the mere giving of votes, no matter how great
the disadvantage in the manner of giving them might be, and
no matter how much the law might afterwards be neglected
or violated, which was thus pretended to be made in common.
But how false and deceptive are all such ideas ! True liberty
consists in the security of persons and property, so that
every man, while he respects the persons of others, and
suffers them to enjoy in quietness the fruits of their industry,
is certain that he himself will be permitted to enjoy the same
blessings at the hands of his fellow-citizens. To concur by
our votes in the enactment of laws, is to enjoy a certain
degree of power; to live in a state, where the laws are equal
for all, and where they are sure to be executed with moderation and fairness, is to be free. But that is a wretched servitude, call it by what name you will,—democracy or aristocracy, a republic or a despotism,—where the laws are partial,
uncertain, fluctuating, and feebly and irregularly administered.

The relation of debtor and creditor in the Roman commonwealth was one of extreme hardship and severity.
Mammon prevailed as much in ancient Rome as in some

modern countries. Avarice raged like a fiery furnace in the bosom of patrician creditors. Private rapine was added to political ambition. The laws allowed exorbitant interest for the use of money. An insolvent debtor might by the decree of the judge, be delivered into the hands of his creditor, by whom he might be scourged, tortured, or put to death at discretion; the most aristocratic and detestable law ever known among men. The severity of the actual law was very oppressive, but it was aggravated by being altogether one-sided; for when a patrician was in pecuniary difficulty, his clients were under obligation to assist him, whereas plebeians, being obliged for the most part to borrow from patricians, enjoyed no such advantage. So tenacious were these haughty and avaricious nobles of all the rigor of their power over debtors, that Veturius, the son of a consul, who had been reduced by poverty to the necessity of borrowing money, was delivered up to his creditor, who exacted from him all the services of a slave, the senate refusing to grant any relief. This law was so execrable, so diabolical, one might almost say, that an attempt to get rid of it at almost any rate would have been a virtue.

The oppressions growing out of this law were the occasion of instituting the office of tribunes of the people. And what did the Roman people gain by this institution? In reality very little. The first tribunes can scarcely be called a magistracy even of the commonalty. Certainly they were not a magistracy of the state. Neibuhr represents their position as analogous to that of a modern ambassador, whose duty it is in a foreign state to protect the subjects of his own sovereign. The Roman tribunes had not sufficient power for the effective protection of the commonalty. They had only enough to head every popular tumult, and to blow into a flame every spark of popular discontent. If the number had been three hundred, instead of three, and they had formed a representative assembly, with power to propose laws, deliberate, amend, and improve, that would have been a real advance, and would have constituted an effective balance. But the tribunes had no right to propose any law, or move any resolution. They could only forbid such measures as they deemed injurious. The legislative authority vested in the people was not delegated to their tribunes. These functionaries had power to conclude nothing. The people reserved to themselves the right of ratifying any resolutions taken by them. This circumstance rendered the institution of tribunes in the issue totally ineffectual; for the advantages which accrue to the people from the appointment of representatives are quite inconsiderable, unless they at the same time wholly entrust to them their legislative authority. In the present case, the Roman people, fondly cherishing a chimerical appearance of sovereignty, endeavored to settle, with a hundred thousand votes, things, which would have been better settled by the votes of their representatives, and so defeated the very object of their appointment. But how and why? Thus. The consuls, senators, dictators, and other great men of the state, whom, as De Lolme aptly says, the people were prudent enough to fear, and simple enough to believe, continued to mix with them, and play off their political artifices. They made speeches; changed at pleasure the place and form of the public assemblies; dissolved the comitia, whenever it suited their purposes, under pretext that the auspices were unfavorable; conferred upon the consuls, when they despaired of success by other means, absolute power over the lives of the citizens; or even appointed a dictator, in whom all the powers of the state were centred. Sometimes they falsely accused the tribunes before the assembly itself; at other times, they artfully slandered them in private, and so deprived them of the confidence of the Romans. In this manner the people were brought to see, without concern, the murder of Tiberius Gracchus, a true patriot, a virtuous citizen, and the only Roman, who truly loved them. In this manner Caius Gracchus, who could not be deterred, even by his brother's fate, from imitating his brother's generosity, saw himself in the end so utterly forsaken by the people, that not one of them would lend him a horse to fly from the fury of the nobles. Often the patricians fomented divisions among the plebeians, and kept moderate men from attending the comitia by rendering them scenes of tumult and confusion. In a word, that nothing might be wanting to their aristocratic insolence, they sometimes falsified the number of votes in declaring them, and even carried off the urns, into which the citizens were to cast their suffrages. And all these things happened, not in those degenerate ages, when one half of the people were made to arm themselves against the other in the comitia, but in what is commonly esteemed the best period of the republic, the times immediately preceding and following the third Punic war. If, when the tribuneship was instituted, a representative assembly of the commonalty had been formed, with powers corresponding to those of the English house of commons or the American house of representatives, how different would have been the history of Roman liberty! The distinction between a representative constitution and a popular constitution is well stated by De Lolme. According to him, a representative constitution places the remedy in the hands of those who feel the disorder, while a popular constitution places the remedy in the hands of those who cause it. In the former case, the care of repressing the invasions of power is committed to the men who suffer from them, in the latter, to the men who practise them.

But there was a deeper and more radical defect in the Roman constitution ; a defect inherent in political organizations of that sort ; a defect, which struck at the very vitals of the public liberty. The tribunes were faithless to their trust, and, human nature remaining as it is, they could scarcely be otherwise. Under a constitution like that of Rome, it was impossible that the people should have faithful defenders. They could not show a preference for a man, without attacking his virtue. They could not elevate him, without losing him. They could not lavish their favors upon him, without sending him to swell the number of their enemies. As soon as their favorites saw themselves in a condition to control power, they became, from that very circumstance, its defenders. They were beyond the reach of oppressions themselves; why should they care to restrain them? By so doing they would but lessen a power which they hoped would one day be their own. How could it be expected, that men, who aspired to be praetors, consuls, and senators, would be zealous to limit the powers belonging to those offices? In point of fact, they were not; and their long contest with the patricians was not a struggle for general liberty, but a scramble for dignities, emoluments, and power. This was the only end they ever pursued with sincerity and perseverance. They never employed the power of the people for things really beneficial to the people. They never set bounds to the exorbitant and despotic power of the magistrates. They never repressed that class of citizens, who, however great their crimes, knew how to secure an immunity from punishment. They never sought to regulate the judicial power. But these are precautions, without which nations may struggle to the end of time, and they will never attain true liberty. The judicial power especially is a sure criterion of the goodness of government; and this, at Rome, was always a mere instrument of tyranny. Consuls, praetors, dictators, tribunes, and senators seem all to have been clothed with the power of life and death. While such infamous monsters as Verres and Piso were for the most part secure against the danger of punishment, they themselves could, through mere wantonness and cruelty, cause the inferior citizens of Rome to be scourged with rods, and even put to death upon the cross. And what can we say of the personal rights of the weaker members of society, in a state where the law regarded children as things rather than as persons, as a part of the furniture of the family mansion, which, like any other part of it, the head of the family might remove, sell, or destroy, at his discretion; where a father, through sheer caprice, could compel his married daughter to repudiate a husband, whom she tenderly loved, and whom he himself had approved; and where a wife was considered, in the eye of the law, as the daughter of her husband, who might retain or dismiss her at pleasure, and, for certain offences, might even take her life?

Very high encomiums have been bestowed upon the tribunal of censors at Rome by Montesquieu, Rousseau, and most other writers, who have treated of the Roman affairs. More just appears to me the opinion of De Lolme, who considers it a piece of state-craft, like those described above, invented by the patricians, as an additional means of securing their own authority. It was founded on a principle similar to that advocated by Sir Thomas More, in his Account of Utopia, the happy region; though not carried to the extreme of that writer, whose ravings, in many parts of his work, can hardly be matched out of bedlam; for he made it a capital crime in the people even to talk of the conduct of their rulers. Still, the power of the censors, under the Roman constitution, in its own nature altogether arbitrary, was at the same time wide in its range, and excessive in degree. Among other discretionary powers, entrusted to them, was that of determining the social standing of every member of the state; that of punishing with the brand of ignominy (nota censoria) every moral baseness which could not be reached by the law, as disaffection towards parents, alienation between husbands and wives, harshness towards neighbors, excessive luxury, idleness, and the like; and, by the Ovinian law, that even of filling vacancies in the senate. These were, indeed, vast and terrific powers; and all of them, as may be seen at a glance, well adapted to advance the interests of the aristocracy, and to diminish and restrain the privileges of the people. Certainly the existence of a censorial power in a state is of very great importance. It is a power capable of producing excellent effects. It may even be said to be essential to liberty. But the exercise of it, unlike that of the legislative power, ought to be left to the people themselves. "The sentiments of the people are the only thing in question here. It is, therefore, necessary, that the people should speak for themselves, and manifest their sentiments. A particular court of censure would frustrate the intended purpose. It is attended, besides, with very great inconveniences. As the use of such a court is to determine upon those cases which lie out of the reach of the laws, it cannot be tied down to any precise regulations. As a further consequence of the arbitrary nature of its functions, it cannot even be subjected to any constitutional check; and it continually presents to the eye the view of a power entirely arbitrary, and which, in its different exertions, may affect, in the most cruel manner, the peace and happiness of individuals. It is attended, moreover, with the very pernicious consequence, that, by dictating to the people, their judgments of men and measures, it takes from them the freedom of thinking, which is the noblest privilege, as well as the firmest support of liberty." (De Lolme.) The true ends of the censorial power were better secured, and with less danger to liberty, as I shall show hereafter, under the Hebrew constitution, by the institution of the prophetical office, and still better, under the English and American constitutions, by a free press. How terrible the censorial power, exercised by the Hebrew prophets, was to tyrants, we see in the history of Ahab; how formidable the power of a free press is to our own rulers, every day attests. The right, so constantly and freely used among us, of openly canvassing and arraigning the conduct of public men, dispels the halo of greatness which surrounds them, brings them down to the level of the rest of the people, and strikes a salutary terror into their

minds, whenever they feel tempted to overstep the bounds of
a lawful authority, and abuse the trusts confided to them by
their fellow-citizens.

If we examine the revolutions, which happened at Rome,
we shall find them uniformly terminating in settlements,
which inured to the benefit of the few, while the interests of
the many received but little attention. Thus, the only consequence of that great revolution, by which the kings were
driven from Rome, was, that the powers, lately exercised by
them, were transferred to the senators, by whom the revolution
had been instigated. The cause of public liberty gained
nothing. Indeed, it was rather damaged than otherwise.
Power was stretched even beyond its former tone; a fact
more than intimated by Livy, when he says, in allusion to
the consuls, that the people now had two kings, instead of
one. In like manner, the commotion, in which the people
withdrew in a body from Rome, and posted themselves on a
hill beyond the Anio, ended in nothing but the advancement
of a few particular persons, under the title of tribunes. The
grievances, which had caused the commotion, remained
unredressed; and the most that the tribunes did with them, was
to use them as an instrument in advancing their own personal
views. Even the code of the twelve tables, which the people
procured at the greatest cost and pains, was, as to the framing
of it, wholly in the hands of the patricians, and left the
power of the senate and consuls as undefined as before. The
revolution, whereby the decemvirs were expelled from power,
on account of their capricious and wanton abuse of it, issued
but little better for the cause of the people. The tribunes
did, undoubtedly, by means of it, obtain many additional
privileges, and got a law passed, to the effect, that the resolutions of the comitia tributa, in which they had the right to
propose new laws, should be binding upon the whole
commonwealth. This is well described by Livy as acerrimum
telum, a most active and powerful weapon; and most actively

and efficaciously did they use it, till the consulship, the
praetorship, the censorship, the priesthood, the senatorial
dignity, and all the other offices of executive power, were
within their grasp. This was the goal, at which they were
constantly aiming. This was what they meant in all their
proposals for relieving the people of their debts, for diminishing the rate of interest, and for dividing among the people
the lands taken from the enemy. These were all equitable
and excellent proposals; but, unfortunately for the people,
as made by their tribunes, they were only pretences, devised
to cover and conceal schemes of personal ambition. To these
selfish views and aims they continually made the cause of the
people subservient. That this is not mere assertion, but fact,
we have clear proof in the manner in which they procured
for themselves the right of admission to the consulship.
Availing themselves of what was called an interregnum, that
is, a time when there happened to be no magistrates in the
state but themselves, they brought three propositions before
the comitia of the tribes, viz. one for regulating the rate of
interest, another for limiting the quantity of land that could
be held by a citizen, and a third requiring that one of the
two consuls should be taken from among the plebeians. The
tribes voted in favor of the first two measures, but against
the last. The tribunes declared, that the three bills must be
accepted or rejected together. The most violent commotions
followed, and lasted through an entire year. The tribunes
clung to the consulship, and at length triumphed. Livy
truly observes, that, on this occasion, it was quite manifest
which of the laws in question were most agreeable to the
people, and which to those who proposed them. The tribunes
were so intent upon personal advantages, that they were
willing to sacrifice to them the most weighty interests of their
constituency. "A few tribunes, indeed, did at times apply
themselves seriously, out of real virtue and love of their
duty, to remedy the grievances of the people; but their

fellow tribunes, and the whole body of those men, upon whom the people had, at different times, bestowed consulships, aedileships, censorships, and other dignities without number, united together with the utmost vehemence against them; and the real patriots, as Fulvius and the Gracchi, constantly perished in the attempt." (De Lolme.)

If the laws concerning the liberty of the citizens were imperfect in themselves, the execution of them was still more defective. Soon after the expulsion of the kings, a law was passed, confirming the right of the citizens,—a right previously enjoyed by them,—of appealing to the people from decrees of death passed upon them. The consuls, however, paid little attention to such appeals, but as we learn from Dionysius and Livy, sported with the lives of the citizens in the most arbitrary manner. The same law was introduced into the twelve tables; but it was as little respected by the decemvirs, and the magistrates who succeeded them, as it had before been by the consuls. About a hundred and forty years later, this law concerning an appeal to the people was enacted for the third time; but to no better purpose than on the previous occasions. It was continually violated by the different magistrates of the republic; and once the senate, of its own authority, ordered four thousand citizens to be put to death, despite the urgent remonstrances of the tribunes against so summary and severe an exercise of public justice. According to the constitution, no war could be waged, without the sanction of the people in the curiae or centuries. But instances occur, in which the senate alone declared war, levied armies, and carried on hostilities. Neibuhr is of the opinion, that the agrarian law was actually passed under Spurius Cassius; but if so, it is certain, that the people did not enjoy the benefit of it. Nor did the magistrates content themselves with perpetrating acts of injustice in their political capacity. They added the most shameless extortions. First they plundered the provinces. But Italy itself did not escape.

The disease at length reached the very heart of the republic. And here a new disorder arose. The judges proved as corrupt, as the magistrates had been oppressive. As early as the times of the Gracchi, it had become a general complaint, that no man, who had money, could be brought to punishment. Cicero says, that in his time, the same opinion was universally received; and his orations abound with lamentations over the levity and infamy of the public judgments.

Thus, on a review and recapitulation of what has been said concerning the Roman constitution, it appears, that the principal assembly of the people, the comitia centuriata, was constituted in such a manner, as to give a preponderating influence to rank and riches; that an exact and well defined division of powers was wanting; that there was no adequate system of checks and balances; that the patricians were at the greatest pains to give the people wrong notions of liberty; that a tyrannical and frightful power was exercised by creditors over debtors; that the tribuneship was radically defective in its constitution; that, by the use of a great variety of artifices, the senators and great men of the state held the people always under their control; that the tribunes themselves were not faithful defenders of liberty, but continually betrayed those who confided in them; that the judicial power was a mere instrument of tyranny; that the senate, consuls, and dictators possessed an arbitrary power over the lives of the citizens; that the tribunal of censors was a mere piece of state-craft, devised as an additional prop to patrician and senatorial power; that almost all the revolutions and public commotions at Rome ended in advancing the power and interests of the few, while the grievances of the many remained unredressed; and that imperfect as the laws concerning the liberty of the citizens were, the execution of them was still more defective. Let any one attentively consider these things, and say, whether popular liberty in ancient Rome was any thing more than a name, a dream, a gilded blind, cunningly contrived to conceal from vulgar eyes the real tyranny of aristocratic rulers.

I deny not that there were elements in the Roman, Grecian, Egyptian, and even Asiatic polities, worthy of praise and imitation. But the point which I have aimed to establish is this,—that civil liberty, founded on equal rights, and acting through the popular will, was a blessing unknown to the whole ancient gentile world. When we turn from the dreary prospects, on which our eyes have rested through this chapter, where tyranny rules, the hour and the scene each moment is imbued in blood, to the green vales and vine-clad hills of Palestine, we shall see millions of freemen reposing, in happiness and security, beneath the sheltering aegis of a polity, stamped, in its every lineament, with the signatures of its divine original. This favored people were not more distinguished, during their journeyings and encampments in the wilderness, by the mysterious shechinah, which shot its fiery splendors up to mid-heaven, symbolizing the divine presence among them, than they afterwards were by their civil constitution; a constitution containing the elemental principles of all just, wise, and equal legislation, and bearing indubitable marks of a divine wisdom in its formation.

CHAPTER IX.

Geographical Limits and Population of Palestine.*

THE principal passages in the Pentateuch and other historical books of the Old Testament, relating to the boundaries of the holy land, are the following :—Gen. 15 : 18–21. Exod. 23 : 31. Numb. 34 : 1–29. Deut. 1 : 6–8. 11 : 24. Josh. 11 : 16–17. 13 : 1–7. 19 : 24–31. 15 : 47. Judg. 1 : 31. 2 Sam. 8 : 3. 1 Kings 4 : 21–24. 2 Chron. 8 : 1–6. 9 : 26. The reader is requested, before he proceeds further, to peruse these passages, and compare them together. On a careful examination of them, the first thing, which strikes the mind, is an apparent inconsistency in their statements respecting the eastern and southern limits of the Israelitish territories. In the thirty-fourth chapter of Numbers, where the boundary line is described with great minuteness, the river Jordan is mentioned as the east border; and an irregular curve, extending across the desert, from the southern extremity of the Dead Sea to the river of Egypt, forms the south border. But in all the other passages, where the boundaries are spoken of, viz. Gen. 15, Exod. 23, Deut. 1, 11, 2 Sam. 8, 1 Kings 4, and 2 Chron. 8, 9,—eight passages in all,—the Euphrates is mentioned as the eastern limit; and in Exod. 23 : 31, the bounds of Israel are spoken of as stretching to the southward, as far as the Red Sea.

* See on the subject of this chapter Mich. Com. on the Laws of Moses, Arts. 19–28.

But there is no real contradiction. The boundary of the holy land, which the Israelites were to divide, after expelling the inhabitants, was one thing; the boundary, beyond which they were not permitted to extend their conquests eastward, was another. Jordan was the former; Euphrates the latter. The intervening territory was not necessarily to be occupied, exclusively, by the Israelites; but was to serve as a pasture-ground for their cattle; the greater part of it, indeed, being fit for no other purpose. The appointment of the Euphrates as a boundary included in it a prohibition to the Israelites against extending their dominion beyond it; which, in point of fact, they never did, not even in the reign of David, although he obtained important victories over the kings of Mesopotamia. Palestine proper, that country which was to be the fixed abode of the Hebrews, lay west of the Jordan. Moses laid no claim to the territories east of that river. The Israelites were forbidden, without provocation, to molest the Moabites and Ammonites, the children of Lot, and to drive them from their lands. *   Even the Amorites, a Syrian tribe descended from Canaan, were not dispossessed of their territories, nor was the purpose of dispossessing them entertained, till Sihon, their king, without provocation on the part of the Hebrews, marched an army beyond his frontier, and commenced hostilities against them. In this attack, the Amorites were unsuccessful; and, by right of conquest, Moses seized upon their territories, and appropriated them to the use of the chosen people.† The same thing afterwards happened to the Edomites, whose country lay to the south of the land of Israel. Their conduct was such as to give just cause of war; and David took occasion thence to conquer their territories, and annex them to the Israelitish dominions.‡ This extended the boundary of Israel, on the

* Deut. ii. 9. Judg. xi. 15.   † Numb. xxi. 21–25.
‡ 2 Sam. viii. 14. 1 Chron. xviii. 13.

south, to the Red Sea, agreeably to a divine promise,* and gave to the Hebrews the ports of Aela and Eziongeber.

The case, then, appears to be this. 1. The Hebrews were to drive out the Canaanitish nations, inhabiting the country lying between the Mediterranean sea and the river Jordan, and between the river of Egypt and the mountains of Lebanon. This region was to be their peculiar inheritance. This was the land of promise, and was to be, in a preëminent sense, the holy land. Accordingly, we find, that a remarkable distinction was always made between the country lying to the east, and that situated to the west of the Jordan. The latter was, even by the tribes inhabiting the former, ever accounted more sacred than their own.† 2. The Israelites were permitted to make conquests of the surrounding regions, when provoked to war by the nations occupying them. These conquests might be extended as far as to the river Euphrates, should there be just occasion for so doing. 3. Beyond this boundary, the Hebrews were not permitted to pass, under any provocation, nor for any purpose, to make conquests and annexations. The permission to go so far was tantamount to a law against going any farther.

Let us now, as far as we are able, trace the limits of the Hebrew dominions, as they were at their widest extent, or as they were intended to be, if the Israelites had obeyed the divine command respecting the extermination of the Canaanites.

The western boundary was to be the great sea, that is, the Mediterranean. The boundary was to commence, where the south border touches the sea, viz. at the river of Egypt, and to stretch northward to a great distance. How far, however, is a question still in dispute. All agree that it extended to Achzib, or Ecdippa, a little above the thirty-third degree of north latitude, and about fifteen miles to the north of Acco, the Ptolemais of the Greeks, and the Acre of the Turks. It

* Exod. xxiii. 31.　　　　† Josh. xxii. 24, 25.

was of great importance to the Hebrews, that this last mentioned place should be embraced within their territories. It is the Gibraltar of Palestine. Its possession is decisive of the fate of the country. Whoever holds it is master, or may easily make himself master of all Palestine. The whole course of history, ancient and modern, evinces this fact. The reason is plain. From this city, the vast and fertile plain of Esdraëlon extends, in a southerly direction, from the Mediterranean to the Jordan, dividing Palestine into two unequal halves. In this plain have been fought nearly all the great battles, which have decided the fate of the country. Here Sisera fell, and his army was routed and slain.* Here Saul lost his crown and his life together.† Here king Josiah was defeated and slain.‡ And here, during the crusades, the bloodiest and most decisive battles were fought. This plain was the chief theatre of those holy wars.

But the real boundary here never corresponded to the boundary contemplated by the law. The people of Israel did not expel the Philistines, agreeably to the divine command. David was the first who executed what the lawgiver required on this head; and even he rather subdued than exterminated these strange nations. The clear possession of this coast is of great importance to a state established in Palestine, even though it do not engage in commerce; for without it the boundary can never be secure. As long as the Philistines continued to occupy but a small tract of the coast, the Israelites were never at rest. Sometimes they were even brought under the Philistine yoke, as we see from the books of Judges and Samuel.

As it regards that part of the coast, which extends northward, from Achzib to Zidon, the learned are not agreed, whether the sea was here to form the Israelitish boundary, or whether a narrow strip of territory was to be left to the undisturbed possession of the Sidonians. The majority of

* Judg. iv.   † 1 Sam. xxxi.   ‡ 2 Kings xxiii. 29.

biblical scholars hold to the first of these opinions. The arguments, which they bring in support of it, are weighty and strong. The principal passages, bearing upon the point, are the following :—Josh. 13 : 6. 19 : 28, 29. Judg. 1 : 31. By consulting these places, it will be seen, that "all the Sidonians" were included among the people to be driven out of their territories by the Israelites; that the border of Asher was to extend "unto great Zidon," and "the strong city Tyre;" and that tribe is censured for not "driving out the inhabitants of Zidon."

Michaelis dissents from this opinion, and maintains, on the contrary, that the narrow strip of coast, between mount Hor and the sea, extending from Achzib to Sidon, about half a degree of latitude in length, was to be left to the Phenicians, who were the actual possessors of it at the time of the conquest. The arguments, by which he defends this position, are plausible, if not convincing. They are as follows : 1. This coast was never in the possession of the Hebrews. They never made any attempt to conquer it,—not even in the reigns of David and Solomon. 2. These two monarchs lived in the closest friendship with the kings of Tyre; nor is the alliance between them, though often referred to in scripture, ever mentioned with disapprobation. 3. In all the catalogues given by Moses himself, whether longer or shorter, of the nations to be expelled by the Israelites, the Sidonians are never included. 4. The boundary line of the tribe of Asher, traced by Joshua, seems to confirm this view. It first touches the sea near mount Carmel and the river Belus. Thence the boundary line runs landward a great way to the north; then turns southward, passing Sidon and Tyre, apparently without reaching the sea in this quarter; and, finally, comes to touch the coast again near Achzib. Whence it would seem that the small tract of coast north from Ecdippa, which we call Phenicia, was to remain in the indisputed possession of the original proprietors. 5. This little country would be more valuable to the Israelites, if it remained in the possession of the Phenicians, than if they conquered and annexed it to their own dominions. It would have been of no great use to them, if incorporated into their territory, since they were not to be a trading people. But if the trading people, who inhabited it, had been driven out, and the maritime commerce, which the Israelites could not carry on themselves, had totally ceased, they would have lost a most valuable market for their surplus corn, wine, oil, and other commodities, which they exported by means of the Phenicians, together with the caravan trade from Arabia to Phenicia, which must have been very profitable. The loss of these markets would, at the same time, have been the loss of their chief motives to industry, agriculture, and manufactures. Neither could there be much danger to the Israelites in suffering this little stretch of coast to continue in possession of the Phenicians, since their boundary here was quite secure by means of mount Lebanon, at whose foot the sea flowed. The inhabitants of so small a tract of coast could not become very formidable, especially as their devotion to commerce would naturally lead them to cultivate relations of amity and peace with foreign nations. 6. In the blessings of Jacob, it is actually represented as a fortunate circumstance for Zebulon, that he was to have his inheritance on a sea coast, well frequented by ships, and not far from Sidon.

This theory is plausible, and the arguments brought to sustain it not destitute of force. Still, as the learned commentator himself confesses, it is pressed with great difficulties. The strongest objection is drawn from the passage in Judg. 1 : 31, where it is represented as a fault in Asher, that he " did not drive out the inhabitants of Zidon." From this it would seem, that he should have done so, and have taken possession of it himself. Michaelis ingenuously owns, that he knows not what satisfactory answer to make to this objection. To escape from difficulty, he suggests an emendation, perhaps I might better say, a mutilation of the text. He conjectures, that the words "inhabitants of Zidon" are an interpolation, though he pretends no other authority for the criticism, than the strength of the argument for excluding Sidon from the territories of Israel. This is a bold liberty, and not to be tolerated, except in a case of absolute necessity. Whether or not the present is such a case, the reader will judge for himself.

The southern boundary of Israel, according to the statute contained in the thirty-fourth chapter of Numbers, was to extend from the Mediterranean sea, at the point where the river of Egypt empties into it, to the southern extremity of the Salt, that is, the Dead sea. What stream is meant by the river of Egypt, is a point much disputed by biblical geographers. Some consider it a rivulet, which falls into the sea at El-Arisch, the ancient Rhinocolura. Others regard it as a stream, which empties into the Sirbonic lake, or gulf, near Calich. Others, still, understand by it the eastern, or Pelusic branch of the Nile. Dr. Hales* has given the subject an extended examination, and has exhibited strong proofs of the correctness of the last mentioned of these opinions. The statements of Herodotus and Pliny favor this view. The former† mentions mount Casius, lying between Pelusium and the Sirbonic lake, as the boundary between Egypt and Palestine; and the latter‡ reckons the Sirbonic lake itself as the boundary. Between these two points, the river of Egypt and the southern extremity of the Dead sea, the boundary fixed by the law of Moses, ran, in an irregular curve, through various places, whose names will be found in Numbers 34 : 3–5. The position of most of these places has never been determined with exactness; and of course the curvatures of the boundary line cannot be laid down with certainty.

The nearest neighbors of the Israelites, on this side, were

* Anal. Chron. V. 1, pp. 413, 414. † L. 3, C. 5.
‡ Nat. Hist. 1. 5, C. 13.

the Edomites. They were descendants of Esau (called also Edom*), and of course nearly related to the Israelites. They had a fertile country and lived under a settled government. Then came the Amalekites, Geshurites, and other wild Arab tribes. These were fierce, warlike, marauding nations, who lived by plundering their neighbors, and making slaves of their young women. With such people, no settled peace could be had. Moses, therefore, took advantage of an unprovoked attack of the Amalekites to incorporate into his code a law for their extermination. This procedure has drawn down upon him very bitter reproaches. Yet he ought not to be blamed for it, for prudence required, that the desert should be cleared of such neighbors. Their unprovoked and repeated injuries gave the Hebrews a just right to exterminate them. It was no more unjust in Israel to proceed in this manner towards the Amalekites than it would be in the United States to destroy a nest of pirates, that had taken possession of some neighboring island, for greater convenience of preying upon the property and lives of our citizens.

We must not suppose, that these Arab tribes had accurately defined limits and fixed habitations. Such a notion would often involve us in great perplexity in reading the Bible. They were wandering herdsmen, just as the Arabs of our day are. They pastured their sheep and cattle, wherever convenience dictated. They had no right of property in the soil. There might be encampments of Amalekites, Midianites, and other nomadic tribes, with their flocks and herds, all on the same plain, and within short distances of each other. Nay, they might even be mingled together, as we see the Kenites were with the Amalekites; for Saul, when about to attack the latter, sent to request, that the former would withdraw, for a time, from that quarter.† We can hence easily see how Balaam, from the heights of Moab, could see so many different nations.‡ They were not whole nations, but hordes of the

---

* Gen. xxxvi. 43.   † 1 Sam. xv. 6.   ‡ Numb. xxiv.

various nations, whose fates he predicted, when he cast his eye upon their several encampments, scattered over the wide desert below.

Even Edom, though under a regular government, had not its boundaries perfectly defined. The history of the march of the Israelites shows this. The territories of Edom extended from the southern border of Palestine to the Red Sea, and included the seaport town of Eziongeber. Now, in going from Sinai to the eastern shore of the Jordan, it is necessary to cross this region somewhere. Yet Moses did not traverse the country of Edom, but went round it.* This makes it clear, that there could not have been an accurately defined boundary, but that uncultivated and unappropriated wastes must have overspread the country.

The southern boundary of Israel did not always continue what it was made by the law recorded in Numb. 34. God, through his servant Moses, promised the chosen people, that their bounds should be from the Red Sea to the sea of the Philistines.† This looks like a permission, when a just provocation should afford the occasion, to conquer the Idumean territory, and appropriate it to their own use; which was actually done in the reigns of David and Solomon. The father conquered and annexed to the Israelitish dominions the whole country, even to the Red Sea; and the son made the Idumean ports of Aela and Eziongeber, on that sea, the seat of . an extensive, rich, and flourishing commerce. Some learned men believe, that the ships of Solomon, starting from this point, circumnavigated Africa. But this is a matter, which does not belong to the present inquiry.

The eastern boundary of what was strictly the holy land was the river Jordan. But the permitted boundary, and, for a considerable time, the actual boundary, was the river Euphrates. In point of fact, the Jordan never formed the bounding line of the Israelites on the east. A vast extent of

---

* Numb. xxxiii. 35–37.   † Exod. xxiii. 31.

country, forming the kingdoms of Sihon and Og, which was peculiarly adapted to the rearing of cattle, became the possession of Reuben and Gad, who were rich in herds. The Amorites, a Canaanitish nation, then held possession of the land of Gilead. This was conquered by the half tribe of Manasseh, who obtained it for a habitation.* How far the inheritance of these tribes extended to the eastward, is the question now in hand. In maps, these countries are confined within narrow limits, and are kept at a great distance from the Euphrates. The question is, did they not approach nearer to that river than is commonly supposed? This question is lucidly treated by Michaelis, the substance of whose article in relation to it, is embodied in the following paragraphs.

It seems almost certain, that mount Gilead, properly so called, from which the whole country had its name, lay far without the space, which the common maps of Palestine include, and was, in fact, at no great distance from the Euphrates. Of this any one will convince himself, who will take the trouble to weigh the history of Jacob's flight from Haran. Laban overtook him on the tenth day. Let it be remembered, that Haran is several days' journey to the east of the Euphrates; that an immense stretch of country lies between the upper part of that river and the lower part of the Jordan; and that Jacob was encumbered with vast herds of cattle, camels, sheep, and goats, with their young, besides wives, children, and servants. Ten or fifteen miles a day would be good travelling, under such circumstances. Who can believe, that Jacob could have approached the mouth of the Jordan in ten days? Yet Laban overtook him on mount Gilead. The inference is clear, that this mountain could not have had the position usually assigned it; but must have been in the neighborhood of the Euphrates. How far the land of Gilead may have stretched beyond the peaks of the

* Numb. xxxii. 39–42.

25

mountain, and whether it extended quite to the Euphrates, it is impossible to determine. Indeed, of the eastern and northern boundaries of the lands belonging to the two and a half tribes, we know almost nothing. The city of Kirjathana, which Moses assigned to the tribe of Reuben, in the opinion of Michaelis, lay only one day's journey from Palmyra.

Whether, in the time of Moses and Joshua, the tribes on the further side of Jordan pastured their herds as far eastward as the Euphrates, or not, they certainly did afterwards; and that before the time of David.* This fact has not been much noticed, because it is recorded in a book, which, consisting in great part of dry catalogues of names, is comparatively but little read. On this account, many remarkable historical occurrences, related in it, are commonly overlooked. But in 1 Chron. 5, 9, it is expressly said that the posterity of Reuben dwelt eastward, as far as the river Euphrates, because their cattle were multiplied in the land of Gilead. A very surprising history is added in vv. 10–22. It is to the following effect. The two and a half trans-jordanic tribes, in the days of Saul, made war with four powerful Arabian nations, among whom were the Hagarites, whose country bordered on the Persian gulf. They gained a decisive victory, took a hundred thousand captives, and an immense quantity of cattle and sheep, drove out the former inhabitants, and " dwelt in their steads, throughout all the east of Gilead, till the captivity.† Thus it appears, that these conquests, reaching to the banks of the Euphrates and the shores of the Persian gulf, were maintained from the reign of Saul to the time of the Assyrian captivity; a period of nearly three hundred years.

David not only rendered these possessions more secure, but extended the Israelitish dominions in that direction by still further conquests. Solomon, his son and successor, built

* 1 Chron. v. 9, 10.

† Vv. 10, 22. A statement, which affords pretty strong ground for believing, that the land of Gilead actually extended to the Euphrates.

Tadmor,* by the Greeks called Palmyra, which was not more than a day's journey from the Euphrates. It is also related of him, that " he had dominion over all the region on this side the Euphrates, from Tiphsah, (without doubt the ancient Thapsacus on that river,) even to Azzah, over all the kings on this side the river."†

Towards the south, also, the eastern boundary of Israel extended pretty far eastward, and lay in part beyond the land of Moab. Maon, which belonged to the tribe of Judah, even in the days of Joshua,‡ and where Nabal dwelt,§ is described by Abulfeda as the farthest city of Syria towards Arabia, and as six days' journey from the sea, and two beyond Zoar. Even in those eastern deserts, the Israelitish state could boast some wealthy and powerful citizens. Three private persons in Gilead were in such circumstances as, at their own expense, to supply David's whole army with food and other necessaries.‖ Nor is this matter of wonder, since the rearing of cattle, especially in such extensive pastures, tends to produce greater riches, than the cultivation of paternal fields.

Michaelis has an elaborate article on the northern boundary of the Israelites. He regards it as extending, in a serpentine line, from the Euphrates to the Mediterranean, in such a way, that Palmyra was on the south, and Damascus on the north side of it, and reaching the sea somewhere about the thirty-sixth degree of north latitude. For a detail of the argument, by which this line is established by the learned commentator, the reader is referred to the original work.

It thus appears, that the Israelitish boundaries, at their widest actual or intended extent, embraced a territory, from six to eight degrees of latitude in length, and as many of longitude in breadth ; a territory of not less than one hundred million acres. It is true, that large portions of this territory consisted of mountains and deserts. Much of it was fit only

* 1 Kings ix. 18. 2 Chron. viii. 4.   † 1 Kings, iv. 24.
‡ Josh. xv. 55.   § 1 Sam.xxv. 2.   ‖ 2 Sam. xvii. 27, 29.

for pasturage, and much of it was good for nothing at all. Still it is likely, that one half of it, or fifty million acres, was capable of cultivation. At a moderate computation, the lands to be divided among the Israelites, on both sides of Jordan, in the lifetime of Joshua, must have amounted to twenty-five million acres. This, distributed among six hundred thousand citizens, would give to each about forty-two acres. Let us still reduce this quantity one half, and even then each house-holder would have a farm of twenty-one acres.* I have no doubt, that this is below the amount actually divided. Yet, assuming it as the amount, let us see what can be said as to the capability of the land of promise maintaining so great a number of people, as were to live upon it.

My first remark here is, that Palestine was an extremely fertile country, the glory of all lands in the richness of its soil. Moses distinctly so represents it; and his representation is confirmed by the testimony of Josephus,† Tacitus,‡ the great Arabian geographer Abulfeda,§ and the best modern travellers, particularly Dr. Shaw.‖ The whole country was one vast and busy workshop of rural industry, abounding in all the productions of the tropical and temperate zones. It was cultivated like a garden. The sides of the mountains were terraced, even to their summits, and the cold rocks were covered with soil by the hand of industry. No judgment can be formed of its pristine fertility, from the state, to which it has been reduced, by eighteen centuries of tyranny and de-vastation. Yet even now intelligent travellers represent the soil of Palestine as unusually rich and productive.

In the second place, all the Israelites had always the right

---

* Curius Dentatus, as Pliny informs us, looked upon that Roman as a pernicious citizen, who was not content with seven acres of land, and did not find it sufficient for his subsistence. At one time, the Roman law did not allow more than that to each citizen.

† Jewish War, L. 3, C. 3.   ‡ Hist. L. 5, C. 6.

§ Tabulae Syriae, p. 9.   ‖ Travels, pp. 336, 337.

of pasturage in the deserts, and thither they were accustomed
to drive their flocks and herds, to graze upon the fertile spots,
which, like innumerable islands, dot the sandy wastes of
Arabia. The consequence of this was, that every Israelite
had all his fields for cultivation. Palestine could thus support a much greater population than a country equally good,
in which large portions of the farms are necessarily used for
pasturage. I am enabled to illustrate this point, from the
state of things in the place where I write, the township of
East Hampton, on the eastern extremity of Long Island. The
inhabitants of this township have pasture grounds, to the
extent of nine thousand acres, on the high lands of Montauk,
where thousands of sheep, cattle, and horses find abundance
of excellent pasturage, during the spring, summer, and
autumn. This leaves the people at liberty to cultivate a much
larger proportion of the remaining land, than they would
otherwise be able to do. And, were it not that there are
other large tracts, fit only for the growth of wood, on account
of the lightness of the soil, I am persuaded, that the territory
would sustain a population nearly double that, which the
same number of acres would support, under the ordinary
system of farming, where each particular farm must supply
pasturage to the flock and the herd. Palestine enjoyed two
advantages over this place, viz., first, in having an unlimited
quantity of pasturage in the deserts and mountains, and,
secondly, in the superior mildness of its winters, which took
away the necessity of providing any great amount of fodder.
On both these accounts, a still larger proportion of the land
could be appropriated to the sustenance of man; and in the
same proportion its power of supporting a numerous population would be increased.

In the third and last place, a country of equal fertility in a
southern latitude will support more inhabitants than in a
northern one. And this for several reasons. As 1. Large

tracts of land are required to furnish the fuel necessary for a cold country; while, in a warm climate, but little wood is needed for fuel. Hence the spaces, which, in the former, must be devoted to the growing of wood, can be used for tillage in the latter. In point of fact, the article of wood was very scarce in Palestine. 2. A much greater amount of clothing is consumed in cold than in warm countries. Consequently, in a northern climate, a vast quantity of land must be taken up in producing cotton, flax, and wool, which, in a southern one, can be devoted to the raising of bread stuffs. 3. In a country of the latitude of Palestine, and one which, like that, is cultivated as a garden, the land may be cropped several times within the year, which adds immensely to its capability of sustaining human life. This, indeed, is an advantage, for which Moses expressly celebrates Palestine.* 4. The same number of people consume less food in a warm country, than in a cold one. Men must be temperate in a hot climate, if they would keep their health. They seldom eat meat, but live mostly on vegetables. Chardin represents the inhabitants of northern Europe as beasts of prey, in comparison with the Asiatics. The nearer we approach the equator, the more abstemious we find the people. There are millions of people in India, who live on the value of a penny a day. Even in Europe, there is a sensible difference between the inhabitants of the north and the south. A Spaniard will subsist for a week on what a German would eat at a meal. The luxury of an Englishman displays itself in the number of dishes and the quantity of solid meats on the table; that of an Italian, in sweetmeats and flowers.† But 5. It is more important to observe, that the industry of husbandmen in countries, where rain seldom falls, and the fields must be watered artificially, surpasses any thing that our farmers exhibit. In such countries, they learn to make use of every foot of

* Deut. xxxiii. 14.   † Rouss. Soc. Cont. L. 3, C. 8.

land. They cover the naked rocks with soil, and raise walls to prevent showers from washing it away. Numerous examples of this are seen in Switzerland. Maundrell, in his travels, discovered many traces of this laudable economy in the ancient cultivation of the holy land.

Thus far the argument has been conducted solely on grounds of reason. It has been of an a priori character. But does the history of agriculture furnish no facts, bearing upon the present inquiry? Yes, many and important ones. From the evidence given in 1843 before the committee on allotments of land in the British parliament, it appears, that a hundred and twelve bushels of wheat had been obtained from an acre of land dug with the spade; that the average profit derived from cottage allotments was at the rate of a hundred dollars an acre; and that one man on the eighth of an acre of very indifferent land had grown a crop worth twenty-five dollars, or at the rate of two hundred dollars per acre.* Mr. Thornton, in his Plea for Peasant Proprietors, says, that a Flemish farmer of six acres of moderate land obtains from two acres and a half as much grain, potatoes, butter, pork, and milk, as are required for the consumption of himself, his wife, and three children, and sells the produce of the remaining three acres and a half.† The twenty-five millions of acres, which, on a moderate estimate, were, or should have been, distributed among the Israelites, on the conquest of Canaan, if parcelled out into estates of six acres each, would have supported four million families engaged exclusively in agriculture, and at least as many more occupied in other pursuits. That is to say, this territory would have furnished sustenance to a population of forty millions. And when at its greatest extent, the land of Israel must have been capable of maintaining double that number of inhabitants.

* Cited in the N. A. Rev. for July, 1848.   † Ibidem.

Surely, in this view of the case, which is rational and solid, all difficulty as to the Israelitish territory being able to support the largest population ever assigned to it, vanishes. Indeed, the difficulty never could have arisen, except upon the ground of a twofold error; the error of confining the holy land within too narrow limits, and the error of underrating the productive capability of a given quantum of soil.

BOOK II.

ORGANIC LAW OF THE HEBREW STATE.

CHAPTER I.

Fundamental Principles.

It is the proper function of the sciences to arrive at general principles; that is to say, primary, or general facts, in which all secondary, or particular facts are included. Gravitation may serve as an illustration of my meaning. By this one simple principle, astronomy explains all the complex laws of the celestial harmony.

In political, as well as physical science, there are certain great principles, true or false, from which, in any given case, all the numerous details of social organization flow.* Every state is based upon some fundamental ideas; and the study of those ideas is the most important object of inquiry in the study of its constitution. No social system can be understood without a knowledge of its fundamental principles. The Hebrew government, like all others, was founded upon certain great maxims of policy, to the development and elucidation of which the reader's attention is now invited.

The first and most essential of these fundamental principles was the unity of God.†

To some it may have an odd sound, to hear announced, as

---

* Salvador's Histoire des Institutions de Moïse, l. 1, p. 63.
† Deut. vi. 4.

a principle of political science, what we are apt to regard as
a mere religious dogma. But this can arise only from a want
of due reflection on the subject. When Moses made his appearance in the world, idolatry had crept in on every side.
It was firmly established in all nations. With its long train
of moral and social evils, it had become the common sentiment and common practice of mankind. It had gained the
credit of a settled truth, and the authority of an undoubted
principle of common sense. There was not a civil constitution then in being, which was not based upon the assumed
truth of polytheism. The Israelites themselves had become
so infected with it, that all the miracles wrought for their
deliverance, were not sufficient to cure their superstition, and
keep them steadfast to the worship of the true God.

A civil constitution, inseparably interwoven with the worship of the one living God, was, as far as we can judge, an
indispensable agency in enabling, perhaps I ought rather to
say, in compelling the Hebrews to answer their high destination. By this means, the worship of the true God would be
made imperishable, so long as the nation continued a nation.
By this means, it would happen, that religion and the political existence of the people must be annihilated together.
Whatever reason, therefore, there was for desiring the overthrow of idolatry, there was the same reason for incorpo-
rating the idea of the divine unity into the political structure
of the Hebrew commonwealth.

Such a politico-religious constitution could then be introduced without difficulty, since it was in accordance with the
political ideas of the times. Religious prodigies were as
familiar as civil edicts, and as constantly bore their share in
the administration of public affairs. All the ancient lawgivers called in the aid of religion to strengthen their respective polities. Thus did Menes in Egypt; Minos in Crete;
Cadmus in Thebes; Lycurgus in Sparta; Zaleucus in Locris;
and Numa in Rome.

But the procedure of Moses differed fundamentally from that of these heathen legislators. They employed religion in establishing their political institutions, while he made use of a civil constitution as a means of perpetuating religion.* Thus Moses made the worship of the one only God the fun- damental law of his civil institutions. This law was to remain forever unalterable, through all the changes, which lapse of time might introduce into his constitution. Thus was the Jewish lawgiver enabled to secure a result of indis- pensable necessity to human virtue and happiness; a result, which, as far as we can see, could have been attained in no other way.

In this procedure Moses has shown himself one of the greatest benefactors of mankind. The pernicious influence of polytheism will be more fully exhibited in our chapter on the Hebrew theocracy. Let it suffice for the present to observe, that the superstitions connected with it are a prolific source of immorality, crime and misery. But it is to be carefully noted, that it is one thing to make the single article of the worship of one God the first principle of a civil polity; and it is another and totally different thing to make the numerous articles of a religious creed, and their maintenance among the people, the object and scope of political arrangements. Moses framed no symbolic books for the people to subscribe; nor did he publish any mere theolo- gical dogma, the belief of which was to be enforced by civil penalties. Such was the structure of the Hebrew state, as will be explained in the next chapter, that idolatry became, under its constitution, a civil crime. No mere private opinion, however, nothing but the overt act of idolatry, was

* It is not meant to be asserted here, that Moses did not also employ religion in establishing his political institutions, but merely to direct attention to the fact, that with the heathen legislators religion was the means, and government the end, while with him government was the means, and religion the end.

punishable, under the laws of Moses, by the civil authorities.*

A second fundamental principle of the Hebrew government was national unity.

This idea was, in that age, as new and startling as the doctrine of the divine unity. The most ancient sages made
their ideas of the material universe the type of their political
and social institutions. The Egyptian priests regarded the

---

*Mich. Com. on the Laws of Moses, Arts. 32, 33, 34, and 245. The politi-
cal prohibition of idolatry, under the sanction of civil punishment, was
not, as we shall see in the next chapter, founded on the doctrine of the
true God, considered as a theological dogma, but on the principle that
Jehovah, having delivered the Israelites from slavery, and made them a
nation, was, by their own free choice, constituted civil head of their commonwealth. He was, therefore, to be honored as their king, as well as
their God. Even on the assumption of the truth of idolatry, on the supposition that there actually were other gods, this principle bound every
subject of the Israelitish government to worship none but the God of
Israel. Still, it was not opinions that were prohibited, but actions. But,
words may be political actions. Blackstone, indeed, (B. 4. C. 6.) lays
down the doctrine, that words spoken amount only to a high misdemeanor,
and no treason; for the words may be spoken in heat, without any intention, or they may be mistaken, perverted, or misremembered by the
hearers. But he adds, that words set down in writing constitute an overt
act of treason, for scribere est agere. But by the law of Moses, words
spoken against the divine King of Israel were considered as compassing,
that is, designing and aiming at the overthrow of the government. They
were an overt act of treason, which was punished capitally. Hence blasphemy was a state crime; and I have no doubt, that to speak any evil of
the God of Israel, or to deny his existence, was blasphemy, within the
meaning of the statute. This law extended to foreigners, as well as to
natives, Numb. 15 : 15. While Moses provided, that strangers, who took
refuge in the land of Israel, should be treated with justice and kindness,
he gave no protection or privilege to any foreign religion. He prohibited
absolutely all manner of idolatry. Still, if the stranger was, in his heart,
a friend of paganism, Moses did not authorize any inquiry into his private
opinion. Such an inquisitorial procedure was foreign both to his temper
and his legislation. His laws gave no sanction to it. They were framed
against actions, not ideas.

universality of things as composed of two distinct essences;
the one intellectual and active, the other physical and passive.* This philosophic dogma had a predominating influence on the civil state. In the political system framed by
them, the spiritual essence of the universe was the symbol of
the sacerdotal aristocracy; while the baser material essence
represented the common people. Thus the higher and lower
classes, the nobility and commonalty, were separated by a
gulf, as impassable as that which divides the inhabitants of
different planets.

Moses, endowed with a capacity and animated with a principle higher than any preceding philosopher or statesman,
rejecting this doctrine of dualism in the formation of his
commonwealth, substituted in its place the principle of national unity. His, however, was not that species of unity,
which the world has since so often seen, in which vast multitudes of human beings are delivered up to the arbitrary
will of one man. It was a unity, effected by the abolition of
caste; a unity, founded on the principle of equal rights; a
unity, in which the whole people formed the state, contrary
to what happened in Egypt, where the priesthood was the
state, and contrary to the celebrated declaration of a French
monarch,† who avowed himself to be the state.

Let us glance at the decalogue ‡ to ascertain, if possible,
its relation to this question of the unity of the Hebrew state.
These ten precepts belonged not simply to the department of
ethics among the Hebrews. They were civil, as well as
moral laws. They were intended to serve as the basis of the
whole system of civil legislation. They have suggested to
modern legislators the first idea of the declaration of the
rights of man.

Mark the expressive form given to the preamble of these
laws. It is as significant as it is laconic. "I am Jehovah
THY God, which brought THEE out of the house of bondage."

* Herod. l. 2.   † Louis XIV.   ‡ Ex. xx.

Here the Hebrews are addressed as one man; and so they are throughout the enactment of this fundamental code. It is Israel, it is the entire people, to whom the lawgiver speaks. Here is no distinction of castes. Here is no appropriation of dignities to one class; no hereditary inferiority assigned to another. The priesthood had not at this time been instituted, nor the tribe of Levi set apart to its peculiar functions. This tribe formed, it is true, a kind of literary aristocracy, and its dignities and duties were hereditary. Still, as will be shown in our chapter on the Levitical order, it was far from constituting a nobility, in the modern acceptation of that term. The same fundamental rights are recognized as belonging to all; the same fundamental duties as binding upon all. The whole law is in the interest of the whole people.* Social distinctions, therefore, whenever they arise, must rest upon the natural basis of superior intelligence and worth.

Another of those great ideas, which constituted the basis of the Hebrew state, was liberty.

Liberty is a word often uttered, but seldom understood. It is the theme of much glowing declamation, but of little sober inquiry. Poets and orators have eulogized the charms of liberty; demagogues use the word every day, as an instrument of political advancement; yet few, comparatively, investigate or comprehend its nature. Civil liberty, the liberty of a community, is a severe and restrained thing. The fundamental idea of it is that of protection in the enjoyment of our own rights, up to the point where we begin to trench upon the rights of others. It is natural liberty, so far restrained, and only so far, as may be necessary for the public good. Every law, which abridges personal freedom, without a corresponding general advantage, is an infringement of civil liberty. But it is no infringement of liberty to restrain the freedom of individuals, when the public good requires it. On the contrary, civil liberty implies, in the very notion of it,

* Maimon. More Nevochim, pt. 3. C. 34.

authority, subjection, and obedience. Montesquieu has well defined it, when he says, that it " consists in the power of doing what we ought to will, and in not being constrained to do what we ought not to will."* Liberty is a right of doing what the laws permit. ' If one citizen might do what they forbid, all might do it, which would be anarchy. True liberty would expire in such a state of things.

This rational, restrained, regulated liberty was amply secured by the Hebrew constitution. In the preamble to the ten commandments,† before cited, God expressly declares, that he had brought his people out of the "house of bondage." In another place he says : " I have broken the bands of your yoke, and made you go upright."‡ These expressions, rendered into their modern equivalents, mean : " I have delivered you out of a state of servitude, and constituted you a nation of freemen." " Is Israel a slave ?" cries Jeremiah,§—his heart bursting with sadness at the contrast between the freedom secured by the constitution of his country and the vassalage imposed upon his countrymen by foreign arms.

The learned Fleury‖ has declared his opinion on this point in unequivocal terms. "The Israelites," he says, " were perfectly free. They enjoyed the liberty cherished by Greece and Rome. Such was the purpose of God." Montesquieu¶ makes a reflection, which is applicable here. He says, that countries are not cultivated in proportion to their fertility, but to their liberty. Tried by this test, the freedom of Palestine will bear a favorable comparison with that of any nation in any age of the world ; for never was territory more highly cultivated, or more productive, than that of the chosen tribes, in the palmy days of their history.

The freedom, secured by the polity of Moses, will more

* Spirit of Laws, B. 11, C. 3.   † Ex. xx. 2.   ‡ Levit. xxvi. 13.
§ Levit. ii. 14.   ‖ Manners of the Israelites, C. 20.
¶ Spirit of Laws, B. 18, C. 3.

fully appear, as we advance in our inquiries. There is no doubt, that the constitution was as free as it could be, consistently with its own safety and stability; and it is probable, that the Hebrew people enjoyed as great a degree of personal liberty, as can ever be combined with an efficient and stable government.

A fourth fundamental principle of the Hebrew constitution was the political equality of the people.

This was absolute and entire. I lay down the following proposition broadly and without qualification. The members of the body politic, called into being by the constitution of Moses, stood upon a more exact level, and enjoyed a more perfect community of political rights, dignities, and influence, than any other people known in history, whether of ancient or modern times.

A few words will place this point in a clear and convincing light.

It is a principle of political philosophy, first announced by Harrington,* and much insisted upon by Lowman† and the elder Adams,‡ that property in the soil is the natural foundation of power, and consqeuently of authority. This principle will not now be disputed. Hence, the natural foundation of every government may be said to be laid in the distribution of its territories. And here three cases are supposable, viz. the ownership of the soil by one, the few, or the many. First, if the prince own the lands, he will be absolute; for all who cultivate the soil, holding of him, and at his pleasure, must be so subject to his will, that they will be in the condition of slaves, rather than of freemen. Secondly, if the landed property of a country be shared among a few men, the rest holding as vassals under them, the real power of government will be in the hands of an aristocracy, or nobility, whatever authority may be lodged in one or more persons, for the sake of greater unity in counsel and action.

* Oceana, p. 37.   † Civ. Gov. Heb. C. 2.   ‡ Defence, Letter 29.

But, thirdly, if the lands be divided among all those who compose the society, the true power and authority of government will reside in all the members of that society ; and the society itself will constitute a real democracy, whatever form of union may be adopted for the better direction of the whole, as a political body. Under such a constitution, the citizens themselves will have control of the state. They will not need to have this power conferred upon them by express grant. It will fall into their hands by the natural force of circumstances, by the inevitable necessity of the case. There is no truth in political science more easy to comprehend, more open to the view of all, or more certainly known in universal experience, than that the men who own the territories of a state will exercise a predominating influence over the public affairs of such state.* This is agreeable to the constitution of human nature, and is confirmed by the concurrent testimony of all history.

The provision of the Hebrew constitution in reference to the ownership of the soil, is that of my third supposition. Moses ordered, that the national domain should be so divided, that the whole six hundred thousand free citizens should have a full property in an equal part of it.† And to render this equality solid and lasting, the tenure was made inalienable, and the estates, thus originally settled upon each family, were to descend by an indefeasable entail, in perpetual succession.‡

The principle which lies at the bottom of this argument for

* England, it must be owned, is an exception to this remark. But this is owing to peculiar circumstances. The enormous debt of England has created a species of property called funded property,—which has all the stability of landed possessions, and which is much more diffused among the people. The vast commercial and manufacturing wealth of England is another cause of the diminished political influence of land. Hence the predominant influence is no longer in the territorial property. The funded property prevails over the landed, the boroughs over the counties.

† Numb. xxxiii. 54.   ‡ Levit. xxv. 23.

the political equality of the Hebrew citizens, is strongly developed, in its application to our own country, by one of our ablest political writers. " The agrarian in America," says the elder Adams,* " is divided into the hands of the common people in every state, in such a manner, that nineteen twentieths of the property would be in the hands of the commons, let them appoint whom they might for chief magistrate and senators. The sovereignty, then, in fact as well as theory, must reside in the whole body of the people; and even an hereditary king and nobility, who should not govern according to the public opinion, would infallibly be tumbled instantly from their places." Such was the opinion of Mr. Adams in regard to the nature and operation of this principle. He held, that the sovereignty of a state is an inseparable attribute of property in the soil. Lord Bacon and Harrington were of the same opinion. The former uses property and dominion as convertible terms ;† and the latter says expressly, that empire follows the balance of property, whether lodged in one, few, or many hands.‡

The details of the agrarian law of Moses will occupy our attention in a subsequent part of this treatise. The reader, however, is desired to mark, in passing, a few points in it, evincing its great wisdom. It made extreme poverty and overgrown riches alike impossible, thus annihilating one of the most prolific sources as well as powerful engines of ambition. With the denial of the means of luxury, it took away all the ordinary incitements to it, in the example of a titled and wealthy aristocracy. It gave to every member of the body politic an interest in the soil, and consequently in the maintenance of public order and the supremacy of law, which

---

Defence, Letter 29.

†' How shall the plough, then," he says, " be kept in the hands of the owner, and not mere hirelings ? * * *   How, but by the balance of dominion, or property ?"

‡ Prerogative of Pop. Gov. C. 3.

he had not even the power to part with. It made the virtues of industry and frugality necessary elements in every man's character. Its tendency was to secure to all the citizens a moderate independence, and to prevent those extremes of opulence and destitution, which are the opprobrium of modern civilization. Great inequality of wealth in a nation is a great evil, to be avoided by the use of all just and prudent means. It was a leading object with Moses to give to his constitution such a form, as would tend to equalize the distribution of property. Under his polity, the few could not revel in the enjoyment of immense fortunes while the million were suffering from want. Misery was not the hereditary lot of one class, nor boundless wealth of another. The government watched over all, and cared for all alike. No citizen could justly charge his poverty to its neglect.

The agrarian of Moses elevated labor to its just dignity, and removed the odium, which adhered to it in all other ancient states. It is an error, into which our best informed political writers have fallen, to suppose, that, for the first time in the history of the world, labor has taken its true position in our country. It was as much fostered by the government, it was as generally practised, and it was as honorable among the ancient Hebrews, as it is even in New England. St. Paul says, " if any man will not work, neither shall he eat."* This saying of the apostle was but the reflection of a common Hebrew sentiment, and shows in what estimation labor was held by that people. Intelligent labor, manly labor, independent labor, labor thinking, and acting, and accumulating for itself, was the great substantial interest, on which the whole fabric of Hebrew society rested. Such was Hebrew labor, and such the position assigned to it by the Hebrew lawgiver.

But, not content with establishing originally a full equality among the citizens, the constitution of Moses made provision for its permanent continuance. With such jealous care did

* 2 Thess. iii. 10.

it watch, that the people might never moulder away, and be lost to the state in the condition of slaves, that it provided for a general periodical release of debts and servitudes;— partially by the institution of the sabbatical year, but more completely by that of the jubilee. No matter how often the property had changed hands, at the return of the jubilee year, it was restored, free of encumbrance, to the original owners or their heirs.* The Israelite, whom calamity or improvidence had driven abroad, needed no longer to wander for want of a home of his own to welcome him. This was a wise, as well as benevolent provision of the constitution. It was admirably suited to preserve a wholesome equality among the citizens. The rich could not accumulate all the lands. The fiftieth year, beyond which no lease could run, was always approaching, with silent, but sure tread, to relax their tenacious grasp. However alienated, however unworthily sold, however strongly conveyed to the purchaser an estate might be, this long-expected day annulled the whole transaction, and placed the debtor in the condition, which either himself or his ancestor had enjoyed. At the return of this day, the trumpet peal was heard, in street and field, from mountain top and valley, throughout the length and breadth of the land.† The chains fell from the exulting slave. The burden of debt, like that of Bunyan's Pilgrim, rolled off from shoulders, long galled by its pressure. The family mansion and the paternal estate again greeted eyes, from which misfortune, through many a weary year, had divorced them. The inequalities of condition, which the lapse of half a century had produced, once more disappeared. Garlands of flowers crowned all brows; and the universal gladness found vent in music, feasting, and merriment.‡

---

* Levit. xxv. 10, 13. † Ibid. xxv. 9.

‡ Godwyn's Moses and Aaron, l. 3. c. 10. Jahn's Bib. Arch. Sect. 351. A reflection of Lord Bacon, in his History of Henry VII. (p. 72.) is pertinent here. He is commending the wisdom of the law, which required,

A magistracy elected by the people, the public officer chosen by the public voice, was another of those great principles, on which Moses founded his civil polity.

The magistrates are not properly the ministers of the people, unless the people elect them. It is, therefore, a fundamental maxim in every popular government, that the people should choose their ministers, that is to say, their magistrates. The people need councillors of state and executive officers, as much as monarchs, perhaps even more than they. But they cannot have a just confidence in these officers, unless they have the choosing of them. And the people, in every nation capable of freedom, are well qualified to discharge this trust. Facts, obvious to sense, and to which they cannot be strangers, are to determine them in their choice. The merits of their neighbors are things well known to them. " Should we doubt of the people's natural ability in respect to the discernment of merit, we need only cast an eye on the continual series of surprising elections made by

" that all houses of husbandry, that were used with twenty acres of ground, or upwards, should be maintained and kept up forever, together with a competent proportion of land, to be used and occupied with them, and in no ways to be separated from them." On this he observes : " The houses being kept up, did of necessity enforce a dweller, and the proportion of land for occupation being kept up, did of necessity enforce that dweller not to be a beggar or cottager, but a man of some substance. This did wonderfully concern the might and manhood of the kingdom, to have farms, as it were, of a standard sufficient to maintain an able body out of penury ; and did, in effect, amortize [transfer as an inalienable possession] a great part of the lands of the kingdom unto the hold and occupation of the yeomanry, or middle people, of a condition between gentlemen and cottagers, or peasants. Thus did the king sow hydra's teeth, whereupon, according to the poet's fiction, should rise up armed men for the service of the kingdom." This observation of a wise and able politician sets in a striking light the wisdom of this part of the Hebrew constitution. If the law, on which Bacon is here commenting, " did wonderfully concern the might and manhood of the kingdom," how much more the agrarian of Moses!

the Athenians and Romans, which no one surely will attribute to hazard."* The people, therefore, though in the mass incapable of the administration of government, are, nevertheless, capable of calling others to this office. They are qualified to choose, though, as a general thing, not qualified to be chosen. "In their sentiments," said the great Edmund Burke, "the people are rarely mistaken."

The election by the Hebrew people of Jehovah himself to be the civil head of their state, is a point, which has been already established, in the introductory essay.† The proofs need not be repeated here. No fact can be plainer, or more certain, than that the judges, instituted at the suggestion of Jethro, were chosen by the suffrages of all Israel. The direction of Moses to the people, upon that occasion, is very explicit. His words are, "Take you wise men, and understanding, and known among your tribes, and I will make them rulers over you."‡ The meaning is, "Do you elect the proposed officers, and I will commission and induct them into office." It is very observable, that these magistrates were to be taken "out of all the people," and not from any privileged class. The only qualifications for office required were, that they should be "able men, such as fear God, men of truth, hating covetousness,"§ "wise men, and understanding, and known among their tribes." The possession of these high attributes was enough; no other patent of nobility was required. Mr. Jefferson's test of official competency is expressed in the three interrogatories, "Is he honest? Is he capable? Is he faithful?" If he had added a fourth, "Does he fear God?" he would have had the Mosaic test to a tittle. Moses demanded four qualifications in a civil ruler, viz. ability, integrity, fidelity, and piety.

When the land of Canaan was to be divided among the tribes, Joshua addressed all Israel thus: "Give out from

* Montesq. Sp. of Laws, B. 2. C. 2.   † Pp. 47, 48.
‡ Deut. i. 13.   § Exod. xviii. 21.

among you three men from each tribe, and I will send them,"* &c. "Give out from among you;" that is, "Select, choose for yourselves." When Jephthah was made judge, it is expressly said, "The PEOPLE made him head and captain over them."† These instances, and others which might be cited, prove, that the great principle, that rulers should be elected by the ruled, that authority should emanate from those over whom it is to be exercised, was fully embodied in the Hebrew constitution.

A principle, closely allied to this, viz. that the people should have an authoritative voice in the enactment of the laws, is another of those great ideas, which underlie the Hebrew government; and this principle, like the preceding one, is fundamental in every popular government.

When Moses, on descending from the mount, rehearsed to the people the laws which he had received from the Lord, with one voice, they answered and said, " All the words that the Lord has said, will we do."‡ What is this, but an acceptance by the nation of the constitution proposed to them? The Hebrew constitution was adopted by the Hebrew people, as truly as the American constitution was adopted by the American people. "This adoption, by the Jewish nation, of the laws, which Moses brought from God, was repeated at the death of Moses, and by a statute, once in seven years was to be repeated ever after by the assembled nation. So that, from generation to generation, once in seven years, the tribes met in a great national convention, and solemnly ratified the constitution. They took what might be called the freeman's oath to observe that constitution."§ The government, then, was, in a solid and just sense, a government of the people; for the magistrates were chosen by their suffrages, and the laws were enacted by their voice.

---

* Josh. xviii. 4. † Judges xi. 11.

‡ Exod. xix. 8. § Beecher's Works, vol. 1, p. 179.

The responsibility of public officers to the people was the seventh fundamental maxim of the Hebrew polity.

In proof of this the reader is referred to the closing scene of Samuel's public administration. The aged statesman resigns his authority to the convention of the people, by whom it had been conferred. History records no sublimer or more touching scene. He calls upon his constituents, if any had been injured by his public acts, or knew of any abuse of the trusts confided to him, to step forward and accuse him. With one voice they reply, " Thou hast injured, oppressed, defrauded none."*

Several incidents, related in the history of the kings, confirm this view. When Saul was chosen king, a writing, limiting the royal prerogative, was prepared by Samuel, and deposited in the sanctuary, where reference might afterwards be made to it, in case of royal usurpation.† A similar writing was exacted of his successors.‡ Solomon, during the latter period of his life, had reigned as a despot. When his son mounted the throne, Judah and Benjamin were the only tribes, which acknowledged him. The other tribes offered to submit to his authority, on conditions which were not accepted. But when the young king rejected their terms, they rejected him, chose a sovereign for themselves, and established a separate kingdom.§ These instances show, that the people held their rulers to a stern responsibility for the manner in which they discharged their public trusts.

All this was the action of the republican spirit of the nation; a spirit, inspired, cherished, and sanctioned by the constitution. Who can doubt whether it was a constitution, intended for a free and self-governing community?

A cheap, speedy, and impartial administration of justice was another of those great ideas, on which Moses founded his civil polity.

* 1 Sam. xii. 1-5.   † Ibid. x. 25.
‡ 2 Sam. v. 3; 1 Kings xii. 4; 2 Kings xi. 17.   § 1 Kings xii. 1-20.

Under the Hebrew constitution, the poor and the weak were not to be the victims of the rich and the strong. The small as well as the great * were to be heard, and equal justice awarded to all, without fear or favor. That terrible and ruinous evil, " the law's delay," was unknown to the Hebrew jurisprudence. Courts of various grades were established, from high courts of appeal down to those ordained for every town. " Judges and officers shalt thou make thee in all thy gates,"† was the constitutional provision on this subject. To what a minute subdivision the judiciary system was carried, appears from the ordinance, which required, that there should be " rulers over thousands, rulers over hundreds, rulers over fifties, and rulers over tens, who should judge the people at all seasons.‡ Care was thus taken, that in suits and proceedings at law, every man should have what was just and equal, without going far to seek it, without waiting long to obtain it, and without paying an exorbitant price for it. Certainly, with a judiciary constituted in this manner, justice could be administered promptly, while provision was made against the evils of hasty decisions, in the right of appeal to higher courts ; in important cases, even to the venerable council of seventy, composed of the wisest, the gravest, the ablest, the most upright, and trustworthy men in the nation.§

Another vital principle of the Hebrew constitution was peace.

A thirst of conquest, and the foul passions, which it implies and engenders, had no place in the legislator's own bosom, and were utterly repugnant to the spirit of his legislation. It was a prime object of his polity to discountenance and repress a military spirit in the nation.

In the first place, his constitution made no provision for a standing army ; and a soldiery under pay was an innovation

* Deut. i. 17.　　　† Deut. xvi. 18.　　　‡ Ex. xviii. 21.
§ Deut. vii. 8, 9.

long posterior to the time of Moses. The whole body of
citizens, holding their lands on condition of military service,
when required,* formed a national guard of defence. Thus
the landholders (and every Israelite was a landholder) formed
the only soldiery, known to the Mosaic constitution.

In the second place, the intensely agricultural character of
the Hebrew government served to impress upon it an almost
equally pacific character. Light and darkness are scarcely
more repugnant to each ther, than husbandry and war.
Among the ancient Germans, as we learn from Tacitus and
Cæsar, the chiefs, in the general council of the nation, made
an annual distribution of the lands in the country. The motive prompting to such a procedure was, that the thoughts of
the people might not be diverted from war to agriculture.
Deeply did those sagacious chieftains feel, for clearly did
they perceive, that permanent landed possessions, improved
habitations, and a too curious attention to domestic conven-
iences and comforts, would beget in the tillers of the soil an
affection for the spots they cultivated, which would produce
sentiments and manners, quite repugnant to their own
schemes of conquest and military aggrandizement.

Thirdly, the use of cavalry, at once the effect and, the
cause of a passion for war, was prohibited by the constitution.† On the occasion of a certain victory, when a large
number of the enemy's horses had fallen into his hands,
Joshua was directed by the oracle to " hough," or hamstring
them, that is, to cut their thigh sinews.‡ This was practised

* Judges v. 23.   † Deut. xvii. 16.

‡ Joshua xi. 6. The object of "houghing" the horses was not, as most
expositors, following Kimchi and Bochart, have represented, to merely
lame them in the hind legs and let them go, but to kill them. A horse
can be hamstrung in an instant, and, as the operation cuts the artery of
the thigh, he soon dies of the wound, by bleeding to death. This plan is
still sometimes used by military commanders to render horses, which have
been taken in battle, and cannot be carried away, unserviceable to the
enemy.

on similar occasions, even as late as the reign of David.* The law against multiplying horses appears to have been faithfully observed, till the proud ambition of Solomon swept away this, in common with many other wholesome provisions of the national constitution. In governments, which have made conquest a leading object of pursuit, the principal military force has consisted in cavalry, and this especially in rude societies. In the infancy of the military art, the superiority of cavalry over infantry is very conspicuous. The fate of battle depended on that part of the army, which fought on horseback, or in chariots. It is obvious, that no founder of an empire, in those early ages, who intended his people for a career of conquest and military grandeur, would or could have dispensed with cavalry in his armies. The fact that Moses forbade the use of this species of force, is a proof that he designed his people for peaceful pursuits, and not for military glory.

But Moses had another motive for his prohibition of cavalry. The political equality of all the citizens, as we have seen under a former head, was a darling object with him. But in all ancient nations, where cavalry was employed, the horsemen, being necessarily the wealthier members of the community, became also the more powerful. The system threw the chief political power into the hands of a few rich citizens, who could afford to mount and bring into the field themselves and their dependants. This naturally tended to the establishment of monarchical and aristocratical governments. Moses could not but perceive this tendency, and on this account, as well as on account of his repugnance to an aggressive military policy, he excluded a mounted soldiery from the forces of the republic. It is remarkable, how speedily the substitution of the monarchical for the republican form of polity, led to the introduction and use of cavalry in the Israelitish armies.

* 2 Sam. viii. 4.

Fourthly, according to the testimony of Josephus, it was required, except in the case of the Canaanitish nations, that, previous to actual hostilities, heralds should be sent to the enemy with proposals of peace; and not until negotiation had failed, was force to be called in. This testimony is confirmed by a law contained in Deuteronomy 20 : 10. Considerable light is also thrown upon the point, by what I will venture to call a state paper of Jephthah. * It is a letter of instructions to his ambassadors, directing them as to the manner in which they should conduct a negotiation with the king of the Ammonites. The instructions are drawn up with an ability, force, and skill, which would not discredit any statesman of modern times.

Another proof of the repugnance of Moses to aggressive wars, and of the peaceful spirit of his general policy, may be drawn from the law of the Hebrew festivals. Thrice every year all the males were required to repair to the capital.† With such a law in operation, how could a nation engage in schemes of foreign conquest? The idea seems little less than preposterous.

Finally, this view of the pacific character of the Hebrew constitution is strengthened by a forcible argument of Michaelis,‡ in which that learned writer undertakes to prove, that the sin of David in numbering the people, which has so puzzled the commentators, consisted, not in any ambitious motions, hid in the secret chambers of his own heart, but in openly aspiring at the establishment of a military government, and in attempting, with that view, to subject the whole nation to martial regulations, to form a standing army, and so to break down and ride over one of the fundamental provisions of the constitution,—the many successful wars which he had carried on having, in all likelihood, filled his mind with the spirit of conquest.

* Judges xi. 12–27.   † xxxiv. 23.
‡ Com. on the Laws of Moses, Art. 174.

In beautiful harmony with the peaceful genius of his institutes, was the conduct of Moses, whenever he wished to
march through the territories of other nations. Unlike the
mere military chieftain of ancient times, whose sole aim was
conquest and plunder, he always asked permission to do so,
promising to abstain from treading down the cornfields, and
to pay for every thing he consumed, not accepting even
water. Sihon himself was not conquered and despoiled of
his territories, because of his refusal to grant a passage
through them, nor because he marched an army of observation toward his frontier, for the Edomites had done the same
before, but because he proceeded beyond his frontier into the
wilderness, and, without provocation, attacked the Israelites
first.*

Let us pause here, for a moment, to contemplate the remarkable phenomenon, offered to our observation. What do
we behold? A man, whose deep sagacity, under the guidance of a divine illumination, " discerned the hollowness of
martial glory, in an age when battles were the business and
delight of nations; when hardly any thing was respected,
either in societies or men, in comparison with military fame;
and when public virtue and civil wisdom dwindled into
nothing before the splendid sins of war."† In such an age,
his penetrating genius saw, that the true elements of public
prosperity lay in the path of public tranquility; and that
the greatness of a nation consisted not in standing armies, in
memorable victories, or in uncounted acres; but in the calm
virtues of industry, frugality, and beneficence; in the blood-
less triumphs of disciplined intelligence; in the mild dignities,
which play around the domestic circle; and in the amount
of individual prosperity and happiness, spread through the
homes and hearts of the land. And was he not right in this
estimate? Of all the evils, which afflict humanity, the
greatest in magnitude, the most injurious in its moral influ-

* Numb. xx. 14–21; xxi. 21–23.   † Christian Examiner for Sept. 1836.

ences, the most repugnant to christianity, and the most expensive of money, is war. How, then, can we sufficiently admire the wisdom of a lawgiver, who, in an age of barbarism and war, established a government upon the broad principles of equity and peace? In vain does the imagination essay to follow, in all their amplitude and variety, the streams of happiness, which shall gush forth, as from a thousand fountains, when war shall never again unfurl his crimson banner to the breeze, nor imprint his bloody footsteps upon the earth. Then shall religion, learning, social order, and regulated liberty become the inheritance of the race. Humanity shall receive purer impulses. Arts shall flourish, and science extend her enriching victories. Plenty and contentment shall become the general lot. Piety, that plant of renown, the fairest flower that bloomed in the abode of primeval innocence, shall again strike deep its roots into the human heart. And the broad earth, now scathed and blighted by the curse of its offended maker, shall again smile in the freshness and beauty of Eden.

The doctrine that agriculture constitutes the best basis of the prosperity and happiness of a state, was the tenth fundamental principle of the Mosaic polity.

Moses labored to impress upon his people the conviction, that their country was best adapted to agriculture, and that agriculture was most favorable to its true and lasting prosperity.* He represented it as a land flowing with milk and honey; a land of brooks of water, of fountains, and of depths that spring out of valleys and hills; a land of wheat, and barley, and vines, and fig-trees, and pomegranates; a land of oil-olive and honey; a land that drank liberally of the river of heaven, and wherein bread should be eaten without scarceness.† Nothing can be plainer, than that it was on agriculture alone, taken in its broadest sense, so as to include the culture of vineyards, olive grounds, and gardens, that Moses

---

* Christian Examiner for Sept. 1836.   † Ex. iii. 8 : Deut. i. 25, viii. 7–10.

saw fit to lay the foundation of the Israelitish state.* By a provision in the constitution, before explained, no Israelite could be born, who did not inherit a piece of land from his progenitors.

Country life has inspired the genius, and tuned the lyre, of many a rural bard. Their smiling pictures have lent new charms to nature herself, and have inspired, in many hearts, a taste for rural scenes and labors. But agriculture presents itself to us under a point of view more positive and practical.† It is the parent art, the paramount interest, of civilized society. The great pursuit of man is agriculture. It is the nurse of the human race. It has principles which elevate it to the rank of a science, a noble and comprehensive science. In the improvement of domestic animals and the fertilization of soils, the most abstruse principles of physiology and chemistry must be consulted. The principles of natural philosophy, also, have an equal relation to agriculture; for there is not a change of the seasons or the wind, there is not a fall of rain or of snow, there is not a fog or a dew, which does not affect some one or more of the manifold operations of the farmer.‡ The relation of science to agriculture is close and vital. It is an error to suppose, that the whole education of a farmer consists in knowing how to plough and sow and reap, the rest being left to the earth, the seasons, good fortune, and providence. The nature of soils and plants, the food they require, and the best methods of supplying it, are objects worthy of an earnest study. In a word, farming is a science, whose principles must be investigated, mastered, and skilfully applied, in order to insure profitable crops. There is no other pursuit, in which so many of the laws of nature must be understood and consulted, as in the cultivation of the earth.

What, then, shall we think of those ancient nations, which

* Mich. Com. on Laws of Mos. Art. 41.
† Salv. Hist. Inst. Mos. l. 3. C. 4.
‡ Wadsworth's Add. to the N. Y. Ag. Society.

treated agriculture as a servile profession, and refused to the tillers of the soil a rank among the citizens of the state? What shall we say of those Greek philosophers and legislators, who abandoned to slaves and the dregs of the people the culture of the lands? Both Plato* and Aristotle† required slaves to till the land. In many of the states of Greece, agriculture was a servile profession. The inhabitants of conquered countries were compelled to practise it, while the citizens found employment in gymnastic and military exercises, forming, as Montesquieu says, a society of wrestlers and boxers. Thus the soil was tilled by the Helots among the Lacedaemonians, by the Periecians among the Cretans, by the Penestes among the Thessalians, and by other conquered people in other republics.‡

Not thus did the Hebrew lawgiver think and act. He made agriculture the great channel of Hebrew industry. Doubtless, the circumstances of the Hebrew people and the grand design of their polity had an influence over this direction. Still, it cannot be doubted, that Moses regarded agriculture as, in itself, the most useful and the most honorable of employments.

The honor accorded by a lawgiver to any pursuit is a sure test of the esteem in which he holds it; and the most effectual means of causing any branch of industry to flourish among a people, is to honor it. Apply this test to agriculture among the Hebrews, and what is the result? We see the same men passing from the labors of the field to the exercise of the highest public functions, and returning again to their

* De Legibus, 1. 5.

† Pol. 1. 7, C. 10. It is true, indeed, that Aristotle, in another place, says, that the best republics were those, in which the citizens themselves tilled the land; but this, as Montesquieu observes, was brought about by the change of the ancient governments, which were become democratic; whereas, in earlier times the cities of Greece were subject to an aristocratic government.

‡ Montesquieu's Spirit of Laws, B. 4, C. 8.

private toils. Even after his elevation to the royal dignity, Saul goes back to the labors of husbandry.* Elijah casts his prophetic mantle upon Elisha, when the latter is engaged in ploughing.† David is taken from the sheepfold, to fill the throne of his country, and to become the leader and shepherd of the people.‡ The highest proof of the devotion of a people to agriculture, and of its flourishing condition, is the increase of population; since, among an agricultural people, this will generally be in proportion to the increased means of subsistence. But nowhere, in the whole history of mankind, has an equal extent of territory given birth and sustenance to a population, as numerous as that of ancient Palestine.§ The figures of the prophets attest the zeal of the Hebrews in preparing their soil, in removing stones and weeds and in surrounding their fields with walls and hedges.

Small proprietorships and the cultivation of all the territories of the state by the actual owners, was the policy of the Hebrew laws. Let us inquire into the effect of this policy on the social condition and general welfare of a country.

Under the system of small ownerships, Attica reached the height of her prosperity, but when Herodes Atticus became universal proprietor, she sank to poverty and misery. We look at Rome under Servius, and we see a vast body of small proprietors, enriching themselves by the cultivation of their own lands.‖ We look again, and see universal poverty. Immense tracts are now in the hands of the Scipios and Pompeys, who have replaced the numerous small, but pros-

---

*1 Sam. xi. 5. †1 Kings xix. 19.
‡1 Sam. xvi. 11, 12. § See B. 1, C. 9, of this work.
‖ Curius Dentatus once said to his soldiers, when they insisted on a larger division of the conquered lands: "God forbid, that a citizen should look upon that as a small piece of land, which is sufficient to support a man." (Plutarch's Lives.) He declared that man a pernicious citizen, who did not find seven acres sufficient for his subsistence. Seven acres was the number fixed by law for each Roman on the expulsion of the kings. (Pliny in Anthon's Class. Dict. Art. Curius.)

27

perous proprietors. The same scenes have, in modern times, been re-enacted in the south of Spain. When the industrious Moors held that country, the lands were divided and worked by the owners, who enriched both themselves and the state. But since these industrious cultivators of their own estates have been succeeded, in the ownership of the soil, by a few princely grandees, the most fertile territories, which the sun visits in his course, are abandoned, I had almost said, to sterility and desolation.* Thus has it been everywhere and always. General wealth and comfort have increased in proportion to the division of the land.

The condition of the several sections of our own country confirms this view. Where do we see competence, domestic comfort, industry, intelligence, and manly dignity most extensively diffused among the masses? In those portions, where the land is divided into small farms, and every man works his own estate. The introduction of slavery into Georgia was owing to the system of large proprietorships. The fatal influence of cultivation by tenantry compelled a resort to slave labor, at a time when slavery was abhorrent to the feelings of. the inhabitants, as well as to the principle on which the colony had been founded.†

But the most remarkable exemplification of the fruits of the two systems of large and small proprietorships is seen in the comparative condition of England and France. In the united kingdom of Great Britain and Ireland, with a population of twenty-six millions, the number of landed proprietors does not exceed eighty-five thousand. In France, with a population of thirty-four millions, the landholders are five and a half millions. Yet the aggregate wealth of Britain is greater than that of France. The rental of the former country exceeds that of the latter by about one-third.

The effect of this state of things on the social condition

---

* Carey's Past, Present, and Future, C. 4.
† North American Review for July, 1848.

of the two countries is well worthy of our study. Great
Britain has a million and a half of public paupers, or one in
eleven of her whole population; and she expends thirty-five
millions of dollars annually for their maintenance. France,
with double her population, has only a little more than a
third of this number, or one in fifty of her whole population;
and the sum expended on their support is less than two million dollars per annum, being about one twentieth of the cost
of English pauperism. Great Britain and Ireland together
contain fourteen millions of human beings, whose utmost
possible earnings fall short, by about one fourth, of what it
would cost her to maintain the same persons in the poor-
houses, notwithstanding a rigid system of economy is practised in those establishments. The consequence of all this is,
that the body of the British working people is fast sinking
into a state, to which there has hardly ever been a parallel.
At Stockport Assizes, in the autumn of 1841, a father and
mother were arraigned and convicted of poisoning three of
their children, to defraud a burial society of 3l. 8s., due on
the death of each child. It was whispered at the time, that
the public authorities hinted that this case might not be a
solitary one, and perhaps it would be best not to probe matters too deeply in that direction. "Such instances are like
the highest mountain apex emerged into view, under which
lies a whole mountain region not yet emerged." Statements,
like those contained in this paragraph, would be incredible,
if their authenticity did not rest on unimpeachable testimony.* The English nation is richer than any nation ever
was before; and yet half her people are starving. The fable
of Tantalus is here a reality. With a soil blooming in
beauty and waving with yellow harvests, with a commerce
whitening every sea, with workshops studding all her terri-

---

* The authorities relied on for these statements are parliamentary reports, cited in three several articles in the North American Review for
the years 1847 and 1848.

tory, with industrial implements and mechanical skill un-matched, and in the midst of plenty such as earth has seen never, her people perish from hunger. It is as if some de-mon had covered the land with his enchantments.

Let us now turn our regards to France, to see the effect of the opposite system of agriculture; that system in which the lands are minutely subdivided, and, for the most part, worked by those who own them. The French people are less edu-cated, less intelligent, less skilful, and less industrious, than the English. They ought, therefore, to be in circumstances of greater destitution and misery; and they undoubtedly were so, before the revolution of 1789. At that time the minute division of landed property commenced. Since then, wages have slowly, but steadily increased, and the social condition of the people has advanced in the same ratio. Rye and wheat flour have superseded buckwheat and oatmeal. The dress of the laboring classes has improved. Their houses are better built, better lighted, better warmed, and better furnished. And, while the rate of wages has increased, bread and clothing have been cheaper; which is a sure proof of the growing prosperity and comfort of the common peo-ple. There is pauperism in France undoubtedly; but in the rural districts it is trifling, and the whole amount is but little, when compared with the enormous aggregate of. it in England.*

Whence this difference? What is the cause of the general misery of the laboring classes in England, and the general well-being of the same classes in France? They have their roots in the respective systems of landed property in the two countries. To a great extent, they are the result, in the one case, of large, in the other, of small proprietorships. The average size of landed estates in England is eight hundred and eighty acres, while in France it is only twenty acres.

"The profit of the earth is for all" was a Hebrew maxim,

which grew into a proverb. The monopoly of the soil is a sore evil. It makes the many the slaves of the few. It produces ignorance, improvidence, destitution, turbulence, and crime. It is essential to the progress of man, that he be unshackled, that his faculties have free play. But this can never be, unless the earth be owned by those who till it. Ownership of the soil will give tone to the mind, vigor to the body, and earnestness to industry. As well might one circle an oak with iron bands, and expect it to unfold its majestic proportions, as to cramp the human mind by unequal institutions and an oppressive distribution of land, and then expect a full development of its powers, and a happy state of society. " As the attraction of gravity is the great principle of motion in the material world, so the possession of the earth in fee simple by the cultivator, is the great principle of action in the moral world. Nearly all the political evils, which have afflicted mankind, have resulted from the unrighteous monopoly of the earth; and the predicted renovation can never be accomplished, until, to some extent, this monopoly has passed away, and the earth is extensively tilled by the independent owners of the soil."*　Great proprietorships are the scourge of any country. All history attests this truth. The multiplication of farms, and their cultivation by the actual owners, is the dictate of true political wisdom. It is this, which peoples the country, and even the cities. It is this, which elevates the masses. It is this, which confers dignity upon the common people. It is this, which stimulates industry, quickens genius, and developes the resources of a state. It is this, which gives true freedom and independence to a nation. And this, to the broadest extent ever known in practical legislation, was the policy of Moses.

These observations will, perhaps, be sufficient to establish

---

* Beecher's Works, vol. 1, p. 318.

the wisdom of the Hebrew constitution in its partition of the territories of the republic. Let us now see what can be said in regard to the policy of founding a state on agriculture alone. I shall say nothing here of the special design of the Hebrew institution, but shall confine my inquiries to the point of general legislative policy.

It must be confessed, as Michaelis* has observed, that the extreme indifference of Moses to foreign and maritime commerce is not a little remarkable. To some of the politicians of our day, this will seem little short of an absurdity. Yet it may be, that some erroneous notion lies at the bottom of their wonder. The wealth acquired by Holland and Great Britain, by means of foreign trade, is so striking, that many are apt to imagine, that commerce alone is the true source of national prosperity, and that it is the greatest benefit which a legislator can confer upon a people. The mere name commerce fascinates their imagination, and seems almost to incapacitate them for sober reflection and comparison. In the delirium of their golden dreams, they forget, that it may prove the ruin of both public and private prosperity; as when too many superfluous commodities are imported, and the nation is thereby plunged into the mire of foreign indebtedness.

A main cause of the overvaluation of commercial as compared with agricultural pursuits, I imagine to be this, that the gains of commerce lie more upon the surface, and are more open to the general observation, while those of agriculture are of a retiring nature, and seldom obtrude themselves on public notice. It will not, therefore, be impertinent to enter somewhat into detail on this point, with the view of showing the superior importance of the cultivation of the earth, as a means of national prosperity, and so of vindicating the wisdom of Moses in founding upon it his civil polity.

Great Britain is the most commercial nation on the globe.

* Com. on Laws of Mos. Art. 39.

Her trade with the United States is nearly twofold that which she carries on with any other country. Yet the entire annual movement of this commerce both ways about equals in value the crop of oats and beans in the former country. The whole foreign commerce of Britain, in pursuit of which she over spreads the ocean with her fleets, and plants her colonies in the most distant islands, is actually less in value, than the annual grass crop of the British isles.* The breadstuffs, annually extracted from our own soil, amount to more than eight hundred million bushels, and their value is triple that of the aggregate exports and imports of the whole country. Our grass crop exceeds in value the whole outward and inward movement of our foreign commerce. The annual Indian corn crop of Tennessee and Kentucky reaches one hundred and twenty million bushels, and is worth as much as all our exports to Great Britain and France. What is not a little remarkable, the corn crop of these two states exactly equals, while the agricultural productions of the single state of New York greatly exceeds in value, the entire cotton crop grown in all the states and territories of this union.†

The instability of commercial pursuits, and the greater certainty of the ultimate rewards of agricultural labor, are worthy of consideration here. The prizes in commerce are comparatively few. While one man rises, multitudes sink. The late Mr. Gallatin instituted researches upon this point, and arrived at results, which seem almost incredible. I have scarcely the courage to repeat them, even under the shelter of such a name. According to this distinguished statesman and philosopher, the fortunate individuals, who attain wealth

* Address of Edward Everett before an Agricultural Meeting in England.

† These statistics may not be exactly accurate at the present time. The paragraph containing them was written in 1842, and its statements are founded on the Report of the Patent Office for the previous year.

by trade and commerce, are less than ten per cent of the whole number, who engage in such pursuits.

The physical and moral influences of agriculture ought not to be overlooked, in estimating the wisdom of a lawgiver, who has seen fit to found his polity upon it. It is the nurse of health, industry, temperance, cheerfulness, and frugality; of simple manners and pure morals; of patriotism and the domestic virtues; and, above all, of that sturdy independence, without which a man is not a man, but the mere slave, or plaything, of his more cunning fellows. Agriculture tends to produce and cherish a spirit of equality and sympathy. Buying and selling are the chief business of cities, the giving and receiving of wages a transaction of hourly occurrence. This produces a collision of interests and feelings, which necessarily begets a spirit of caste, and checks the current of sympathy. But there are comparatively few of these repelling influences in country life. The man who owns fifty acres, and the man who owns a thousand, live side by side, on terms of mutual esteem and friendship. Both, if they are equally entitled to it, have an equal share in the public respect. Both feel and own the bond, that unites them in the cultivation of the earth.

Agriculture begets and strengthens love of country. The heart of the husbandman is bound to the fields, on which he bestows his labor. The soil, which responds to his industry by clothing itself in beauty and riches, has a place in his affections. Especially, the circumstance, that his possession has come down to him through a long line of honored ancestors, greatly strengthens the attachment, which he feels both to his home and his country.*

The agricultural interest is, in the highest degree, conservative in its nature and action. It is the great antagonist of that mad spirit of radicalism and revolutionary innovation, which is the most terrible enemy of popular institutions.

* Mathew's Bib. and Civ. Gov. Lect. 2.

This has long ago been observed by Aristotle. "Husbandry," he says, "is the best stuff of a commonwealth, such a
one being the most devoted to liberty, and the least subject
to innovation or turbulence." The same thing is noticed by
Harrington. "Tillage," he observes, "bringing up a good
soldiery, brings up a good commonwealth; for where the
owner of the plough comes to have the sword too, he will
use it in defence of his own. The plough in the hands of the
owner produces the most innocent and steady genius of a
commonwealth."*

It is in the scenes and occupations of country life, that the
mind is most tranquil, sober, and unclouded. It is in such
an atmosphere, that it can discern most clearly the relations
of things, and look beyond the events of a day. From amid
the deep calm of rural pursuits, free states have drawn many
of their most illustrious patriots and civilians.† The influence
of agriculture, therefore, is rather favorable, than adverse, to
those exalted and commanding civil qualities, which form
the consummate statesman. A Hebrew farmer was summoned from the quiet of a pastoral life on the distant plains
of Midian, to become the founder and lawgiver of a mighty
republic. A Roman farmer was called from his plough to
the helm of state, at a crisis of imminent peril to his country's welfare. And an American farmer led the revolutionary armies to victory, and secured for his grateful and
admiring countrymen the blessings of liberty, independence,
and self-government.

In a word, this great business, the cultivation of the earth,
lies, so far as any branch of human industry can be said to
lie, at the foundation of all that is important and valuable in
civil society. And if, as Mr. Webster‡ once said, if it was
for his sins that man was condemned to till the ground, it

* Oceana, p. 30.   † Mat. Bib. and Civ. Gov. Lect. 2.
‡ Address at Rochester to the N. Y. Agricultural Society.

was the most merciful judgment that almighty benignity could have inflicted upon him.

I promised, in considering the expediency of founding a state on agriculture, to confine myself to the point of general legislative policy. Let me recal that promise, so far as just to advert to the more immediate reasons, which may be supposed to have moved Moses to give no encouragement to commerce. They were probably such as these : 1. Commerce would tend to counteract the first and highest principle of his polity, since it would lead the Israelites to contract intimacies with foreign nations, which could hardly fail to draw them into idolatry. 2. It would entice too many citizens to leave their own country and settle in foreign lands, which would weaken the sentiment of patriotism, and at last cause them to forget their relations and their home. The merchant is, in some sense, a citizen of the world, and has no such ties, either of interest or affection, binding him to his native land, as the man, who lives upon his hereditary farm. 3. It would introduce luxurious tastes and habits, before the nation was rich enough to bear the expense of their indulgence. Commerce is more apt to be hurtful, than beneficial, in the infancy of a state. 4. Maritime commerce would be likely to stir up enemies, against whom they could not successfully contend, without special divine assistance, which it would be irrational to expect, when engaged in pursuits, prejudicial to true religion. It would, in all probability, have embroiled them with the Sidonians and Tyrians, just as, in modern times, we have seen France incurring the irreconcileable enmity of England and Holland, by the establishment of an East India trading company. 5. The vicinity of these two commercial nations, and the constant passage of Asiatic trading caravans to Egypt, secured to the Israelites all the most important advantages of foreign commerce.*

I should, however, fail to do justice to the Mosaic legisla-

* See on this subject Mich. Com. on the Laws of Mos. Art. 39.

tion, if I were to leave this topic, without adverting to one branch of commerce, with which no nation can dispense without essential detriment to its prosperity—I mean a domestic trade, carried on between the different parts of the same country. For such an internal commerce, provision was made in the national festivals, whereby thrice every year the entire male population of Palestine was assembled at Jerusalem. Religious conventions of the kind have generally been made subservient to the purposes of commerce. The fairs, so common in Germany, originated at public masses, to which the people flocked from every quarter. The holy pilgrimages to Mecca gave a strong impulse to the commerce of Arabia. In a similar way the interests of internal trade were consulted in the institutes of Moses. Yet it was done in such a manner, that the carrying of it on could not become a distinct employment, but would merely occupy the weeks of leisure from the toils of agriculture :—before the harvest at the feast of the passover ; after harvest at the feast of pentecost ; and on the conclusion of the vintage, at the feast of tabernacles.*

As for foreign commerce, to expand a little hint contained in the last paragraph but one, the country of the Hebrews was so situated, that they could enjoy its advantages, without engaging in it themselves. The Phenician cities, Tyre and Sidon, were on their borders, ready to supply them with all they wanted in return for their agricultural productions. The rich caravans of the desert continually swept by them, affording them, without expense or hazard to themselves, the benefit of the enterprize of foreign nations. Moses endeavored to make his countrymen content under their vines and fig trees, and to convince them, that in these unambitious cares and labors they would find the most solid prosperity and happiness. And was he not right in this judgment? It is true, that his hopes were disappointed. This unaspiring

* Mich. Com. on the Laws of Mos. Art. 39.

employment was too quiet for his countrymen, when war was
the business of the rest of the world. But the event proved
the truth of his principles and predictions. Solomon laid
Ophir and Tarshish, the East and West Indies of his day,
under contribution. He had his harbors in the Mediterranean
and the Red Sea. He built Tadmor in the desert, now a
marble wilderness, as a station for his caravans. Wealth
flowed in through a thousand channels. But as the prophetic
eye of Moses had foreseen, and his prophetic voice forewarned,
it proved the ruin of his country. It became a golden weight,
which ground its free institutions to the dust.*

But, although Moses made no laws favoring foreign commerce, his legislation was far from being chargeable with the
illiberality of the Greek and Roman laws, or the bigotry of
the early canonists. The profession of a shopkeeper was
infamous among the Greeks, as it obliged a citizen to wait on
a slave or a stranger.† This was more than the haughty
spirit of Grecian liberty could brook. Hence Plato, in his
laws,‡ makes it a criminal offence in a citizen to concern himself with trade, and orders such an one to be punished. The
civil law treated commerce as a dishonorable occupation, and
forbade the exercise of it to persons of birth, rank, or fortune.
The Claudian law forbade the senators to have any ship at
sea, which held more than forty bushels.§ The canon law
went farther still, and declared commerce inconsistent with
christianity. At the council of Melfi, under Pope Urban II.
in the year 1090, the canonists decreed, that it was impossible, with a safe conscience, to exercise the trade of a merchant.
The decree was to the effect, that a merchant could rarely, if
ever, pursue a conduct pleasing to God; that no christian
ought to become a merchant; and that if any of the faithful

* See an able article on Moses and his Institutions in the Christian Ex-
aminer for Sept. 1836.
† Montesq. Sp. of Laws, B. 4, C. 8.
‡ B. 2.   § Liv. B. 21.

meddled with merchandise, he should be excluded from the pale of the church.*

Again, the Hebrew state was founded on the industry of all the citizens. This was the eleventh of those fundamental principles, which lay at the basis of the constitution.

This idea has been partially developed already; but it was so vital to the Hebrew legislation, that it deserves a distinct consideration. We have seen that a leading object of Moses was to make the country of the Hebrews a vast and busy scene of rural industry. Now, the culture of the earth requires a great number and variety of implements; and a soil of but moderate fertility will afford sustenance to a much larger population than is required for its tillage. In these two ideas, behold the germ of an effective system of mechanical industry, and a powerful stimulus to the cultivation and development of mechanical skill.

The lawgiver's first care was the cultivation of the land; his next to provide, that the people might be conveniently and comfortably lodged. He enjoined upon all to labor, that they might not only eat and be satisfied, but that they might also build goodly houses, and dwell therein.† The counsel of Solomon was but an echo of this Mosaic law: " Prepare thy work without, and make it fit for thyself in the field; and afterwards build thine house."‡

. The various objects of necessity, convenience, and luxury, enumerated in the sacred books, prove to us, that industry and the arts were far from being in a depressed state among the Hebrews. They made divers stuffs of wool, cotton, goat's hair, and some say of silk.§ The art of dyeing was in use among them, and reached a high perfection. Their principal colors were blue, crimson, purple, and yellow, which were obtained from vegetables, fishes, and minerals. They labored especially to impart a snowy whiteness to their fabrics used

* Blackstone's Com. B. 1. C. 7.
† Deut. viii. 12.   ‡ Prov. xxiv. 27.   § Ex. xxxix.

for clothing. Rich stuffs, interwoven with threads of gold, and adorned with fringes of variegated colors, presented to the eye designs of various sorts.*

In the construction of the tabernacle, we read of fine twined linen, and of broad tapestries, covered with beautiful figures of delicate workmanship, and joined to each other by clasps of gold. The details in Exodus respecting the proportions of the various pieces, which formed the carpentry of this portable temple, and the numerous articles which constituted its furniture, indicate the use of a great number of instruments, proper for dividing and measuring.†

Together with the arts of carpentry, founding and pottery, the Israelites brought from Egypt the art of engraving precious stones, the art of working metals, the art of inlaying in gold, and the art of moulding. The curtains of the tabernacle with their ornaments, the ark overlaid with gold, the mercy-seat with its cherubim, the table of show-bread with its furniture, the golden candlestick, the vail, the altars of burnt offering and incense, the ephod, with its curious girdle, the breastplate with its mysterious urim and thummim, the priestly vestments, and all the other paraphernalia of the royal tent, must have required, for their construction, a high degree of mechanical ingenuity.‡

In the reign of Solomon the arts shone out in full effulgence. The temple, the royal palaces, their rich furniture, superb gardens, beautiful works in gold and ivory, splendid concerts of vocal and instrumental music, roads multiplied and handsomely paved, towns and fortresses built and repaired, and the great marble city of Palmyra, starting into life like a vision of beauty, attest the encouragement afforded to the arts by that munificent monarch.§

The indignant rebuke of the prophet Amos to the rich and luxurious idlers of his day, is a proof both of the progress of

* Salv. Inst. de Moïse, l. 3, c. 5.   † Ibid. l. 3, c. 5.
‡ Ibid. l. 3, c. 5.   § Ibid, l. 3, c. 5.

Jewish art and of the stern demand for labor, which the Jewish law made upon all. " Woe to them that are at ease in Zion ; * * * that lie upon beds of ivory, and stretch themselves upon their couches, and eat the lambs of the flock, and the calves out of the midst of the stall ; that chant to the sound of the viol, and invent to themselves instruments of music, like David ; that drink wine in bowls, and anoint themselves with the chief ointments ; but they are not grieved for the affliction of Joseph."*

Isaiah, complaining of the luxury of the daughters of Zion, enumerates more than twenty articles of their toilet, all costly or elegant, which are as clear an indication of the state of Jewish art, as they are of the pride and ostentation of the Jewish ladies : " In that day the Lord will take away the bravery of their tinkling ornaments about their feet, and their cauls, and their round tires like the moon, the chains, and the bracelets, and the mufflers, the bonnets, and the ornaments of the legs, and the headbands, and the tablets, and the ear-rings, the rings and the nose jewels, the changeable suits of apparel, and the mantles, and the wimples, and the crisping pins, the glasses and the fine linen, and the hoods and the vails."†

At the time of the captivity, artists abounded in Jerusalem. Of ten thousand heads of families, carried to Babylon at the first invasion, one thousand were workmen in wood and in metals. Winkelman, in his history of art, has made the following observation on this fact : " We are but slightly acquainted with art among the Hebrew people ; nevertheless, it must have reached a certain degree of perfection, at least in design and finish. Among the artists whom Nebuchadnezzar carried captive from the single city of Jerusalem, were a thousand, skilled in inlaid work. It would be difficult to find as many in the largest of our modern cities."‡

It is sometimes made matter of reproach against the He-

* Amos vi. 1-6.   † Is. iii. 18-23.   ‡ Salv. l. 3, c. 5.

brews, that they left none of those great monuments like the pyramids and temples of Egypt, which struggle successfully against the devastations of time. How little do such persons appreciate the true grandeur of nations! There were not slaves in Palestine to erect such ostentatious structures; and free labor employs itself about things more useful. Voltaire himself takes notice of this fact. He regards the pyramids as a proof of the slavery of the Egyptians; and says that nothing could constrain a free people to rear such masses. The temple, the palace of their heavenly king, is the only monumental edifice, of which the memory has been preserved. This shared the fate of the Jewish people; and, after having served as a fortress in the last efforts of liberty, the nation and the temple fell together.*

Since that day the fate of the Jewish people has been one of almost unmingled bitterness. "Scattered and pealed" has been deeply engraved upon its forehead. But they have always displayed much of the energy, activity, and industrious application to business, which distinguished their remote ancestors. This even their worst enemies have been compelled to acknowledge. An old Spanish chronicler, with an ingenuousness which would be amusing, if it did not recal painful memories, says of them : " This portion of humanity was at least good to awaken industry and to pay imposts."†

How far these permanent elements of industry may have been the result of the exact and positive spirit of their ancient law, it is impossible now to trace with distinctness. I do not affirm, but I suggest for reflection, whether the economy, the ability, the tenacity, and the energy of the modern Jews, are not due to some profound cause, which is to be sought in the great principles of their original institution.

Again, the inviolability of private property, and the sacredness of the family relation, are principles, which entered essentially into the Hebrew constitution.

* Salv. l. 3, c. 5.   † Ibid. l. 3, c. 5.

It cannot be necessary to adduce, at any length, the proof of this proposition, for no one can open the Pentateuch, without meeting it on every page. The whole scope of the second table of the decalogue is to guard the institution of the family and the institution of property. The right and the advantage of private property are everywhere assumed by Moses. To facilitate its increase, to regulate its use, and to provide for its distribution are leading objects of his law. In this the Hebrew legislator does but echo a sentiment common to all just and wise lawgivers. A political community could not be organized, except' upon a basis of individual property and right. This is the only bond, strong enough to hold such an association together. Not even a savage tribe could live together without property. The ownership by each member of the body politic of his tools, arms, clothing, and habitation, is essential to the rudest form of civil society. None would be willing to till the ground, if others had an equal right with him to gather the harvest. None would even erect a hut, if his next neighbor might enter and take possession the moment it was finished. If the idle and the industrious, if those who waste and those who save, have the same rights, and are to share alike in the fruits of the earth and the products of labor, then prudence, frugality, thrift, and provision for the future become simple impossibilities. All this is recognized in the legislation of Moses. That legislation has no sympathy with a social theory, which has of late gained some currency in the world; a theory, which places activity, industry, ability, and virtue, upon the same level with indolence, idleness, incapacity, and vice; a theory, which begins by offering a premium for ignorance and incompetency, and which must end in the annihilation of all industry, all emulation, and every opening faculty. Neither has the legislation of Moses any sympathy with another principle, which has a prevalence perhaps still more extensive,—I mean the principle of a separation of the pecuniary interests of the husband and wife.

28

The husband and wife are regarded by the Mosaic law as one person, having, as it were, but one soul, one interest, one will. Doubtless the doctrine, that the man is the head of the woman, and that the property of the latter becomes, as a result of the nuptial tie, part and parcel of that of the former, is sometimes productive of much hardship and suffering; but who, that reflects on the frailties and passions of human nature, can doubt, that the contrary doctrine, adopted and applied as a practical principle of legislation, would be attended with evils far greater, both in number and magnitude?

The spirit of the Mosaic law is opposed to the modern radicalism of woman's rights; a radicalism, which boldly avows its purpose of "subverting the existing order of society and dissolving the existing social compact." Moses did not favor the manhood of woman. "Unto the woman he said, * * * thy desire shall be to thy husband, and he shall rule over thee."* Paul interprets this precept, when he says of women, "It is not permitted to them to speak in the churches; but they are commanded to be under obedience, as also saith the law."† He speaks in the very spirit of Moses, when he says, "The man is the head of the woman;"‡ "wives, submit yourselves unto your own husbands;"§ "Adam was first formed, then Eve."‖ Man has a mission, and so has woman, to which the wisdom that never errs, has adapted the bodily and mental constitution of each. Man's mission is to subdue and till the earth, to cultivate the mechanic arts, to make roads and dig canals, to carry on commerce, to encounter the perils and fatigues of war, to institute and administer government, to be the shield of woman in moments of danger and sudden alarm, in a word, to perform the rough business of life,—that which requires physical strength and endurance. Woman's mission, while it has no less of dignity, is very different from this. It is to be the light and joy of the house-

* Gen. iii. 16.   † 1 Cor. xiv. 34.   ‡ Ibid. xi. 3.
§ Eph. v. 22.   ‖ 1 Tim. ii. 13.

hold, to nourish and train the immortal children within its precincts, to mould the whole mass of mind while in its most plastic state, to fill the throne of the heart, to be the priestess in the sanctuary of home, to be the comfort and support of man in seasons of sorrow and of suffering, to move in the realm of ignorance and want, to shine, to cheer, and to bless in all the varied ministrations of sympathy and love, from the cradle to the grave. What purer, nobler, holier realm can she desire? "The true nobility of woman is to keep her own sphere, and to adorn it." *

Another essential principle of the legislative policy of Moses was the sanctity of human life.

No legislation of antiquity approaches that of the Hebrew lawgiver, in its solicitude to guard the lives of men. The prohibition against killing was one of the ten precepts, which formed what may be called the magna charta of the Hebrew state.† The crime of murder was punished with death. There was no redemption. It was declared, that the land could not be purged of the stain of blood, except by the blood of him who had shed it.‡ Even an ox, which had gored a man to death, and, by parity of reason, any other animal, as a goat, a dog, or a horse, that had killed a person by pushing, biting, or kicking, was to be stoned;§ not, indeed, to punish the beast, but the owner, and so to oblige him to be careful in preventing his oxen, dogs, and other domestic animals, from injuring his neighbors. The flesh of the goring ox could not be eaten,‖ a prohibition which served to keep up a wholesome horror of murder, at the same time that it punished the man by the total loss of his beast. A man, who built a house, was required to make a battlement, or balustrade, to the roof.¶ If he neglected to do this, and a person fell from the roof in consequence, and was killed, the owner of the house brought bloodguiltiness upon himself; he was considered in the light

* Mrs. Sigourney.   † Ex. xx. 13.   ‡ Num. xxxv. 33.
§ Ex. xxi. 28.   ‖ Ibid. xxi. 28   ¶ Deut. xxii. 8.

of a murderer.*　A very peculiar statute concerning homicide by an unknown person is recorded in Deut. 21 : 1–9.　This statute will be particularly examined in a subsequent part of this work, and I forbear, therefore, a detail of its provisions at the present time.　By consulting the passage, the reader will perceive, that the elders, or magistrates, of the nearest city were obliged to purge themselves and their city of the murder, and make a solemn avowal, that they were ignorant of the perpetrator of it.　He will perceive also, that, in the absence of the press, nothing could be better fitted than the ceremonies ordained to give publicity to the murder, and to make every one, who had any knowledge of the matter, give information concerning it.　There can be no doubt, that the investigation instituted by the laws of Moses over the body of a person, who had come to his death by means unknown, is the origin of the coroner's inquest in modern times.　No ancient law made such provision for the detection of secret murders as this of Moses.　That of Plato, which is regarded as the best, simply ordained, that if a man was found dead, and the murderer could not be ascertained, proclamation should be made, that he should not come into any holy place, nor into any part of the whole country; for if he were discovered and apprehended, he should be put to death, be thrown out of the bounds of the country, and have no burial.†　These provisions of the Mosaic code to beget an abhorrence of murder, and to guard the lives of the citizens, are very remarkable.　They evince a humanity in Moses, unknown to all other ancient legislators.　They must have tended, in a high degree, to introduce a horror of shedding human blood, and to give intensity to the idea of the sacredness of human life.

A fifteenth fundamental principle of the Hebrew government was education; the education of the whole body of the

* Deut. xxii. 8.　　　　　　　† Plato de Leg. 1. 9.

people; especially, in the knowledge of the constitution, laws and history of their own country.

An ignorant people cannot be a free people. Intelligence is essential to liberty. No nation is capable of self-government, which is not educated to understand and appreciate its responsibilities. In a republican government, the whole power of education is required.* Upon this principle Moses proceeded in the framing of his commonwealth.

The details of the arrangements for the education of the Hebrew people, contained in the Pentateuch, are but scanty. We are, therefore, greatly in the dark, as to the specific means employed. So far, however, is clear, that the Mosaic law required, that the greatest pains should be taken to mould the minds, the principles, the habits, and manners of the young. Parents were, again and again, commanded to teach their children, from infancy, all the words of the law, and all the glorious facts of their national history. They were enjoined to talk of them, when they sat in the house, and when they walked by the way, when they lay down, and when they rose up.† The whole system of legislation was crowded with commemorative rites and festivals. Into the meaning of these, it was taken for granted, that the young would inquire, and it was ordained, that their curiosity should be satisfied by the explanations of their sires.‡ The passover reminded them of the wonders of the exode; the pentecost, of the terrific splendors, which accompanied the giving of the law; the feast of tabernacles, of the hardships and miraculous supplies of the wilderness; and the monumental heap of stones at Gilgal, of the standing of the waters of Jordan upon an heap, to afford a passage to their forefathers. Even the borders of their garments, their gates, the frontlets between their eyes, and the posts and lintels of

* Montesq. Sp. of Laws, B. 4, c. 5.   † Deut. vi. 7.

‡ Ex. xiii. 14, 15.

their doors, were to become their teachers by the laws and maxims which were inscribed upon them.*

It is hence plain, that Hebrew parents were required, not only to teach their children orally, but also to impart to them the arts of reading and writing. Since they were commanded to write them, they must themselves have learned the art of writing; and since they were to write them for the use of their children, these must have been taught the art of reading. There is reason to believe, that the ability to read and write was an accomplishment, more generally possessed by the Hebrews, than by any other people of antiquity.† This was certainly the case in the time of our Savior. In his addresses to the common people, he constantly appealed to them in such words as these: " Have ye not read what Moses saith? Have ye not read in the scriptures ?"‡ Such language implies an ability, on the part of the people, to examine the scriptures for themselves. The same thing is indicated by a fact, stated by the evangelical historian concerning the inscription placed over the head of Jesus at his crucifixion: " This title then read many of the Jews."§ The writings of Josephus are crowded with testimonies as to the great care of the Hebrews in the education of their children. He says, among other things, that first of all they are taught the laws, as best fitted to promote their future happiness; that the people weekly assemble to hear them read, and to learn them exactly ; and, to crown all, he adds, somewhat hyperbolically, no doubt, that, "if any one do but ask any of our people about our laws, he will more readily tell them all than he will tell his own name." " We find it to be the uniform testimony of Jewish writers, that the school was to be found in every district throughout the nation, and under the care of

---

* Deut. vi. 8, 9.   † Mathew's Bible & Civ. Gov. Lect. 4.
‡ Mat. xii. 3. xix. 4. xxi. 16. xxii. 31. Mark ii. 25. xii. 10, 26. Luke vi. 3.
§ John xix. 20

teachers, who were honored alike for their character and station."* Maimonides, in his treatise on the study of the law,
says: "Every Israelite, whether poor or rich, healthy or sick,
old or young, is obliged to study the law; and even if so poor
as to be maintained by charity, or beg his bread from door
to door, and have wife and children, he must devote some
time to the daily and nocturnal meditation of it." He asks,
" How long ought a man to pursue the study of the law?"
and replies, " Till death."

An important function of the Levites was to superintend
the education of the people. The proofs of this proposition
will be submitted in a subsequent chapter. For the present,
I merely advert to the fact, in passing, that, in the reformation undertaken by Jehoshaphat, that excellent prince, in the
true spirit of the Mosaic institution, commanded the priests
to go through the land, and teach the people, city by city,
the laws of Moses.† Several of the leading political principles of Plato, as I have shown in the first book,‡ were
borrowed from the Hebrew lawgiver; but in no other point
did his republic so closely resemble the Jewish, as in this,
that he enjoined it upon all the citizens to learn accurately
the laws.

In full harmony with the spirit of the Mosaic laws, and
indeed as a natural result of their operation, higher seminaries of learning, under the name of " schools of the
prophets,"§ were introduced and established among the
Hebrews. These institutions were presided over by men
venerable for their age, character, ability and learning. The
notices of these schools in the sacred books are rather scanty,
and this has given rise to various opinions concerning them.
From their name some have conjectured, that they were

* Mathew's Bib. & Civ. Gov. Lect. 4.
† 2 Chron. xvii. 8, 9.   ‡ Chap. 7.
§ 1 Sam. xix. 18.   2 Kings ii. 3, 5.

places of instruction in the art of prophecy. This absurd fancy was borrowed by Spinoza from the rabbins, and by him handed down to his followers ; whence these sage logicians have inferred, that prophecy was among the practical arts of the Hebrews, as much as carpentry, or engraving. But of this we may be certain, that the schools of the prophets were seminaries of prophets, meaning by this term inspired men, only in so far as that those who were best instructed in the divine law, being best fitted to convey God's commands to the people, would, for that reason, be most likely to be chosen by him for that purpose. In opposition to the opinion of Spinoza, Bishop Warburton argues,* with no little force, in support of the opinion, that they were seminaries designed chiefly for the study of the Jewish law. It is probable, however, that they were not devoted exclusively to that department of study, but embraced within their scope other branches of knowledge, which were reckoned among the pursuits of learning in that day. They corresponded to the colleges and universities of modern times. They must have exercised a powerful influence on the mind and manners of the Jewish people. It was in the schools of the prophets, that David imbibed that love for the religious and civil laws of his country, which glowed so intensely in his bosom, which sparkled in his inimitable lyrics, which became so copious a spring of blessing to his nation, and which won for himself the exalted title of the "man after God's own heart ;"† not morally and religiously, for that no man has ever yet been, but, as the whole scope of the passage shows, the man after God's heart as a civil ruler, a man imbued with the spirit, and devoted to the maintenance, of the national constitution.

There was a peculiarity in the Mosaic system of education, which deserves our notice. It did not overlook the fact, that

* Divine Legation.   † 1 Samuel xiii. 14.

every man has what Dr. Arnold calls two businesses; his particular business, as of a farmer, merchant, lawyer, or the like, and his general business, that which he shares in common with all his fellow-citizens, his business as a man and a citizen. Most modern systems of education take but little notice of this distinction. They go upon the presumption that, if a man learns his particular business well, a knowledge of his general business will come of itself, or be picked up by the way. Not such was the view of Moses. He seems rather to have thought, that every man would be impelled to make himself master of his particular business, since his bread depended on it; but that the knowledge of his general business, the want of which is less keenly felt, would be a more fit subject of legal provision. He intended, that all his people should share in the management of the public affairs. He meant each to be a depositary of political power. But he looked upon power as a solemn trust, and thought it incumbent on a legislator to take care that those who hold it, should know how to discharge its duties. Hence, in legislating on the subject of education, he appears chiefly anxious to have his people instructed in the knowledge of their general business, that is, their duties as men and citizens. He belonged neither to that class of political philosophers, who desire to see the mass of the people shut out from all political power, as always and under all circumstances unfit to exercise it, nor to that class, who wish to see the power of the masses increased, irrespective of their ability to discharge so important a trust beneficially to the community. In his educational scheme, power and knowledge went hand in hand. The possession of the latter was regarded as essential to the right use of the former.

The old Romans have received the highest praises, because, conscious of the importance of imparting to the rising generation an early knowledge of the laws, they made the twelve tables one of the first elements of public instruction, requiring

the youth to commit to memory their entire contents. They
were sensible, that what is learned at so early a period is not
only likely to be long remembered, but is almost sure to command respect and veneration. But Moses gave a broader
application to this principle than it ever received among the
Roman people. The education, enjoined by Moses, was not,
as among them, merely of the children of the highborn and
the rich, but of all ranks and conditions. It was a fundamental maxim of his policy, that no citizen, not even the
lowest and the poorest, should grow up in ignorance. How
much does he deserve the gratitude of mankind for so noble
a lesson! In proportion as this idea enters into the constitution of a state, tyranny will hide its head, practical equality
will be established, party strife will abate its ferocity, error,
rashness, and folly will disappear, and an enlightened, dignified, and venerable public opinion will bear sway.

Upon the whole, it may be affirmed, that in no part of the
Hebrew constitution does the wisdom of the lawgiver shine
with a more genial lustre, than in what relates to the education of the young. The provisions of the constitution on this
point cannot be regarded otherwise than as the dictate of a
wise, liberal, and comprehensive statesmanship; for, surely,
it is in the highest degree desirable, that every citizen should
be acquainted with the laws and constitution of his country.
Patriotism itself is but a blind impulse, if it is not founded
on a knowledge of the blessings we are called upon to secure,
and the privileges which we propose to defend. It is political ignorance alone, that can reconcile men to the tame surrender of their rights; it is political knowledge alone, that
can rear an effectual barrier against the encroachments of arbitrary power and lawless violence.*

In full accordance with the spirit of the Mosaic legislation,
is the beautiful prayer of David, "that our sons may be as

* See this topic handled in a masterly manner by Robert Hall in one of
his Reviews; I cannot now recal which.

plants grown up in their youth ; that our daughters may be as corner-stones, polished after the similitude of a palace." Such was the political philosophy of the founder of the Hebrew state, and such was the practice of those statesmen in after times, who adhered most closely to the spirit of his institutions. From a survey of the whole matter, the conclusion seems warranted, that the education of the Hebrew people, conducted mainly, though not wholly, under the domestic roof, was, nevertheless, a national education, and worthy of the imitation of other nations. Especially does it deserve to be studied and copied, so far as that branch of education is concerned, which consists in development, as distinguished from instruction. The Hebrew law required an early, constant, vigorous, and efficient training of the disposition, judgment, manners, and habits both of thought and feeling. The sentiments, held to be appropriate to man in society, were imbibed with the milk of infancy. The manners, considered becoming in adults, were sedulously imparted in childhood. The habits, regarded as conducive to individual advancement, social happiness, and national repose and prosperity, were cultivated with the utmost diligence. The greatest pains were taken to acquaint the Hebrew youth with their duties, as well as their rights, both personal and political. In a word, the main channel of thought and feeling for each generation was marked out by the generation which preceded it, and the stream for the most part flowed with a steady current.

Such a system of mental and moral culture as that for which the Hebrew constitution made provision, could not be without rich fruits. The result was, that the nation reached a high point of literary attainment and distinction. Under their most splendid and munificent monarch, the Hebrews enjoyed what may be called the golden age of their literature. "Solomon and his court were, in their day, the great centre of attraction for those of all nations, who loved and honored knowledge. His wisdom excelled all the wisdom of the east country, and all the wisdom of Egypt. He spake of trees, from the cedar in Lebanon even unto the hyssop that springeth out of the wall; he spake also of beasts, and of fowl, and of creeping things, and of fishes. His songs were a thousand and five, and his proverbs three thousand. And while he excelled in the wide fields of natural science, poetry, and ethics, the temple, which still bears his name, stood before the world a monument of skill and taste, which rendered it in after ages the original model of grace, majesty, and grandeur in architecture. Such gifted luminaries in the intellectual world do not shine alone. They usually belong to a constellation, and the king who sets such an example, is not likely to be without followers. There was, indeed, one cardinal feature in the Hebrew polity, which was pre-eminently favorable, at all times, to the cultivation of knowledge. By divine appointment the whole tribe of Levi was set apart for the service of religion and letters; and while many were employed before the altar and in the temple, others were devoted to study; many of whom, especially in the reign of Solomon, reached a high name both for their attainments in the science of their age, and the fidelity with which they made their learning available for the benefit of the people. Thus was produced that happy conjunction in the history of knowledge, when learning bestowed honor on the learned, and the learned brought honor on learning; when the highest attainments were deemed of value, not according as they gave distinction to him who had reached them, but according as they tended to improve and to bless the whole family of man. Among the Hebrews there was no monopoly of knowledge by a favored few. Intelligence was general in the degree and of the kind adapted to the various pursuits and duties of those among whom it was spread. The tongue and the pen of even learned royalty were industriously employed in giving to knowledge that condensed and practical form, which might bring it within the reach of all, and make it available for the advantage of all; of the shepherd and vine-dresser, as well as of the sons of the prophets."*

Another of those great ideas, on which Moses founded the Hebrew government, was union.

I refer here, not so much to those civil ties which bound the people together in one body politic, as to that oneness of hearts, opinions, and manners, which forms the strongest bond of society, and is the firmest rampart of its defence. This sympathy of souls, and the interchange of social charities springing from it, though not the primary object, was yet an excellent incidental advantage, of the equal distribution of property, heretofore noticed. The nation was thus composed of a brotherhood of hardy yeomen, no one of whom could become either very rich or very poor, or could have anything in his outward circumstances greatly to excite the envy or the contempt of the others. How well suited such a condition of things was to make solid friendships, let the opinions of all antiquity, from Aristotle to Cicero, as well as those of every succeeding age, attest.

The system of education, in vogue among the Hebrew people, tended powerfully to the same result. To this cause Josephus, with much plausibility, traces that unanimity of sentiment concerning God and morals, which, he says, so remarkably distinguished his nation, that even the women and servants spake the same things.

To the same effect was the incessant inculcation of kindness and charity, not only towards one another, but also to strangers, enforced by the oft repeated admonition, "Ye know the heart of a stranger, for ye were strangers in the land of Egypt."† "If," says the venerable patriarch, whose history, there is reason to believe, Moses introduced to the knowledge of his countrymen, if he was not himself the author of it, "if I have withheld the poor from their desire,

* Mathew's Bible and Civil Government, Lect. 4.   † Ex. xxiii. 9.

or have caused the eyes of the widow to fail; if I have
eaten my morsel alone, and the fatherless have not eaten
thereof; if I have seen any perish for want of clothing, or
any poor without covering ; if I did despise the cause of my
man-servant or my maid-servant, when they contended with
me; what then shall I do when God riseth up; and when he
visiteth, what shall I answer him ? Did not he that made
me in the womb, make him ? and did not one fashion us ?"†
How beautifully does this acknowledgment of brotherhood
with paupers and bondmen, from one of the most illustrious
princes of his age, and this warm gush of charity towards
every creature, wearing the human form, and crushed
beneath the burden of human sorrows, contrast with that
utter want of sympathy for man as man, which characterized
all the ancient systems both of government and philosophy !
The " odi profanum vulgus et arceo" of Horace,—that bitter
scorn and supercilious contempt of the profane herd,—was
but the echo of a mode of thinking and feeling, well nigh
universal among the learned and the great of his day.
Much of Greek, and nearly all of Roman letters, breathes a
proud oblivion and contempt of the common people. The
scornful sentiment of the Roman poet, cited above, " hate
for the profane rabble," is but too faithfully reflected from
the pages of ancient scholarship.

But, after all, the great and sufficient means of cementing
the bond of sympathy and friendship among the Hebrews,
were the three annual festivals, at which the males must, and
the females might, assemble at Jerusalem. The divine wisdom has a reach, a compass, a manifold fulness in its plans,
which the shortsighted policy of man would in vain labor to
imitate. Thus it was in the institution of these solemnities.
While the primary end of their appointment was of a religious nature, another and a most important one was the promotion of that fraternal esteem and charity, so congenial

* Job. xxxi. 13 seqq.

both to the character of Moses and the temper of his laws.
This was the opinion of Maimonides. "The festival days,"
says he,* "were appointed generally for purposes of joy, and
because such public assemblies promote that union and
affection, which are necessarily required under all civil and
political governments."

From a similar motive sprang the national games of Greece,
so celebrated in ancient story; and the institution of those
assemblies has ever been looked upon as a master stroke of
policy and prudence. The Greek nation, as observed by
Goguet,† composed of a multitude of small states, jealous
and envious of each other, had need of some common centre,
where all might occasionally find themselves united and commingled. This is precisely what happened in these games,
whither repaired an incredible number of spectators from all
parts of Greece. By this concourse was formed a bond of
correspondence, a sort of confraternity, among all the citizens
of the different Grecian cities. The Greeks, at these times,
appeared to be, in a manner, inhabitants of the same place;
they offered in common the same sacrifices to the same deities, and participated in the same pleasures. By this means
grudges were calmed; animosities stifled; and quarrels
terminated. They had also an opportunity, in these grand
assemblages, of effacing those prejudices, which are commonly kept up only by not knowing the persons, against
whom they are entertained.

Whatever advantages, of this nature, Greece derived from
the institution of her games, the same flowed, in a still higher
degree, to the Hebrews from their national festivals. By
being thus brought frequently into contact, on an equal footing, they were reminded of their common origin and their
common objects. The fact was brought home vividly to

* More Nevochim, C. 18.

† Origin of Laws. I cannot cite the chapter, because I am not now
where I can have access to the work.

their thoughts, that they were sons of the same father, worshippers of the same God, and heirs of the same promises. Persons of distant towns and different tribes met together on terms of brotherhood and fellowship; and old relations were renewed, and new ones formed. Thus the twelve petty states would become more and more closely connected, and would be, not merely nominally, but really, and from social love, united into one great people.

How strong the cementing power of these solemn convocations was actually found to be, plainly appears, in the motive, which prompted the politic and crafty Jeroboam, on the revolt of the ten tribes from the successor of Solomon, to set up the golden calves at Dan and Bethel : " Jeroboam said in his heart, Now shall the kingdom return to the house of David. If this people go up to do sacrifice in the house of the Lord at Jerusalem, then shall the heart of this people turn again to their Lord, even unto Rehoboam, king of Judah, and they shall kill me, and go again unto Rehoboam, king of Judah."*

Here we have a clear proof, that the separation of the ten tribes from the tribe of Judah, under Rehoboam and Jeroboam, could not have been permanent, had not the latter abrogated one part of the law of Moses relative to the festivals. This shows, in a very striking manner, how naturally one common place for national festivals has the effect of preventing, or healing, any such political breaches; and that the legislator, who should be desirous of inseparably uniting twelve small states into one great nation, could not adopt a more effectual plan for that purpose, than that which Moses pursued in the case of the tribes of Israel.†

To bring the illustration of this point somewhat more closely to ourselves, what is it, let me ask, that constitutes the strongest bond of union between the people and states of our own confederacy? Is it a common ancestry? Is it the property we all claim in the public annals of the country ? Is it the cementing power of our revolutionary struggle ? Is it even our national constitution, that precious legacy, bequeathed to us by the wisdom of our patriot sires ? These things, doubtless, have their influence, nor is it a feeble one; but not one, nor all of them combined, are adequate to the result. What, then, is that mysterious, cohesive power, which holds us together, and which alone can hold us together, as one people ? It is our migratory habits. It is our universal fondness for travel. It is the fact, that each of us has a parent, a child, a brother, a sister, in the distant north, the extreme south, the far-off west. It is the certainty that none of us can find ourselves in a railway car, or steamboat, on any of the iron roads or majestic rivers of this broad empire, without meeting, or making, an acquaintance or a friend. It is the cheap postage system, which enables heart to speak to heart, between the most distant points, without taxing even the poor with an expenditure out of proportion to their means. It is the magnetic telegraph, which transmits the messages of business and of affection, with lightning rapidity, from one extremity of the country to the other. It is our numerous watering places, where the inhabitants of the north, the south, the east, and the west, find themselves once a year, like the ancient Greeks at their games, and like the ancient Hebrews at their festivals, united and commingled,—sitting at the same table, bathing in the same waters, drinking at the same springs, inhaling health from the same breezes, engaging in the same sports, mingling in the same social circles, and joining in the song and the joke and the laugh together. It is these influences, and such as these, that bind us more firmly as a people into one common brotherhood, than would a cordon of paper constitutions long enough to encircle the globe.

A well adjusted system of checks and balances between the several powers of government was another fundamental principle of the civil polity of Moses. To form a free government, it is necessary to combine the several powers of it, to adjust them to each other, to regulate, temper, and set them in motion, to give, as Montesquieu expresses it, ballast to one, in order to enable it to resist another. This is a masterpiece of legislation, never produced by hazard, and seldom attained by prudence. It is exactly here, that the point of greatest difficulty with a legislator lies. This will afford scope for the exercise of all his genius, however comprehensive, sagacious, and commanding it may be. It is here that we see the proudest triumph of the British and American constitutions. Here also, as it seems to me, is the chief defect of the constitution of the new French republic. There is no division of powers in it. There is no balance, no check. All the authority of the state is collected into one centre, the single assembly.; and the constant tendency will be to a similar centralization of power in that body. It will be well if the system does not degenerate into the government of an irresponsible junto of master spirits, or even into the despotism of one man, bold enough, and popular enough, to seize the reins of supreme power.*

Unfortunately, history is but too full of proofs, that restless and ambitious spirits, who do not hesitate to seek personal aggrandizement, in the confusion, if not the ruin of their country, are the growth of all ages and nations. It is well observed by Lowman,† that there are two principal methods of preventing the evils of ambition, viz. either to take away the usual occasions of ambitious views, or else to make the execution of them difficult and improbable.

The Hebrew constitution, it may be boldly affirmed, made

---

* This was written in 1849. I do not expunge it, because nothing has occurred since to change my opinion of the constitution, as it stood at that time. If the usurpation of Louis Napoleon does not confirm it, as least it is not against it.

† Civil Gov. of the Hebrews, c. 6.

both these provisions, in a manner equal, if not superior, to
any known constitution of government in the world. Its
very foundation, as we have seen, was laid in a rigid equality
of all the citizens, effected by a perfectly equal division of
the national domain; which division, moreover, a fundamental ordinance of the constitution made perpetual. Such,
then, was the peculiar character of the agrarian of the Hebrews, that, on the one hand, few could acquire the means of
bribery to any considerable extent; and, on the other, there
could hardly, at any one time, be many indigent persons to
be corrupted. The power in the hands of so large a number
of freeholders was so much greater than the power in the
hands of one, or of a few men, that it is impossible to conceive how, without first destroying some of the fundamental
provisions of the constitution, ambition and tyranny could
accomplish their nefarious designs.

But, besides cutting off the usual occasions and incitements
to ambition, the constitution made all factious attempts so little
likely to succeed, as to be next to impracticable. The powers
of each department of the government, as will more clearly
appear from our analysis of the constitution in the following
chapters, were so balanced by the powers of the other departments, that, without the concurrence of all, it was well
nigh impossible for any one part to draw to itself any considerable preponderance of authority over the others. The
authority of the judge was checked by that of the senate of
princes; the power of the senatorial council was balanced by
that of the judge and the popular assembly; while the whole
was tempered and restrained by the oracle of their heavenly
king. Whoever will attentively consider the true plan and
arrangement of the government, will acknowledge, that it
must have been exceedingly hard, if not absolutely impracticable, for any person, tribe, magistrate, or public council, to
invade the property of the citizens, or overturn the liberties
of the state.

But it has been repeatedly charged against the institutes of Moses, that they were purposely contrived to draw all the wealth and power of the nation into the hands of the Levites; and that, therefore, the chief danger to the popular liberty arose out of the constitution of that tribe. Never was so malignant an accusation raised upon so slender a foundation. On the contrary, the organization and disposition of the tribe of Levi was contrived with consummate wisdom, both to impart a vital action to the whole system, and, at the same time, to act as a balance wheel to regulate its motions.

Let us sift a little the charge against this part of the constitution, and see to what it amounts.

There are two principal sources of political, as of personal, power,—knowledge and property. It is undeniable, that the Levites were the scholars of the nation; and it is readily granted, that, if to this advantage they had united an independent government, such as the other tribes enjoyed, and an equal possession of territory, there would have been a continual and dangerous tendency to the accumulation of property and power in their hands. But Moses committed no such capital mistake, as such an organization would argue. His constitution, at one blow, deprived the Levites of a united and independent government, and rendered them incapable of holding landed property. According to an ancient prophecy of their great progenitor, they were "divided in Jacob and scattered in Israel." They were distributed into cities, allotted to them throughout the territories of all the other twelve tribes.

By this arrangement both the estates and the persons of the Levites were given into the hands of the remaining tribes, as so many hostages for their good behavior. They were so separated from each other, that it was impossible for them to form any dangerous combinations among themselves, or to afford mutual assistance in the execution of any ambi-

tious projects. Upon suspicion of any factious attempts on
their part, it was in the power of the other tribes, not only
to put a stop to their whole livelihood, but also to seize upon
all their persons at once.

Hence it may be perceived, that, whatever influence the
constitution conferred upon the Levites to do good, the same
constitution took away from them all power to endanger the
peace, or the liberties of their country. Never, certainly, did
any other constitution watch, with such eagle-eyed jealousy,
to preserve the people from the dangers of ill-balanced
power, or guard the public liberty with so many and so admirably contrived defences against the projects of factious
and restless ambition. Most justly does Lowman take notice
how much these provisions of the Hebrew government to
prevent the occasions of faction excel all the constitutions of
the famed Spartan lawgiver for the same purpose, so much
celebrated by Grecian authors. Nor would they, he adds,
have missed their praise, had they been published by a
Lycurgus, a Solon, a Numa; or, indeed, by any body, but
Moses. The more we examine into the Mosaic plan of government, and the more reflection we bestow upon it, the
more shall we be convinced of the admirable equilibrium of
its powers, and the more shall we feel its fitness for the
efficient preservation of the public liberty.

The necessity of an enlightened, virtuous, salutary public
opinion, is the last of those great ideas, which I shall notice
as lying at the basis of the Hebrew constitution.

Public opinion is an instrument of mighty power; and it
is none the less powerful, because its operation is silent and
unperceived. It is a great and pervading principle of action
among men. No human being is beyond the reach of its influence. The despot moderates his tyranny in obedience to
its mandates. The legislator respects its authority in making
laws. The politician seeks to turn it to account in promoting
his schemes of personal advancement. A disregard of it cost

Charles I, of England, his head, and drove Charles X, of France, from his throne. Ignorance or contempt of it has prostrated monarchs, overthrown governments, and drenched the plains of Europe and America in fraternal blood. Yet how benign it may be made in its operation and effects!—not like those destructive engines, with which the walls of hostile cities are battered down, but like those happier contrivances, by which the waters of rivers are diverted from their channels, and conveyed to the orchards, gardens, and cornfields of the neighboring valleys, which thus become indebted to them for their fertility and their beauty, for the riches, which reward the husbandman's toils, and the bloom and fragrance which regale his senses. Public opinion is " the empire of mind instead of brute force, and will always prevail, when intelligence is generally diffused, and thought is free and untrammelled. Mere statute law is comparatively powerless, if public opinion is against it. Civil liberty, too, even if acquired to-day, may be lost to-morrow, unless there is accompanying it a sound public opinion, growing out of general intelligence, and an elevated tone of moral sentiment among the mass of the people. Hence the great importance of those regulations in a community, which tend to improve the standard of public sentiment."* No legislator ever understood this principle better than Moses, and none ever applied it with a wiser forecast. Undoubtedly the most efficient means employed by him to form a just, pure, wise, and vigorous public opinion, was the system of education, which he established among the people, and which has been already described. But Moses introduced into his code many other regulations, which had a strong tendency to that end, even if such was not their primary intention. Let the reader consult Ex. 22: 21–24, Deut. 24: 6, 10, 19–22, Ex. 23: 4, Deut. 22: 6, 24: 14, Levit. 19: 32, and Ex. 23: 1. Dr. Spring† takes notice of the precepts

---

* Mat. Bib. & Civ. Gov. Lect. 4.
† Obligations of the World to the Bible, Lect. 3.

here referred to, and denominates them great moral axioms, designed to form the moral sensibilities of the Hebrews by a standard refined and honorable, to guard them against unnatural obduracy, and to be a sort of standing' appeal to the tenderness and honor of men in all their mutual intercourse. Dr. Matthews* speaks of them as " statutes by which the national mind in the Hebrew commonwealth was trained to a high standard of public sentiment, imparting to all classes a sensibility to the proprieties of life, and a spontaneous regard to its relative duties, which,. in some degree, render a people a law unto themselves. To produce and perpetuate such a governing power, the power of opinion, is the very essence of wise legislation ; and, in proportion to its strength and prevalence among a people, will the foundations of civil freedom be strong and enduring." This was the steady aim and suc-' cessful endeavor of the Jewish lawgiver.

Such, then, as I conceive, were the great ideas, the fundamental principles, which lay at the basis of the Hebrew state. The unity of God, the unity of the nation, civil liberty, political equality, an elective magistracy, the sovereignty of the people, the responsibility of public officers to their constituents, a prompt, cheap, and impartial administration of justice, peace and friendship with other nations, agriculture, universal industry, the inviolability of private property, the sacredness of the family relation, the sanctity of human life, universal education, social union, a well adjusted balance of powers, and an enlightened, dignified, venerable public opinion, were the vital elements of the constitution of Moses. What better basis of civil polity, what nobler maxims of political wisdom, does the nineteenth century offer to our contemplation, despite its boast of social progress and reform ? The institutions, founded on these maxims, tower up, amid the barbaric darkness and despotisms of antiquity, the great beacon light of the world, diffusing the radiance of a political philosophy,

* Bib. & Civ. Gov. Lect. 2.

full of truth and wisdom, over all the ages, which have succeeded that, in which they were first promulgated to mankind.

CHAPTER II.

The Hebrew Theocracy.

In order to lay down a true plan of the Hebrew government, it will be necessary to inquire whether, besides the common ends of government,—the protection of the life, liberty, property, and happiness of the governed,—the lawgiver had any special views in its institution. If so, the government would naturally be adjusted to those ends ; and it can hardly be understood, without a knowledge of the particular views, which it was intended to answer. Now it is certain, that such special designs entered into the mind of the Jewish lawgiver, and modified his system of government.

By the free choice of the people,* Jehovah was made the civil head of the Hebrew state. Thus the law-making power and the sovereignty of the state were, by the popular suffrage, vested in him. It is on this account, that Josephus,† and others after him, have called the Hebrew government a theocracy. Theocracy signifies a divine government. The term is justly applied to the Mosaic constitution. Yet there is danger of being misled by it, and thence of falling into error respecting the true nature and powers of the Hebrew government. It may be too broadly applied. There was a strong infusion of the theocratic element in the Hebrew constitution. Still it was but an element in the government; and not the whole of the government. In other words, the

* See the Int. Essay.   † Against Apion, 1. 1.

Hebrew government was not a pure theocracy. It was a theocracy, but a theocracy in a restricted sense. Every student of the Hebrew history knows, that the Hebrew people, like other nations, had their civil rulers, men who exercised authority over other men, and were acknowledged and obeyed as lawful magistrates.*

What, then, was the true province of the theocracy? What were its leading objects? These objects, as I conceive, without excluding others, were chiefly two. One was to teach mankind the true science of civil government. It corresponds with the goodness of God in other respects, that he should make a special revelation on this subject. I hold it to have been an important part of the legislation of the Most High, as the lawgiver of Israel, to show how civil authority among men should be created, and how it should be administered, so as best to promote the welfare and happiness of a nation; and also how the relations between rulers and ruled should be adjusted and regulated. But another object of the theocratic feature of the Hebrew government, and the leading one undoubtedly, was the overthrow and extirpation of idolatry. The design was, first, to effect a separation between the Israelites and their idolatrous neighbors, and, secondly, to make idolatry a crime against the state, that so it might be punishable by the civil law, without a violation of civil liberty. A fundamental purpose of the Mosaic polity was the abolition of idolatrous worship, and the substitution in its place, and the maintenance, of true religion in the world. The only agency, adequate to the production of this result, as far as human wisdom can see, was this very institution of the Hebrew theocracy.

The design of the present chapter is to examine and unfold the true nature and bearing of this element of the Hebrew constitution.

In Exodus 19 : 4–6, we find this remarkable and important

* Mathews' Bib. and Civ. Gov. Lect. 1.

record. God there addresses the Israelites thus :—" Ye have
seen what I did unto the Egyptians, and how I bare you on
eagles' wings, and brought you unto myself. Now, therefore,
if ye will hear my voice indeed, and keep my covenant, then
ye shall be a peculiar treasure unto me above all people ; for
all the earth is mine, and ye shall be unto me a kingdom of
priests, and an holy nation."

The nature of this covenant is still more clearly disclosed
in a further account of it, in the twenty-ninth chapter of
Deuteronomy. " Ye stand this day," says Moses in an address to his countrymen, " your captains of your tribes, your
elders and your officers, and all the men of Israel ; that ye
should enter into covenant with Jehovah thy God, and into
his oath that he maketh with thee this day, that he may
establish thee this day for a people unto himself ; (for ye
know how we have dwelt in the land of Egypt, and how we
came through the nations that ye passed by, and ye have
seen their abominations and their idols, wood and stone,
silver and gold, which were among them;) lest there should
be among you man, or woman, or family, or tribe, whose
heart turneth away from Jehovah our God, to go and serve
the gods of those nations."

Here we have what Lowman,* not inaptly, calls the original contract of the Hebrew government. Two principles constitute the sum of it; viz. 1. the maintenance of the worship
of one God, in opposition to the prevailing polytheism of the
times ; and 2. as conducive to this main end, the separation
of the Israelites from other nations, so as to prevent the
formation of dangerous and corrupting alliances.

Without stopping to inquire critically into the meaning of
the several expressions here employed, the general sense of
the transaction is plainly to this effect :—If the Hebrews
would voluntarily receive Jehovah for their king, and would
honor and worship him as the one true God, in opposition to

* Civ. Gov. of the Heb. C. 1.

all idolatry, then, though God, as sovereign of the world, rules over all the nations of the earth, he would govern the Hebrew nation by laws of his own framing, and would bless it with a more particular and immediate protection.

This view is confirmed by the testimony of St. Paul, if bishop Warburton* has correctly interpreted a passage in his letter to the Galatians.† Speaking of the law of Moses, the apostle says, "It was added because of transgressions." It was ADDED. To what was it added? To the patriarchal religion of the unity, says the learned prelate. To what end? Because of transgressions; that is, according to the same authority, the transgressions of polytheism and idolatry; into which the rest of mankind were already absorbed, and the Jews themselves were hastening apace.

To this agrees the opinion of Maimonides,‡ the most learned and judicious of the Hebrew doctors. He observes, that the first intention of the Mosaic law, as is clearly evident from many parts of the scriptures,§ was to eradicate idolatry, and to obliterate the memory of it, and of those who were addicted to it; to banish every thing that might lead men to practise it, as pythons, soothsayers, diviners, enchanters, augurs, astrologers, necromancers, &c.; and to prevent all assimilation to their practices. He assigns this general reason for many of the laws, that they were made to keep men from idolatry, and from such false opinions and practices, as are akin to idolatry,—incantations, divinations, soothsaying, passing through the fire, and the like.

Idolatry had now reached its most gigantic height, and spread its broad and deadly shadow over the earth. To preserve the doctrine of the unity, in the midst of a polytheistic world, was the fundamental design of the Mosaic polity.

---

* Div. Leg. B. 5, S. 1.   † iv. 21.

‡ Townley's More Nevochim of Maimonides, C. 3.

§ See the Pentateuch *passim*, and many other places in the Old Testament.

To this all other purposes, however important in themselves, or useful in their general action, were both subordinate and subservient. If this were a design worthy the wisdom and goodness of God, none of the means adapted to promote it, can be beneath his contrivance, or can, in the least degree, derogate from the dignity and perfection of his nature.

This single observation sweeps away at once the foundation of most of the silly ridicule, with which infidels have amused themselves, in their disquisitions on these venerable institutes. Statutes, which, at first sight, and considered apart from their true relations and intentions, seem frivolous, and unworthy the wisdom and majesty of God, assume quite a different air, and appear in a light altogether new, when viewed as necessary provisions against the danger of idolatry.

Let me illustrate this observation with a few examples. In the nineteenth chapter of Leviticus,* we find the following law: " Ye shall not round the corners of your heads, neither shalt thou mar the corners of thy beard." This law has called forth many a sneer from men, who, without any remarkable claim to such a distinction, arrogate to themselves the exclusive title of free thinkers. But to those who really think with freedom and candor, it will appear a direction, not only proper, but important, when it is known, that it was aimed against an idolatrous custom, which was extensively prevalent, when the law was given. Herodotus says, that the Arabians cut their hair round in honor of Bacchus, who is represented as having worn his in that manner,† and that the Macians, a people of Lybia, cut their hair so as to leave a rounded tuft on the top of the head,‡ just as the Chinese do at the present day. Bochart,§ cited by Patrick,‖ notes, that the Idumaeans, Moabites, Ammonites, and other inhabitants of Arabia Deserta, are called " circumcised in the cor-

* v. 27.   † Lib. 3. C. 8.   ‡ Lib. 4. C. 175.
§ Canaan, l. 1. C. 6.   ‖ In loc.

ners," that is, of the head. The hair was much used in divination among the Greeks. Homer represents it as a common custom for parents to dedicate the hair of their children to some god; which, when they came to manhood, was cut off, and offered to the deity. In accordance with this custom, Achilles, at the funeral of Patroclus, cut off his golden locks, which his father had dedicated to the river god Sperchius, and cast them into the flood.* Virgil represents the topmost lock of hair as sacred to the infernal gods.† Idolatrous priests, ministers of a false religion, made the mode of cutting the hair and beard, forbidden by Moses, essential to the acceptable worship of the gods, and efficacious in procuring the several blessings prayed for by the worshippers. It was to eradicate idolatry, which was, so to speak, the hinge on which the whole law turned, that Moses introduced this prohibitory statute into his code.

In the twenty third chapter of Exodus,‡ the following statute occurs: " Thou shalt not seethe (boil) a kid in his mother's milk." Dr. Clarke§ thinks, that the sole design of this law was to inculcate a lesson of humanity. It is probable, however, that it was directed against an ancient custom of idolatry. Dr. Cudworth ‖ cites a manuscript comment of a Karaite Jew on this place, to the effect, that the ancient heathen were accustomed, when they had gathered in all their fruits, to take a kid, and boil it in the dam's milk, and then, in a magical way, to sprinkle with it their trees, fields, gardens, and orchards, thinking thereby to make them more fruitful. Spencer ¶ has shown that the same idolatrous custom, prompted by a similar motive, prevailed among the ancient Zabii.

---

* Hom. Il. 1. 23. vv. 124 seqq.

† Aen. 1. 4. vv. 698 seqq. See also Dr. A. Clarke's Commentary on Levit. xix. 27.

‡ v. 19.　　　　　　　　　　　§ In loc.

‖ Discourse on the Lord's Supper, p. 36.　　¶ De Legibus Hebraeorum.

A similar reason there was for the statute, which forbade the wearing of "garments mingled of linen and woollen."* Maimonides† informs us, that he found it enjoined in old magical books, that the idolatrous priests should clothe themselves in robes of linen and woollen mixed together, for the purpose of performing their religious ceremonies. A divine virtue was attributed to this mixture. It was supposed that it would make their sheep produce more wool, and their fields better harvests.

On the same ground rested the law, which enjoined, that " the woman shall not wear that which pertaineth unto a man, neither shall a man put on a woman's garment." ‡ Maimonides§ found it commanded in the books of the idolaters, that men in the worship of Venus, the Astarte or Ashtaroth of the Phenicians, should wear the dress of women, and that women, in the worship of Mars, the Moloch of the east, should put on the armor of men. Macrobius‖ cites the old Greek author Philocorus, as saying, concerning the Asiatics, that, when they sacrificed to their Venus, the men were dressed in women's apparel, and the women in men's, to denote that she was esteemed by them both male and female. It was a common practice of idolatry to confound the sexes of the gods, making the same deity sometimes a god, and sometimes a goddess. The Cyprians represented their Venus with a beard and sceptre, and of masculine proportions, but dressed as a woman. The Syrians worshipped her under the form of a woman, attired as a man. At Rome, they had both a male and female Fortune; also, as Servius and Lactantius tell us, an armed Venus. This doctrine of a community of sexes in their gods, led the idolaters to confound, as far as possible, their own sex, in their worship of them.

* Levit xix. 19.   † Townley's More Nev. c. 12.
‡ Deut. xxii. 5.   § More Nev. c. 12.
‖ L. 3, c. 8, cited by Townley in his 33d Note on Maimon. Mor. Nev. Also by Lowman on Civ. Gov. of the Hebrews, C. 1.

Hence the custom, so widely diffused, of men and women wearing a habit different from that of their sex, in performing religious rites. Julius Firmicus describes this manner ot worship as common among the Assyrians and Africans. From them it passed into Europe. It was practised in Cyprus, at Coos, at Argos, at Athens, and other places in Greece.* At Rome, it does not appear ever to have become a common practice, but we read of Clodius dressing himself as a woman, and mingling with the Roman ladies in the feast of the Bona Dea.†

The law, which prohibited the sowing of a field with mixed seeds,‡ was based on a like reason. It is true, that Michaelis§ and Dr. Clarke‖ regard this prohibition as simply a prudential maxim of agriculture, designed to make the Israelites careful to have their seed as pure as possible, and so to prevent the evils of negligent and slovenly farming. More reasonable appears the opinion of Maimonides,¶ Spencer,** and Patrick,†† who regard the statute in question as directed against idolatry, the very name and memory of which the Mosaic law sought to blot out and destroy. Maimonides interprets Levit. 19 : 19, as forbidding the grafting of one species of tree into another, and says, that the prohibition was designed to guard the Israelites against a most abominable and corrupting practice of idolatry. The Zabii performed this kind of grafting, especially of olives into citrons, as a religious rite, accompanying it, at the moment of insertion, with the most indecent actions.‡‡ Dr. Spencer observes, that

* See Young on Idolatrous Corruptions in Religion, vol. 1, pp. 97–105.
† Dr. A. Clarke in loc.   ‡ Levit. xix. 19. Deut. xxii. 9.
§ Comment. on the Laws of Moses, Art. 268.   ‖ In loc.
¶ More Nev. by Townley, C. 12.   ** De Leg. Heb. l. 2. c. 18.
†† Comment. on Deut. xxii. 9.
‡‡ The words of Maimonides are :—"Oportere, ut cùm una species in aliam inseritur, surculum inserendum manu sua tenet formosa quaedam puella, quam praeternaturali ratione vir quidam vitiet et corrumpat, ipsaque congressûs hujus tempore plantulam illam arbori infigat."

it was a rite of idolatry to sow barley and dried grapes together. By this action the idolaters consecrated their vineyards to Ceres and Bacchus, and expressed a dependence on
these deities for their fruitfulness. It was, in effect, a renunciation of the care and blessing of the true God, and a declaration of their hope in the favor of . idol gods. Bishop
Patrick well remarks, that if the Israelites had followed this
custom, it would have made the corn and the grapes, that
sprang up from such seed, impure, because polluted by idolatry.

These laws, and others which infidelity has dared to reproach and ridicule as frivolous, did the divine wisdom enact,
in order to eradicate idolatry, and establish the fundamental
truths of the existence and unity of the living God. The
design of them was, to keep the Israelites from walking in
the ordinances and manners of the nations, which were cast
out before them.* And to this end they were well adapted.
It was essential, that the idolatrous ceremonies of the gentiles
should be prohibited, because, if they had been permitted,
they could not fail to lead to idolatry.

We find a very remarkable law in Leviticus xvii. 1–7. It
forbids, even on pain of death, the killing of any animal for
food, during the abode of the Israelites in the wilderness,
unless it was at the same time brought to the altar, and
offered to the Lord. This certainly appears, at first view,
not only harsh and rigorous, but even unjust and tyrannical.
But it was aimed against idolatry, which, as we shall soon
see, was treason in the Hebrew state, and therefore justly
punishable with death. The statute is thus translated by
Michaelis :†—" Whoever among the Israelites killeth an ox,
sheep, or goat, either within or without the camp, and bring-
eth it not before the convention-tent, to him it shall be
accounted bloodguiltiness; he hath shed blood, and shall be
rooted out from among his people; and this, in order that

* Lev. xviii. 3, xx. 53.   † Mich. Comment. Art. 244.

the children of Israel may bring to the door of the convention-tent their offerings which they have hitherto made in the
field, and give them unto the priest, to be slain as feast
offerings in honor of Jehovah; that his priest may sprinkle
the blood on the altar of Jehovah, and burn the fat as an
offering perfume in honor of him; and that no man may
any more make offerings to satyrs, running after them with
idolatrous lust." "The reason and design of this law," observes the same writer,* "we have no need to conjecture;
for Moses himself expressly mentions it. Considering the
propensity to idolatry, which the people brought with them
from Egypt, it was necessary to take care lest, when any one
killed such animals as were usual for sacrifices, he should be
guilty of superstitiously offering them to an idol. This pre-
caution was the more reasonable, because, in ancient times,
it was so very common to make an offering of the flesh it
was intended it eat. And hence arose a suspicion, not very
unreasonable, that whoever killed animals, usually devoted
to the altar, offered them of course; and, therefore, Moses
enjoined them not to kill such animals otherwise than in
public, and to offer them all to the true God; that so it
might be out of their power to make them offerings to idols,
by slaughtering them privately, and under the pretence of
using them for food." This law was expressly repealed on
the entrance of the nation into the promised land,† when
the enforcement of it would have become a hardship and a
tyranny.

There is a part of the Mosaic code, to which I must call the
reader's attention in this connexion; I mean that which concerns clean and unclean meats. The law upon this point has
ever been most open to the ridicule of unbelievers. It descends to so minute a detail, that men, ignorant of its true
nature and end, have, on account of its apparent unfitness to
engage the concern of God, hastily concluded against its

* Ibid. Art. 244.   † Deut. xii. 15.
30

divine original. But if they would but take the trouble to
reflect, that the purpose of separating one people from the
contagion of universal idolatry was a design not unworthy of
the governor of the universe, they would see the brightest
marks of divine wisdom in an institution, which took away
from that people the very grounds of all commerce, whether
of trade or friendship, with foreign nations. Doubtless the
design of this institution, as of most others in the Mosaic
system, was manifold. Among the ends to be answered by
it, a not unimportant one was to furnish the chosen tribes a
code of wholesome dietetics. That considerations of this
nature entered into the legislator's mind, is the unanimous
opinion of the best interpreters, both Jews and Christians.
Maimonides[*] labors, with great zeal and learning, to prove the
correctness of this view of the law. Dr. Adam Clarke[†]
speaks of the animals denominated unclean as affording a
gross nutriment, often the parent of scorbutic and scrofulous
disorders, and of those called clean as furnishing a copious
and wholesome nutriment, and free from all tendency to gen-
erate disease. M. de Pastoret,[‡] a celebrated French writer,
notices the constant attention of Moses to the health of the
people, as one of the most distinguishing traits in his character as a legislator. The flesh of the prohibited animals, that
of the swine especially, was certainly calculated to aggravate,
if not to produce, that shocking malady, the leprosy, which
was endemic in the east, and prevailed, to a frightful extent,
among the inhabitants of Palestine. Purposes of a moral
nature, also, entered, beyond all question, into the general
design of the law. The distinction of meats tended to promote the moral improvement of the Israelites by impressing

[*] See his More Nevochim in various places.

[†] Commentary in loc.

[‡] Moyse, considéré comme Legislateur et comme Moraliste, C. 7. Cited
by Townley in the Dissertations prefixed to his Translation of the More
Nevochim.

their minds with the conviction, that as they were a "peculiar," so they ought to be a "holy nation;" by prohibiting the eating of flesh, whose gross and feculent nature might stimulate vicious propensities; and by symbolizing the dispositions and conduct to be encouraged and cultivated, or to be abhorred and avoided. Dr. Townley* cites, as concurring in this view, Levi Barcelona, Eusebius, Origen, Justin Martyr, Tertullian, and others.

But, though this law aimed to promote the health and morals of the Hebrews, such considerations did not exhaust the scope and intention of it. Its leading design was to counteract idolatry, by separating the Israelites from their idolatrous neighbors, and so preventing the infection of their example in religion and manners. This opinion does not rest on mere conjecture; nor even on the basis of logical deduction from admitted premises. The main intention of the law is unequivocally declared in the 20th chapter of Leviticus:† "Ye shall not walk in the manners of the nations which I cast out before you; * * * ye shall therefore put difference between clean beasts and unclean, and between unclean fowls and clean; * * * and ye shall be holy unto me."

The wisdom of this provision, considering the end in view, is most admirable. "Intimate friendships," observes a sagacious writer,‡ "are in most cases formed at table; and with the man with whom I can neither eat nor drink, let our intercourse in business be what it may, I shall seldom become as familiar as with him, whose guest I am, and he mine. If we have, besides, from education, an abhorrence of the food which each other eats, this forms a new obstacle to closer intimacy. Nothing more effectual could possibly be devised to keep one people distinct from another. It causes the difference between them to be ever present to the mind, touching, as it does, upon so many points of social and every day con-

* Fourth Diss. prefixed to his Trans. of the Mor. Nev.   † Vv. 23-26.
‡ Mich. Com. Art. 203.

tact. It is far more efficient, in its results, as a rule of distinction, than any difference in doctrine or worship, that men
could entertain. It is a mutual repulsion, continually ope-
rating. The effect of it may be estimated from the fact, that
no nation, in which a distinction of meats has been enforced
as part of a religious system, has ever changed its religion."

It is perfectly evident from the history of the Israelites,
that their entire isolation from other nations was the only
means, save a miraculous control of their understanding and
will, of abolishing idolatry among them. Polytheism was
then the universal religion of mankind; and the Jews, as
Michaelis* has observed, often appear to have had their heads
turned, and to have been driven, as if by a sort of phrensy,
to the belief and worship of many gods.

Yet this circumstance, strange as it now appears, when
duly considered, forms no just ground even of wonder;
much less, of any supercilious self-complacency on our part.
Opinions are extremely infectious, as we ourselves have but
too many proofs, in the thousand extravaganzas of the times.
Let us not flatter ourselves, that, had we lived then, we should
have been superior to the most absurd and besotted follies.
Even Solomon, a learned man and a philosopher, to say
nothing of his inspiration, incredible as it seems to us, built
idol temples, and sacrificed to strange gods. The Jews in
our day are exposed to a similar influence from christianity,
which is powerfully felt by them. Their peculiarities are
invaded by christian institutions and manners. In our country,
for example, the festival of Christmas is extensively observed
by them, though it is, strictly speaking, no more a part of
their religion or manners, than the festival of Baal-peor. I
was myself once invited to the celebration of this festival in
a Jewish family. On my venturing to call the attention of
my host to the incongruity of such an observance by a Jew,
he admitted it, and added, that he had said the same thing to

* Mich. Com. Art. 32

his children that very morning, when they had asked him for Christmas presents. Their reply to him was, "that all children received presents that day, and they wanted them as well." This conversation let much light into my mind on the defection to idolatry of the ancient Israelites.

Another point. Those who wonder at the frequent lapses of this people, forget, that idolatry did not consist simply in the worship of those " dead things called gods of gold and silver," or of " some vile beast laid over with vermilion set fast in a wall." On the contrary, idolatry touched all the infirmities of the human heart. The splendid festival of the idol-worshipper veiled the most voluptuous practices, and initiated into the most infamous mysteries. The heart of the Israelite was of flesh, sensual and carnal, like that of other men. Idolatry was an appeal to his susceptibility of sensual impressions and pleasures. It was a stealth into dark and voluptuous rites. It offered a ready aliment to the secret and wavering passions of the rebellious Hebrews. Hence their frequent lapses into the vilest rites of their idolatrous neighbors, despite the clear proofs, with which they had been favored, of the unity and sovereignty of the divine being.* That madness of debauchery, which was exhibited in the city of Gibeah,† reveals the true source of so obstinate an attachment to the idolatry, which consecrated such vices.

The idolatry of the ancient Israelites had, moreover, this material circumstance of mitigation. They never, at the very height of their polytheistic madness, formally renounced the worship of Jehovah. The follies of idolatry are endless ; and among them, a leading one was the belief in what Warburton calls " gentilitial and local gods." The former accompanied the nations, by whom they were worshipped, in all their migrations ; the latter were immoveably fixed to the spots, where they were adored ; or, as the learned prelate‡ has

* D'Israeli's Genius of Judaism, C. 4.
† Judg. xix. 22–25.   ‡ Divine Legation, B. 5, S. 3.

quaintly expressed it,—" the one class were ambulatory, the other stationary."

This principle led to an intercommunity of worship; so that the adoption and worship of a new deity was by no means looked upon as a necessary renunciation of those worshipped before. Thus it is recorded of the mixed rabble of idolators, with whom the king of Assyria, after the conquest and removal of the ten tribes, had peopled Samaria, that " they feared Jehovah, and served their own gods."* So also Sophocles makes Antigone say to her father, that " a stranger should both venerate and abhor those things, which are venerated and abhorred in the city where he resides." Celsus gives as a reason for such complaisance, the doctrine, that the several parts of the world were, from the beginning, parcelled out to several powers, each of whom had his own peculiar allotment and residence. It was the same idea, that led Plato to adopt and advocate the maxim, that nothing ought ever to be changed in the religion we find established in a country.

In accordance with this principle, the Israelites combined the worship of idols with the worship of the true God, who, in amazing condescension, assumed the title of a tutelary local God, and chose Judaea as his peculiar regency.† Thus, when the people " made a calf in Horeb,"‡ it was evidently designed as a representative of the God who had wrought deliverance for them ; for Aaron proclaimed a feast to Jehovah, not to Isis or Osiris. So Jeroboam, when he set up the golden calves at Dan and Bethel,§ does not give the slightest intimation of a formal intention to renounce the worship of Jehovah. And Jehu, one of his successors, while he still persists in the sin of Jeroboam, the son of Nebat, that is, in the worship of the calves, actually boasts of being a zealot

* 2 Kings xvii. 33.   † Warburton's Div. Leg. B. 5. S. 3.
‡ Exod. xxxii. 4; Ps. cvi. 19.   § 1 Kings xii. 28–33.

for Jehovah.* Instances of the like nature are scattered throughout the Old Testament Scriptures; and they prove conclusively, as Warburton† has observed, that "the defection of Israel did not consist in rejecting Jehovah as a false god, or in renouncing the law of Moses as a false religion; but in joining foreign worship and idolatrous ceremonies to the ritual of the true God. To this they were stimulated, as by various other motives, so especially by the luxurious and immoral rites of paganism."

These observations naturally lead us to the inquiry, whether the suppression of idolatry was a design worthy to engage the care of the divine mind; in other words, whether idolatry was a matter of mere harmless speculation, or a fountain of dangerous immoralities, and a prolific source of evils to the human race, whenever and wherever it has prevailed.

The religious sentiment has ever been paramount, either for good or for evil, in its action both upon societies and individuals. " Wherewith shall I come before Jehovah, and bow myself before the high God; shall I come before him with thousands of rams, or with ten thousands of rivers of oil; shall I give my firstborn for my transgression, the fruit of my body for the sin of my soul?"‡—is the piercing cry, which our universal nature has sent up to heaven, in all ages of the world. Let the thirty thousand gods of the Greeks and Romans, the costly temples reared for their worship, and the countless hecatombs that smoked upon their altars; let the long and painful pilgrimages of whole armies of devotees to the shrine of their idolatry, and their innumerable and cruel self-tortures, inflicted in the vain hope of thereby securing the divine favor; above all, let the rivers of human blood, shed to glut the rapacity of some sanguinary deity, which have drenched the soil of every nation under heaven, —attest the truth of this observation.

* 2 Kings x. 16.   † Div. Leg. B. 5. S. 3   ‡ Mic. vi. 6, 7.

"Religion," says Coleridge,[*] "true or false, is, and ever has been, the centre of gravity in a realm, to which all other things must and will accommodate themselves." The sense which mankind have ever entertained of the power of the religious principle in moulding human character, plainly appears in the pains taken by the ancient lawgivers to impress upon those for whom they legislated, an idea of their inspiration by some deity. Minos, lawgiver of the Cretans, often retired to a cave, where he boasted of having familiar conversations with Jupiter, whose sanction he claimed for his legislation. Mneves and Amasis, renowned legislators of Egypt, attributed their laws to Mercury. Lycurgus claimed the sanction of Apollo for his reformation of the Spartan government. Pythagoras and Zaleucus, who made laws for the Crotoniates and Locrians, ascribed their institutions to Minerva. Zathraustes, lawgiver of the Arimaspians, gave out that he had his ordinances from a goddess adored by that people. Zoroaster and Zamolxis boasted to the Bactrians and the Getae of their intimate communications with goddess Vesta. And Numa amused the Romans with his conversations with the nymph Egeria.

These facts demonstrate a universal persuasion of the controlling energy of the religious sentiment over men's minds and practices. It cannot, indeed, be otherwise than that the ideas which men entertain of the gods they worship, should constitute a capital element in the formation of their moral character. Like gods, like worshippers. It is vain to expect, that the virtue of the devotee will exceed the virtue of the divinity. The worshippers of a bloody Mars, a thievish Mercury, an incestuous Jupiter, and a voluptuous Venus, could hardly help being sanguinary, dishonest, and licentious.

> "Gods partial, changeful, passionate, unjust,
> Whose attributes were rage, revenge, and lust,"

[*] Manual for Statesmen.

could never become the authors of the opposite virtues in those by whom they were adored. Whatever sanctions they might annex to their laws, their example would always prove more powerful than their terrors.

Plato excluded poets from his republic, dismissing even Homer, with a garland on his head, and with ointment poured upon him. His object, in this otherwise unaccountable rigor, was, that they might not corrupt the right notions of God with their fables. If we consider the absurdity, as well as the immorality, of their fictions, we shall hardly be disposed to blame him. They distinguished the gods in their places and ways of living, in the same manner as they would different sorts of animals. Some they placed under the earth ; some in the sea; some in woods and rivers; and the most ancient of them all they bound in hell. Some are set to trades ; one is a smith; another is a weaver; one is a warrior, and fights with men; others are harpers; and others, still, delight in archery and the chase. Gods of the sea, the rivers, the woods, the hills, and the valleys; gods of smithery, music, and the chase; gods of wine, war, and love; —what more besotted could be imagined ? The father of the gods himself is fast bound by the fates, so that he cannot, contrary to their decrees, save his own offspring. Not seldom does he resort to policy and craft, nay to the basest disguises and hypocrisies, to accomplish his purposes, which are often of the most shameful nature. Storm, darkness, fear, rage, madness, fraud, and the vilest passions were invested with divinity. Unbounded lusts and disgraceful amours were ascribed by the poets to almost all the gods. There was scarcely a member of the Olympian senate, who would now be admitted to decent society among mortals. No wonder that Plato shut out from his commonwealth a class of writers, whose extravagant and teeming fancy he regarded as the source of these monstrosities.

It was a principle of polytheism, that the supreme God,

after he had made the world, retreating, as it were, wholly into himself, had committed the government of it to subordinate deities, and did not interfere in the regulation of human affairs. Thus the temporal blessings of health, long life, fruitful seasons, plenty, safety, victory over enemies, and such like advantages, were to be sought from these demons, or idols. And these blessings were to be obtained, and the opposite evils averted, not by the practice of virtue and beneficence, but by the use of some magical ceremonies, or by the performance of certain senseless and barbarous rites of worship. That this was a fundamental doctrine of idolatry, we have undoubted proofs, both from sacred and profane writers. King Ahaz, in 2 Chronicles,* says, " Because the gods of the kings of Syria help them, therefore will I sacrifice to them, that they may help me." The prophet Hosea† represents the Jews of his time as saying, " I will go after my lovers (the idol gods), that give me my bread and my water, my wool and my flax, mine oil and my drink." To a reproof from Jeremiah for their idolatry, they replied : " As for the word that thou hast spoken unto us in the name of the Lord, we will not hearken unto thee. But we will certainly do whatsoever thing goeth forth out of our own mouth, to burn incense unto the queen of heaven, and to pour out drink-offerings unto her, as we have done, we, and our fathers, our kings, and our princes, in the cities of Judah, and in the streets of Jerusalem : for then had we plenty of victuals, and were well and saw no evil. But since we left off to burn incense to the queen of heaven, and to pour out drink-offerings unto her, we have wanted all things, and have been consumed by the sword and by the famine."‡ Here they aver, in substance, that as long as they had worshipped the queen of heaven, all had gone well with them, and her, therefore, they would worship, and to her sacrifice, in spite of his admonitions. To the like purport is the decla-

* xxviii. 23. † ii. 5. ‡ Jer. xliv. 16–18.

ration of Plato. In his work De Anima Mundi, speaking of
the punishment of wicked men, he says; "All these things
hath Nemesis decreed to be executed in the second period by
the ministry of vindictive terrestrial demons, who are overseers of human affairs ; to which demons the supreme God
hath committed the government of this world."

But was not this a harmless philosophical dogma? By no
means. It was a doctrine, not more false in point of fact,
than pernicious in its results. It was a denial of the providence of God. The disbelief of this great truth gave plausibility, attractiveness, and energy to the whole system of
idolatry. The supreme being was thought to be too exalted
in his dignity to take any concern in human conduct, too remote from this sublunary scene to regard its vicissitudes with
any interest, too much absorbed in the contemplation of his
own infinite perfections to care for the perfection of inferior
beings, too much engrossed in the enjoyment of his own independent happiness to feel any desire for the happiness of
creatures. Hence his existence came to be, either totally
forgotten, or regarded with indifference. However the case
might have been with a few philosophic and contemplative
minds, to the generality of mankind the true God was as
though he were not. They referred not their conduct to his
direction, for his power had nothing to do with their happiness or misery. He had delegated to demons the government
of this world. The agency of these inferior beings controlled
its affairs ; their will determined the blessings or calamities
of life. While, therefore, it was wise and safe to neglect the
supreme being, it was unwise and unsafe to treat with a like
indifference the subordinate deities, to whom he had committed the administration of human affairs.* Thus men
came to think, that they were not to expect the blessings of
life from the favor of the one true God, by imitating his
purity and goodness; but from a Jupiter, stained with

* See on this subject Graves on the Pent. Pt. 2, Lect. 1.

crimes that would doom a mortal to the gibbet or the penitentiary; from a Mercury, a thief and a patron of thieves; from a Bacchus, the god of drunkenness; from a Mars, the instigator of war and bloodshed; or from a Venus, the patron ess of all manner of voluptuousness and debauchery. Hence they became, almost necessarily, as corrupt in practice, as they were erroneous and grovelling in their opinions. The principles of moral goodness were well nigh extinguished in the human heart, and the practice of the moral virtues had almost disappeared from the earth. And intemperance, ferocity, lust, fraud, and violence might have brought a second deluge upon the race, had not the truth of God stood pledged against the repetition of so dire a calamity.

But further, and worse. Idolatry did not simply lead to vicious practices, it even consecrated vice in its sacred rites. Incredible as it may seem, uncleanness formed a part of the religious worship paid to the gods. Persons of both sexes prostituted themselves in honor of Venus, Priapus, Astarte, Baalpeor, and other filthy and loathsome deities. Of these obscene rites, as constituting a part of the religion of idolaters, we have the clearest proofs in authors of undoubted credit. Strabo* informs us, that a single temple at Corinth maintained more than a thousand religious prostitutes. Herodotus† tells us, that women of this description abounded among the Phenicians, Babylonians, and other eastern nations. He even says, that by an express law, founded on an oracle, it was ordained, that all the women of Babylon should, at least once in their lives, repair to the temple of Venus, and prostitute themselves to strangers. Strangely enough as it seems to me, an eminent and for the most part judicious author,‡ has labored to prove, that this custom must have been conducive to the virtue of chastity. Facts, however, contradict the theory of this learned writer. Babylon,

---

* Geog. l. 8. † Lib. 1. c. 187.
‡ Goguet in his Origin of Laws.

by the testimony of both sacred and profane authors, was one vast sink of pollution. Its inhabitants made a particular study of all that could delight the senses, and excite and gratify the most shameless passions. The women of Cyprus sacrificed their chastity before marriage, to Venus.* The Egyptians had religious prostitutes, who were consecrated to Isis.† The Isiac rites, transported to Rome, became a mere cloak for licentiousness. Tiberius caused the images of Isis to be thrown into the Tiber. But her worship was too alluring to be suffered to die out and disappear. It was, therefore, subsequently revived in full force, and Juvenal speaks of it in an indignant strain.‡ Selden, De Diis Syriis, has fully shown the impurities of the ancient idolatrous worship. Bacchus, Osiris, and Ceres were adored with rites, which modesty forbids to explain.§ That these religious obscenities were practised in the days of Moses, is manifest from the history of the Israelites, who committed fornication with the daughters of Moab.‖ The immorality was perpetrated at a sacrificial festival, the Moabitish women exposing themselves in honor of Baal-peor, who was the same as the Priapus of the Romans. It is further evident from a law of Moses, forbidding a father to prostitute his daughter, " to cause her to be a whore."¶ This law must be understood as prohibiting the exposure of a daughter as an act of religion, for surely no man, not even the vilest and most abandoned, could prostitute a child to purposes of common whoredom.

The necessary consequences of religious doctrines and ceremonies, like those described in the preceding paragraph, was the extinction of all true religious principle, and even of

* Justin l. 18. c. 5. Herod. l. 1. c. 187.
† Lewis's Antiq. of the Heb. Rep. B. 5, c. 1.
‡ See Anthon's Class. Dict. Art. Isis, and the authorities referred to by him.
§ See Lowman on Civ. Gov. Heb. c. 1.
‖ Num. xxv. 1-3.   ¶ Levit. xix. 29.

all the principles of moral virtue and goodness. They gave intensity to the depraved appetites of human nature. They put the bridle upon the neck of lust, and caused men to run riot in every species of impurity.

But the ancient mythologists represented their deities under, if possible, a still more malign and repulsive light. The learned professor Meiners* says, that the more ancient Greeks imagined their gods to be envious of human felicity. Whenever any extraordinary success attended them, they were filled with terror, lest the gods should bring upon them some dreadful evil. Herodotus† attributes to Solon, in his interview with Croesus, the formal declaration,—"The gods envy the happiness of men." The Egyptian monarch Amasis grounds the withdrawment of his friendship from Polycrates, tyrant of Samos, on the notoriously envious nature of the divine being.‡ The sage Artabanus warns Xerxes, that even the blessings which the gods bestow, are derived from an envious motive.§ A similar doctrine prevailed at Rome, agreeably to which the great Fabius, as Livy informs us, remonstrated with the Roman people against an election to the consulship in his old age, urging, among other reasons, that some divinity might think his past successes too great for mortal, and turn the tide of fortune against him. In accordance with this doctrine, we find even the reflecting Tacitus expressing the opinion, that the gods interfere in human affairs but to punish.‖

As a necessary consequence, almost the whole of the religion of the ancient pagan world consisted in rites of deprecation. Fear was the leading feature of their religious impressions. Hence arose that most horrid of all religious ceremonies,—the rite of human sacrifice. Of this savage custom, archbishop Magee, in one of the notes appended to his Discourses on

---

* Historia Doctrinae de vero Deo, p. 208.　† L. 1. C. 32.
‡ Herod. l. 3. C. 40.　§ Ibid. l. 7. C. 46.
‖ "Non esse curae deis *securitatem* nostram, esse *ultionem*."

Atonement and Sacrifice,* asserts and proves, that there is no
nation mentioned in history, which we cannot reproach with
having, more than once, made the blood of its citizens to
stream forth, in holy and pious ceremonies, to appease the
divinity, when he appeared angry, or to move him, when he
appeared indolent.

" Conformably with this character of their gods," adds the
same learned prelate, " we find the worship of many of the
heathen nations to consist in suffering and mortification, in
cutting their flesh with knives, and scorching their limbs with
fire. The cruel austerities of the gymnosophists, both of
Africa and India; the dreadful sufferings of the initiated
votaries of Mithra and Eleusis; the frantic and savage rites of
Bellona; and the horrid self-mutilations of the worshippers of
Cybele,—but too clearly evince the dreadful views entertained
by the ancient heathens of the nature of their gods."

Undoubtedly, then, it became the wisdom, the justice, and
the goodness of the one true God, to check these spreading
and direful evils; to bring men back from their polytheistic
follies to the belief and worship of himself; and to let them
know, that he had not parted with the administration of
providence, nor given over the disposal of temporal blessings
to any subordinate beings whatsoever; so that health, plenty,
and all kinds of prosperity were to be sought from him alone,
and expected as the sole gift of his sovereign bounty. And
here we may take notice, in passing, of an opinion of Origen,
in which Spencer and others of the learned concur, that it was
a very wise procedure in Moses to enforce the observance of
his laws by the hope of temporal good and the fear of temporal
evil. Such hopes and fears were, if not a source of idolatry,
at least a means of strengthening it. The Hebrew lawgiver
turned this battery, if I may be allowed the expression, against
the enemy. In the name of Jehovah, Israel's divine king, he
promised temporal blessings to the obedient, and threatened

temporal calamities to the disobedient. Thus the very things, which before had been motives to idolatry, now became motives and aids to true religion. It may be said without irreverence, that a sort of necessity was laid upon the true God to proceed in this manner. How could he effectually check the propensity to idolatry; how could he show, that he had not delegated to demons the government of the world; how could he vindicate his own incommunicable sovereignty and omnipotence, but by doing, in reality, what the false gods pretended to do?

Upon the same principle it was, I think, that prophecy, in the more restricted sense of foretelling future events, was so much employed under the Hebrew government. The ability to peer into the future was claimed by the ministers of the ancient idolatrous worship; and the people, confiding in their pretensions, consulted them upon all occasions. To meet and overcome the power of superstition in that direction, it would seem natural, and, indeed, almost necessary, that the true God should show, by infallible tokens, that the past, the present, and the future were all one to him.

But the pestilent virus of idolatry was too deeply seated to be eradicated by such agencies as these. The question, then, naturally arises: What just and rational means were adequate to the suppression of it? Opinions are not to be bound by legal enactments; and to enforce mere theological dogmas by the arm of the civil law, would be a gross breach of civil liberty. It would be strange indeed, if a code, to which the world is indebted for most of the true principles of civil freedom, violated that freedom, in a fundamental article of it. And, in truth, however certain ignorant or prejudiced writers may have represented the matter, the constitution of Moses is chargeable with no such inconsistency.

How, then, was Moses able to suppress idolatry, without infringing the principle here announced? By the introduction of the theocratic system into his inspired legislation. " One

God only shalt thou serve," was the first great principle of the Hebrew polity. To the end that this fundamental truth of religion might become a vital element of Hebrew thought, faith, and manners, the one true God became also the covenanted king, the civil head of the Hebrew state. Thus to the Israelite the Deity was both a celestial and a terrestrial sovereign, his God and his king. Viewed as to a main design of it, then, the theocracy was a divine constitution, employed the more effectually to supplant idolatry, without a violation of that precious principle of civil liberty, that mere opinions, whether theological, ethical, or political, were not to be cramped and restrained by the pains and penalties of the civil law.

"The records of the Hebrew polity," observes Coleridge,* with a just discrimination, "are rendered far less instructive as lessons of political wisdom by the disposition to regard the Jehovah in that universal and spiritual acceptation, in which we use the word as christians; for relatively to the Jewish polity the Jehovah was their covenanted king."

What, then, was the theocracy? God condescended to assume the title and relation to the Hebrew people of chief civil ruler. He stablished a civil sovereignty over them. He issued his edicts as a civil magistrate. The manner in which the compact, giving reality to this relationship, was formed, deserves particular notice. It is detailed in the nineteenth chapter of Exodus. Moses, acting under a divine commission, proposed to the nation the question, whether they would receive Jehovah for their king, and submit to his laws? The suffrage of the people appears to have been entirely free in this matter. By their own voluntary consent Moses made God their king. Thus idolatry and every thing leading to idolatry or growing out of it, became a crime against the state,—became, in fact, "crimen laesae majestatis," high treason, or rebellion. As such, it was justly

* Manual for Statesmen.

31

punishable with death,—all governments agreeing in this, that treason is the highest of civil crimes. The punishment of idolatry by law had, then, plainly, this capital quality of justice, that it was punishing the act of those who had chosen the government under which they lived, when freely proposed to them. Their own suffrages had made it a political offence. Hence idolatry is called by the Hebrew writers "the trangression of the covenant." It was a breach of the fundamental compact between the Hebrew people and their chosen king. The theocracy made religious apostacy a state crime, which it could not be, without infringing liberty, under any other constitution.

It is a material consideration, that Moses nowhere deduces God's right to give laws to the Hebrew nation from his being the one only God, but from his having by miraculous interpositions and works of power, laid the foundation of their state. In confirmation of this view, the reader's attention is invited to a remarkable passage in Deuteronomy.* I give the passage, as translated by Michaelis :† "When thy son asketh thee in after times, whence come all the statutes and laws, which Jehovah thy God hath given thee? thou shalt say to him, we were in Egypt slaves to the king; but Jehovah, with a strong hand brought us out of Egypt, and did before our eyes great miracles, whereby he punished the Egyptians, and Pharoah and his house ;· and he brought us out, to give us the land, which he had by an oath promised to our fathers : Therefore he commanded us to keep all these laws." Here the right of legislating for the Hebrews is, in express terms, grounded on the favors which God had bestowed upon them, and not upon his absolute sovereignty as creator and universal lord.

What God says to the Israelites in Exod. 20: 2, 3, is to the same effect: "I am Jehovah, thy God, which have brought thee out of Egyptian bondage; thou shalt have no

* vi. 20–24.   † Com. Art. 34.

gods before me." It would have been quite consonant with sound theology to say : " I Jehovah am God alone ; therefore thou shalt have no gods but me." This fundamental article of religion is taught in many parts of the Mosaic writings. But the opinions of the Israelites were not to be fettered by legal enactments ; and yet idolatry must be prohibited on pain of civil punishment. God, therefore, as Michaelis has observed, addressed a people strangely prone to polytheism, to this effect :—" Lest you should absurdly suppose, that there are many gods, who can hear your prayers and recompense your offerings, know that I alone have delivered you from Egyptian tyranny ; have made you a people; and am the author and founder of your state : Therefore let no gods but me be worshipped among you."*

But it ought never to be forgotten, that, although God, by what he wrought for the Israelites, had acquired all the right to be their sovereign, that any man could possibly have, still he neither claimed nor exercised that right in an arbitrary and despotic way. Moses, by his direction, permitted the people freely to choose whether they would accept Jehovah as their king, and obey the laws which he might give them. When they had formally assented to this, God was considered as their king, but not before. The whole world, indeed, was under his moral rule; his dominion as creator embraced all the tribes of earth ; but Israel was his peculiar property, whose people had chosen him for their king. The passages of scripture to this effect are surprizingly pointed and striking. The history of the election by the Israelites of Jehovah to be the head of their state, contained in the nineteenth chapter of Exodus, has been before explained and commented on at length.† Other passages are no less remarkable. Thus, in Deut. 33 : 5, it is said " God was king in Jeshurun, WHEN the heads of the people, and the tribes of Israel were gathered

* Com. Art. 33.   † See pp. 47, 48 of this vol.

together."* This seems a plain reference to the account in Exodus, and as plain an intimation, that God was made king. by the vote of the assembled nation. So when the Israelites first desired a man for a king, God said to Samuel, "They have not rejected thee, they have rejected me, that I should not reign over them."† Again, when they were to receive this king, the record is, "Thus saith Jehovah, God of Israel, I brought up Israel out of Egypt, and delivered you out of the hand of the Egyptians, and out of the hand of all kingdoms, and of them that oppressed you ; and ye have this day rejected your God, who himself saved you out of all your adversities and your tribulations, and ye have said unto him, Nay, but set a king over us."‡

What is the issue ? We have seen the monstrous doctrines, pollutions, and crimes of idolatry. We have seen the justice, wisdom, and goodness of the purpose to put a stop to such dreadful evils. We have seen the nature and ground of God's claim to the sovereignty of the Hebrew state. We have seen, that the government was a voluntary compact between the sovereign and the citizens. We have seen, that idolatry under this constitution was a state crime, was in fact high treason. We have seen, that the whole scope and hinge of the Hebrew polity was the overthrow of idolatry, and that the theocratic element was introduced into it expressly to further that design. Let the reader consider and weigh these things, and, if he be

---

* The common version makes Moses king in Jeshurun. But Kennicott, Michaelis, Adam Clarke, and other distinguished Hebrew scholars, are of the opinion, that the word Moses crept into the text by mistake of some transcriber, and was not in the original, as written by Moses himself. Dr. Clarke, with his usual curtness and vigor, pronounces the sense yielded by our translation "most absurd." Dr. Kennicott's argument in support of the opinion, that God, and not Moses, is the real subject of the proposition, is forcible and conclusive ; but it is hardly worth while to trouble the reader with philological discussions of that nature. See Clarke in loc., Kennicott's first Dissertation, and Michaelis's Commentaries, Art. 34.

† 1 Sam. viii. 7.   ‡ Ibid. x. 18, 19.

candid and unbiased, if his mental vision be not warped and clouded by prejudice, he will own, that to have imposed the penalty of death upon the worship of false gods can no longer appear in the light of inquisitorial tyranny.

It will be proper to conclude this chapter with a brief sketch of the religious and moral doctrines of judaism.*

There is one God, says the Jewish lawgiver, and there is none besides him. He is the sole object of religious trust and worship. Himself the supreme being, and the necessary source of all other beings, there is no other that can be compared with him. A spirit, pure, immense, infinite,—no material form can be a fit symbol of his nature. He framed the universe by his power ; he governs it by his wisdom; he regulates it by his providence. Nothing escapes his omniscient glance; nothing can resist his almighty power. The good and evil of life are alike dispensed by his righteous hand.

A public worship of this God is instituted. Ministers to preside over it are appointed. Sacrifices and offerings and a splendid ceremonial are established. But all this pomp is nothing in his eyes, unless prompted and animated by the sentiments of the heart. The worship which he demands, before all and above all, is the acknowledgement of our absolute dependence and of his supreme dominion ; gratitude for his benefits ; trust in his mercy ; reverence for his authority ; love towards his excellence ; and submission to his law.

What purity and beauty in the moral doctrines of this code! Equity, probity, fidelity, industry, compassion, charity, beneficence ;—in a word, every thing that makes men respectable in their own eyes, every thing that can endear them to their fellows, every thing that can assure the repose and

* See on this subject " Lettres de quelques Juifs Allemands et Polonais à M. de Voltaire." The valuable substance of the first Letter is embodied in these closing sentences.

happiness of society,—are placed among the number of human duties.

Where else, in all antiquity, are to be found ideas of God and his worship, so just and sublime; religious institutions, so pure and spiritual; ethical doctrines, so conformable to the sentiments of nature and the light of reason? Recal the picture, presented in a former part of this chapter, of the religious and moral condition of the ancient world. What false and grotesque notions of the divine nature! What extravagant, impure, and cruel rites! What objects of adoration! From the heavenly orbs to the meanest plant, from the man distinguished for his talents or his crimes to the vilest reptile,—everything has its worshippers. Here, chastity is sacrificed in the temples. There, human blood flows upon the altars, and the dearest victims expire amid flames, kindled by superstition. Again, nature is outraged by beastly amours, and humanity brutalized by vices that cannot be named without offence. Everywhere, the people are plunged into a frightful ignorance, and the philosophers themselves grope in doubt and uncertainty.

Wherefore this difference? But one cause, adequate to the result, can be assigned. All the pagan nations had for their guide only the feeble and tremulous light of human reason. Among the Hebrews, a higher, even the pure and eternal reason, had pierced the darkness, scattered its shades, and poured a divine illumination into the mind of prophet, priest, lawgiver, judge, and king. Thus was the intellect of the nation enlightened, and its heart purified. Thus were its manners humanized; its morals elevated; its institutions liberalized. Thus was the nation educated for its great mission of guidance and of blessing to all the nations of the earth, in all the periods of their history.

The Hebrew government was a government of tutelage. No form of polity has ever approached it in grandeur, purity, simplicity, and beneficence. Had men been more perfect, it would have stood forever. But human inconstancy wearied even of a perfect government; mortal passions corrupted even a divine institution; and the commonwealth of Israel, like the empire of Rome, at length fell beneath the weight of its own vices, and disappeared from the brotherhood of nations. It lives only in history, a monument at once of the divine goodness and equity.

CHAPTER III.

General Idea of the Hebrew Constitution.

THE political equality of the people, without either nobles or peasants properly so called, was, as we have seen,[*] a fundamental principle of the Mosaic constitution. This could not but give the state a strong democratic tendency. Nor is it matter of surprize, that on this foundation Moses established a commonwealth, rather than a monarchy.[†] On this point, there is scarcely a dissenting voice among all the learned men, who have written upon these institutions. Mr. Horne[‡] does but echo the general opinion, when he says, that "the form of the Hebrew-republic was unquestionably democratical."

Moses did not, indeed, by an unchangeable law, enact, that no alteration should ever be made in the form of government. On the contrary, his prophetic eye foresaw, that the time would come, when his countrymen, infected and dazzled

---

[*] Bk. 2, c. 1, p. 400.   [†] Mich. Com. on the Laws of Moses.
[‡] Introduction, vol. 2, Pt. 2, c. 1.

by the example of the surrounding nations, would lose their
relish for republican simplicity, and would demand the splendors of a throne and a court. But it was not his wish, that
they should have a king. ·Upon this point he reasoned ; he
dissuaded ; he expostulated ; he warned. The spirit of his
law was strongly against monarchy ; and all, who afterwards
maintained that spirit, were equally strong against it. This
was the case with Gideon, who indignantly rejected the offer
of a crown. This was the case with Samuel, that model of a
popular magistrate. He remonstrated, solemnly and eloquently, with the people, against their rash determination to
have a king. He told them, that they were fastening upon
themselves an oriental despotism ; that their kings would
rule them with a rod of iron : and that they would repent of
their rashness, when it was too late. The truth is, that all
who followed the maxims of the founder of the state, set
their faces against usurpation, and maintained the rights of
the people at all hazards, and in the most disastrous times.*

Foreseeing, however, that all his admonitions would, in the
end, prove unavailing, Moses enacted a fundamental law to
define and limit the power of the future kings. This law is
found in the 17th chapter of Deuteronomy. Despotism
seems to be the native growth of the east. Man there,
cradled in servitude, becomes fitted to listen to his fate, in
the mandates of a tyrant. The climate dissolves the energy
of the heart, and hence the people of the east have always
been mere children in respect of political institutions. Indolence loves to gaze, and hence they have ever been delighted
with the trappings of royalty, and have been prone to look
on an earthly king with a veneration approaching to idolatry.
The pomp of their sovereign feeds their vanity ; his power is
their pride. They have no notion of popular freedom.
Hence a chief magistrate, subject to the laws of his people,
a constitutional king, is a conception, foreign to all their

* Chr. Exam. for Sept. 1836.

habits of thought and feeling. In Egypt, Moses had witnessed the abuse of the regal power; in the wilderness, he had
observed the tyranny of the petty despots in the neighbor- !
hood of Israel. Hence the enactment of the law referred to
above. The particular provisions of this law will be ex
amined in another chapter. I will only observe now, in
passing, that they were such as to insure, whenever the anticipated change in the form of polity should take place, the
existence of a constitutional monarchy. The king, permitted
by Moses to the folly of his countrymen, was, in truth, what
a late monarch in France* claimed to be, a " citizen king ;"
a popular magistrate, rather than an arbitrary sovereign. If
the Hebrew statesman could not wholly resist the proclivity
of his nation to the regal form of government, he at least,
with prescient wisdom, limited the power intrusted to the
hands of royalty. In this he shows how thoroughly his own
spirit was impregnated with democratic principles, how deep
was his hatred of tyranny, and how ardent and irrepressible
his sympathy for the rights, the liberty, and the happiness of
man.†

Considerable difference of opinion exists among the learned
in regard to the number and nature of the departments of the
Hebrew government, and the officers by whom the administration of public affairs was conducted. The mixture of civil
and military authority, which marks this constitution, the
blending of the legislative and judicial functions in the same
assembly, the union of various and, according to our way of
thinking, somewhat incongruous powers in the priesthood,
the apparent chasms‡ in the Mosaic legislation arising from
the frequent retention by Moses of ancient consuetudinary

---

* Louis Philippe.

† See on this subject D'Israeli's Genius of Judaism, c. 4.

‡ I say "apparent chasms," because what are chasms to us were not so
to the Israelites, being supplied by a then well known law of usage; a
' lex non scripta," corresponding to the common law among us.

laws, without any formal introduction of them into the body of his own laws, and the extreme brevity of the history of the Israelitish state, as contained in the sacred books, are the causes of that obscurity, which has operated to produce this diversity of opinion. As far as I have been able to satisfy my own mind, the following statement embodies the radical features of this ancient and venerable polity.*

Each of the Israelitish tribes formed a separate state, having a local legislature and a distinct administration of justice. The power of the several states was sovereign within the limits of their reserved rights. Still, there was both a real and a vigorous general government. The nation might have been styled the united tribes, provinces, or states of Israel. The bond of political union between the sovereign states appears to have been fourfold. In other words, there were four departments of the Hebrew government: viz. the chief magistrate, whether judge, high priest, or king; the senate of princes; the congregation of Israel, the popular branch of the government; and the oracle of Jehovah, a most interesting and singular part of the political structure. The form of a legal enactment might have run somewhat after this fashion:—"Be it enacted by the senate and congregation of Israel, the judge approving, and the oracle concurring." There was a judiciary system, in which causes of a sufficient magnitude could be carried up, through courts of various grades, till they came, for final adjudication, before a supreme national court, which held its session in the capital of the nation. Finally, on the one hand, the organization of the tribe of Levi gave vitality to the whole system, acted as a counterpoise to the democracy, and restrained its excesses, while, on the other, the prophetical order maintained the rights of the people, and formed a powerful barrier against the encroachments of arbitrary power.†

---

* Lowman on the Civ. Gov. Heb. C. 8.

† I do not here cite the particular Scriptures in support of these views.

A knowledge of the polity of the Hebrews prior to the time of Moses will help us in understanding his constitution, since he retained in it many of the ancient laws and institutions, sometimes unaltered, sometimes slightly modified. The simplicity of ancient manners rendered complicated methods of government unnecessary. The form actually employed by most nations in the earliest times, appears to have been patriarchal. To this rule the Hebrew polity does not form an exception. Abraham, Isaac, and Jacob governed their families with an authority well nigh unlimited. Their power over their households was little short of a sovereign dominion. They were independent princes. They acknowledged no subjection, and owed no allegiance, to any sovereign. They formed alliances with other princes.* They treated with kings on a footing of equality.† They maintained a body of servants, trained to the use of arms; were the chiefs, who led them in war; and repelled force by force.‡ They were the priests, who appointed festivals, and offered sacrifices. § They had the power of disinheriting their children,‖ of sending them away from home without assigning any reason,¶ and even of punishing them capitally.**

The twelve sons of Jacob ruled their respective families with the same authority. But when their descendants had become numerous enough to form tribes, each tribe acknowledged a prince as its ruler.†† This office, it is likely, was at first hereditary in the eldest son, but afterwards became elective. When the tribes increased to such an extent, as to embrace a great number of separate households, the less powerful ones united with their stronger relatives, and ac-

since the passages on which they rest will be often referred to in the subsequent detail of the Hebrew institutions.

* Gen. xxi. 22 32.   † Gen. xiv. 24. xxxiv. 6–19.
‡ Gen. xiv. 13–16.   § Gen viii. 20. xxii. 13. Job i. 5.
‖ Gen. xlix. 3, 4. 1 Chron. v. 1 ¶ Gen. xxi. 14.
** Gen. xxxviii. 24.   †† Numb. 1.

knowledged them as their superiors. In this way, there arose a subdivision of the tribes into collections of households. Such a collection was technically called a family, a clan, a house of fathers, or a thousand.* This last appellation was not given, because each of these subdivisions contained just a thousand persons, or a thousand households; for, in the nature of things, the number must have varied, and in point of fact, it is manifest from the history, that it did. As the tribes had their princes, so these clans, families, or thousands had their respective chiefs, who were called heads of houses of fathers, heads of thousands, and sometimes simply heads.† Harrington denominates these two classes of officers phylarchs, or governors of tribes, and patriarchs, or governors of families. Both, while the Israelites were yet in Egypt, were comprehended under the general name of elders.‡ Whether this name was a title of honor, like that of sheik (the aged) among the Arabs, and that of senator among the ancient Romans, or whether it is to be understood, according to its etymology, as denoting persons actually advanced in years, is uncertain; probably, however, the former is the true sense of the term. These princes of tribes and heads of thousands, the elders of Israel, were the rulers of the people, while they remained still subject to the power of the Pharoahs, and constituted a kind of " imperium in imperio." Of course they had no written constitution, nor any very formal code of laws, but governed by custom, reason, and the principles of natural justice. They watched over and provided for the general good of the community, while the affairs of each individual household continued under the control of its own father. For the most part, it may be supposed, only those cases, which concerned the

* Judges, vi. 15. 1 Sam. x. 19–21. xxiii. 23. Numb. xxvi. 5–50.
† Numb. xvii. 3. xxv. 15. Joshua xxii. 14. xxiii. 2.
‡ Exod. iii. 16. iv. 29.

fathers of families themselves would come under the cognizance and jurisdiction of the elders.

Such was the patriarchal form of government. It was
found among all the branches of Abraham's posterity;—
Ishmaelites, Edomites, and Israelites alike. Each of these,
like the ancient Germans, the Roman gentes, and the Scottish
clans, kept together in a body, according to their tribes and
families. Every tribe formed a little commonwealth, having
its own particular interests; while all united became a great
republic, with a common weal. Thus we find the Ishmaelites
governed by twelve princes, according to the number of Ish-
mael's sons.* Their descendants, the Beduin Arabs, have
preserved the patriarchal polity to this day. They call their
princes emirs, and their heads of clans sheiks,—elders,—
under which latter designation, the Hebrews included both
these orders of rulers. In like manner, the Edomites had
what the sacred historian calls kings, but under them, again,
stood a multitude of chiefs, styled princes, who ruled over so
many clans.† The same arrangement took place among the
Israelites. That there were twelve great tribes is known to
all. That the tribes were governed, each by its own prince,
that they were subdivided into clans, or groups of related
families, having also their respective chiefs, and that these
princes of tribes and chiefs of clans received the common
appellation of " elders of Israel," will be evident to any one,
who will take the trouble to compare the first chapter of
Numbers with Exod. 3: 16, 4: 29, and 6: 14, 15.

Another order of officers, who, in the end, came to possess
great dignity and power, likewise sprang up among the Hebrews, while yet in Egypt. These were the shoterim, in our
version rendered " officers." That they were different from
the judges is certain, since Moses ordained, that, when the
Israelites came into the promised land, they should appoint

* Gen. xxv. 16.   † Gen. xxxvi.

both judges and shoterim in every city.* What the duties
of these functionaries were, there is not much difficulty in
determining. The emirs among the Arabians, a people very
nearly related to the Hebrews, and retaining many of the
ancient customs common to all the descendants of Abraham,
have their secretaries, a class of officers evidently very similar to the Israelitish shoterim. The most important business
of the shoterim was to keep the genealogical registers; to
record accurately the marriages, births, and deaths among the
people; and probably, as they kept the rolls of families, to
apportion the public burdens and services on the people
individually. Modern governments, indeed, have no office
exactly corresponding to this, because they do not regulate
their affairs in this genealogical manner; they do not take
the census of the people by families. But among a people
like the Israelites, whose ideas were altogether clannish, a
people, with whom all hereditary succession and all posthumous fame depended on genealogical descent, this must have
been an office at least as important as that of a judge. The
proof that this office existed in Egypt, is clear and certain;
for the Hebrew shoterim were employed, under the direction
of Hebrew overseers, to apportion and press forward the
labors, exacted from the people.† It is likely, that originally
the princes of tribes and chiefs of families performed the
duties of genealogists, but that afterwards, to ease themselves,
they employed secretaries to do the work for them, who came
at length to constitute a distinct order of magistrates, under
the name of shoterim.‡

* Deut. xvi. 18. "Judges and officers (shoterim) shalt thou make thee
in all thy gates."

† Exod. v. 6, 10, 14, 15.

‡ See on this subject, Michaelis's Commentaries on the Laws of Moses,
Arts. 46–51; Jahn's Hebrew Commonwealth, B. 2. Sect. 8; Lowman on
the Civil Government of the Hebrews, c. 5; Lewis's Antiquities of the
Hebrew Republic, B. 1. C. 4; Harrington's Commonwealth of Israel, chaps.

Such was the polity, which Moses found established among his countrymen, when he returned to Egypt, after a forty years' residence in Midian. The time had now come, when, agreeably to the divine purpose, the chosen people were to be delivered out of the hand of their oppressors, and put in possession of the land of promise. They were no longer to pursue the nomadic life of their ancestors, but were to be settled, as an agricultural people, in fixed habitations. As a nation, they were designed to answer very important purposes in the divine plan. It was, therefore, necessary, that they should receive new political institutions, suited to their new circumstances and high destination. To this end Moses led them to the foot of Sinai, where the tribes freely elected Jehovah to be their king, a solemn compact was formed between the sovereign and the people, and the civil constitution was settled upon this foundation.* Thus Jehovah, in accordance with the prevalent notion of those ages, condescended to be the national and tutelar deity of the Hebrews; his worship was made the fundamental law of the state; and idolatry became a political crime.

But the theocratic element in this constitution did not make a fourth form of government, in addition to the three forms, with which the world is familiar. It was not a political constitution, fundamentally different from the monarchical, aristocratical, democratical, and mixed forms of polity.† Warburton‡ has shown, that the theocracy continued to the coming of Christ. But during the period intervening between the establishment of the constitution by Moses and the birth of the Messiah, the government underwent many

---

1, 2; Salvador's Histoire des Institutions de Moïse et du Peuple Hébreu, B. 2. C. 2; and Horne's Introduction to the Critical Study and Knowledge of the Holy Scriptures, vol. 2, Pt. 2, c. 1.

  * Ex. 19. Jahn's Heb. Com. B. 2, S. 8.

  † Mich. Com. Art. 35.   ‡ Div. Leg. B. 5, S. 3.

changes, and assumed a variety of forms. It was democratical till the time of Saul, monarchical from his accession to the throne till the captivity, and aristocratical after the restoration of the Jews to their own country; but through all these revolutions it retained the theocratic feature. We may, therefore, proceed in our study of this constitution, and in the attempt to present a true analysis of it, just as we would perform a similar labor in reference to the constitution of Rome, or of England.

The patriarchal polity, of which a brief sketch is given above, Moses retained unaltered. The subdivision of tribes into collections of families remained as it had been before. At the time of the exodus, the larger clans of this sort, exclusive of the tribe of Levi, amounted to fifty-eight, and their chiefs, in conjunction with the twelve princes of tribes, formed a council of state, consisting of seventy members.* It is evident, however, that the principle of subdivision was carried much farther than a perusal of the twenty-sixth chapter of Numbers would at first lead us to suppose. There must have been a division, not noticed by the historian, according to which the collections of families were far more numerous, and of course the number of heads of families far greater, for no less than two hundred and fifty chiefs of this rank joined the rebellion of Korah.† The princes of tribes and chiefs of families were the natural representatives of the people and magistrates of the state.‡ They commanded their respective tribes in war, and guided their counsels in peace. They appear to be alluded to in the song of Deborah as those who " ride on white asses and sit in judgment;" a passage in which, I am inclined to think, there is a reference to this union in their persons of civil and military authority. Whether these officers were elective or hereditary seems hard to determine. Harrington§ considers them hereditary.

---

* Numb. xxvi.   Exod. xxiv. 1.   † Numb. xvi. 2.

‡ Jahn's Heb. Com. B. 2, S. 11.   § Com. Is. C. 2.

Jahn* inclines to regard them as elective. Lowman† doubts. Michaelis‡ can find no trace of the manner in which they were chosen. I rather think that Jahn is right. At least it is certain, that the office was not strictly hereditary in the first-born of the tribe or the family. This is plain from the case of Nahshon. Though he was prince of Judah, he was not the heir-male of the tribe. He was the son of Aminadab, the son of Ram, who was a younger son of Hezron, the son of Pharez, himself a younger son of Judah, the original patriarch of the tribe.§ This certainly is not a proof that the office was elective, but it looks that way; and the analogy of other offices in the Hebrew government strengthens the probability.

Another order of functionaries, retained by Moses, was that of the shoterim, translated in our bible "officers." In Num. 11 : 16, and Deut. 29 : 10, they are named in connection with the elders, that is, the princes of tribes and heads of families. They were, therefore, magistrates and representatives of the people. However obscure and uninfluential their office might have been originally, it gradually acquired importance, till it came at length to be one of great dignity and authority. We have seen before, that they were the keepers of the genealogical tables. In Egypt, they were charged with seeing, that every Israelite delivered the required number of bricks. ‖ It was their business to give their discharge to citizens, who were by law exempt from military duty.¶ Another function appertaining to them was to communicate to the people the orders of the general respecting military affairs.** From the shoterim and elders together, as being persons of the highest respectability, the supreme senate of seventy was to be chosen.†† We find them repeat-

---

* Heb. Com. B. 2, S. 11,   † Civ. Gov. Heb. C. 5.
‡ Com. on the Laws of Moses, Art. 46.   § 1 Chron. ii.
‖ Exod. v. 10 seqq.   ¶ Deut. xx. 5–9.   ** Josh. i. 10.
†† Numb. xi. 16.

32

edly mentioned as forming a part of the legislative assemblies
of the nation.* And in the time of the kings, we find the
chief shoter, though not a military commander, exercising a
general superintendence and control over the whole army.†
When the nation was settled in Palestine, the shoterim were
distributed into every city, and performed the duties of their
office for the city and its surrounding district.‡ They could
not properly discharge their functions without having accurate catalogues of the names of the Hebrews, with a record
of the age, pecuniary ability, and domestic circumstances of
each individual master of a household. There appears evidently to have been a chief genealogist, who was the president
of the whole order, and exercised a general superintendence
over the affairs entrusted to them. Several of these chiefs
are mentioned by name under the kings.§ In 1 Chron. 24 :
6, and Jer. 52 : 25, mention is made of a " principal scribe
of the host," that is, a chief shoter, " who mustered the people of the land " for war. How the shoterim were chosen
the history does not distinctly inform us. There is little difficulty, however, in gathering from what it does say concerning them, that the office was elective. While the Hebrews
dwelt in Egypt, and before the Levites had been set apart
from the other tribes, and consecrated to letters and religion,
they must either have been selected out of every clan, or,
more probably perhaps, chosen from the whole tribe, irrespective of families, according to the opinion entertained of
their fitness for the office. After the Levites had become
fairly installed in their office, as the learned class, the genealogists were generally taken from among them.‖ " This was
a very rational procedure, as the Levites devoted themselves

* Deut. xxix. 10. xxxi. 28. Josh. viii. 3. xxiii. 2.

† 2 Chron. xxvi. 11.   ‡ Deut. xvi. 18.

§ 2 Sam. viii. 17. xx. 25. 2 Kings xxv. 19. 1 Chron. xxiv. 6. 2 Chron.
xxvi. 11. Jer. lii. 25.

‖ 1 Chron. xxiii. 4. 2 Chron. xix. 11. xxxiv. 13.

particularly to study; and, among husbandmen and unlearn-
ed people, few were likely to be so expert at writing, as to be
entrusted with the keeping of registers so important."*

The magistracies, thus far noticed, formed a part of the
polity of the Hebrews, before the exodus from Egypt. But,
by the advice of Jethro, which was confirmed by their king
Jehovah, Moses instituted a new order of rulers, which must
now be explained.† Although in Egypt the Hebrews had a
sort of political government among themselves, yet it is not
to be supposed, that they would be permitted to hold regular
courts for the trial of civil causes. Hence they had no judges
in their bondage, being subject to Egyptian magistrates in
that capacity. On their leaving Egypt, Moses took the whole
judicature upon himself, and was for some time sole judge.
But this was too much for mortal strength, and, from the little
attention that could be given to each individual case, not
altogether consistent with the public interest. His father-in-
law, who appears to have been a man of great judgment and
wisdom, convinced him of this, and by his advice he instituted judges. The principle, on which he arranged the institution, was a remarkable one, and must have been suggested
by the military divisions of the people. He appointed judges
for thousands, hundreds, fifties, and tens; in all about seventy-
eight thousand six hundred.‡ There was a regular gradation
of rank among these judges, and, in all probability, such a
subordination of the inferior to the superior, that the cases
which the judges of tens found too hard for them, they
referred to the judges of fifties; in the same manner, the cases
which these latter found too difficult to decide, they passed
over to the judges of hundreds; questions too intricate or too
important in the opinion of the judges of hundreds for their
determination, they carried up to the judges of thousands;

* See on the office of the shoterim Mich. Com. Art. 51, and Jahn's Heb.
Com. B. 2, S. 11.
† Exod. xviii.   ‡ Exod. xviii. 25.

who, in their turn, referred difficulties too great for their resolution to Moses, or, after his death, to the supreme judicial
authority, in whomsoever lodged. The principle of this judiciary system was, that the administration of justice should be
brought to every man's door, and of course that it should be
prompt and cheap; notwithstanding which, care was taken
to avoid the evils of hasty and partial decisions, by the right
of appeal to tribunals of a higher grade, when the case was
of sufficient magnitude to warrant such a resort. This principle was retained in the judicial system of the nation, after
its settlement in Palestine. But the system itself necessarily
underwent some modifications. It could not remain exactly
as it was; for the people no longer lived together, as in the
wilderness. On their taking possession of the promised land,
judges, as well as shoterim, or genealogists, were to be appointed in every city,* who were to discharge the duties of
their respective offices for the city and the surrounding district. Yet even the plan proper for Israel as an army march-
ing was not altogether unsuited to their settlement in permanent habitations, as tribes and families. The military division
might have its counterpart in a civil division into counties,
centuries, and decuries. The old Saxon constitution of sheriffs
in counties, hundreders or centgraves, in hundreds, and deci-
ners in decennaries, was formed upon this model. Lord
Bacon† is of the opinion, that king Alfred took this frame of
government from the laws of Moses. Whether the judges
were to be natives of their respective cities, or even of the
tribe in whose territory the cities were situated, or whether
the fittest persons were to be chosen, without regard to tribe,
family, or residence, does not appear from the history. The
latter supposition is rendered probable by the fact, that in
after times the office was very generally filled by Levites.‡

* Deut. xvi. 18.
† On Eng. Gov. P. 1. p. 70. cited by Lowm. on Civ. Gov. Heb. C. 9.
‡ 1 Chron. xxiii. 4: xxvi. 29–32. 2 Chron. xix. 8–11.

This might, not improbably, have been the intention of Moses, which he did not seek to render effective by any legal enactment, as foreseeing, that the thing would happen naturally, since the Levites, devoted to learning by the very constitution of their tribe, would best understand the laws of the land. Besides, it is quite conformable to the ideas of those times, and not foreign to the notions and manners of the east in all ages, that the judicial and sacerdotal offices should be united in the same persons. Among the ancient Egyptians, the priests were the usual administrators of justice.* The Arabs resorted to the temples and the priests for justice. Before the time of Mahomet, they even carried on law-suits before their gods. This he prohibited;† but to this day, the seat of justice is commonly called by the Arabs God's tribunal; and the usual form of citation is, "Thou art invited to the tribunal of God."‡

The chief function of the Israelitish judges was to administer justice between man and man.§ It is possible, and, looking to the general spirit and frame of the Hebrew constitution, not improbable, that they united some degree of military power to their civil authority. They are mentioned as among the persons summoned by Joshua to the legislative assemblies.‖ It is hardly probable, however, that the seventy two thousand judges of tens and fifties had seats and voices in these diets. It is more likely, that only those of hundreds and thousands, perhaps even only the latter of these classes, are to be understood, when judges are mentioned as constituting a part of the public deliberative assemblies of the Hebrews.¶

* Jablonski's Pantheon, p. 102 of the Prolegomena, cited by Mich. Art. 49.

† Koran, Sura iv. 61–64 and v. 46–55.

‡ Arvieux's Travels through Palestine in Mich. Com. Art. 49.

§ Deut. xvi. 18.   ‖ Josh. xxiii. 2, xxiv. 1.

¶ On the subject of the Heb. Judges see Mich. Com. Art. 49; Jahn's

The judicial office among the Hebrews was elective. Josephus says so expressly, though with hardly greater plainness than Moses. "Take you wise men, and understanding, and known among your tribes, and I will make them rulers over you,"* were the lawgiver's words to his countrymen, when he instituted the office. The only function which he here claims for himself, is that of commissioning those whom the people should elect. Even the supreme judge was chosen by the free suffrages of the people. The historian distinctly informs us, that " the people made Jephthah head and captain over them."† Four stages may be noted in the proceedings relating to Jephthah ;—the preliminary discussion, the nomination, the presentation to the people, and the installation.‡ The enemy was encamped in Gilead. At this point, the people and their rulers, assembled in convention on the plain, said to one another, " Who shall be our chief, to lead us against the foe ?" This was the discussion, in which every citizen seems to have had the right to participate. In the exceedingly brief history of the affair, it is not expressly stated, but it is necessarily implied, that Jephthah, of Gilead, a man of distinguished military genius and reputation, was nominated by the voice of the assembly. But this able captain had been some years before driven out from his native city. It was necessary to soothe his irritated spirit. To this end the elders went in person to seek him, laid before him the urgent necessities of the state, softened his anger by promises of preferment, and brought him to Mizpeh. Here, manifestly, they made a formal presentation of ·him to the people, for it is added, " the people made him head and captain over them." That is, they completed the election by giving him their suffrages, recognizing him as their leader,

Heb. Com. B. 2, S. 11; Lowm. Civ. Gov. Heb. c. 9; and Harrington on the Com. of Israel, c. 2.

* Deut. i. 13.

† Judg. xi. 11.　　　　　　　‡ Ibid. x. 17, 18, and xi. 1–11.

and installing him in his office. Here, then, we have, 1. The free discussion of the people in a popular assembly concerning the selection of a leader ; 2. The nomination of Jephthah by the meeting to be chief; 3. The elders' presentation of him to the people for their suffrages ; and 4. His inauguration as prince and leader of Israel. It is to the analysis of such incidental relations as this scattered here and there through the history, that, in default of a more exact account of the primitive order of things, we are compelled to resort, in our study of the Hebrew constitution, for much of the information, which it would be gratifying to find in a more detailed and systematic form.

The magistrates, then, in every tribe were a prince of the tribe, chiefs of families or clans, genealogists, and judges. " Each of these classes of magistrates had its own peculiar duties. The judges administered justice. The genealogists kept the genealogical tables, in which they occasionally noted the most remarkable occurrences of their times. The historical notices contained in the first book of Chronicles, and which are not found in the books of Moses, were probably derived from these tables.*   The heads of families, with the prince of the tribe, had charge of· the general concerns of each tribe, and to them the judges and genealogists were in some degree subordinate. In Palestine these magistrates were distributed into the several cities, and those who resided in the same city, composed the legislative assembly of that city and the surrounding district. When the magistrates of all the cities belonging to any one tribe were collected, they formed the supreme court, or legislative assembly, of the tribe. In like manner, the magistrates in several different tribes might assemble in one body, and legislate conjointly for all those tribes which they represented. When the magistrates of all the tribes met together, they formed the general legislature of the whole nation. Though there

* 1 Chron. iv. 21-23, 39-45. v. 10, 19-22. vii. 20-24.

was no pecuniary emolument attached to these offices, they conferred great dignity and authority upon those who held them."*

Such is a brief view of the magistracies, instituted or confirmed by the Mosaic constitution. Let us now direct our attention to the tribes themselves in their individual capacity, in their relation to one another, and in their legislative functions.

It is agreed, on all hands, by those who have written on the Hebrew institutès, that each tribe formed a separate state. Each composed an entire political community, in some respects independent of the others. Each was under its own proper government, administered its own affairs by its own representative assemblies and magistrates, and claimed and exercised many of the rights of sovereignty. Its local legislation and municipal arrangements were in its own hands. "Dan," says the venerable patriarch Jacob, "shall judge his people, as one of the tribes of Israel." On this, bishop Sherlock,† an author of great learning and judgment, observes: "It is evident, that every tribe had its own prince and judge, and that every prince or head of a tribe judged his own people; consequently every tribe had a sceptre and lawgiver, as well as the tribe of Judah." In other words, every tribe had its own proper staff of command and a distinct administration of justice.‡ The princes of the tribes, chiefs of families, judges, and genealogists governed the tribes of Israel, as distinct and independent sovereignties. The tribes were all equal in respect of political dignity and right. The sovereignty of Simeon, which numbered but twenty-two thousand men capable of bearing arms, was as complete as that of Judah, which had seventy-six thousand. No one tribe had any political superiority or right of command over any other. This is plain from the

* Jahn's Heb. Com. B. 2. S. 11.   † Dissertation 3.
‡ Lowm. Civ. Gov. Heb. c. 5.

fact, that on the death of Joshua, the people inquire of God, "who should go up for them against the Canaanites?" * This question could not have been asked, if any one tribe had had the right of precedency and government over the rest. The answer was, "Judah shall go up."† Judah thus acquired the right of leading by a decision of the oracle; a clear proof, that such a right did not otherwise belong to that tribe.

The powers reserved to the separate tribes, and freely exercised by them, were very great. We find them often acting like independent nations. This was the case not only when there was neither king nor judge, in the land, but even under the government of the kings. They levied war and made peace, whenever it seemed good to them. Thus we find Joshua exhorting his brethren, the children of Joseph, to make war against the Perizzites;‡ and Zebulon and Naphthali uniting to fight against Jabin.§ We see the tribe of Dan, singly and of its own proper motion, attacking and destroying the people of Laish, and afterwards taking possession of their city and the surrounding country. A very remarkable record of this kind is contained in the fifth chapter of 1 Chronicles.‖ It is there related, that the tribes beyond Jordan, even in the reign of Saul, carried on, upon their own responsibility, a most important war. Yet so little interest was taken in it by the other tribes, that the author of the book of Samuel has not so much as alluded to it in his history of that prince; though, in a military point of view, it was a far more brilliant affair than all his martial achievements together. Four nations were leagued together against the trans-jordanic tribes in this war. The booty taken from the enemy was immense;— fifty thousand camels, two hundred and fifty thousand sheep, two thousand asses, a hundred thousand prisoners of war; and of slain, the historian says, "there fell down many." The

* Judg. i. 1.   † Ibid. i. 2.
‡ Josh. xvii. 15.   § Judg. iv. 10.   ‖ Vv. 18-23.

entire territories of these nations came into the possession of the Hebrews as the fruit of this contest, "and they dwelt in their steads until the captivity." As late as the reign of Hezekiah, we see the tribe of Simeon waging two successful wars,—one against the inhabitants of Gedor, and the other against the remnant of the Amalekites,—and that without aid or authority from its neighbor republics.*

Some occurrences of a different kind, in the history of the kings, will further illustrate the powers, which the constitution conferred upon the separate tribes. By divine direction, David had been anointed king in the life-time of Saul.† That unction, however, did not inaugurate him as king, nor confer any authority upon him. It was rather a prophecy in action, foreshadowing his future elevation to the throne. Therefore, when Saul had fallen in battle, David returned, as a private person, to one of the cities of Judah. There he awaited the action of the people in his behalf. At first he became king of Judah alone, and that by the free choice of the citizens of that tribe.‡ In the message, which he sent to the inhabitants of Jabesh-Gilead, thanking them for their kindness to Saul, he does not arrogate any right of command over them, nor address them in quality of sovereign. He simply informs them, that the men of Judah had chosen him for their king, thus virtually inviting them to follow the ex-

---

* 1 Chron iv. 41–43.

† 1 Sam. xvi. 13. Dr. Clarke, in his note on 2 Sam. ii. 4, remarks: "David was anointed before by Samuel, by which he acquired *jus ad reg-num*, a right TO the kingdom; by the present anointing he had *jus in regno*, authority OVER the kingdom."—"The invisible king directed the prophet Samuel to assure the throne privately by a prophetic anointing to David, the youngest son of Jesse, a citizen of Bethlehem." Jahn's Heb. Com. B. 4, S. 28. It will be seen, that the views of these eminent scholars accord with those expressed in the text as to the nature and object of David's unction by Samuel.

‡ 2 Sam. ii. 1–4.

ample.* Meanwhile, the other eleven tribes had anointed
Ishbosheth, the son of Saul, as their king.† It is evident,
that David did not regard that as an illegal act on their part,
for he limited his hostile movements simply to defending himself, when attacked by the armies of Ishbosheth. Joab, his
general-in-chief, had no orders to attack the troops of his rival,
or to maintain his own claim to the throne by force of arms.
Ishbosheth reigned two years without any rupture with David
or his men; nor did the civil war commence, till Abner, captain of his host, crossing over Jordan with his forces, provoked an encounter. Joab, in a conference with Abner, intimated that he would not have attacked the adherents of
David's rival, unless he had been provoked to it; thus clearly
showing that his orders were to act only on the defensive.‡
One after another, the eleven tribes came into the interest of
David; and at length the whole nation chose him for their
king, and made a league with him, that is, proposed a capitulation limiting the royal prerogative, to which he solemnly
assented; after which he was anointed sovereign of all Israel,
as having been elected by the voice of the people to that high
dignity.§

The many and heavy exactions, to which the people had
been subjected during the reign of Solomon, had greatly ex-
asperated their minds. Towards the close of his life, their
complaints became loud and bitter. On his death, they proposed to his son Rehoboam, certain new stipulations, with a
view to lighten the public burdens. Their request, though
reasonable, was insolently and contemptuously rejected by the
fiery young monarch. Thereupon ten of the tribes refused
their allegiance to the new government, and chose a king of
their own. It would almost seem as if this was not an act of

* 2 Sam. ii. 5–7.   † Ibid. ii. 8–9.
‡ Ibid. ii. 12–29. See especially v. 27, as confirming the last statement
in the text.
§ 2 Sam. chaps. iii. iv. v. and xii.—particularly the last.

rebellion, but the exercise of a reserved right; for Judah was forbidden by the Lord to make war upon the ten tribes. At any rate, an instantaneous revolt of this kind could not have occurred, unless the Israelites had been governed, as Michaelis expresses it, " tribe-wise," each tribe being a little republic, and having its own leading men, according to whose views the rest of the people regulated their conduct.

From the above detail it appears, that " the Hebrew constitution authorized each tribe to provide for its own interests; or, if the strength of any one of them was insufficient for the purpose, to unite with some of the other tribes, and make common cause with them. We frequently find several tribes thus acting in concert. Judah and Simeon united in their war against the Canaanites; as did also Ephraim and Manasseh. The tribes of Zebulon and Naphthali united with Barak to oppose the army of Jabin. Manasseh, Asher, Zebulon, and Naphthali, chose Gideon for their leader against the Midianites. The tribes east of Jordan made choice of Jephthah for their general to carry on a war against the Ammonites. In later times, and during the reign of Saul, the same tribes made war upon the Hagarites, the Ituraeans, the Nobadites, and the Naphishites. Upon the death of Saul, eleven tribes remained faithful in their allegiance to his family, and seven years intervened before they submitted to David. After the death of Solomon, ten tribes revolted from the house of David, and elected Jeroboam for their king. In short, any tribe, or any number of tribes united, exercised the power of convening legislative assemblies, passing resolves, waging wars, making treaties, and electing for themselves chiefs, generals, regents, and kings."*

---

* Jahn's Heb. Com. B. 2, S. 13. The passages on which Dr. Jahn relies for the statements made in this extract are,—Judg. i. 1-3, 22. vii. 23, 29 viii. 1-3. xi. 1-11. 1 Chron. v. 10, 18, 19. 2 Sam. iii. 17. 1 Kings, xii. 1-24.

In such a constitution of the tribes, various disturbing
forces could not but exist; and the history informs us of the
action of these antagonistic forces upon several occasions.
Rivalries would naturally spring up among twelve sovereign
states so closely connected with each other. Lesser interests
would sometimes stand in the way of the general welfare.
Hence arose jealousies, which sometimes issued in fierce,
sanguinary, and protracted civil wars.* All this we may readily believe from the examples of Holland, Switzerland, the United States, and especially of the German empire, which, from
the inequality of its constituent parts, is perpetually dis-
tracted by divisions, and has often been the scene of intestine
hostilities. Nothing, then, could be more probable than
sectional jealousies and rivalries among the constituent
members of the Hebrew commonwealth; and Michaelis has
well remarked,† that two cases may be supposed, in which
they would certainly break out, and display all their mischievous effects:—1. If any two tribes became more powerful
than the others, in which event they would regard each other
with suspicion and hatred; and 2. If any one tribe acquired
considerable ascendancy over the rest, of which the consequence would be, the excitement of their universal envy and
opposition. The learned commentator adds, that both these
cases actually occurred in the Israelitish republic; a fact of
so much importance, that it may be said to form the key to
the whole Hebrew history. The Israelites entered Palestine
with a force of six hundred thousand citizens, capable of
bearing arms, exclusive of the tribe of Levi. Of course, the
medium strength of the tribes would be about fifty thousand.
Those tribes, which exceeded that number, would be accounted
strong; and, in like manner, those which fell below it, would

* Judg. xii. 1-6.   xx. 1-48.   2 Sam. iii. 1.   1 Kings xii. 16-24.

† Commentaries on the Laws of Moses, Art. 46;—an article to which I
acknowledge my indebtedness in illustrating this part of my subject, since
I have embodied the valuable substance of it in these paragraphs.

be deemed weak. It may gratify the reader to see the comparative strength of the tribes, at this time, brought into one
view. This is done in the following statement, in which
fractions of thousands are omitted for the sake of brevity.
The tribe of Joseph numbered eighty-five thousand; Judah,
seventy-six thousand; Issachar, sixty-four thousand; Zebulon,
sixty thousand; Asher, fifty-three thousand; Dan, forty-six
thousand; Benjamin, forty-five thousand; Naphtali, forty-five
thousand; Reuben, forty-three thousand; Gad, forty thousand;
and Simeon, twenty-two thousand.* It will not escape the
notice of the reader, that one tribe, that of Simeon, was very
weak; that two, Joseph and Judah, were very powerful;
while the others did not vary materially from the average
strength. The tribe of Joseph was, indeed, divided into two
half-tribes; but it was still, and even as late as near the close
of Joshua's administration, regarded and spoken of as one
tribe.† Ephraim, however, in consequence of the prophetic
blessing of Jacob, and the predictions concerning his future
extraordinary increase,‡ though as yet numerically weak, in
comparison with Manasseh, was regarded as his superior, and,
indeed, obtained a certain preëminence over all the other
tribes. From this time, therefore, we find a perpetual emulation and rivalry existing between the two tribes of Ephraim
and Judah. This sentiment of jealousy, sometimes reaching
even to hatred, displayed itself on all occasions; and allusions to it are not infrequent in the prophetical writings.§ It
is very distinctly recognized by Isaiah,‖ when, foretelling the
peaceful effect of Messiah's reign, he says, " And the envy of
Ephraim shall depart, and the enemies of Judah shall be cut
off. Ephraim shall not envy Judah, and Judah shall not vex
Ephraim." The prophet predicts a state of harmony and

* Numb. xxvi.   † Josh. xvii. 17.   ‡ Gen. xlviii. 15–20.
§ Judg. viii. 1. xii. 1. 1 Kings xi. 26; xiv. 30; xv. 16. Ps. lxxvii.
9–11, 60, 67, 68. Is. xi. 13. Jer. iii. 18. Ez. xxxvii. 16–19. Hos. i. 11.
‖ xi. 13.

peace by declaring, that the hereditary and proverbial enmity of Judah and Ephraim shall cease.** Thoughout the entire
Hebrew history, from the exodus to the captivity, these two
were regarded as the leading tribes of Israel. In the wilderness, Moses gave the precedence of all the tribes to Judah,
in assigning to it the most honorable place in the army, whether in the camp or on the march.† But after his death, two
events occurred, which tended greatly to the exaltation and
preëminence of Ephraim. That tribe had the good fortune
to give to the nation a chief magistrate in the person of
Joshua, and also to have the tabernacle, the palace of their
invisible, heavenly king, set up in Shiloh, a place within the
territory of Ephraim.‡ Both these circumstances advanced
the honor of the tribe ; and the latter, by promoting trade
and marriages, gave it no inconsiderable advantages, in respect of the increase of wealth and population. From
that time, the ambition of Ephraim knew no bounds. The
jealousy of the Ephraimites towards the other tribes appears
in their conduct to Gideon and Jephthah.§ Their special
jealousy of Judah showed itself in their refusal to submit
to David, after the death of Saul ; ‖ in their adherence to
Absalom, when he revolted against his father ; ¶ and in the
readiness with which they joined in the revolt of Jeroboam,
who was himself of the tribe of Ephraim.** The author of
the seventy eighth Psalm†† represents Ephraim as having been
the chief tribe, and God as having rejected it for its political
and religious apostacy, when the tabernacle and the kingdom
were transferred to Judah. Even while Ephraim continued
the most influential tribe, Judah enjoyed a more extensive
sway, than the other tribes to the west of the Jordan. When

* Alexander on Isaiah,—note on Ch. xi. 13.
† Num. ii. 3. x. 14.   ‡ Josh. xviii. 1. 1 Sam. iv. 3.
§ Judg. viii. 1. xii. 1.   ‖ 2 Sam. ii. 8, 9.   ¶ Ib. xviii. 6.
** 1 Kings xi. 26. xii. 16. See Alexander's note on Is. xi. 13.
†† vv. 9–11, 60, 67, 68.

the monarchy was substituted for the democracy, a king was elected from Benjamin, the youngest and weakest of all the tribes. This seems to be a perfect levelling.of the tribes. Apparently no preference was given to any of them, on account of any preëminence in dignity, or power, supposed or real. If, however, we look a little below the surface of things, we shall judge otherwise. We must bear in mind how exceedingly genealogical and clannish was the way of thinking among the Hebrews. This will throw no little light upon the point. As Benjamin and Joseph were sons of the same mother, the Benjamites regarded themselves as in some sense belonging to the tribe of Joseph. Of this we have a certain proof in the fact, that Shimei, though a Benjamite, said, that he was the first man of all the house of Joseph to meet king David, when he returned victorious, after crushing the rebellion of Absalom.* Hence, even when Benjamin was advanced in the person of Saul to the leadership of Israel, Ephraim still enjoyed a certain preëminence. In the 80th Psalm, composed about this time, Ephraim, Benjamin, and Manasseh are mentioned as the chief tribes, Ephraim being placed before the other two. The rivalship between the tribes continued, with unabated force, during the reign of Saul. That king had but little authority in the tribe of Judah; for, when he was pursuing David with the bitterest enmity to take his life, David had little difficulty in eluding him, by fleeing from place to place within the limits of that tribe. And when at last he fled into the land of the Philistines, there does not appear to have been any necessity for his doing so. He might have remained where he was, without much peril of a capture. On the other hand, Saul, as king, was very partial to his own kindred, including, beyond a doubt, the children of Joseph, as well as those of Benjamin. Upon them he conferred most of the offices within the gift of the crown. This he openly acknowledged, and made

* 2 Sam. xix. 20.

it the ground of a claim to their gratitude and support.* When Saul fell in battle, eleven of the tribes, doubtless under the lead of Ephraim, adhered to his family, and chose Ishbosheth for their king. Judah alone recognized David as their sovereign. But David was a man of consummate ability and great nobleness of character. He acted with prudence, moderation, and magnanimity. These are qualities, which never fail to excite the admiration and love of the people. They so won upon the tribes of Israel, that, by degrees, they all voluntarily submitted themselves to his rule. It was the surrender of their hearts rather than of their arms. The civil and military talents of David were equal to each other, and both were of the highest order. Under his administration, the territories of the state were greatly enlarged; its wealth and power were increased; and its renown was spread far and wide. Its name struck terror, not only into the petty tribes in its immediate neighborhood, but into the great nations dwelling on the shores of the distant Euphrates. The tribe of Judah now became exceedingly powerful. Its numbers were incredibly multiplied, the effect not merely of the natural increase of population, but also of the multitude of foreigners, who flocked to its capital, and became proselytes to the Jewish religion. Even before this time, the other tribes had begun to be called by the common name of Israel.† Thenceforward Israel came to be their ordinary designation, and they were animated by a common jealousy of the tribe of Judah.‡ It was in this sentiment, that the roots of that unnatural rebellion excited by Absalom, found a congenial soil. The extraordinary success of that patricidal revolt has been the puzzle of many, and is wholly inexplicable, except as the result of a deeply seated and long cherished animosity on the part of the other tribes towards the tribe of Judah. This animosity even broke out,

* 1 Sam. xxii. 7.   † 2 Sam. ii. 9.
‡ 2 Sam. xix. 11, 40–43.   xx. 1, 2.
33

and raged violently, on the king's return. A strife arose between Judah and the other tribes, as to which should recal
him to the throne, and it came near ending in a revolt of the
eleven tribes from David.* The power and splendor of the
tribe of Judah culminated in the reign of Solomon. David
and Solomon, kings of the house of Judah, were no common
men. For seventy three years did the other tribes submit to
their government, awed by the splendor of their genius, the
force of their character, and the vigor of their rule. But the
fire was all the while glowing under the ashes, and waited
but an occasion to burst forth in fierce and devouring flames.
That occasion was found in an imprudent declaration of Rehoboam, the son and successor of Solomon, on his accession to the
throne. Ten of the tribes, led by Jeroboam, an Ephraimite,
revolted, shook off their allegiance to the kings of Judah, and
set up a separate kingdom, with Jeroboam for their king.†
He takes but a superficial view of the Hebrew history, who
regards the conduct of Rehoboam, however unwise or even
unjust it might have been, as the cause of this schism. It
was but the occasion, the pretext. The cause was the old
grudge of Ephraim against Judah. The separation was not
a sudden occurrence; it was not fortuitous; it was but the
natural result of causes, which had long been working. It is
very remarkable, that, of all the kings who reigned over
Israel, although they were very far from succeeding one
another in the line of hereditary descent, there was not one
that did not belong to Ephraim; so that, with the single exception of Saul, all the Hebrew kings were natives of one or
other of the two rival tribes.

As the result either of an admirable stroke of policy on the
part of David, or of an equally admirable good fortune,
Benjamin, after the separation, remained united to Judah, and
the two tribes ever afterwards formed one kingdom. The
event, to which I refer, was the choice by David of the city

* 2 Sam. xix. 9–14. 40–43. xx. 1, 2.   † 1 Kings xii. 1–20.

of Jerusalem for his residence and capital. This city was
within the territory of Benjamin, but it lay close to the confines of Judah, and had long been inhabited by members of
the latter tribe, as well as of the former. David's selection
of it for the royal residence was well calculated to flatter the
pride of the Benjamites, and unite them more closely to his
family. It appears to have had the effect to extinguish the
jealousy, which Benjamin, in common with Ephraim, had felt
towards the tribe of Judah. At all events, its issue was, as
stated above, to link the fortunes of these two tribes together
in indissoluble bonds.

Such, then, were the jealous rivalries, which, sometimes
more and sometimes less active, we find always subsisting
among the tribes of Israel; and such the bitter fruits, which
they produced. But it was not ambition alone, which disturbed the peace of the nation, and caused the blood of the
citizens to stream forth in civil strife. Great as the reserved
rights of the tribes were, they occasionally magnified them
beyond their just bounds and betrayed a strong disposition to
nullify the laws of the general government. But such a procedure was at the peril of the tribe engaging in it. In the
book of Judges* we have a painfully interesting account of
an act of nullification on the part of Benjamin; wherein we
see, that the authority of the national law was vindicated by
the other tribes with a severity, bordering on barbarism. The
tribe of Benjamin was prophetically described as a ravening
wolf;†—a figure highly descriptive of its fierce and warlike
character. The case, to which I refer, was this. A Levite
and his wife were travelling peaceably through the territories
of Benjamin. At Gibeah, some demons in the form of men,
called by the historian "sons of Belial," abused the latter in
such a way as to cause her death. The Levite appealed for
retribution to the tribes in a general court. With the exception of Benjamin, they assembled at once in convention at

* Chaps. xix, xx. † Gen. xlix. 27.

Mizpeh. There, the states-general, in regular session, heard the appeal to their justice. They carefully examined into the facts of the case. They found certain of the inhabitants of Gibeah guilty, not only of a violation of the rights of hospitality and humanity, and of a riotous breach of the peace, but moreover, which, in a national point of view, was of greater importance, of a breach and violation of the common right of the tribes to a safe passage through the whole country. It was, therefore, not so much an injury to any private persons, as to the tribes of Ephraim and Judah, to which the Levite and his wife belonged. Indeed, it was an injury to all the tribes in common, since the case of Ephraim and Judah might become the case of any of them. No man in all Israel could have any security in travelling, if such open outrage and violence were suffered to go unpunished. But the tribes were independent of each other. No one tribe had jurisdiction over any of the rest. Benjamin was a sovereign state. Neither Judah nor Ephraim could, by the constitution, call the inhabitants of Gibeah to account. This was, therefore, a case calling for the interposition of the states-general. Yet even they could not proceed directly against the guilty parties. That would have been in derogation of the sovereignty of Benjamin. Therefore, having by investigation satisfied themselves of the facts in the case, they sent a summons to the tribe of Benjamin to deliver up the delinquents, that they might be dealt with according to law. Benjamin declined a compliance with this summons, and determined rather to dissolve the union of the states than submit to the will of the nation, though expressed in a deliberate, dispassionate, and constitutional manner. This changed the entire case. It was no longer the murder of a private person by some ill-disposed individuals of the city of Gibeah, but an open rebellion of the whole tribe of Benjamin. The authority of the national union was opposed and set at naught. And, not content with refusing to give up the murderers to justice, Benjamin raised an army to protect them, and levied war against all Israel. The rest of the tribes declared them in a state of rebellion, and proceeded against them accordingly. So stubborn and unbending was the spirit of the nullifying tribe, that the national army was twice defeated. But in the third battle Benjamin was routed, with the loss of twenty-five thousand men; and there was no danger of the offence being repeated, for the offending city was levelled with the ground, the country was made a wilderness, and six hundred men, posted on the inaccessible rock of Rimmon, were all that remained of the contumacious tribe.*

From this history of the Benjamite rebellion the passage is natural to a consideration of the union of the tribes in a general government; for, while the history illustrates the distinct nationality and independent spirit, I might amost add the turbulent temper, of the separate tribes, it affords, at the same time, a proof and an example of the reality, strength, and vigor of the national administration. The central government was not a mere confederacy of states. Such an organization would have been too feeble, and too tardy in its action, for the elements, which it was intended to control. It was a GOVERNMENT in the proper sense of the term, and not a CONFEDERATION. Moses drew up a constitution, which applied, not merely to each tribe as a distinct political body, but also to the individuals in the tribe. He made it bear on every individual in every tribe, thus giving to each a personal interest in the national concerns, and making him as much a member of the nation, as he was of his own tribe.† The tribes formed but one nation. And though they had separate interests, as being in some respects independent states, they had also general interests, as being united in one body politic. They had much in common to

* Lowm. Civ. Gov. Heb. C. 14.   Chr. Exam. No. 76.
† Chr. Exam. No. 76.

draw them together in bonds of brotherhood, and strengthen
the ties of political union;—a common ancestor, the illustrious depositary of promises appertaining to all the tribes
alike; a common God, who was their chosen and covenanted
king; a common tabernacle and temple, which was the royal
palace; a common oracle, the urim and thummim; a common high priest, the prime minister of the king; a common
learned class, who possessed cities in all the tribes; a common faith and worship, which at the same time differed fundamentally from that of all other contemporaneous nations;
and a common law of church and state.* Thus, while each
Hebrew was strongly concerned to maintain the honor of his
tribe, the constitution of the general government gave him an
equal interest in the honor of his country.

Thus we see, that the constitution was so contrived, that,
notwithstanding the partial independence and sovereignty of
the separate tribes, each, as constituting a part of the national
union, had a kind of superintendence over all the rest, in
regard to their observance of the law. Any of the tribes
could be called to an account by the others for an infraction
of the organic law: and, if they refused to give satisfaction,
they might be punished by war. † Obedience to the states-
general, in whom the tribes were united into one government,
was a fundamental obligation of every member of the national union. On this point the constitution was imperative.
Disobedience to their orders, a rebellious opposition to their
authority, was an act of high treason;—the greatest crime
that can be committed, since it is an injury, not to any one
man, or any number of private persons, but to the whole
society, and aims at subverting the peace and order of the
government, on which the property, liberty, happiness,. and
life of the citizens depend.‡

Let me adduce two proofs of this obligation on the part

* Jahn's Heb. Com. B. 2. S. 13.   † Ibid. Judg. xx.
‡ Lowm. Civ. Heb. c. 14.

of the tribes to submit to the will of the nation, as embodied in the resolves of the general government.

The first is taken from a record, which I find in the thirty-sixth chapter of Numbers.* By a law, passed some time before, constituting daughters, in default of sons, the legal heirs of their fathers, it would happen, that the inheritance of the daughters of Zelophehad, who belonged to the tribe of Manasseh, if they married into another tribe, would be transferred from their own to their husband's tribe. This, should it ever occur, Manasseh thought would be a hardship and a wrong. What course did that tribe pursue? She did not attempt to rebel against the authority of the nation, and nullify the laws of the land. She brought the case before the national legislature, and sought relief through its action. She appealed to the justice of the nation in congress assembled, just as the states of our union do. Her petition was respectfully considered, and a law was enacted in accordance with its prayer. By this law, heiresses were

---

* The critical reader, who examines the references to see whether they sustain the text, might, on a cursory perusal of the chapter here cited, be inclined to think, that in the view presented in this paragraph, too much is rested on assumption. A deeper study of the subject, however, will be apt to change such an impression. For, first, either the first eleven verses of the 27th chapter should come in before this chapter, or this chapter should come in immediately after those eleven verses, since, as Dr. Clarke says, both certainly make parts of the same subject, and there it is expressly said, that the matter was brought "before Moses, and before Eleazar the priest, and before the princes, and before all the congregation," and by them referred to the oracle. Secondly, even in this chapter, the chiefs of Manasseh are related to have laid their petition before Moses and the princes, who may here very well be taken, in a general sense, to mean the whole diet. And, thirdly, even if this chapter stood wholly disconnected with the 27th chapter, and neither the diet nor any part of it had been mentioned at all, still the analogy of numerous other cases in the Hebrew history would authorise us to assume, that the matter had been, in due form, laid before the states-general of Israel, and by them solemnly adjudicated.

required to marry in their own tribes, that no part of the ancient inheritance might be alienated from the original family. It is plain, that, if the decree of the nation had been different from what it was, Manasseh's duty would have been submission. Resistance and nullification would have been in derogation and contravention of rightful authority.

The second proof of the duty of obedience on the part of the tribes to the decrees of the general government, I derive from the history of the wrong done by certain Benjamites to a Levite, who was passing through their territory, taken in connexion with the national proceedings, which followed thereupon.* The states-general immediately convened at Mizpeh, and passed a resolve, calling upon the local government of Benjamin, to deliver up the offenders, that they might be dealt with as their conduct deserved. This order Benjamin refused to obey. What said the national government? Did it say, that Benjamin, being a sovereign state, had a right to interpret the constitution for herself, and to act her own pleasure in the matter? Far from it. It declared, that she had been guilty of an infraction of the organic law, and an act of treason against the state. And the nation proceeded at once to vindicate her own sovereignty and supremacy. There was no coaxing, no truckling, no faltering. Not honied words, but hard blows, promptly administered, and with a terrible energy and rapidity of repetition, were the means employed to sustain the majesty of the government and the authority of the law.

It thus appears that the Hebrew tribes were, in some respects, independent sovereignties, while, in other respects, their individual sovereignty was merged in the broader and higher sovereignty of the commonwealth of Israel. They were independent republics, having each a local government, which was sovereign in the exercise of its reserved rights; yet they all united together and formed one great republic,

* Judg. xix. 20.

with a general government, which was sovereign in the highest sense. The constitution of Israel had, in this respect, a similitude to our own, which will strike every reader. It may also be considered as in some measure resembling that of Switzerland, where thirteen cantons, of which each has a government of its own, and exercises the right of war, are nevertheless united into one great state, under a general government. Thus all the Israelitish tribes formed one body politic. They had one common weal. They held general diets. They were bound to take the field against a common enemy. They had at first general judges, and afterwards general sovereigns. And even when they had no common head, or, as the sacred historian expresses it, when there was neither king nor judge, a tribe guilty of a breach of the fundamental law, might be accused before the other tribes, who, as we have seen, were authorized to carry on war against it as a punishment. It is evident, that the tribes were sometimes without a general chief magistrate. The constitution, as explained above, makes it quite conceivable, that the state might have subsisted and prospered without a common head. Every tribe had always its own chief magistrate; subordinate to whom again, were the chiefs of clans, the judges, and the genealogists; and if there was no general ruler of the whole people, there were twelve lesser commonwealths, whose general convention would deliberate together, and take measures for the common interest. The head might be gone, but the living body remained. Its movements would be apt to be slower and feebler; yet, as the history of the Benjamite rebellion* teaches us, they did not always want either promptness or energy.†

As the twelve tribes, though independent and sovereign

---

* This is said to have happened (Judg. xix. 1), when "there was no king in Israel;" i. e. when the tribes had no common head, no general chief magistrate.

† Mich. Com. Art. 46.

for local purposes, yet formed but one political body for the care and promotion of the common weal, they would naturally have general legislative assemblies, who would, as occasion required, meet together and consult for the good of the nation at large. This we find to have been actually the case.* The law can neither enact, interpret, nor execute itself. For the discharge of these functions there is required a certain number of citizens, organized into one or more bodies, and forming a legislative, judicial, and executive corps. Conringius,† bishop Sherlock,‡ and Lowman§ totally misconceive and misrepresent the Hebrew constitution, when they deny, that it lodged any proper legislative power in the national diet, or states-general of Israel. Their error arises from a misinterpretation of Deut. 4 : 1, 2. "Now, therefore, hearken, O Israel, unto the statutes and unto the judgments which I teach you, for to do them, that ye may live and go on, and possess the land, which the Lord God of your fathers giveth you. Ye shall not add unto the word which I command you, neither shall ye diminish aught from it, that ye may keep the commandments of the Lord your God, which I command you." The same thing is repeated in Deut. 12 : 32. "What thing soever I command you, observe to do it; thou shalt not add thereto, nor diminish from it." From these precepts, the learned authors, cited above, erroneously conclude, that no proper legislative authority or power was confided by the constitution to the general assemblies of Israel. There is, undoubtedly, a sense, in which the law was perpetual and unchangeable, viz. in its principles. The principles of a pure and absolute justice remain always the same; and new developments of those principles, made necessary by new circumstances, do not change, even in modifying them, the truth of former developments. It would be absurd in a

* Exod. xix. 7, 8. Numb. i. 16, xvi. 2, x. 2–4, xxvii. 2, xxxvi. 1. Deut. xix. 10. Josh. xxiii. 2, xxiv. 1. Judg. xx. 2.

† De Rep. Heb. S. 10.   ‡ Dissert. 3.   § Civ. Gov. Heb. C. 7.

legislator, in giving a code of laws to a people, to take away
from them the power of enacting new laws, as new manners
and new conditions of the body politic required them. The
command of Moses in this case must be understood as addressed to individuals, and as announcing to them, that they
must observe the whole law, without adding to it, or taking
from it, on their private authority. When he speaks to the
national assemblies, to all Israel, his language is altogether
different. Then, on the contrary, he commands to seek justice, to provide for the public welfare, to pursue (go on in)
the way of equity, otherwise called "the way of the Lord,"
without turning to the right hand or to the left; that is,
without departing from the fundamental principles, laid
down in the constitution. Thence the Hebrew doctors derive
the maxim, assented to by the great Selden, "From the
senate [the national diet] proceeds the law to all Israel."*

The great principle of legislation, which pervades the Hebrew constitution, is, that the general will, the common consent of the citizens, freely and clearly expressed in regularly constituted assemblies, is necessary to give birth to law.
This principle Moses seems to have regarded, if not as an
essential, at least as an important bond of social order, and a
great source of strength to the body politic. Hence at Sinai
he obtained the assent of the people, through their elders, to
the proposition of Jehovah to be their king and to the laws
which he should dictate.† Again, after numerous laws had
been given, and while the Hebrews still remained encamped
at the foot of mount Sinai, he called the diet together anew,
rehearsed "all the words of the Lord and all the judgments,"
and proposed a fresh vote upon them, whereupon the people,
by their representatives, signified their unanimous approval,
and formally enacted them into laws. Not content with even

* Mischna, vol. 4, c. 10, and Selden de Synedriis, cited by Salvador, in
Hist. des Inst. de Moïse, 1. 1, c. 2.

† Exod. xix. 3-8.

this expression of the popular will, he caused them all to be written out, engrossed as it were, and the next day, after offering a solemn sacrifice accompanied by various imposing and impressive ceremonies, he read them in the audience of the assembly, and required another formal assent. This last act was strictly of the nature of a compact between Jehovah as sovereign and the Hebrews as subjects; and it is expressly called so by Moses.* In like manner a short time before his death, when the code had been completed, he assembled the national legislature, and submitted the whole body of laws to their approval, and caused them to renew the compact with their king.† Surely, never did legislator attach a higher importance to the general will, or take more pains to obtain a full, free, and fair expression of it.

This great principle of popular consent, as the basis and nerve of legislation, received fresh confirmation, on various memorable occasions, in the subsequent history of the commonwealth. After the passage of the Jordan, Joshua assembled the states-general of Israel, agreeably to an express injunction of Moses, and caused the nation to renew its vote in favor of the code, which had been framed for it.‡ Near the end of his life, this same Joshua, a worthy successor of Moses, as having no small share of his ability, and as being deeply penetrated with his spirit, convened the representatives of the nation at Shechem, recounted the leading events of their history, and made them re-elect Jehovah for their king, renew the compact with him, and give their assent once more to the laws, which he had ordained.§ On the return of the Jews from Babylon and the re-establishment of their republic, the law was publicly proclaimed for many successive days, and a solemn formula was drawn up, in which the assent and sanction of the nation might be expressed. To this document twenty-three priests, seventeen Levites, and forty-four chiefs

---

* Exod. xxiv. 3–8.   † Deut. xxix. 9–13.

‡ Josh. viii. 30–35.   § Ibid. xxiv.

of the people,—eighty-four leading men in all,—signed their names, and affixed their seals. The rest of the people gave their assent to the covenant and the statutes, in a manner somewhat less formal, but no less binding.*

These facts are a demonstration, that the principle in question entered essentially into the constitution of Moses, and into the practice of the nation. They put the seal of authenticity upon it. Bossuet himself, a man of vast genius, but whose social relations made him too much the friend of absolute power, and from whom nothing but the force of truth could have drawn such an expression of opinion, recognizes this fact in the following terms: "God, through the agency of Moses, assembles his people, proposes to them the law, which establishes the rights of the nation, both sacred and civil, public and private, and causes them to give their assent thereto in his presence. The entire people expressly consent to the compact. Moses receives this compact in the name of the people, who had given it their assent."† Again: "All who have spoken accurately concerning the [Hebrew] law, have regarded it, in its origin, as a solemn pact and treaty, by which individual men agree together in reference to what is necessary to form themselves into a civil society."‡

But since Jehovah is the creator of men, and can lay upon them whatever obligations he pleases, since he needs not human assent to strengthen his authority, why should he propose laws, instead of imposing them? Why should he exact the free concurrence of individuals? If his word is truth, expressing both that which is, and that which ought to be, to what end should serve the approval of a multitude? To this I reply as follows: First, God did not give laws to the Hebrews as their creator, but as their deliverer and the founder of their state. Secondly, an important purpose of the Hebrew polity was to teach mankind the real nature of civil govern-

* Neh. viii. 18; ix. 38; x. 1–29.

† Politique Sacrée, l. 1. Art. 4.   ‡ Ibid.

ment, and the true source of political power; whence it necessarily follows, that the authority of Jehovah, as civil head
of the Hebrew state, must be drawn from the same fountain,
rest upon the same basis, and be regulated by the same principles, as the authority of a human ruler, standing in the
same relation to a civil community. Thirdly, several valuable political advantages, even with Jehovah himself for king,
resulted from the assent of the people to the code. As 1.
The law then became not simply a rule, but a rule clothed
with the consent of all. It was the expression, not of an
absolute power, but of the general will; or rather, to speak
more philosophically, it was the expression of political truth,
sanctioned by the general will. A rule arbitrarily imposed,
however good it may be, tends to despotism; and a thing,
wrong in itself and contrary to the eternal principles of justice, though sanctioned by the voice of the whole world, can
never be a law to bind the conscience. 2. The consent of the
people to the public compact had the effect of obliging each
individual towards all the rest. And 3. It had the further
effect of binding the moral person called the state, which was
formed by this union, to the infinite and unchangeable being;
the Hebrews, on their part, promising to shun whatever was
hurtful, and to submit to whatever was useful, to the body
politic, and Jehovah, on his, engaging to recompense their
fidelity with prosperity and happiness.

It has been well remarked by Salvador,* that no other
nation offers the example of a compact so wise and so sublime. He adds the opinion, which is worthy of being
pondered, that it is the essential cause of the strong power of
cohesion, developed by the political association of the Hebrews, inspiring prophets, full of genius, with the thought,
that, as long as the laws of nature shall endure, Israel and
his law shall never pass away. Such, then, is the principle

* Hist. des Inst. de Moïse, 1. 1. C. 2. The whole of the chapter on the
formation of the law, is well worthy of the reader's attention.

of the Hebrew legislation, viz. that law must rest upon the foundation of the general will, the consent of the nation freely and clearly expressed.

The legislative assemblies, created by the constitution of Moses, were of two kinds,—an upper and a lower house. The former was a select assembly, called commonly the princes, elders, or senators of Israel; and was convened by the sound of a single trumpet. The latter was a larger and more popular assembly, called the congregation of Israel; and the signal for calling it together was the blowing of two trumpets.* These were the signals while Israel was an army, and abode in the wilderness; but after the nation was settled in Canaan, either they met at stated times, or heralds must have been employed to convey the summons for assembling to the persons having a seat in the diet. "These general assemblies were convened by the chief magistrate of the commonwealth, by the commander of the army, or by the regent; and, when the nation had no such supreme head, by the high priest, in his capacity of prime minister to the invisible king. The great assembly mentioned in the twentieth chapter of Judges, was undoubtedly convoked by the high priest Phinehas, who was so zealous for the honor of Jehovah.† It was to these assemblies, that Moses immediately addressed himself, and to them he delivered the precepts, which he received from Jehovah. The magistrates, particularly the genealogists, then communicated to the people the precepts and orders of Moses, each one to the families under his immediate direction. In like manner, the commands of the generals and the resolves of the assemblies were made known to the people, who were sometimes assembled ready to receive these communications; or if not, were called together by the proper officers. The legislative assemblies exercised all the rights of sovereignty.

* Numb. x. 2–4.
† Numb. x. 2–4. Josh. xxiii. 2. xxiv. 1. 1 Sam. xi. 14. Judg. x. 27, 28.

They declared war, made peace, formed alliances, chose generals, chief judges or regents, and kings. They prescribed to the rulers whom they elected the principles by which they were to govern. They tendered to them the oath of office, and rendered them homage."*

I forbear for the present all investigation of the vexed question as to who were entitled to seats in the national legislature, reserving such inquiries, till I come to treat, in detail, of the different branches, which composed it.

I have already spoken of the inferior courts among the Hebrews, by which the local administration of justice was conducted. But the judiciary system could not be complete, without a supreme judicature, which, accordingly, we find to have been established by the constitution. The provision for this court is in the following words : "If there arise a matter too hard for thee in judgment, between blood and blood, between plea and plea, and between stroke and stroke, being matters of controversy within thy gates (i. e. in the inferior, local courts) ; then thou shalt arise, and get thee unto the place which the Lord thy God shall choose ; and thou shalt come unto the priests the Levites, and unto the judge that shall be in those days, and inquire ; and they shall show thee the sentence of judgment."† The priests the Levites and the judge here evidently mean a national council or court. The phrase cannot be understood of the whole tribe of Levi, but must be interpreted of such priests and Levites only, as had some commission to give judgment in the place, which Jehovah should choose. They were not priests and Levites in general, but chosen members of a national tribunal. It was not, indeed, made necessary by any provision of the constitution or any direction of law, that the priests or Levites

* Jahn's Heb. Com. B. 2. S. 14. Exod. xix. 7, xxiv. 3–8, xxxiv. 31. xxxv. 1. Josh. ix. 15–21. Judg. xx. 1–13, 18, 28. xxi. 13 seqq. 1 Sam. x. 24. xi. 14, 15. 2 Sam. iii. 17–21. v. 1–3. 1 Kings xii.

† Deut. xvii. 8, 9.

should be in this tribunal at all; yet, on account of their learning and knowledge of the laws, they would naturally be esteemed best qualified to be chosen to interpret them. This supreme judicature, composed of persons of the greatest ability, experience, and learning in the laws, was not only highly important and useful, as a court of appeal in adjudicating difficult cases, and those in which great interests were at stake between individuals; but it was absolutely indispensable for the decision of controversies, which might arise between different tribes. As no one tribe had any authority or jurisdiction over any other, such controversies could be decided only by some common judge. The tribes, as sovereign states, were subject to no lower court, than the supreme judicial council of the whole nation. What concerned one tribe was by no means to be determined by the judges of another.* It is hardly necessary to add, that the judgment of this court was final. Hence it was enacted: "Thou shalt do according to the sentence, which they of that place which the Lord shall choose (the supreme court) shall show thee; and thou shalt observe to do all according to all that they inform thee; according to the sentence of the law which they shall teach thee, and according to the judgment which they shall tell thee, thou shalt do; thou shalt not decline from the sentence which they shall show thee, to the right hand nor to the left." †

From this general view of the Hebrew constitution, a brief reference to the tribe of Levi can by no means be omitted. This was the learned class, a kind of literary aristocracy. The members of this tribe were devoted to the tabernacle and the altar, that is, politically speaking, to be the ministers and courtiers of the king Jehovah. They performed, not only the rites of religion, but also the duties of all those offices of state, for which learning was necessary. They

* Lowm. Civ. Gov. Heb. c. 5. Selden de Synedr. l. 3. c. 4.
† Deut. xvii. 10, 11.

were by birth devoted to the cultivation of the sciences, especially the science of government and jurisprudence. They were to study the book of the law; to make, preserve, and disseminate correct copies of it; to instruct the people both in human and divine learning; to test the accuracy of weights and measures; to exhort the soldiers, and inspire them with courage, when about to engage in battle; to perform the duty of police physicians; to determine and announce the moveable feasts, new moons and intercalary years; to discharge the functions of judges and genealogists; with a variety of other duties. * Consequently they were to be theologians, jurists, lawyers, historiographers, mathematicians, astronomers, surveyors, teachers, orators, and medical practitioners. " What fruits might not such a plant have borne, if the priests and Levites had faithfully accomplished the purposes of their appointment!"†

The prophetical, not less than the Levitical order, among the Hebrews, had very important relations to the civil state. The prophets were the popular orators of the Israelitish commonwealth. They were not, as has been, with different views and for different ends, alleged by the church of Rome and the school of Voltaire, an appendage of the priesthood. On the contrary, they were quite independent of the sacerdotal order, and of the royal power as well.‡ In the public assemblies on the sabbath, the new moon, and in the solemn convocations, the prophets, observes Calmet,§ harangued the people, and freely reproved the disorders and abuses, which showed themselves in the nation. They were true patriots, who spoke the truth, without disguise and without fear, to

* Numb. xviii. 2–1. Lev. xxv. 8, 9. Deut. xvii. 9. xx. 2–4. xxxi. 11–13. Lev. xiii. 14. 1 Chron. xxiii. 4. 2 Chron. xvii. 7–9. xix. 8. xxxiv. 13. Mal. ii. 7.

† Jahn's Heb. Com. B. 2. S. 12.

‡ Eichhorn cited by Salvador, l. 2, c. 3.

§ Dissert. sur les Ecoles des Hébreux, S. 11.

people, priests, senators, princes, and kings. We have an instance of this in the indignant rebuke of Isaiah, chap. 1 : 21–24 : " How has she become an harlot, (faithless to her compact with Jehovah,) the faithful city, full of justice, righteousness lodged in it, and now murderers. Thy silver is become dross, thy wine weakened with water. Thy rulers are rebels, and fellows of thieves, every one of them loving a bribe and pursuing rewards. The fatherless they judge not, and the cause of the widow cometh not unto them. Therefore, saith the Lord, Jehovah of hosts, the mighty one of Israel, I will comfort myself of my adversaries (literally, from them, i.e. by ridding myself of them) and I will avenge myself of my enemies."*

Thus it appears, from all which has gone before, that the nature of the public functions, prescribed in the Hebrew constitution, flow from the nature of things. The first want of a state, as of every organized, living being, is self-preservation. To meet this want, the constitution institutes certain functionaries, not only to strengthen the union of the tribes, but also to preserve, in its integrity, both the letter and the spirit of the fundamental law, and to teach it incessantly to the people. Such are the Hebrew priests and Levites. Next, the body politic wants a supreme legislative council, to watch over its wants, to direct its general movements, to shape its policy, and to modify old laws and enact new ones, as the exigency of times and occasions demands. For this the constitution provides in the assemblies composing the states-general of Israel. The third fundamental necessity of a nation is that of having the civil relations of the citizens maintained agreeably to the rules laid down in the law. The constitution satisfies this requirement by a judiciary system, which brings the administration of justice to every man's door, and makes it at once cheap and speedy, taking care, however, to prevent the evils of crude, hasty, and interested

* Alexander's Translation, Earlier Prophecies, pp. 16, 17.

decisions, by a system of appeal through courts of various grades, up to the supreme judicature, which holds its sessions in the capital of the republic. Again, the state requires, that its force be wisely and effectively directed against its public enemies. This care the constitution devolves upon the chief magistrate of Israel. Finally, it is necessary to the best welfare of a state, that men of lofty genius, men endowed with sagacity to discover the connexion between an existing evil and antecedent acts of folly or injustice, men inspired with great ideas, political or moral, should be able freely to utter their thoughts, and boldly to censure both magistrates and people. This necessity the Hebrew constitution meets by its institution of the prophetical order; an institution, which, in those remote ages, admirably supplied the want of a free press, and must have contributed, powerfully and effectively, to the formation of a public opinion, wise, just, pure, and dignified.

Before concluding this chapter, let us glance at the government of the individual tribes and cities.

Each tribe was a reproduction, a miniature copy, as it were, of the nation. It would naturally happen, that the government and functionaries of the former would correspond, in all important respects, to the latter. Nor have we any reason to doubt, that such was the case. This at least is the general opinion of the learned. As all Israel had a council of elders and a representative congregation of the people, so each tribe had its senate of princes and its popular assembly. All the tribes together formed a sort of federative republic, in which nothing could be done or resolved without the general consent of their respective representatives, and in which each individual tribe had a constitution formed upon the model of the national constitution.

As the general government was the type of the provincial governments, so these furnished the model of the city administrations. Every city had its bench of elders, distinct

from its judges and genealogists.* Thus the cities, like the
nation and the tribes, had an upper and a lower house, a board
of aldermen and a board of assistant aldermen. These municipal assemblies managed the public business of the cities,
as the assemblies of the tribes administered the general affairs
of the tribes, and the assemblies of the commonwealth those
of all Israel. Numerous proofs of this constitution of the
city governments occur in the sacred books. That every
city, with its surrounding district, was to have a board of
judges and genealogists, we have already seen.† That a
board of elders was superadded to this as a part of the municipal administration, the evidence is equally clear. The
men of Succoth having offended Gideon, when pursuing the
routed Midianites, on his return from the battle he caught a
young man of the place, and compelled him to give to him
in writing a list of the princes and elders of his city.‡ In
the law concerning the expiation of an uncertain murder,
the two boards are mentioned in connexion, and yet plainly
distinguished from each other; for it is said, "Thy elders and
thy judges shall come forth."§ In like manner, when, on the
return of the Jews from Babylon, the matter concerning the
unlawful marriages was in hand, "the elders of every city
and the judges thereof" are related to have appeared, with
the transgressors, before "the rulers of all the congregation."||
The author of the book of Judith speaks of a council of ancients in Bethulia, and of three mayors, or governors, to
whom the executive function was committed. He also mentions one of the governors, Ozias, as having made a feast to
the elders.¶

To these municipal assemblies it belonged to direct the
public affairs of the cities by their council and authority, and

* Deut. xxi. 1 seqq. Judg. xi. 5, 6, 11. viii. 6, 14. Ruth iv. 4, 9. Ezra x. 14, and many other scriptures.

† Deut. xvi. 18.   ‡ Judg. viii. 6, 14.   § Deut. xxi. 2.

|| Ezra x. 14.   ¶ Judith vi. 14–21.

to interpret the law in whatever related to the interests of their respective cantons. Salvador* thinks, that like the censors at Rome and the ancients of Sparta and Athens, they watched over the public manners and morals. Seated without parade at the city gate, or beneath the shade of trees, they lent the ear, he says, to the aggrieved citizens, to the weeping wife, to the oppressed slave, to the poor, the stranger, the orphan, and the widow. If their complaints admitted of legal redress, they proclaimed and enforced the law; if not, they became the counsellors and comforters of the afflicted. By their efforts, a rigorous father was softened; a wandering son was reclaimed and brought back to the paternal mansion; and families, rent by discord, were re-united in peace. On the sacred days, the presence of the rulers, reverently listening to the reading of the law and the exhortations of the orators, impressed upon the youthful citizens the importance of the subjects handled, and communicated to the assemblies a calm, thoughtful, and dignified air.

Thus flowed the current of affairs, during those long periods of repose enjoyed by Israel, despite the powerful enemies by which the nation was surrounded. Such was the simple but energetic polity, which impressed upon the soul of the Hebrews memories never to be effaced, and which, in spite of many odious actions, produced by the barbarism of the times, imparts a charm to their sacred books, unknown to other compositions; a charm, which neither distance of time nor diversity of manners has power to dissolve, or even to weaken.

* Hist. des Inst. de Moïse, l. 2. c. 2.

CHAPTER IV.

The Hebrew Chief Magistrate.

MOSES did not, by an express law, unalterably determine in what sort of magistrate the supreme executive authority of the Israelitish state should be lodged. On the contrary, he provided beforehand, in his constitution, for a change in the form of the government and the title and prerogatives of its head, without subjecting the nation to the horrors of a civil war. And the change from the republican to the regal form was, in a subsequent age, actually accomplished without bloodshed or commotion, an event hardly paralleled by any other in history. Still, Moses was far from being indifferent in regard to the name and powers of the civil head of the state. His chief magistrate was a republican president, who had the title of judge, or rather, as Jahn says, governor, and was elective by the people.

A strange notion in regard to the chief magistracy of Israel has been entertained by several very learned authors; viz. that it was the design of Moses, that the nation should, if possible, do without a chief executive officer. Such appears to have been the opinion of Harrington,* Fleury,† Lewis,‡

* Commonwealth of Israel, C. 3.
† Manners of the Ancient Israelites, C. 23.
‡ Antiquities of the Heb. Rep. B. 1, C. 4.

Michaelis,* Smith,† and Dupin.‡ Their idea would seem
to have been, that, considering how difficult it is to control
power once entrusted to the hands of an individual, the lawgiver of Israel wished to have the ends of an executive answered in his republic, without setting apart a single person
for that tempting distinction, trusting that, on emergencies,
men would appear, who could discharge the duty required
by the occasion, without any other commission, than their
own preëminent qualifications, instinctively acknowledged by
the public voice. In the view of these writers, the judges
were all extraordinary magistrates, not unlike the dictators
in ancient Rome.

I have called this a strange opinion, because a state without
a chief magistrate, is as monstrous as a body without a head.
But I must add, that, notwithstanding the great names, by
which it is supported, it appears to me wholly without foundation. If I look either to the conduct or the laws of Moses,
I can discover no ground for such an idea. Let us first take
his acts for our guide in the study of this point. Moses himself was, unquestionably, the chief magistrate of the Hebrew
state. Now, when he had finished his course, and the time
of his departure was at hand, about to yield up the authority,
which he had so long and usefully exercised, he was mainly
anxious to provide a suitable successor in that office ; a man
of courage, prudence, piety, and other needful gifts of government.§ He was to be one, who should go out and come
in before them ; that is, he was to have the command of their
armies in war, and the direction of their civil affairs in peace.
As to the opinion, that this was to be an extraordinary magistracy, it is pure assumption. No intimation is given,
that it was to last only during the conquest and settlement of
Canaan. The reason assigned by Moses for his anxiety in
the matter, viz. that the congregation of Jehovah be not as

* Comment. on the Laws of Moses, Art. 53.   † Hebrew People, C. 3.
‡ Hist. of the Canon, B. 1, C. 3.   § Numb. xxvii. 15–17.

sheep that have no shepherd, seems to me to settle the question beyond doubt or cavil. Sheep without a shepherd would be as appropriate a symbol of Israel without a chief magistrate after the settlement of Canaan, as before it. This reason for the office of leader or head, viz. its great usefulness or importance to the well-being of the body politic, which are inherent and permanent qualities, stamps it as an essential and standing part of the constitution. And this is conformable to the general sentiment and practice of mankind. The wisest nations have ever deemed it convenient to have a first magistrate, either hereditary or elective, either for life or a term of years, who should be the commander in chief of their armies, and who should preside over the civil administration. No otherwise can the force of a nation be properly employed for its protection, and its laws duly executed.

But, again, if we look at the laws of Moses, we shall come to the same conclusion, viz. that the opinion I am combatting is without any solid foundation. Michaelis* says truly, that Moses gave no law, imposing an obligation on the people to choose one universal magistrate of the whole nation. Yet he at least does that which is equivalent; he manifestly takes it for granted, that the nation would have such a magistrate. Thus in Deut. 17 : 9, the judge of the whole republic is mentioned in connexion with the high priest; and that, not as a military, but as a civil functionary. In the twelfth verse of the same chapter, the word judge is used as a title of supreme authority. A still more decisive passage occurs in 2 Sam. 7 : 11. It is an address, which Jehovah, by the mouth of the prophet Nathan, made to king David, concerning his intention to build him a house. The divine speaker, in a distinct allusion to the chief magistrates of Israel, prior to the institution of monarchy, says expressly: " I COMMANDED judges to be over my people Israel.". Upon the whole, there can be no reasonable doubt, that, as the Lacedaemonians had their

* Art. 53.

kings, the Athenians their archons, and the Romans their consuls, so, according to the constitution of Moses, the Hebrews were to have their general judges, or governors of the whole republic. As to what is alleged by some, as a ground of belief that Moses did not intend to have an unbroken succession of chief magistrates, that, prior to the establishment of monarchy, there were times, when the nation was without a civil head, and that the authority of some of the judges did not extend to all Israel, but was limited to particular tribes, that is undoubtedly true. But it is a fact, which may be accounted for on more rational grounds, than the theory of these writers. It was the result of a neglect, rather than an observance, of the Mosaic constitution ; a neglect, in all probability, occasioned by the jealous rivalry between the different tribes, as explained in the last chapter.

In order to a just understanding of the frame and operation of the Hebrew government, it is material to inquire, both what were the powers, and what the limitations of power, appertaining to this magistracy. If we would conceive justly of the office, we must study it, as it was instituted and exercised by Moses and Joshua, in whose history alone we may expect to find an exact and true account of it, since, after the death of the latter, this part of the constitution was very soon altered or neglected, there being no regent or judge in the land.*

The supreme authority of the Hebrew state was in Jehovah. God himself was properly king of Israel. With respect to this divine king, Moses, as Conringius† says, might not improperly be called his viceroy. It is evident from the whole history, and therefore particular citations are not necessary to prove, that Moses was clothed with very ample powers. He had authority to convene the states-general of Israel, to preside over their deliberations, to command the army, to appoint officers, and to hear and decide civil causes.

* Judg. xix. 1.   † De Rep. Haebr. p. 249, cited by Lowman, C. 10.

But it may be alleged, and it is certainly true, that Moses had an authority depending, in a peculiar manner, on God himself. Let us, therefore, look at this office of chief magistrate, as exercised by Joshua. We find a somewhat detailed account of it, in the narrative of his appointment as the successor of Moses. The historian says :* "And the Lord said unto Moses, Take thee Joshua the son of Nun, a man in whom is the spirit, and lay thine hand upon him: and set him before Eleazar the priest, and before all the congregation : and give him a charge in their sight. And thou shalt put some of thine honor upon him, that all the 'congregation of the children of Israel may be obedient. And he shall stand before Eleazar the priest, who shall ask counsel for him after the judgment of urim before the Lord : at his word shall they go out, and at his word they shall come in, both he, and all the children of Israel with him, even all the congregation. And Moses did as the Lord commanded him : and he took Joshua, and set him before Eleazar the priest, and before all the congregation. And he laid his hands upon him, and gave him a charge, as the Lord commanded by the hand of Moses."

We learn, still more clearly, the nature of this part of the Hebrew constitution, from the history of Joshua's accession to the government. "Now, after the death of Moses, the servant of the Lord, it came to pass, that the Lord spake unto Joshua, the son of Nun, Moses's minister."† The object of this address was to encourage him to take upon himself the government of the Israelites.‡ Thereupon the new regent immediately issues his orders :§ "Then Joshua commanded the officers of the people, saying, Pass through the host and command the people, saying, Prepare you victuals : for within three days ye shall pass over this Jordan, to go in to possess the land which the Lord your God giveth you to possess it." Then he summoned the tribes, who had received their inherit-

* Numb. xxvii. 18–23. † Josh. i. 1. ‡ Ibid. i. 2–9.
§ Ibid. i. 10, 11.

ance east of the Jordan, and directed them to accompany their brethren, and assist them in taking possession of their portion on the western side of that river.* Their reply was remarkable, and deserves to be inserted at length; as we distinctly see from it their conception of the nature and extent of the authority, which was vested in Joshua:—† "And they answered Joshua, saying, All that thou commandest us, we will do, and whithersoever thou sendest us, we will go. According as we hearkened unto Moses in all things, so will we hearken unto thee: only the Lord thy God be with thee, as he was with Moses. Whosoever he be that doth rebel against thy commandment, and will not hearken unto thy words in all that thou commandest him, he shall be put to death: only be strong and of a good courage."

These are the principal passages, relating to the office of chief magistrate among the Hebrews, as it was exemplified in the history of the first two judges. A critical analysis of them establishes several important conclusions.

1. The Hebrew judges held their office for life. There was, unquestionably, a disadvantage attendant upon this arrangement. On the death of a judge, the supreme executive authority ceased. This often led to anarchy, or at least to great disorders, in consequence of a delay in electing a successor. In virtue of the English maxim of law, that the king never dies, all the rights of the sovereign, on his demise, instantly vest in his heir. Perhaps, however, the disadvantage, resulting from the adoption of the opposite principle in the Hebrew polity, was more than counterbalanced, by its preventing a degenerate heir, or successor, from giving to idolatry the support of his influence.‡

2. The office was not hereditary. Moses took no steps to perpetuate this magistracy in his family, or to leave it as an hereditary honor to his posterity. He did not even seek to confine it within his own tribe. All he desired, in his suc-

---

* Josh. i. 12–15.   † Ibid. i. 16–18.   ‡ Jahn's Heb. Com. B. 3. S. 22.

cessor, was a man fit for the office; a man, in whom was the spirit of prudence, courage, and the fear of God, with all the other gifts of government, necessary in an upright, patriotic, zealous, and able chief magistrate. Joshua, the immediate successor of Moses, was of the tribe of Ephraim; Othniel was of Judah; Ehud, of Benjamin; Deborah, of Naphtali; Gideon, of Manasseh; and Samuel, of Levi. The other judges were of several different tribes; and, they being dead, their children remained among the common people; and we hear no more of them. " Let the supreme authority be given to the worthiest," is the voice of reason. " Let the supreme authority be given to the worthiest," is echoed back by the Mosaic constitution, as face answers to face in water, and the heart of man to man.

3. The chief magistracy of Israel was elective. The oracle, the high priest, and all the congregation, are distinctly recorded to have concurred in the elevation of Joshua to this office.* Jephthah was chosen to the chief magistracy by the popular voice.† Samuel was elected regent in a general assembly of Israel.‡ And, for aught that appears, the other judges were raised to this office by the free, unsolicited choice of the people.

4. The authority of these regents extended to affairs of war and peace. They were commanders in chief of the military forces of the Israelites, and chief judges in civil causes. That Moses united these functions in his person, is undisputed. He administered justice, as well as commanded armies. That Joshua did the same, that his authority was, in these particulars, of an equal extent, is also clear. Moses was directed to put some of his honor upon him, that all the congregation of the children of Israel might be obedient.§ What does this mean, but that, as suggested by bishop Patrick, Moses communicated to Joshua some of his own authority,

---

* Numb. xxviii. 19, 22.   † Judg. xi. 4–11.
‡ 1 Sam. vii. 5–8.   § Numb. xxviii. 20.

and made him an associate in the government? But the
point is yet clearer from the words, in which the trans-
jordanic tribes recognized Joshua's authority : " All that thou
commandest us we will do, and whithersoever thou sendest
us we will go. According as we hearkened unto Moses
in all things, so will we hearken unto thee."* This is explicit and unequivocal. The authority of Joshua was co-
extensive with that of Moses, and comprehended civil as well
as military affairs. Most of the succeeding judges had been
at the head of armies; had delivered their country from
foreign oppression ; and were elevated to the chief magistracy
in reward of their military exploits. Eli and Samuel, however, certainly were not military men. Deborah was judge,
and held her court under a palm tree, before she planned the
war against Jabin.† Of Jair, Ibzan, Elon, and Abdon, it is
uncertain whether they ever held any military command.
The judges are mentioned in the Mosaic law, in connection
with the high priest, as arbiters of civil controversies.‡ The
command of the army cannot, therefore, be considered as the
peculiar, much less the exclusive function of these magistrates. They appear rather to have been appointed for the
general administration of public affairs. It is true, that martial achievements were, in several instances, the means, by
which men raised themselves to the rank of judges ; but the
present inquiry is, not how the office was obtained, but for
what ends it was instituted.§

The authority of the judge was, without doubt, very great.
As general, he had the chief command of the army ; as civil
head of the state, he convened the senate and congregation,
presided in those assemblies, proposed the public business,
exercised a powerful influence over their deliberations, and,
in all things, acted as viceroy of Jehovah, the invisible king
of Israel. He was the fountain of justice, and the executive

* Josh. i. 16, 17.   † Judg. iv. 4, 5.   ‡ Deut. xvii. 9, 12.
§ Jahn's Heb. Com. B. 3, S. 22.

power of the government was principally lodged in his hands.*

5. A contumacious resistance of the lawful authority and orders of the Hebrew judges, was treason. This is plain from the address of the eastern tribes to Joshua, in formally recognizing him as the head of the nation, and promising allegiance to his government. " Whosoever he be," they say, " that doth rebel against thy commandment, and will not hearken unto thy words, in all that thou commandest him, he shall be put to death."† It is, perhaps, still plainer from Deut. 17: 12 : "The man that will do presumptuously, and will not hearken unto * * * * the judge, even that man shall die." And this was consonant to reason and justice ; for, the chief authority, both in military and civil affairs, being vested in him, he embodied and represented the majesty of the state. Rebellion against him was rebellion against the supreme power. It was a violation of all order and government, an attempt to frustrate the will of the nation, an act of mutiny and sedition ; offences, which, in all governments, have been regarded and treated as capital crimes.

6. The authority of the Israelitish regents was not unlimited and despotic. It was tempered and restrained by the oracle. This is distinctly affirmed, in the history of the appointment of Joshua to the chief magistracy, as the successor of Moses.‡ It is there said, that he should stand before Eleazar the priest, who should ask counsel for him, after the judgment of urim before the Lord. This implies an obligation to follow the counsel, when given. This use of the oracle throws light on some parts of the Hebrew history, which are commonly not well understood. In particular, it suggests the reason why the Israelites were so often conquered and oppressed by their enemies. It was either because of their rashness in trusting to their own wisdom, without asking

* Lowm. on Civ. Gov. Heb. C. 10.

† Josh. i. 18.   ‡ Numb. xxvii. 21.

counsel of the oracle, or because of their neglect to follow the counsels, which they received from it. In either case, the behavior of the Hebrews could not be otherwise than highly criminal, under this constitution ; and, of course, highly provoking to their divine king. The power of the Hebrew chief magistrates was further limited by that of the senate and congregation. In ordinary cases, it would seem, they were not bound to consult the states-general. It was enough, if these did not remonstrate against the measures of the judge ; a procedure to which they were by no means backward in resorting, whenever, in their judgment, occasion required it. But, in important emergencies, they summoned a general assembly of the rulers, to ask their advice and consent. This we find to have been repeatedly done by Moses, Joshua, and Samuel.

Still another limitation to the authority of the Hebrew judges was in the law itself. Their power could not be stretched beyond its legal bounds. This is pretty plainly intimated, in the address of the people to Joshua, on his accession to the chief magistracy. They say, in effect, that they would be obedient to him, provided he himself would obey the law of Jehovah, and follow the path traced out by his servant Moses.* This magistracy was always in subjection to the law, nor, as far as appears from the history, did any of the judges ever abuse the power committed to them, unless we except Gideon, who, through his own superstition, gave some slight encouragement to idolatry. As it is a maxim of the British monarchy, that the law maketh the king,† so it was a principle of the Hebrew commonwealth, that the law made the judge ; and as, under the English constitution, he is not king, where will and pleasure rule, and not the law ;† so, under the Israelitish constitution, he would not long have continued judge, who, trampling on the law, should have made his own will the rule of his administration.

* Josh. i. 17.   † Blacks. Comment. B. 1. c. 6.

The observation may appear singular, yet I believe it to be true, that the constitution of Carthage throws light on this part of the constitution of Israel. " The history of the Carthaginians," observes Michaelis,* " will here assist us in forming more accurate ideas of this chief magistrate of the Israelitish republic, and in comparing his office with a well known European one. In the Hebrew language, a judge is called schofet. The Carthaginians, who were descendants of the Tyrians, and spoke Hebrew, called their chief magistrate by that name. But the Latins, who had no such *sch*, as we have, wrote the word with a sharp *s*, and, adding a Latin termination, denominated them suffetes. By the historian Livy, they are compared to the Roman consuls. In book 28, chap. 38, he says, ' Ad colloquium suffetes eorum, qui summus Poenis est magistratus, cum quaestore elicuit.' There, however, he is speaking, not of the suffetes of the city of Carthage itself, but of inferior ones. But in book 30, chap. 7, he mentions the former in these words : ' Senatum suffetes, quod velut consulare apud imperium erat, vocaverunt.' Now such were the judges of Israel, whose history is recorded in the book called by their name."

No salary was attached to the chief magistracy in the Hebrew government. No revenues were appropriated to the judges, except, perhaps, a larger share of the spoils taken in war, and the presents, spontaneously made to them, as testimonials of respect.† No tribute was raised for them. They had no outward badges of dignity. They did not wear the diadem. They were not surrounded by a crowd of satellites. They were not invested with the sovereign power.‡ They could issue orders ; but they could not enact laws. They had not the right of appointing officers, except perhaps in the army. They had no power to lay new burdens upon the people in the form of taxes. They were ministers of justice,

* Comment. Art. 53.   † Judg. viii. 24. 1 Sam. ix. 7. x. 27.

‡ Pastoret, Histoire de la Legislat. t. 3. pp. 79 seqq.

protectors of law, defenders of religion, and avengers of
crime; particularly the crime of idolatry.* But their power
was constitutional, not arbitrary. It was kept within due
bounds by the barriers of law, the decisions of the oracle,
and the advice and consent of the senate and commons of
Israel. They were without show, without pomp, without
retinue, without equipage; plain republican magistrates.
" They were not only simple in their manners, moderate in
their desires, and free from avarice and ambition, but noble
and magnanimous men, who felt that whatever they did for
their country, was above all reward, and could not be recompensed; who desired merely to promote the public good;
and who chose rather to deserve well of their country, than
to be enriched by its wealth. This exalted patriotism, like
every thing else connected with politics in the theocratical
state of the Hebrews, was partly of a religious character;
and those regents always conducted themselves as the officers
of God. In all their enterprises, they relied upon him, and
their only care was, that their countrymen should acknowledge the authority of Jehovah, their invisible king. Still,
they were not without faults; neither are they so represented
by their historians. These relate, on the contrary, with the
utmost frankness, the great sins, of which some of them were
guilty. They were not merely deliverers of the state from a
foreign yoke, but destroyers of idolatry, foes of pagan vices,
promoters of the knowledge of God, of religion, and of morality; restorers of theocracy in the minds of the Hebrews;
and powerful instruments of divine providence in the promotion of the great design of preserving the Hebrew constitution, and, by that means, of rescuing the true religion from
destruction."†

Such was the chief magistrate of Israel, as created by the
constitution of Moses. It will be interesting and not unimportant, to inquire into the state of the country, during the

---

* Calmet's Dict. Art. Judges.   † Jahn's Heb. Com. B. 3. S. 22.

government of the judges. Very grave errors on this point, and such as are calculated to discredit the wisdom of this constitution, have been committed by authors, otherwise candid and learned. It has been by no means uncommon to represent the four hundred and fifty years, during which this consular magistracy lasted, as times of imbecility, confusion, anarchy, barbarism, and crime. Harrington * speaks of the Israelitish commonwealth, during this period, as " without any sufficient root for the possible support of it, or with such roots only as were full of worms " Lowman † speaks of " the weak state of the Hebrews," and Smith, ‡ of " the moral and social deterioration of the people," during the same period. Nothing can be more unfounded, or unjust, than such representations. This error is probably grounded on another, viz. that of regarding the book of Judges as a complete history of the times of the judges. But such it manifestly is not. The book is exceedingly fragmentary as a narrative, being made up rather of heads of history, than history itself. It is aptly characterised by Jahn § as " a mere register of diseases, from which, however, we have no right to conclude, that there were no healthy men, much less that there were no healthy seasons; when the book itself, for the most part, mentions only a few tribes, in which the epidemic prevailed, and notices long periods, during which it had universally ceased." If any one will attentively read over the book of Judges, and take the trouble to compare the times of oppression and adversity with those of independence and prosperity, he will find the duration of the former less than one-fourth that of the latter. The entire history of one hundred and twenty years of this period is contained in these two brief records :—" The land had rest forty years ;"‖ " the land had rest four score years." ¶ Surely, Othniel,

---

* Commonwealth of Israel, c. 3.   † Civ. Gov. Heb. c. 10.
‡ Heb. Peop. c. 3.   § Heb. Com. B. 3. S. 23.
‖ Judges iii. 11.   ¶ Ibid. iii. 30.

Ehud, and Shamgar must have governed with prudence and ability, since all the time of their administration was prosperous and peaceable, both within and without. It is quite apparent, therefore, that the Israelites experienced much more of prosperity than of adversity in the time of the judges. Under their government, the nation enjoyed periods of repose, happiness, and plenty, of which the history of other ancient nations affords but few examples. Wherefore, then, change the republican to the regal form? Pride and folly prompted the revolution; a revolution, soon repented of with bitter but unavailing regrets; a revolution, in which lay buried the seeds of despotism and ultimate dissolution.

This magistracy of judge, regent, or consul, was the true primitive arrangement of the Hebrew constitution. This the wisdom of the divine lawgiver appointed as one of the bonds, whereby the tribes were to be united in the power of their arms, in their national councils, and in the administration of justice. If Moses, in framing his polity, had stopped here, it would have been necessary for any one, in analyzing and describing it, to arrest himself at the same point. But since he provided for the establishment of the regal form of government among the Hebrews, whenever they should tire of republican simplicity, and since he enacted a fundamental law to define and limit the power of the future kings, the study of the Hebrew chief magistracy involves an examination of the regal office; nor would the analysis of the Mosaic constitution be complete without it. To this labor, therefore, I now address myself.

The law, referred to in the last paragraph, is in these words :—

" When thou art come into the land, which the Lord thy God giveth thee, and shalt possess it, and shalt dwell therein, and shalt say, I will set a king over me, like as all the nations that are about me : Thou shalt in any wise set him king over thee whom the Lord thy God shall choose : one from among thy brethren shalt thou set king over thee :

thou mayest not set a stranger over thee, which is not thy brother. But he shall not multiply horses to himself, nor cause the people to return to Egypt, to the end that he should multiply horses: forasmuch as the Lord hath said unto you, Ye shall henceforth return no more that way. Neither shall he multiply wives to himself, that his heart turn not away: neither shall he greatly multiply to himself silver and gold. And it shall be when he sitteth upon the throne of his kingdom, that he shall write him a copy of this law in a book out of that which is before the priests the Levites. And it shall be with him, and he shall read therein all the days of his life: that he may learn to fear the Lord his God, to keep all the words of this law and these statutes, to do them: that his heart be not lifted up above his brethren, and that he turn not aside from the commandment to the right hand or to the left: to the end that he may prolong his days in his kingdom, he, and his children, in the midst of Israel."*

Agreeably to the provisions of this enactment, the nation was at liberty, whenever it thought fit, to institute the regal form of government; the king was to be chosen by the concurrent voice of the people and the oracle; the sovereign must be a native Israelite; the multiplication of horses was interdicted to him; he was not to have many wives; he might not accumulate and hoard large treasures; he was to be the defender of religion; the law must be the rule of his government; he must regard his people as brethren and equals; and, upon these conditions, the throne was to be hereditary in his family. I propose briefly to illustrate each of these particulars.

1. Monarchy was permitted to the Israelites. Moses was not ignorant of the temper of the orientals. He knew their strong propensity to kingly government, which, at a later period in the world's history, was remarked by the Greeks and Romans. He well understood, also, the general mutability of human affairs. On these grounds, he anticipated, and the law under consideration presupposes, what afterwards took place, a desire in the Hebrew people to have a king, in

* Deut. xvii. 14–20.

imitation of the polity of other eastern nations. For the gratification of this desire in a peaceful way, Moses provided in this law. Among the immediate causes of this change in the Hebrew constitution, we may probably, without error, enumerate the effeminacy and cowardice of the people, the disunion and jealousy of the tribes, the formidable power of the Ammonites and the Philistines, from whose incursions the eastern and southern tribes were constant sufferers, the fear that, after the death of Samuel, being left without a supreme regent, and consequently becoming disunited, they would fall a prey to these terrible enemies, the degeneracy of Samuel's sons, the example of all their neighbors, the idea of the greater respectability of a nation with a king at its head, the desire or the necessity of being always ready for war, a want of faith and constancy in the Hebrew mind, and, more than all perhaps, a weak longing after the pomp and glitter of royalty. But, whatever the cause might be, the change was made. It conduces not a little to the honor of the Hebrews, that they effected it in accordance with the principles of theocracy, and without bloodshed. This is a clear proof, that the time of the judges was neither an impious nor a barbarous age.*

2. The right of election was left to the people; subject to this limitation, however, that they were not to appoint any one as king, who was not chosen by God. At first view, the two parts of this proposition appear contradictory to each other. But the difficulty vanishes, when it is understood as simply implying, that the oracle and the states-general must concur in the choice. In some of our state legislatures, United States senators are elected by a separate vote of each house, in which case the two houses must be of accord, or there is no election. The case was analogous in the election of an Israelitish sovereign. The people and the oracle must concur. A fair interpretation of the statute itself will lead

* Jahn's Heb. Com. B. 3, ss. 24, 25. Mich. Comment. Art. 54.

to this conclusion. "Thou shalt in any wise set him king over thee, whom the Lord thy God shall choose : one from among thy brethren shalt thou set over thee : thou mayest not set a stranger over thee, which is not thy brother."* That the oracle was to be consulted in the election, this passage places beyond doubt. That the people also were to have a voice in the transaction, it makes almost equally clear. The earnest cautions, addressed to them in reference to the choice of a sovereign, would be absurd, if all liberty of action were absolutely taken from them, and they were simply to receive one, arbitrarily imposed upon them by the will of another.

But the meaning of the statute may be best studied in the actual application of it. In this, as in other instances, the history throws light upon the code. In regard to the institution of the monarchy, and Saul's elevation to the throne, let any one attentively read that part of the first book of Samuel, which is contained in chaps. 8–11, and he will find set forth in it the following facts. Samuel convoked the general diet of Israel at Mizpeh. There, after recounting the Lord's past mercies to them, he reminded them, that in demanding a king, they had rejected Jehovah; who had himself saved them out of all their adversities. He then called them to present themselves before the Lord by their tribes. On the application of the sacred lot, the tribe of Benjamin was taken. Afterward, in a similar manner, the family of Matri was taken; and then, in the same way, Saul, the son of Kish, was selected. Samuel then presented the nominee of the oracle to the representatives of the people for their approval and confirmation. Many of them, probably a majority, gave an affirmative vote. But a powerful minority opposed his investiture with the royal authority, on the ground, that they did not believe him possessed of sufficient military talent and experience to lead the Israelitish armies to victory. The narrative inclines me to think, that Saul was not inaugurated and

* Deut. xvii. 15.

invested with the kingly power on this occasion. The circumstances, which seem to me to render this a probable opinion, are the following. Saul assumed neither the state nor the authority of a king; but went back to his agricultural pursuits in Gibeah, as aforetime. No tribute was levied for him, nor any arrangement made for supporting the regal dignity. He received gifts from only a few, while by many he was openly contemned. The mass of the people paid him scarcely any deference at all. Samuel did not let go the reins of government, nor resign his power as chief magistrate of Israel; for his authority was joined to that of Saul in summoning the Israelites to the assistance of Jabesh-gilead, against Nahash, king of the Ammonites. In this war, Saul exhibited military talents of a high order. Nor were the moderation and clemency, displayed by him, at its close, towards those who had opposed his elevation to the throne, less signal. His valor, prudence, and magnanimity completely won the confidence and the heart of the nation. Samuel, taking advantage of this favorable temper of the people, convened a general assembly at Gilgal, proposed Saul as king a second time, and obtained a unanimous vote in his favor. Then, for the first time, it is said, that they, that is, the people, made Saul king, and gave themselves up to great and general rejoicings. Immediately after his inauguration, Samuel formally resigned his office as judge, surrendering his authority into the hands of the people, from whom he had received it, and by whom he was honorably exonerated from all charge of blame in his public administration, and the fullest testimony was borne to the purity of his official conduct. Josephus* says, that, on the occasion of Saul's election and inauguration at Gilgal, Samuel anointed him a second time. This seems not improbable, though the circumstance is not mentioned by the sacred historian; for the first anointing was a private transaction, and he was not anointed, when elected by the lot. From this

* Antiq. l. 6. C. 5.

time Saul assumed the reins of government, and was regarded as the lawful sovereign of Israel.

How clearly do we see from this detail, that the choice of a king in Israel was neither in the oracle nor the people separately, but in both conjointly; since the decision of the former did not take effect, till it was ratified and confirmed by the action of the latter. How manifest is it, that the miraculous designation of magistrates in the Hebrew commonwealth, was never understood to exclude the free suffrage of the people in their election. If these things still seem to any irreconcilable, we are able to adduce examples of their co-existence even out of the history of heathen states. It is related by Livy* of Tarquinius Priscus and Servius Tullius, that, before they were raised to the regal dignity at Rome, the one had his hat taken off, borne aloft into the air, and fitly deposited again in its place, by an eagle; and the other had a flame resting on his head, which, after being for some time an object of terror to the beholders, glided off, on his awaking out of sleep, without leaving any trace of its presence on his person. By these portents it was believed, that each of them was designated of the deity to be king. Still, neither by themselves nor others were they interpreted as giving them a right to the throne, much less as excluding the popular suffrage from their election, or authorizing the opinion that any man ought to be king of Rome, whom the people had not first chosen to reign over them. Certainly I would not be understood, from this illustration, as intending to compare the vain prodigies of the heathens with the true miracles of the Israelites. Yet it should be remembered, that each people had a like opinion of each. God raised up judges for his people Israel. That the scripture plainly asserts. But to infer from hence, that the people did not elect them, would be false reasoning, since the fact is unquestionable, that they did. So, that God elected Saul to be

* Lib. 1, c. 34, 39.

king of Israel, is certain. Yet it is just as certain, that the people did, none the less for that, themselves elect him likewise. The one certainly is as strong as the other.*

The history of David's elevation to the throne still further illustrates the meaning of the statute under consideration. The house of Saul had, by God's command, on account of his infractions of the law, been excluded from the succession.† The prophet Samuel had, by direction of the oracle, privately anointed David, as the successor of Saul.‡ The subsequent history shows, that that unction did not, of itself alone, confer a full and valid title to the crown of Israel. When Saul had been slain in a battle with the Philistines, an Amalekite stripped him of his crown, and brought it to David.§ Did David consider himself entitled to wear it? By no means. He assumed neither the crown itself, nor the authority, of which it was the symbol. He returned, with his followers, to the city of Hebron, as a private citizen. In that capacity, he abode there for some time, until, as the historian states, "the men of Judah (the citizens, the people of that tribe) came and anointed David king over the house of Judah."‖ Thus did David, by the joint act of the oracle and the people, become king of Judah. The other eleven tribes raised Ishbosheth, a son of Saul, to the sovereign power, and adhered to him for seven years.¶ Did David, for that, regard them as guilty of treason? Not in the least. Yet that would have followed inevitably, if his unction by Samuel had given him a legal right to the throne of all Israel. David defended himself, (as who would not?) when attacked by the army of Ishbosheth ;** but he made no attempt to reduce the eleven tribes to allegiance to his government by force of arms. When at length they submitted themselves to his sceptre, their submission was voluntary. They freely chose him for

---

* Harrington's Com. Isr. c. 2.   † 1 Sam. xv. 11, 26, 28.
‡ 1 Sam. xvi. 13.   § 2 Sam. i. 10.
‖ 2 Sam. ii. 1–4.   ¶ Ibid. ii. 8, 11.   ** Ibid. ii. 12–30.

their king; yet, in doing so, it is remarkable that they distinctly recognized the part which the oracle had previously taken in his election.* Here, again, we perceive the concurrence of the oracle and the people, in the choice of a person to fill the throne of Israel.

It is probable, as we shall see in the sequel, that David, when he was made king, reserved the right of naming his successor. But, notwithstanding this, it is clear, that a general diet was held; that Solomon was formally proposed to them; and that they, by their free suffrages, confirmed the royal nomination.† It was not till after this vote, that Solomon was anointed and inaugurated, and the people gave themselves up to the festivities, suited to the occasion. The history adds: "Then (i. e. after his election by the congregation) Solomon sat on the throne of the Lord as king, instead of David his father, and prospered; and all Israel obeyed him. And all the princes, and the mighty men, and all the sons likewise of king David, submitted themselves unto Solomon the king."‡ Manifestly, this submission and obedience were rendered to him, as having been constitutionally elected to the regal office.

3. The Hebrew sovereign was to be a native Hebrew citizen; he was to be elected from his brethren; no foreigner was to sit on the throne of Israel. This was a politic and patriotic law. A foreigner might change the constitution, or raise up a faction in direct opposition to the national interest.§ Foreigners were heathens, and would be more inclined than Israelites to violate the fundamental law of the state, by the introduction of idolatry. But this law was grossly misinterpreted in the later periods of the Jewish history. It was understood as forbidding, on the part of the Hebrews, submission to those foreign powers, under whose dominion they had been brought, through the overruling providence of

* Ibid. v. 1-3.   † 1 Chron. xxix. 20-22.
‡ Ibid. xxix. 23, 24.   .   § D'Israeli's Genius of Judaism, c. 4.

God. It was on the ground of this misinterpretation of the law, that the Jews proposed that insidious question to our Lord, "Is it lawful to give tribute to Caesar, or not?"* for they were at that time under a foreign power, Judea being a Roman province. If he had said yes, they in-tended to destroy him through the charge of subverting this law of Moses; if he had answered no, they meant to crush him by the power of Rome. But the law had, in real-ity, no reference to such a case. It referred to free elections. Moses speaks only of kings chosen by the Israelites themselves. A law, such as the later Jews conceived this to be, would inevitably have led to the annihilation of a conquered people. The conquerors, unable to trust their fidelity or rely upon their allegiance, would be driven to the necessity, either of putting them all to the sword, or scattering them by slavery. The Hebrew prophets interpreted the law quite differently from the Hebrew zealots. Jeremiah and Ezekiel exhorted their countrymen, when now a conquered people, to submit quietly to the Chaldeans, and conduct themselves as loyal subjects of the Babylonish government.†

4. The Hebrew king was not to multiply horses. As the Israelites made no use of horses in agriculture, and but little as beasts of burden, employing for these purposes oxen and asses, and as they made most of their journeys on foot, and of course did not need them for travelling, this must be un-derstood as a prohibition against maintaining a strong force of cavalry. For defence cavalry was unnecessary. On the west Palestine had the sea. On the north, its barrier was a range of lofty and almost impassable mountains, where a mounted soldiery would be of little use. To the east and south, it was bounded by vast deserts, where an enemy's ca-valry could not subsist, for want of forage. The only object, therefore, for which an Israelitish sovereign could desire to

---

* Matt. xxii. 17.

† Mich. Com. Art. 54.   Jahn's Heb. Com. B. 3, S. 25.

keep any considerable force of this description, would be to make foreign conquests. But it was against the whole scope of the Mosaic law, nay, subversive of its fundamental purpose, that the Hebrews should be conquerors of foreign countries, and their king a universal monarch. And as the keeping of a strong body of horse could hardly fail to engender a spirit of foreign conquest, it was expressly interdicted to the head of the state. He was especially forbidden to attempt the conquest of Egypt in order to obtain horses

5. The Israelitish sovereign was still further forbidden to marry many wives; so early were women dreaded as the corrupters of royalty. I look upon this law as a prohibition against keeping a numerous harem, or a state seraglio; that inseparable accompaniment of eastern despotism. Besides the inherent tendency of the thing to render kings effeminate, and dissolve their hearts in indolence and pleasure, there was a special reason against it in the Israelitish polity. It is incident to the keeping of a harem as a matter of royal state, that the monarch seek out and collect together the most beautiful women of all nations. But all other nations at that time were idolaters. Moses dreaded the influence of heathen beauties upon the religious principles and character of the Hebrew kings. He feared that it would lead to the introduction and practice of idolatry. How reasonable his fears were, the history of Solomon affords a memorable and melancholy proof. His harem contained a thousand women, many of whom were Moabites, Ammonites, Edomites, Zidonians, and Hittites, besides the daughter of Pharoah; "strange women." His wives turned away his heart after other gods. He appears to have built temples for them all, and himself joined in paying divine honors to Ashtoreth, and Milcom, and Chemosh, and Molech. The conduct of Solomon places in a very striking light the wisdom of this statute; at the same time that it shows, that none of the laws of Moses were less observed than this. It shows further, that the spirit of monar-

chy, at least in the form in which it has always been found in the east, was repugnant to the genius of the Mosaic legislation.

6. The king was not greatly to multiply to himself silver and gold. Moses dreaded wealth, not less than women, as tending to the corruption of royalty. The possession of great treasure naturally leads to luxury, which is an enemy to virtue. It is, moreover, in a monarch, a great engine of despotism. He may use it for crushing the liberties of the people. The hoarding up of large treasures by the sovereign tends to obstruct the circulation of money, discourage industry, and . impoverish his subjects. The Israelitish king, observes Lewis,* " was allowed to lay up money in the treasury at the temple, for the occasions of the state, but was forbidden to fill his own coffers for his private interest, lest he should squeeze his subjects, and exact more of them than they were able to bear.". There is, undoubtedly, as Michaelis† has noticed, a wide and obvious difference between these two sorts of treasure. That laid up in the public treasury, the king could not use, without the consent of the other branches of the government. Of course, he could not pervert it to purposes of tyranny, on pretence of applying it to the public service. David had collected large treasures for the sanctuary.‡ According to the common reckoning, they amounted, in round numbers, to four thousand three hundred and five million dollars, a sum almost beyond belief. Michaelis (in his Commentary on the Age anterior to the Babylonish Captivity, § 7.) estimates the shekel at one tenth the value usually assigned to it. This would reduce the amount to four hundred and thirty millions. But Kennicott§ is of the opinion, that, in the enumeration, a cypher too many has crept in.. Cutting off that, there still remain forty three mil-

* Antiq. Heb. Repub. B. 1. c. 5.

† Com. on Laws of Moses, Art. 54.

‡ 1 Chron. xxii. 14.   § Dissert. 2. p. 354.

lion dollars, which, says Michaelis, for David's time, is still a very great treasure, and only to be accounted for, from the plunder of so many nations.

7. The sovereign of Israel must be the defender of religion. Judaism could exist only in a constant triumph over idolatry. " By the fundamental law of the Hebrew commonwealth, the king was forbidden to introduce any new mode of religious worship. Neither could he, like the kings of other nations, perform the functions of a priest, unless he was of the tribe of Aaron, as was the case with the Asmonean princes. On the contrary, he was required to reign as the representative and vassal of Jehovah, to promote the institutions of religion as a matter of obedience to him, and to attend to the declarations of the prophets, as his ambassadors." *

8. The law, and not the king's own will and pleasure, was to be the rule of his administration. This point was made very prominent in the statute, as the reader will perceive by recurring to it. The king was required to make, or cause to be made, an accurate transcript of the law out of the book, which was before the priests the Levites; that is, probably, the autograph, kept in the tabernacle. This he must have with him continually, and read therein all the days of his life, to the end that he might learn to keep all the words of this law and these statutes, to do them. He might not "turn aside from the commandment (the constitution and the laws) to the right hand or to the left." From this we see, that the laws were supreme. The kings were as much bound to observe them, as the private citizens. They had no power to make or repeal a single statute. We have here a perfect exemplification of a government of laws. The constitutional king of Israel could not assume and exercise arbitrary power, without first trampling under foot the fundamental law of the state. Moses made him simply the first citizen. He aimed also at making him the wisest, the purest, and the best.

* Jahn's Heb. Com. B. 4. S. 26.

9. The king must be gracious and condescending towards
his subjects. His heart must not be lifted up. He must look
upon his people, not only as equals, but as brethren. We
find the best kings cherishing this sentiment, and acting
upon it. When David addressed the states-general, he rose
before them, and used this affectionate compellation : " Hear
me, my brethren, and my people."* On this foundation the
Hebrew doctors have established the rule, that the king must
render honor to the general assembly ; when it presents
itself before him, he must rise from his seat, and receive it
standing.†

10. All the above conditions being observed by him, whom
the Israelites should choose for their king, the throne was to
be hereditary in his family. This is plain from the concluding words of the statute, which are as follows : " To the end
that he may prolong his days in his kingdom, he and his
children, in the midst of Israel." Moses enjoins it upon the
king to keep the laws, that he and his posterity may long fill
the throne. But it is quite as important to observe, that,
although the sceptre was hereditary, it was not inalienable.
It might be taken from one family and given to another, by
the concurrent will of Jehovah and the Hebrew people.
Nay, it certainly would be thus transferred, if the king failed
to govern according to the laws. The Hebrew crown, then,
was elective, not in the sense that every individual king was
to be chosen, but only, when occasion required, some particular family. " Consequently, while the reigning family did
not violate the fundamental laws, they would continue to
possess the throne ; but if they tyrannized, they would forfeit
it. Moses, who gave this injunction, knew certain elective
monarchies, where every individual king was chosen, as in
Poland. The kingdom of Edom in his time was undoubtedly

* 1 Chron. xxviii. 2.
† Schickard de Jur. Reg. Haebr. p. 91, cited by Salvador, L. 6, c. 2.

of this description ; for of eight kings, we find not one, who was the son of his predecessor."*

Thus we perceive, that the Israelitish kings were not absolute and unlimited sovereigns ; they were constitutional monarchs.† Besides that original and fundamental law, which we have just been examining, a special capitulation was sworn to by the kings of Israel. The compact between Saul and the Hebrew people, made when he was chosen to the royal dignity, was drawn up by Samuel. That writing, in which doubtless were specified the rights of the king, was carefully deposited in the sanctuary.‡ Of its contents, however, the bible does not inform us. Still, there can be no doubt, that the limitations of the royal power, fixed by it, were numerous and important. This is the more probable, as we find several of the kings of Israel, whose sway was much less limited than that of Saul, yet subject to very great restrictions.

When the eleven tribes submitted to David, we again find express mention made of a compact between him and the people, called a league, or covenant ;§ yet, as in the former case, we are ignorant of its specific provisions. There is probable ground for the conjecture, that it gave to the king the right of naming for his successor whichever of his sons he might think most capable of filling the throne beneficially to the nation ; for this right David not only exercised, but all Israel conceded it to him ; insomuch that Bathsheba, instructed by Nathan, said to him : " The eyes of all Israel are upon thee, that thou shouldest tell them who should sit on the throne of my lord the king after him."‖ And we find, that the bare word of the king, in the last extremity of old age,

---

* Mich. Com. Art. 54.

† The remaining part of this chapter is, for substance, though much condensed, and otherwise not a little modified, taken from articles 55–60 of the Commentaries of Michaelis.

‡ 1 Sam. x. 25.   § 2 Sam. v. 3.   ‖ 1 Kings i. 20.

was sufficient to place Solomon on the throne, in opposition
to the wishes of the eldest brother, the general of the army,
and the high priest, and to prevent the coronation of Adonijah, even although the ceremony had been commenced.*
This right of setting aside the first born by the arbitrary will
of the king is not usual in hereditary monarchies, and therefore it is probable, that it was conferred upon David by the
terms of the capitulation.

The ten tribes proposed to Rehoboam some new stipulations, with a view to abridge the royal prerogative, as exercised by Solomon. This was, in fact, a new capitulation,
offered to the young monarch by a people yet in possession
of their liberty. The king despotically refused their terms.
Thereupon the ten tribes refused their allegiance to him, and
chose a king for themselves, who, no doubt, acceded to the
wishes of the people, and promised to abide by the stipulations required.†

When Joash was anointed king, mention is again made of
a covenant between him and the people.‡ But here, again,
the history gives us no certain information concerning its
contents. Yet there is no doubt, that the design of the
people, in imposing this capitulation upon their king, was to
bring the royal prerogative, stretched beyond all bounds in
the preceding reigns, within something like the original
limits, affixed to it by the law of Moses.

Upon the whole, it is quite clear, that the king of Israel
was not an unlimited monarch, as the defenders of the divine
right of kings, and of the passive obedience of subjects, have
been accustomed to represent him.§ How could he be so,
when every tribe was under its own chief, had its own government and common weal, and even exercised the right of
war?|| Saul, the first of the kings, appears to have had very
little power. In the beginning of his reign (if his reign

---

* 1 Kings i. 25–27.   † 1 Kings xii. 1–20.   ‡ 2 Kings xi. 17.
§ See Filmer *passim*. || See the last chapter.

commenced at his first election, according to the common opinion, which, however, I doubt, for reasons previously assigned,) he still pursued the business of husbandry, apparently laboring with his own hands.* Afterwards, his army, even in the field, shared with him many of the rights of the supreme power.† In the reign of David, such was the power of this army, that he found it prudent to allow two murders, perpetrated by its general, Joab, to go unpunished, though he did so with extreme reluctance. In this, we may perhaps think, that we perceive the marks of a military government, where the army is omnipotent, and while it renders the king independent of the people, still keeps him in subjection to itself. But this was by no means the case. For, in the first place, the army was the people; and both Harrington‡ and Lowman§ are of the opinion, that its officers were, to a great extent at least, the deputies who composed the general diets of Israel. But, secondly, the military was so in subjection to the civil power, the king and the army were so limited by the liberty of the people, that the king appears not even to have had the right to demand of the cities of Israel the opening of their gates to his troops. The story, contained in 2 Sam. 20 : 1–20, seems to warrant this conclusion. Sheba, a rebel, had thrown himself into the city of Abel. Joab besieged it by David's orders. The citizens declared that they had no share in the rebellion. They did not, however, on that account, open their gates to Joab ; but they sent him the rebel's head, and he quietly retired with his troops. Even Solomon, who carried the royal prerogative to a great height, and ruled quite after the manner of a despot, built cities of his own for his cavalry and his chariots, not venturing to quarter them on the people. In the latter times, from the reign of Hezekiah, we find the kings still more circumscribed in their power, by their privy council.

---

* 1 Sam. xi. 5. † Ibid. xiv. 44, 45.

‡ Commonwealth of Israel, C. 2. § Civ. Gov. Heb. C. 8.

But notwithstanding the limitations of the royal prerogative, imposed by the law of Moses and the jealousy of the
people, there was yet, as Samuel had forewarned his countrymen there would be, a strong tendency to despotism, in the
government of the Israelitish kings. Their will often became
law, even in matters of the highest importance. How tyran-
nically did Saul act towards David, and those eighty priests,
whom he caused to be put to death, without the shadow of a
trial or a crime!* In the condemnations and pardons, pronounced by David, we also perceive the decisions of despotic
authority. Solomon went still greater lengths in this respect,
even to the deciding on life and death by his bare will and
word.†

The notion, that the king in person should be the supreme
judge, a doctrine peculiarly Asiatic, tended strongly to promote
the despotism of the Israelitish monarchs. Of the king, therefore, as chief judge, it will be necessary to speak somewhat
in detail. It is one of the first ideas of the orientals respecting their king, and what they naturally expect of him, that
he should himself administer justice. Hence we are not sur-
prised to find it related by Herodotus, that the Medes once
obtained a king from the following circumstance. A man,
who had great reputation for wisdom and integrity, and to
whom almost all were wont to resort as an arbiter in cases of
dispute, refused at last, from the neglect of his domestic concerns occasioned by it, to decide upon their quarrels, or to
listen to their applications for that purpose; and thus he
forced them to choose him for their king. The more ancient
nations are, and the nearer to their origin, the more prevalent
do we find this idea of a king. Indeed, while nations are
yet in their infancy, and the number of the people small, it is
easier to act upon this doctrine. The king of a thousand families may do what to the king of a million would be impossible.
In a great nation, the king cannot, in his own person, exer-

* 1 Sam. xxii. 17, 18.   † 1 Kings ii. 25.

cise the office of judge, without materially injuring the general interests of the citizens. He cannot have time to inform himself sufficiently of such a multiplicity of lawsuits, as he must be called upon to decide. Hence, either many a liti-gant will not obtain a hearing at all, or causes in general will not be sufficiently investigated, and arbitrary and unrighteous decisions will follow. The mischief is still greater, when the king is very gracious, and gives free access to all his subjects. In that case, he is apt to be overwhelmed with trifles, and villainy takes advantage of his goodness, to effect the ruin of the innocent and the simple. On the other hand, if his subjects have not free access to him, another evil arises, of no less magnitude; for then his ministers may be guilty of the grossest injustice and oppression, and yet the sovereign know nothing about it. In Asia, it is more practicable for the king to be judge in his own person, than in Europe, because there, justice is, in general, very summary, and independent of settled forms. Still, this does not make it less liable to abuse, nor the actual abuse less mischievous in its consequences.

If the first kings of Israel assumed the office of judge, the fault lay in the manners of the east. Moses is not responsible for it. He did, indeed, ordain, that the king should be a daily student of his law, but not that he should discharge the office of a universal judge. It is, undoubtedly, highly useful to a king to be acquainted with civil law, that he may keep his eye on his subordinates, and know whether they decide conformably to it. In this view, it would appear, Moses desired, that the king should not be ignorant of jurisprudence; but he did not mean to constitute him the daily judge of his people. Let the following circumstances be considered. Moses himself found, by experience, that it was beyond his power to determine all the disputes among the people, and, therefore, he appointed other judges of various grades; yet, in matters, which could not be decided by written law, known usage, or manifest equity, he established an appeal to himself, that, on such occasions, he might consult God, and enact new laws by his direction.* Could he, then, have thought of imposing on the kings a burden, which he was himself unable to bear? The king was not a prophet; neither did he, like Moses, enjoy the privilege of immediate intercourse with God. Consequently he could not, by a direct consultation with the unerring one, pronounce an infallible judgment. The high priest, according to the constitution of Moses, was the supreme jurist. Certainly, the legislator, who devoted one whole tribe to the study of jurisprudence, and constituted its head the supreme legal authority, could never have intended, that the king, occupied, as he must be, with the cares of government, and with the conduct of wars, should, in addition, be overwhelmed with the investigation of lawsuits, which could not, as a consequence, fail to be decided too much in the summary style of military procedure.

All this was, undoubtedly, in the plan and intention of Moses. Yet, on its actual institution, and as matter of fact, the Israelitish monarchy was not, in this respect, thus wisely regulated. Without inquiry, without trial, without the intervention of any impartial tribunal, Saul condemned to death eighty innocent priests, and, among them, the high priest himself, together with their wives and children.† David was far from being a tyrant; yet, on some occasions, he had recourse to judicial procedure equally summary, and without allowing other judges to interfere.‡ Even his acts of grace took place without those preliminary and circumstantial inquiries, which, in governments not despotic, are deemed necessary to render them valid, and to prevent artifice and fraud from abusing the royal clemency, to the scandal of justice and the prejudice of the country. Of this, a memorable instance is afforded in the pardon of the supposed son

---

* Exod. xviii. Numb. xv. 32–36.

† 1 Sam. xxi. 11–19.

‡ 2 Sam. i. 5–16. iv. 9–12. xiv. 4–11. 1 Kings ii. 5–9.

of the widow of Tekoah.* Had the king instituted the least inquiry into the facts of the case, he could not have been inveigled into a condemnation of himself.

In the time of this king, the defect, which had thus attended the administration of justice, broke out into a formidable evil. As long as David was king of Judah alone, it was not beyond his power, in some measure at least, to execute the office of judge. But when he became king of all Israel, and his known humanity and love of justice probably induced too many of his subjects, all of whom had free access to his presence, to bring their causes immediately before him, he found himself overpowered with business, and the course of law became tedious, to a degree till then unknown in the east. The complaint does not appear to have been, that unjust decisions were rendered; but that, for want of time to hear them, even clear cases could not be decided. It is probable, that the course of law was still rapid, in comparison with what it is with us; but Asia is so much accustomed to summary justice, that the least delay there seems a great grievance. It was not imputed to negligence in David, that he did not do more than one man could do; and the tears with which Jerusalem, where he was best known, accompanied him in his flight from Absalom, impress us with a favorable idea of his previous government. Absalom, however, availed himself of the opportunity, which the tediousness of justice presented him, to seduce the affections of the people from his father. He placed himself at the entrance of the palace, and questioned the complainants, who came from the provinces to the capital, concerning their suits. Having heard their statements, he told every one that his case was clear, and that it was greatly to be regretted, that the king, oppressed with business, would appoint no one to listen to complaints. At the same time, he expressed a wish, that the king would commit the task to him, in which case

* 2 Sam. xiv. 4–11.

every man might look for speedy justice.* By this artifice, for which a departure from the true intent of the Mosaic constitution furnished the occasion, he excited a general rebellion, which was attended with much bloodshed. Without any battle, the universal discontent of the tribes drove David from the throne; nor did he recover it, till the blood of many citizens was spilt. It is not mentioned in the history, what measures the king took after his restoration, to correct those defects in judicial procedure, which had almost cost him his crown. We know, however, that, in the latter part of his reign, he appointed several thousands of Levites as judges.† With these he probably filled some of the higher tribunals, which administered justice in the king's name. The Levites in the provinces are expressly said to have had charge of all matters pertaining to God and the king.‡ Of course, they must have had power to administer justice in the king's name.

Notwithstanding this, however, the king seems to have reserved the right of pronouncing arbitrary sentence, even in cases where life was concerned. The innocent blood, which Manasseh and Jehoiakim are said to have shed,§ renders this more than probable. It is true that blood may be unjustly shed, with all the forms of law, as in the case of Naboth.‖ But such instances are rare. If a tyrant shed much innocent blood, it affords ground of presumption, that he has the power of pronouncing on life and death in himself. At least European kings, even the most absolute of them, are prohibited from shedding much innocent blood; except, indeed, in the case of the hundreds of thousands, whom they sacrifice in unjust wars.

The mention of war naturally suggests the inquiry, how far the power of the Israelitish sovereigns extended in mili-

* Sam. xv. 2-6.
† 1 Chron. xxiii. 4. xxvi. 29-32.
‡ 1 Chron. xxvi. 30, 32.
§ 2 Kings xxi. 16. xxiv. 4.
‖ 1 Kings xxi. 1-14.

taiy matters. On this point, the sacred book leaves us very much in the dark. Whether the king could, of himself alone, and without consulting the states-general, proclaim war, and conclude peace, is a point, which must be reckoned among the chasms in our knowledge of Hebrew law. Here it would seem, the jus publicum of the Israelites was itself defective, because, on the first choice of a king, they had no ancient usage to guide them; and Moses, who did not himself establish a monarchy, but only permitted its future establishment, had said nothing on this point, but left all to the determination of the Israelites. It is certain, that Saul made his first war, without consulting the people.* The case, however, was one of peculiar urgency; so much so, that he may almost be said to have been forced into hostilities, in defence of the threatened liberties of the Gileadites.† From this case, therefore, nothing positive can be inferred in regard to the general right of the Hebrew sovereigns concerning war.

The royal prerogative extended to ecclesiastical affairs. Indeed, the rights of the kings in reference to matters of this nature, were so great as to excite our wonder, especially when we consider, that the priests and Levites, as a sort of nobility, were intended to balance the power of the kings. They could condemn even the high priest himself to death. Not only did Saul,‡ in his rage and madness, do this; but Solomon§ speaks as if he could have done it, and, out of pure clemency, was satisfied with deposing him. The kings exercised the right of reforming abuses in religion, and gave attention to the management of public worship, as the most efficacious means of promoting religion and morality, and so of securing the obedience of the people to the supreme, invisible, divine Sovereign of Israel. Of this exercise of the royal prerogative, we have many examples, of which none

* 1 Sam. xi. 7.   † 1 Sam. xi. 2.
‡ 1 Sam. xxii. 17, 18.   § 1 Kings ii. 26, 27.

are more memorable, than those of David and Hezekiah. It was altogether suitable to the Hebrew constitution, in which the worship of one only God was the fundamental principle. Under that constitution, false religion was treason to the state, and it was proper, that the kings should have the power of exterminating so dangerous an enemy.

Among the prerogatives of the Hebrew sovereigns must also be placed the right of pardon. That this power should exist somewhere in the state, is highly expedient, and even necessary. A civil law, without all possibility of dispensation, would be subject to very great inconveniences; and would be the occasion of sometimes inflicting very grievous wrong. Without a power of sometimes remitting punishments, innocence might suffer by the very law, which was made for its protection. That the right of pardon was exercised by the Israelitish kings, is beyond a doubt. Nor was the exercise of it always the effect of mere partiality, but of principle and a consideration of circumstances. David not only pardoned his son Absalom, but, in a supposed case, which was laid before him, he granted a murderer his life, who was represented to have killed his brother, because the mother herself interceded in his behalf, and his father's race would have been extinct, had he suffered the penalty of the law.*

I now pass to a consideration of the royal revenues. Moses left no ordinance concerning them. With regard to what later laws and usages introduced on this head, the following particulars may be gleaned from the books of the Old Testament. The several branches of the king's revenue were, presents; tithes; royal demesnes; bond service; the right of pasturage in the Arabian deserts; the spoils of vanquished enemies; the tribute of conquered nations; and, in the end, the profits of a lucrative foreign commerce.

1. Presents. Long before the time of the kings, and even

* 2 Sam. xiv. 4–21.

before the age of Moses, there sprung up in the east a custom, often mentioned in the Persian history, and noticed by
Asiatic travellers, that whoever paid a visit to a person of
higher rank, carried with him a suitable present.   Joseph, as
prime minister of Egypt, received such a present from his
brethren.*   Saul did not presume to wait on Samuel, the
judge, without a present.†   This was, therefore, the most
ancient source of a king's revenue, prior to all tributes and
demesnes.   That Saul actually enjoyed a revenue of this
kind is certain.‡   Whether the tax continued to be paid to
his successors, does not appear.   There is no trace of it after
the reign of Saul.   It is not improbable, that David abolished
so unseemly an impost, and admitted every petitioner into
his presence, without subjecting him to any expense.

2. Tithes.   In 1 Sam. 8 : 15–17, mention is made of the
tenth of the produce of the fields, the vineyards, and the
flocks, as the right of the future king.   This, on his actual
appointment, was the third tenth which every Israelite had
to pay.   The first was given to the Levites ;§ the second was
appropriated to the sacrifice-feasts, to which were invited
priests, Levites, friends, orphans, and strangers.‖   None but
a very fruitful country could have borne the burden of an
impost to the extent of three tenths of its produce.

3. Royal demesnes.   Samuel mentions a demesne, to which
the king would have a right; for, says he, " he will take your
fields, and your vineyards, and your oliveyards, even the best
of them, and give them to his servants ;"¶ i. e. in lieu of salaries.   This seems inconsistent with the Mosaic law, which
divided the whole of Palestine among the Israelites, and prohibited the alienation of their land.   Nevertheless, it is certain, that the king had a demesne.**   It is likely, that at first

* Gen. xliii. 11–25.   † 1 Sam. ix. 7.   ‡ 1 Sam. x. 27, xvi. 20.
§ Numb. xviii. 21–32.   Levit. xxvii. 30–33.
‖ Deut. xii. 17–19.   xiv. 22–29.   xxvi. 12–15.
¶ 1 Sam. viii. 14.   ** Eccl. ii. 4–6.   1 Chron. xxvii. 26–31.

the kings took possession only of the spots, which had not been previously appropriated and improved, of which there might be found a considerable number, particularly beyond Jordan, and about the rills in the Arabian deserts. Still, that will not sufficiently explain the passage, cited a little above; for it is there said, the king would take the best parts of every sort of landed property.

We must, therefore, seek some other mode of providing him with demesnes. It is certain, that the kings exercised the right of bestowing the inheritance of state criminals upon other persons.* It is not improbable, that they availed themselves of the same right, to increase the royal demesnes by confiscations. Indeed, we have an instance of this, in the case of Nabal, who was stoned on a false charge of treason, and his estate annexed to the king's demesnes.† This mode of increasing their lands must have formed a strong temptation to wicked kings, to put innocent persons to death for pretended crimes, in order to seize and appropriate their property. Need we wonder, that, in the Hebrew history, we find so frequent mention of the shedding of innocent blood?

All this is confirmed, and rendered certain, by what we find in Ezekiel. That prophet was favored with a vision of the future reformation of the Israelitish church and state.‡ In it he tells us, that the prince will then have his own portion, which he must neither alienate nor enlarge. It is very distinctly enjoined upon the king not to take the people's inheritance away from them by oppression, and not to thrust them out of their possessions. It is further enjoined upon him not to give lands to his family out of the people's portions, but out of his own. This clearly indicates the practices, and, I may add, the abuses, of preceding times.

The olive and sycamore grounds, in that part of the territory of Judah, which lay nearest the sea, and was called the

---

* 2 Sam. xvi. 4.   † 1 Kings xxi. 15, 16.
‡ Ezek. xlv. 7, 8.   xlvii. 16–18.

lowlands, belonged to the king's demesnes. It is distinctly stated, that David placed one officer over the trees in that district, and another over the oil-stores.*

That the kings assigned a part of the royal demesnes to their servants, in lieu of salary, appears unquestionable.† At a time, when the sovereign could be possessed of but little money, this was the natural way of maintaining and rewarding his servants.

4. Bond service. For the cultivation of their lands, the Israelitish kings, governing a country where slavery was permitted, would naturally require servile labor. Accordingly, we find bond service mentioned by Samuel among the royal rights, established by usage among the neighboring kingdoms, and which would be claimed and exercised by the Hebrew sovereigns, whenever monarchy should be instituted.‡ In process of time, these services seem to have been increased and altered, so that they became very burdensome and very distasteful to the Israelites.§ It was probably this, which gave occasion, first to the complaints, and then to the rebellion, in the reign of Rehoboam.

5. The right of pasturage in the Arabian deserts. This right belonged to the king, in common with his subjects. We find David taking advantage of this privilege, and keeping large herds of cattle, sheep, goats, asses, and camels, partly in Sharon, and partly in Arabia; the greater part of them, no doubt, in the latter place.‖ Among the officers, who had charge of them, two Arabians are mentioned, Obil, the Ishmaelite, superintendant of the camels, and Jaziz, the Hagarite, superintendant of the sheep.

6. The spoils of vanquished enemies partly flowed into the royal treasury.¶

7. Among the royal revenues must be reckoned the tribute

* 1 Chron. xxvii. 28.   † 1 Sam. viii. 14. xxii. 7.
‡ 1 Sam. viii. 12, 16.   § 1 Kings v. 17, 18.
‖ 1 Chron. xxvii. 29–31.   ¶ 2 Sam. viii. iii. 12.

paid by conquered nations. These are often mentioned under the name of gifts.*

8. Commerce. Solomon discovered a new source of royal revenue, which must have been very productive. He engaged in an extensive and lucrative foreign commerce, trading chiefly in gold, silver, precious stones, spices, linen, and horses.†

CHAPTER V.

The Hebrew Senate.

THIS was another department of the Hebrew government, and one of the bonds of union between the tribes of Israel. The study of this part of the constitution is not without its difficulty. The persons composing the senatorial council, the powers vested in it, and the functions discharged by it, are points involved in no little obscurity. All the information, which I find in the sacred books, touching this subject, is embodied in the present chapter.

· According to the Hebrew polity, as we have seen,‡ every tribe, and even every city, had its senate of princes, or elders, as well as a more popular assembly. Some such institution seems to be essential in every well-balanced government. A council of sages, venerable on account of their age, wisdom, and dignity, is necessary to check the rashness and haste of popular assemblies. Accordingly, we find, that free governments have always had senates of some kind, to balance the power of the people, to prepare matters of public business, and

* 1 Kings iv 21. Ps. lxxii. 10. 2 Sam. viii. 6.   † 1 Kings x.   ‡ B. 2. C. 3.

to propose measures of state, in some degree of maturity, for the action of the more popular branch of the government.* That the commonwealth of Israel had a council of this sort, does not admit of a reasonabla doubt. This is rendered certain by the frequent mention in the Hebrew history of the princes and elders of Israel, and the distinction, many times made, between the princes and the congregation. We are now to inquire when this body was instituted, what it was, and how long it continued.

Bertram† has well observed, that the number of seventy elders, appointed by the law of God, was not so much a new institution, as the continuation of a former usage; as God rather confirmed than new instituted many things at Mount Sinai, which were ancient customs of the fathers. Bishop Sherlock‡ also takes notice, "that every tribe had its own princes and judges," even while they yet remained in Egypt. When Moses was first sent to the children of Israel, to inform them, that Jehovah had visited them, and seen what was done unto them in Egypt, he was commanded to gather the elders of Israel together, and deliver the message to them.§ This direction was punctually followed, for it is said: "Moses and Aaron went and gathered the elders of the children of Israel."‖ It is a material observation here, that, besides the princes of tribes, explicit mention is made, in the same period of the Hebrew history, of the heads of families, or clans.¶ Of these, as we learn from a subsequent part of the history,** there were fifty-eight, who, being added to the twelve princes of the tribes, make up the number seventy.

There is little doubt, that, even before the exodus of Israel out of Egypt, these chiefs of tribes and heads of clans formed a council of state, a kind of provisional senate. They were

* Lowm. Civ. Gov. Heb. c. 9.
† De Rep. Hebr. p. 51, cited by Lowm. c. 9.
‡ Dissert. 3.   § Exod. iii. 16.   ‖ Exod. iv. 29.
¶ Exod. vi. 14 seqq.   ** Numb. xxvi.

regarded and addressed as persons of chief dignity in their respective tribes. That they were clothed with some sort of authority, is evident from what one of the Hebrews said to Moses : " Who made thee a prince and a judge over us ?"* It is, moreover, apparent, that these dignitaries formed an organized body, in whose counsels and resolutions the tribes themselves were united into one nation ; since Moses addressed them, not as princes of particular tribes, but as elders of Israel.† It deserves, also, particular attention, that when the Israelites left Egypt, it was in hosts, or by their armies, that they did it.‡ They did not go as a confused and disorderly rabble, but marched in battalions, each under its own officers and its own standard. This observation, though of little moment in itself, is, nevertheless, important for the inference, which it supports. Let it be remembered, that the Israelites left Egypt in great haste. Now, it would have been impossible for them to go in hosts, or squadrons, if there had not been persons, previously known and recognized as commanders. They could not otherwise have known under what standard they were to march, or by what particular officers they were to be led. Obviously, it would not have been practicable to organize an army of two and a half million people, at the instant of departure. It would seem, therefore, that, while the Israelites were yet in Egypt, the princes of tribes must have been acknowledged as general officers of the tribes, and the chiefs of families as subordinate officers, commanding their respective clans.§ It was, in all likelihood, the same seventy, who, at the giving of the law, were summoned to go up unto the Lord, with Moses and Aaron.|| What places it out of all doubt, that these officers were an organized body, and acted as a council of state, or senate of sages, is a law contained in the tenth chapter of Numbers.¶ Moses is there directed to make two silver trumpets. When both of them

* Exod. xi. 14.   † Exod. xii. 21, 28.   ‡ Exod. xii. 41, 51.
§ Lowm. Civ. Gov. Heb. c. 9. || Exod. xxiv. 1.   ¶ Vv. 1–4.

were blown, the whole congregation was to assemble; when
only one of them, the princes and heads of the thousands of
Israel were to come together for the despatch of public
business. But this law was given, before the body, which is
the principal subject of this chapter, was called into being,
and, indeed, before the events occurred, which were the special occasion of its institution.

The Israelites lay encamped at the base of Mount Sinai for
the space of a year. At the end of that time, the trumpets
sounded, the cloud was taken up from off the tabernacle of
testimony, and the children of Israel took their journeys out
of the wilderness of Sinai. Their first halting place was the
wilderness of Paran.* Here the people complained bitterly
for want of flesh. Their murmurs displeased the Lord, and
his anger was kindled greatly. Moses also was displeased,
and greatly afflicted at so unpromising a state and prospect
of affairs. He, in his turn, complained, that he found the
burden of government too heavy for his individual strength.
" I am not able," says he, "to bear all this people alone,
because it is too heavy for me." By divine direction, and in
order to alleviate the weight of the burden, that oppressed
him, Moses instituted a council of seventy elders, who might
share his functions, support his authority, and promote his
views.† It was a supreme senate, designed to take part with
him in the government. As it consisted of persons of age,
worth, experience, and respectability, it would serve materially to support his power and influence among the people
in general. It would unite a number of powerful families
together, from their being all associated with Moses in the
government, and would materially strengthen the union of
the tribes.‡

A detailed account of the origin of this body is given in
the eleventh chapter of Numbers. The general mode of or-

---

* Numb. x. 11–13.   † Numb. xi.
‡ Mich. Comment. Art. 50.
37

ganization is related in these words :*—" And the Lord said
unto Moses, Gather unto me seventy men of the elders of
Israel, whom thou knowest to be the elders of the people, and
officers over them : and bring them unto the tabernacle of the
congregation, that they may stand there with thee. And I
will come down and talk with thee there ; and I will take of
the spirit which is upon thee, and will put it upon them : and
they shall bear the burden of the people with thee, that thou
bear it not thyself alone. And Moses went out, and told the
people the words of the Lord, and gathered the seventy men
of the elders of the people, and set them round about the tabernacle. And the Lord came down in a cloud, and spake
unto him, and took of the spirit that was upon him, and gave
it unto the seventy elders : and it came to pass, that when the
spirit rested upon them, they prophesied, and did not cease.
But there remained two of the men in the camp, the name of
the one was Eldad, and the name of the other Medad : and
the spirit rested upon them; and they were of them that
were written, but went not out unto the tabernacle : and they
prophesied in the camp."

" Three things," says Salvador,† " are here worthy of note.
The candidate for the senatorial office must be a man of the
people ; he must be an elder of the people ; and he must have
been previously elevated by the voice of the people to some
public trust." That is to say, he must be a tried man ; a man
in whom the people put confidence after trial ; and a man of
experience in public affairs.

The seventy senators, chosen from among the elders and
officers, were to be brought to the tabernacle of the congregation, that they might stand there with Moses. In other
words, they were to be solemnly inaugurated, and consecrated
to this service, that they might be a permanent council, to
assist Moses in the government of the people. To give the
greater weight to their decisions, God promises, that he would

---

* Vv. 16, 17, 24–26.   † Hist. Inst. de Moïse, 1. 2. C. 2.

talk with Moses, to declare, suggests bishop Patrick,* that he appointed them to be assistants to Moses in the government. The further promise was added, that the Lord would take of the spirit, which was upon Moses, and would put it upon them; that is, as again suggested by bishop Patrick,* he would confer upon these men wisdom, judgment, courage, and other needful gifts of government, with which Moses was endowed. To give assurance of the fulfilment of this promise, it came to pass, that, when the spirit rested upon them, they prophesied. The spirit of prophecy was a manifest token, that they were chosen by God to be coadjutors of Moses, that they were approved by him, and that they had received from him a spirit of government.†

Yet these men were not chosen by God alone. The people concurred in the election. This is very evident from the history cited above. The names of the candidates are there said to have been written, or inscribed; a very important statement. In what ·manner were they inscribed? The text does not inform us; and the field is left open to conjecture. Let it be premised here, that, as the senators were to bear the common burden of government with Moses, which concerned all the tribes, and that they were specially intended to prevent mutiny and sedition, it would be highly suitable, that there should be an equal number from each tribe, and that they should be persons, whom the tribes themselves approved. On this point, Hebrew and christian writers are unanimous. I now return to the question, How were the names of the candidates inscribed? Did Moses himself write the names of the persons, whom he judged competent and qualified for the senatorial office, and submit them to the approval of the tribes? This would have been to deprive the tribes of one of their fundamental rights, that of designating their own magistrates. Besides, Moses was not charged with appointing the senate, but with assembling it.

* In loc.   † Lowm. Civ. Gov. Heb. C. 9.

It is not probable, therefore, that this is what is meant by their names being written. Did the citizens, then, of the respective tribes, themselves elect, by ballot, the persons, whom they believed most worthy of the dignity, and best fitted to discharge its functions usefully? This supposition seems the most reasonable. In the selection and appointment of magistrates, Moses demanded, not simply wise men, but such as were known among the tribes. How could this demand be answered, otherwise than by a manifestation of individual opinion? The history of the Acts of the Apostles sheds light upon this point, and lends confirmation to this conjecture. The apostles incorporated the principles of the Mosaic constitution into their spiritual society. Needing certain functionaries, they convene the whole body of the disciples, and after the example of their ancient lawgiver, they say to them: "Look ye out seven men, of honest report, and full of wisdom."* The proposition pleased the assembly. Thereupon, they themselves selected the functionaries, as suggested; and the apostles, in accordance with a long established national usage, inducted them into office by the solemn imposition of hands.† Here, again, I observe by the way, we see the concurrence of the oracle and the people in the election of civil rulers.

Such, then, was the general spirit of the law. Without insisting on the correctness of this or that particular mode of selection, the fundamental principle, which is well worthy to arrest our attention, is plain and obvious. The law institutes a great national council, or senate, composed, not of priests, but of civilians; not of men belonging to privileged classes, or possessing vast estates, but of men wise, prudent, able, of good repute, fearing God, and already skilled in affairs of state; not politicians merely, but statesmen, sages, patriots. The name of seniors, or senators, belonged to the members of the great council. It is probable, that men of advanced age

* Acts. vi. 3.   † Salvador, l. 2. c. 2.

were commonly chosen into it; yet young men, of superior endowments, sometimes gained admission. This we learn from the speech of such an one in the Wisdom of Solomon,* who boasts, that in spite of his youth, he had obtained an honorable distinction for wisdom among the senators.

The design and functions of this institution are points of chief importance in this inquiry. The law declares, in general terms, that the senators were to bear the burden of the people with Moses, that he might not bear it alone. By this can hardly be meant the ordinary administration of justice, for provision had been made for that in the institution of the Jethronian judges. So far, therefore, as the senate was to assist Moses in judiciary matters, it could only be in those greater and more important causes, which were to be brought before him on appeal, or those difficult questions, which the judges of the inferior courts themselves referred to him. But this was not the principal end of its institution. The occasion of its appointment is a proof of this. It was instituted to crush a rebellion. But for such an end, of what use would a mere court of judicature be? On the other hand, a council of sages, a supreme senate, composed of men venerable for their age, and of approved wisdom and integrity, would be of the greatest efficacy. There can be no doubt, therefore, that these seventy were to be permanent assistants of Moses in his councils. They were to aid him with their advice on all occasions, to preserve peace and good order among the people, to strengthen the sentiment of loyalty to the constitution, and to prevent those mutinies and seditions, which, if permitted to break out and rage, would in the end prove fatal to the government and the nation. "In this view," observes Lowman,† "the seventy elders will appear to be designed, not only as a standing court of law and equity, to assist Moses as judge in causes of greater consequence, and in appeals, but to assist the judge with their ad-

* C. 8. V. 10. seqq.   † Civ. Gov. Heb. c. 9.

vice on every occasion. This was properly to bear the burthen of the people together with Moses, that he might not
bear it himself alone. For now the judge would not bear all
the envy or ill will of the people, when dissatisfied or uneasy
with any part of the administration; for the common people,
though they know very little of the reasons of any administration, are yet apt to think every thing wrong, that does not
please them, or which is attended with difficulties to themselves or the public. Now, a council of seventy persons, of
the most approved wisdom and integrity, would at least share
this burthen among them all, instead of throwing the whole
on one man. And it would be, moreover, an ease to the
judge's own mind, and make him more resolved in any
counsel to be taken or executed, when it should be with the
advice and approbation of a multitude of counsellors, in
which there is wisdom and safety. And, finally, it was
proper to give authority and respect to such orders as should
be made by advice of persons, whom the people themselves
had approved and chosen, as eminent for their wisdom and
integrity. Consider, then, this court as a standing senate,
always at hand, or as a constant privy council to the judge,
and we have a most wise provision for the easier and better
government of the whole nation; and this will make a considerable part of the states-general of the united tribes."

Still, it must be borne in mind, that the senate was not the
government; it was only a constituent part of the government. It was but the council of the nation; the head, as it
were, of the general diet. In all important questions, its
decisions were to be submitted to the congregation, which,
by its approbation, enacted them into laws. Of this we have
a clear proof in the twentieth chapter of Judges, where the
ancients are recorded to have called upon the general assembly of the people to deliberate upon a matter, and give their
decision. Even when the Hebrews demanded a king, they
were far from wishing to change this part of the constitution.

Hence it has been observed by the abbé Guénée,* that " it was always the duty of the king to govern the nation according to the laws. Their authority was neither despotic nor arbitrary. The senate, composed of the most distinguished members of all the tribes, served him as a council. He took their advice in all important affairs; and if any thing occurred, in which the interest of the whole nation was concerned, the congregation, that is to say, the assembly of the people, was convoked. The senate proposed, the congregation decided, and the king executed." A memorable example of this we have in 1 Chron. 13 : 1–8. David, after consulting with his counsellors of state, in regard to the removal of the ark, refers the final decision of the question to the congregation of Israel. They, upon deliberation, approve and enact. Immediately thereupon, David proceeds to execute the decree. But it must not be inferred from hence, that the general assembly never took the initiative, much less that it had not the right of so doing. Moses tells the Hebrews, that on a certain occasion he made a proposition to them, which they approved and accepted; whereas, on another occasion they proposed a certain measure to him, which, meeting his cordial approbation, he accepted and executed.†

Such, then, were the leading powers of the Hebrew senate. Let us inquire by what limitations they were confined within their just bounds. The Jewish law opposed itself invincibly to the existence of great landed proprietors, and thus prevented the members of the senate from uniting the influence of vast territorial estates to that which they derived from their office. The senator received no salary for his services. His age and the conditions of eligibility to the senatorial dignity served as a guaranty of his integrity. The decrees to which he contributed, extended to his children, his friends, and himself. Out of the senatorial seat, he was but a simple

* Lettres de quelques Juifs à Voltaire, tom. 2, lettr. 2.
† Deut. i. 13, 22, 23.

COMMENTARIES ON THE

Israelite. The office was not hereditary; and the son of a senator was no more, in the eye of the law, than the son of the humblest citizen. These, however, were rather moral than legal restraints. But the sacerdotal magistracy, engaged by its very nature to the guardianship of the law; the prophets, those stern state censors and moralists, who launched the most unsparing denunciations against all, who in any way abused the trusts confided to them; the decisions of the oracle; and the necessity of the intervention of the congregation of Israel in important questions, furnished guaranties, of a positive and effective character, against the usurpation and tyranny of the Hebrew senate. Here is a system of moral and legal restrictions upon power, to which it would be difficult to find a parallel in other governments. The remark of Blackstone respecting the English constitution, is equally applicable to the Hebrew polity, viz. that every branch of it supports and is supported, regulates and is regulated, by the rest. The senate, the congregation, the chief magistrate, the oracle, the Levitical order, and the prophetical office, constituted so many checks upon each other's power, so many dykes and embankments to restrain the exercise of tyranny, so many combined forces to give the machine of government a safe direction, and cause it to move in the line of the public liberty and happiness.

It has been a question with some, whether the senate of seventy, instituted by Moses on the occasion of the rebellion in Paran, continued permanent. Calmet* endeavored to discredit the continued existence of this council. In this opinion he is followed by Michaelis.† But the common and more probable opinion is, that it was a permanent body. Bossuet‡ says: "To maintain the law in its vigor, Moses formed an assembly of seventy counsellors, which may be termed the senate of Israel, and the perpetual council of the nation."

* Dissert. sur la Police des anciens Hébreux.
† Hist. Univ. Pt. 2, § 3.   ‡ Comment. Art. 50.

The abbé de Fleury* observes: "As often as mention is made in the scripture of assemblies and public affairs, the elders (or senators) are put in the first place, and sometimes named alone. Thence comes the expression in the Psalms, exhorting to praise God in the congregation of the people, and in the seat of the elders, that is, the public council." There is, indeed, a strong antecedent probability against the abolition of this council on the death of Moses; for, as Basnage† well suggests, "if that great legislator needed such a council, during his life, it must have been still more necessary to those who succeeded him in the administration of the republic." Salvador‡ has an able if not a convincing argument, to prove, that the senate is often designated in the sacred books by the name of its president, or of the general judge, in the same manner as the senate of Venice was called "most serene prince." Thus, when the Hebrews say, that a man judged Israel, he thinks the expression signifies, that he governed in concurrence with the senate. The argument, by which he supports this view, is not without force; but the reader, who would judge of it, is referred to the original work. Undoubtedly, the senate underwent many changes in the progress of time. It would be interesting, but it does not belong to my present work, to trace these revolutions. I, therefore, dismiss the subject with the remark, that, what-ever vicissitudes it experienced, it appears always to have maintained its existence.

A difficulty will have occurred to the reflecting reader, as he has followed me through the above detail. The chapter professes to treat of the Hebrew senate; but, in reality, it has exhibited two distinct councils, one instituted in Egypt, and the other in the wilderness, without attempting to adjust or explain their relation to each other. This is a difficulty, not a

* Manners of the Anc. Israelites, c. 21.
† Histoire des Juifs, 1. 2, c. 2.
‡ Hist. des Inst. de Moïse, 1. 2. c. 2.

little formidable in appearance. Which of these was the senate of Israel? Did the latter supersede the former? Or did they co-exist, and in that case, was there any union between them? I have little doubt, that Lowman* has hit upon the true solution of the difficulty, and I shall here condense the view, which he has taken of this part of the Hebrew constitution. His idea is, that the original senate, composed of the princes of tribes and heads of families, continued to exist, after the institution of the sanhedrim. The grounds of this opinion are as follows: When the children of Reuben and Gad came with a petition to have their settlement assigned them on the east of Jordan, they came and spake unto Moses and Eleazar the priest, and unto the princes of the congregation.† Though this was long after the institution of the sanhedrim, yet the princes of the congregation are assembled to consider the proposal; as they had been before in the case of female succession,‡ and as they were afterwards upon the regulation of the marriage of heiresses.§ When Joshua made a league with the Gibeonites, it was confirmed by the princes of the congregation.|| Other instances of the like nature might be cited, but let these suffice. Now, as these persons are described by the titles of princes and chief fathers of the children of Israel, it is plain, that the same persons must be meant, who were princes of tribes and heads of families before the institution of the sanhedrim, and whose rank and authority were not taken away by the formation of that court. They were still the great council or senate of the nation. But what, then, becomes of the sanhedrim, instituted by Moses? Both classes of officers are spoken of in such a way, as to show, that they were employed in the great affairs of the nation. Why, then, may we not conceive of the sanhedrim as a select senate, a sort of privy council, while all the princes of Israel still had session

* Civ. Gov. Heb. c. 9.   † Numb. xxxii. 1, 2.   ‡ Ibid. 27.
§ Ibid. 36. || Joshua ix. 15.

and vote in the great and general council of the nation, which, when assembled, was called by the ancient style, the princes of the congregation. This may be the reason, why the elders of the sanhedrim have so little apparent notice taken of them; for, when the general national senate was assembled, they were considered only as particular members of it.

Lowman conceives, that the constitution of the old parliament of Paris may give a pretty accurate idea of the senate of Israel. The kings assembled the great men of the kingdom, and these assemblies were called the king's court or parliament. The great men, who attended these assemblies were styled barons of the kingdom, and afterwards peers of France. They were the bishops, dukes, earls, and all the great tenants, who held immediately of the crown; but as it was not easy to examine fully many of the affairs, which came before them, the kings gave commission to men of abilities, to assist with their care and counsels; and these counsellors were called masters of parliament. In the parliament of Paris, then, all the peers of France had session and vote, but the ordinary business was transacted by a select number of counsellors. Somewhat after this manner, it is most likely, the senate of Israel was constituted. The elders of the sanhedrim formed a select council, to assist the chief magistrate on ordinary occasions; but on occasions of greater moment, and especially when the states-general were convened, the national senate of Israel consisted of princes of the tribes, heads of families, and elders of the sanhedrim. But however this might be, and whoever the persons were who composed the great council of the Hebrew nation, it is clear and undoubted, that, under the style of princes, chief fathers, or elders, there was a senate of the whole republic, who assisted the judge with their advice in affairs of moment. And this was a second bond of political union between the tribes.

CHAPTER VI.

The Hebrew Commons.

IN treating this subject, three inquiries present themselves, viz. 1. Whether a house of commons, or popular assembly, formed a part of the Hebrew constitution? 2. If so, who composed it? 3. What were its powers?

The first of these interrogatories must be answered in the affirmative. It is an undoubted fact, that there was a popular branch in the Hebrew government. This body was called by different titles, as the congregation, the congregation of Israel, all the assembly, all the children of Israel, and the whole congregation of the Lord. Moses was directed to make two silver trumpets, and the following law was enacted respecting the use of them. "And when they shall blow with them, all the assembly shall assemble themselves to thee at the door of the tabernacle of the congregation. And if they blow but with one trumpet, then the princes, which are heads of the thousands of Israel, shall gather themselves unto thee."* Other scriptures might be cited, but this passage alone is decisive; and, indeed, there is no · dispute on this point among those who have written on the Hebrew institutions.

In regard to the second question, viz. as to who composed the congregation, there is less unanimity of opinion. Lowman† does not doubt, from its being described in expressions so full and emphatic, as " all the congregation of Israel,"

* Numb. x. 2–4.   † Civ. Gov. Heb. c. 8.

"the whole congregation of Jehovah," and the like, that
every free Israelite had a right to vote in this assembly.
Harrington* is of the same opinion. He says: "While the
whole people was an army, Moses could propose to them in
body, or under their staves, or standards of their camps; then
he needed not, and so he used not, any representative." Both
these writers think, that there were different manners of
holding this assembly, the people sometimes voting in mass,
and sometimes by deputies. The abbé Guénée† holds the like
view. "The assemblies under Moses," he observes, "while
the Hebrews formed one great army, very much resembled
the assemblies of the people at Athens, at Lacedaemon, and
at Rome; but afterwards, it would seem, they were often
composed of deputies, or representatives of the people, not
unlike the parliaments of England and the states of Holland."
Salvador,‡ the learned Jewish author, is of the same way of
thinking. He regards it as the inalienable right of every
Hebrew citizen to have session and vote in the general assembly, basing it, however, upon the false principle, borrowed
from Rousseau,§ that the people, properly so called, have that
in common with the Deity, that they cannot be rigidly represented but by themselves. Jahn‖ also expresses the opinion,
that, at least upon very important occasions, as many of the
common people as chose to attend, took part in the deliberations and resolves of this body.

I cannot concur in the view of these learned men. More
just and scriptural appears to me the opinion of Michaelis,¶
that the Hebrew people never voted as a pure democracy, but
always, in the wilderness as well as after their settlement in
Canaan, by known and authorized representatives. His ar-

* Commonwealth of Israel, c. 3.
† Lettres de quelques Juifs à Voltaire, Pt. 4. L. 2. Note.
‡ Hist. des Insts. de Moïse, l. 2. c. 2.
§ Contr. Soc. l. 4. c. 15.   ‖ Heb. Com. B. 2. S. 14.
¶ Art. 45.

gument in support of this view seems to me conclusive ; and
I therefore present it in his own words : " From various passages in the Pentateuch, we find that Moses, at making
known any laws, had to convene the whole congregation of
Israel ; and in like manner, in the book of Joshua, we see,
that when diets were held, the whole congregation were assembled. If on such occasions every individual had had to
give his vote, everything would certainly have been democratic in the highest degree ; but it is scarcely conceivable how,
without very particular regulations made for the purpose,
(which, however, we nowhere find,) order could have been
preserved in an assembly of six hundred thousand men, their
votes accurately numbered, and acts of violence prevented.
If, however, we consider that, while Moses is said to have
spoken to the whole congregation, he could not possibly be
heard by six hundred thousand people, (for what human
voice could be sufficiently strong to be so?) all our fears and
difficulties will vanish ; for this circumstance alone must convince any one, that Moses could only have addressed himself
to a certain number of persons, deputed to represent the rest
of the Israelites. Accordingly, in Numb. 1 : 16, we find
mention of such persons. In contradistinction to the common
Israelites, they are there denominated ' those wont to be called
to the convention.' In the 16th chapter of the same book,
ver. 2, they are styled ' chiefs of the community, that are
called to the convention.' I notice this passage particularly,
because it appears from it, that two hundred and fifty persons
of this description, who rose up against Moses, became to
him objects of extreme terror ; which they could not have
been, if their voices had not been, at the same time, the
voices of their families and tribes. Still more explicit, and
to the point, is the passage, Deut. 29 : 9, where Moses, in a
speech to the whole people, says, ' Ye stand this day all of
you before the Lord your God, your heads, your tribes, (that
is, chiefs of tribes,) your elders, your scribes, all Israel, in

fants, wives, strangers that are in your camp, from the hewer of wood, to the drawer of water.' Now, as Moses could not possibly speak loud enough to be heard by two millions and a half of people, (for to so many did the Israelites amount, women and children included,) it must be manifest, that the first-named persons represented the people, to whom they again repeated the words of Moses. Whether these representatives were on every occasion obliged to collect and declare the sense of their constituents, or whether, like the members of the English house of commons, they acted in the plenitude of their own power for the general good, 'without taking instructions from their constituents, I find nowhere expressly determined ; but, methinks, from a perusal of the Bible, I can scarcely doubt, that the latter was the case. Who these representatives were, may, in some measure, be understood from Josh. 23: 2, and 24: 1. They would seem to have been of two sorts. To some, their office as judges gave a right to appear in the assembly ; and these were not necessarily of the same family in which they exercised that office. Others, again, had a seat and a voice in the diet, as the heads of families."

But the particular constitution of the popular branch of the Hebrew government, as to the persons composing it, is a matter comparatively indifferent. The material part of the inquiry, which will be found eminently worthy of our attention, relates to the functions, which that body exercised. These were of a grave and important kind, and such as to evince the supremacy of the popular will under this constitution. A few instances, chosen out of many, will illustrate the powers confided to this department of the government. We shall find them broad and comprehensive, extending to the election of magistrates, the management of foreign relations, the adjudication of civil and criminal causes, and the care of ecclesiastical affairs.

In the nineteenth chapter of Exodus, we have a deeply in-

teresting account of the manner in which God was chosen
king of the Hebrew people, and the laws adopted, which he
proposed for their government. Moses, having received a
commission to make the proposition to the nation, " came
and called for the elders of the people, and laid before their
faces all these words, which Jehovah commanded him. And
all the people answered together, and said, all that Jehovah
hath spoken we will do. And Moses returned the words of
the people unto Jehovah." Here we have an account of the
form in which questions were proposed and resolved in the
national legislature. It is the just and philosophical remark
of Lowman on this passage, that legal forms explain the true
powers of any part of a constitution much better than general
arguments. Let the reader observe how closely this form of
voting resembles that called a rogatio among the Romans.
A proposal from the senate to the people was in these words ;
" Is it your will, O Romans, and do you resolve it ?" To
which the response, if affirmative, was : " We will, and resolve it." In the above election, the elders only are mentioned by name; but it is manifest from the expression, " all
the people answered and said," that it was the act of the
general diet of Israel. The term elders was not restricted to
any one class of functionaries, and it is certainly sometimes
applied to the members of the popular branch. And here, I
may observe by the way, we have another proof, that the
congregation was a representative body, and not the whole
body of the people. It was certainly a select assembly,
which, on this occasion, responded to the proposal of Moses ;
yet it is stated in the broadest terms, " all the people answered."

The appointment of Joshua to be the successor of Moses
appears, from the record·of it in the twenty-seventh chapter
of Numbers, to have been made, or at least confirmed, by the
popular vote in the national diet. He was to be set before
" all the congregation ;" and, when thus proposed, he appears

to have been elected by their vote to the chief magistracy of Israel.

So also Saul, though designated to the regal office by the lot, was nevertheless chosen king by the great national diet, —the congregation of the people. Afterwards, to quiet the dissatisfaction of certain malecontents, Samuel summoned the people by their representatives to Gilgal, " to renew the kingdom there ;" that is, to elect Saul king a second time. " And all the people went to Gilgal," says the historian, " and there they made Saul king before the Lord in Gilgal."* When Adonijah, in anticipation of his father David's death, endeavored to seize upon the supreme authority, the latter, by a royal edict, caused Solomon to be proclaimed king. But he immediately summoned the parliament of the realm, and proposed Solomon as his successor; and the history adds, " They made Solomon, the son of David, king the second time. * * * Then Solomon sat on the throne, * * * and all Israel obeyed him,"—evidently as being the sovereign of their own choice.† Josephus informs us that, when Moses announced the appointment of Aaron to the priesthood by Jehovah, he took pains to impress the assembly with a sense of his brother's great merits ; whereupon, he adds, the He- brews gave their approbation to him whom God had ap- pointed. Jeroboam is expressly said to have been made king by the congregation of Israel.‡

These instances sufficiently evince the authority of the popular voice, through its representatives, in the election of the national rulers.

The management of the foreign relations of the nation belonged, in part, to the congregation. This is evident from what occurred in the case of the Gibeonites, soon after the passage of the Jordan. Joshua, deceived by their plausible tale, made with them a treaty of peace, which was confirmed

* 1 Sam. x. 17–27. † 1 Chron. xxix. 22, 23.
‡ 1 Kings xii. 20.

by the oath of the senate of princes. But when the imposition was discovered, the congregation was loud in its complaints, and could with difficulty be induced to give, its assent
to the arrangement. It seems a fair inference from this relation, that a convention of peace, though made by judge and
senate, still needed the ratification of the people, in their
national assembly, in order to its full and binding authority.

The jurisdiction of the congregation extended also to civil
causes. The question of female succession, in default of male
heirs, was, by petition from the daughters of Zelophehad,
laid before Moses, the priest, the princes, and all the congregation. Their father, they alleged, had died without sons;
and their request was, that they might be constituted his
heirs. The question, being a novel one, was referred, by the
other departments of the government, to the oracle. The response was, that the demand of the young women was reasonable, and ought to be granted. Thereupon a decree was passed
to that effect, and a law was enacted to settle the matter of
female succession for all after ages. Here, by the way, we
have the union of the tribes in the four departments of the
government pretty plainly referred to. Here is the chief
magistrate of the nation. Here is the oracle of Jehovah.
Here is the senate of princes. And here, finally, is the congregation of all Israel.* The body, before which this question was brought, was an assembly of the states-general of
Israel, composed of judge, senate, and commons; and the history of the affair shows plainly, that questions of this nature
were properly, according to the Hebrew constitution, brought
before them. ,

To the congregation belonged likewise the right of taking
cognizance of criminal matters. It was expressly charged
with judging between the slayer and the avenger of blood:
"Then the congregation shall judge between the slayer and
the revenger of blood according to these judgments: And the

* Numb. xxvii. 1-9.

congregation shall deliver the slayer out of the hand of the revenger of blood, and the congregation shall restore him to the city of his refuge, whither he was fled : and he shall abide in it unto the death of the high priest, which was anointed with the holy oil."* It matters not whether the congregation here spoken of was provincial or national; for, whatever rights vested in the lower assembly, would undoubtedly inhere in the higher.

An instance of the power of the Hebrew commons in criminal questions occurs in the history of Saul, and is too interesting to be passed in silence.† Upon a certain occasion, Saul had given an order, forbidding his army to taste food, during a day's encounter with the Philistines. Whoever violated the prohibition was devoted to certain death by the oath of the king. Jonathan, to whose prudence and valor, under God, the victory was entirely owing, ignorant both of the order and the anathema, and worn down with the fatigues of battle, had eaten a little wild honey. Upon his confession of the fault, Saul fiercely exclaims, "God do so to me, and more also; for thou shalt surely die, Jonathan." This is very positive, and seems irreversible. Yet the people step in, and say, " Shall Jonathan die, who hath wrought this great salvation for Israel ? God forbid ! As Jehovah liveth, there shall not an hair of his head fall to the ground. So the people rescued (literally redeemed) Jonathan." Bishop Patrick truly observes on this place, that the people did not rescue Jonathan by violence or force. Yet his further opinion, and that of the learned Grotius, that the rescue was effected by petition, seems not at all consistent with the expressions employed. " As Jehovah liveth, there shall not an hair of his head fall to the ground," has very little the sound of an humble request to a master. It is more like the voice of conscious authority, clear and strong in the expression of an undoubted right. Neither is the expression, " redeemed Jonathan," properly

* Numb. xxxv. 24, 25.   † 1 Sam. xiv. 42 seqq.

descriptive of an act of mutiny and rebellion. There remains, then, but the conclusion, that it was an exercise of rightful authority, whereby the unconscious offender was pardoned, and the sentence of death reversed, in the general court of Israel. It is thus that Lowman interprets the procedure.*

Ecclesiastical affairs were, also, to some extent at least, subject to the jurisdiction and control of the Hebrew commons. When David wished to remove the ark to Jerusalem, he would not do so, without a formal vote of the congregation to that effect.† On the accession of Solomon to the throne, when Abiathar was deposed from the office of high priest, and Zadok elevated to that dignity, it was "all the congregation," the great assembly of the people, that established the latter in the high-priesthood, and caused him to receive the sacerdotal unction, which constituted a chief part of the inaugural ceremony.‡

In the brief digest of the English constitution, which Montesquieu has given in the sixth chapter of the eleventh book of his Spirit of Laws, he makes the following remark: "Whoever shall read the admirable treatise of Tacitus on the manners of the Germans, will find, that it is from them the English have borrowed the idea of their political government. This beautiful system was invented first in the woods." On referring to the passage in Tacitus, cited by the learned jurist, it will be found, that the historian says :— "Ordinary affairs were treated in the council of chiefs ; great affairs, in the assembly of the people ; yet so that those matters, on which it belonged to the people to decide, were debated by the chiefs."§ On this Salvador ‖ has well observed, that Montesquieu might have traced the idea of the English constitution to a higher source, and made it rest upon bases

* Civ. Gov. Heb. C. 8.
† 1 Chron. xiii. 2–4.   ‡ 1 Chron. xxix. 20–22.
§ De Morib. Germ. § 15.   ‖ Hist. des Insts. de Moïse, l. 2. c. 2.

more sacred in the eyes of modern nations. This beautiful system of government invented in the woods indeed! Its true source is the inspired legislation of Moses. Besides their military chiefs (the council to which Tacitus referred), the Hebrews had a senate of civilians, as well as a house of commons. They recognized three distinct crowns;—the crown of the priests, the crown of the law, and the crown of the king; in other words the sacerdotal or conservative power, the legislative power, and the executive power. Besides, how many of the English have ever read Tacitus? Whereas the bible, found in every house, has exercised the greatest influence over their manners and institutions, and has produced more than one point of resemblance between the ancient people of Israel and the first nation of modern times, which has comprehended the whole power of law, and has founded its polity on the principle, that laws ought to govern, rather than the will and pleasure of the prince.

CHAPTER VII.

The Hebrew Oracle.

THE fact that the original sovereignty of the Hebrew state, though by the free consent and suffrage of the people, was vested in Jehovah, distinguished this government from all others, ever known among men. This circumstance would naturally lead us to look for some peculiarity of organization in the political structure. Nor does the history of the government, contained in the writings of its founder, disappoint such expectation. This organic peculiarity appears in the oracle of Jehovah, as an essential part of the civil constitution.

We have already seen,[*] that there was a strong theocratic element in the Israelitish constitution; so strong, indeed, that the government has been commonly called a theocracy. In what manner and through what agencies, did this element in the government make itself practically felt? The general answer to this question is :—It was by means of the oracle of Jehovah. With the view of shedding, if possible, some light on this obscure but interesting point, I propose to inquire briefly into the nature and functions of the Hebrew oracle, to institute a comparison between it and the oracles of pagan antiquity, and to vindicate the wisdom and benevolence of such an institution, against the sneers and sophistries of infidelity, by showing its admirable adaptation to the infant state of the world and the church.

The oracle played a conspicuous and most important part in the establishment and administration of the Jewish theocracy. That incomparable summary of the Mosaic code, and of all moral duty,—the decalogue,—was uttered, amid terrific thunderings and lightenings, from the mysterious symbol of the Divinity, in an articulate voice, which reached every ear, and penetrated every heart, and awed every understanding, of the mighty multitude, that crowded around the base of mount Sinai. So also all the rest of the political, civil, moral, and religious laws of the Hebrews were dictated by the oracle, though they were afterward, as observed by Dr. Spring, in his " Discourses on the Obligations of the World to the Bible," passed upon and adopted by the legal assemblies of the nation. The oracle, in the form of the cloudy pillar, regulated the motions of the Israelitish armies: " For when the cloud was taken up from the tabernacle, the children of Israel journeyed ; and when the cloud rested, there the children of Israel pitched their tents ; at the com-

* B. 2, C. 2.

mand of Jehovah they journeyed, at the command of Jehovah they pitched."* How far the oracle directed the military
affairs of the Hebrews, plainly appears in the history of the
Canaanitish wars, and particularly in the story of the siege
and capture of Jericho.† In the earlier periods of the commonwealth, the oracle was constantly appealed to on questions of civil and ecclesiastical law, in settling principles of
state policy, and generally in affairs of moment, appertaining
to the public administration. "In the time of Moses," observes Michaelis,‡ "the oracle was unquestionably very conspicuous. God himself gave laws to the Israelites; decided
difficult points of justice; was constantly visible in the pillar
of cloud and fire; and inflicted punishments, not according
to the secret procedure of providence, but in the most manifest manner." The constitution of the Hebrew judges, both
higher and lower, the election of civil rulers, the cognizance
of many causes, some in the first instance, and others on
appeal, were branches of the sovereignty of Jehovah, as king
of Israel. The use of the oracle in deciding difficult cases
in law, is the more worthy of note, as it serves to explain the
constitution with respect to appeals. It was thus that the
oracle decided the question, how persons defiled by a dead
body should keep the passover.§ Thus also the oracle determined the question of female succession, in the case of the
daughters of Zelophehad.‖ And thus it was the oracle,
again, which declared the punishment of sabbath breaking.¶
Hence it may be seen, that the last resort both in civil and
criminal cases, especially when new and difficult questions
were involved, was in the oracle, and not in the opinion of
the high priest alone, nor of the judge alone, nor of both conjointly with the senate and congregation, unless they were
fully agreed. If a difficulty arose, the last appeal was to the
oracle; in whose decision, the high priest did not give his

* Numb. ix. 17, 18.		† Josh. vi.		‡ Comment. Art. 35.
§ Numb. ix. 6–10.		‖ Numb. xxvii. 1–9.		¶ Numb. xv. 32–36.

private judgment, but the oracle itself gave final judgment in the case.*

The person charged with consulting the oracle, was the high priest. An objector may here ask : " Did not this open the door to corruption? Might not an ambitious pontiff abuse such a trust to unrighteous ends?" This difficulty may be best met by explaining to whom the consultation of the oracle was permitted; the occasions on which it might be consulted; and the probable manner of the consultation.

The oracle could not be interrogated by any mere private individual; not even by the high priest himself, in his personal capacity. This was permitted only to the chief magistrate, or other high functionary of the government. The occasions, on which the advice of the oracle could be asked, must be of a public nature. The matter of consultation must relate to a question of public policy, of public morals, or of religious faith. Neither could the consultation take place in a clandestine way. The person, proposing the question to the high priest, remained with him during the ceremony. Josephus affirms, that any person who chose might be present on such occasions.† This would be an effectual guard against collusion, and an ample guarantee for the fairness of the transaction. The office of the high priest, in this particular, was that of a mediator, or middle man. He was herein simply the channel of communication between the Hebrew state and its Divine head. It is remarkable, that there is not an instance on record, in the Jewish annals of a high priest, who abused this trust to unworthy objects.

The opinion of learned and judicious authors, as to the manner of taking the sense of the oracle, is this : The high

* See Lowm. on Civ. Gov. Heb. c. 11.

† See in confirmation of these views Numb. xxvii. 21, and Prideaux's Connex vol. 1, p. 155 seqq. with the authorities cited by him. Also Josephus Antiq. l. 3, c. 10.

priest clothed in his pontifical garments, and having on the breastplate of judgment, in which were the mysterious urim and thummim, symbolical of the clearness and fulness of the oracular responses, presented himself before the veil of the tabernacle, over against the mercy seat,—the immediate residence of the Divine presence. The magistrate, who came to consult the oracle, stood directly behind him, and propounded the question, which was repeated by the priest. The answer was returned in an audible voice, in terms explicit, direct, and unambiguous. This explains the reason why the holy of holies, where the mercy seat stood, is so often called the oracle. It was because from thence, God returned answers to those, who came to ask counsel of him, on behalf of the public conscience, or the public administration.

That the responses were returned in an articulate voice, seems probable from several expressions of holy writ. When the ten commandments were given on Sinai, it is said, that " God SPAKE all these words."* In regard to the subsequent laws, it is declared that " Jehovah SPAKE unto Moses, saying."† When Moses went into the tabernacle to learn the divine will, it is recorded of him that " he heard the voice of one SPEAKING to him from off the mercy seat.‡ Similar forms of expression are used in reference to the like occasions in after ages, from all which the conclusion seems warranted, that the responses of the Hebrew oracle were rendered in an audible voice, and without secrecy, craft, or ambiguity of any kind.§

I have said above, that the person charged with consulting the oracle was the high priest. The observation, however, ought not to be omitted, that there were two ways, in which the oracle expressed its will, in one of which the high priest

* Exod. xx. 1.   † Exod. passim.   ‡ Numb. vii. 89.
§ Numb. ix. 9. Judg. i. 1–2. xx. 18, 23, 28. 1 Sam. x. 23; and many other places.

had no share. This was by a voice from the shekinah directly. It was in this way that the ten commandments were given, in which case the oracle was heard by the whole Hebrew nation. In this manner, also, the other civil ·laws, given at Sinai, were dictated to Moses. What the exact nature of the phenomenon, called the shekinah, was, we cannot with certainty determine. " We can only say, that it appears to have been a concentrated glowing brightness, a preternatural splendor, an effulgent something, which was appropriately expressed by the term glory ; but whether, in philosophical strictness, it was material or immaterial, it is probably impossible to determine."

But notwithstanding this, it still remains true, that the ordinary mode of consulting the oracle, was through the high priest, by urim and thummim. It is not material to the illustration of this part of the Israelitish constitution, that we should know precisely what these terms mean. Yet it may gratify the reader to be informed of the several opinions, entertained by the learned on this point. All that the scripture says concerning urim and thummim, is, that they were something put by Moses into the breast-plate of the high priest. The breast-plate was a piece of cloth doubled, of a span square, in which were twelve precious stones, set in sockets of gold, and having the names of the twelve tribes of Israel engraved on them. In this, then, the urim and thummim were placed. Four principal opinions have obtained as to what they were. The first is that they were two small images, which, enclosed within the fold of the breast plate, gave out the oracular answers. This is the idea of Philo Judaeus, in which he has been followed by later writers. But it is too heathenish a conceit to be for a moment entertained. It has been well characterized as " a Talmudical camel, which no one in his wits can ever swallow." A second opinion is, that the urim and thummim consisted in a peculiar radiance, or shining light, with which certain of the letters, en-

graven on the breast-plate, were invested, when a question
had been put; so that these luminous characters, being properly arranged, gave the answer to the inquiry. This was
the notion of Josephus. Dr. Prideaux has triumphantly
refuted it; but his answer is too long to be inserted here. A
third opinion is that of Michaelis, in which he is followed by
Jahn. These writers think, that the urim and thummim
were simply a sacred box. They suppose it probable, that
three stones were used, one of them marked with an affirmative; a second, with a negative; and the third, *blank;*—
and that Moses commanded these to be kept within the
doubling of the breast-plate of the priest. This of course
would require the question always to be put in such a way,
that it could be answered with a simple yes or no. But
there are various responses in the scriptures, inconsistent with
the truth of this theory; especially that contained in 2 Sam.
5 : 23, 24, where explicit and detailed directions are given.
The fourth opinion is that of Prideaux, who thinks that by
urim and thummim we are not to understand any thing
visible and corporeal, but only a divine virtue and power,
given to the breast-plate in consecration, of obtaining oracular answers from God, whenever counsel was asked of him
by the high priest, in the prescribed manner. Amid this
conflict of opinion, one thing seems sufficiently evident, that
the answers were rendered in an audible voice, and that the
breast-plate, bearing the names of the twelve tribes, invested
the high priest with his true representative character, and
thus enabled him successfully to ask counsel of God.*

In comparing the Hebrew oracle with the oracles of paganism, my remarks will embrace the period of their respective
institution; the times, occasions, and conditions of consulting

* See on this subject Lowm. on Civ. Gov. Heb. c. 11; Prideaux's Connex.
Vol. 1. pp. 155–160; Mich. Comment. Art. 52; Jahn's Archaeol. Art. 369;
Smith's Heb. Peop. p. 533; and Calmet's Dict. Art. Urim and Thummim.

them; the machinery of consultation; and the nature of the responses uttered by each.

Infidel writers have represented the Hebrew oracle as a mere imitation of those of pagan institution; a graft from one system of imposture, into another but little better. Morgan says, that " while the Jews were in Egypt, they had been dazzled by the infallible declarations of Jupiter Ammon." Sir Isaac Newton, however, places the birth of Ammon more than 400 years after the Exodus of Israel out of Egypt. These are the words of this illustrious chronologist : " The year before Christ 1002, Sesac reigned in Egypt. He erected temples and oracles to his father in Thebes, Ammonia, and Ethiopia; and thereby caused his father to be worshipped as a god in those countries. This was the original of the worship of Jupiter Ammon, and the first mention of oracles I meet with in profane history. The Greeks, in their oracles, imitated the Egyptians; for the oracle of Dodona, which was the oldest in Greece, was set up by an Egyptian woman after the example of the oracle at Thebes."* Thus it appears, according to this high chronological authority, that, instead of the Jewish oracle being an imitation of the pagan oracles, the reverse was the fact. The latter drew their original from the former.

The Hebrew oracle could be consulted at all times, when the occasions of the state required; the Grecian, only on particular days of a particular month in the year. It is obvious to remark, what an advantage this gave to the priests of those lying divinities to anticipate the questions to be proposed, and to frame skilful and deceptive replies.

The Hebrew oracle could be consulted only by some high public functionary, and when questions of moment, relating to the government of the republic, demanded resolution. The Grecian oracles refused not their utterance to any persons,

---

* Empire of Egypt, p. 207.

nor upon any occasion, provided only that the fee was sufficiently ample to cause them to break silence.

This leads me to remark upon another distinction between
the two institutions. No money was ever received for consulting the Jewish oracle. The offer of it would have been
an insult to him, whose voice was heard in its responses.
The Grecian oracles were sources of vast revenues to the priests.
The wealth of the Delphian oracle exceeded that of the most
opulent states and princes. Its treasury blazed with uncounted
jewels, and groaned beneath the masses of gold and silver
that filled its capacious vaults.

Another point of difference appears in the machinery of
consultation, and the character of the responses. Nothing
can be more simple than the method of consulting the divine
oracle; nothing less ambiguous than its answers. But what
endless mystery, and mummery, and cumbrous rites of divination, accompanied the responses of the heathen oracles!
These were always so contrived as to be susceptible of a
double interpretation. In proof of this, the reader's attention is directed to the response of the Delphian oracle to
Crœsus, the powerful monarch of the Lydian empire, respecting the issue of his war with Cyrus. Its purport was, that
he should overturn a great empire, and that the Persians
would not conquer him, till they had a mule for their prince.
History has recorded the result. The wily priests had well
considered their answer. They knew nothing of the issue.
How could they? But they must clutch the treasures of
Lydia's richest sovereign. To this end, they must flatter his
pride. And they must maintain the credit of their oracle,
whichever way fortune might decide the contest. With
demoniac cunning did they frame the response to answer all
these ends. When the unhappy Lydian, lured to his ruin by
their lying flatteries, dared to reproach them with their deception, with insulting scorn they replied:—" Ungrateful fool!
you have overturned a great empire, even that over which

606 COMMENTARIES ON THE

you reigned, and your throne and sceptre have been wrested
from you by the mule of our oracle, even Cyrus, who, his
father being a Persian and his mother a Median, fills the
measure of its import." Behold the system! Behold the
commentary! Each worthy of the other, and both of that
infernal craft and policy, in which they had their origin.
One hardly knows against whom to feel the greater indignation; whether against the contrivers of such a system of
delusion, or the bold blasphemer, who dares to liken it to
that oracle of eternal truth, whose immaculate responses
were fitly symbolized by a legend, which signifies, " LIGHTS
AND PERFECTIONS."

Infidels have indulged in a superabundance of malignant
and silly ridicule over this divine oracle; but with their usual
want of inquiry and reflection. I admit, that it is an extraordinary institution. I admit, that it is altogether without
a parallel in the history of the world. But this is no argument against either the fact or the wisdom of it. No other
civil society has ever been formed for precisely the same objects, nor existed under exactly the same circumstances. No
other civil polity ever proposed, as its main end, the overthrow of idolatry, the preservation of true religion in the
world, and the education of mankind for a more spiritual and
universal dispensation of grace. Add to this, that the human
race was then, as it were, in its infancy and nonage. It had
but few abstract ideas. It was, for the most part, confined
in its mental operations to sensible objects. In such a state
of things, philosophy itself would teach us to look for just
such an institution as the Hebrew oracle. And when we
find it making its appearance in the Jewish church, enlightened reason is prepared to exclaim in the language of revelation, " Oh the depths of the riches both of the wisdom and
knowledge of God."

The oracle was the institution of all others, adapted to the
mental condition, habits, and needs of the Hebrew people.

It operated as a salutary check to the ignorance and rashness of both rulers and people. By powerfully impressing the imagination through the senses, it supplied the place of a strong, realizing conception of an infinite and omnipresent spirit, which was wanting in that minority and pupilage of the nation. It served to detach their affections and their trust from the pompous and alluring idolatries of their heathen neighbors. This sensible manifestation of the Deity, —the cloud of glory shooting up to mid-heaven in a column of massy splendor, or resting in luminous folds over the mercy-seat in the holy of holies,—is so far from being incredible, that, while scripture affirms its truth, reason and philosophy declare its expediency. The divine oracle with its attendant visible glories,—the ark, the mercy-seat, the cherubim, the luminous cloud, the breastplate of judgment, with its mystical urim and thummim, and the audible responses of the Deity,—formed a school, designed, with admirable wisdom and condescension, for tutoring the infant intellect and heart of the world, and training them up to a full spiritual maturity and strength. "To pour contempt, therefore, on these extraordinary appearances, as absurd and romantic fables, would be as unphilosophical and as ungrateful, as it would be for a child, when arrived at manhood, to censure and despise those condescending methods, by which parental wisdom and love had moulded and carried forward his childhood to manly vigor and understanding."* Let us not be guilty of the folly, the injustice, we may say, of measuring the intellectual and religious wants of a comparatively rude and infant state of society, by those of our own more cultivated, more enlightened, more spiritual, more manly, and christian age of the world. And while we admire the beauties of the dawn, and adore the wisdom and benevolence of those early pencillings of spiritual light, let us rejoice and

* Tappan's Jewish Antiquities, Lect. 6.

be grateful, that the full-orbed sun has arisen upon us in all his splendor.

"In the oracle, then," to conclude this chapter in the words of Lowman,* "we see a considerable part of the Hebrew constitution to direct the councils of the united tribes, the political wisdom of which is seldom remarked in the civil government of that nation. There was a congregation of all Israel, or assembly of the people, that all things might be done with general consent. There was a senate of wise and able persons, to prepare things by previous deliberation and consultation, that things might not be concluded rashly in a popular assembly, before they were maturely considered and examined by men of wisdom and experience. There was a judge to assemble the states-general on proper occasions, to preside in their assemblies, and to command the armies of the united provinces, and to see the national resolutions duly executed. And finally, here was an oracle, which was to be consulted by the high priest on great occasions, that no rash resolutions of the people, senate, or judge, might be brought into execution, in cases of moment and difficulty; but they were to ask counsel of God, or to obtain the royal assent of Jehovah, as king of Israel, by his oracle. This was a wise provision, to preserve a continual sense in the Hebrew nation of the principal design of their constitution, to keep them from idolatry and to the worship of the one true God, as their immediate protector; and that their security and prosperity depended upon adhering to his counsels and commands."

* Civ. Gov. Heb. c. 11.

CHAPTER VIII.

The Hebrew Priesthood.

I USE the term priesthood here in an enlarged sense. I include, under that designation, the whole tribe of Levi, as possessing a sacerdotal or sacred character. It is of this tribe, that I now propose to treat, in its constitution, its functions, and its revenues. No part of the Mosaic institution has been, either more grossly misunderstood, or more wickedly misrepresented. It is proper, therefore, to examine it, in the relations just indicated.*

The tribe of Levi had an organization quite different from that of the other tribes. These were settled in distinct provinces, and had each a government of its own. This had no landed property, did not live together, and was without an independent government. Its members were dispersed through all the territories of Israel; drew their livelihood from the other tribes; and were subject to the government of the province, in which they lived.

How this happened, it is interesting to inquire. On the departure of the Israelites from Egypt, all their first-born males were sanctified to the Lord, and destined to the altar. But

* On the subject of this chapter, see Lowm. Civ. Gov. Heb. c. 6; Cunaeus de Repub. Hebr. l. 2. c. 1; Mich. Comment. Art. 52; Jahn's Heb. Com. b. 2. § 12; Salv. Inst. de Moïse, l. 2. c. 1. and l. 3. c. 3; Fleury, Manners of the Israelites, Pt. 2. c. 22, and Pt. 4. c. 5; Lewis's Antiq. Heb. Rep. b. 2; and Harrington's Commonwealth of Israel, b. 2. c. 2.

39

the difficulty of obtaining from each family its first-born son, the difficulty of detaching them from their private interests, as citizens of such a tribe or such a town, rendered this mode impracticable. Moses, therefore, without in the least changing the original principle, substituted, for this service, the tribe of Levi, in place of all the first-born. But why was this tribe chosen? And, of all its members, why did Aaron and his sons obtain the priesthood? Two circumstances dictated the preference of the tribe of Levi, the smallness of its numbers, and the zeal which it had displayed in punishing the Israelites for their idolatry in the matter of the golden calf. The talent, eloquence, and eminent public services of Aaron, which had already won the admiration and gratitude of his countrymen, pointed him out as the person most worthy of being raised to the second dignity in the state.

It is remarkable, and deserves attention, as showing the democratic character of this government, that the tribe of Levi, though designated by Jehovah to the service of the temple, received its legal institution from the Hebrew people, as represented in the states-general of Israel. In the first instance, Moses, with the senate and the congregation, consecrated the high priest and his associates, thus evincing, that it belonged to the general diet to choose the chief pontiff from among the priests most distinguished for their ability and merit, and to establish him in his charge.* Afterwards, the whole assembly of the children of Israel was convoked to induct the Levitical order into their office. The people, by their representatives, laid their hands upon the Levites, and the high priest consecrated them in the name of the children of Israel, as an offering freely made by them to Jehovah their king.†

From the above detail it appears, that the designation and institution of the high priest belonged, not to the council of priests, but to the senate, and must receive the confirmation

* Levit. viii. 2–5. † Numb. viii. 5–22.

of the people through their deputies. But this will still more clearly appear from some examples in the Israelitish history. Aaron had four sons. Two of them died without issue. Of the other two, Eleazar obtained the high-priesthood.* But this dignity was not necessarily hereditary in his family, for, under the judges, it passed into the family of his brother. As to the motive for this change, and the manner in which it was made, the bible is silent. But it informs us distinctly of the circumstances, which restored the dignity to the family of Eleazar. Abiathar, having taken part against Solomon, was deposed, and Zadoc elevated to the pontificate in his place. By whom was this done? It was the congregation of Israel, that chose, anointed, and established Zadoc in this office.† Josephus cannot be accused of partiality to democratic ideas, and still less of depreciating the rights of the priests ; yet he admits, that this dignity was, and of right ought to be, conferred by the people. When the nephew of the high priest Onias publicly reproaches his uncle with his conduct, he tells him, that it is strange that, having been elevated by the people to the honor of the high-priesthood, he should have so little concern for the welfare of his country.‡ It was the people, who gave the pontificate to Judas Maccabeus.§ It was the people, again, who conferred the same dignity upon his brother Simon.‖ In short, the great principle of the ancient Hebrews, in which we recognize the germ of the modern idea of the three powers, was, that there were three crowns in Israel, viz. the crown of royalty, the crown of the priesthood, and the crown of the law. The first was bestowed upon David and his descendants; the second was given to Aaron and his sons; but the third, which was superior to both the others, was the inheritance of all Israel. The king, the priest, the judge, all the magistracies, were the creatures of the law ; and the law was enacted by

* Numb. xx. 26.   † 1 Chr. xxix. 22.   ‡ Antiq. l. 12. c. 4.
§ Antiq. l. 12. c. 10.   ‖ 1 Macc. xiv. 35.

the people. The constitution, in its parts, was pervaded with the democratic spirit.

I pass now to the inquiry concerning the functions of the sacerdotal tribe. Morgan and other skeptical writers have wished to discover in the Levites a government of priests, intent solely on the enjoyment of sovereign power, and the exorbitant enrichment of their own order. But this idea is without foundation, and against truth, being wholly repugnant to the genius and scope of the institution.

The Levites were not a mere spirituality. Certainly they were the ministers of religion, and charged with all the functions appertaining to the public worship of Jehovah. But so close was the relation between the law and the religion of the Hebrews, that all ecclesiastical persons were at the same time political persons. The entire tribe of Levi was set apart to God, the king of this commonwealth. Politically speaking, they were Jehovah's ministers of state. Hence this tribe, as constituted by Moses, was not only a priesthood, appointed to the service of the altar, but also a true temporal magistracy, having important and vital civil relations. The burden of government was, in great measure, laid upon its shoulders. Besides performing the ceremonies of public worship, it was destined to preserve in its integrity, and to interpret in the seat of justice, the text of the fundamental laws; to teach these laws to all Israel; to inspire the people with a love for them; to oppose all its own authority and influence against any and every attempt to overthrow them; and to bind firmly together all the parts of the body politic.

Let the reader transport himself, in imagination, to the age when Moses lived; let him look at the circumstances, in which he found himself; let him consider the difficulties to be overcome by him;—and this institution will readily become its own interpreter.

In the midst of men ignorant, debased by slavery, and prone to superstition; in the midst of twelve distinct repub-

lics, governed by their own assemblies, senates, and magistrates, Moses felt deeply the necessity of some means, both of
elevating the people and of uniting in close and strong bonds
all these different parts of the body politic,—some means,
which would continually recal their regards to the same end,
•and prevent the evils, to which federative republics are so liable, where the individual interests of the several members
are apt to overpower and bear down the general interest and
welfare. To obtain this agency, Moses gave to the tribe of
Levi the particular organization, under which we find it. He
distributed it throughout all the other twelve tribes, and assigned to it certain specific duties. The high priest, as president of the tribe and supreme interpreter of the text of the
law, had his permanent residence at the capital of the nation.
Thus the centre of the particular system of conservatism and
union corresponded with the centre of the republic itself.
From this centre, the system spread itself out to the utmost
extremities of the nation. Every where its influence was
exerted to inspire a love of law and order; to promote peace;
to cement the bonds of social and political union; to insure
a constantly progressive civilization; in a word, to place continually before the eyes of all their countrymen that law, to
which their own individual interest and happiness were indis-
solubly united.

Let us look at another difficulty, which met the Jewish
lawgiver in the framing of his constitution, and particularly
in the organization of this magistracy. The individuals to
compose it must be taken from among men, who, instead of
watching over the preservation of the text of the law, would
quite as likely hasten to change it according to their own
caprices, and, instead of teaching it to others, would themselves, perhaps, tear and lacerate its provisions, beyond the
possibility of recovery. To parry this danger, and at the
same time to establish the institution upon natural guaranties,
Moses had recourse to the power of private interest. By

making the functions of the Levites hereditary, he was enabled to unite their essential interests to those of the other tribes, by a combination, which would, as it were, compel them to fulfil the objects of their charge. He excluded them from all inheritance in the soil of Israel, and made them wholly dependent, in their private interests, upon the rest of the people. Thus the Levite would be led to attach himself to the law, on which his own livelihood depended. He would seek the peace and welfare of the state, because they were the necessary conditions of his own. Self-interest would prompt him to respect the law, in order that others might respect it. Self-interest would lead him to publish it, that the precepts which consecrated his own right, might not be forgotten. Self-interest, in fine, would cause him to watch over its entire execution,—thus making of this tribe, a true and powerful instrument of conservatism.

But while the tribe of Levi, as it came from the hand of Moses, constituted a true civil magistracy, it was far from being, as Morgan would have us believe, the tyrant of the state. No; the state had but one master under the constitution of Moses, and that was the law. To this the sons of Levi were as much bound to submit, as the other citizens. " Lex major sacerdotio,"—the law is greater than the priesthood,—was the principle of the Hebrew polity. How vast, how radical, herein, the difference between the priesthood of Egypt and the priesthood of Israel ! The former made the laws themselves, changed them at will, and concealed the books in which they were written from all profane eyes. The latter were simply charged with preserving the laws intact, with keeping them constantly exposed to the eyes of the people, and with teaching them all to all exactly.

If Moses, as is alleged, had really intended to form a government of priests, clothed with absolute powers, would he, being of a sane mind, have pursued the course that he did ? Would he have begun, by stripping the priests of the power conferred by territorial estates? Would he have continued, by depriving them of the authority derived from the command of the military forces of the nation? Would he have ended, by withholding from them the influence, which illusion always enables the knowing to wield over the ignorant? Moses was no stranger to these things. He had seen them all, and he had seen their almost omnipotence, in Egypt. These are capital points in the argument; and it is idle to attempt either to deny or evade their force. Moses took away from his priesthood the power derived from property; the power derived from military command; the power derived from illusions. What, then, did he leave it? Nothing but the power of the law; a law, which they did not make, which they could not change, and which they were themselves bound to obey. Here, surely, is no basis of tyranny. Here is no foothold for despotism. Here is no germ or aliment of ecclesiastical oppression. The Hebrew priests could become despots and tyrants, only by overthrowing the constitution, which gave them being, and on which their whole livelihood depended.

One of the most important of the civil functions of the sacerdotal order, under the Hebrew constitution, was that of acting as judges. This required for its performance a large proportion of its members. No less than six thousand of them, in the time of David, acted as judges and genealogists. " The declaration of Moses on this point," says Michaelis, " is perfectly clear, Deut. 21 : 5. ' On the mouth of the priest shall every controversy and every stroke depend.' It was, in an especial manner, the business of the priests, in all disputes of a more serious nature, to pronounce the final decision, and lay down the law, much in the same manner as it is of our judicial faculties and tribunals of appeal." The words of Moses in his valedictory ode and benediction to Israel, (Deut. 33 : 9, 10.)—" He who said unto his father and to his mother, I have not seen him, neither did he acknowl-

edge his brethren, nor knew his own children, and shall
teach Jacob thy judgments, and Israel thy law,"—must undoubtedly be meant of teaching these laws in the seat of
judgment; inasmuch as the expressions employed refer to
that impartiality, which is so essential an attribute of a good
judge.

The Levites were also the literati of all the faculties.
They were by birth obliged to devote themselves to the
sciences. They formed a sort of literary aristocracy, whose
influence was intended to counteract the hasty measures,
likely to result from the strongly democratic character of the
government. They acted as physicians, as teachers, as
transcribers of books, as writers of contracts and other law
papers, as chroniclers and historians, as astronomers, and as
mathematicians employed in the service of the state.

The tribe of Levi, then, comprehended the learned of all
names; the sages and professors of law and jurisprudence;
of medicine and physiology, of the physical and mathematical sciences; in short, of all the so called liberal arts and
sciences, the possession and application of which constitute
the civilization of a country. It was to be the chief instrument of a continuing and progressive mental, moral, and
religious culture of the people. Its business was to produce,
preserve, and perfect all the necessary sources and conditions
of national civilization; to form and train up the people of
the country to be obedient, free, useful citizens and patriots,
living to the benefit of the state, and prepared to die for its
defence.

Such, in a political point of view, were the noble functions,
such the strongly conservative character of the sacerdotal
order, under the Mosaic constitution. Yet the Hebrew
priesthood was far from having obtained a range of powers,
equal in extent and magnitude to that embodied in the college of Roman pontiffs. Within the jurisdiction of this latter
body were included, besides what belonged to religious

affairs, adoptions, marriages, funerals, wills, oaths, consecra-
tions, the care of the public annals, the arrangement of the
calendar, and, in concurrence with the jurisconsults, the determination of the rules and forms of judicial procedure.*
The revenues of the tribe of Levi next claim our attention.†
These were undoubtedly liberal; but they have been greatly
overrated and overstated by men, who would neither weigh
the advantages they gave up in return, nor take the trouble
to inform themselves of the real nature, extent, and value of
their services to the state. Morgan, in particular, has indulged in the wildest and most extravagant calculations, and,
as Michaelis says, has called falsehood to his aid, with a view
to exaggerate the amount of the already too great income of
his supposed spirituality. What, then, was the provision,
which the law made for the priests and Levites, as near as we
can ascertain it from the history? The tribe of Levi, at the
time of the enumeration in the wilderness, contained twenty-
two thousand males, or, probably about twelve thousand
arrived at adult age. The other tribes numbered six hundred thousand, capable of bearing arms. Consequently, the
Levites constituted about a fiftieth part of the whole nation.
Besides cities to dwell in, this tribe was to receive a tenth of
all the produce of the land, both of fruit and cattle. From
this it would appear, that the income of each individual
Levite was equal to the average income of five other Israelites. But if we should conclude from hence, that this was
the actual proportion, we should deceive ourselves.

A variety of circumstances tended to diminish the tithe
accorded to the Levites. 1. They were themselves obliged to

* Terrasson, Hist. de la Jurispr. Rom. Berryat-Saint-Prix, Hist. du
Droit Rom. cited by Salv. 1. 2, c. 1.

† I make a general reference here to the passages, which relate to this
subject, viz. Numb. xviii.; Lev. ii. vii. and xxvii. 30–33; Exod. xxiii. 19;
Deut. xxvi. 2–10; Exod. xiii. 13, and xxx. 11 seqq. Lev. xxiii. 19, 20;
Deut. xviii. 4: Exod. iv. 20.

hand over a tenth of it to the priests. 2. The whole land of
Israel was not tithable; no woodlands, no timber, paid any
tithe at all. 3. Even the cattle, which constituted an important, if not indeed the most important part of the Israelitish
husbandry, paid only a tithe of the young. When the tenth
lamb, calf, kid, &c. were paid as tithe, the remainder of the
flock and the herd paid nothing more, in wool, milk, butter,
or flesh. Hence it is plain, that the whole country of the
Hebrews by no means paid a tenth of its produce to the Levites. The greater part of the soil, indeed, as all the woodlands and pasture grounds, either paid nothing at all, or so
slight a percentage, as to be really of little account. 4. The
rendition of the tithes was left entirely to the conscience and
the loyalty of each individual Israelite. No compulsory process could be instituted to compel a payment of them; neither
did the priests or the magistrates have any superintendence
or oversight of the matter. It will readily be imagined, that
the law must have been often but partially complied with,
and sometimes wholly eluded. That this was actually the
case, appears from a command issued by king Hezekiah,*
and from the censures addressed by the prophets to the Hebrew people.† 5. If one or more of the tribes abandoned
themselves to idolatry, the Levites lost the revenues accruing
to them from such tribes. This undoubtedly often happened.
The condition of the Levites could not have been one of much
prosperity or abundance, at the time of the idolatry of Micah,
when one of them, belonging to the tribe of Judah, was
obliged to go about the country, seeking for some employment,
and was glad to find it, even in the service of an idolatrous
Israelite, on condition of receiving his food, one suit of
clothes, and ten shekels of silver, (about five dollars) by the
year. A memorable example of the loss of revenue to the
sacerdotal tribe from religious apostacy, we have in the history of the reign of Jeroboam, when the Levites driven out

* 2 Chr. xxxi. 4.   † Jer. viii. 10: Mal. iii. 8.

from their habitations to make room for idolatrous priests,
took refuge in Judah and Jerusalem.* 6. Another considerable subtraction must be made from the income of the Levites, if an opinion of Joseph Scaliger and Salvador† is well
founded. 1 am not, indeed, convinced, that their idea is correct; neither am I convinced, that it is erroneous. I shall,
therefore, state the opinion, which they have advanced, and
leave the reader to examine and judge for himself. It is well
known, that, besides the tithe for the support of the Levites,
the Israelites were required to pay a second tithe, which,
however, was not properly of the nature of a tax, since it was
to be consumed by the people themselves, at the offering-
feasts and other entertainments, in the place which the Lord
should choose, to put his name there. To these, besides other
friends, they were admonished to invite Levites, widows,
orphans, strangers, poor people, and their own servants, thus
giving them an occasional season of festivity. There is also,
apparently, mention made of a third tithe for every third
year, to be expended in similar festive entertainments at
home.‡ Three opinions have obtained respecting this last
mentioned tithe. One is, that it was really an additional tithe,
distinct from the other two. For this notion, however, there
does not appear to be any sufficient foundation. The second
opinion, which, as it is the more common, seems, I confess, to
be the more probable, is, that what seem to be two tithes,
were in reality one and the same, and the law in Deut. xiv.
28, 29, is merely a direction, requiring that so much of the
second tithe as should not have been consumed in offering-
feasts at the place of the altar, should, during the third year,
be expended in similar entertainments at home. The third
opinion is that of Scaliger and Salvador, referred to above.

* 2 Chr. xi. 13, 14.
† De Decimis, in the Coll. of Sacr. Crit. p. 211, Hist. des Insts. de Moïse,
l. 3. C. 3.
‡ Deut. xiv. 28, 29 : xxvi. 12.

It is, that every third year the tithe of the Levites did not belong to them exclusively, but was to be shared by them with three other classes of persons, viz. widows, orphans, and strangers. Upon the whole, it is manifest, that the income of a Levite must have fallen very far below that of five common Israelites.

But it may be suggested, that very important elements have been omitted in making the above estimate. I reply, that so far as the Levites proper are concerned, nothing has been excluded. The priests enjoyed other revenues, to which I am now going to turn my attention. In the first place, they had a tenth of the tithe of the Levites. Then there were the first fruits of the earth ; the firstlings of cattle; the redemption money for the first-born of men ; portions of every sacrifice, of which the blood came not into the holy of holies ; all things devoted ; all matters of vow ; the skins of the burnt offerings ; and some other minor sources of income.* I do not mention the half-shekel poll tax, ordered at the numbering of the Israelites in the wilderness, because I am convinced that that was paid but once prior to the captivity, and that the Jews under the second temple, in making it an annual tribute, went beyond the requisition of the law of Moses.

The items of income, enumerated above, undoubtedly formed a very considerable sum total, which came into the hands of the priests. The question is, did it all belong to them as their private property, which they were at liberty to expend in whatever way they pleased ? The thing is impossible ; and those who think so, err egregiously. They confound two things, which are distinct in themselves and ought to be carefully distinguished, the minister and the ministry ; and they imagine analogies between the Hebrews and other nations, which have no existence, except in their own fancy. The tabernacle first, and the temple afterwards, were not,

---

* Numb. xxviii. 5-32, and Leviticus passim.

like our churches, wholly religious in their design and use. On the contrary, they had a character and a purpose eminently political. Public worship was certainly performed there. But there also the states-general held their sessions; and there the national treasure was kept. The Israelite, who consecrated any thing to Jehovah, must not be supposed to have devoted it to the priest in person, but simply to have made use of his ministry to convey it into the sacred treasury, which was no other than the national treasury. Not to the priests themselves, therefore, but to Jehovah, belonged whatever came into their hands. A liberal sum was, doubtless, allowed for the support of their families; but, after this had been taken out, the rest became a part of the public treasure.

This is what I had to say on the constitution, the functions, and the revenues of the sacerdotal tribe among the Hebrews. Three considerations the Levites rendered to the rest of the Israelites for whatever they received from them. 1. The tribe of Levi gave up to the other tribes their whole share of the promised land, except so much as was sufficient to afford them a place of habitation. 2. They parted with the right of an independent government, such as the other tribes enjoyed, and completely sunk their political existence. 3. They gave up themselves to the national service, as ministers of religion, ministers of state, magistrates, teachers of the people, and literati of all the faculties, as explained in a former part of this chapter; services the most laborious, responsible, and useful to the commonwealth. For all this, they received a simple annuity, liberal it may be, but depending solely upon the national faith for its payment, while they divested themselves of all power of re-entry in case of non-payment. Let the benefits surrendered and the services performed be weighed in just balances, and the rent-roll of the tribe of Levi will appear rather below than above the demands of reason and justice.

CHAPTER IX.

The Hebrew Prophets.

THE right understanding of the prophetical office among
the Hebrews will throw much light on the Mosaic constitution, and strikingly evince the popular character of the Israelitish government.   On this point, far be it from me to disturb the faith, which we have inherited from our fathers, or
to unsettle, in any mind, the received opinion concerning the
true divine inspiration of the Hebrew prophets.   I receive,
with implicit and unquestioning faith, the testimony of Paul,
that "all scripture is given by inspiration of God,"* and
the testimony of Peter that "holy men of God spake as they
were moved by the Holy Ghost."†   Nevertheless, to foretell
future events, and to impart religious truth and spiritual lessons, were not the whole duty and office of a prophet, under
the constitution of Moses.

Doubtless, the most important functions of the Hebrew
prophets were, in the strict sense, religious in their character.
The office of the prophets was much more like that of our
modern clergymen, than was the office of the priests, who
had, in fact, but few points of resemblance to the ministry
instituted by Christ.‡   The prophets were the preachers of

---

* 2 Tim. iii. 16.   † 2 Pet. i. 21.

‡ A single fact is decisive of this, viz. their living in cities by themselves. How could christian pastors discharge their appropriate functions,
how could they fulfil the command to watch for souls, if they dwelt in

the ancient church. According to Augustine,* they were the philosophers, divines, instructors, and guides of the Hebrews in piety and virtue. These holy men were the bulwarks of religion against the impiety of princes, the wickedness of individuals, and every kind of immorality.† But by far the most important part of their commission was to foretell the coming and kingdom of the Messiah, with their attendant circumstances, and, by slow degrees, yet with constantly increasing clearness, to acquaint their countrymen with the approaching change of their economy, and with the nature of the new, more spiritual, and universal dispensation, which was to succeed it.‡

Still, as hinted above, the duties of the prophets were not wholly religious. Their relation to the civil state was not, indeed, fixed by any constitutional provision, or legal enactment. They did not form a component part of the political system.§ They were not a branch of the machinery of government. Yet their authority and influence in affairs of state was by no means inconsiderable. They were, so to speak, the privileged state-moralists, guardians, and popular orators of the republic. Coleridge‖ speaks of them as uniting the functions and threefold character of the Roman censors, the tribunes of the people, and the sacred college of augurs. The historian Schlosser¶ says: "We hear, in the prophets, the voice of true patriots, who, standing upon a provision of the law of Moses, spake the truth to the people, to the priests, and to the kings." Horne** speaks of them as possessing great authority in the Israelitish state, and as highly esteemed by the pious sovereigns, who undertook no important affairs

isolated towns, twenty, thirty, or fifty miles apart, instead of living as now among their respective flocks ?

* De Civitat. Dei, l. 18. c. 21.

† Horne's Int. Pt. 5. c. 4.   ‡ Warburton's Div. Leg. l. 3. Appendix.

§ J. A. Alexander's Earlier Prophecies of Is. Intr. p. 16.

‖ Manual for Statesmen.   ¶ Cited by Salv. l. 2. c. 3.   ** Pt. 5. c. 4.

without consulting them. Alexander* represents their influence in the government as very powerful, not indeed by official, formal action, but as special divine messengers, whose
authority could not be disputed or resisted by any magistrate,
without abjuring the fundamental principles of the theocracy. Milton† compares them to the orators of the Greek
democracies. The lines which this sage and learned poet
puts into the mouth of our Savior, both from their truth and
appositeness, deserve to be cited here.

> " Their orators. thou then extoll'st, as those
> The top of eloquence ;—statists, indeed,
> And lovers of their country, as may seem ;
> But herein to our prophets far beneath,
> As men divinely taught, and better teaching
> The solid rules of civil government,
> In their majestic, unaffected style,
> Than all the oratory of Greece and Rome.
> In them is plainest taught and easiest learnt,
> What makes a nation happy, and keeps it so,
> What ruins kingdoms and lays cities flat."

Nobly said, and truthfully too ! The prophetical writings
abound with the finest lessons of political wisdom. I know
of no compositions more worthy of the profound study of
statesmen and legislators, than the writings of the Hebrew
prophets. In seven verses of his forty-seventh chapter, beginning at the seventh verse, the prophet Isaiah, as Coleridge
has observed, revealed the true philosophy of the French revolution of 1789, more than two thousand years before it
became a sad, irrevocable truth of history. A collection of
political maxims, forming an excellent manual for statesmen,
might be culled from the books of the Hebrew prophets ; a
collection, which would surprise even diligent students of the
scriptures by the number, the variety, the purity, and the
deep and comprehensive wisdom of its counsels.

* Earl. Proph. Is. Int. p. 12.   † Paradise Regained.

But it is time to look at the institution of the prophetical office, as it is related in the Hebrew history. The record is contained in Deut. 18 : 9-22. I cite the passage in a somewhat abbreviated form, retaining, however, all the material parts of it. " When thou comest into the land which Jehovah, thy God, giveth thee, thou shalt not learn to do after the abominations of those nations. There shall not be found among you any * * * * that useth divination, or an observer of times, or an enchanter, or a witch, or a charmer, or a consulter with familiar spirits, or a wizard, or a necromancer. * * * * Jehovah, thy God, will raise up unto thee a prophet from the midst of thee, of thy brethren, like unto me; unto him ye shall hearken. * .* * * But the prophet, which shall presume to speak a word in my name, which I have not commanded him to speak, or that shall speak in the name of other gods, even that prophet shall die. * * * When a prophet speaketh in the name of Jehovah, if the thing follow not, nor come to pass, that is the thing which Jehovah hath not spoken, but the prophet hath spoken it presumptuously : thou shalt not be afraid of him."

On this passage I offer the following observations.

1. At the time when this law was given, it was the custom of mankind to pry into future events. No propensity was stronger or more general than this; and religion was universally regarded as the means of gratifying this curiosity. Indeed, it was looked upon as a chief service, which religion owed to her votaries, to give them information concerning the future. The nations, by whom the Hebrews were surrounded, had their various ways of peering into futurity, some of which are enumerated in this law. If no means had been provided, whereby the Israelites could foreknow things to come, it would have been very difficult, considering the prying curiosity of those early ages, to keep them from despising their own religion, and resorting to the divinations of

40

their idolatrous neighbors. All this is noticed by Origen,* as a ground of necessity for the establishment of the prophetical office in the Hebrew commonwealth. To keep the Israelites from being carried away by the torrent of superstition, which overflowed and corrupted the nations, true religion was provided with an institution, which should really furnish that knowledge, which false religion pretended to give. A constant succession of true prophets would be a powerful means of weaning God's people from superstitious practices, and of keeping them from consulting diviners to discover what should befal them. And this is precisely what God promises in the passage under consideration.

2. This interpretation, which is the obvious and natural one, confutes that which restricts the words to a prophecy respecting the Messiah. Some interpreters do so restrict their import, because they are expressly applied to our Savior by Peter.† Certainly the passage has reference to Christ, since the apostle affirms it. But who is ignorant of the fulness of meaning, which often inheres in the words of holy scripture? Bishop Middleton has well expressed the principle, which is applicable here. He observes, that there are many passages in the Old Testament, which are capable of a twofold application; being directly applicable to circumstances then past, or present, or soon to be accomplished; and indirectly to others, which divine providence was about to develope under a future dispensation. Bloomfield,‡ while pointing out the peculiar resemblances between Moses and Christ, admits that, after all, this reference may not have been directly in view, and accordingly, that this may be of the number of those passages, to which bishop Middleton refers, as being capable of a twofold application. Dr. J. A. Alexander§ says, that one of the most plausible interpretations of this passage is, that it contains the promise of a con-

* Contra Celsum, l. 1.   † Acts iii. 22.   ‡ In loc.
§ Introduction to Earl. Proph. Is. p. 12.

stant succession of inspired men, of which succession Christ himself was to be the greatest. The word plausible here is' rather ambiguous ; but it is evident, that the learned professor inclines to the belief, that the interpretation is just, as well as plausible. This is the decided opinion of Michaelis,* in which I fully concur. Beyond a doubt, there is a double reference in the passage, viz. to the Messiah, and to the whole line of divinely inspired prophets under the Hebrew theocracy. One of these references did not suit the purpose of Peter, while the other did. He takes that which is in point, without alluding to that which is not. But his use of the one reference is not, upon any just principles of interpretation, exclusive of the other. If a single prophet only is intended, and that one the Lord Jesus Christ, the context seems to be without meaning, and the whole passage out of joint. The words, then, are to be regarded as a record of the institution of a permanent order of men in the Israelitish commonwealth, of whom Jesus Christ, as he would resemble Moses in being the minister of a new dispensation and in his intimate communication with God, would at the same time be the greatest and the most illustrious.

3. Two tests only of the truth or falsity of the claim to prophetical inspiration are here recognized, viz. first, whether the prophet spake in the name of Jehovah or of false gods ; and, secondly, whether or not a future event, foretold by him, happened according to his word. Miracles could not be demanded of him in proof of a divine commission to speak in the name of Jehovah. The power of working wonders did not inhere in his official designation. As long, therefore, as a pretending prophet was not convicted of being a lying prophet, he was to be tolerated, and was to go unpunished, although he should have threatened calamity or even destruction to the state. Whoever prophecied in the name of the true God, must be borne with, until an unfulfilled prediction

* Comment. Art. 36.

proved him to be an impostor.* The trial of Jeremiah, as related in the twenty-sixth chapter of his prophecies, casts a strong light upon this subject. He had publicly foretold the destruction of Jerusalem. For this he was seized, and arraigned before the princes, or senate, as worthy of death. He offered no other defence than that the Lord had sent him to speak as he had, and he was willing to die in attestation of the truth of what he affirmed; only he added, by way of warning, that, if they put him to death, they would surely bring innocent blood upon themselves. He had done nothing, which, by the law of Moses, merited death, or even censure. He had predicted evil to the state, but that was not a crime, unless he had spoken it presumptuously. He might, indeed, be a false prophet, in which case he would be worthy of death; but as yet there was no proof of it. If it was not a crime to be a prophet, it was not a crime to predict calamity, for nations do not always experience good fortune. It was his duty to foretell the truth, just as it had been revealed to him, whether it was agreeable or disagreeable. It is remarkable, that there were prophets among his accusers; how many is not stated, but apparently not a few. The court, after hearing the case, rendered a judgment of acquittal, on the ground both of law and precedent. They aver, in their judgment, that Jeremiah had spoken in the name of Jehovah, as the law required, and that the fact of his foretelling evil cannot be imputed as a crime, since other prophets had done the same without rebuke, of which they cite a memorable instance. And so the case was dismissed, and the accused set at liberty. The history of the procedure is very interesting, and the reader is requested to peruse it for himself.

4. So far as the right of interdiction by man was concerned, this law gave a very broad liberty to the exercise of the prophetical office. Undoubtedly there could be no right,

* Mich. Comment. Art. 36.

in the sight of God, to assume this office, without a true
divine commission and a supernatural divine inspiration.
But, so far as his fellow-citizens were concerned, every man,
whatever his birth, tribe, calling, or fortune might be, could
say, "1 am a prophet." He could proclaim to the people
the consequences of their iniquities, and freely censure the
conduct of the magistrates, of the priests, of the senators, of
the kings, of all. He could speak, preach, exhort, reprove,
and fulminate; and no man had the right to close his mouth.
On the contrary, both citizens and rulers were bound to listen
to him, when his voice was raised against corruptions and
abuses, and in favor of the just and the right.* There is no
need to cite examples of the boldness and energy, with which
the prophets reproved the sins of all, from the highest to the
lowest. Nathan dared to say to David, "Thou art the
man."† Isaiah addressed the rulers as rebellious, as com-
panions of thieves, as loving bribes, and as following after
rewards.‡ Ezekiel speaks of the princes as resembling
wolves ravening for their prey, in their eagerness to shed
blood and get dishonest gain.§ Zephaniah represents the
princes of Israel as roaring lions, her judges as evening
wolves, her prophets as treacherous persons, and her priests
as doing violence to the law.‖ Malachi charges upon the
whole nation the crime of robbing God.¶

5. This liberty, however, was restrained by a severe penalty,
to be inflicted upon the false prophet. The prophet, who
presumed to speak without a commission from God, was to be
punished with death. The falsity of his claim to the prophetic
inspiration could be evinced by proving, either that he had
prophecied in the name of strange gods, or that he had uttered
a prediction, which was falsified by the event. The reader,
who would see the justice of so severe a penalty fully
vindicated, is referred to articles 252 and 253 of Michaelis's

* Salv. l. 2, c. 3.   † 2 Sam. xii. 7.   ‡ Is. i. 23.
§ Ezek. xxii. 27.   ‖ Zeph. iii. 3, 4.   ¶ Mal. iii. 8.

Commentaries on the Laws of Moses. The assumption of the prophetic office without authority was a species of treason in the Israelitish state; and besides this, mischiefs of a fearful magnitude flowed both from the public predictions of false prophets, and from the secret practice of superstitious arts, such as fortune-telling, astrology, and divinations of all sorts.

6. The passage under consideration affords solid ground for belief in the supernatural inspiration of the true prophets of Jehovah. What legislator, not bereft of the last spark of justice and humanity, would punish with death a mere error in judgment? Yet this charge is in effect brought against Moses by those, who represent the Hebrew prophets as nothing more than sagacious men, whose natural perspicacity enabled them to foresee and predict future events; men endowed, in a superior degree, with the faculties of reason, imagination, and genius. Could there be a clearer proof, if not that the prophets were supernaturally inspired, at least that Moses and his countrymen thought so? Unless, indeed, we are willing to suppose, that the lawgiver himself rather deserved the punishment, which he threatened against the violators of his law.

Upon the whole, there can be no doubt, that the prophetical office was designed to be a great and influential element in the Hebrew government. The seventy elders, chosen as assistants to Moses in the valley of Paran, were divinely inspired men, and spake to the people under the influence of the Holy Spirit. From the very foundation of the state, teachers supernaturally enlightened were appointed to instruct the people in religion, virtue, and law; and, in the darkest periods of the Hebrew history, God left not himself without inspired witnesses to the truth. At length there appeared what have been called schools of the prophets, that is, companies of young men, taught and disciplined under the direction of Samuel and other aged prophets, who succeeded him. Not that the art of prophecy became a branch of Hebrew education. Three principal objects, we may reasonably conjecture, the youths, who frequented these schools, had in view,—the improvement of their minds, growth in piety, and knowledge of the Mosaic law. From among the persons thus disciplined and instructed, the prophets were ordinarily, though not uniformly, selected by God, who communicated to them, in addition to the qualifications for the prophetical office thus acquired, the gift of inspiration. It was of the utmost importance, that the prophets should have an ample and accurate acquaintance with the laws of Moses; and it was, on many accounts, better that they should acquire this by their own study, than by immediate inspiration.

It would naturally be expected, that, under a law like that which we have been examining, the prophets, true and pretended, would form a numerous body in the state. And such was undoubtedly the case. Every city had its prophets, who, says Calmet,* in the public assemblies on the sabbath, at the new moons, and in the solemn convocations, preached to the people, and reproved the various disorders and abuses, which appeared in the nation. Ezekiel has indicated, in a manner extremely elegant and poetical, the duties of a prophet, under the Mosaic economy.† The prophets served as a counterpoise to the influence of the priests, the magistrates, and the senate itself, which rarely omitted, on important occasions, to call for the advice of one or more of the most renowned of these inspired men.

Among such a crowd of popular preachers and orators, it will readily be imagined, that multitudes were mere pretenders; and that there was but a feeble minority of divinely commissioned prophets. The mass spake without divine light and guidance. Profaning the name of Jehovah, and sacrificing the welfare of the state to their private interests, they ignominiously sold both their consciences and their discourses. Every page of the prophetical writings proves this. "Thy

* Dissert. on the Schools of the Hebrews, § 11.
† Ezek. xxxiii. 2, seqq.

prophets," cries Jeremiah, "have seen vain and foolish things for thee; and they have not discovered thine iniquity, to turn away thy captivity." In the same strain, Ezekiel inveighs against the prophets who daubed with untempered mortar, and divined lies; and he speaks of a conspiracy of prophets, who ravened the prey like a roaring lion, and filled their hands with treasure and precious things. But what if some abuses grew out of the prophetical institution? It is better, as Salvador says, to give free course to torrents of vain words, than to arrest a single one, about to be uttered by a true messenger from heaven.

CHAPTER X.

Conclusion.

In the foregoing pages, I have offered an analysis of the Hebrew constitution, such as I conceive it to have been, when it came from the hand of the inspired Hebrew lawgiver. The constitution contained a provision that, when the Israelites came into the promised land, it should be submitted to the people, and formally accepted by them all. They were to be assembled in an amphitheatre formed by two mountains,—Ebal, a bleak, frowning rock, towering on one side, and Gerizim, springing up covered with verdure and beauty on the other. The one height was a prophetic monument of the prosperity and loveliness, which would follow the observance of these institutions; the other, of the barrenness and desolation, which a disregard of the constitution would inevitably bring upon the nation. There the tribes, when the proper time came, were ranged in order, and listened to its provisions; and there they signified their acceptance of it, by an act of free choice, which was binding on them and their children for ever.* The Hebrew constitution, in its substance and its forms, in its letter and its spirit, was eminently republican. The power of the people was great and controlling. This point is clear, even on a superficial examination of the subject. But not only so; it had also important and striking analogies with our own constitution, and with that other free constitution, from which ours, in its most essential features, was taken; a constitution, which Montesquieu erroneously represents as drawn from the woods of Germany, but which Salvador, and truly without doubt, regards as derived from the Hebrew fountains. Whoever attentively considers the Hebrew and British constitutions, and still more the Hebrew and American constitutions, cannot but be impressed with the resemblance between them. Their fundamental principles are identical; and many of the details of organization are the same or similar. The rights of every person in the Hebrew state, from the head of the nation to the humblest stranger, were accurately defined and carefully guarded. Even Ahab, an unprincipled tyrant, dared not invade the field of a vine-dresser, though the want of it was so keenly felt as to make him refuse his ordinary food; and his still more tyrannical and unprincipled queen, Jezebel, knew no method of compassing the same end, but through the perverted forms of law and justice.† Every man was, in a political sense, on an equality with the most exalted of the nation. The rulers were raised to the dignities which they enjoyed, by the free suffrages of their fellow citizens. The laws, though proposed by God, were approved and enacted by the people, through their representatives, in the states-general of Israel. The Israelites exercised the right of meeting in primary assemblies, of discussing questions of public

* See Chr. Exam. for Sept. 1838. † 1 Kings xxi.

policy, and of petitioning their rulers for the redress of grievances. Every Hebrew citizen was eligible to the highest
civil dignities, even to that of the royal purple. The whole
nation constituted a republic of freemen, equal originally
even in property, equal in political dignity and privilege,
equal in their social standing, and equally entitled to the
care and protection of the government.

The Hebrew polity was essentially a system of self-government. It was the government of individual independence,
municipal independence, and state independence,—subject
only to so much of central control, as was necessary to constitute a true nationality, and to provide for the general
defence and welfare. Centralization was eminently foreign
to its spirit. The local governments loom out under the
Mosaic constitution; the central government is proportionably overshadowed. Herein the Hebrew constitution remarkably resembles our own, and as remarkably differs from
other ancient polities. All the ancient Asiatic governments,
and most of the European, were great centralizers. With
them, almost every thing originated and terminated in a
centre. The Greek democracies can scarcely be regarded as
an exception to this rule; the Roman commonwealth certainly was not.

Public opinion was a powerful element in the Hebrew
government. This gave shape and force both to the national
and provincial administrations. Let any one read the Hebrew history with this in his mind, and he will see proofs of
it in every page. If called upon for a single decisive proof
of the strength of the popular will under this constitution, I
would select the change in the government from the republican to the regal form. Samuel was against this change.
The oracle was against it.* The council of Moses was
against it. The opinion and practice of a long line of illustrious chiefs were against it. It is a reasonable presumption,

* The oracle did, indeed, give its assent; but reluctantly.

that a strong party of the wisest spirits of the state was against
it. Yet the change was made. How and why? The people
willed it; the people decreed it; and so it was. What more
pregnant argument could there be of the authority and energy,
with which the collective will of the nation uttered and enforced its resolves? The quiet submission of the whole nation
to the will of the majority, after the intense excitement of the
struggle, through which it must have passed, reminds me
more strongly than any thing else in history, of a presiden-
tial election among ourselves, which is ever accompanied
with a like convulsion of the public mind, and a like subsequent acquiescence and repose of the defeated party.

It is an admitted fact, that the tendency of all the modern
improvements in government is to equalize the conditions of
men, and so to bring about that general social intercourse, by
which many of the most important principles and habits are
formed and fixed, and the masses of society are elevated,
humanized, and refined. To secure these great ends, many
bloody wars have been waged, and countless treasures expended. But all these struggles and expenditures have not
yet, in the particulars just indicated, brought modern society
to that point, where Moses fixed his people, in an age, when
even the Greeks and the Romans were still savages and barbarians. Privileged classes, enjoying the benefit of milder
laws and special exemptions, were unknown to the Mosaic constitution. Neither patent of nobility nor benefit of clergy
found any place among its provisions. And civil liberty,
according to the notion of it presented in the excellent defi-
nitions of Blackstone, Paley, and other approved writers on
public law, that it is no other than natural liberty, so far restrained by human laws (and no farther), as is necessary and
expedient for the general advantage of the public; that it is
the not being restrained by any law, but what conduces in a
greater degree to the public welfare; and that it consists in
a freedom from all restraints, except such as established law

imposes for the good of the community ;—liberty, I say, thus regulated by law, with the superadded idea, that the restraining laws should be equal to all, was as fully developed and secured by the Hebrew constitution, as by any other known system of government in the world. The great natural rights of personal security, in respect to life, limb, health, and reputation ; of personal liberty, in respect to locomotion, residence, education, and the choice of occupation ; and of private property, in the free use, enjoyment, and disposal of all acquisitions, without any control or diminution, save by the laws of the land,—were recognized and guarded, in the amplest manner, by the laws and constitution of Moses. And these absolute and paramount rights were protected, and their inviolability maintained, by other subordinate rights :— the right of representation in the congregation of Israel; the right of a speedy and impartial administration of justice through the courts; and the right of petitioning the public authorities for the redress of wrongs, where other means of establishing the right were inadequate to the purpose. Such were the liberties of a Hebrew citizen ; such the barriers, by which they were defended ; such the inestimable system of public polity and law, which spread its ample and beneficent protection over the humblest and meanest, as well as the most exalted and honored member of the commonwealth of Israel.

The two greatest interests of a state, and yet the two interests most difficult to be harmonized,—permanence and progress,—were as wisely provided for and as effectually secured by the Mosaic system of government, as by any other civil constitution in the world : the former, by its regulations respecting the distribution and tenure of landed property ; the latter, by the three annual assemblages of the nation, whereby there was kept up a continual circulation of ideas between all parts of the country : and both, by the institution of the Levitical order, which was at once conservative and progressive; conservative, by its duty to teach, interpret, and maintain the laws; progressive, by its obligation to devote itself to the cultivation of science and letters.

Is it not a fact well worthy to arrest attention, that, in the midst of barbarism and darkness, hearing no sounds but those of violence, and seeing no soil which was not drenched with blood, a legislator should have founded a government on principles of peace, justice, equality, humanity, liberty, and social order, carried out as far as in the freest governments, now existing among men? This would be an inexplicable mystery, on any other theory than that of a supernatural revelation to the lawgiver. The reality of the divine legation of Moses might be rested on this argument alone. And whoever holds to the divinity of his mission, and therefore necessarily believes, that a constitutional and representative democracy is a form of government, stamped with the seal of the divine approbation, while the monarchy was a concession to the folly of the people, will thence derive a new and forcible argument to cherish and defend the precious charter of our own liberties, since its type and model came originally from the depths of the divine wisdom and goodness.

I have sometimes imagined all the legislators of America gathered into one vast assemblage, and the Jewish lawgiver appearing suddenly in their midst. "Gentlemen," he might say to them, "at length my word is fulfilled. What you boast of doing now, I accomplished, as far as in me lay, in a distant age. I broke the doors of the house of bondage, and proclaimed the principle of universal equality among men. I substituted for castes and privileged classes, a nation of freemen, and for arbitrary and capricious impositions, the reign of law, equal and universal. I preferred peace to war, general competence and happiness to the false glory of arms, substantial blessings to airy nothings. My highest efforts were constantly directed to procure for all the citizens the greatest equality practicable, both of the labors and enjoyments of life; for the whole commonwealth of Israel, lands well cultivated, good habitations, rich herds, and a population healthy, numerous, enlightened, pious, and contented. It is false, what ignorance and irreligion have charged against me, that I held in abhorrence, after the example of Egypt, foreign nations. No other legislator in the world has ever shown to the stranger an equal justice, an equal tenderness, with myself. Nor is this all: I earnestly labored to secure a universal intellectual equality. Far from being jealous of the superiority, which God and the discipline of my faculties had given me, I nourished the animating hope, that all the lights, which I possessed, would one day become the common property of all, even the humblest of my fellow-creatures. LAWS,—not men,—were the rulers of my republic; CONSENT, — not force, — the basis of my government. Conquests, and servitude; magnificent palaces, and servitude; boundless luxury, and servitude; brilliant spectacles, and servitude; a certain amount of science, and still servitude;—behold a brief but true picture of the governments, by which I was surrounded. It is a libel upon my name and memory to charge me with having framed my institutions upon the model of those stupendous systems of fraud and tyranny. By the wisdom of my counsels and the energy of my policy, I overthrew, at a blow, the whole degrading apparatus of political jugglery and priestly despotism. I reduced the speculative ideas of my own and the preceding ages to a single sublime principle of simplicity. I recognized the happiness and well-being of the people, as the one supreme law of political philosophy. By the institutions founded upon this principle, I impressed a new character upon my age and species; I gave a new impulse to man, both in his individual and social energies; I fixed upon my labors the indestructible seal of a divine wisdom and beneficence. Forward, then, gentlemen, without fear or faltering, in the doctrine of Jehovah,—in those great principles of free and equal government, which, taught by the Divine Spirit, I first promulgated to the world; and to which, after so many ages of tyranny and misgovernment, you have at length returned. Cling to these principles, legislators of a world that had no being when I founded my republic. Give them a broader development, a higher activity; and the civilization, the prosperity, the happiness flowing from them, shall outstrip your fondest hopes, and more than realize the brightest vision of bard or prophet."

Such is the spirit that speaks to us, of this distant age and clime, in the Mosaic constitution. It is a spirit of faith, hope, charity. There are some, who entertain apprehensions concerning the issue of our political experiment, and who doubt the capacity of the people for self government. For myself, I have no such fears. My faith in our institutions has been strengthened by my study of the Hebrew constitution. I have seen with surprize and delight, that the essential principles of our constitution are identical with those of a political system, which emanated from a superhuman wisdom, and was established by the authority of the supreme ruler of the world. I accept this knowledge as a pledge, that these principles are destined, in the good providence of God, to a universal triumph. Men are capable of governing themselves; such is the decision of the infinite intelligence. Tyranny will every where come to an end; humanity will recover its rights; and the entire race of mankind will exult in the enjoyment of freedom and happiness. Futurity is big with events of momentous import; events, I verily believe, compared with which the grandest and the sublimest, hitherto inscribed upon the rolls of fame, are but as insignificant trifles. But this better future, for which our nature sighs, and to which it is evidently tending, " is not a tree transplanted from paradise, with all its branches in full fruitage. It was not sowed in sunshine. It is not in vernal breezes and gentle rains, that its roots are fixed, and its growth and strength

insured. With blood was it planted. It is rocked in tempests. Deep scars are on its trunk, and the path of the
lightning may be traced among its branches." But, through
storm and darkness, amid blood and carnage, the political
redemption of our race holds on its course. Liberty and
law, christianity and science, religion and learning are yet to
enjoy a universal triumph, to sway a universal sceptre. The
day is to come, when human nature, relieved from the pressure imposed upon it by the abuses of ancient dynasties,
shall start afresh, with unimpeded and elastic tread, on its
destined race of improvement and perfectibility. Thanks be
to God for that rainbow of promise, with which the civil
polity of Moses has spanned the political heavens!

THE END.

www.ingramcontent.com/pod-product-compliance
Lightning Source LLC
Chambersburg PA
CBHW020409100426
42812CB00001B/257